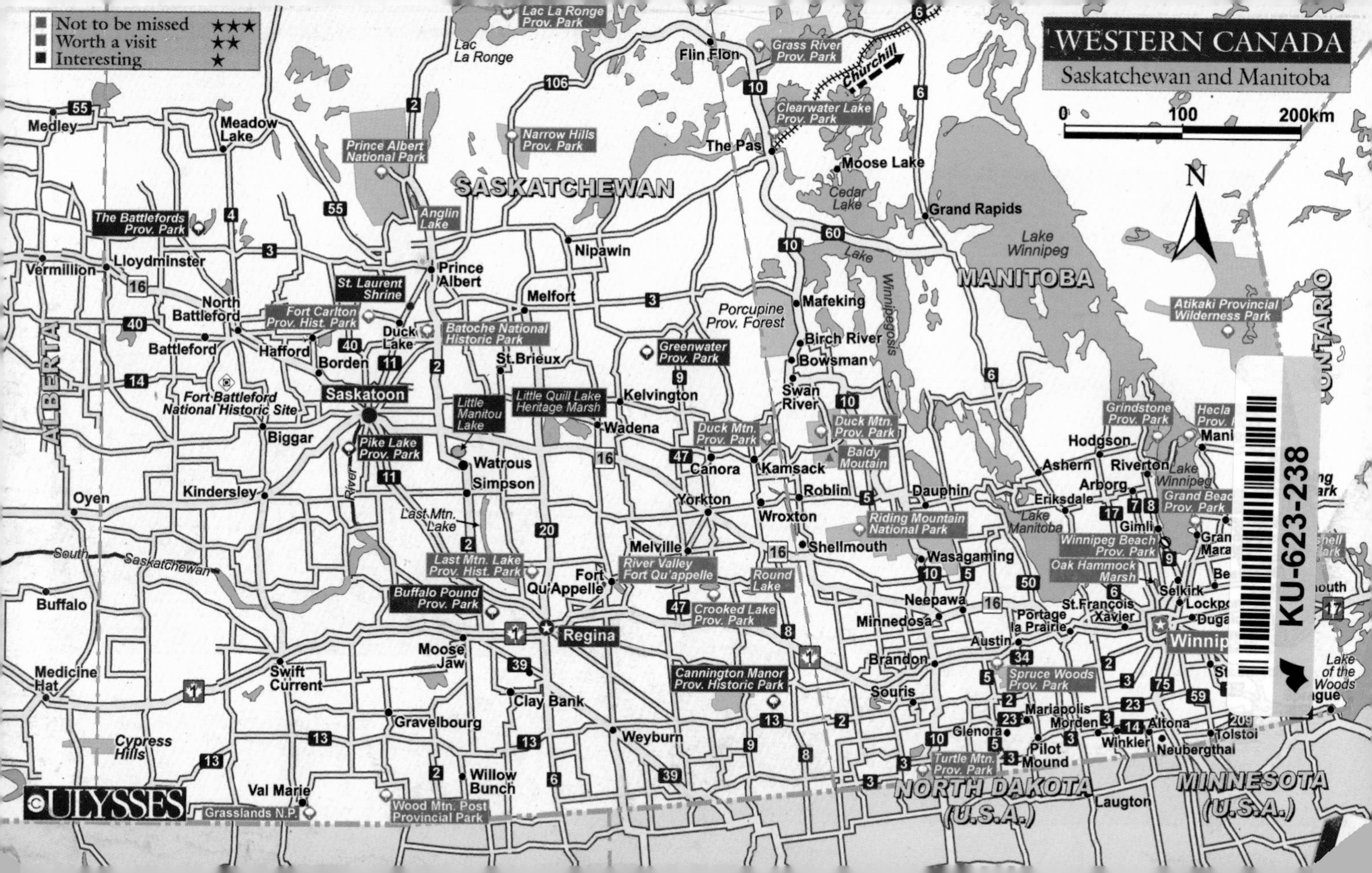
WESTERN CANADA
Saskatchewan and Manitoba
0 100 200km
N
Not to be missed ★★★
Worth a visit ★★
Interesting ★
SASKATCHEWAN
MANITOBA
ALBERTA
ONTARIO
NORTH DAKOTA (U.S.A.)
MINNESOTA (U.S.A.)
Lac La Ronge
Lac La Ronge Prov. Park
Flin Flon
Grass River Prov. Park
Churchill
Clearwater Lake Prov. Park
The Pas
Moose Lake
Cedar Lake
Grand Rapids
Lake Winnipeg
Lake Winnipegosis
Atikaki Provincial Wilderness Park
Medley
Meadow Lake
Narrow Hills Prov. Park
Prince Albert National Park
Anglin Lake
The Battlefords Prov. Park
Nipawin
Vermillion
Lloydminster
Prince Albert
St. Laurent Shrine
Melfort
Mafeking
Porcupine Prov. Forest
North Battleford
Fort Carlton Prov. Hist. Park
Duck Lake
Batoche National Historic Park
Birch River
Battleford
Hafford
Borden
Greenwater Prov. Park
Bowsman
St.Brieux
Swan River
Fort Battleford National Historic Site
Saskatoon
Kelvington
Little Manitou Lake
Little Quill Lake Heritage Marsh
Wadena
Duck Mtn. Prov. Park
Grindstone Prov. Park
Hecla Prov. Park
Biggar
Pike Lake Prov. Park
Watrous
Baldy Moutain
Hodgson
Ashern
Riverton
Lake Winnipeg
Canora
Kamsack
Arborg
Grand Beach Prov. Park
Oyen
Kindersley
Simpson
River
Yorkton
Roblin
Dauphin
Eriksdale
Last Mtn. Lake
Wroxton
Riding Mountain National Park
Lake Manitoba
Gimli
Shellmouth
Winnipeg Beach Prov. Park
South Saskatchewan
Melville
Last Mtn. Lake Prov. Hist. Park
River Valley Fort Qu'appelle
Round Lake
Wasagaming
Oak Hammock Marsh
Fort Qu'Appelle
Selkirk
Buffalo
Buffalo Pound Prov. Park
Crooked Lake Prov. Park
Neepawa
St.François Xavier
Minnedosa
Portage la Prairie
Regina
Moose Jaw
Austin
Winnipeg
Brandon
Medicine Hat
Swift Current
Cannington Manor Prov. Historic Park
Spruce Woods Prov. Park
Lake of the Woods
Souris
Clay Bank
Mariapolis
Gravelbourg
Morden
Altona
Glenora
Tolstoi
Weyburn
Winkler
Neubergthai
Cypress Hills
Pilot Mound
Turtle Mtn. Prov. Park
Willow Bunch
Val Marie
Laugton
Grasslands N.P.
Wood Mtn. Post Provincial Park
©ULYSSES
KU-623-238

Sunset over Vancouver, a prosperous, modern city.
- *Walter Bibikow*

Nature and the ocean are never far away in Vancouver, even in the heart of the city.
- *Michel Gascon*

Western Canada

3rd Edition

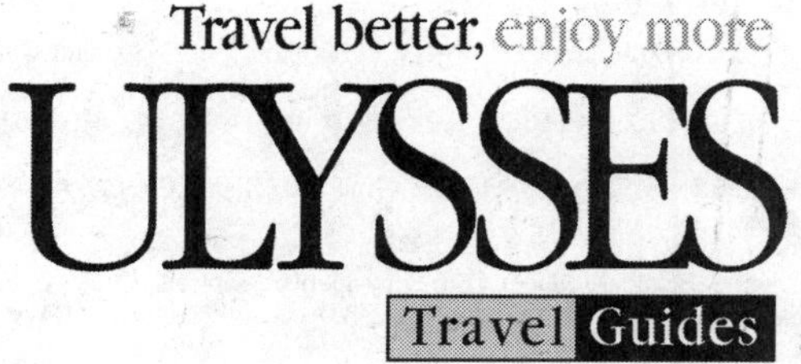

Research and Writing
Alexis de Gheldere
Paul-Éric Dumontier
Stéphanie Heidenreich
Paul Karr
Pierre Longnus
Jennifer McMorran
Lorette Pierson
François Rémillard
Clayton Anderson

Publishers
Daniel Desjardins
Stéphane G. Marceau

Project Director
Pascale Couture

Project Coordinator
Jacqueline Grekin

Editing
Jacqueline Grekin
Tara Salman

Translation
Myles McKelvey
Tracy Kendrick
Eric Hamovitch
Danielle Gauthier
Emmy Pahmer

Illustrations
Lorette Pierson
Myriam Gagné
Jenny Jasper

Photography
Cover Page
George Hunter
Inside Pages
M. Michaelnuk
(Megapress Images)
Walter Bibikow
Michel Gascon
Derek Caron
Sean O'Neill
Tibor Bognar
Troy and Mary Parlee

Page Layout
Typesetting
Clayton Anderson
Jenny Jasper
Elyse Leconte
Julie Brodeur
Final Layout
Jenny Jasper

Cartographers
Patrick Thivierge
Yanik Landreville

Computer Graphics
Stéphanie Routhier

Artistic Director
Patrick Farei (Atoll)

Distributors

AUSTRALIA: Little Hills Press, 11/37-43 Alexander St., Crows Nest NSW 2065, ☎ (612) 437-6995, Fax: (612) 438-5762

CANADA: Ulysses Books & Maps, 4176 Saint-Denis, Montréal, Québec, H2W 2M5, ☎ (514) 843-9882, ext.2232, 800-748-9171, Fax: 514-843-9448, info@ulysses.ca, www.ulyssesguides.com

GERMANY and **AUSTRIA**: Brettschneider, Fernreisebedarf, Feldfirchner Strasse 2, D-85551 Heimstetten, München, ☎ 89-99 02 03 30, Fax: 89-99 02 03 31, cf@brettschneider.de

GREAT BRITAIN and **IRELAND**: World Leisure Marketing, Unit 11, Newmarket Court, Newmartket Drive, Derby DE24 8NW, ☎ 1 332 57 37 37, Fax: 1 332 57 33 99, office@wlmsales.co.uk

ITALY: Centro Cartografico del Riccio, Via di Soffiano 164/A, 50143 Firenze, ☎ (055) 71 33 33, Fax: (055) 71 63 50

PORTUGAL: Dinapress, Lg. Dr. Antonio de Sousa de Macedo, 2, Lisboa 1200, ☎ (1) 395 52 70, Fax: (1) 395 03 90

SCANDINAVIA: Scanvik, Esplanaden 8B, 1263 Copenhagen K, DK, ☎ (45) 33.12.77.66, Fax: (45) 33.91.28.82

SPAIN: Altaïr, Balmes 69, E-08007 Barcelona, ☎ 454 29 66, Fax: 451 25 59, altair@globalcom.es

SWITZERLAND: OLF, P.O. Box 1061, CH-1701 Fribourg, ☎ (026) 467.51.11, Fax: (026) 467.54.66

U.S.A.: The Globe Pequot Press, 246 Goose Lane, Guilford, CT 06437-0480, ☎ 1-800-243-0495, Fax: 800-820-2329, sales@globe-pequot.com

OTHER COUNTRIES: Ulysses Books & Maps, 4176 Saint-Denis, Montréal, Québec, H2W 2M5, ☎ (514) 843-9882, ext.2232, 800-748-9171, Fax: 514-843-9448, info@ulysses.ca, www.ulyssesguides.com

Canadian Cataloguing in Publication Data (see page 7)

Printed in Canada
ISBN 2-8946244-x

"Then the locomotive whistle sounded again and a voice was heard to cry: "All aboard for the Pacific." It was the first time that phrase had been used by a conductor from the East... The official party obediently boarded the cars and a few moments later the little train was in motion again, clattering over the newly laid rail and over the last spike and down the long incline of the mountains, off towards the dark canyon of the Fraser, off to broad meadows beyond, off to the blue Pacific and into history."

Pierre Berton
The Last Spike

Table of Contents

Symbols

(ship symbol)	Ulysses's Favourite
☎	Telephone Number
⇄	Fax Number
≡	Air Conditioning
⊗	Fan
≈	Pool
ℜ	Restaurant
⊛	Whirlpool
ℝ	Refrigerator
K	Kitchenette
⌂	Sauna
⊘	Exercise Room
tv	Colour Television
pb	Private Bathroom
sb	Shared Bathroom
bkfst incl.	Breakfast included in price of room

ATTRACTION CLASSIFICATION

★	Interesting
★★	Worth a visit
★★★	Not to be missed

The prices listed in this guide are for the admission of one adult.

HOTEL CLASSIFICATION

The prices in the guide are for one room, double occupancy in high season.

RESTAURANT CLASSIFICATION

$	$10 or less
$$	$10 to $20
$$$	$20 to $30
$$$$	$30 and more

The prices in the guide are for a meal for one person, not including drinks and tip.

All prices in this guide are in Canadian dollars unless otherwise stated

Write to Us

The information contained in this guide was correct at press time. However, mistakes can slip in, omissions are always possible, places can disappear, etc. The authors and publisher hereby disclaim any liability for loss or damage resulting from omissions or errors.

We value your comments, corrections and suggestions, as they allow us to keep each guide up to date. The best contributions will be rewarded with a free book from Ulysses Travel Guides. All you have to do is write us at the following address and indicate which title you would be interested in receiving (see the list at the end of guide).

Ulysses Travel Guides
4176 Rue Saint-Denis
Montréal, Québec
Canada H2W 2M5
www.ulyssesguides.com
E-mail: text@ulysses.ca

"We acknowledge the financial support of the Government of Canada through the Book Publishing Industry Development Program (BPIDP) for our publishing activities".

We would also like to thank SODEC (Québec) for their financial support.

Canadian Cataloguing in Publication Data

Main entry under title:

Western Canada

(Ulysses Travel Guide)
Translation of: Ouest Canadian
Includes index
ISSN 1486-3480

ISBN 2-89464-244-X

1. Canada, Western - Guidebooks. 2. British Columbia - Guidebooks.
3. Alberta - Guidebooks. I. Series

FC3202.09313 917.1204'3 C99-301660-X
F1060.4.09313

List of Maps

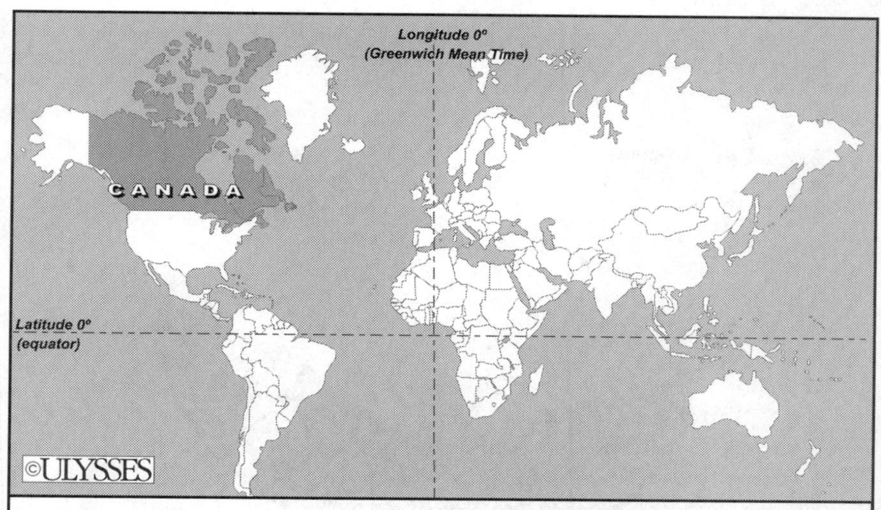

Where is Canada?

WESTERN CANADA	
British Columbia	**Alberta**
Capital: Victoria Population: 3,900,000 inhab. Area: 950,000 km²	Capital: Edmonton Population: 2,600,000 inhab. Area: 661,000 km²
Saskatchewan	**Manitoba**
Capital: Regina Population: 990,000 inhab. Area: 651,900 km²	Capital: Winnipeg Population: 1,114,000 inhab. Area: 649,950 km²

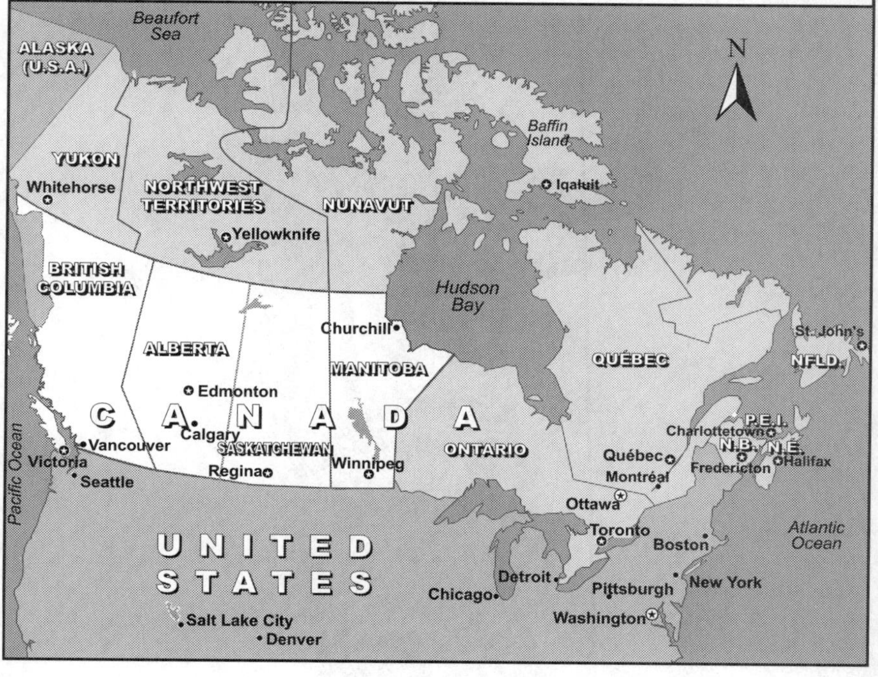

Beaufort Sea
ALASKA (U.S.A.)
N
Baffin Island
YUKON
Whitehorse
NORTHWEST TERRITORIES
NUNAVUT
Iqaluit
Yellowknife
BRITISH COLUMBIA
Hudson Bay
Churchill
St. John's
ALBERTA
QUÉBEC
NFLD.
MANITOBA
Edmonton
C A N A D A
P.E.I.
Charlottetown
Calgary
N.B.
N.E.
Vancouver
SASKATCHEWAN
ONTARIO
Québec
Halifax
Victoria
Winnipeg
Fredericton
Seattle
Regina
Montréal
Pacific Ocean
Ottawa
Toronto
Atlantic Ocean
UNITED STATES
Boston
Detroit
New York
Chicago
Pittsburgh
Washington
Salt Lake City
Denver

Portrait

Western Canada is a difficult region to pin down. Some define it as British Columbia and Alberta, some as everything west of Ontario (the generally accepted centre of Canada), while still others would further divide that version of Western Canada into the Prairies, the mountains and the coast.

The version of Western Canada described in this guidebook adopts the wider definition, including the provinces of British Columbia, Alberta, Saskatchewan and Manitoba, so that we may introduce you to the range of landscapes found across this part of Canada.

The fabulous chain of mountains, the Rocky Mountains, is an easy focus for any trip to this part of the world but what trip to Canada's west would be complete without also experiencing Calgary and the world-famous Stampede, the rolling plains, magnificent lakes and rivers, of southern Alberta, Saskatchewan and Manitoba or for that matter the metropolis of the Pacific, Vancouver, the stunning coastline, Gulf Islands or the fruit-bearing valleys of Southern British Columbia?

This region has only been known to Europeans for the last 200 years. In fact, the sons of the French explorer La Vérendrye did not set eyes on the Rocky Mountains until the end of the 18th century, and England's George Vancouver only explored the Pacific coast and Columbia River in the last decade of the same century. White settlement of the region is even more recent, going back just over 100 years in Alberta, which, like Saskatchewan, has only existed as a province since 1905. Aboriginal peoples have inhabited this territory for at least 11,000 years, but never in large numbers; there were only 220,000 of them in all of Canada when explorer Jacques Cartier arrived in 1534.

Geography

This guide covers the four most westerly provinces of Canada: British Columbia, located on the Pacific coast and covered by vast mountain chains; Alberta, which begins on the eastern slopes of the Rocky Mountains and extends into the vast Canadian prairies, Saskatchewan, and finally Manitoba, which borders the central province of Ontario. These provinces are bordered to the south by the U.S. states of Washington on the coast, and heading eastwardIdaho, Montana, North Dakota and Minnesota. British Columbia borders Alaska to the northwest and the Yukon to the north. The northeastern corner of British Columbia and the entire northern border of Alberta and Saskatchewan are shared with the Northwest Territories, while Manitoba's northern border is shared by the newly created Inuit territory of Nunavut.

British Columbia is the largest of these provinces with an area of 950,000km^2. And Alberta, Saskatchewan, and Manitoba cover some 650,000km^2.

Carved out by countless fjords and dotted with hundreds of islands, British Columbia's jagged coastline is 7,000km long, not counting the shores of the islands. The largest of these is Vancouver Island, about the size of the Netherlands and home to the provincial capital, Victoria. Despite its name, the city of Vancouver is not on the island but rather lies across the Strait of Juan de Fuca, on the mainland. The Queen Charlotte Islands lie to the north. The maritime nature of the province is foremost in many minds, but in actuality three quarters of the province lie an average of more than 930m above sea level, and a 3,000m-high barrier of mountains is visible from the coast. A succession of mountain ranges stretches from west to east, all the way to the famous Rocky Mountains, whose summits reach up to 4,000m. This chain was named for its bare, rocky eastern slopes.

During the Precambrian era, the Pacific Ocean covered most of Western Canada. Over a period of about 500 million years, the ocean advanced and receded, depositing sediment on the Precambrian rock of the Canadian Shield, one of the oldest rock formations on earth. Microscopic organisms in the sea died, creating enormous amounts of decaying organic matter, at the source of Alberta's huge oil deposits. By the Cretaceous period, some 75 million years ago, the Arctic Ocean had flooded most of Alberta, creating a vast inland sea known as the Bearpaw.

Dinosaurs thrived along the shores of this subtropical sea and along the rivers that emptied into it. They lived there for millions of years, until about 70 million years ago when the Pacific Plate collided with the North American Plate and was forced upwards, forming the mountain ranges of present-day British Columbia and western Alberta. This gradually altered the climate, cooling things down and eventually killing off the dinosaurs around 63 million years ago. Then, about a million years ago, four polar ice caps advanced across the region, eroding the mountain ranges and carving out the rivers and lakes that make up the present landscape as they receded.

These rivers divide the province of Alberta into regions. The Mackenzie, Peace and Athabasca Rivers make the land arable as far as the Boreal forests of the north and eventually empty into the Arctic Ocean. The North Saskatchewan and Red

Deer Rivers provide most of the irrigation for Alberta farms, and empty into Hudson Bay, along with the South Saskatchewan, Oldman and Bow Rivers.

Flora and Fauna

There is a section devoted specifically to the flora and fauna of the Rockies at the beginning of the chapter describing that region (see p 287)

Despite the limited extent of the plains in British Columbia, 60% of the province's territory is covered by forest. The forest growing along the coast, on the Queen Charlotte Islands and on the west coast of Vancouver Island is so lush that it is called the northern rain forest, the counterpart of the tropical rain forest. Douglas firs and western red cedars abound, as does the Sitka spruce. The Douglas fir can grow to up to 90m in height and 4.5m in diameter. This forest receives up to 4,000mm of rain per year and many of its trees are more than 1,000 years old, though most of the ancient Douglas firs were cut down in the last century. Much higher and drier, the province's interior is home to vast pine, spruce and hemlock forests.

Larches grow in the subalpine forests found at higher altitudes. The larch is the only coniferous tree in Canada that loses its needles in the fall, after they turn yellow. They grow back in the spring.

Sheltered by Vancouver Island, the southern Gulf Islands have a relatively dry, mild climate. You'll even find certain varieties of cacti here, including the prickly pear. Flowers bloom in this area all year round, especially in the months of April and May.

Coyote

The prairies stretch from southeast Alberta to Ontario. Grasses cover the land, except along the rivers, where cottonwood and willows trees grow. Cacti are also common here. The prairies rise and become hilly as you head west into the foothills, where aspen, white spruce, lodgepole pine and Douglas fir trees grow.

Wolf

A belt of aspen parkland acts as a transition zone between the grasslands of the south and the Boreal forest of the north. Aspen and grasslands cover most of this area.

Beyond this, more than half the territory is covered with Boreal forest dotted with lakes, bogs, and marshland. In the northern mixed forest, it is not uncommon for an invasion of parasites, a heavily logged area, or a forest fire to spawn a pioneer forest which will initiate the regeneration of the original forest. White spruce, lodgepole pine and balsam fir are the most common trees. Finally, parts of this region are strewn with bushes bearing raspberries and Saskatoon berries.

Wildlife abounds throughout Alberta and travellers with cars should look out for muledeer and white-tailed deer. Even just outside the city of Calgary these animals can often be found close to highways. Pronghorns scampering across grasslands are a common sight, and coyotes and occasionally wolves can also be spotted near highways, especially farther north. Black bears are found in forested areas throughout the province, while grizzly bears inhabit Waterton Lakes National Park along with cougars and bighorn sheep.

Warmed by the Japanese current, the waters of the Pacific maintain a higher temperature than those of the Atlantic which are cooled by the Labrador current. As a result, this region features very distinctive marine life. For example, this is the only place in Canada where sea otters are found, even though they were almost completely exterminated by hunting. Sea lions are also indigenous to the Pacific coast.

The Northern sea lion is often the subject of fishers' griping, since it is the main predator of salmon. It is true that some sea lions can weigh up to a tonne and never seem to stop eating, but many other animals feast on the abundant salmon on the coast and in the rivers where they spawn. Grizzly bears, for example, gather for a feast when the rivers are teeming with salmon, and gourmets that they are, eat only the roe and the head! Wolves, black bears, raccoons, gulls and bald eagles eat the leftovers.

Grizzly Bear

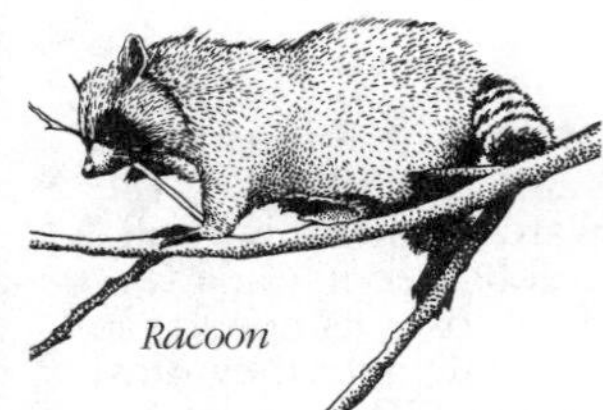

Racoon

Speaking of bald eagles, the Pacific coast is home to Canada's largest population of these majestic birds, which have all but disappeared from the Atlantic coast.

Countless orcas inhabit the waters around Vancouver Island and are commonly spotted from the ferries that link this island with the mainland. They are the only marine mammals that eat warm-blooded animals like seals, belugas and other smaller whales, which probably explains their more common appellation, killer whales.

With the arrival of fall, certain marine mammals, like the grey whale, migrate from Alaska to Baja California in Mexico. They make their way back up to Alaska in the winter.

Large numbers of cougars (see p 288) inhabit British Columbia's forests, particularly on Vancouver Island, where they feed on Columbia blacktail deer.

An impressive variety of birds and mammals inhabits Alberta. Some of the more noteworthy winged species are bald eagles found around the northern lakes, prairie and peregrine falcons, which can often be seen in and around the plains either diving for prey or waiting patiently on a fence post by the highway. Finally, the migratory path of the trumpeter swan passes through Alberta.

Bald Eagle

To the delight of anglers, the lakes and rivers of this region are teeming with countless freshwater fish, including eight different varieties of trout.

History

The First Inhabitants

The region's first human inhabitants are believed to have arrived at least 11,000 years ago when the Wisconsin glacier receded, though they may have arrived on the American continent earlier. These people found large numbers of buffalo and other game animals here, as well as berries and roots. They did not waste any of these resources, using hides for clothing, storage and shelter, bones as tools, horns for spoons, antlers for handles, plants for medicines, sinew for thread and clay for pottery.

There is some doubt, however, as to whether native civilization on the West Coast First Nation's with these same vast waves of immigration. According to one theory, the ancestors of the West Coast tribes came here more recently (around 3000 BC) from islands in the Pacific. Proponents of this hypothesis base their argument on Aboriginal art, traditions and spoken languages, which are not unlike those of the indigenous peoples of the Pacific islands.

In the 18th century, five First Nation's families occupied the area between Hudson Bay and the Rocky Mountains. The part of the Canadian shield covered by vast forests is Ojibway land. The Assiniboins occupied the plains and prairies and the Western Crees lived in the forests and plains south of present-day Manitoba and Saskatchewan. Southwest of these two groups lived the Blackfoot and in the far north, the Athapaskans.

The arrival of the European colonists drastically disrupted these nations. They were either brought into direct conflict with the colonists or other displaced Aboriginal groups, or were affected by the ensuing profound changes in the environment, such as the near extinction of the Prairie buffalo herds.

Buffalo

The arrival of traders around Hudson Bay introduced items like metal tools and weapons to some of Alberta's First Nations before they had even laid eyes on a single European. The horse was unknown to Alberta's First Nations, and its arrival in the early 1700s following the Spanish conquest of Mexico changed their hunting methods forever. The traditional buffalo jump, during which buffalo were herded over a cliff to their death, thus became obsolete.

Canadian history is marked by a series of treaties between First Nations and Europeans. In the West, the first treaties were drawn up in the 19th century the Aboriginal peoples had, seeing themselves on the brink of assimilation, to give up much of their land to the Crown. This is when the first reserves were created, which, to this day, are still home to many First Nation's peoples.

When the first Europeans arrived on the coast in the 18th century, the territory that was to become British Columbia was occupied by Nootka, Coast Salish, Kwakiutl, Bella Coola, Tsimshian, Haida and Tlinkit. Tagish, Tahltan, Testsaut, Carrier, Chilcotin, Interior Salish, Nicola and Kootenays occupied the interior. Slavery seems to have been practised among the Interior Salish, who had three social classes.

The region that would become Vancouver was inhabited by the Salish. Like their compatriots, they favoured this region for its remarkably mild climate and abundance of belugas, salmon, seals, fruit and other resources. This beneficial environment, combined with the barrier formed by the nearby mountains, enabled the coastal nations to thrive. Not only was their population quite large, but it was also significantly denser than that of other First Nations in central and eastern Canada.

In 1820, there were some 25,000 Salish living on the shores of the Fraser River, from its mouth south of Vancouver all the way up into the Rockies. Like other native tribes, the Salish were sedentary and lived in villages of red cedar longhouses. They traded with other natives along the coast during potlatches, festive ceremonies lasting weeks on end and marked by the exchange of gifts.

Fur and Exploration

In 1670, the territory now known as the prairies, made up of the provinces of Manitoba, Saskatchewan and Alberta, was ceded by the British Crown to the Hudson's Bay Company (HBC), which took over the economic and political administration of the region.

The HBC controlled trade in Rupert's Land, which encompassed all land that drained into Hudson Bay, therefore covering much of present-day Canada. In 1691, Henry Kelsey, an employee of the company was the first to set sight on the eastern boundary of Alberta. HBC traders, however, had competition from French fur trappers, known as *voyageurs*, who headed inland to the source of the fur instead of waiting for the natives to bring the pelts to the trading posts. Encouraged by favourable reports, independent fur traders in Montreal formed the North West Company in 1787, and then founded the first trading post in Alberta, Fort Chipewyan, on Lake Athabasca.

These trading posts eventually came to serve as bases for exploration and in 1792 Alexander Mackenzie crossed Alberta by the Peace River, becoming the first man to reach the Pacific overland. The trading companies' sole interest in the West lay in the fur trade, which continued unabated, even receiving a boost when the North West and Hudson's Bay Companies merged in 1821. By the late 1860s, however, beaver stocks had begun to dwindle, and merchants turned their attention to buffalo.

Beaver

After only 10 years of buffalo hunting and trading, there were almost no more of these majestic animals which had once roamed wild. This had dire consequences for the Aboriginal peoples, who depended on the buffalo for their survival and were ultimately left with no choice but to negotiate treaties with Canada, give up their land and move onto reserves.

Furthermore, the fur-trading companies were only interested in fur and offered nothing in the way of law enforcement. Whisky traders from the United States were thus drawn north to this lawless land. With dwindling buffalo herds, Aboriginal peoples were exploited and generally taken advantage of by the Americans, not to mention the deleterious effect the whisky trade had on them. Uprisings, including the Cypress Hills Massacre (see p 405), prompted the formation of the Northwest Mounted Police and the March West began. Starting from Fort Garry in Winnipeg, the police crossed the plains lead by James Macleod. Their presence got rid of the whisky traders at Fort Whoop-Up in 1874, and they then set about establishing four forts in southern Alberta, including Fort Macleod and Fort Calgary.

The fur trade being the principle activity of the HBC, the Company did all it could to discourage colonization in the region, so that they could pursue their activities unimpeded. At the time, the United States had just ended its civil war and was clearly interested in conquering the British part of North America, present-day Canada. They had purchased Alaska from Russia in 1867, and in 1868, Minnesota drew up a resolution favouring the annexation of the Canadian prairies.

These vague American impulses were enough to worry the leaders of the fledgling Canadian Confederation (1867) who negotiated with Great Britain and the Hudson's Bay Company to acquire the Northwest Territories (which at the time included present-day Alberta, Saskatchewan, Manitoba and the Northwest Territories) in 1868 without so much as consulting the people who had settled there, for the most part French-speaking Metis. These people resisted and prevented the governor appointed by Canada from taking power.

Their leader, Louis Riel, tried to obtain a land title for his people, but the Canadian government paid no attention. With his troops, he then declared himself leader of Manitoba and forced Ottawa to negotiate. Finally, on July 15, 1870, the bilingual province of Manitoba was created. Its territory, not much larger than present-day Belgium, was small, and, except for some control over land development and natural resources, it had little of the power the other provinces had. These circumstances have continued to influence relations between the federal and provincial governments of what would one day be the Prairie provinces of Manitoba, Saskatchewan and Alberta.

Some 15 years later, the Metis called back their exiled leader to confront a similar situation, this time in Saskatchewan. Ottawa was faring better this time and sent troops to quash the rebellion. Under of an old British law, Riel was found guilty of treason and hung.

The Isolation of the Pacific Coast

The 18th century saw an increase in exploration and colonization all over the world by European sea powers, but there was an immense area that still seemed inaccessible: the far-off and mysterious Pacific Ocean. Some of the many peoples inhabiting its shores were completely unknown to French, Spanish and English navigators. The Panama Canal had not yet been dug, and sailing ships had to cover incredible distances, their crews braving starvation, just to reach the largest of the Earth's oceans.

In 1792, English explorer James Cook's compatriot George Vancouver (1757-1798) took possession of the territory surrounding the city that now bears his name for the King of England, thereby putting an end to any claims the Russians and Spaniards planned to make. The former would have liked to extend their empire southward from Alaska, while the latter, firmly entrenched in California, were looking northward. Spanish explorers had even made a brief trip into Burrard Inlet in the 16th century. This far-flung region was not coveted enough to cause any bloody wars, however, and was left undeveloped for years to come.

The Vancouver region was hard to reach not only by sea, but also by land, with the virtually insurmountable obstacle of the Rocky Mountains blocking the way. Imagine setting out across the immense North American continent from Montreal, following the lakes and rivers of the Canadian Shield, and exhausting yourself crossing the endless Prairies, only to end up barred from the Pacific by a wall of rock several thousand metres high. In 1808, the fabulously wealthy fur merchant and adventurer Simon Fraser became the first person to reach the site of Vancouver from inland. This belated breakthrough had little impact on the region, though, since Fraser was unable to reach any trade agreements with the coastal nations and quickly withdrew to his trading posts in the Rockies.

The Salish thus continued to lead a peaceful existence here for many more years before being disrupted by white settlers. In 1808, except for sporadic visits by Russians, Spaniards and Englishmen looking to trade pelts for fabrics and objects from the Orient, the Aboriginal people were still living according to the traditions handed down to them by their ancestors. In fact, European influence on their lifestyle remained negligible until the mid-19th century, at which point colonization of the territory began slowly.

In 1818, Great Britain and the United States created the condominium of Oregon, a vast fur-trading zone along the Pacific bounded by California to the south and Alaska to the north. In so doing, these two countries excluded the Russians and the Spanish from this region once and for all. The employees of the North West Company combed the valley of the Fraser River in search of furs. Not only did they encounter the coastal Aboriginals, whose precious resources they were depleting, but they also had to adapt to the tumultuous waterways of the Rockies, which made travelling by canoe nearly impossible. In 1827, after the Hudson's Bay Company took over the North West Company, a large fur-trading post was founded in Fort Langley, on the shores of the Fraser, some 90km east of the present site of Vancouver, which would remain untouched for several more decades.

Unlike the Prairies, which were simply annexed to the Canadian Confederation in 1868, British Columbia was already a British colony and was thus able to negotiate its entrance into confederation. Isolated on the Pacific coast, British Columbia's principal trading partner was California. As its population grew with the gold rush of the 1850s, certain residents even dreamed of creating an independent country. But these hopes were dashed at the end of this prosperous period, when in 1871, British Columbia's population was only 36,000. Great Britain had already joined its colony on Vancouver Island with British Columbia in anticipation of their eventual integration into the new Canadian Confederation.

Due to American protectionism, local industrialists and merchants could not distribute their products in California, while Montréal was too far away and too hard to reach to be a lucrative market. The only favourable outlets, therefore, were the other British colonies on the Pacific, which paved the way for Vancouver's present prosperity.

With a promise from Canada that a Pan-Canadian railway would reach the coast by 1881, British Columbia joined confederation in 1871. However, all sorts of problems delayed the construction of the railroad, and in 1873, as a severe recession gripped Canada, causing major delays in the railway, British Columbia threatened to separate. It wasn't until November 7, 1885 that the railway from Montréal to Vancouver was finally completed, four years late.

Expanding Confederation

As the railway expanded, more and more farmers settled in the region known as the Northwest Territories, which had no responsible government on the provincial level. You will recall that Canada had annexed the territories (Prairies) without giving them provincial status, except for a small parcel of land, which became the province of Manitoba. Inevitably, Canada had to create the provinces of Alberta and Saskatchewan and enlarge the province of Manitoba in 1905.

Most settlers arrived in Alberta when the Canadian Pacific Railway reached Fort Calgary in 1883 and eight years later in 1891 when the Grand Trunk Railway's northern route reached Edmonton. Ranchers from the United States and Canada initially grabbed up huge tracts of land with grazing leases that, in the case of the Cochrane Ranch, west of Calgary, occupied 40,000ha. Much of this open range land was eventually granted to homesteaders.

To easterners, the West was ranches, rodeos and cheap land, but the reality was more often a sod hut and loneliness. Though a homestead could be registered for $10, a homesteader first had to cultivate the land, and own so many head of cattle. But the endless potential for a better future kept people coming from far and wide. Alberta's population rose from 73,000 in 1901 to 375,000 in 1911.

Hard Times

Life in Western Canada was hard around the turn of the century. The coal mines of Alberta and British Columbia were the most dangerous in the Americas: by the end of the century there were 23 fatal accidents for every million tonnes of coal extracted, while in the United States there were only six. In British Columbia, a strike by 7,000 miners looking to improve their working conditions lasted two years, from 1912 to 1914, and finally had to be broken by the Canadian army.

For the farmers who came here to grow wheat, the high cost of rail transport, lack of rail service, low wheat prices and bad harvests, along with duties too high to protect the fledgling industry in central Canada, all came together to make for miserable and desperate times. Certain arrangements improved the situation, like the establishment in 1897 of the Crow's Nest Pass rate for grain transport.

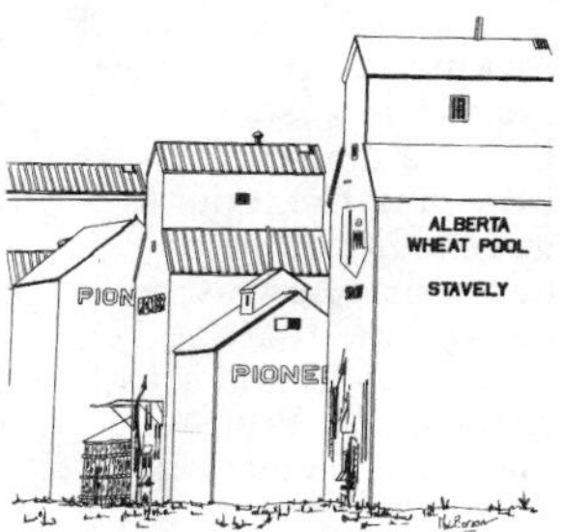

The First World War created a temporary boom, which lasted until 1920, causing a rise in the price of raw materials and wheat. The workers remained dissatisfied, though, and in 1919, the workers' unions of the West created their own central union, the One Big Union. As supporters of Russian Bolsheviks, the union's goal was to abolish capitalism. However, a general strike in Winnipeg, Manitoba quickly created a rift between the workers with respect to their objectives, and demonstrated Canada's determination not to let the country adopt Marxist ideology.

The 1920s again proved prosperous for the West, and Alberta and the prairie provinces, whose economies were essentially agricultural at the time, were able to finish clearing their territory.

The great crash of 1929 had a profound effect on Western Canada, in particular the Prairie provinces, which saw their agricultural revenues drop by 94% between 1929 and 1931! And the fact that their farms specialized almost exclusively in wheat made the situation even worse.

This period was marked by the evolution of two Western Canadian political movements, both of which remained almost

Prairie Cathedrals

There used to be a grain elevator and a town every 16km along the railway line that follows Highway 61, and throughout the Prairies for that matter.

The old elevator system was established in the 1880s and based on the premise that a farmer and his horse-drawn carriage could only haul grain a distance of 16km in one day. Long-haul trucks put an end to the need for so many elevators and the phasing out of a government transportation subsidy has forced the construction of a new generation of elevators.

The more sophisticated "high throughputs" can hold more grain, handle the drying and cleaning and load the grain more quickly into the railcars. As a result, grain elevators are being torn down so quickly that they will be extinct within 25 years, maybe sooner. The prairie towns that once depended on the elevators for the better part of their tax base are also losing a significant part of their histories.

The Provincial Museum of Alberta is searching for old photographs to preserve these cathedrals before the 1,153 elevators that still stood in the Prairies in the summer of 1997 are gone.

exclusively local, the Social Credit and the Co-operative Commonwealth Federation (CCF).

The doctrine of the Social Credit, which supported the small farmers' and workers' stand against the capitalist ascendancy by providing interest-free credit, reached its height under William Aberhart, who was elected premier of Alberta in 1935. His government dared to defy the capitalist system like no Canadian government ever had before (or has since). In 1936, Alberta refused to redeem any bonds, unilaterally cut the interest it was paying on its loans in half, started printing its own money, prohibited the seizure of assets for non-payment and even went so far as to force provincial newspapers to print the government's point of view. One by one, these Albertan laws were voided by the federal government or the Supreme Court of Canada, but Aberhart was so successful in making the population believe it was the victim of a conspiracy involving the federal government and capitalists that he was re-elected in 1940. He died in 1943 and was replaced by Ernest Manning, elected in 1944.

Manning got the party in order and eliminated all the anti-capitalist rhetoric from the party line. He dealt with all the controversy surrounding Alberta's debt, enabling the province to benefit once again from investment capital.

In 1947, large oil deposits were discovered, and from then on the province enjoyed unprecedented prosperity, thanks to royalties and foreign investment in the gas and petroleum industries.

The CCF, for its part reached its pinnacle in 1933 when it became the official opposition in British Columbia. An

Portrait

Preston Manning: Western Politics

Preston Manning, son of Ernest C. Manning, Premier of Alberta for 25 years, was born and raised on a dairy farm east of Edmonton. After working as a research and management consultant, Preston Manning founded the Reform Party in 1987 and lead it to an overwhelming success in the West in the 1993 and 1997 federal elections. With a platform based essentially on cost-cutting, Manning found tremendous support among westerners, who have always felt neglected by Ottawa and were fed up with federal over-spending. Many easterners find the Reform Party's raison-d'être to be divisive and not conducive to solving the country's constitutional crisis. Furthermore, its desire to cut funding for bilingual services and stories that do not quite mesh with the nice image of Canada as a multicultural country certainly haven't made Manning many friends among French-speaking Canadians.

outgrowth of the Socialist Party, workers' unions and farmers' associations, the party was never elected to power, but nevertheless influenced the political agenda and gave rise to the New Democratic Party (NDP).

At the beginning of the 20th century, Vancouver's economic focus shifted from Gastown to the Canadian Pacific Railway yards. Nevertheless, most local residents still earned their livelihood from the lumber and fishing industries and lived in makeshift camps on the outskirts of town. Economic ups and downs caused by the opening of the Panama Canal (1914), the end of World War I and the crash of 1929 plagued British Columbia, as the country began to focus its energies on its status as the railway terminal of Canada.

The Modern Era

Neither the Social Credit nor the CCF, two western parties, ever came to play an important role in federal politics. The arrival of John Diefenbaker, the first Canadian prime minister from the West, only further marginalized the two parties. Under Diefenbaker, a true representative of the West (Saskatchewan), as well as under the leadership of his successor, Lester B. Pearson, who truly understood the need to give the provinces more powers, the demands of the West almost seemed a thing of the past. They came to the fore once again, however, during the 1970s, when the oil crisis caused world markets to reel. Residents of oil-rich Alberta took particular offense at Prime Minister Trudeau's various attempts to weaken the provinces by imposing unpopular policies such as the transfer of control over natural resources to the federal government.

At the end of the 1970s, the oil boom, combined with an economic slowdown in Ontario and Québec, gave Alberta almost total employment and made it the province with the highest revenue per capita. This record performance cost Alberta some credibility when it came to its demands for larger control of its oil and gas. The split between the province and the federal government widened, and in the 1980 federal elections, the Liberal Party, the party ultimately brought to power, failed to elect any members of parliament from British Columbia or Alberta. The Liberals thus led the country until 1984 without any representation from these two provinces.

The National Energy Program tabled by the Trudeau government was the straw that broke the camel's back as far as Albertans were concerned. Under this program, the federal government was to claim a greater and greater share of the price of Canadian oil and natural gas, leaving only a very marginal amount of the profits generated by the explosion of the world markets for the provinces and producers. This appropriation by the federal government of natural resources that had been regulated and private since Confederation was strongly repudiated by Alberta and was one of the reasons, along with the repatriation of the Constitution without the consent of Québec in 1982, for the federal Liberals' defeat in the 1984 election. In the early '80s, separatist movements in Alberta succeeded in gaining the support of 20% of the population and in electing a member to the Alberta legislature in 1981.

Pierre Trudeau's Liberal government, which had led Canada almost continuously for 17 years, was succeeded by the Progressive Conservative government of Brian Mulroney, which did away with the much hated National Energy Program. Mulroney was unable, however, to maintain the support of westerners beyond his second mandate. The reasons for this are the same ones that cost him the federal elections of 1993: an inability to reduce the deficit left by the Trudeau government, large-scale corruption and discontent with many of his major decisions, including free trade with the United States and the Meech Lake constitutional accord.

Drawing on Western Canada's sense of alienation and the extreme-right's disappointment with the weakness of the Mulroney government, Preston Manning, an Albertan, founded the Reform Party in Vancouver in 1987. This party advocates, among other things, a smaller, less costly federal government and the reduction of federal expenditures. Westerners massively supported the Reform Party during the 1993 and 1997 elections.

Alberta's Legislature

At the same time, Quebecers massively supported the Bloc Québecois party, which favours an independent Québec. In the 1993 election the Bloc formed the official opposition in the federal parliament, while in 1997, the position was taken over by Reform, which maintained its popularity in the West and also gained ground in other regions of Canada. This last election, and the parliamentary distribution that resulted, illustrate the regionalism that exists in Canada and the potential risk of disintegration.

Talk of British Columbia separating first surfaced in the late 1980s and has resurfaced many times since. As a province whose economic well-being is more dependent on Asia than on the rest of Canada, it is naturally less interested in what goes on in Ottawa. This is further emphasized by the fact that its industries are heavily based on the exploitation of natural resources, and that these are for the most part provincially regulated, except fisheries. And the feeling goes both ways; Ottawa is not implicated in and therefore rarely spends much time on B.C. issues; its endless constitutional wrangling is that much more resented by British Columbians.

The New Democratic Party (NDP), a social-democratic party, is the governing party of three of the four western provinces, which indicates that following a difficult economic period, many Canadians are preoccupied by social issues.

The government of British Colombia is led by Ujjal Dosanjh, the first Indo-Canadian premier in Canada, who was elected NDP party leader in February 2000. Saskatchewan's NDP government has been led by Roy Romanow for several years and Gary Doer is head of Manitoba's NDP government.

Alberta is presently led by one of the most right-wing governments in Canada, Ralph Klein's Conservatives. They have chosen to concentrate on cutting the deficit, and so far the population is grateful that at least Alberta's debt has stopped growing.

The Canadian Political System

The constitutional document that forms the basis of the Canadian Confederation of 1867, the British North America Act, established a division of power between the two levels of government. This means that in addition to the Canadian government, located in Ottawa, each of the 10 provinces has its own government capable of legislating in certain areas. The Confederative Pact originally allowed for a decentralized division of powers, however, over the last 50 years, the Canadian government has tended away from this decentralization in areas traditionally within the jurisdiction of the provinces, thereby creating tensions between the two levels of government.

Based on the British model, Canada's political system, like those of the provinces, gives legislative power to a parliament elected by universal suffrage according to a single ballot vote with a simple majority. This method of voting usually leads to an alternation of power between two political parties. Besides the House of Commons, the federal government also consists of an Upper Chamber and the Senate, whose real powers are presently being curtailed and whose future remains uncertain.

The Economy

Alberta and British Columbia are the richest provinces in Canada, with a gross domestic product (GDP) of $30,000 and $27,000 per resident, respectively, compared to $22,200 for all of Canada. However, because of their smaller populations, their total GDP is less than Ontario's, even when added together.

Alberta, Saskatchewan and Manitoba are important grain producers; the Prairies produce almost all of Canada's wheat.

Manitoba's economy is not only agriculture-based but has a strong service sector and mining industry; 75 % of its mining concentrates on metals such as copper and zinc, and the province is the world's leading producer of nickel.

In addition to wheat, Saskatchewan grows canola, rye, oats, barley and flax. Its land feeds pigs and large herds of cattle and the dense northern forests keep the timber industry strong. Saskatchewan's subsoil is rich in minerals, such as petroleum, uranium, coal, natural gas and it is one of the largest exporters of potash.

Alberta is also the province with the most cattle ranches. Some 4 million head of cattle represent the largest portion of Alberta's agricultural output. These ranches are concentrated in the southern half of the province and in the foothills of the Rockies, where dry conditions and steep slopes make for poor farming conditions.

Although the oil boom is over, the petroleum industry is still vital to Alberta's economy, representing more than 10% of the GDP. Tourism, natural gas, coal, minerals, forestry and agriculture complete Alberta's economic pie.

In British Columbia, only 2% of the territory is used for agriculture, but it is carried out very efficiently. Dairy and poultry farms make up the majority of the province's agricultural production, while the cultivation of small fruits, vegetables and flowers represents an important share as well. Orchards fill the Okanagan Valley, while vast sheep and cattle ranches stretch across the centre of the province.

Forestry remains British Columbia's most important economic activity, representing more than 30% of the province's GDP. Mining is next, and tourism now occupies third place.

The Population

In the huge land mass that makes up Western Canada, the total population wavers around 8.8 million. While most have British, French or First Nations origins, many come from Asian or European families who immigrated here in the early 20th century or since.

Saskatchewan has a total population of 1,019,500. This province stands out from other Canadian provinces in that most of its population has origins other than British, French or First Nations. A substantial part of the population has German, Ukranian, Scandinavian, Dutch, Polish or Russian origins.

Sixty per cent of Manitoba's 1,138,934 inhabitants live in or around the capital. Interestingly, it is home to the largest Ukrainian cultural centre outside of the Ukraine. There is also an important Mennonite community, not to mention the 115,000 Metis and First Nations people.

The majority of Alberta's 2.7 million inhabitants lives in the southern part of the province, while 20% of the population lives in rural areas. Greater Edmonton has more than 873,000 residents, about 624,000 of whom live in the city itself; Calgary has 790,000 residents. Alberta's population is among the youngest in the western world; nearly two-thirds of the population is under 40 years of age

Alberta's, largest ethnic group is represented by descendants of homesteaders from the British Isles lured to the province at the turn of the century. The second largest group consists of Germans who migrated over a longer period. German Hutterites today live in closed communities throughout central and southern Alberta. They are recognizable by their particular, traditional dress. Ukrainians are the third largest group. They left their homeland, attracted by the promise of free land. The fourth largest ethnic group is French. Early French fur traders and missionaries were actually the first permanent settlers in the province. Other large ethnic groups include Chinese, Scandinavian and Dutch.

British Columbia has 3.9 million inhabitants, more than half of whom live in Greater

Vancouver; which has a population of 1.9 million; the city itself numbers 543,000. Victoria has 76,000 people and the provincial capital region 333,000. Over 90% of the province's territory belongs to the provincial government.

Even early on, British Columbia had a multi-ethnic population, but in the wake of the colonial era, residents of British descent still formed a large majority. A number of Americans came here during the gold rush, and soon after, the first wave of Chinese immigrants established Vancouver's Chinatown, which grew considerably after the completion of the Canadian Pacific railway (1886), a good part of which was built by Asian labourers. Before long, a Japanese community was born, further diversifying the city's "Pacific" profile. Today, Vancouver has over 200,000 residents of Asian descent.

British Columbia's cultural mosaic became that much richer in the 20th century, when immigrants from Europe (especially Germany, Poland, Italy and Greece) began arriving. In 1989, Vancouverites of British descent made up only about 30% of the total population. The French Canadian population, which has always been small in British Columbia, stands at about 29,000 (1986), while the Aboriginal population has dwindled to 12,000 (1991).

Only a small minority of westerners are able to express themselves in both of Canada's official languages, English and French. The English language dominates in this part of Canada. There is, however, a significant French presence in the province of Manitoba.

The West was settled in a few short years by people from a variety of ethnic backgrounds, and with no forerunners to either absorb or alienate them, these newcomers found that geography and history had created a Western Canadian subculture. They have always been inspired by their common future, rather than by their disparate pasts.

First Nations

After coming within a hair's breadth of vanishing completely, due to the illnesses to which they were exposed through their contact with European settlers in the late 19th century, the First Nations of the West are now seeing a substantial growth in their population. In 1870, there were fewer than 80,000 Aboriginals in British Columbia. In 1934, illnesses like scarlet fever, tuberculosis and smallpox, against which their immune system had not developed any antibodies, drove their population below 24,000. It has since climbed back up to nearly 100,000, accounting for about 3% of the province's total population.

Though the Aboriginal population is growing considerably, it would be incorrect to speak of a real "renaissance", since a number of nations, like the Coast Salish, who once inhabited the Vancouver region, have vanished forever, taking their rites and traditions along with them. Other communities have become highly visible, but their future is still uncertain. For example, the Haida of British Columbia, known for their beautiful totem poles, only number 2,500 (1991). In Alberta, there are 25,000 Cree, 11,000 Blackfoot and 4,500 Dakota but only 800 Sarcee and just 25 Sawridge.

Two thirds of western Aboriginals live on reservations. Some of these pieces of land are the size of Switzerland, while others aren't even as big Manhattan. A notable case in point is the Capilano reservation in North Vancouver, which barely covers three blocks and is completely surrounded by the city. The reservations were created by the Indian Act, adopted in 1867 by the federal government of Canada, and do not always correspond to the traditional territory of the various nations. Some have been laid out on the sites of former Catholic and Protestant missions, while others were stuck in remote and sometimes inhospitable locations. All the reservations are administered by a band council answerable to the Canadian Ministry of Indian and Northern Affairs.

Aboriginals living on reservations are entitled to certain privileges. They pay no income taxes, nor any goods and services taxes. They also have the right to free education from primary school through university. Finally, health-related expenses such as eye exams, glasses and dental care are paid by the State. Until the 1950s, the Indian Act also attempted to strip Aboriginal people of their traditional culture, by forbidding their languages, ceremonies and rituals were forbidden. Children were separated from their families and sent to boarding schools, where they were forced to learn and speak only English and to wear western clothing, to the extent that when the families were reunited, the parents and the children could no longer understand each other.

Since 1960, the Aboriginals of British Columbia have been struggling to revive their culture and traditions. The Haida artists of the Queen Charlotte Islands have become known around the world by organizing totem pole- and dug-out-canoe-carving festivals (Capilano Park Festival). In addition, a number of Nations have become involved in protecting the province's magnificent forests, viewed by some as a place of peace and harmony and by others as raw material waiting to be turned into shingles, furniture and paper. The demonstrations organized to preserve the old-growth forests of Vancouver Island have been marked by numerous clashes, pitting natives and ecologists on one side against loggers and big business on the other.

The Aboriginals of the Prairies face a gloomier situation than their British Columbian compatriots. Relegated to bleak lands in the late 19th century, after giving up their vast ancestral hunting grounds, these former nomads, who were forced to settle in one place, never really adapted to their new way of life. Serious drug and alcohol problems are undermining these Aboriginal individuals and communities, as can be seen, for example, on the streets of downtown Winnipeg.

The gradual disappearance of traditional grounds has given rise to aggressive territorial claims in most of Canada's provinces. With the help of the Assembly of First Nations, made up of several band chiefs, the First Nations are trying to advance their cause with government authorities, both federal and provincial.

Arts and Culture

Many Canadians have ambiguous feelings when it comes to their U.S. neighbours. American popular culture is omnipresent in their everyday lives. It is fascinating, but also troubling, and much time and energy is invested in defining just what distinguishes Canadian culture from that found south of the border. Nevertheless, countless extremely talented artists of all kinds have gained international renown and have established cultural trends that are uniquely Canadian.

The Canadian Radio-television and Telecommunications Commission (CRTC) supervises all types of broadcasting in Canada, ensuring, among other things, Canadian content. For example, non-Canadian songs are limited to 18 airings per week. Though this may seem restrictive, it has gone a long way to promoting Canadian music and television in all its forms and languages, and to ensuring that Canadian artists get a fair chance in an area that is all too often dominated by the sleeping giant to the south.

In the following pages we have identified some of the distinctive elements of the culture of this young region, in the hopes that travellers will be tempted to learn more during their visit.

Aboriginal Culture

Totemic culture is surely one of the greatest legacy of Canada's First Nations. This culture reached its height at the middle of the 19th century, and it is easy to imagine the wonder that the sight of 30 to 40 totem poles along the rivers leading to each Aboriginal village must have engendered in the first Europeans to settle in British Columbia. The totems were not revered like idols but featured elements relating to Aboriginal beliefs. The celebrated British Columbian painter Emily Carr (see below) visited many native villages, and some of her most beautiful paintings were inspired by totemic culture.

Unfortunately, totem poles do not stand up well against the ravages of weather, and the only ones that have survived to this day are those that have been preserved in parks and museums. Aboriginal art has always been linked to the beliefs of its producers, which were consistently viewed with suspicion by European missionaries, who did all they could to convert Aboriginal people. This ultimately led to a loss of interest in their art among Aboriginals themselves. Efforts were made in the1960s and 1970s to revive First Nations' cultures in northwestern British Columbia with the KSAN project, centred in the village of Hazelton (see p 261).

Visual Arts

Emily Carr

At the beginning of this century, Emily Carr, who had travelled extensively throughout British Columbia, produced magnificently beautiful paintings reflecting the splendid landscapes of the Pacific coast and revealing certain aspects of Aboriginal spirituality. Her blues and greens portray the captivating atmosphere of British Columbia. Several rooms at the Vancouver Art Gallery (see p 73) are devoted exclusively to her work. A pioneer of the West Coast art scene, she was followed by such great artists as Jack Shadbolt and Gordon Smith, whose work illustrates the unique vision that all inhabitants of this region have of the landscapes that surround them.

Chinese-Canadian Art

Canadians of Chinese extraction are the largest ethnic group in British Columbia. They are divided into two distinct groups. On the one side, there are the Cantonese, who settled in Canada after the construction of Canadian Pacific's transcontinental railroad at the end of the 19th century. These individuals suffered from poverty and pervasive racism until the 1960s, and were long restricted to thankless jobs. On the other side, there are the wealthy immigrants from Hong Kong, who display an almost arrogant confidence in re-establishing themselves and all their money in Canada.

This duality is reflected in the many and varied works of art produced by the Chinese-Canadian community. In addition, certain artists of Chinese origins want to develop their individual style and no longer wish to be associated with a particular ethnic group. One example is Diana Li's work *Communication* (from the exhibition Self not Whole, presented at the Chinese Cultural Centre in Vancouver in 1991). Other artists are more concerned with exorcising past injustices suffered by the Chinese community, like Sharyn Yuen, whose installation entitled *John Chinaman* (1990) looked back on the dismal lot of Chinese-Canadians living in the 1920s.

Literature

One of the earliest pieces of literature from the Canadian West is *David Thompson's Narrative of his Explorations in Western North American 1784-1812*. Earle Birney was born in Alberta, and was brought up there and in British Columbia. His belief that geography links people to their history is evident in his poetry and its attempts to define the significance of place and time.

Born in 1920 in the Yukon, which was overrun by gold-diggers in the 19th century, to a father who participated in the Klondike gold rush, Pierre Berton lived in Vancouver for many years. He has written many accounts of the high points of Canadian history including *The Last Spike* which recounts the construction of the pan-Canadian railway across the Rockies all the way to Vancouver.

Renowned for her powerful paintings of Canada's Pacific coast, Emily Carr wrote her first book at the age of 70, just a few years before her death. The few books she wrote are autobiographical works, which vividly portray the atmosphere of British Columbia and exhibit her extensive knowledge of the customs and beliefs of the First Nations.

Robert Kroetch and Rudy Wiebe are two of Alberta's most well-respected writers. Kroetch is a storyteller above all, and his *Out West* trilogy offers an in-depth look at Alberta over four decades. *Alberta* is part travel guide, part wonderful collection of stories and essays, and captures the essence of the land and people of Alberta. *Seed Catalogue* is another of his excellent works.

Rudy Wiebe is not a native Albertan but spent most of his life there. He was raised as a Mennonite, and the moral vision instilled in him by his religious background is the most important feature of his writing. *The Temptations of Big Bear*, for which he won the Governor General's Award, describes the disintegration of native culture caused by the growth of the Canadian nation.

Nancy Huston was born in Calgary, where she lived for 15 years. More than 20 years ago, after a five-year stay in New York City, she decided to relocate to Paris, where she finished her doctoral studies in semiology under the tutelage of Roland Barthes. After winning the Governor

General's Award in 1993 for her novel *Cantique des Plaines* (*Plainsong* in English) she became a major contributor to French-language literature. Since then she has published, among other works, *Tombeau de Romain Gary*, another brilliant work.

The writings of Jane Rule, an American who has lived in British Columbia since 1956, reflect a mentality that is typical of both the American and Canadian west. However, she is better known for her efforts to bridge the gap between the homosexual and heterosexual communities. Other notable western writers include poets Patrick Lane from British Columbia and Sid Marty from Alberta. Douglas Coupland is perhaps the province's best-know contemporary writer. (see inset)

Vancouver playwright George Ryga's play *Ecstasy of Rita Joe* marked a renewal for Canadian theatre in 1967. This work deals with the culture shock experienced by Aboriginal communities, who are inherently turned towards nature yet existing in a dehumanized western society. Albertan Brad Fraser's powerful play *Unidentified Human Remains or the True Nature of Love* analyzes contemporary love in an urban setting. The play was adapted for the cinema by Denys Arcand under the title *Love and Human Remains*.

Music

Western Canada is a cultured place with orchestras, operas and theatre. British Columbia, and more particularly cosmopolitan Vancouver has produced a variety of significant mainstream stars. Bryan Adams was actually born in Kingston, Ontario, but eventually settled in Vancouver. This Grammy-nominated rock 'n' roll performer is known the world over. Grammy-winner Sarah McLachlan, herself born in Halifax, Nova Scotia, now calls Vancouver home and has set up her own record label, Nettwerk, in the city.

In the case of Alberta, however, country music is perhaps more representative of the culture. This music has recently experienced a revival, entering the mainstream and moving up all sorts of country charts as well as pop charts. Calgarian Wilf Carter became famous in the United States as a yodelling cowboy. More recently k.d. lang, of Consort, Alberta became a Grammy-winning superstar. In her early days with the Reclines she was known for her outrageous outfits and honky-tonk style, but of late, her exceptional voice and blend of country and pop are her trademarks. A rarity in show business, she has always had the courage to be open about her homosexuality. Alberta also has its share of more mainstream stars, among them Jann Arden.

Loreena McKennitt, whose recordings featuring haunting Celtic melodies, have sold by the million in over 40 countries, was born and raised in Morden, Manitoba. She currently lives in Stratford, Ontario. Chantal Kreviazuk, a Juno-award- (Canadian equivalent of the Grammy) winning songstress and pianist, hails from Winnipeg, as do the Crash Test Dummies, whose first hit was the catchy *Superman's Song* in 1991.

As for Saskatchewan, its most famous daughter by far is popular folk singer Joni Mitchell. Born Joan Anderson in Fort McLeod, Alberta, Mitchell grew up in Saskatoon, Saskatchewan before heading south of the border, where she found fame and fortune.

Architecture

The sharp geographical contrast – it could even be called a clash – between British Columbia and the Prairies has led to the development of two very different styles of architecture - as is true of the other arts as well. The blanket of forests and mountains that covers two thirds of the Canadian West, combined with the coastal climate, which is much milder than in the rest of Canada, is juxtaposed with the bare Prairies, where the climatic conditions are among the harshest in Canada, and the deep snow is blown by violent winds during the long winter months.

The Aboriginal people were the first to adapt to these two extremes. Some developed a sedentary architecture with openings looking out onto the sea and the natural surroundings; others, a nomadic architecture designed primarily to keep out the cold and the wind. Thanks to the mild climate along the coast and the presence of various kinds of wood that were easy to carve, the Salish and the Haida were able to erect complex and sophisticated structures. Their totem poles, set up in front of longhouses made with the carefully squared trunks of red cedars, still stood along the beaches of the Queen Charlotte Islands near the end of the 19th century. These linear villages provided everyone with direct access to the ocean's resources. The ornamentation of the houses, sometimes reminiscent of Polynesia, indicates possible links between the Aboriginal peoples of British Columbia and the inhabitants of those faraway islands.

On the other side of the Rocky Mountains, the Prairie peoples turned the hides of bison to good account, using them to make clothing, build homes and even to make shields with which to defend themselves. Their homes, commonly known as tipis, could be easily taken down and packed up for transportation. They consisted of a thin cone-shaped structure made with the woody stems of shrubs and covered with hides sewn together with animal tendons.

The first Europeans to exploit the natural resources of the Canadian West took refuge in palisaded forts that doubled as fur trading posts during peacetime. They erected these rectangular structures between the mountains and the plains during the first half of the 19th century to protect themselves from warlike Aboriginals. Some interesting reconstructions can be found in a number of places.

On the West Coast, peace and easy living provided a fertile environment for the introduction of Loyalist architecture from Upper Canada, as evidenced by Victoria's St. Ann Schoolhouse (1848) and Wentworth Villa (1862). These structures are shingled and painted white, and have sash windows with small panes of glass. During the second half of the 19th century, this type of building quickly gave way to elaborate Victorian architecture, which made maximum use of the region's abundance of soft wood, which was easy to cut and turn mechanically.

Numerous sawmills in British Columbia started producing Gothic Revival balconies, Renaissance Revival cornices, Second Empire dormer windows and Queen Anne gables. California, located a few hundred kilometres to the south, left its mark starting in 1880, with the appearance of multiple oriels on British Columbia's facades.

Emily Carr House

Empress Hotel

These big, multi-level windows project out over the sidewalks, thus letting in lots of natural light.

With Canadian Pacific's construction of a transcontinental railroad and the opening of coal mines in Alberta and British Columbia, all sorts of new towns sprang up, each with its own destiny in store. During their first years of existence, all of them had boomtown architecture, characterized by rows of buildings with prefabricated wooden structures, often imported from eastern Canada, and a false front that concealed a smaller interior. Some of these façades were adorned with a prominent cornice or a whimsically shaped parapet.

The inauguration of the transcontinental railroad was also marked by the dismissal of the thousands of Chinese-born workers who had helped build it. These people settled in the towns of the West Coast, where they developed a hybrid architecture, adding deep Cantonese loggias and tiled roofs with turned-up edges to North American buildings (Chinese School of Victoria, 1909). This curious mixture marked the beginning of an oriental influence that continues to be felt to this day throughout the region.

In 1890, anxious to rid themselves of their backward, uncouth Far West image, the fledgling towns of the West destined for a bright future started using local and imported stone (red sandstone from Scotland, beige sandstone from Calgary, grey granite from Québec, limestone from Indiana) and adopting the Richardsonian Romanesque Revival style, in fashion in the rest of North America at the time. Calgary's Stephen Avenue Mall is still lined with these massive, rustic stone buildings, which are adorned with multiple arches framed by small columns with medieval-looking capitals. In the same spirit, but more Beaux-Arts in style, Vancouver, which only had 120,000 inhabitants in 1912, became the home of the tallest skyscraper in the British Empire (Sun Tower).

Upon completing its transcontinental railway in 1886, Canadian Pacific began building a nationwide network of luxury hotels and took particular interest in the Canadian West from the outset. It erected hotels and train stations in the Château style, which over the years became the company's trademark and the country's "national" style.

Banff Springs Hotel

The Banff Springs Hotel, erected in 1903, and the Empress Hotel in Victoria (1908), both graced with tall, sloping roofs and adorned with Renaissance details, at once reminiscent of the manors of Scotland and the châteaux of the Loire, are the finest examples.

These palaces contrast sharply with the modest Prairie farmhouses hastily erected by immigrants from Central Europe, large numbers of whom settled all over the Prairies in the early 20th century. The lines of some of these houses, now either abandoned or converted into museums, were vaguely inspired by the traditional architecture of old German, Hungarian, Polish and Ukrainian villages. In those days, the rural landscape was punctuated with thatched and orange-tiled, hipped roofs. In villages, it was not unusual to see wooden churches topped with onion domes.

Since then, Alberta's cattle ranches and farms have become gigantic businesses. The owner's house, often covered with standard white aluminum siding, is surrounded by several modern farm buildings, also covered with metal. The centres of these villages are no longer dominated by the bell tower of the local church, but rather by the huge grain elevators next to the railroad tracks.

At the beginning of the 20th century, British Columbia residents of English and Scottish extraction began developing a taste for the temperate natural environment in which they were living, and also seem to have become infatuated with the first part of their province's name. Lovely landscaped gardens full of flowers that couldn't survive anywhere else in Canada became all the rage, particularly in Vancouver and Victoria. In the midst of these magnificent green spaces, huge Tudor Revival and Arts and Crafts houses were built. These two styles originated in the so-called "back to basics" movement led by British immigrants.

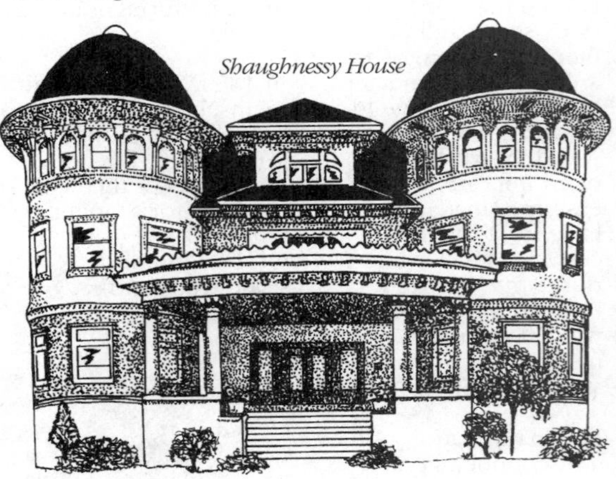
Shaughnessy House

The Tudor Revival style was inspired by the manors built in the English countryside under the reign of Henry VIII, and was characterized by the use of red-brick facing, bay windows with stone mullions and surbased gothic arches.

The Arts and Crafts movement, which could be described as both a craze for rural British crafts and a rejection of the industrialization of big cities, produced an organic architecture featuring extensions covered with different materials, ranging from half-timbering to walls made of stones from the beach. Everything was skillfully designed to produce an overall effect of great charm. The Vancouver architects Maclure and Fox excelled in this domain (Walter Nichol House, 1402 The Crescent, Shaughnessy Heights, Vancouver).

The public buildings erected during the same period, shaped more by their function, are more urban in style. Here, too, however, the emphasis was on British styles and architects. Sir Francis Rattenbury, who designed Victoria's Legislature and Vancouver's former courthouse (now the Vancouver Art Gallery), was the leading light of this prosperous era.

Sinclair Centre

Due to the severe economic crisis that hit British Columbia and the Prairies in the 1920s and 1930s, Art Deco, popular at the time in the rest of the western world, did not make much of an appearance here. There are, however, a few noteworthy examples of this style, including St. James Anglican Church (Adrian Gilbert Scott, 1935) and especially the Marine Building (McCarter and Nairne, 1929), both in Vancouver.

The end of World War II marked the beginning of a new era of unprecedented prosperity throughout the region. The birth of the oil industry in Alberta and the migration of thousands of Canadians to the West Coast, lured by the wonderfully mild climate and remarkable quality of life here, stimulated architectural research. Vancouver soon became one of the country's principal testing grounds for modern architecture. Influenced once again by nearby California, as well as by the Japan of the shoguns and by Haida art, West Coast architects started moving in a new direction.

Using wood, and then concrete, individuals like Robert Berwick, C.E. Pratt, Ron Thom and more recently Arthur Erickson designed buildings according to the elementary post and beam method, and erected them on the Coast Mountains. The pure lines of these structures blend into the luxuriant greenery that envelops the communal rooms, while the wall-to-wall picture windows that fill in the voids highlight the panoramas of the Pacific Ocean (Robert Berwick, Berwick House, 1560 Ottawa Avenue, Vancouver, 1939; Erickson and Massey, Gordon Smith house, The Byway, Vancouver, 1965). Until that time, only houses in the fishing ports of Vancouver Island had had any openings looking out onto the sea.

In Alberta, the prosperity of the 1970s and 1980s led to massive development in the cities of Edmonton and Calgary. Skyscrapers sprang up like mushrooms, changing both skylines considerably in just a decade. In Calgary, a network of skywalks known as the "+15" was put in place, so that office workers and shoppers could make their way from one building to another despite the winter cold. In addition, the sprawling suburbs of the two rival cities gobbled up several kilometres of the surrounding countryside. Both places are steeped in mainstream North American culture, as evidenced so clearly by the enormous West Edmonton Mall, where the "teachings" of Disneyworld and Las Vegas blend together in a whirl of gaudy commercialism.

However, since 1985, individuals like Douglas Cardinal, an Aboriginal architect from Red Deer, have been trying to develop a style more in harmony with the particularities of the Alberta plains. The undulating shapes of Cardinal's buildings, which look as if they have been sculpted by the violent winds that sweep the Prairies, have gained international recognition (Canadian Museum of Civilization, Hull, Quebec 1989). In the same spirit, Robert Leblond's design for the interpretive centre of Head-Smashed-In Buffalo Jump (see p 394) blends seamlessly into the land on which it is built.

Two events also drew the world's attention to the region in the 1980s. Expo '86 left Vancouver with a magnificent convention centre (see p 71) shaped like a sailing ship, while Calgary equipped itself with a saddle-shaped stadium, appropriately called the Saddledome (opened in 1983; see p 368) for the 1988 Winter Olympics. Both buildings clearly illustrate that the interaction between architecture and geography endures to this day in the Canadian West.

Canada Place

Practical Information

Information in this chapter will help visitors better plan their trip to Western Canada.

Entrance Formalities

Passport

For a stay of less than three months in Canada, a valid passport is usually sufficient for most visitors and a visa is not required. American residents do not need passports, though these are the best form of identification. A three-month extension is possible, but a return ticket and proof of sufficient funds to cover this extension may be required.

Caution: some countries do not have an agreement with Canada concerning health and accident insurance, so it is advisable to have the appropriate coverage. For more information, see the section entitled, "Health," on page 46.

Canadian citizens who wish to enter the United States, to visit Alaska or Washington State for example, do not need visas; neither do citizens of the majority of Western European countries. A valid passport is sufficient for a stay of less than three months. A return ticket and proof of sufficient funds to cover your stay may be required.

Extended Visits

Visitors must submit a request to extend their visit **in writing**, **before** the expiration of their visa (the date is usually written in your passport) to an Immigration Canada office. To make a request you must have a valid passport, a return ticket, proof of sufficient funds to cover the stay, as well as the $65 non-refundable filing-fee. In some cases (work, study), however, the request must be made **before** arriving in Canada.

Customs

If you are bringing gifts into Canada, remember that certain restrictions apply.

Smokers (*minimum age is 18 in Manitoba, Saskatchewan and Alberta, 19 in British Columbia*) can bring in a maximum of 200 cigarettes, 50 cigars, 400grams of tobacco, or 400 tobacco sticks.

For wine and alcohol the limit is 1.1litres; in practice, however, two bottles per person are usually allowed. The limit for beer is 24 355-ml size cans or bottles.

Plants, vegetation, and food: there are very strict rules regarding the importation of plants, flowers, and other vegetation; it is therefore not advisable to bring any of these products into the country. If it is absolutely necessary, contact the Customs-Agriculture service of the Canadian embassy before leaving your country.

Pets: if you are travelling with your pet, you will need a health certificate (available from your veterinarian) as well as a rabies vaccination certificate. The vaccination must have been administered at least 30 days before your departure and should not be more than a year old.

Tax reimbursements for visitors: it is possible to be reimbursed for certain taxes paid on purchases made in Canada (see p 55).

Embassies and Consulates

Canadian Embassies and Consulates Abroad

AUSTRALIA
Canadian Consulate General
Level 5, Quay West,
111 Harrington Rd
Sydney, N.S.W. Australia 2000
☎ ***(612) 364-3000***
⇄ ***(612) 364-3098***

BELGIUM
Canadian Embassy
2 Avenue de Tervueren,
1040 Brussels
☎ ***(2) 741-0611***
⇄ ***(2) 741.06.19***

DENMARK
Canadian Embassy
Kr. Bernikowsgade 1, DK=1105
Copenhagen K, Denmark
☎ ***(45) 12.22.99***
⇄ ***(45) 14.05.85***

FINLAND
Canadian Embassy
Pohjos Esplanadi 25 B, 00100
Helsinki, Finland
☎ ***(9) 171-141***
⇄ ***(9) 601-060***

GERMANY
Canadian Consulate General Internationales Handelzentrum
Friedrichstrasse 95, 23rd Floor
10117 Berlin, Germany
☎ ***(30) 261.11.61***
⇄ ***(30) 262.92.06***

GREAT BRITAIN
Canada High Commission
Macdonald House, One Grosvenor Sq., London W1X 0AB
England
☎ ***(171) 258-6600***
⇄ ***(171) 258-6384***

ITALY
Canadian Embassy
Via Zara 30, 00198 Rome
☎ ***(6) 44.59.81***
⇄ ***(6) 44.59***

NETHERLANDS
Canadian Embassy
Parkstraat 25, 2514JD The Hague, Netherlands
☎ ***(70) 361-4111***
⇄ ***(70) 365-6283***

NORWAY
Canadian Embassy
Oscars Gate 20, Oslo 3 Norway
☎ ***(47) 46.69.55***
⇄ ***(47) 69.34.67***

PORTUGAL
Canadian Embassy
MCB Building, Avenida
Liberdade no. 144, 2nd and 3rd floors, 1200 Lisboa
☎ ***213474892***
⇄ ***213476466***

SPAIN
Canadian Embassy
Edificio Goya, Calle Nunez de Balboa 35, 28001 Madrid
☎ ***(1) 423.32.50***
⇄ ***(1) 423.32.51***

SWEDEN
Canadian Embassy
Tegelbacken 4, 7th floor, Stockholm, Sweden
☎ ***(8) 613-9900***
⇄ ***(8) 24.24.91***

SWITZERLAND
Canadian Embassy
Kirchenfeldstrasse 88, 3000
Berne 6
☎ ***(31) 357.32.00***
⇄ ***(31) 357.32.10***

UNITED STATES
Canadian Embassy
501 Pennsylvania Ave. NW
Washington, DC, 20001
☎ ***(202) 682-1740***
⇄ ***(202) 682-7726***

Canadian Consulate General
Suite 400 South Tower, One CNN Center, Atlanta, Georgia, 30303-2705
☎*(404) 577-6810*
☎*(404) 577-1512*
⇌*(404) 524-5046*

Canadian Consulate General
Three Copley Place, Suite 400
Boston, Massachusetts, 02116
☎*(617) 262-3760*
⇌*(617) 262-3415*

Canadian Consulate General
180 N Two Prudential Plaza
Stetson Ave., Suite 2400 Chicago, Illinois, 60601
☎*(312) 616-1860*
⇌*(312) 616-1877*

Canadian Consulate General
St. Paul Place, Suite 1700
750 N. St. Paul St., Dallas, Texas 75201
☎*(214) 922-9806*
⇌*(214) 922-9815*

Canadian Consulate General
600 Renaissance Center
Suite 1100, Detroit, Michigan 48234-1798
☎*(313) 567-2085*
⇌*(313) 567-2164*

Canadian Consulate General
300 South Grande Ave.
10th Floor, California Plaza
Los Angeles, California, 90071
☎*(213) 687-7432*
⇌*(213) 620-8827*

Canadian Consulate General
Suite 900, 701 Fourth Ave. S
Minneapolis, Minnesota
55415-1899
☎*(612) 333-4641*
⇌*(612) 332-4061*

Canadian Consulate General
1251 Avenue of the Americas
New York, New York 10020-1175
☎*(212) 596-1600*
⇌*(212) 596-1793*

Canadian Consulate General
One Marine Midland Center
Suite 3000, Buffalo, New York
14203-2884
☎*(716) 852-1247*
⇌*(716) 852-4340*

Canadian Consulate General
412 Plaza 600, Sixth and Stewart Sts., Seattle, Washington 98101-1286
☎*(206) 442-1777*
⇌*(206) 443-1782*

Foreign Consulates in Western Canada

Australia

Australian Consulate:
888 Dunsmuir St., Vancouver
BC, V6C 3K4
☎*(604) 684-1177*

Belgium

Honourary Consulate of Belgium:
Birks Place, Suite 570, 688 West Hastings, Vancouver, BC
V6B 1P4
☎*(604) 684-6838*

Honourary Consulate of Belgium:
107-4990 92nd Ave., Edmonton
AB, T6B2V4
☎*(780) 496-9565*

Honourary Consulate of Belgium:
Winnipeg
☎*(204) 261-1415*

Denmark

Danish Consulate:
1235 11th Ave. SW, Calgary, AB
T3C 0M5
☎*(403) 245-5755*

Royal Danish Consulate:
10235 101 St. NW, Suite 1112
Edmonton, AB, T5J 3G1
☎*(780) 426-1457*

Danish Consulate:
1801 Hamilton St.
Regina, SK
☎*(306) 787-4750*

Honourary Consulate of Denmark:
239 Aubert, Winnipeg, MB
R2H 3G8
☎*(204) 233-8541*

Finland

Consulate of Finland:
1188 Georgia St. W., Apt. 1100
Vancouver, BC, V6E 4A2
☎*(604) 688-4483*

Consulate of Finland:
10303 Jasper Ave. NW
Suite 1130, Edmonton, AB
T5J 1Y5
☎*(780) 426-7865*

Honourary Consulate of Finland:
Winnepeg, MB
☎*(204) 837-6466*

Finnish Consulate:
2010 11th Avenue, Regina, SK
S4P 0J3
☎*(306) 565-5111*

Germany

Consulate General of Germany:
World Trade Centre, 999 Canada Place, Suite 704, Vancouver, BC
V6C 3E1
☎*(604) 684-8377*

Consulate General of Germany:
3127 Bowwood Dr. NW, Calgary
AB, T3B 2E7
☎ ***(403) 247-3357***

Honourary Consul of Germany:
8003 102 St. NW, Suite 201
Edmonton, AB, T6E 4A2
☎ ***(780) 434-0340***

Honourary Consulate of Germany:
1200 Pembina, Winnipeg, MB
R3T 2A7
☎ ***(204) 475-3088***

German Consulate:
3534 Argyle Rd., Regina, SK
S4S 2B8
☎ ***(306) 586-8762***

Great Britain
British Consulate General:
111 Melville St., Suite 800
Vancouver, BC, V6E 3V6
☎ ***(604) 683-4421***

ITALY
Consulate General of Italy:
1200 Burrard St., Suite 705
Vancouver, BC, V6Z2C7
☎ ***(604) 684-7288***
⇄ ***(604)685-4263***

Consulate General of Italy:
1900 Merrill Lynch Tower
Edmonton, AB, T5J 2Z2
☎ ***(780) 423-5153***

Honourary Consulate of Italy:
1044 Wilkes, Winnipeg
R3P 1C1
☎ ***(204) 488-8745***

NETHERLANDS
Consulate General of the Netherlands:
475 Howe St., Suite 821, Vancouver, BC, V6C 2B3
☎ ***(604) 684-6448***

Consulate General of the Netherlands:
10214 112 St. NW, Edmonton
AB, T5K 1M4
☎ ***(780) 428-7513***

Consulate of The Netherlands:
304 Eight Ave. SW, Suite 708
Calgary, AB, T2P 1C2
☎ ***(403) 266-2710***

Consulate of The Netherlands:
2432 14th Ave., Regina SK
S4P 0Y3
☎ ***(306) 522-8081***

Honourary Consulate of The Netherlands:
69 Shorecrest, Winnipeg, MB
R3P 1N9
☎ ***(204) 487-1211***

NORWAY
Royal Norwegian Consulate General:
1200 Waterfront Centre
200 Burrard St., Vancouver, BC
V6C 3L6
☎ (604) 682-7977
⇄ (604) 682-8376

Royal Norwegian Consulate:
P.O. Box 577, CDN Victoria, BC
V8W 2P5
☎ ***(604) 384-1174***
⇄ ***(604) 382-3231***

Royal Norwegian Consulate:
1753 North Tower, Western Canadian Place, 707 8th Ave. SW, P.O. Box 6525, Station D
Calgary, AB, T2P 3G7
☎ ***(403) 263-2270***
⇄ ***(403) 298-6081***

Royal Norwegian Consulate:
2310 80th Ave. NW, P.O. Box 5584, Edmonton, AB, T5C 4E9
☎ ***(780) 440-2292***
⇄ ***(780) 440-1241***

PORTUGAL
Consulate of Portugal
700 Pender St. W.
Vancouver, BC, V6C 1G8
☎ ***(604) 683-3674***

Honorary Consulate of Portugal
167 Lombard Ave.,
Winnipeg, MB, R3B 0T6
☎ ***(204) 943-8941***

SPAIN
Consulate General of Spain:
There is no Spanish consulate in Western Canada. If you have any inquiries, contact the consulate general in Toronto:
200 Front St. W., Toronto, Ont.
M5V 3K2
☎ ***(416) 977-1661***
⇄ ***(416) 593-4949***

SWEDEN
Consulate of Sweden:
1188 Georgia St. W., Apt. 1100
Vancouver, BC, V6E 4A2
☎ ***(604) 683-5838***

Consulate of Sweden:
1039 Durham Ave. SW, Calgary
AB, T2T 0P8
☎ ***(403) 541-0354***

Consulate of Sweden:
10104 103rd Ave. NW,
Suite 2500, Edmonton, AB
T5J 1V3
☎ ***(780) 421-2482***

Consulate of Sweden:
2550 15th Ave., Suite 325,
Regina, SK, S4P 1A5
☎ ***(306) 359-3300***

SWITZERLAND
Consulate General of Switzerland:
999 Canada Place, Vancouver
BC, V6C 3E1
☎ ***(604) 684-2231***

Honourary Consulate of Switzerland:
1245 Henderson, Winnipeg, MB R2G 1M1
☎ ***(204) 338-4242***

UNITED STATES
U.S. Consulate General:
1095 West Pender, Vancouver BC, V6E 2M6
☎ ***(604) 685-4311***

U.S. Consulate General:
625 Macleod Trail SE
Suite 1050, Calgary, AB T26 4T8
☎ ***(403) 266-8962***
⇌ ***(403) 264-6630***

Tourist Information

Each of the four provinces covered in this guide has a Ministry of Tourism in charge of promoting tourism development in its respective province. Tourist information is distributed to the public by regional offices. You can get details on the sights, restaurants and hotels in the region. Besides these numerous information centres, most large cities also have their own tourism associations. These offices are open year-round, whereas the regional offices are generally only open in the high season. The addresses of the various regional tourist information offices are located in the "Practical Information" section of each chapter.

Before Leaving

The following provincial tourism offices will gladly mail you general information on their province, or consult their Internet sites:

Super, Natural British Columbia (*Box 9830, Station Province-Government, Victoria, V8W9W5,* ☎ *1-800-663-6000, www.travel.bc.ca*) can provide information on and reservations for travelling in British Columbia.

Tourism British Columbia
Parliament Buildings
Victoria BC V8V 1X4
☎ ***800-HELLO-BC toll free in North America***
☎ ***(250) 387-1642***
☎ ***(604) 435-5622 Vancouver***
www.tourismkiosk.com
www.travel.bc.ca

Travel Alberta
Box 2500
Edmonton, Alberta
T5J 2Z1
☎ ***(403) 297-2700***
⇌ ***(403) 297-5068***
info@travelalberta.com
www.travelalberta.com

Travel Manitoba
155 Carleton St., 7th Floor
Winnipeg, MB, R3C 3H8
☎ 800-665-0040
☎ (204) 945-3777
www.travelmanitoba.com

Tourism Saskatchewan
1900 Albert St., Suite 500
Regina, SK, S4P 4L9
☎ (306) 787-2300
☎ 877-2ESCAPE
⇌ ***(306) 787-5744***
www.sasktourism.com

Canada:
www.city.net/countries/canada

Getting to Western Canada

By Plane

From Europe

There are two possibilities: direct flights or flights with a stopover in Montréal, Toronto or Calgary. Direct flights are, of course, much more attractive since they are considerably faster than flights with a stopover (for example expect about nine hours from Amsterdam for a direct flight compared to 13 hours). In some cases, however, particularly if you have a lot of time, it can be advantageous to combine a charter flight from Europe with one of the many charter flights within Canada from either Montréal or Toronto. Prices for this option can vary considerably depending on whether you are travelling during high or low season.

The major airlines flying to western Canada are **Air Canada, KLM**, **Air France** and **British Airways.**

For more information:
Air Canada
☎ ***800-361-8620*** (from Europe)
☎ ***888-247-2262*** (from Canada and the United States)

Practical Information

From the United States

American Airlines, Delta Airlines, Northwest Airlines, United Airlines, Air Canada and their affiliates offer daily direct or connecting flights between major US. and western Canadian cities.

From Oceania

Air Canada, in cooperation with United Airlines, offers three daily flights from Sydney to Vancouver via Los Angeles or San Francisco; one continues on to Calgary.

Quantus flies twice daily between Sydney and Los Angeles, from where there are connector flights to Vancouver and other western Canadian cities.

Air Canada Offices

AUSTRALIA
Level 12 - 92 Pitt St., Sydney
☎(61-2) 9232 5222
Inwats: 1-300 656 232
⇌(61-2) 9223 7606

NEW ZEALAND
Dingwall Building 3/F
87 Queen Street, Auckland
☎(64-9) 379 3371
⇌(64-9) 302 2912

From Asia

Both Air Canada and Canadian International offer direct flights between Vancouver and Hong Kong.

Air Canada Offices

HONG KONG
Room 1601-4 Wheelock House
20 Pedder Street Central
☎(852) 2522 1001
⇌(852) 2810 1117

Within Canada

Air Canada has just bought Canadian International, but both are being administered as separate entities until spring 2000. With their respective local partners (**Air BC** offers flights within Alberta and British Columbia, as does Canadian Airlines' regional partner, **Canadian Regional**), these companies offer regular and connecting flights to Western Canada. Daily flights to the cities of Vancouver, Victoria, Edmonton and Calgary as well as many other cities are offered from all the major cities in the country. Flights from eastern Canada often have stop-overs in Montréal or Toronto. For example Air Canada flies to Vancouver, Calgary, Edmonton and Victoria 14 times a week. During the high season, the charter companies such as **Air Transat, Royal** and **Canada 3000** offer flights to Vancouver and Calgary. These flights are subject to change regarding availability and fares.

Air Canada

☎888-247-2262
(Canada and the United States)

Canadian International

All Provinces and Territories
☎800-665-1177

Hearing Impaired (TTY)
☎800-465-3611
(Continental US/Canada)

U.S.A
(Including Hawaii)
☎800-426-7000

Airports

Vancouver International Airport (***☎604-276-6101, www.yvr.ca***) is served by flights from across Canada, the United States, Europe and Asia. Nineteen airline companies presently use the airport. The airport is located 15km from downtown. It takes about 30min to get downtown by car or bus. A taxi or limousine will cost you about $25-$30, or you can take the **Airporter** (*☎604-946-8866 or 800-688-3141*), which offers shuttle service to the major downtown hotels, the bus depot and the ferries (*$10 one-way or $17 return; departures: every 15min from 6:30am to 12:10am*). To reach downtown by public transit take Bus #100 for downtown and points east and Bus #404 for Richmond, Delta and points south. Take note: even if you have already paid various taxes included in the purchase price of your ticket, Vancouver International Airport charges every passenger an **Airport Improvement Fee (AIF)**. The fee is $5 for flights within B.C. and to the Yukon, $10 for flights elsewhere in North America, and $15 for overseas flights; credit cards are accepted, and most in-transit passengers are exempted. Besides the regular airport services (*duty-free shops, cafeterias, restaurants, etc.*) you will also find an exchange office. Several car rental companies also have offices in the airport, including **Avis, Thrifty, National, Hertz, Alamo Rent-a-Car** and **Budget**.

Victoria International Airport (☎*250-953-7500*) is 27km from downtown Victoria and the second largest airport in British Columbia. There is an exchange office open from 6am to 9pm. Several car rental companies, including Avis, Budget, Hertz and National Tilden have offices at the airport. Taxis and limousines can bring you downtown for about $38. The **AKAL Airport Shuttle** (☎*250-386-2525*) provides transportation to the major downtown hotels. The cost is $13 one-way or $23 return for adults.

Calgary International Airport (☎*403-735-1200*) is the largest airport in the province of Alberta and the fourth busiest in Canada. There is a currency exchange office open from 6am to 9pm. Taxis and limousines can take you downtown for about $25, while the **Airport Direct** (*every day 5am to midnight;* ☎*888-642-5252*) shuttle bus takes passengers downtown. Several car-rental companies have offices at the airport, including Avis, Thrifty, Dollar, Hertz, Budget and Tilden.

Two shuttles run between Calgary International Airport and Banff, Lake Louise and Jasper: **Brewster** (☎*800-661-1152 or 403-221-8242, www.brewster.ca*) charges $36 to Banff, $41 to Lake Louise and $71 to Jasper, all one-way, and the **Banff Airporter** (☎*888-449-2901 or 403-762-3330*) charges $34 one-way to Banff.

Calgary International Airport charges an Airport Improvement Fee (AIF) of 10$.

Edmonton International Airport (☎*780-890-8382 or 800-268-7134, www.edmontonairports.com*) is the second largest airport in the province. A taxi or limousine from the airport downtown is about $30, while the **Sky Shuttle** (☎*780-465-8515 or 800-268-7134*) costs $11 one-way or $18 return. It passes every 20min on weekends and every 30min during the week. Several car-rental companies have offices at the airport. They include Avis, Thrifty, Budget, National Tilden and Hertz. Edmonton International Airport recently began collecting an **Airport Improvement Fee (AIF)**. It is payable when you clear security in cash (CA or US) or by credit cards, debit cards or travellers cheques. The cost is $5 for passengers travelling withing Alberta and $10 for those leaving the province. Passengers in transit are not charged.

To get to Saskatoon's **John Glk Diefenbaker Airport** (☎*306-975-8900*), head directly north of the city approximately 7km. A chain of motels marks the approach. It is about a $12 taxi ride from downtown. There is no shuttle bus.

Regina Airport (☎306-761-7561) lies just 5km southwest of the city; a cab costs about $10. The shuttle bus goes to the hotels (*$7; 6pm to 1am*)

Winnipeg International Airport (www.waa.ca) is situated surprisingly close to the downtown area, only about 5km away. The two major Canadian airlines (Air Canada and Canadian International) have offices inside the airport.

By Train

Travellers who are not rushed for time may want to consider the train, one of the most pleasant and impressive ways to discover Western Canada. Via Rail Canada is the only company that offers train travel between the Canadian provinces. This mode of transportation can be combined with air travel (various packages are offered by Air Canada and Canadian Airlines) or on its own from big cities in Eastern Canada like Toronto or Montreal. This last option does require a lot of time however, it takes a minimum of five days to get from Montreal to Vancouver. The transcontinental railway passenger service runs three times a week. Note that it does not travel through Calgary, it follows a more northern route through Edmonton and Jasper and then on to Vancouver.

The CANRAILPASS
☎888-842-7245
www.viarail.ca
This pass offers unlimited travel in economy class for a period 12 days in one month. This package is an economical way of seeing the country.

Beginning on April 26, 2000, the **Rocky Mountaineer** (*☎800-665-7245, www.rkymtnrail.com*) will offer service between Vancouver and Banff, with some magnificent scenery along the way. Different discounts are offered.

BC Rail (*1311 West First St., North Vancouver, ☎604-984-5246*) trains travel the coast. Schedules vary depending on the seasons.

There is daily service aboard Amtrak's **Mount Baker International** from Seattle, Washington, to Vancouver; the trip takes 3hrs and follows a scenic route. For reservations or information call **Amtrak US Rail** at ***1-800-USA-RAIL*** or ***1-800-872-7245*** (*toll-free in North America*).

See the "Finding Your Way Around" sections throughout this guide for train station addresses.

By Car

The best way to see Western Canada at your own pace is by car, especially when you consider the excellent road conditions and the price of gas, which is as little as one-third the price in Europe. An extensive network of roads links the United States and Canada as well as the eastern provinces with the rest of the country. The most famous of these is by far the impressive Trans-Canada Highway which links Saint John's in Newfoundland with Victoria in British Columbia.

Driver's licenses from western European countries are valid in Canada and the United States. While North American travellers won't have any trouble adapting to the rules of the road in Western Canada, European travellers may need a bit more time to get used to things.

Here are a few hints:

Pedestrians: Drivers in Western Canada are particularly courteous when it comes to pedestrians, and willingly stop to give them the right of way, even in the big cities, so be careful when and where you step off the curb. Pedestrian crosswalks are usually indicated by a yellow sign. When driving, pay special attention that no one is about to cross near these signs. Turning right on a red light when the way is clear is permitted in Western Canada.

When a school bus (usually yellow in colour) has stopped and has its signals flashing, you must come to a complete stop, no matter what direction you are travelling in. Failing to stop at the flashing signals is considered a serious offense, and carries a heavy penalty.

Table of distances (km/mi)

Via the shortest route

Vancouver (BC)	Red Deer (AB)	Prince Rupert (BC)	Prince George (BC)	Penticton (BC)	Medicine Hat (AB)	Lethbridge (AB)	Kamloops (BC)	Jasper (AB)	Grande Prairie (AB)	Fort St. John (BC)	Edmonton (AB)	Campbell River (BC)	Calgary (AB)	Banff (AB)	
															Banff (AB)
														130	Calgary (AB)
													281	1068	Campbell River (BC)
												1477	278	408	Edmonton (AB)
											655	1456	1290	881	Fort St. John (BC)
										207	447	1636	1470	674	Grande Prairie (AB)
									395	603	365	1240	1075	278	Jasper (AB)
								661	1057	970	898	579	413	489	Kamloops (BC)
							843	632	949	1157	502	1422	1256	354	Lethbridge (AB)
						165	906	695	1012	1219	564	1485	1319	416	Medicine Hat (AB)
					967	904	247	722	1118	1189	959	646	481	550	Penticton (BC)
				733	1070	1007	514	374	542	455	740	1001	835	653	Prince George (BC)
			733	1461	1804	1741	1242	1108	1276	1189	1474	708	989	1387	Prince Rupert (BC)
		1652	918	815	421	358	754	543	582	790	135	1334	1168	265	Red Deer (AB)
	1102	941	769	415	1253	1190	347	1009	1404	1224	1245	233	967	836	Vancouver (BC)
106	1168	989	835	481	1319	1256	413	1075	1470	1290	1311	271	1033	902	Victoria (BC)

Example: The distance between Jasper (AB) and Penticton (BC) is 722 km.

Wearing of seatbelts in the front and back seats is mandatory at all times.

Almost all highways in Western Canada are toll-free, and just a few bridges have tolls. The speed limit on highways is 100km/h. The speed limit on secondary highways is 90km/h, and 50km/h in urban areas.

Gas Stations: Because Canada produces its own crude oil, gasoline prices in Western Canada are much less expensive than in Europe, and only slightly more than in the United States. Some gas stations (especially in the downtown areas) might ask for payment in advance as a security measure, especially after 11pm.

Winter driving: Though roads are generally well plowed, particular caution is recommended. Watch for violent winds and snow drifts and banks. In some regions gravel is used to increase traction, so drive carefully.

Always remember that wildlife abounds near roads and highways in Western Canada. It is not unheard of to come face to face with a deer only minutes from Calgary. Pay attention and drive slowly, especially at nightfall and in the early morning.

If you do hit a large animal, try to contact the **Royal Canadian Mounted Police (RCMP)**. Dial ***0*** or ***911*** to reach the police.

Certain roads in northern British Columbia and Alberta are not paved. Make sure you rent the appropriate vehicle (4-wheel drive, high clearance) if you plan on covering any rough terrain.

Car Rentals

Packages including air travel, hotel and car rental or just hotel and car rental are often less expensive than car rental alone. It is best to shop around. Remember also that some companies offer corporate rates and discounts to auto-club members. Some travel agencies work with major car rental companies (Avis, Budget, Hertz, etc.) and offer good values; contracts often include added bonuses (reduced ticket prices for shows, etc.).

When renting a car, find out if the contract includes unlimited kilometres, and if the insurance provides full coverage (accident, property damage, hospital costs for you and passengers, theft).

Certain credit cards, gold cards for example, cover the collision and theft insurance. Check with your credit card company before renting.

To rent a car you must be at least 21 years of age and have had a driver's license for at least one year. If you are between 21 and 25, certain companies (for example Avis, Thrifty, Budget) will ask for a $500 deposit, and in some cases they will also charge an extra sum for each day you rent the car. These conditions do not apply for those over 25 years of age.

A credit card is extremely useful for the deposit to avoid tying up large sums of money.

Most rental cars come with an automatic transmission, however you can request a car with a manual shift.

Child-safety seats cost extra.

See the "Finding Your Way Around" sections throughout this guide for local car rental outlets.

Accidents and Emergencies

In case of serious accident, fire or other emergency dial ☎***911*** or ***0***. If you run into trouble on the highway, pull onto the shoulder of the road and turn the hazard lights on. If it is a rental car, contact the rental company as soon as possible. Always file an accident report. If a disagreement arises over who was at fault in an accident, ask for police help.

By Ferry

BC Ferries serves 47 ports of call on 25 routes throughout coastal British Columbia. The crossings between Vancouver Island and B.C.'s Lower Mainland take between 90min and 2hrs. Shorter hops include service to the Gulf Islands, and to communities along the Sunshine Coast, northwest of Vancouver. For more of a cruise experience, you can travel British Columbia's majestic Inside Passage, from Port Hardy at the northern end of Vancouver Island to Prince Rupert. Reservations are a must for this trip and for the 8hr crossing from Prince Rupert to the Queen Charlotte Islands. BC Ferries has introduced a new summer route between Port Hardy and Bella Coola. This area is called the Discovery Coast Passage, because it reveals a part of the province that until now was difficult to reach.

For information on all these routes contact:

BC Ferries
☎1-888-BCFERRY
250-386-3431 or
604-669-1211
⇄250-381-5452
www.bcferries.bc.ca

Also see the appropriate "Finding Your Way Around" sections in this guide.

By Bus

Extensive and inexpensive, buses cover most of Canada. Except for urban transportation, there is no government run-service. Several private companies service the country.

Greyhound Canada
☎1-800-661-8747
www.greyhound.ca
Greyhound services all the lines in Western Canada in cooperation with local companies like Orléans in Québec. Here are some sample one-way fares:

Calgary to Vancouver:
$116, $233 return
Calgary to Regina:
$90, $183 return
Regina to Winnipeg:
$60, $120 return

See the "Finding Your Way Around" sections throughout this guide for local bus stations.

Smoking is forbidden on all lines and pets are not allowed. Generally children five years old or younger travel for free and people aged 60 or over are eligible for discounts.

An economic way of travelling long distances by bus in Canada is with the International Coach Pass, a package offering discounts on selected trips between seven days and two months.

Insurance

Cancellation

Your travel agent will usually offer you cancellation insurance when you buy your airline ticket or vacation package. This insurance allows you to be reimbursed for the ticket or package deal if your trip must be cancelled due to serious illness or death.

Theft

Most residential insurance policies protect some of your goods from theft, even if the theft occurs in a foreign country. To make a claim, you must fill out a police report. It may not be necessary to take out further insurance, depending on the amount covered by your current home policy. As policies vary considerably, you are advised to check with your insurance company. European visitors should take out baggage insurance.

Health

This is the most useful kind of insurance for travellers, and should be purchased before your departure. Your insurance plan should be as complete as possible because health care costs add up quickly. When buying insurance, make sure it covers all types of medical costs, such as hospitalization, nursing services and doctor's fees. Make sure your limit is high enough, as these expenses can be costly. A repatriation clause is also vital in case the required care is not available on site. Furthermore, since you may have to pay immediately, check your policy to see what provisions it includes for such situations. To avoid any problems during your vacation, always keep proof of your insurance policy on your person.

Climate and Packing

Climate

The climate of Western Canada varies widely from one region to another. The Vancouver area benefits from a sort of micro-climate thanks to its geographic location between the Pacific and the mountains. Temperatures in Vancouver vary between 0°C and 15°C in the winter and much warmer in the summer.

The high altitudes of the Rocky Mountains and the winds of the Prairies make for a varied climate throughout the rest of the region. Winters are cold and dry and temperatures can drop to -40°C, though the average is about -15°C. Winters in southern Alberta are often marked by the phenomenal Chinook wind which can melt several feet of snow is a matter of hours. Summers are dry, with temperatures staying steady around 25°C on the plains and lower in the mountains.

Winter

December to March is the ideal season for winter-sports enthusiasts (skiing, skating, etc.). Warm clothing is essential during this season (coat, scarf, hat, gloves, wool sweaters and boots). Winnipeg and Saskatoon are the coldest cities in Canada in winter. Vancouver on the other hand, has a particularly wet winter so don't forget your raincoat. In southwestern British Columbia the mercury rarely falls below 0 C°.

Spring and Fall

Spring is short (end of March to end of May) and is characterized by a general thaw leading to wet and muddy conditions. Fall is often cool. A sweater, scarf, gloves, windbreaker and umbrella will therefore come in handy.

Summer

Summer lasts from the end of May to the end of August. Bring along T-shirts, lightweight shirts and pants, shorts and sunglasses; a sweater or light jacket is a good idea for evenings. If you plan on doing any hiking, remember that temperatures are cooler at higher altitudes.

Health

General Information

Vaccinations are not necessary for people coming from Europe, the United States, Australia and New Zealand. On the other hand, it is strongly suggested, particularly for medium or long-term stays, that visitors take out health and accident insurance. There are different types so it is best to shop around. Bring along all medication, especially prescription medicine. Unless otherwise stated, the water is drinkable throughout British Columbia and Alberta.

During the summer, always protect yourself against sunburn. It is often hard to feel your skin getting burned by the sun on windy days. Do not forget to bring sun screen!

Canadians from outside British Columbia or Alberta should take note that in general your province's health-care system will only reimburse you for the cost of any hospital fees or procedures at the going rate in your province. For this reason, it is a good idea to get additional private insurance. In case of accident or illness make sure to keep your receipts in order to be reimbursed by your province's health care system.

Emergencies

In case of emergency (police, fire department, ambulance), dial ☎*911*.

Accommodations

A wide choice of types of accommodation to fit every budget is available in most regions of Western Canada. Most places are very comfortable and offer a number of extra services. Prices vary according to the type of accommodation and the quality/price ratio is generally good, but remember to add the 7% GST (federal Goods and Services Tax) and the provincial sales tax of 7% in British Columbia and Saskatchewan, and 6% in Manitoba; Alberta has no provincial sales tax, though there is a 5% tax on lodging. The GST is refundable for non-residents in certain cases (see p55). A credit card will make reserving a room much easier, since in many cases payment for the first night is required.

Many hotels offer corporate discounts as well as discounts for automobile club (CAA, AAA) members. Be sure to ask about these special rates, as they are generally very easy to obtain. Furthermore, check in the travel brochures given out at tourist offices as there are often coupons inside.

Hotels

Hotels rooms abound, and range from modest to luxurious. Most hotel rooms come equipped with a private bathroom. There are several internationally reputed hotels in Western Canada, including several beauties in the Canadian Pacific chain.

Inns

Often set up in beautiful historic houses, inns offer quality lodging. These establishments are plentiful and usually more charming and picturesque than hotels. Many are furnished with beautiful period pieces. Breakfast is often included.

Bed and Breakfasts

Unlike hotels or inns, rooms in private homes are not always equipped with a private bathroom. Bed and breakfasts are well distributed throughout Western Canada, in the country as well as the city. Besides the obvious price advantage, is the unique family atmosphere. Credit cards are not always accepted in bed and breakfasts.

Motels

There are many motels throughout the province, and though they tend to be cheaper, they often lack atmosphere. These are particularly useful when pressed for time.

Youth Hostels

Youth hostel addresses are listed in the "Accommodations" section for the cities in which they are located.

University Residences

Due to certain restrictions, this can be a complicated alternative. Residences are generally only available during the summer (mid-May to mid-August); reservations must be made several months in advance, usually by paying the first night with a credit card.

This type of accommodation, however, can be less costly than the "traditional" alternatives, and making the effort to reserve early can be worthwhile. Visitors with valid student cards can expect to pay approximately $25 plus tax. Bedding is included in the price, and there is usually a cafeteria in the building (meals are not included in the price).

Camping

Next to being put up by friends, camping is the most inexpensive form of accommodation. Unfortunately, unless you have winter-camping gear, camping is limited to a short period of the year, from June to August. Services provided as well as prices vary considerably, from $8 to $20 or more per night, depending on whether the site is private or public.

Restaurants

There are several excellent restaurants throughout western Canada. The local specialties are without a doubt Pacific salmon and Alberta beef. Every city has a wide range of choices for all budgets, from fast food to fine dining.

Prices in this guide are for a meal for one person, excluding drinks and tip.

$	***less than $10***
$$	***$10 to $20***
$$$	***$20 to $30***
$$$$	***more than $30***

In most cases there is no cover charge, aside from the occasional mandatory coat-check. However, expect to pay a few dollars to get into discos on weekends. The legal drinking age is 19 in British Columbia and Saskatchewan and 18 in Alberta and Manitoba; if you're close to that age, expect to be asked for proof.

Wine, Beer and Alcohol

The legal drinking age is 19 in British Columbia and Saskatchewan and 18 in Alberta and Manitoba. Beer, wine and alcohol can only be purchased in liquor stores run by the provincial governments.

Shopping

What to Buy

Salmon: you'll find this fish on sale, fresh from the sea, throughout the coastal areas of British Columbia.

Western wear: Alberta is the place for cowboy boots and hats and other western leather gear.

Local crafts: paintings, sculptures, wood-working items, ceramics, copper-based enamels, weaving, etc.

Native Arts & Crafts: beautiful sculptures made by Aboriginal artists from different types of stone, wood and even animal bone are available, though they are generally quite expensive. Make sure the sculpture is authentic by asking for a certificate of authenticity issued by the Canadian government.

Wine: British Columbia has a well established wine industry. Vineyard tours are possible and the wines can be purchased throughout the province.

Mail and Telecommunications

Canada Post provides efficient mail service across the country. At press time, it cost $0.46 to send a letter anywhere in Canada, $0.55 to the United States and $0.96 overseas. Stamps can be purchased at post offices and in many pharmacies and convenience stores.

Telecommunications

There are two area codes in Alberta: **403** for Calgary and southern Alberta and **780** for Edmonton, central and northern Alberta.

There are two area codes in the province of British Columbia. The area code for the lower mainland and Vancouver is **604**; the area code for Vancouver Island, eastern, central and northern British Columbia is **250**.

The area code for Manitoba is **204** and **306** for Saskatchewan.

Long-distance charges are cheaper than in Europe, but more expensive than in the U.S. Pay phones can be found everywhere, often in the entrances of larger department stores, and in restaurants. They are easy to use and most accept credit cards. Local calls to the surrounding areas cost $0.25 for unlimited time. 800 and 888 numbers are toll free.

BC Tel (in British Columbia), Telus (in Alberta), SaskTel (in Saskatchewan) and MTS (in Manitoba) sell local- and long-distance phone cards in various denominations for use in pay phones, or you can use coins. Bell Canada also sells cards for local- and long-distance calls, available in most variety stores, newspaper stands, etc. Many pay phones also take credit cards.

Calling Abroad

When calling abroad you can use a local operator and pay local phone rates. First dial 011 then the international country code and then the phone number, except for the United States for which you simply dial 1 the area code and the phone number.

Country Codes

United Kingdom	**44**
Ireland	**353**
Australia	**61**
New Zealand	**64**
Belgium	**32**
Switzerland	**41**
Italy	**39**
Spain	**34**
Netherlands	**31**
Germany	**49**

Another way to call abroad is by using the direct access numbers below to contact an operator in your home country.

United States:

AT&T
☎ ***1-800-CALLATT***

MCI
☎ ***1-800-888-8000***

Britain:

British Telecom Direct:
☎ ***1-800-408-6420 or 1-800-363-4144***

Australia:

Australia Telstra Direct:
☎ ***1-800-663-0683***

New Zealand:

New Zealand Telecom Direct:
☎ ***1-800-663-0684***

Money and Banking

Currency

The monetary unit is the dollar ($), which is divided into cents (¢). One dollar=100 cents.

Bills come in 2-, 5-, 10-, 20-, 50-, 100-, 500- and 1000-dollar denominations, and coins come in 1- (pennies), 5- (nickels), 10- (dimes), 25-cent pieces (quarters), and in 1-dollar (loonies) and 2-dollar coins.

Exchange

Most banks readily exchange U.S. and European currencies but almost everyone of these will charge a commission. There are, however, exchange offices that do not charge commissions and keep longer hours. Just remember to ask about fees and to compare rates.

Exchange Rates

$1 CAN	=	$0.68 US	$1 US	=	$1.45 CAN
$1 CAN	=	0.43 £	1£	=	$2.29 CAN
$1 CAN	=	$1.13 Aust	$1 Aust	=	$0.88 CAN
$1 CAN	=	$1.41 NZ	$1 NZ	=	$0.71 CAN
$1 CAN	=	$0.71 EURO	$1 EURO	=	$1.40 CAN
$1 CAN	=	1.57 fl.	1 fl.	=	$0.64 CAN
$1 CAN	=	1.14 SF	1 SF	=	$0.87 CAN
$1 CAN	=	118 BF	10 BF	=	$0.37 CAN
$1 CAN	=	1.39 DM	1 DM	=	$0.71 CAN
$1 CAN	=	118 PTA	100 ITL	=	$0.84 CAN
$1 CAN	=	1376 ITL	1000 PTA	=	$0.73 CAN

Traveller's Cheques

Traveller's cheques are accepted in most large stores and hotels, however it is easier and to your advantage to change your cheques at an exchange office. For a better exchange rate, buy your traveller's cheques in Canadian dollars before leaving home.

Credit Cards

Most major credit cards are accepted at stores, restaurants and hotels. While the main advantage of credit cards is that they allow visitors to avoid carrying large sums of money, using a credit card also makes leaving a deposit for a car rental much easier and some cards, gold cards for example, automatically insure you when you rent a car (check with your credit card company to see what coverage it provides). In addition, the exchange rate with a credit card is generally better. The most commonly accepted credit cards are Visa, MasterCard, and American Express.

Banks

Banks can be found almost everywhere and most offer the standard services to tourists. Visitors who choose to stay in Canada for a long period of time should note that non-residents cannot open bank accounts. If this is the case, the best way to have money readily available is to use traveller's cheques. Withdrawing money from foreign accounts is expensive. However, several automatic-teller machines accept foreign bank cards, so that you can withdraw directly from your account. Money orders are another means of having money sent from abroad. No commission is charged but it takes time. People who have resident status, permanent or not (such as landed immigrants, students), can open a bank account. A passport and proof of resident status are required.

Taxes

The ticket price on items usually does not include tax. There are two taxes, the GST. (federal Goods and Services.Tax) of 7%, which is payable in both provinces, and the P.S.T. or Provincial

Sales Tax of 7% in British Columbia and Manitoba, and 6% in Saskatchewan; Alberta has no provincial sales tax. They are cumulative and must be added to the price of most items and to restaurant and hotel bills. Some hotels charge an additional 8% provincial room tax.

There are some exceptions to this taxation system, such as books, which are only taxed with the GST and food (except for ready made meals), which is not taxed at all.

Tax Refunds for Non-Residents

Non-residents can obtain refunds for the GST paid on purchases. To obtain a refund, it is important to keep your receipts. Refunds up to $500 are obtained instantly from participating duty-free shops when leaving the country or by mailing a special filled-out form to **Revenue Canada**.

For information, call:
☎***1-800-66-VISIT***
(***1-800-668-4748***) in Canada, or
☎***(902) 432-5608*** from outside Canada.

Tipping

In general, tipping applies to all table service: restaurants, bars and night-clubs (therefore no tipping in fast-food restaurants). Tips are also given in taxis and in hair salons.

The tip is usually about 15% of the bill before taxes, but varies, of course, depending on the quality of service.

Business Hours

Stores

Stores are generally open the following hours:

Mon to Wed
10am to 6pm
Thu and Fri
10am to 9pm
Sat
9am or 10am to 5pm
Sun
noon to 5pm

Well-stocked convenience stores that sell food are found throughout Western Canada and are open later, sometimes 24hrs a day.

Banks

Banks are open Monday to Friday from 10am to 3pm. Most are open on Thursdays and Fridays until 6pm or even 8pm. Automatic teller machines are widely available and are open night and day.

Post Offices

Large post offices are open Monday to Friday from 9am to 5pm. There are also several smaller post offices located in shopping malls, convenience stores, and even pharmacies; these post offices are open much later than the larger ones.

Holidays

The following is a list of public holidays in the four western provinces. Most administrative offices and banks are closed on these days.

January 1 and 2

Easter Monday

Victoria Day:
the 3rd Monday in May

Canada Day:
July 1st

Civic holiday:
1st Monday in August

Labour Day:
1st Monday in September

Thanksgiving:
2nd Monday in October

Remembrance Day:
November 1

Christmas Day:
December 25

Advice for Smokers

As in the United States, cigarette smoking is considered taboo, and it is being prohibited in more and more public places, such as in most shopping centres, on buses and in government offices.

Most public places (restaurants, cafés) have smoking and non-smoking sections. However, the city of Vancouver has recently passed a by-law prohibiting smoking in all restaurants. Cigarettes are sold in bars, grocery stores, newspaper and magazine shops.

Safety

If you take the normal precautions you take at home, there is no need to worry about your personal security. If trouble should arise, remember to dial the emergency telephone number ☎***911***.

Disabled Travellers

Major western Canadian cities have special transportation and facilities for disabled travellers. We have indicated the establishments that are equipped for the handicapped with the ♿ symbol.

For more information, contact the following organizations:

Canadian Foundation For Physically Disabled Persons:
731 Runnymede
Toronto, Ontario
☎***(416) 760-7351***

Disabled Peoples International:
3516 42A Ave. NW
Edmonton, Alberta
☎***(780) 462-4853***

Children

As in the rest of Canada, facilities exist in Western Canada that make travelling with children quite easy, whether it be for getting around or when enjoying the sights. Generally children under five travel for free, and those under 12 are eligible for fare reductions. The same applies for various leisure activities and shows. Find out before you purchase tickets. High chairs and children's menus are available in most restaurants, while a few of the larger stores provide a babysitting service while parents shop.

Calgary was the only city in North America to have a "Child Friendly Business Accreditation Program". Its website (www.childfriendly.ab.ca) provides a list of child-friendly businesses and services, as rated by kids themselves!

Seniors

Seniors get various discounts on transportation and entertainment. Ask around or contact the **Canadian Association of Retired Persons** (*27 Queen E, Toronto, ON, M5C 2M6, 416-363-8748, www.fifty-plus.com*)

Gay And Lesbian Life

In 1977, Québec became the second place in the world, after Holland, to include in its charter the principle of not discriminating on the basis of sexual orientation. Other Canadian provinces later followed suit (most recently Alberta).

Canadians are generally open and tolerant towards homosexuality. Over the years, legislation, particularly at the federal level, has been reformed, to an extent, in favour of gays and lesbians, thus reflecting changing attitudes in society, especially in Québec, Ontario and British Columbia. However, the government sometimes seems to be living in the dark ages when Canada Customs does everything in its power to ban the importation of Marcel Proust's novels in English Canada! Little Sisters bookstore in Vancouver has been putting up a brave legal battle against these inspectors who believe they are the authority on censorship.

Generally speaking, rural areas tend to be more homophobic and Western Canada is not as tolerant of gays and lesbians. Yet, the Prairies have their share of queer celebrities, including country-singer, k.d. lang. Vancouver has the largest established gay communities in Western Canada. It is mainly in the West End.

For more information on gay and lesbian life:

British Columbia

Little Sister Book and Art Emporium
1221 Thurlow St., Vancouver
☎ ***(604) 669-1753 or 800-567-1662***
⇄ ***(604) 685-0252***

Lesbian & Gay Counselling & Consulting Services:
Vancouver
☎ ***(604) 222-7807***

Gay Lesbian Transgendered Bisexual Community Centre:
1170 Bute, Vancouver
☎ ***(604) 684-4901/5307/6869***

Alberta

Gay & Lesbian Community Centre Of Edmonton
10612 124 St. NW, Suite 103
Edmonton
☎ ***(780) 488-3234***

Gay & Lesbian Community Services
223 12 Ave. SW, Suite 205A
Calgary, Alberta
☎ ***(403) 234-8973/9752***
glcsa@canuck.com

Saksatchewan

Gay & Lesbian Community of Regina
2070 Broad St., Regina, Saskatchewan
☎ ***(306) 569-1995***

Manitoba

Rainbow Resource Centre
#1-222 Osborne St. S.
☎ ***(204) 284-5208 or (204) 474-0212***
⇄ ***(204) 478-1160***

Gay/Lesbian Info Line
☎ ***(204) 284-5208 or 888-399-0005***
⇄ ***(204) 478-1160***

Weights and Measures

Although the metric system has been in use in Canada for several years, some people continue to use the Imperial system in casual conversation.

Miscellaneous

Time Zone

Western Canada covers two different time zones: **Mountain Time** and **Pacific Time**. Alberta is therefore two hours behind Eastern Standard Time, while British Columbia is three hours behind. Continental Europe is nine hours ahead of British Columbia and eight hours ahead of Alberta. The United Kingdom, on the other hand is eight and seven hours ahead respectively. **Daylight Savings Time** (+ 1 hour) begins the first Sunday in April.

Illegal Drugs

Recreational Drugs are against the law and not tolerated (even "soft" drugs). Anyone caught with drugs in their possession risk severe consequences.

Electricity

Voltage is 110 volts throughout Canada, the same as in the United States. Electricity plugs have two parallel, flat pins, and adaptors are available here.

Laundromats

Laundromats are found almost everywhere in urban areas. In most cases, detergent is sold on site. Although change machines are sometimes provided, it is best to bring plenty of quarters (25¢) with you.

Movie Theatres

There are no ushers and therefore no tips.

Museums

Most museums charge admission. Reduced prices are available for people over60, for children, and for students. Call the museum for further details.

Newspapers

Each big city has its own major newspaper:

Vancouver
Vancouver Sun
Vancouver Province

Calgary
Calgary Sun
Calgary Herald

Edmonton
Edmonton Journal

Regina
The Leader Post

Winnipeg
Winnipeg Free Press

The larger newspapers, for example *The Globe and Mail*, are widely available, as are many international newspapers.

The Airlines

Air Canada	1-800-222-6596
Canadian Airlines	1-800-665-1177
Delta Airlines	1-800-221-1212
Northwest Airlines	1-800-225-2525
American Airlines	1-800-433-7300
US Airways	1-800-428-4322
KLM	1-800-361-1887
Lufthansa	1-800-563-5954
British Airways	1-888-334-3448
Air France	1-800-667-2747
Qantas	1-800-227-4500
Air New Zealand	1-800-663-5494

Pharmacies

In addition to the smaller drug stores, there are large pharmacy chains which sell everything from chocolate to laundry detergent, as well as the more traditional items such as cough drops and headache medications.

Restrooms

Public washrooms can be found in most shopping centres. If you cannot find one, it usually is not a problem to use one in a bar or restaurant.

The four provinces of Western Canada boast vast, untouched stretches of wilderness protected by national and provincial parks, which visitors can explore on foot, by bicycle or by car.

You'll discover coasts washed by the waters of the Pacific Ocean (Pacific Rim and Gwaii Haanas National Parks), vast rain forests harbouring centuries-old trees (Vancouver Island), majestic mountains that form the spine of the American continent (Banff, Jasper, Kootenay and Yoho National Parks) and some of the world's richest dinosaur-fossil beds in the Badlands of the Red Deer River Valley (Dinosaur Provincial Park) vast stretches of forest, prairies and lakes (Prince Albert National Park; Lac La Rouge Provincial Park; Grasslands National Park) beaches (Grand Beach Provincial Park) and vast northern expanses of rivers, lakes and lush forests (Grass River Provincial Park).

The following pages contain a description of the various outdoor activities that can be enjoyed in these unspoiled areas.

Parks

In Western Canada, there are 11 national parks, run by the federal government, and more than 400 provincial parks, each administered by the government of the province in question. Most national parks offer facilities and services such as information centres, park maps, nature interpretation programmes, guides, accommodation (B&Bs, inns, equipped and primitive camping sites) and restaurants. Not all of these services are available in every park (and some vary depending on the season), so it is best to contact park authorities before setting off on a trip. Provincial parks are usually smaller, with fewer services, but are still attractively located.

A number of parks are crisscrossed by marked trails stretching several kilometres, perfect for hiking, cycling, cross-country skiing and snowmobiling. Primitive camping sites or shelters can be found along some of these paths. Some of the campsites are very rudimentary, and a few don't even have water; it is therefore essential to be well equipped. Take note, however, that in the national parks in the Rocky Mountains, wilderness camping is strictly forbidden due to the presence of bears and other large animals. Since some of the trails lead deep into the forest, far from all human habitation, visitors are strongly advised to heed all signs. This will also help protect the fragile plant-life. Useful maps showing trails, camping sites and shelters are available for most parks.

National Parks

There are eleven national parks in Western Canada: Glacier National Park (British Columbia), Yoho National Park and Kootenay National Park (in the Rockies, in British Columbia), Mount Revelstoke National Park (in the Columbia River Valley in British Columbia), Pacific Rim National Park (on Vancouver Island), Gwaii Haanas (in the Queen Charlotte Islands), Waterton Lakes National Park (on the U.S. border in Alberta), Banff National Park and Jasper National Park (in the Rockies), Elk Island National Park (east of Edmonton) and finally Wood Buffalo National Park (in Northern Alberta, on the border with the Northwest Territories). In addition to these parks, the Canadian Park Service also oversees a number of national historic sites, which are described in the "Exploring" section of the appropriate chapters.

For more information on national parks, you can call ☎800-651-7959, visit the Parks Canada Internet site at ***www.parkscanada.pch.gc.ca*** or contact the regional offices by mail:

Parks Canada Western Region
Room 552, 220 Fourth Ave. SE, Calgary, AB, T2G 4X3
☎***(403) 292-4401*** or ***800-748-7275***
⇄***(403) 292-4242***

Parks Canada Prairie and Northern Region
457 Main St.,
Winnipeg, MB
R3B 3E8

Provincial Parks

Each of the two provinces manages a wide variety of parks; there are more than 400 in all. Some of these are small, day-use areas, while the larger ones offer a broader scope of activities. These parks provide visitors with access to beaches, campsites, golf courses, hiking trails and archaeological preserves. Throughout this guide, the most important parks are described in the "Parks and Beaches" section of each relevant chapter. For more information on provincial parks, contact:

British Columbia

BC Parks
2nd Floor, 800 Johnston St., Victoria
mailing address:
Box 9398, Stn Prov Govt, Victoria V8W 9M9
☎***250-387-5200***

Alberta

Environmental Protection and Natural Resources administer the provincial parks, but travellers are better off contacting **Travel Alberta** at ☎***800-661-8888*** for information.

Saskatchewan

Travel Saskatchewan
☎***800-667-7191***

Manitoba

Travel Manitoba
☎***800-665-0204***
www.travelmanitoba.com

Summer Activities

When the weather is mild, visitors can enjoy the activities listed below. Anyone intending to spend more than a day in the park should remember that the nights are cool (even in July and August) and that long-sleeved shirts or sweaters will be very practical in some regions. In June, and throughout the summer in northern regions, an effective insect repellent is almost indispensable for an outing in the forest.

Hiking

Hiking is an activity open to everyone, and it can be enjoyed in all national and most provincial parks. Before setting out, plan your excursion well by checking the length and level of difficulty of each trail. Some parks have long trails that require more than a day of hiking and lead deep into the wild. When taking one of these trails, which can stretch dozens of kilometres, it is crucial to respect all signs.

To make the most of an excursion, it is important to bring along the right equipment. You'll need a good pair of walking shoes, appropriate maps, sufficient food and water and a small first-aid kit containing a pocket knife and bandages.

Bicycling

Visitors can go bicycling and mountain biking all over Western Canada, along the usually quiet secondary roads or the trails criss-crossing the parks. The roads offer prudent cyclists one of the most enjoyable means possible to tour these picturesque regions. Keep in mind, however, that distances in these vast provinces can be very long.

If you are travelling with your own bicycle, you are allowed to bring it on any bus; just be sure it is properly protected in an appropriate box. Another option is to rent one on site. For bike rental locations, look under the heading "**Bicycling**" in the "Outdoor Activities" section of the chapters on each province, contact a tourist information centre or check under the "Bicycles-Rentals" heading in the *Yellow Pages.* Adequate insurance is a good idea when renting a bicycle. Some places include insurance against theft in the cost of the rental. Inquire before renting.

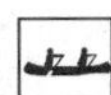

Canoeing

Many parks are strewn with lakes and rivers which canoe-trippers can spend a day or more exploring. Primitive camping sites have been laid out to accommodate canoers during long excursions. Canoe rentals and maps of possible routes are usually available at the parks' information centres. It is always best to have a map that indicates the length of the portages in order to determine how physically demanding the trip will be. Carrying a canoe, baggage and food on your back is not always a pleasant experience. A 1km portage is generally considered long, and will be more or less difficult depending on the terrain.

Beaches

Whether you decide to stretch out on the white sand of Long Beach on Vancouver Island, or prefer the more family-oriented atmosphere of Qualicum Beach, with its calm waters, or Wreck Beach, the driftwood-carvers' rendez-vous, you'll discover one of Western Canada's most precious natural attractions, British Columbia's Pacific Coast. Swimming is not always possible, however, because of the heavy surf and cold water temperatures. Alberta even has some lovely beaches lining crystal-clear fresh water lakes.

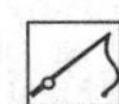

Fishing

In the West, anglers can cast their line in the ocean or in one of the many rivers and lakes. Don't forget, however, that fishing is a regulated activity. Fishing laws are complicated, so it is wise to request information from the two provinces ahead of time and obtain the brochure stating key fishing regulations. Furthermore, keep in mind that there are different permits for fresh water and salt water fishing. Most permits or licenses can be purchased at major sporting-goods stores.

For more information on salt water fishing, contact:

Federal Department of Fisheries and Oceans
555 West Hastings St. Vancouver, BC V6B 5G3
☎(604) 666-5835

For more information on fresh water fishing, contact:

B.C. Ministry of Environment Lands and Parks 2nd Floor, 800 Johnston St., Victoria, BC, V8V 1X4
☎(604) 582-5200

Alberta Fish and Wildlife Services
Main Floor, North Tower, Petroleum Plaza, 9945 108th St., Edmonton, AB T5K 2G6

Saskatchewan Environment and Resource Management
3211 Albert St.,
Regina, SK
S4S 5W6
☎(306) 787-2700
www.serm.gov.sk.ca

Manitoba Conservation
Box 20, Saulteaux Cr.
Winnipeg, MB
R3J 3W3
☎(800) 214-6497
www.gov.mb.ca/natres

As a general rule, however, keep in mind that:

- it is necessary to obtain a permit from the provincial government before going fishing

- a special permit is usually required for salmon fishing

- fishing seasons are established by the ministry and must be respected at all times

- the seasons vary depending on the species

Fishing is permitted in national parks, but you must obtain a permit from park officials beforehand (see regional office addresses in this chapter, or in the parks section of the chapter on the provinces); for more information, look under the "Fishing" heading in the "Outdoor Activities" section of the relevant chapter.

Bird-Watching

The wilds of Western Canada attract all sorts of birds, which can easily be observed with the help of binoculars. Some of the more noteworthy species that you might spot are hummingbirds, golden eagles, bald eagles, peregrine falcons, double-crested cormorants, pelicans, grouse, ptarmigans, countless varieties of waterfowl, including the mallards, barnacle geese, wild geese, trumpeter swans (which migrate from the Arctic to Mexico) and finally the grey jay, a little bird who will gladly help himself to your picnic lunch if you aren't careful. For help identifying them, purchase a copy of *Peterson's Field Guide: All the Birds of Eastern and Central North America*, published by Houghton Mifflin. Although parks are often the best places to observe certain species, bird-watching is an activity that can be enjoyed throughout Alberta and British Columbia.

Whale-Watching

Whales are common along the coasts of British Columbia. Visitors wishing to catch a closer view of these impressive but harmless sea mammals can take part in a whale-watching cruise or go sea-kayaking. The most commonly sighted species are orcas (also known as killer whales), humpbacks and grey whales. These excursions usually start from the northeastern end of Vancouver Island, in the Johnstone Strait, or from Long Beach. Ensure that the company you organize your tour with is a reliable one that respects the space and safety of the whales.

Seal-Watching

Seals are also found along British Columbia's coasts, and anyone wishing to observe them from close up can take part in an excursion designed for that purpose. Occasionally, attracted by the boat, these curious mammals will pop their heads out of the water right nearby, and gaze, with their big, clack eyes, at the passengers.

Golf

Magnificent golf courses, renowned for their remarkable natural settings, can be found throughout British Columbia and Alberta. Stretching along the ocean, or through narrow mountain valleys, these courses boast exceptional views and challenging holes.

Grey Whale

A few courses have been laid out in provincial parks (in Kananaskis Country) and near the parks of the Rockies (in the valley of the Columbia River), where peace and quiet reign supreme and luxurious hotels are just a short distance away.

Horseback Riding

Trail riding through the Canadian Rockies is a unique experience. You can sleep under the stars and get a taste of the cowboy and pioneer ways of life. A ranch vacation is another exciting introduction to life in the west.

The relevant chapters contain some suggestions for pack-trip outfitters and ranches. For more information call the relevant provincial travel office.

Winter Activities

In winter, most of Western Canada is covered with a blanket of snow creating ideal conditions for a slew of outdoor activities. Most parks with summer hiking trails adapt to the climate, welcoming cross-country skiers. This largely mountainous region boasts world-class resorts that will satisfy even the most demanding skiers.

Cross-Country Skiing

Some parks, like those in Kananaskis Country and in the Rocky Mountains, are renowned for their long cross-country ski trails. The cross-country skiing events of the 1988 Winter Olympics were held in the small town of Canmore, Alberta. Daily ski rentals are available at most ski centres.

Downhill Skiing and Snowboarding

Known the world over for its downhill skiing, the mountains of Western Canada attract millions of downhill skiers and snow-boarders every year. The most popular ski hills are around Banff and Jasper and outside of Vancouver at Whistler and Blackcomb.

Fans of powder skiing are whisked to the highest summits by helicopter, and deposited there to enjoy the ski or snowboard of their lives.

Snowmobiling

This winter activity has many fans in the West. Each province is criss-crossed by thousands of kilometres of trails.

In British Columbia, the **BC Snowmobile Federation** (☎ *250-942-4603*) can provide further information on the provincial trail system, clubs and events. Alberta does not have one organization responsible for the activity. Your best bet is to contact **Travel Alberta** ***☎800-661-8888.*** Don't forget that a permit is required. It is also advisable to take out liability insurance. The following rules should respected at all times: stay on the snowmobile trails; always drive on the right side of the trail; wear a helmet; all snowmobiles must have headlights.

Vancouver ★★★

is truly a new city, one framed by the mighty elements of sea and mountains.

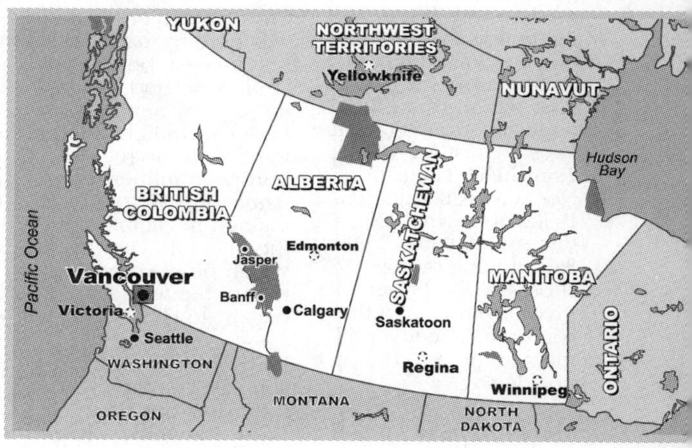

As part of one of the most isolated reaches on the planet for many years, the city has, over the last 100 years, developed close ties with the nations of the largest ocean on Earth, and is one of the most multicultural metropolises of the Pacific Rim. Its history is tied to the development of British Columbia's natural resources. Most residents were lured here by the magnificent setting and the climate, which is remarkably mild in a country known for its bitter winters and stifling summers. Vancouver, where Asia meets America, is a city well worth discovering.

Geography

Pacific-minded though it is, Vancouver does not actually face right onto the ocean, but is separated from the sea by Vancouver Island, where Victoria, the capital of British Columbia, is located. Vancouver, the province's economic hub, lies on the Strait of Georgia, an arm of the sea separating Vancouver Island from the mainland. Its population is scattered across two peninsulas formed by Burrard Inlet to the north and False Creek to the south.

Point Grey, the larger, more southerly peninsula, is home to the University of British Columbia and sprawling residential neighbourhoods. On the smaller peninsula to the north, visitors will discover a striking contrast between the east end, with its cluster of downtown skyscrapers, and the west end, occupied by the lovely, unspoiled woodlands of Stanley Park. Vancouver is only about 30km from the U.S. border (and less than 200km north of Seattle).

Vancouver boasts an exceptionally mild climate, with average temperatures of 3°C in January and 17°C in July. There is very little snow, though there is a lot of rain (annual average: 163 days of precipitation) and the summers are temperate and sunny. Clouds that form over the ocean are blown inland by westerly winds, when they hit the Coast Mountains they precipitate causing generally grey weather.

History and Economy

When the first Europeans arrived here in the late 18th century, the region that would become Vancouver was inhabited by the Salish First Nation (the other linguistic groups on the Pacific coast are Haida, Tsimshian, Tlingit, Nootka-Kwakiutl and Bellacoola). In 1820, there were some 25,000 Salish living on the shores of the Fraser River, from its mouth south of Vancouver all the way up into the Rockies.

The voyages of French navigator Louis Antoine de Bougainville and English explorer James Cook, removed some of the mystery surrounding these distant lands. After Australia (1770) and New Zealand (1771), Cook explored the coast of British Columbia (1778). He did not, however, venture as far as the Strait of Georgia, where Vancouver now lies.

In 1792, Cook's compatriot George Vancouver (1757-1798) became the first European to trod upon the soil that would give rise to the future city. He was on a mission to take possession of the territory for the King of England.

The Vancouver region was hard to reach not only by sea, but also by land. A belated breakthrough by Simon Fraser in 1808 had little impact on the region. European influence on native lifestyle remained negligible until the mid-19th century, at which point colonization of the territory began slowly.

In 1827, after the Hudson's Bay Company took over the North West Company, a large fur-trading post was founded in Fort Langley, on the shores of the Fraser, some 90km east of the present site of Vancouver, which would remain untouched for several more decades.

The 49th parallel was designated the border between the United States and British North America in 1846, cutting the hunting territories in half and thereby putting a damper on the Hudson's Bay Company's activities in the region.

It wasn't until the gold rush of 1858 in the hinterland that the region experienced another era of prosperity. When nuggets of the precious metal were discovered in the bed of the Fraser, upriver from Fort Langley, a frenzy broke out. In the space of two years, the valley of the golden river attracted thousands of prospectors, and makeshift wooden villages went up overnight. Some came from Eastern Canada, but most, including a large number of Chinese Americans, were from California.

In the end, however, it was contemporary industrialists' growing interest in the region's cedar and fir trees that led to the actual founding of Vancouver. In 1862, Sewell Prescott Moody, originally from Maine (U.S.A), opened the region's first sawmill at the far end of Burrard Inlet, and ensured its success by creating an entire town, known as Moodyville, around it. A second sawmill, called Hastings Mills, opened east of present-day Chinatown in 1865. Two years later, innkeeper Gassy Jack Deighton arrived in the area and set up a saloon near Hastings Mills, providing a place for sawmill workers to slake their thirst. Before long, various service establishments sprang up around the saloon, thus marking the birth of Gastown, later Vancouver's first neighbourhood.

In 1870, the colonial government of British Columbia renamed the nascent town Granville, after the Duke of Granville. The area continued to develop, and the city of Vancouver was officially founded in April 1886. It was renamed in honour of Captain George Vancouver, who made the first hydrographic surveys of the shores of the Strait of Georgia. Unfortunately, a few weeks later, a forest fire swept through the new town, wiping out everything in its way. In barely 20 minutes, Vancouver was reduced to ashes. In those difficult years, local residents were still cut off from the rest of the world, so the town was reconstructed with an eye on the long term. From that point on, Vancouver's buildings, whether of wood or brick, were made to last.

The end of the gold rush in 1865 led to a number of economic problems for the colony of British Columbia. In 1871, British Columbia agreed to join the Canadian Confederation on the condition that a railway line linking it to the eastern part of the country be built.

Recognizing the potential of this gateway to the Pacific, a group of businessmen from Montréal set out to build a transcontinental railway in 1879. Canadian Pacific chose Port Moody (formerly Moodyville) as the western terminus of the railway. On July 4, 1886, the first train from Montréal reached Port Moody after a tortuous journey of about 5,000km.

A few years later, the tracks were extended 20km to Vancouver in order to link the transcontinental railway to the new port and thereby allow greater access to the Asian market. This change proved momentous for the city, whose population exploded from 2,500 inhabitants in 1886 to over 120,000 in 1911! Many of the Chinese who had come to North America to help build the railroad settled in Vancouver when the project was finished; they were soon joined by Asians from Canton, Japan and Tonkin. The city's Chinatown, which grew up between Gastown and Hastings Mills, eventually became the second largest in North America after San Francisco's.

At the beginning of the 20th century, the city's economic activity gradually shifted from Gastown to the Canadian Pacific Railway yards, located around Granville Street. Within a few years, lovely stone buildings housing banks and department stores sprang up in this area. In 1913, the city was much like a gangling adolescent in the midst of a growth spurt. It was then that a major economic crisis occurred, putting an end to local optimism for a while. The opening of the Panama Canal (1914) and the end of World War I enabled Vancouver to emerge from this morass, only to sink right back into it during the crash of 1929. During World War II, residents of Japanese descent were interned and their possessions confiscated. Paranoia prevailed over reason, and these second- and sometimes even third-generation Vancouverites were viewed as potential spies.

Nevertheless, the city's dual role as a gateway to the Pacific for North Americans and a gateway to America for Asians was already well established, as evidenced by the massive influx of Chinese immigrants from the 19th century onwards and the numerous import-export businesses dealing in silk, tea and porcelain. The name Vancouver has thus been familiar throughout the Pacific zone for over a century.

With the explosive economic growth of places like Japan, Hong Kong, Taiwan, Singapore, the Philippines, Malaysia and Thailand, especially in regards to exportation, Vancouver's port expanded at lightning speed. Since 1980, it has been the busiest one in the country; 70.7 million tonnes of merchandise were handled here in 1991.

Vancouver (especially the downtown core) has enjoyed continued growth since the late 1960s. Even more than San Francisco or Los Angeles, Vancouver has a strong, positive image throughout the Pacific. It is viewed as a neutral territory offering a good yield on investments and a comfortable standard of living.

Finding Your Way Around

By Car

Vancouver is accessible by the **Trans-Canada Highway 1**, which runs east-west. This national highway links all of the major Canadian cities. It has no tolls and passes through some spectacular scenery. Coming from Alberta you will pass through the Rocky Mountains, desert regions and a breathtaking canyon.

The city is generally reached from the east by taking the "Downtown" exit from the Trans-Canada. If you are coming from the United States or from Victoria by ferry, you will enter the city on Hwy. 99 North; in this case expect it to take about 30min to reach downtown.

Car Rental Companies

Tilden
1128 W. Georgia St.
☎***685-6111***
☎***800-227-7368***
☎***800-CAR-RENT***
at the airport
☎***273-3121***

Budget
450 W. Georgia St.
and at the airport
☎***668-7000***
☎***800-268-8900***
(from Canada)
☎***800-527-0700***
(from the US)

ABC Rent-a-Car
255 W. Broadway
☎***873-6622***
☎***800-464-6422***

Thrifty
1400 Robson St.
☎***681-4869***
at the airport
☎***276-0800***

Avis
757 Hornby St.
and at the airport
☎***606-2847***

Exotic Car and Motorcycle Rentals
1820 Burrard St.
☎***736-9130*** or ***644-9128***

Dollar Rent-a-Car
☎***800-800-4000***

Lo-Cost Rent-a-Car
☎***689-9664***

By Plane

Vancouver International Airport

Vancouver International Airport is located 15km from downtown. Besides the regular airport services (duty-free shops, cafeterias, restaurants, etc.) you will also find an exchange office. Several car-rental companies also have offices in the airport. It takes about 30min to get downtown by car or bus. A taxi or limousine will cost you about $25-$30. To reach downtown by public transit take bus #100 for downtown and points east and bus #404 or #406 for Richmond, Delta and points south.

Take note: even if you have already paid various taxes included in the purchase price of your ticket, Vancouver International Airport charges every passenger an Airport Improvement Fee (AIF). The fee is $5 for flights within B.C. and to the Yukon, $10 for flights elsewhere in North America, and $15 for overseas flights; credit cards are accepted, and most in-transit passengers are exempted.

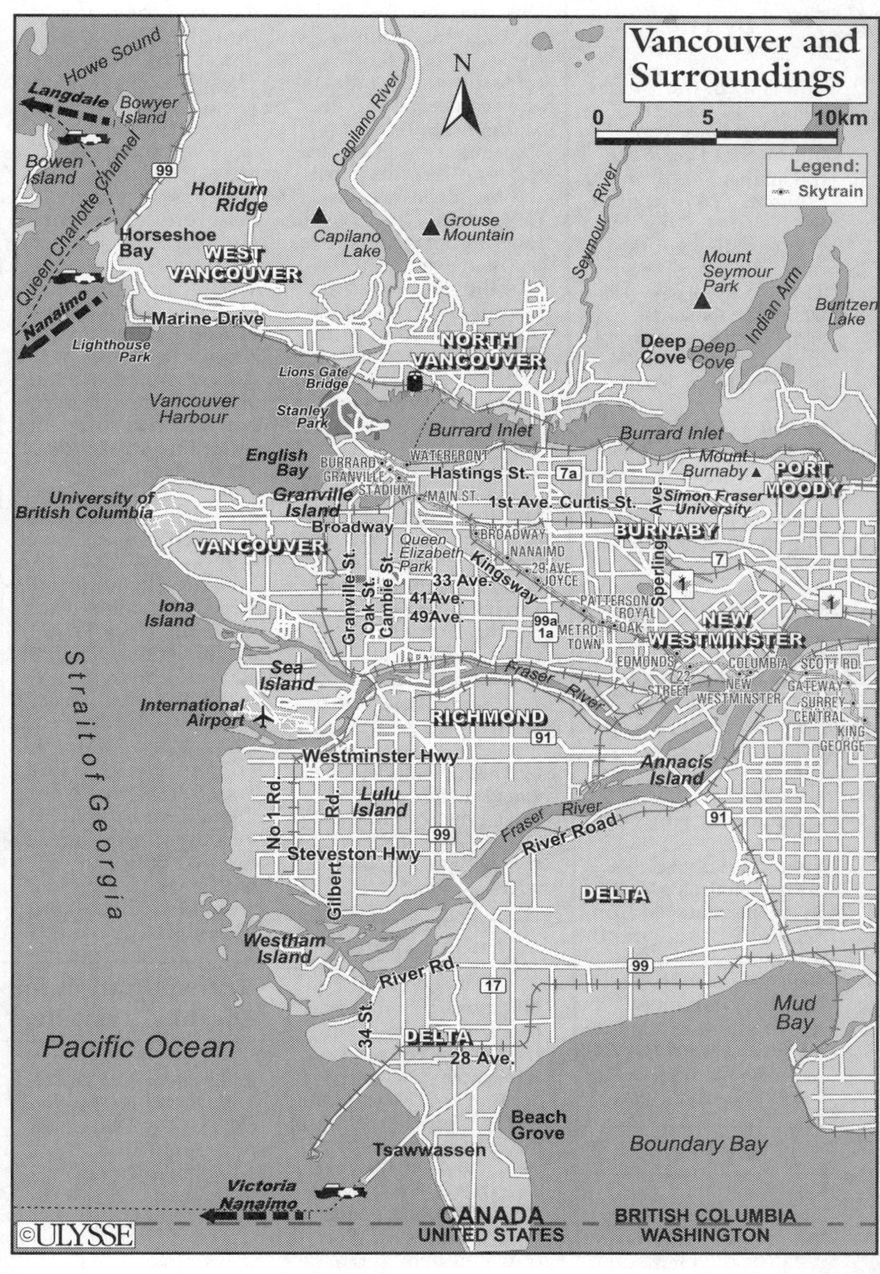

Vancouver and Surroundings
N
0
5
10km
Legend:
Skytrain
Howe Sound
Langdale
Bowyer Island
Bowen Island
Queen Charlotte Channel
99
Holiburn Ridge
Capilano River
Capilano Lake
Grouse Mountain
Seymour River
Horseshoe Bay
WEST VANCOUVER
Mount Seymour Park
Indian Arm
Buntzen Lake
Nanaimo
Marine Drive
Lighthouse Park
NORTH VANCOUVER
Deep Cove
Deep Cove
Lions Gate Bridge
Vancouver Harbour
Stanley Park
Burrard Inlet
Burrard Inlet
English Bay
BURRARD
WATERFRONT
GRANVILLE
STADIUM
Hastings St.
7a
Mount Burnaby
PORT MOODY
University of British Columbia
Granville Island
MAIN ST.
1st Ave.
Curtis St.
Sperling Ave.
Simon Fraser University
Broadway
BROADWAY
BURNABY
VANCOUVER
Queen Elizabeth Park
NANAIMO
Kingsway
29 AVE
JOYCE
7
Granville St.
Oak St.
Cambie St.
33 Ave.
41 Ave.
49 Ave.
1
1
Iona Island
PATTERSON
ROYAL OAK
METRO TOWN
99a
1a
NEW WESTMINSTER
EDMONDS
22 STREET
COLUMBIA
NEW WESTMINSTER
SCOTT RD.
GATEWAY
SURREY CENTRAL
KING GEORGE
Strait of Georgia
Sea Island
Fraser River
International Airport
RICHMOND
91
Westminster Hwy
Annacis Island
No 1 Rd.
Gilbert Rd.
Lulu Island
Fraser River
River Road
91
99
Steveston Hwy
DELTA
Westham Island
99
River Rd.
17
Mud Bay
34 St.
Pacific Ocean
DELTA
28 Ave.
Beach Grove
Boundary Bay
Tsawwassen
Victoria
Nanaimo
CANADA
UNITED STATES
BRITISH COLUMBIA
WASHINGTON
©ULYSSE

By Train

Trains from the United States and Eastern Canada arrive at new intermodal **Pacific Central Station** *(Via Rail Canada, 1150 Station St., ☎800-561-8630)* where you can also connect to buses or the Skytrain. The cross-country Via train, **The Canadian** arrives in Vancouver three times a week from Eastern Canada.

BC Rail *(1311 West First St., North Vancouver, ☎984-5246)* trains travel the northern west coast. Schedules vary depending on the seasons.

During the summer, the **Great Canadian Railtour Company Ltd**. offers **Rocky Mountain Railtours** *($725 per person, $670 per person double occupancy; ☎606-7200 or 800-665-7245, ≠606-7520)* between Calgary and Vancouver.

There is daily service aboard **Amtrak's Mount Baker International** from Seattle, Washington; the trip takes 3hrs and follows a scenic route. For reservations or information call Amtrak US Rail at ***☎800-USA-RAIL*** or ***☎800-872-7245*** (toll-free in North America).

By Ferry

Two ferry ports serve the greater Vancouver area for travellers coming from other regions in the province. Horseshoe Bay, to the northwest, is the terminal for ferries to Nanaimo (crossing time 90min), Bowen Island and the Mainland Sunshine Coast. Tsawwassen, to the south, is the terminal for ferries to Victoria (Swartz Bay crossing time 95min), Nanaimo (crossing time 2hrs) and the Southern Gulf Islands. Both terminals are about 30min from downtown. For information on these routes contact **BC Ferries** *(☎250-386-3431)*.

There is a ferry between Granville Island and the Hornby Street dock; it runs from 7am to 8pm. For information contact **Granville Island Ferries** *(☎684-7781)* or **Aquabus Ferries** *(☎689-5858)*.

By Bus

Greyhound Lines of Canada
Pacific Central Station
1150 Station St.
☎482-8747
☎800-661-8747

Public Transit

BC Transit bus route maps are available from the **Vancouver Travel InfoCentre** *(200 Burrard St., ☎683-2000)* or from the BC Transit offices in Surrey *(13401 108th Ave., 5th floor, Surrey, B.C., ☎800-903-4731 or 540-3450)*. BC Transit also includes a rail transit system and a marine bus. The **Skytrain** runs east from the downtown area to Burnaby, New Westminster and Surrey. These automatic trains run from 5am to 1am all week, except Sundays when they start at 9am. The **Seabus** shuttles runs frequently between Burrard Inlet and North Vancouver.

Tickets and passes are available for **BC Transit**, including Skytrain and Seabus tickets from the coin-operated machines at some stops, in some convenience stores or by calling ***☎261-5100*** or ***521-0400***.

The fares are the same whether you are travelling on a BC Transit bus, the Skytrain or the Seabus. A single ticket generally costs $1.50 for adults and $0.75 for seniors, children and students (must have BC Transit GoCard), except at peak hours (Mon to Fri before 9:30am and 3pm to 6:30pm) when the system is divided into three zones and it costs $1.50 for travel within one zone, $2.25 within two zones and $3 within three zones.

Transportation for Disabled Travellers

Handydart *(300-3200 E. 54th St., ☎430-2692)* provides public transportation for wheelchair-bound individuals. You must reserve your seat in advance.

Vancouver Taxis *(2205 Main St., ☎255-5111 or 874-5111)* also offers transportation for disabled individuals.

By Taxi

Taxis are usually easy to find, either near large downtown hotels or on the main streets such as Robson and Georgia. The following are the main companies:

Yellow Cab
☎681-1111

McLure's
☎731-9211

Black Top
☎731-1111
(wheelchair accessible taxis)
☎871-1111

For Limousines
☎582-5544
☎671-5733

Practical Information

Area Code: 604

Tourist Information

The **Tourism Vancouver Tourist Info Centre** *(May to Sep, every day 8am to 6pm; Sep to May, Mon to Fri 8:30am to 5pm, Sat 9am to 5pm; Plaza Level, Waterfront Centre, 200 Burrard St., V6C 3L6, ☎683-2000, ⇄682-6839, www.tourism-vancouver.org)* provides brochures and information on sights and accommodations for the city as well as for the province.

For information on and reservations for travelling in the rest of the province you can call **Super Natural British Columbia** at ***☎800-663-6000*** or write to them at Box 9830, Station Province-Government, Victoria, V8W 9W5.

Banks and Currency Exchange

Automatic teller machines can be found throughout the city. The following exchange offices are centrally located.

Custom House Currency Exchange
375 Water St.
☎482-6006

International Securities Exchange
1169 Robson St.
☎683-9666

Thomas Cook
701 Granville
☎687-6111

Money Services
Money Mart
☎606-9522
☎606-9612 *(24hrs)*

Post Office

The main post office in Vancouver is located at 349 West Georgia Street.

Exploring

The following nine tours, each covering a different part of Vancouver, will help you fully enjoy the local sights. You can set out to explore the city's streets by taking:

Tour A: Gastown ★

Tour B: Chinatown and East Vancouver ★★

Tour C: Downtown ★★

Tour D: The West End ★

Tour E: Stanley Park ★★★

Tour F: Burrard Inlet ★★★

Tour G: False Creek ★

Tour H: South Vancouver and Shaughnessy ★★

Tour I: The Peninsula ★★★.

Carrall Street serves as the dividing line between east and west in the centre of town (south of False Creek the border between east and west is Ontario Street). It also marks the border between Gastown, to the west, and Chinatown, to the east.

Tour A: Gastown

Just a few steps from downtown, Gastown is best discovered on foot. The area dates back to 1867, when John Deighton, known as Gassy Jack, opened a saloon for the employees of a neighbouring sawmill. Gastown was destroyed by fire in 1886. However, this catastrophe did not deter the city's pioneers, who rebuilt from the ashes and started anew the development of their city, which was incorporated several months later.

In the late 19th century, Gastown's economic development was driven by rail transport and the gold rush. The neighbourhood then became an important commercial distribution centre, but was later abandoned in favour of areas farther west. After a long period of decline, restoration was begun in the mid-1960s and continues to this day. Gastown's streets are now lined with little hotels, trendy cafés, restaurants, art galleries, souvenir shops and gaslit lanterns, and they make for a pleasant stroll.

Start off your tour at the corner of Water and West Cordova Streets, at the west edge of Gastown, which is accessible from the Waterfront station of the Skytrain.

The **Landing** *(375 Water St.)*, with its brick and stone facade, was a commercial warehouse at the time of its construction in 1905; today it is a fine example of restoration. Since the late 1980s, it has housed offices, shops and restaurants.

Walk east along Water Street.

The **Gastown Steam Clock**, at the corner of Cambie Street, uses steam conducted through an underground network of pipes to whistle the hours. In clear weather, this spot affords a stunning view of the mountains north of the city.

Farther along Water Street, you will see the steep roofs of **Gaslight Square** *(131 Water St.)*, a shopping centre laid out around a pretty inner court (Henriquez and Todd, 1975). Nearby are the offices of the **Architectural Institute of British Columbia** ★ *(free; summer Wed to Sun, Sep to May weekends only, 440 Cambie St., Suite 100, schedule and programme, ☎683-8588)*, which offers guided tours of Vancouver during the summertime.

The intersection of Water and Carrall Streets is one of the liveliest parts of Gastown. Long **Byrnes Block** *(2 Water St.)*, on the southwest corner, was one of the first buildings to be erected after the terrible fire of 1886. It was built on the site of Gassy Jack's saloon; a statue of the celebrated barkeep graces tiny **Maple Tree Square**. The thick cornice on the brick building is typical of commercial buildings of the Victorian era. Rising in front is the former **Hotel Europe** *(4 Powell St.)*, a triangular building erected in 1908 by a Canadian hotel-keeper of Italian descent.

Head south on Carrall Street, then turn right onto West Cordova .

Lonsdale Block *(8-28 W. Cordova St.)*, built in 1889, is one of the most remarkable buildings on this street, which is undergoing a beautiful renaissance with the recent opening of several shops and cafés.

Turn left on Abbott Street.

The south end of Abbott Street is dominated by the **Sun Tower** ★ *(100 W. Pender St.)*, erected in 1911 for the *Vancouver World* newspaper. It later housed the offices of the local daily, *The Vancouver Sun*, after which it was named. At the time of its construction, the Sun Tower was the tallest building in all of the British Empire, although it only had 17 floors.

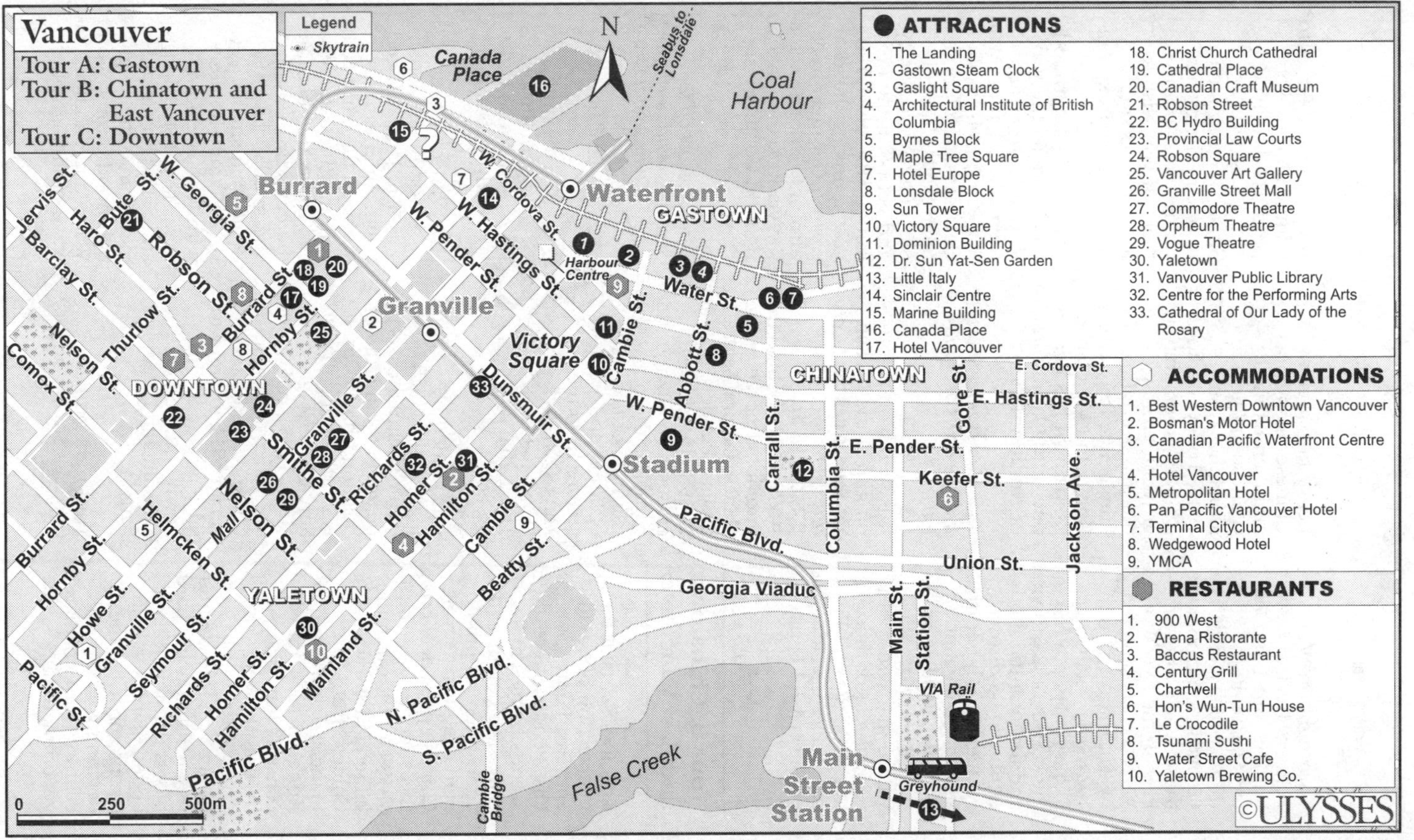

Vancouver
Tour A: Gastown
Tour B: Chinatown and East Vancouver
Tour C: Downtown
Legend
Skytrain
ATTRACTIONS
1. The Landing
2. Gastown Steam Clock
3. Gaslight Square
4. Architectural Institute of British Columbia
5. Byrnes Block
6. Maple Tree Square
7. Hotel Europe
8. Lonsdale Block
9. Sun Tower
10. Victory Square
11. Dominion Building
12. Dr. Sun Yat-Sen Garden
13. Little Italy
14. Sinclair Centre
15. Marine Building
16. Canada Place
17. Hotel Vancouver
18. Christ Church Cathedral
19. Cathedral Place
20. Canadian Craft Museum
21. Robson Street
22. BC Hydro Building
23. Provincial Law Courts
24. Robson Square
25. Vancouver Art Gallery
26. Granville Street Mall
27. Commodore Theatre
28. Orpheum Theatre
29. Vogue Theatre
30. Yaletown
31. Vanvouver Public Library
32. Centre for the Performing Arts
33. Cathedral of Our Lady of the Rosary
ACCOMMODATIONS
1. Best Western Downtown Vancouver
2. Bosman's Motor Hotel
3. Canadian Pacific Waterfront Centre Hotel
4. Hotel Vancouver
5. Metropolitan Hotel
6. Pan Pacific Vancouver Hotel
7. Terminal Cityclub
8. Wedgewood Hotel
9. YMCA
RESTAURANTS
1. 900 West
2. Arena Ristorante
3. Baccus Restaurant
4. Century Grill
5. Chartwell
6. Hon's Wun-Tun House
7. Le Crocodile
8. Tsunami Sushi
9. Water Street Cafe
10. Yaletown Brewing Co.
Canada Place
Coal Harbour
Seabus to Lonsdale
N
Burrard
Waterfront
GASTOWN
Granville
Victory Square
Harbour Centre
Stadium
CHINATOWN
DOWNTOWN
YALETOWN
Main Street Station
VIA Rail
Greyhound
False Creek
Cambie Bridge
Jervis St.
Bute St.
W. Georgia St.
Haro St.
Barclay St.
Robson St.
Thurlow St.
Burrard St.
Hornby St.
Nelson St.
Comox St.
W. Cordova St.
W. Hastings St.
W. Pender St.
Water St.
Cambie St.
Abbott St.
Dunsmuir St.
Granville St.
Smithe St.
Richards St.
Homer St.
Hamilton St.
Mall
Helmcken St.
Howe St.
Seymour St.
Mainland St.
Beatty St.
Pacific Blvd.
N. Pacific Blvd.
S. Pacific Blvd.
Pacific St.
Georgia Viaduc
Carrall St.
Columbia St.
E. Cordova St.
E. Hastings St.
E. Pender St.
Gore St.
Keefer St.
Union St.
Jackson Ave.
Main St.
Station St.
0
250
500m
©ULYSSES

Turn right on West Pender Street to reach Cambie Street and **Victory Square**, in the centre of which stands **The Cenotaph**, a memorial to those who lost their lives in the two World Wars. It was sculpted by Thornton Sharp in 1924. The square acts like a pivot between the streets of Gastown and those of the modern business district. Facing onto the north side is the elegant **Dominion Building ★** *(207 W. Hastings St.)*, whose mansard roof is reminiscent of those found on Second Empire buildings along the boulevards of Paris.

Tour B: Chinatown and East Vancouver

This tour starts at the intersection of Carall and East Pender. On East Pender Street, the scene changes radically. The colour and atmosphere of public markets, plus a strong Chinese presence, bring this street to life. The 1858 Gold Rush in the hinterland drew Chinese from San Francisco and Hong Kong; in 1878, railway construction brought thousands more Chinese to British Columbia. This community resisted many hard blows that might have ended its presence in the province. At the beginning of the 20th century, the Canadian government imposed a heavy tax on new Chinese immigrants, and then banned Chinese immigration altogether from 1923 to 1947. Today, the local Chinese community is growing rapidly due to the massive influx of immigrants from Hong Kong, and Vancouver's Chinatown has become one of the largest in all of North America.

Take East Pender Street into the heart of Chinatown.

It is well worth stopping in at the **Dr. Sun Yat-Sen Garden ★** *(every day 10am to 7:30pm; 578 Carrall St., ☎689-7133)*, behind the traditional portal of the **Chinese Cultural Centre** at 50 East Pender St. Built in 1986 by Chinese artists from Suzhou, this garden is the only example outside Asia of landscape architecture from the Ming Dynasty (1368-1644). The 1.2ha green space is surrounded by high walls which create a virtual oasis of peace in the middle of bustling Chinatown. It is worth noting that Dr. Sun Yat-Sen (1866-1925), considered the father of modern China, visited Vancouver in 1911 in order to raise money for his newly founded Kuomintang ("People's Party").

Turn right on East Cordova Street and south on Gore Street to admire all the exotic products displayed along East Pender Street or enjoy a meal in one of the many Chinese restaurants there. If you wish to leave no stone unturned in your exploration of Vancouver's ethnic neighbourhoods, take Gore all the way to Keefer, turn right, then take a left on Main Street to reach Pacific Central Station (about a 5min walk). Take the Skytrain toward Surrey, and get off at the next station (Broadway). If you're driving, head east on Georgia Street, turn onto Prior Street at the viaduct, then take a right on Commercial Drive.

When you get off the Skytrain, head north up Commercial Drive.

The next part of town you'll pass through is known as **Little Italy**, but is also home to Vancouverites of Portuguese, Spanish, Jamaican and South American descent. In the early 20th century, the Commercial Drive area became the city's first suburb, and middle-class residents built small, single-family homes with wooden siding here. The first Chinese and Slavic immigrants moved into the neighbourhood during World War I, and another wave of immigrants, chiefly Italian, arrived at the end of World War II.

Tour C: Downtown

On May 23, 1887, Canadian Pacific's first transcontinental train, which set out from Montréal, arrived at the Vancouver terminus. The railway company, which had been granted an area roughly corresponding to present-day downtown Vancouver, began to develop its property. To say that it played a major role in the development of the city's business district would be an understatement. Canadian Pacific truly built this part of town, laying the streets and erecting some of the area's most important buildings.

This tour starts at the corner of West Hastings and Richards. Head west on West Hastings, toward the Marine Building, which will be directly in your line of vision. This tour can easily be combined with Tour A, which covers Gastown and ends nearby.

The **Sinclair Centre** ★ *(701 W. Hastings St.)* is a group of government offices. It occupies a former post office, and its annexes are connected to one another by covered passageways lined with shops. The main building, dating from 1909, is considered to be one of the finest examples of the neo-baroque style in Canada.

The **Marine Building** ★★ *(355 Burrard St.)*, which faces straight down West Hastings Street, is a fine example of the Art Deco style, characterized by vertical lines, staggered recesses, geometric ornamentation and the absence of a cornice at the top of the structure. Erected in 1929, the building lives up to its name, in part because it is lavishly decorated with nautical motifs, and also because its occupants are ship-owners and shipping companies. Its facade features terra cotta panels depicting the history of shipping and the discovery of the Pacific coast.

Sinclair Centre

The interior decor is even more inventive, however. The lights in the lobby are shaped like the prows of ships, and there is a stained glass window showing the sun setting over the ocean. The elevators will take you up to the mezzanine, which offers an interesting general view of the building.

Take Burrard Street toward the water to reach **Canada Place** ★★ *(999 Canada Place)*, which occupies one of the piers along the harbour and looks like a giant sailboat ready to set out across the waves. This multipurpose complex, which served as the Canadian pavilion at Expo '86, is home to the city's Convention Centre, the harbour station where ocean liners dock, the luxurious Pan Pacific Hotel and an Imax theatre. Take a walk on the "deck" and drink in the magnificent panoramic view of Burrard Inlet, the port and the snow-capped mountains.

Take Burrard Street back into the centre of town and continue southward to West Georgia Street.

The imposing **Hotel Vancouver** ★*(900 W. Georgia St.)*, a veritable monument to the Canadian railway companies that built it between 1928 and 1939, stands at the corner of West Georgia Street. For many years, its high copper roof served as the principal symbol of Vancouver abroad. Like all major Canadian cities, Vancouver had to have a Château-style hotel. Make sure to take a look at the gargoyles near the top and the bas-reliefs at the entrance, which depict an ocean liner and a moving locomotive.

The 23-storey hotel dwarfs the tiny **Christ Church Cathedral** *(690 Burrard St.)* facing it. This Gothic Revival Anglican cathedral was built in 1889, back when Vancouver was no more than a large village. Its skeleton, made of Douglas fir, is visible from inside. What is most interesting about the cathedral, however, is neither its size nor its ornamentation, but simply the fact that it has survived in this part of town, which is continually being rebuilt.

Flanking the cathedral to the east are the shops and offices of **Cathedral Place** *(925 W. Georgia St.)*, built in 1991. Its pseudo-medieval gargoyles have not managed to make people forget about the Art Deco style Georgia Medical Building, which once occupied this site, and whose demolition in 1989 prompted a nationwide outcry. The **Canadian Craft Museum** *($5; Mon to Sat 10am to 5pm, Sun and holidays noon to 5pm, Thu to 9pm, Sep to May closed Tue; 639 Hornby St., ☎687-8266)* lies behind in a pretty little garden integrated into the project. This small, recently built spot houses a sampling of Canadian handicrafts and a few decorative elements that were part of the Georgia Medical Building.

Head west on West Georgia Street.

Turn left on Thurlow Street and left again on **Robson Street** ★, which is lined with fashionable boutiques, elaborately decorated restaurants and West Coast-style cafés. People sit at tables outside, enjoying the fine weather and watching the motley crowds stroll by. In the mid-20th century, a small German community settled around Robson Street, dubbing it Robsonstrasse, a nickname it bears to this day.

Return to Burrard Street, turn right and continue to Nelson Street.

The former **B.C. Hydro Building** ★ *(970 Burrard St.)*, at the corner of Nelson and Burrard, was once the head office of the province's hydroelectric company. In 1993, it was converted into a 242-unit co-op and renamed The Electra. Designed in 1955 by local architects Thompson, Berwick and Pratt, it is considered to be one of the most sophisticated skyscrapers of that era in all of North America. The ground floor is adorned with a mural and a mosaic in shades of grey, blue and green, executed by artist B.C. Binning.

Walk east on Nelson Street.

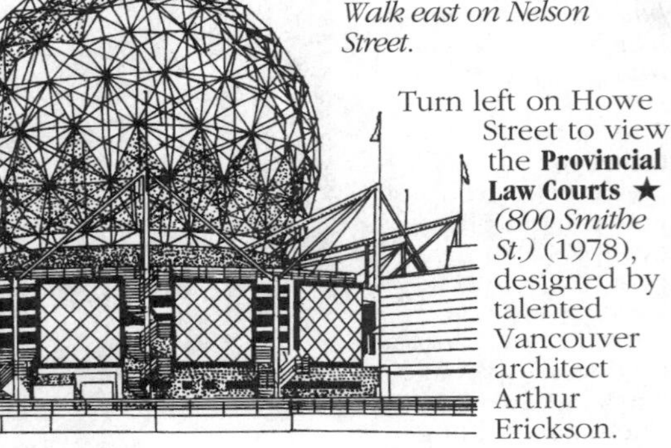

Turn left on Howe Street to view the **Provincial Law Courts** ★ *(800 Smithe St.)* (1978), designed by talented Vancouver architect Arthur Erickson.

The vast interior space, accented in glass and steal, is worth a visit. The courthouse and **Robson Square** *(on the 800 block of Robson St.)*, by the same architect, form a lovely ensemble.

The **Vancouver Art Gallery** ★ *($10; May 3 to Oct 9, Mon to Wed 10am to 6pm, Thu 10am to 9pm, Fri 10am to 6pm, Sat 10am to 5pm, Sun and holidays noon to 5pm, closed Mon and Tue during winter; 750 Hornby St., ☎662-4700)*, located north of Robson Square, occupies the former Provincial Law Courts. This big, neoclassical-style building was erected in 1908 according to a design by British architect Francis Mawson Rattenbury, whose other credits include the British Columbia Legislative Assembly and the Empress Hotel, both located in Victoria, on Vancouver Island. Later, Rattenbury returned to his native country and was assassinated by his wife's lover. The museum's collection includes a number of paintings by Emily Carr (1871-1945), a major Canadian painter whose primary subjects were the Aboriginal peoples and landscapes of the West Coast.

Continue along Howe Street.

Turn right on West Georgia Street, then right again on the **Granville Street Mall** ★, the street of cinemas, theatres, nightclubs and retail stores. Its busy sidewalks are hopping 24hrs a day.

Stroll along the Granville Street Mall heading south towards Theatre Row. You'll pass the **Commodore Theatre** *(870 Granville St.)* and the **Orpheum Theatre** ★*(649 Cambie St., free tour upon reservation ☎665-3050)*. Behind the latter's narrow facade, barely 8m wide, a long corridor opens onto a 2,800-seat Spanish-style Renaissance Revival theatre.

Vancouver Public Library

Designed by Marcus Priteca, it was the largest and most luxurious movie theatre in Canada when it opened in 1927. After being meticulously restored in 1977, the Orpheum became the concert hall of the Vancouver Symphony Orchestra. Farther south, you'll see the vertical sign of the **Vogue Theatre** *(918 Granville St.)*, erected in 1941. Today, popular musicals are presented in its Streamlined Art Deco hall.

Turn left on Nelson and left again on Homer.

Located in the southeast of the downtown area, **Yaletown** was an industrial area when the railways were still king. The growth of the trucking industry shifted business away from Yaletown's big warehouses, and the loading docks of Hamilton and Mainland streets have since been transformed into outdoor cafés and restaurants. A new group of tenants now occupies the old brick warehouses; designers, architects, film production companies and business people in general have brought this area back to life; trendy cafés and restaurants have followed suit.

At the corner of Robson Street is a curious building that is somewhat reminiscent of Rome's Coliseum. It is the **Vancouver Public Library** ★★ *(free admission; year-round, Mon and Tue 10am to 9pm, Wed to Sat 10am to 6pm; Oct to Apr, Sun 1pm to 5pm, closed Sun in the summer; free tours can be arranged, ☎331-4041; 350 W. Georgia St., ☎331-3600).*

This brand-new building is the work of Montréal architect Moshe Safdie, known for his Habitat '67 in Montréal and the National Art Gallery in Ottawa. The project stirred lively reactions both from local people and from architecture critics. The design was chosen after finally being put to a referendum. The six-storey atrium is positively grandiose. The **Ford Centre for the Performing Arts**, completed in 1996, lies just opposite on Homer Street. Among other things, it contains an 1,800-seat theatre, whose orchestra seats, balcony and stage are depicted on the facade, north of the glass cone that serves as the entryway. These two buildings are sure evidence of Vancouver's thriving cultural scene.

Take Homer Street north, then turn right on Dunsmuir Street.

To conclude your tour of downtown Vancouver, stop by the city's Catholic cathedral, the **Cathedral of Our Lady of the Rosary** *(at the corner of Dunsmuir and Richards)*, erected in 1899. The rusticated stone facing and the wood and metal clock towers are reminiscent of parish churches built around the same time in Quebec.

Tour D: The West End and Stanley Park

Excluding Vancouver Island, farther west, the West End is the end of the line, the final destination of that quest for a better life that thousands of city-dwellers from eastern Canada have been embarking upon for generations. Despite all its concrete skyscrapers, the West End has a laid-back atmosphere, influenced both by the immensity of the Pacific and the wisdom of the Orient.

Because of this westward movement, and the fact that there is nowhere to go beyond here, the West End has the highest population per square kilometre of any area in Canada. Fortunately, nature is never far off, what with nearby Stanley Park (see p 74), stunning views of snow-capped mountains from the streets running north-south, or simply the sight of a cackling Canada goose strolling around a busy intersection.

Head west on Davie Street, then left on Bidwell Street to reach **Alexandra Park ★**, which forms a point south of Burnaby Street.

This luxuriant park also offers a splendid view of **English Bay Beach ★★** *(along the shore between Chilco and Bidwell Sts.)*, whose fine sands are crowded during the summer.

After dipping your big toe in the Pacific Ocean (it's that close!), walk up Cardero Street to Robson Street.

Head east on Robson Street, to the **Robson Public Market ★** *(1610 Robson, at the corner of Cardero)*, a bustling indoor market with a long glass roof. You'll find everything here from live crabs and fresh pasta to local handicrafts. You can also eat here, as dishes from all over the world are served on the top floor. A pleasure for both the palate and the eyes!

★★★ Stanley Park

Lord Stanley, the same person for whom ice hockey's Stanley Cup was named, founded Stanley Park on a romantic impulse back in the 19th century, when he was Canada's Governor General (1888-1893). Stanley Park lies on an elevated peninsula stretching into the Georgia Strait, and encompasses 405ha of flowering gardens, dense woodlands and lookouts offering views of the sea and the mountains.

Obviously Vancouver's many skyscrapers have not prevented the city from maintaining close ties with the nearby wilderness. Some species are held in captivity, but many others roam free – sometimes even venturing into the West End.

A 10km water front promenade known as the **Seawall** runs around the park, enabling pedestrians to drink in every bit of the stunning scenery here. The **Stanley Park Scenic Drive** is the equivalent of the Seawall for motorists. The best way to explore Stanley Park, however, is by bicycle. You can rent one from **Stanely Park Rentals** *(corner of West Georgia and Denman, ☎688-5141)* (see p 88).

Another way to discover some of the park's hidden treasures is to walk along one of the many footpaths crisscrossing the territory. There are numerous rest areas along the way.

From West Georgia Street, walk along Coal Harbour toward Brockton Point.

You'll be greeted by the sight of scores of gleaming yachts in the Vancouver marina, with the downtown skyline in the background. This is the most developed portion of the park, where you'll find the **Malkin Bowl**, the **Brockton Oval** and most importantly, the **Totem Poles ★**, reminders that there was a sizeable Aboriginal population on the peninsula barely 150 years ago. The **9 O'Clock Gun** goes off every day at 9pm on Brockton Point (it is best not to be too close when it does). This shot used to alert fishermen that it was time to come in.

Continue walking along Burrard Inlet.

On the left is the entrance to the renowned **Vancouver Aquarium Marine Science Centre ★★★** *($13; Jul and Aug, every day 9:30am to 7pm; Sep to Jun, every day 10am to 5:30pm; ☎659-3474)*, which has the undeniable advantage of being located near the ocean. It displays representatives of the marine animal life of the West Coast and the Pacific as a whole, including magnificent killer whales, belugas, dolphins, seals and exotic fish. The zoo at the back is home to sea lions and polar bears, among other creatures. The nearby **Miniature Railway** is a real hit with kids.

Head back to the Seawall under **Lions Gate Bridge ★★**, an elegant suspension bridge built in 1938. It spans the First Narrows, linking the affluent suburb of West Vancouver to the centre of town. **Prospect Point ★★★**, to the west, offers a general view of the bridge, whose steel pillars stand 135m high. Next, the Seawall passes **Third Beach ★**, one of the most pleasant beaches in the region.

We recommend stopping at the **Stanley Park Tearoom ★** (see Teahouse Restaurant, p 98), located between Third Beach and **Second Beach ★**.

Complete the loop by taking the path to the **Lost Lagoon ★**, which was once part of Coal Harbour but was partially filled in during the construction of Lions Gate Bridge. It is now a bird sanctuary, where large numbers of barnacle geese, mallards and swans can be seen frolicking about.

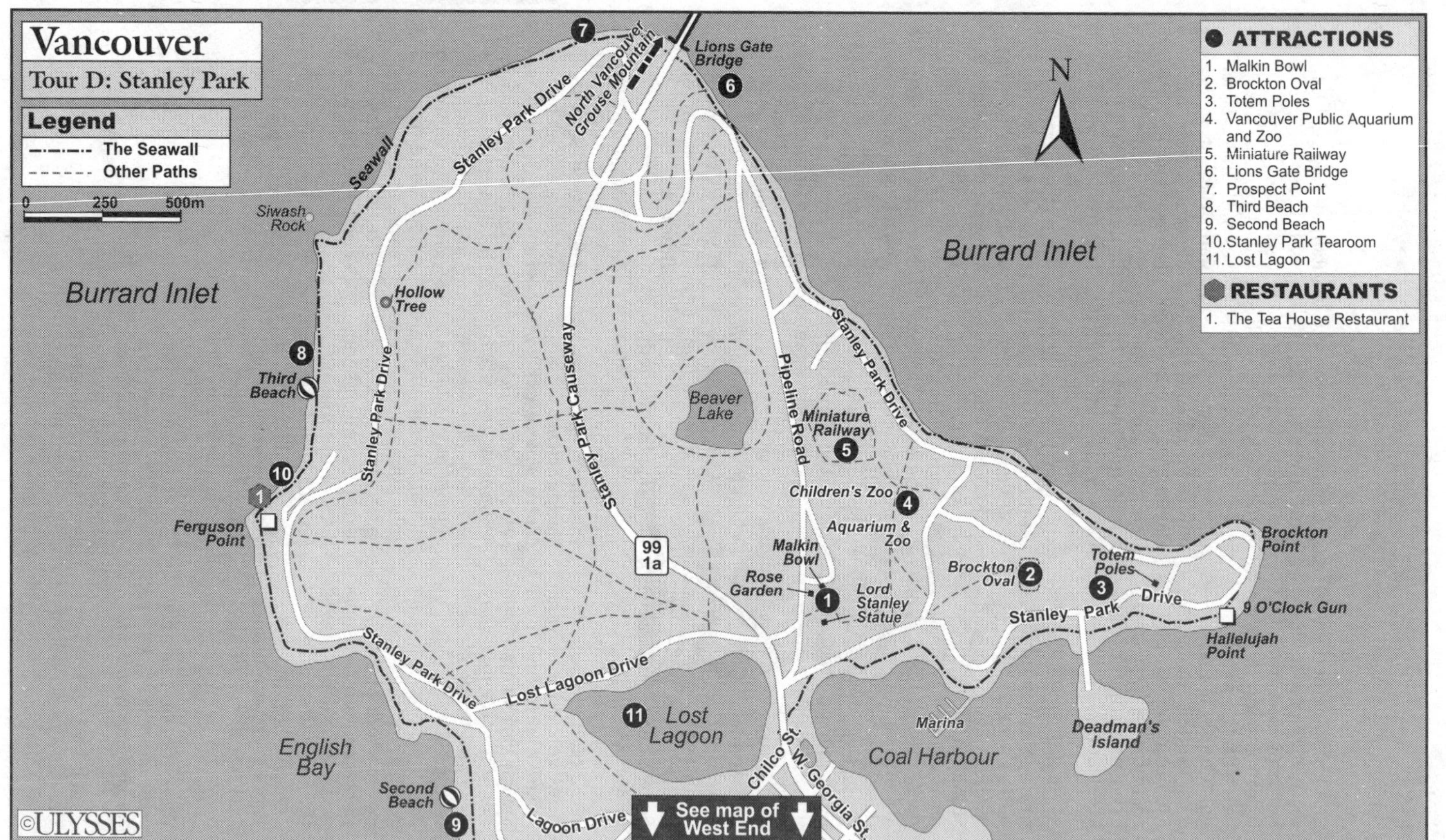
Vancouver
Tour D: Stanley Park
Legend
The Seawall
Other Paths
0 250 500m
ATTRACTIONS
1. Malkin Bowl
2. Brockton Oval
3. Totem Poles
4. Vancouver Public Aquarium and Zoo
5. Miniature Railway
6. Lions Gate Bridge
7. Prospect Point
8. Third Beach
9. Second Beach
10. Stanley Park Tearoom
11. Lost Lagoon
RESTAURANTS
1. The Tea House Restaurant
N
Burrard Inlet
Burrard Inlet
English Bay
Coal Harbour
Seawall
Siwash Rock
Hollow Tree
Third Beach
Ferguson Point
Second Beach
Stanley Park Drive
Stanley Park Drive
Stanley Park Drive
Stanley Park Drive
North Vancouver
Grouse Mountain
Lions Gate Bridge
Stanley Park Causeway
99
1a
Beaver Lake
Pipeline Road
Miniature Railway
Children's Zoo
Aquarium & Zoo
Malkin Bowl
Rose Garden
Lord Stanley Statue
Brockton Oval
Totem Poles
Stanley Park Drive
Brockton Point
9 O'Clock Gun
Hallelujah Point
Deadman's Island
Marina
Lost Lagoon Drive
Lost Lagoon
Lagoon Drive
Chilco St.
W. Georgia St.
See map of West End
©ULYSSES

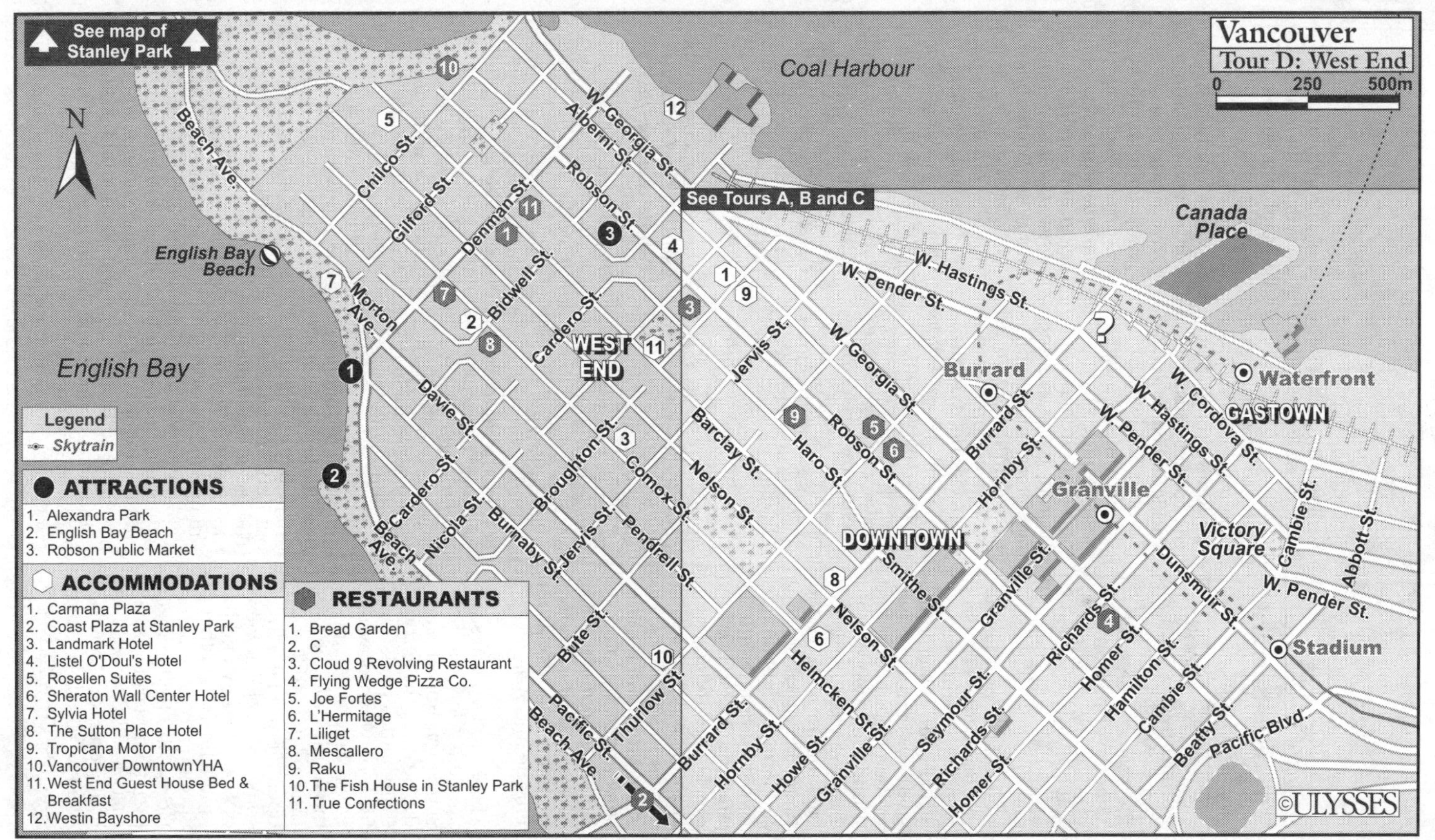

Vancouver
Tour D: West End
0 250 500m
See map of Stanley Park
See Tours A, B and C
Coal Harbour
English Bay
English Bay Beach
Canada Place
WEST END
DOWNTOWN
GASTOWN
Victory Square
Waterfront
Burrard
Granville
Stadium
Beach Ave.
Chilco St.
Gilford St.
Denman St.
Robson St.
Alberni St.
W. Georgia St.
Bidwell St.
Cardero St.
Morton Ave.
Davie St.
Nicola St.
Burnaby St.
Broughton St.
Jervis St.
Comox St.
Pendrell St.
Bute St.
Thurlow St.
Pacific St.
Barclay St.
Nelson St.
Haro St.
W. Pender St.
W. Hastings St.
Burrard St.
Hornby St.
Howe St.
Granville St.
Seymour St.
Richards St.
Homer St.
Helmcken St.
Smithe St.
Hamilton St.
Cambie St.
Beatty St.
Pacific Blvd.
Dunsmuir St.
W. Cordova St.
Abbott St.
Legend
Skytrain
ATTRACTIONS
1. Alexandra Park
2. English Bay Beach
3. Robson Public Market
ACCOMMODATIONS
1. Carmana Plaza
2. Coast Plaza at Stanley Park
3. Landmark Hotel
4. Listel O'Doul's Hotel
5. Rosellen Suites
6. Sheraton Wall Center Hotel
7. Sylvia Hotel
8. The Sutton Place Hotel
9. Tropicana Motor Inn
10. Vancouver DowntownYHA
11. West End Guest House Bed & Breakfast
12. Westin Bayshore
RESTAURANTS
1. Bread Garden
2. C
3. Cloud 9 Revolving Restaurant
4. Flying Wedge Pizza Co.
5. Joe Fortes
6. L'Hermitage
7. Liliget
8. Mescallero
9. Raku
10. The Fish House in Stanley Park
11. True Confections
©ULYSSES

Tour E: Burrard Inlet

Burrard Inlet is the long and very wide arm of the sea on which the Vancouver harbour – Canada's most important port for over 20 years now – is located.

Beyond the port lie the mountainside suburbs of North and West Vancouver, which offer some spectacular views of the city below. Along their steep, winding roads, visitors can admire some of the finest examples of modern residential architecture in North America. These luxurious houses, often constructed of posts and beams made of local wood, are usually surrounded by lofty British Columbian firs and a luxuriant blend of plants imported from Europe and Asia.

There are two ways to take this tour. The first is by foot: hop aboard the Seabus, the ferry that shuttles back and forth between downtown Vancouver and the north shore of Burrard Inlet, enjoy the open air and take in some exceptional views of both the city and the mountains. The other option is to drive across Lions Gate Bridge (see p ?), take Marine Drive east to Third Street and head south on Lonsdale Avenue. The following descriptions refer to the walking tour, unless otherwise indicated.

Start off your tour in front of the Neo-Classical Revival facade of the former **Canadian Pacific Station** ★ *(601 W. Cordova St.)*, which dates from 1912 and was designed by Montréal architects Barrott, Blackader and Webster. This station, Canadian Pacific's third in Vancouver, occupies a special place in the city's history, for before ships arriving from the west took over, trains arriving from the east fuelled the area's prosperous economy. In keeping with the times, the station no longer welcomes trains, but provides access to the Granville terminal of the Seabus. It also provides indirect access to the Waterfront terminal of the Skytrain (at the far end of Howe Street), but that's somewhat of a meagre consolation prize.

Follow the signs for the Seabus. The crossing *($1.50)* takes barely 15min, though you'll wish it were longer. The ferry lands at its northern terminal near the pleasant **Lonsdale Quay Market** ★★, built on a quay stretching out into Burrard Inlet. The cafés surrounding the market offer an unimpeded view of Vancouver and the mountains, as well as all the activity at the nearby port, for the colourful tugboat dock flanks the market to the east. From here, Vancouver really looks like a Manhattan in the making.

If you are travelling by car, return to Marine Drive heading west and go up Capilano Road until you reach the **Capilano Suspension Bridge and Park** *($10; May to Oct 8am to 9pm; Nov to Apr 9am to 5pm; 3735 Capilano Rd., ☎985-7474)*. If you are on foot at Lonsdale Quay Market, take bus number 236 to Edgmont Boulevard. Paths lead to this metal-cabled bridge, suspended 70m above the Capilano River, which replaced the original bridge of rope and wood built in 1899.

Three kilometres to the north is the **Capilano Fish Hatchery** ★ *(free entry; 4500 Capilano Park Rd., ☎666-1790)* the first salmon hatchery in British Columbia. This well-laid-out spot provides visitors with an introduction to the life cycle of the salmon. In the summer, Pacific salmon wear themselves out as they make their way up the Capilano River to reach the reproduction centre, making for an exceptional spectacle for visitors.

At the north end of Nancy Greene Way, there is a **cable car** *($17; summer every day 9am to 10pm, Sat and Sun 8am to 10pm; ☎984-0661)* that carries passengers

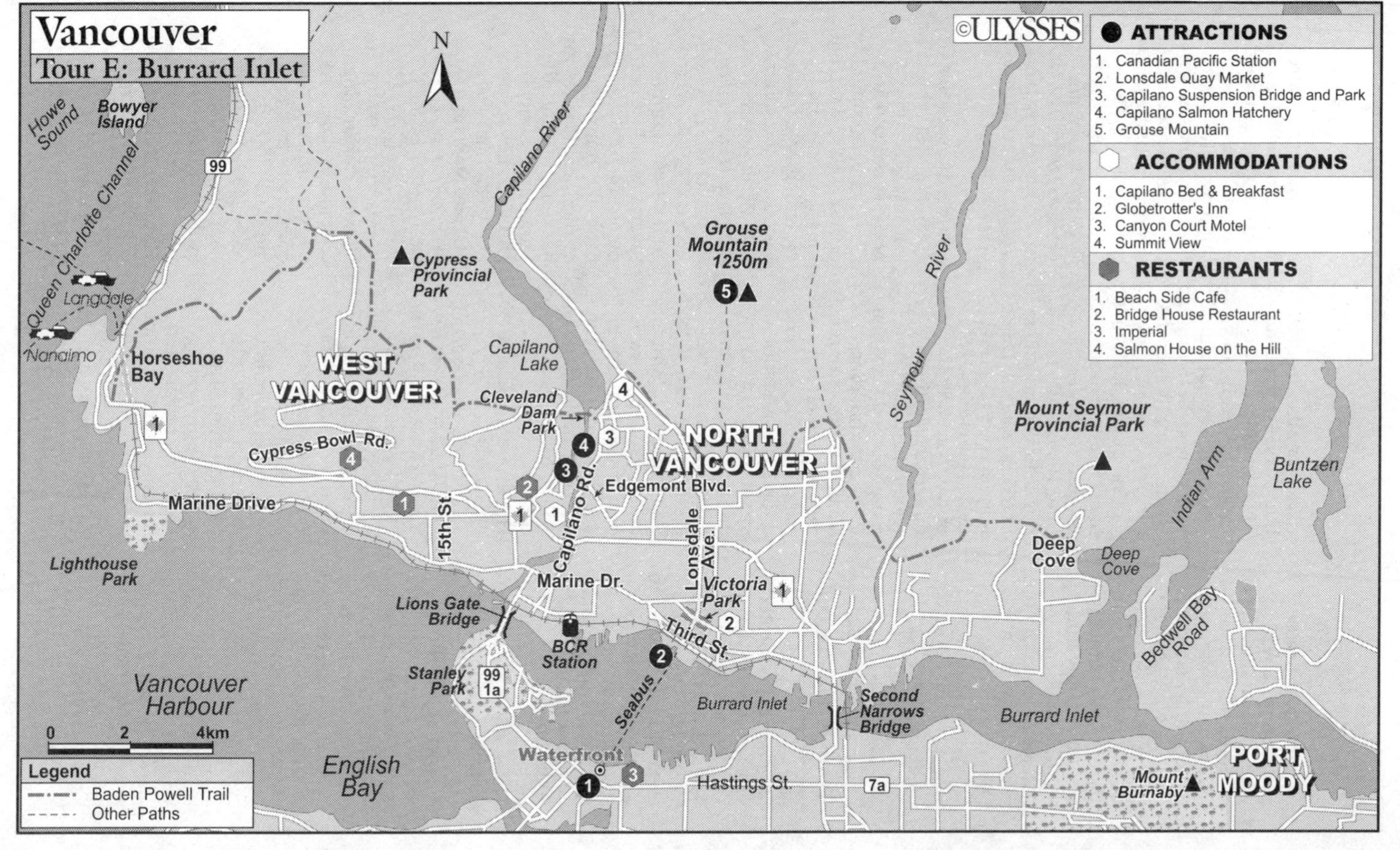

Vancouver
Tour E: Burrard Inlet
©ULYSSES
N
ATTRACTIONS
1. Canadian Pacific Station
2. Lonsdale Quay Market
3. Capilano Suspension Bridge and Park
4. Capilano Salmon Hatchery
5. Grouse Mountain
ACCOMMODATIONS
1. Capilano Bed & Breakfast
2. Globetrotter's Inn
3. Canyon Court Motel
4. Summit View
RESTAURANTS
1. Beach Side Cafe
2. Bridge House Restaurant
3. Imperial
4. Salmon House on the Hill
Howe Sound
Bowyer Island
Queen Charlotte Channel
Langdale
Nanaimo
Horseshoe Bay
Cypress Provincial Park
Capilano River
Grouse Mountain 1250m
Seymour River
Capilano Lake
WEST VANCOUVER
Cleveland Dam Park
NORTH VANCOUVER
Mount Seymour Provincial Park
Cypress Bowl Rd.
Edgemont Blvd.
Capilano Rd.
Marine Drive
15th St.
Lonsdale Ave.
Indian Arm
Buntzen Lake
Deep Cove
Lighthouse Park
Marine Dr.
Victoria Park
Lions Gate Bridge
BCR Station
Third St.
Bedwell Bay Road
Stanley Park
Vancouver Harbour
Seabus
Burrard Inlet
Second Narrows Bridge
Waterfront
English Bay
Hastings St.
PORT MOODY
Mount Burnaby
0 2 4km
Legend
Baden Powell Trail
Other Paths

to the top of **Grouse Mountain ★★★**, where, at an altitude of 1,250m, skiers and hikers can contemplate the entire Vancouver area, as well as Washington State (in clear weather) to the south. The view is particularly beautiful at the end of the day. Wilderness trails lead out from the various viewing areas. During summer, Grouse Mountain is also a popular spot for hang-gliding.

Tour F: False Creek

False Creek is located south of downtown Vancouver and, like Burrard Inlet, stretches far inland. The presence of both water and a railroad induced a large number of sawmills to set up shop in this area in the early 20th century.

These mills gradually filled a portion of False Creek, leaving only a narrow channel to provide them with water, which is necessary for sawing. Over the years, two thirds of False Creek, as explorer George Vancouver had known it in 1790, disappeared under asphalt.

In 1974, when the local sawmills shut down en masse, people began moving into new housing developments, the likes of which were becoming more and more popular around the world by that time. Then, in 1986, False Creek hosted Expo '86, attracting several million visitors here in the space of a few months.

Get off at the Skytrain's Main Street Station, located opposite the long Beaux-Arts facade of **Pacific Central Station** *(1150 Station St.)*. Determined not to be outdone, Canadian National (formerly the Canadian Northern Pacific Railway Company) copied Canadian Pacific by building a second transcontinental railway, which ran parallel to the first and ended at this station, erected in 1919 on the embankment of False Creek. Today, it welcomes Canadian VIA trains and U.S. Amtrak trains, as well as various private trains which use the tracks running through the Rockies for scenic tours.

Head over to **Science World ★** *($11.75 or $14.75 with movie; 1455 Quebec St., ☎443-7440)*, the big silver ball at the end of False Creek. Architect Bruno Freschi designed this 14-storey building as a welcome centre for visitors to Expo '86. It was the only pavilion built to remain in place after the big event. The sphere representing the Earth has supplanted the tower as the quintessential symbol of these fairs since Expo '67 in Montréal. Vancouver's sphere contains an Omnimax theatre, which presents films on a giant, dome-shaped screen. The rest of the building is now occupied by a museum that explores the secrets of science from all different angles.

Walk alongside False Creek to Pacific Boulevard South before plunging into the void beneath Cambie Bridge.

During the summer of 1986, the vast stretch of unused land along the north shore of False Creek was occupied by dozens of showy pavilions with visitors crowding around them. Visible on the other side of an access road, **GM Place** *(Pacific Blvd. at the corner of Abbott, ☎899-7400)* is a 20,000-seat amphitheatre which was completed in 1995 and now hosts the home games of the local hockey and basketball teams, the Vancouver Canucks and Grizzlies respectively. Its big brother, **BC Place Stadium** *(777 Pacific Blvd. N., ☎669-2300, 661-7373 or 661-2122, ⇌661-3412)* stands to the south. Its 60,000 seats are highly coveted by fans of Canadian football, who come here to cheer on the B.C. Lions. Big trade fairs and rock concerts are also held in the stadium.

The beautifully restored **CPR Roundhouse ★** *(at the corner of Davie St. and Pacific Blvd.)*, located opposite, is all

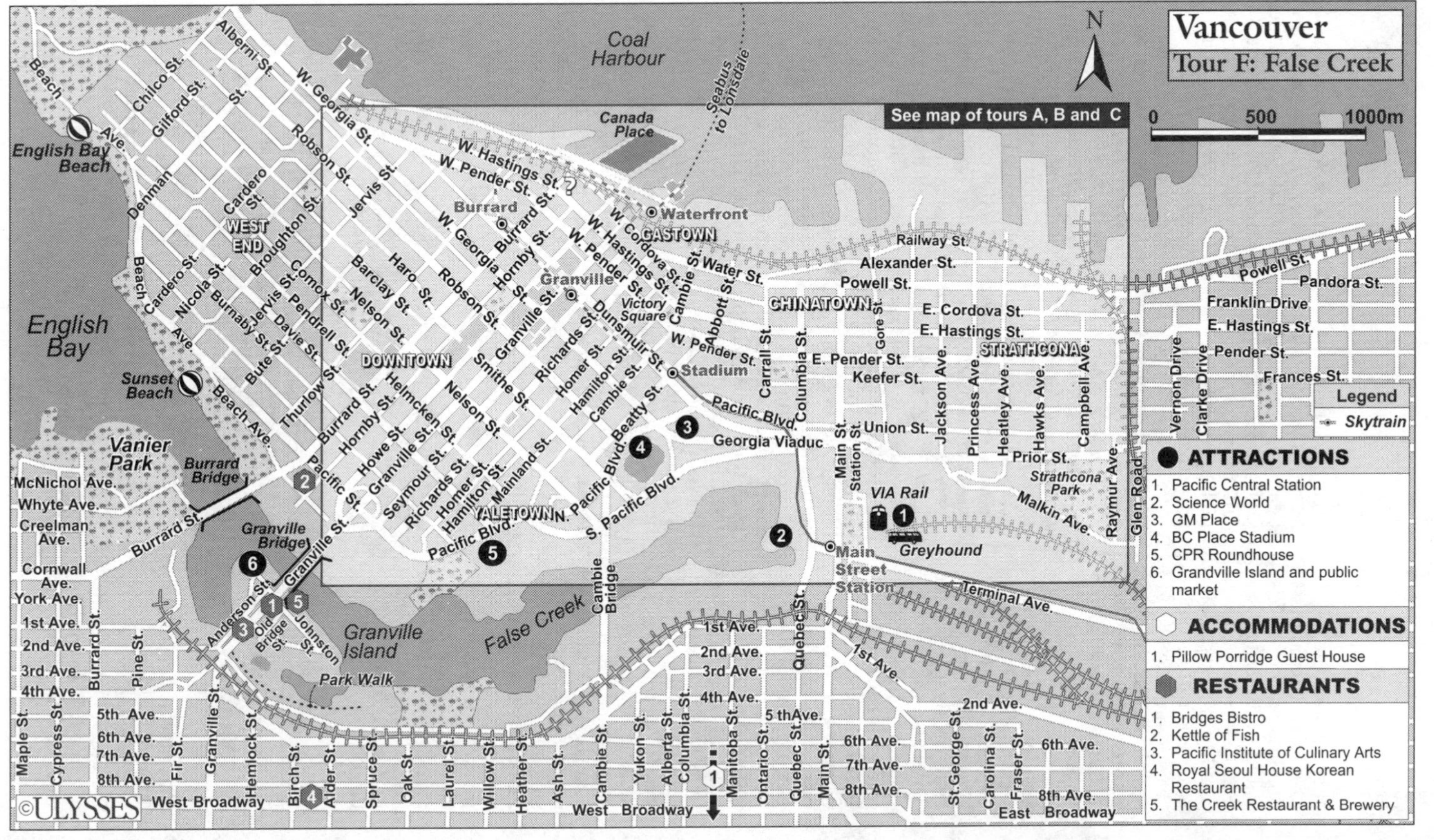

Vancouver
Tour F: False Creek
0 500 1000m
See map of tours A, B and C
Legend
Skytrain
ATTRACTIONS
1. Pacific Central Station
2. Science World
3. GM Place
4. BC Place Stadium
5. CPR Roundhouse
6. Grandville Island and public market
ACCOMMODATIONS
1. Pillow Porridge Guest House
RESTAURANTS
1. Bridges Bistro
2. Kettle of Fish
3. Pacific Institute of Culinary Arts
4. Royal Seoul House Korean Restaurant
5. The Creek Restaurant & Brewery
Coal Harbour
English Bay
False Creek
Granville Island
Vanier Park
WEST END
DOWNTOWN
GASTOWN
CHINATOWN
STRATHCONA
YALETOWN
©ULYSSES

that remains of the Canadian Pacific marshalling yard once located on this site. Erected in 1888, it was used for the servicing and repair of locomotives. Granville Island is visible across the water, as are the new residential areas along False Creek.

Follow Pacific Boulevard under Granville Bridge, then turn left on Hornby Street and right on Beach Avenue. The False Creek ferry docks are nearby; catch a ferry for **Granville Island** and its **public market** ★★. You'll notice the vaguely Art Deco pillars of the Burrard Street Bridge (1930). In 1977, this artificial island, created in 1914 and once used for industrial purposes, saw its warehouses and factories transformed into a major recreational and commercial centre. The area has since come to life thanks to a revitalization project. A public market, many shops and all sorts of restaurants, plus theatres and artists' studios, are all part of Granville Island.

Tour G: South Vancouver

Shaughnessy Heights is an affluent residential enclave, laid out by Canadian Pacific starting in 1907. Extending west of Oak Street, the area boasts elegant avenues lined with beautiful houses and well tended gardens, The Crescent and McRae Avenue are particularly lovely.

Van Dusen Botanical Gardens ★★ *(summer $5.50, winter $2.75; every day, summer 10am to nightfall, call for exact schedule; Apr and Sep 10am to 6pm; Oct to Mar 10am to 4pm; free guided tours every day, 1pm, 2pm and 3pm; 5251 Oak St., ☎878-9274)*. Since Vancouver is so blessed by Mother Nature, a number of lovely gardens have been planted in the area, including this one, which boasts plant species from all over the world. When the rhododendrons are in bloom (late May), the garden deserves another star. At the far end is a housing co-op that blends in so perfectly with the greenery that it looks like a gigantic ornamental sculpture (McCarter, Nairne and Associates, 1976).

Shaughnessy House

Farther east on 33rd Avenue is another magnificent green space, **Queen Elizabeth Park** ★★ *(corner of 33rd Ave. and Cambie St.)*, laid out around the **Bloedel Floral Conservatory** *($3.50; Apr to Sep, Mon to Fri 9am to 8pm, Sat and Sun 10am to 9pm; Oct to Mar, every day 10am to 5pm; at the top of Queen Elizabeth Park, ☎257-8570)*. The latter, shaped like an overturned glass saucer, houses exotic plants and birds. The Bloedel company, which sponsored the conservatory, is the principal lumber company in British Columbia. This park's rhododendron bushes also merit a visit in springtime. Finally, the outdoor gardens offer a spectacular view of the city, English Bay and the surrounding mountains.

One of the other attractions in South Vancouver that visitors with cars can visit is the second biggest **Buddhist temple** in North America *(every day 10am to 5pm; 9160 Steveston Hwy., Richmond, ☎274-2822)*. To get there, take Oak Street southward toward Hwy. 99, which leads to the ferry for Victoria, and get off at the Steveston Highway West exit. Located between the third and fourth streets on your left, this place of worship has free entry.

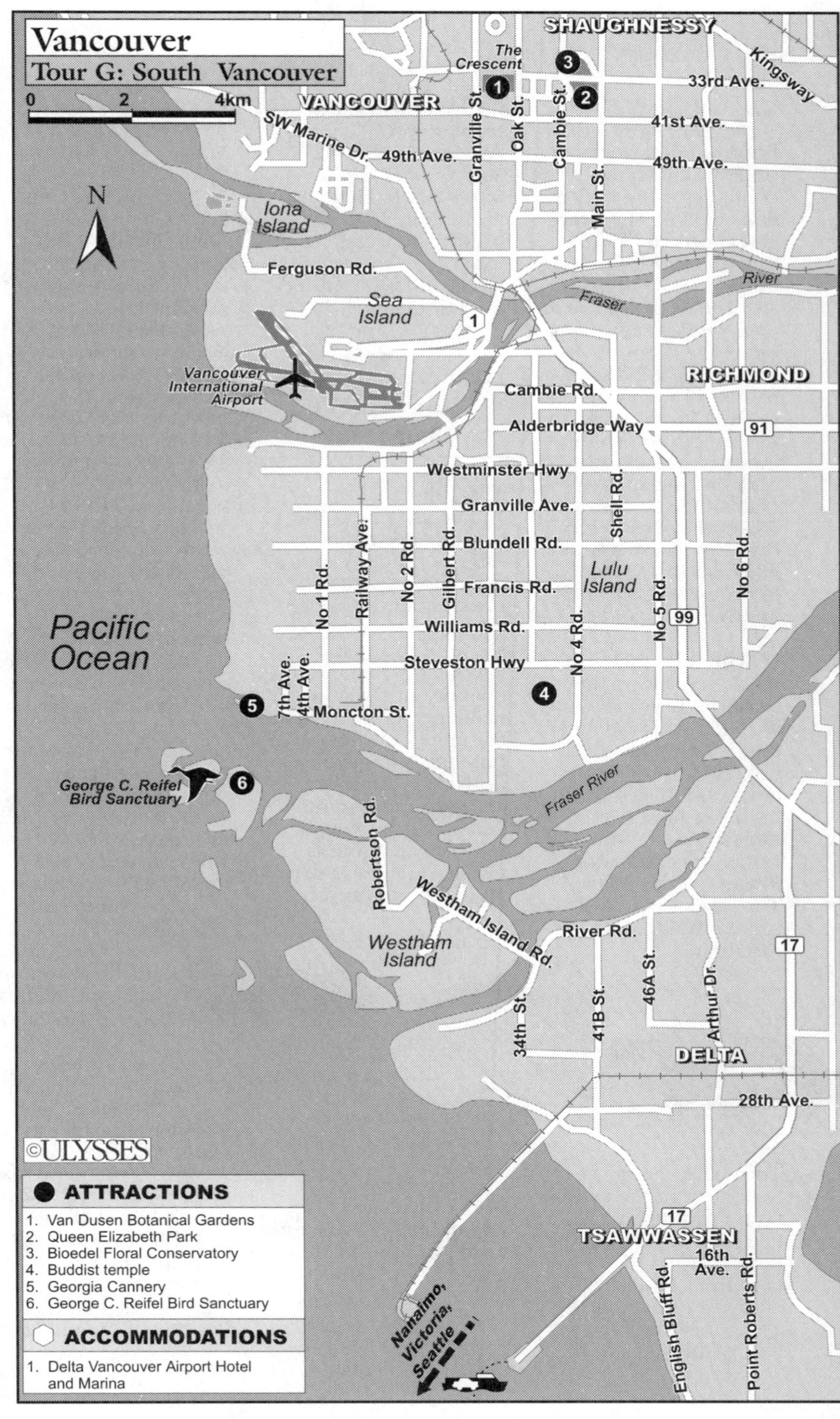

Vancouver
Tour G: South Vancouver
0 2 4km
SHAUGHNESSY
The Crescent
Kingsway
33rd Ave.
VANCOUVER
41st Ave.
SW Marine Dr.
49th Ave.
49th Ave.
Granville St.
Oak St.
Cambie St.
Main St.
N
Iona Island
Ferguson Rd.
Sea Island
River
Fraser
Vancouver International Airport
RICHMOND
Cambie Rd.
Alderbridge Way
91
Westminster Hwy
Granville Ave.
Shell Rd.
Blundell Rd.
Railway Ave.
No 2 Rd.
Gilbert Rd.
No 6 Rd.
Lulu Island
Francis Rd.
No 1 Rd.
No 5 Rd.
99
Williams Rd.
No 4 Rd.
Pacific Ocean
Steveston Hwy
7th Ave.
4th Ave.
Moncton St.
George C. Reifel Bird Sanctuary
Fraser River
Robertson Rd.
Westham Island Rd.
River Rd.
Westham Island
17
34th St.
41B St.
46A St.
Arthur Dr.
DELTA
28th Ave.
©ULYSSES
ATTRACTIONS
1. Van Dusen Botanical Gardens
2. Queen Elizabeth Park
3. Bioedel Floral Conservatory
4. Buddist temple
5. Georgia Cannery
6. George C. Reifel Bird Sanctuary
ACCOMMODATIONS
1. Delta Vancouver Airport Hotel and Marina
17
TSAWWASSEN
16th Ave.
English Bluff Rd.
Point Roberts Rd.
Nanaimo, Victoria, Seattle

Get back on the Steveston Highway heading west, turn left on Fourth Avenue, and continue to the end of this avenue. The **Georgia Cannery** ★ *($5; Jul and Aug, every day 10am to 5pm; May, Jun and Sep, Thu to Mon 10am to 5pm; guided tours every hour; 12138 Fourth Ave., Richmond, ☎664-9009)*, restored by Parks Canada, retraces the history of the fishing industry in Steveston. This historic spot explains the steps involved in conserving fish, especially salmon, and also shows how herring is transformed into pet food and oil.

Leaving this establishment, stay along the seashore by way of the wooden walkway near the fishing boats. Fishing remains an important economic activity in this region. A commercial area with restaurants and shops invites you to relax. The day's catch is served in the restaurants.

Turn back along the Steveston Highway, this time heading east, and take Rte. 99 toward the ferry pier for Victoria; take the Ladner exit after the tunnel. Go along this road and follow the signs to the **George C. Reifel Bird Sanctuary** ★★ *($3.25; every day 9am to 4pm, 5191 Robertson Rd., Delta, ☎946-6980)*. Each year more than 350 species of birds visit this magical spot in the marshlands at the mouth of the Fraser River.

Tour H: The Peninsula

The culture of the Pacific as well as the history and traditions of the Aboriginal peoples are omnipresent throughout this tour, which follows the shore of the vast peninsula that is home to the majority of Vancouver's residents. Posh residential neighbourhoods, numerous museums, a university campus and several sand and quartz beaches from which Vancouver Island is visible on a clear day all make up this tour.

This is a driving tour, as it extends over 15km. The first four attractions are accessible aboard bus # 22 from downtown or by taking bus # 4 directly to the campus of the University of British Columbia.

Exit the downtown area by the Burrard Street Bridge.

Keep right, and immediately after going down the roadway leading off the bridge, take a right on Chestnut Street to get to **Vanier Park**, which is home to three museums. The **Vancouver Museum** ★★ *($8; Jul and Aug, every day 10am to 5pm; Sep to June closed Mon; 1100 Chestnut St., in Vanier Park, ☎736-4431)* forms its centrepiece. This museum, whose dome resembles the headdress worn by the coast Salish First Nation, presents exhibitions on the history of the different peoples who have inhabited the region.

On the same spot is the **Pacific Space Centre** *($12.50; presentations Tue to Sun 2:30pm and 8pm, extra shows Sat and Sun 1pm and 4pm; ☎738-7827)*, which houses the H.R. MacMillan Planetarium and relates the creation of our universe. It has a telescope through which you can admire the stars. The **Maritime Museum** *($6; May to Oct, every day 10am to 5pm; Nov to Apr closed Mon; 1905 Ogden Ave., ☎257-8300)* completes the trio of institutions in Vanier Park. Being a major seaport, it is only natural that Vancouver should have

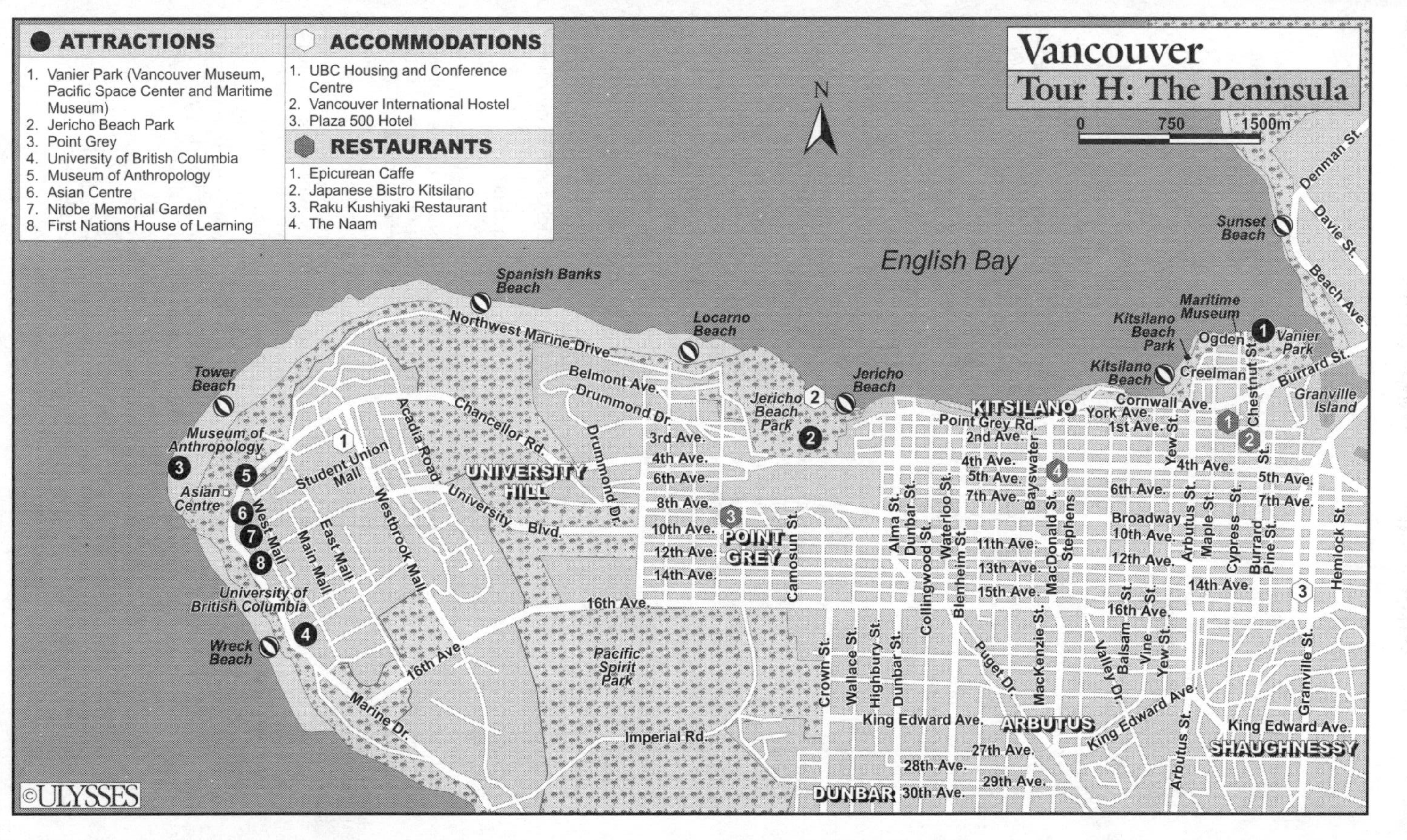

Vancouver
Tour H: The Peninsula
ATTRACTIONS
1. Vanier Park (Vancouver Museum, Pacific Space Center and Maritime Museum)
2. Jericho Beach Park
3. Point Grey
4. University of British Columbia
5. Museum of Anthropology
6. Asian Centre
7. Nitobe Memorial Garden
8. First Nations House of Learning
ACCOMMODATIONS
1. UBC Housing and Conference Centre
2. Vancouver International Hostel
3. Plaza 500 Hotel
RESTAURANTS
1. Epicurean Caffe
2. Japanese Bistro Kitsilano
3. Raku Kushiyaki Restaurant
4. The Naam
N
0
750
1500m
English Bay
Spanish Banks Beach
Northwest Marine Drive
Locarno Beach
Jericho Beach
Jericho Beach Park
Tower Beach
Museum of Anthropology
Asian Centre
Wreck Beach
University of British Columbia
UNIVERSITY HILL
POINT GREY
KITSILANO
ARBUTUS
DUNBAR
SHAUGHNESSY
Pacific Spirit Park
Sunset Beach
Maritime Museum
Kitsilano Beach Park
Kitsilano Beach
Vanier Park
Granville Island
Belmont Ave.
Drummond Dr.
Chancellor Rd.
Acadia Road
Student Union Mall
Westbrook Mall
East Mall
Main Mall
West Mall
University Blvd.
16th Ave.
Marine Dr.
Imperial Rd.
Camosun St.
Crown St.
Wallace St.
Highbury St.
Dunbar St.
Alma St.
Collingwood St.
Waterloo St.
Blenheim St.
Puget Dr.
MacKenzie St.
MacDonald St.
Stephens
Bayswater
Valley Dr.
Balsam
Vine
Yew St.
Arbutus St.
Maple St.
Cypress St.
Burrard
Pine St.
Hemlock St.
Granville St.
King Edward Ave.
Broadway
Cornwall Ave.
York Ave.
Point Grey Rd.
1st Ave.
2nd Ave.
3rd Ave.
4th Ave.
5th Ave.
6th Ave.
7th Ave.
8th Ave.
10th Ave.
11th Ave.
12th Ave.
13th Ave.
14th Ave.
15th Ave.
27th Ave.
28th Ave.
29th Ave.
30th Ave.
Creelman
Ogden
Chestnut St.
Burrard St.
Denman St.
Davie St.
Beach Ave.
©ULYSSES

its own maritime museum. The key attraction is the ***Saint-Roch***, the first boat to circle North America by navigating the Panamá Canal and the Northwest Passage.

Get back on Chestnut Street and turn right on Cornwall Avenue, which becomes a scenic road named Point Grey Road.

You will now pass through **Kitsilano** *(between Arbutus and Alma Sts.)*, bordered to the north by a public beach. This area, whose wooden Queen Anne and Western Bungalow Style houses are typical of the West Coast, was a middle-class neighbourhood in the early 20th century.

Fourth Avenue runs alongside lovely **Jericho Beach Park**, a green space and beach rolled into one at the edge of English Bay. Turn right on Northwest Marine Drive and head west to **Point Grey ★★★**, also known as Pacific Spirit Park, which stretches out into the salt water, offering a full panoramic view of the Strait of Georgia.

The tour continues onto the grounds of the **University of British Columbia ★**, or UBC. The university was created by the provincial government in 1908, but it was not until 1925 that the campus opened its doors on this lovely site on Point Grey. An architectural contest had been organized for the site layout, but the First World War halted construction work, and it took a student demonstration denouncing government inaction in this matter to get the buildings completed. Only the library and the science building were executed according to the original plans. **Set Foot for UBC** *(May to Aug, free tours organized by students, ☎822-TOUR)*.

To this day, the UBC campus is constantly expanding, so don't be surprised by its somewhat heterogeneous appearance. There are a few gems however, including the **Museum of Anthropology ★★★***($6, free admission Tue 5pm to 9pm; in the summer, every day 10am to 5pm, in the winter closed Mon and Dec 25 and 26; 6393 NW Marine Dr.; from downtown, take bus #4 UBC or bus #10 UBC; ☎822-3825)* which is not to be missed both for the quality of Aboriginal artwork displayed here, including totem poles, and for the architecture of Arthur Erickson. Big concrete beams and columns imitate the shapes of traditional Aboriginal houses, beneath which have been erected immense totem poles gathered from former Aboriginal villages along the coast and on the islands. Wooden sculptures and various works of art form part of the permanent exhibition.

On the edge of the West Mall is the **Asian Centre** *(1871 West Mall)*, capped with a big pyramid-shaped metal roof, beneath which are the department of Asian studies and an exhibition centre. Behind the building is the magnificent **Nitobe Memorial Garden ★★** *($4.50 summer, free winter; mid-Mar to mid-Oct, every day 10am to 6pm; winter, Mon to Fri 10am to 2:30pm; ☎822-9666)*, which symbolically faces Japan, on the other side of the Pacific. Farther along, **First Nations House of Learning ★** is a community centre for Aboriginal students that was completed in 1993. It was designed to be a modern version of a Coast Salish Longhouse. The curved roof evokes the spirit of a bird (Larry Macfarland, architect). Totem poles surround the great hall, which can accommodate up to 400 people at a time.

The southwestern edge of the campus harbours a spot unlike any other, **Wreck Beach ★** *(NW Marine Dr. at University St.)*, where students come to enjoy some of life's pleasures. Nudists have made this their refuge, as have sculptors, who exhibit their talents on large pieces of driftwood. Vendors hawk all sorts of items next to improvised fast-food stands. A long stairway, quite steep in places, leads down to the beach.

Outdoor Activities

For general information on all outdoor activities in the Greater Vancouver area, contact **Sport B.C.** *(509-1367 Broadway, Vancouver, V6H 4A9, ☎737-3000)* or the **Outdoor Recreation Council of B.C.** *(334-1367 Broadway, Vancouver, V6H 4A9, ☎737-3058).* Both organizations offer many suggestions and information.

Vancouver Parks & Recreation
☎257-8400
Provides all information on sports and recreation activities.

Calendar of Sports and Cultural Events
24hrs/day
☎661-7373

Swimming

The Vancouver shoreline is in a large part made up of easily accessible sandy beaches. All these beaches lie along English Bay, where it is possible to walk, cycle, play volleyball and, of course, take a dip in the sea to enjoy this environment fully. Stanley Park is fringed by **Third Beach** and **Second Beach**, and then, farther east, along Beach Avenue, by **First Beach** where, on January 1, hundreds of bathers brave the icy water to celebrate the new year. A little farther east, **Sunset Beach** celebrates the day's end with gorgeous sunsets. At the southern edge of English Bay are **Kitsilano Beach**, **Jericho Beach**, **Locarno Beach**, **Spanish Banks Beach**, **Tower Beach** and, finally, **Wreck Beach** at the western edge of UBC campus. Kitsilano Beach is enlivened by beach volleyball tournaments and by an assortment of sports facilities, including a basketball court. Locarno, Jericho and Spanish Banks beaches are quieter spots for family relaxation where walking and reading are key activities.

Hiking

Stanley Park is definitely the best place go hiking in Vancouver, with over 50km of trails through forest and greenery along the sea- and lakeshores, including the **Seawall**, an outstanding 8km trail flanked by giant trees.

If you like gardens and are heading through Chinatown, you won't need a pair of hiking boots to visit the **Dr. Sun Yat-Sen Classical Chinese Garden** *(☎689-7133)*, whose little bridges and trails will guide you through a realm of peace and serenity (see p 70).

Mountain hiking can be done on one of the peaks near the city centre. **Cypress Provincial Park** *(☎924-2200)* north of the municipality of West Vancouver, has several hiking trails.

The hike up **Grouse Mountain ★★★** *(☎984-0661)* is not particularly difficult, but the incline is as steep as 25° in places, so you have to be in good shape. It takes about 2hrs to cover the 3km trail, which starts at the parking lot for the cable car. The view of the city from the top of the mountain is fantastic. If you are too tired to hike back down, take the cable car for the modest sum of $5.

Mount Seymour Provincial Park *(☎986-2261)* is another good hiking locale, offering two different views of the region. To the east is Indian Arm, a large arm of the sea extending into the valley.

A little farther east in this marvellous mountain range on the north shore, magnificent **Lynn Headwaters Park ★★★** is scored with forest trails. It is best known for its footbridge, which stretches across an 80m-deep gorge. Definitely not for the faint of heart! To get there, take Hwy. 1 from North Vancouver to the Lynn Valley Road exit and follow the signs, then turn right on Peters Road.

A 15min **ferry** *(BC Ferries, ☎250-386-3431)* ride from Horseshoe Bay transports you to **Bowen Island ★★★** *(☎947-2216)*, where hiking trails lead through a lush forest. Although you'll feel as if you're at the other end of the world, downtown Vancouver is only 5km away as the crow flies.

Cycling

The region has a multitude of trails for mountain biking. Just head to one of the mountains north of the city. A pleasant 8km ride runs along the Seawall in Stanley Park. Bicycle rentals are available at **Spokes Bicycle Rental** *(1798 West Georgia St., corner of Denman, ☎688-5141)*. Outside Vancouver, you can go cycling in the Fraser Valley, near farms or along secondary roads.

Birdwatching

Birders should make a trip to the **George C. Reifel Bird Sanctuary ★★** *(5191 Robertson Rd., Delta, ☎946-6980)* on Westham and Reifel islands. Dozens of species of migratory and non-migratory birds draw ornithology enthusiasts year-round to see aquatic birds, birds of prey, and many other varieties. Farther south, several species can also be observed at Boundary Bay and Mud Bay, as well as on Iona Island closer to Vancouver, next to the airport.

Canoeing and Kayaking

Those who prefer running white water on canoes or kayaks can contact one of the following agencies, which organize expeditions and will equip you from head to toe: **Whitewater Kayaking Association of B.C.** *(1367 Broadway, Vancouver, V6H 4A9, ☎222-1577)*, or **Canadian Adventure Tours** *(Box 929, Whistler, V0N 1B0, ☎938-0727)*, a good place if you're passing through Whistler.

Canadian River Expeditions *(301-3524 W. 16th Ave., Vancouver, V6R 3C1, ☎938-6651)* allows you to plan an expedition from Vancouver.

Sea To Sky Trails *(105C-11831 80th Ave., Delta, V4C 7X6, ☎594-7701)* is a small adventure travel agency located in a suburb south of Vancouver .

Rafting

Thrill-seekers will certainly appreciate the waterways around Vancouver. A white-water rafting paradise awaits visitors in the heart of Cascade Mountains, a semi-arid region less than 2hrs away from the city by car, on the **Fraser River**, the greatest waterway in British Columbia in terms of flow. Certain parts of the river are sure to make your hair stand on end.

Thompson River (a tributary of the Fraser River) is the best-known for white-water rafting. This beautiful emerald green river runs through a magnificent rocky, arid landscape. Experts say the Thompson River descent is a real roller-coaster ride. Good luck!

Coquihalla River is another interesting and worthwhile destination. This powerful little river runs at the bottom of a deep canyon offering spectacular scenery. Another tumultuous little river, the **Nahatlatch**, is less frequented than its renowned counterparts, but worth considering nonetheless. The rafting river closest to Vancouver is the **Chilliwack**. Despite its proximity to large urban centres, this river runs through a wild landscape. Over the course of the years, it has acquired a solid reputation among kayakers and canoeists.

Fraser River Raft Expeditions *(Box 10, Yale, V0K 2S0, ☎863-2336)* is located in the heart of the Fraser River canyon and specializes in expeditions on the Fraser, Thompson, Coquihalla and Nahatlatch Rivers.

Hyak Wilderness Adventures *(204B-1975 Maple St., Vancouver, V6J 3S9, ☎734-8622)* is a major rafting enterprise with an excellent reputation. It has the practical advantage of having its offices in Vancouver and offers expeditions on the Chilliwack, Fraser and Thompson Rivers.

REO Rafting Adventures *(☎684-4438)* is a big agency that organizes white-water rafting on the Chilliwack, Nahatlatch and Thompson Rivers. Group rates.

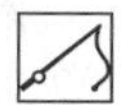

Fishing

Deep-Sea Fishing

Vancouver is the starting point for unforgettable fishing. When it comes to sea fishing, **salmon** reigns supreme. Before casting your line, you must obtain a permit from a specialized outfitter, from whom you can also rent out the necessary equipment: they have boats, know the best locations, supply equipment and often meals, too. Make sure you are dressed appropriately, though. Even when the sun is out, it can get very cold on the open sea. You will find a mine of information in ***BC Sportsfishing*** magazine *(contact Rick Taylor, 909 Jackson Cres., New Westminster, V3L 4S1, ☎683-4871, ⇄683-4318).*

Fresh-Water Fishing

Its infinite number of lakes and rivers ensure that trout fishing in British Columbia is always excellent. Permits are sold in all camping equipment stores as well as at **Ruddik's Fly Fishing** *(1654 Duranleau St., Granville Island, ☎681-3747)*, a good shop for this sport. Thousands of flies for catching every kind of fish in the area can be purchased here. The owner will gladly offer advice. Vancouver is the starting point to equip yourself and make inquiries, though you will have to leave the city to fish on a river or lake. The interior region and Cariboo Country are prime destinations for anglers in Vancouver.

N.B. Salt-water and fresh-water fishing licenses are not interchangeable.

Golf

Vancouver is unquestionably the golf capital of Western Canada, with golf for all tastes and budgets. Golf courses in Vancouver and its surrounding areas are virtually all hilly and offer spectacular views of the ocean and especially the mountains, which loom over all parts of the region. It should be noted that all golf clubs require appropriate attire. Because of the lack of space, there are very few courses in Vancouver itself, but the suburbs boast one at practically every turn.

The **University Golf Club** *(5185 University Blvd., ☎224-1818)* is one of the best-known in town and among the priciest. It is situated a stone's throw from the University of British Columbia (UBC).

The oldest public golf course, the **Peace Portal Golf Course** *(16900 Fourth Ave., Surrey, ☎538-4818)* was founded in 1928 and is open year-round. It lies along Hwy. 99, near the U.S. border, in the suburb of Surrey.

The **Fraserview Golf Course** *(7800 Vivian Dr., ☎327-5616)* is an affordable public golf course, managed by the City (Vancouver Board of Parks and Recreation) and located at the southern tip of Vancouver.

The **Langara Golf Course** *(6706 Alberta St., ☎257-8355)* is also a municipal golf course (Vancouver Board of Parks and Recreation), situated southeast of town.

Gleneagles *(6190 Marine Dr., West Vancouver, ☎921-7353)*, right near the lovely village of Horseshoe Bay and 15min from Vancouver, is a very inexpensive golf course that is sometimes jam-packed on weekends, but the scenery makes playing here worth the wait.

Cross-Country Skiing

Less than a half-hour from Vancouver, three ski resorts welcome snow-lovers from morning to evening. In **Cypress Provincial Park**, on Hollyburn Ridge, Cypress Bowl Ski Areas *(☎926-5612)* offers 25km of mechanically maintained trails suitable for all categories of skiers. These trails are frequented day and evening by cross-country skiers. There are also trails at **Grouse Mountain** *(☎984-0661)* and **Mount Seymour Provincial Park** *(☎986-2261)*.

Downhill Skiing

What makes Vancouver a truly magical place is the combination of sea and mountains. The cold season is no exception, as residents desert the beaches and seaside paths to crowd the ski hills, which are literally suspended over the city. There are four ski resorts close to the city: **Mount Seymour** *($26; 1700 Mount Seymour Rd., North Vancouver, V7G 1L3; Upper Level Hwy. heading east, Deep Cove Exit, information ☎986-2261, ski conditions ☎718-7771, ☎/⇄986-2267)*, a family resort with beginner trails, situated east of North Vancouver, above Deep Cove; **Grouse Mountain** *($28, night skiing $20; 6400 Nancy Greene Way, North Vancouver, ☎984-0661, ski conditions ☎986-6262, ski school ☎980-9311)*, a small resort accessible by cable car, which offers an unobstructed view of Vancouver that is as magnificent by day as it is by night; **Cypress Bowl** *($35, night skiing $23; from North Vancouver, take Trans-Canada Highway 1, heading west for 16km, then follow road signs. Information and ski conditions ☎926-5612)*, a resort for the most avid skiers, also offers magnificent views of Howe Sound and of the city.

Another option is the village-style **Hemlock Valley Resort** *($32, night skiing $11; Hwy. 1 heading east, Agassizou Harrisson Hot Springs Exit, ☎797-4411, ski conditions ☎520-6222, ⇄797-4440, accommodation reservations ☎797-4444)*. Situated at the eastern tip of Vancouver's urban area, in the heart of the Cascade Mountains, this resort boasts an abundance of snow and a spectacular view of Mount Baker in the United States.

As soon as enough snow blankets the slopes, in late November or early December, these four ski resorts are open every day until late at night, thanks to powerful neon lighting. It should be noted, however, that the first three resorts do not provide accommodation.

Of course there are also Whistler and Blackcomb, two great hills easily accessible from Vancouver, see p 214.

Accommodations

Vancouver is a big city with lodgings for all tastes and budgets. All accommodations shown here are well located, within walking distance of bus stops and, in most cases, in or near the downtown area. **Super Natural British Columbia** (☎*800-663-6000*) can make reservations for you.

Tour C: Downtown

Vancouver Downtown YHA
$19 members
$23 non-members
1114 Burnaby St.
V6E 1P1
☎***684-4565***
⇄***684-4540***
Vancouver Downtown YHA is a big hostel (239 beds) right downtown at the corner of Thurlow. Common kitchen and tv room; coin-laundry.

YMCA
$39
sb, tv, K, ≈
955 Burrard St.
☎***681-0221***
⇄***681-1630***
This establishment on the corner of Nelson Street is not actually restricted to men, and families are welcome. The building is brand-new and offers rooms accommodating one to five people.

Best Western Downtown Vancouver
$89
tv
718 Drake St.
corner Granville St.
☎***669-9888***
⇄***669-3440***
Facing Granville Street, this brand-new, comfortable hotel is situated near interesting attractions. If you don't have a car, there's a bus stop just before the entrance to the Granville bridge.

Ramada Vancouver Centre
$90
tv
898 W. Broadway
☎***872-8661***
⇄***872-2270***
Located in the eastern part of Vancouver, this hotel belongs to the Ramada hotel chain, which specializes in accommodations for large groups and families. Comfortable rooms and impeccable, personalized service.

Bosman's Motor Hotel
$139
≡, ≈, *P*
1060 Howe St.
☎***682-3171***
☎***888-BOSMANS***
⇄***684-4010***
Bosman's Motor Hotel is in the heart of the city, close to the National Museum, theatres and beaches. The rooms are spacious and modern.

Terminal City Club
$160
tv, ℜ
837 W. Hastings St.
☎***681-4121***
⇄***681-9634***
The favourite place for business travellers, this luxurious establishment has an elegant style. It has 60 cosy rooms with a cheerful decor. Its poolroom, golf simulator, ocean view and attentive service will make your stay memorable.

Canadian Pacific Waterfront Centre Hotel
$220-$350
tv, ≈, ⏲, ✗, ≡, ⌂, ⊛, *P*, ℜ, ♿
900 Canada Place Way
☎***691-1991***
☎***800-441-1414***
⇄***691-1999***
The Canadian Pacific Waterfront Centre Hotel is a luxury hotel located just a few steps from Gastown. It has 489 rooms.

Wedgewood Hotel
$240
⏲, ⌂, ≡, ℜ
845 Hornby St., V6Z 1V2
☎***689-7777***
☎***800-663-0666***
⇄***668-3074***
The Wedgewood Hotel is small enough to have retained some character and style, in particular the lovely lobby complete with shiny brass accents, cosy fireplace and distinguished art, and large enough to offer a certain measure of privacy and professionalism. This is a popular option for business trips and romantic weekend getaways.

Hotel Vancouver
$340
tv, ≈, ⊛, ⊘, ⌂, ℜ, ℝ, ♞, ♿, *P*
900 West Georgia St.
☎***684-3131***
☎***800-441-1414***
⇄***662-1929***
The Hotel Vancouver belongs to the Canadian Pacific Hotel chain and was built in the 1930s in the château style characteristic of Canadian railway hotels, of which the Château Frontenac in Québec City was a precursor. In 1939 it hosted George VI, the first British monarch to visit Canada. You will find tranquillity and luxury in the heart of downtown near Robson Street and Burrard Street. The hotel has 508 rooms.

Pan Pacific Hotel Vancouver
$410
≡, ⊛, ⊘, *tv*, ≈, ⌂, *P*, ℜ, ♿, ♞
300-999 Canada Place
☎***662-8111***
in Canada:
☎***800-663-1515***
in the US:
☎***800-937-1515***
⇄***685-8690***
The luxurious Pan Pacific Hotel Vancouver is located in Canada Place, on the shore of Burrard Inlet facing North Vancouver, with a good view of port activities. The hotel has 506 rooms, and its lobby, with its marble decor, 20m-high ceilings and panoramic view of the ocean, is magnificent.

Tour D: The West End and Stanley Park

Rosellen Suites
$100
tv, K
2030 Barclay St.
☎***689-4807***
⇄***684-3327***
Located in the heart of the West End near Stanley Park and downtown, these completely furnished suites have one or two bedrooms, kitchenettes and all the modern conveniences. They can be rented on a short- or long-term basis. Cost varies slightly depending upon the length of stay.

Sylvia Hotel
$115
tv, K, ℜ, ♞, *P*
1154 Gilford Street
☎***681-9321***
Located just a few steps from English Bay, this charming old hotel, built in the early 1900s, offers unspoiled views and has 118 simple rooms. People come for the atmosphere, but also for food and drink at the end of the day. For those on lower budgets, rooms without views are offered at lower rates. The manager of this ivy-covered hotel is a Frenchman who is fully and justifiably dedicated to his establishment. Request a southwest-facing room (one facing English Bay) in order to benefit from magical sunsets over the bay.

Tropicana Motor Inn
$139
tv, K, ℜ, ⌂, ≈
1361 Robson St.
☎***687-6631***
⇄***687-5724***
The affordable Tropicana Motor Inn rarely has the "no vacancy" sign up. A great location right in the action on the busy part of Robson probably has something to do with it. It is not a palace, but is perfect for younger travellers and people on a tighter budget.

West End Guest House Bed & Breakfast
$150 bkfst incl.
P, ⊗
no children under 12
1362 Haro St.
☎***681-2889***
⇄***688-8812***
westendguesthouse.com
This magnificent inn set in a turn-of-the-century Victorian house is well situated near a park and near Robson Street. Evan Penner is your host. A minimum two-day stay may apply. The West End Guest House has an excellent reputation. (Nearby, at 1415 Barclay St., is Roedde House, built in Victorian-Edwardian style in 1893 and designed by none other than the architect Francis Rattenbury, who also created the Vancouver Art Gallery, the legislature building in Victoria, and the Empress Hotel.)

Carmana Plaza
$160
tv, K, ⊘
1128 Alberni St.
☎683-1399
⇄683-1391
The Carmana Plaza is a luxurious, all-suite facility. Each suite has a view of the sea or city. Enjoy its numerous amenities, including a kitchen, office and conference rooms for business travellers, exercise room, cleaning service, security guard and parking.

Sheraton Wall Centre Hotel
$160
tv,ℜ, ⊘*, P*
1088 Burrard St.
☎331-1000
⇄893-7123
This hotel has remarkable architecture, a creatively decorated interior, a colourful bar, restaurants with innovative cuisine, a distinguished ambience, a welcoming garden and a sports club.

Chez Phillipe
$175-$225 bkfst incl.
tv, K, P
by appointment only
☎649-2817
Chez Phillipe is located in the heart of Vancouver, in the West End neighbourhood, two steps away from False Creek, in a very holiday-like setting. It's a luxurious apartment on the 17th floor of a modern highrise built at the entrance to the Seawall.To get to Granville Island Market, you have to take a charming little ferry that leaves from the foot of the building and crosses False Creek. A generous breakfast is included in the price and you can even cook for yourself if you like. Guests also have access to a dishwasher, a washing machine and a dryer, as well as a full bathroom with a separate shower and a terrace. By reservation only.

Landmark Hotel
$200
tv, ⊛, ⊘, ℜ, ⌂, ≈, ♿
1400 Robson St.
☎687-0511
☎800-830-6144
⇄687-2801
The Landmark Hotel truly is a landmark with it 40 floors and its revolving resto-bar at the top. The view is fascinating and quite an experience!

Listel O'Doul's Hotel
$200
tv, ℜ, ⌂, ⊛, ♿
1300 Robson St.
☎684-8461
☎800-663-5491
⇄684-8326
The Listel O'Doul's Hotel on Robson also houses a friendly, though slightly noisy, pub and a good restaurant. The service and comfort are indisputable.

The Westin Bayshore
$200-$300
tv, ℜ, ⌂, ≈, *P*
1601 W. Georgia St.
☎682-3377
⇄687-3102
The Westin Bayshore is a very classy place. Its setting is typically "Vancouver" with the surrounding mountains, the proximity of the sea and the city so close by. The 517 rooms each have their own charm, not to mention the stunning views. Staying here is like staying at a tropical resort.

Coast Plaza at Stanley Park
$250-$330
≈, ⌂, *tv,* ⊘, ℜ, *K,* ℝ, 🐕, ♿, *P*
1763 Comox St.
☎688-7711
☎800-663-1144
⇄688-5934
If you are looking for a big, modern, American-style hotel close to the beach, this 267-room establishment is a good choice. The restaurant serves everything, and the food is decent.

Sutton Place Hotel
$265-$415
⊛, ⊘, ≈, ⌂, ℝ, ℜ, ♿
845 Burrard St.
☎682-5511
☎800-961-7555
⇄682-5513
The Sutton Place Hotel, formerly the Meridien, offers 397 rooms and the full range of five-star services normally provided by the top hotel chains. The European decor has been maintained. If you are a chocolate lover, don't miss the chocolate buffet served on Fridays.

Tour E: Burrard Inlet

The Globetrotter's Inn
$18 sb
45$ pb
tv
170 West Esplanade
North Vancouver
☎988-2082
⇌987-8389
The Globetrotter's Inn, in the heart of North Vancouver, near the Seabus and the shops of Marine Drive and the Quay Market, is very affordable. Hostel-style dorm rooms are also available!

Capilano Bed & Breakfast
$60-$175 bkfst incl.
tv
1374 Plateau Dr.
☎990-8889
☎877-990-8889
⇌990-5177
The Capilano Bed & Breakfast is located close to Lions Gate Bridge. Skiers can easily get to Cypress Bowl (15min) and Grouse Mountain (8min). Except during rush hour, the hotel is 5min from Stanley Park, 10min from downtown and Chinatown, and about 25min from the airport. The rooms are attractive, and some have nice views. The complete breakfasts are delicious. Prices for weekly stays can be negotiated and they offer a 20% discount on ski tickets for Grouse Mountain.

Canyon Court Motel
$110
tv, ≡, ≈
1748 Capilano Rd.
North Vancouver
☎/⇌988-3181
The Canyon Court Motel is located right next to the Capilano Suspension Bridge, the Lion's Gate Bridge and the Trans-Canada Highway. It is very comfortable and not too expensive.

Summit View
$110-$150 bkfst incl.
tv, P, ℜ
5501 Cliffridge Pl.
☎990-1089
⇌987-7167
To get here from the Lions Gate Bridge, head toward North Vancouver, turn right on Marine Drive, then, at the first intersection, turn left on Capilano Road, right on Prospect Road, left on Cliffridge Avenue and finally left on Cliffridge Place. To get here from the Second Narrows Bridge, take Hwy. 1 west and exit onto Capilano Road, then continue as above.

Each room has its own character. In the elegant dining room, breakfast and dinner are prepared to order, according to your tastes or diet. Rock-climbing, skiing, fishing, canoeing, swimming and tennis are all possible nearby. The management offers bicycles to help you discover the wonders of the area. Low-season rates are considerably less expensive here.

Tour F: False Creek

Pillow Porridge Guest House
$85-$135 bkfst incl.
tv, ℝ, K,
2859 Manitoba St.
☎879-8977
⇌897-8966
www.pillow.net
The Pillow Porridge Guest House is a residence dating back to 1910, and the decor and ambience attest to it. These complete apartments with kitchens are pleasant and comfortable. Close to a number of ethnically diverse restaurants.

Tour G: South Vancouver

Stay'n Save Inn
$79
tv, K, ℜ
10551 St. Edwards Dr.
near the airport
☎273-3311
⇌273-9522
This decent facility has comfortable rooms (some of which have kitchenettes), and a family-style restaurant.

William House
$95-$190 bkfst incl.
tv
2050 W. 18th Ave.
☎/⇌731-2760
whouse@direct.ca
William House is a beautiful, completely restored country house, in the old area of Shaughnessy, a few minutes from downtown. Luxury suites and rooms offer a pleasantly calm, comfortable environment.

The large garden and yard provide havens from all the noise of the city. Well suited to business people. Prices are negotiable depending on the season and the length of your stay.

Delta Vancouver Airport Hotel and Marina
$150-$300
tv, ≈, ℜ
3500 Cessna Dr., Richmond
☎278-1241
☎800-268-1133
⇄276-1975
The exciting spectacle of planes and seaplanes landing is part of staying at the Delta Vancouver Airport Hotel and Marina. This hotel offers all the amenities you would expect in a hotel of the Delta chain. It is located on the edge of the airport, close to the Fraser River.

Tour H: the Peninsula

Vancouver International Hostel Jericho Beach
$16-$20
men's and women's dormitories
some private rooms
sb, tv, cafeteria from Apr to Oct
1515 Discovery St.
☎224-3208
⇄224-4852
Located in Jericho Park, this youth hostel is open day and night; take UBC bus #4 from downtown to reach it. With Locarno and Jericho beaches nearby, this is a great spot for budget travellers.

UBC Housing and Conference Centre
$22-$105
sb/pb, K, ℝ, P, ♿
5961 Student Union Blvd.
reservation @brock.housing.ubc.ca
☎822-1010
⇄822-1001
In addition to a year-round 48-suite hotel, campus apartments are available from May to August. Inexpensive and well located near museums, beaches and hiking trails, this spot also provides tranquillity.

Johnson House Bed & Breakfast
$80-$155 bkfst incl.
sb/pb
Nov to Feb by request only
2278 West 34th Ave.
Kerrisdale district
☎/⇄266-4175
www.johnsons-inn-vancouver.com
The Johnson House Bed & Breakfast occupies a magnificent, fully renovated house from the 1920s, with an extra floor added. The owners, Sandy and Ron Johnson, carried out the work; they also acquired several antiques that form part of the decor.

Plaza 500 Hotel
$109
tv, ⊘, ℜ
500 W. 12th Ave., corner of Cambie St.
☎873-1811
⇄873-1980
Located 15min by car from downtown just after the Cambie bridge, this beautiful hotel has sumptuous rooms and view of the city. Broadway Street, only 2min away, has a variety of shops, restaurants and bars. The perfect place for large groups or conferences.

Restaurants

Tour A: Gastown

Water Street Café
$
closes at 10pm weekdays 11pm weekends
300 Water St.
☎689-2832
A handsome bistro with big windows facing Gastown. Tables are decorated with pretty lanterns, and service is friendly. The menu centres around pastas prepared in creative ways.

Capone's
$$
1141 Hamilton St.
☎682-7900
This romantic restaurant has a New-Orleans-style atmosphere with a jazz orchestra, and it serves intimate candlelight diners including pizza, pasta or salads, accompanied with a selection of original martinis. Located in the trendy new area of Yaletown.

Top of Vancouver
$$$
Sunday brunch buffet for $26.95
every day 11:30am to 2:30pm and 5pm to 10pm
except Sun brunch at 11am
555 W. Hastings St.
☎669-2220
This restaurant, located atop Harbour Centre (the elevator is free for restaurant patrons), revolves once an hour, giving diners a city tour from high in the air while they eat. Classic West Coast cuisine is served here.

Tour B: Chinatown and East Vancouver

Hon's Wun-Tun House
$
268 Keefer St.
☎688-8303
This restaurant has been a Vancouver institution for more than 20 years. Its reasonably priced dishes, including traditional Chinese specialities, are all excellent. Sample some of the dishes in the noisy, jam-packed, canteen-style atmosphere. Efficient service.

Waa Zuu Bee Café
$
every day 11:30am to 1am
1622 Commercial Dr.
☎253-5299
The Waa Zuu Bee Café is great and inexpensive. The innovative cuisine combined with the "natural-techno-italo-bizarre" decor are full of surprises. The pasta dishes are always interesting.

Santos Tapas Restaurant
$$
1191 Commercial Dr.
☎253-0444
Latinos seem to have a gift for calming the atmosphere with the aromas of their spices and with their music. This is certainly the case here where groups of musicians perform at your table. This restaurant is frequented mostly by Vancouverites.

Sun Sui Wah Seafood Restaurant
$$
every day
3888 Main St., at Third Ave.
☎872-8822
Authentic Chinese food, lobster, crayfish, crab, oysters and, of course, Peking duck.

Cannery Seafood Restaurant
$$$
until 10pm
2205 Commissioner St.
☎254-9606
The Cannery Seafood Restaurant is one of the best places in town for seafood. It is located in the East End in a renovated, century-old warehouse. The view of the sea is fantastic.

Tour C: Downtown

Kitto
$
833 Granville St.
☎687-6622
All kinds of Japanese delicacies, such as *sushi*, *robata* and *yakisoba*. Reasonable prices and fast service.

Arena Ristorante
$$
11:30am to 2:30pm and 5pm to 10pm
300 W. Georgia St.
☎687-5434
The Arena Ristorante serves Italian specialties. The atmosphere is livelier on Friday and Saturday nights when live jazz performances are put on.

Bacchus Restaurant
$$
Wedgewood Hotel
845 Hornby St.
☎689-7777
A lovely, intimate decor, an ambience enhanced by piano music and a cuisine cooked up by an award-winning chef make this restaurant popular with its downtown clientele.

Tsunami Sushi
$$
238-1025 Robson St.
☎687-8744, unit 238
Tsunami Sushi has a revolving sushi bar, much like those in Japan, from which patrons can choose specialties at will. Excellent quality for the price; huge, sunny terrace overlooking Robson Street.

Yaletown Brewing Co.
$$
closed midnight
1111 Mainland St.
☎681-2739
The Yaletown Brewing Co. is a veritable yuppie temple in the post-industrial neighbourhood of Yaletown and

7 095 244 3639

a fun place to spend an evening. Try the pizza from the wood-burning oven.

Century Grill
$$$
1095 Hamilton St.
☎***668-8088***
With a beautiful, luxurious decor, this restaurant, which has a terrace outside, offers dishes made with fresh, local ingredients.

Il Giardino
$$$
1382 Hornby St.
☎***669-2422***
This popular restaurant has a renowned reputation for its attractive Italian-style decor, charming patio, inspired dishes with local and European accents and its vast selection of Italian pasta. Always crowded. Warm, friendly ambience.

Joe Fortes
$$$
777 Thurlow St., at Robson
☎***669-1940***
Joe Fortes is renowned in the West End for its oysters and other seafood. This bistro, with its turn-of-the-century decor and heated upstairs terrace, has an appetizing menu. This is a popular meeting place for successful young professionals.

Le Crocodile
$$$-$$$$
909 Burrard St.
entry by Smithe St.
☎***669-4298***
This establishment is the beacon of French cuisine in Vancouver, as much for the quality of its food as for its service, its decor and its wine list. Lovers of great French cuisine will be spoiled by the choice of red meats and the delicacies from the sea. The salmon tartare is a must – you *are* on the Pacific coast after all!

Chartwell
$$$$
791 W. Georgia St.
☎***844-6715***
Chartwell has won several awards. The service is impeccable and the cuisine has West Coast influences. Located in the Four Seasons Hotel.

Lumière
$$$$
closed Mon
2551 W. Boradway Ave.
☎***739-8185***
Lumière is a favourite with Vancouver residents, especially chefs. The simple, white interior allows the food the shine, and shine it does. The fresh, local ingredients used in each dish make for creative and honest, but very refined cuisine. One winning choice is veal tenderloin with braised turnip lasagna topped off by lemon tarts or chocolate truffles.

Tour D: The West End and Stanley Park

Bread Garden
$
24hrs a day
three locations in the same area
1040 Denman St.
☎***685-2996***
812 Bute St.
☎***688-3213***
2996 Granville St.
☎***736-6465***
These cafés sell bread, pastries and tasty prepared dishes to go, such as quiches, lasagnas, sandwiches, and fruit plates. Good vegetarian selections. You can also enjoy all of these in-house. Good service and low prices. Also located at:
1880 West First Ave., Kitsilano
☎***738-6684***
550 Park Royal N., West Vancouver
☎***925-0181***
4575 Central Blvd., Burnaby
☎***435-5177***

Flying Wedge Pizza Co.
$
Royal Centre
1055 W. Georgia St.
☎***681-1233***
3499 Cambie St.
☎***874-8284***
1937 Cornwall, Kitsilano
☎***732-8840***
Vancouver Airport
☎***303-3370***
Library Square
☎***689-7078***
Pizza lovers, these are addresses to jot down if you're looking for pizza that doesn't remind you of something you ate last week.

You'll get a discount if you bring your own plate, showing that you're ecologically minded.

 **True Confections**
$
until 1am
866 Denman St.
☎682-1292
True Confections is a dessert place par excellence that serves huge slices of cake. Be sure to try the divine Belgian dark-chocolate torte.

Ohana Sushi
$-$$
1414 W. Broadway
☎732-0112
This chain of Japanese restaurants offers excellent dishes at reasonable prices. Service is efficient and pleasant. A fine Asian experience.

Liliget
$$
every day
1724 Davie St.
☎681-7044
Liliget is a First Nations restaurant that offers authentic Aboriginal-style food: salmon grilled on a wood fire, smoked oysters, grilled seaweed and roasted wild duck. Worth exploring.

Mescallero
$$
until midnight weekdays
1am weekends
1215 Bidwell St.
☎669-2399
The Latin-American and Mexican cuisine of Mescallero is served in a pretty setting with a friendly ambience; things get really busy on Saturday evenings.

 **Raku**
$$
838 Thurlow St., north of Robson
☎685-8817
A wealthy young Japanese clientele meets here and fits right in. It has the atmosphere of a noisy bar, but it is an ideal spot to begin a promising evening. The sushi and grilled meats are recommended.

 **C**
$$$
1600 Howe St.
☎605-8263
This Chinese restaurant, whose name evokes the sea, is the talk of the town, and for good reason. The chef has returned from Southeast Asia with innovative and unique recipes. Served on the stroke of 12, the C-style Dim Sum is a real delight. Titbits of fish marinated in tea and a touch of caviar, vol-au-vents with chanterelles, curry shrimp with coconut milk, and the list goes on... All quite simply exquisite. Desserts are equally extraordinary. For those who dare, the crème brûlée with blue cheese is an unforgettable experience. This restaurant is an absolute must.

Le Café de Paris
$$$
751 Denman St.
☎687-1418
The speciality of Le Café de Paris is its *cassoulet* (a stew originating from southwestern France). Many other dishes are inspired from different regions of France. The fries that accompany every dish are excellent. Good wine and prompt service.

The Fish House in Stanley Park
$$$
until 10:30pm
8901 Stanley Park Dr.
☎681-7275
The Fish House in Stanley Park is located in a Victorian house right in the heart of the park and just a few steps from the Seawall. Fine seafood and fish dishes are served in a lovely, opulent decor.

Teahouse Restaurant
$$$
until 10pm
along the Seawall
7501 Stanley park Dr.
☎669-3281
The Teahouse Restaurant serves delicious food and affords stunning views of English Bay from Stanley Park. Call ahead for reservations and for precise directions as it can be tricky to find.

L'Hermitage
$$$-$$$$
every day
1025 Robson St., Suite 115
☎689-3237
The chef-owner Hervé Martin, is an artist when it comes to French cuisine and will tell you stories from his days as the chef of the Belgian Royal Court. Wines from his native region of Burgundy

accompany the finest of dishes, each prepared carefully and with panache. The decor is chic and the service exemplary. The terrace, set back from Robson, is lovely in the summertime.

Cloud 9 Revolving Restaurant
$$$$
until 11pm
1400 Robson St.
☎687-0511
The Cloud 9 Revolving Restaurant is an experience. This resto-bar at the top of the 40-storey Landmark Hotel offers an exceptional view. It takes 80min for the restaurant to rotate 360°. Sunset is particularly picturesque as the sky darkens and the city begins to glow. Try the lamb chops or the salmon.

Tour E: Burrard Inlet

Beach Side Café
$$
11am to 3:30pm and 5:30pm to 11:30pm
1362 Marine Dr.
☎925-1945
The Beach Side Café in West Vancouver is a lovely restaurant with original recipes prepared from local produce, as well as meat and fish dishes.

Bridge House Restaurant
$$
brunch 11am to 2pm
3735 Capilano Rd.
North Vancouver
☎987-3388
In a warm and intimate, English-style setting, this restaurant serves traditional Canadian dishes, homemade pies and warm bread. Reservations recommended.

The Salmon House on the Hill
$$$
every day
2229 Folkestone Way
West Vancouver
☎926-8539
www.salmonhouse.com
The Salmon House offers unique, creative cuisine that focuses on salmon in a superb, Canadian-cedar decor. A view of the ocean, the city and Stanley Park adds to the pleasure of the palate.

Imperial
$$$-$$$$
Mon to Fri 11am to 2:30pm and 5pm to 10pm
Sat and Sun and holidays 10:30am to 2:30pm and 5pm to 10pm
355 Burrard St.
☎688-8191
Located in the Marine Building, an Art Deco architectural masterpiece (see p 71), this Chinese restaurant also has several Art Deco elements, but it is the big windows looking over Burrard Inlet that are especially fascinating. In this very elegant spot, boys in livery and discreet young ladies perform the *dim sum* ritual. Unlike elsewhere, there are no carts here: the various steamed dishes are brought on trays. You can also ask for a list, allowing you to choose your favourites among the 30 or so on offer. The quality of the food matches the excellent reputation this restaurant has acquired.

Tour F: False Creek

Bridges Bistro
$
until 11:30pm
1696 Durenleau St.
Granville Island
☎687-4400
⇄687-0352
The Bridges Bistro boasts one of the prettiest terraces in Vancouver, right by the water in the middle of Granville Island's pleasure-boat harbour. The food and setting are decidedly West Coast.

The Creek Restaurant & Brewery
$$
Granville Island
1253 Johnston St.
☎685-7070
This enormous elegant restaurant has a patio as well as a great view of the False Creek sailing harbour. It offers both simple and more elaborate dishes, all meticulously presented. Open late. Two adjoining bars serve several different kinds of beer, such as the famous Granville Island Pale

Ale, all of which are brewed on the premises. Connected to a nightclub (open on weekends).

Royal Seoul House Korean Restaurant
$$
1215 W. Broadway
☎ ***738-8285*** or ***739-9001***
The Royal Seoul House Korean Restaurant has a large dining room divided into compartments, each of which has a table with a grill for preparing food and can accommodate four or more people. Order your all-you-can-eat meat, fish and seafood buffet, and have fun. Everything here is good, including the service.

Kettle of Fish
$$$
900 Pacific St.
☎ ***682-6661***
Kettle of fish has a cosy winter-garden-style ambience with flowers. The menu includes tasty fish and fresh seafood as well as an excellent wine list. Good service.

Pacific Institute of Culinary Arts
$$$
1505 W. Second Ave.
☎ ***734-4488***
The Pacific Institute of Culinary Arts has a patio and offers a different gourmet menu every day prepared by its students. The dishes are exquisite and the service is excellent.

Tour H: The Peninsula

Gypsy Rose
$
1660 Cypress St.
☎ ***731-3528***
A little cafe situated on a street with many shops, Gypsy Rose offers pastries, light fare and specialities from southern France. Bernard, the friendly manager, is from Marseille.

Naam
$
open 24hrs
2724 W. 4th Ave.
☎ ***738-7151***
The Naam blends live music with vegetarian meals. This little restaurant has a warm atmosphere, friendly service, and is frequented by a young clientele.

Pâtisserie Lebeau
$
1660 Cypress St.
☎ ***731-3528***
This quaint little place, which has a few chairs outside, bakes delicious cakes. It serves up hot waffles for breakfast and scrumptious sandwiches for lunch (such as ham and cheese on a French baguette) accompanied by coffee and a lively atmosphere. Try the Liège waffles. Practice your French with Olivier, the Belgian owner, who makes all the delectable pastry.

Epicurean Caffe
$$
1898 W. First Ave.
corner Cypress St.
☎ ***731-5370***
Owners Dario and his son Christian serve Italian-style cuisine. Chose the dish and the portion you desire on the home-made menu. This quaint little place has a friendly, warm atmosphere and whips up one of the best expressos in Vancouver. Bask in the winter or summer sun at one of the outdoor tables. The motorcycles and bikes parked along the sidewalk are a hot topic of conversation amongst the regulars.

Japanese Bistro Kitsilano
$$
1815 W. First Ave.
☎ ***734-5858***
Japanese Bistro Kitsilano features an all-you-can-eat sushi and tempura buffet. Large terrace; excellent service.

Maria's Taverna
$$
2324 W. Fourth Ave.
☎ ***731-4722***
This pretty little restaurant serves up generous portions of authentic Greek cuisine in a blue-checked decor. The roast lamb is highly recommended.

The Smoking Dog
$$
1889 W. First Ave.
☎ ***736-8811***
The Smoking Dog has a warm, lively atmosphere, lovely decor and reasonable prices for its carefully pre-

pared *table d'hôte*. Exquisite steak, copious salads and creative daily specials. The fries that accompany every dish are golden brown on the outside and tender on the inside. Jean-Claude, the owner, is a friendly *Marseillais*.

Raku Kushiyaki Restaurant
$$-$$$
closed Mon
4422 W. 10th Ave.
☎222-8188
The young chefs of this little restaurant prepare local cuisine served with oriental aesthetic rules in mind; they will help you discover their art. Take a meal for two to appreciate the spirit of this *nouvelle cuisine*, which encourages the sharing of meals among guests. The portions may seem small, but you still come away satiated. Ingredients are chosen according to the seasons, for example wild mushrooms are served accented with garlic, green bell peppers, butter, soya sauce and lime juice. This dish may seem simple, and it is, but the taste of the food is not masked by mediocre sauces. The meat and fish are also treated with subtlety.

Entertainment

ARTS Hotline *(☎684-ARTS)* will inform you about all the shows (dance, theatre, music, cinema and literature) in the city.

The Georgia Straight *(☎730-7000)*. This weekly paper is published every Thursday and distributed free at many spots in Vancouver. You will find all the necessary information on coming shows and cultural events. This paper is read religiously each week by many Vancouverites and has acquired a good reputation.

For information on jazz shows in Vancouver, call the **Jazz Hotline** *(☎682-0706)*.

To book tickets for cultural or sporting events, try the following:

Ticketmaster
☎280-4444

Arts Line
☎280-3311 *(for tickets only)*

Sports Line
☎280-4400

Bars and Danceclubs

Tour A: Gastown

Blarney Stone
216 Carrall St.
☎687-4322
The Blarney Stone is the spot for authentic Irish jigs and reels. The ambience is frenetic, with people dancing everywhere, on the tables, on the chairs... A must-see!

Richard's on Richards
1036 Richard St.
☎687-6794
Richard's on Richards is an institution in Vancouver. People of all ages flock to this chic spot to see and be seen. Theme nights. A must try.

The Purple Onion Cabaret
every day
15 Water St., 3rd floor
☎602-9442
The Purple Onion Cabaret is the mecca of upbeat jazz in Vancouver, with entertainment provided by a disc-jockey or live bands. Cover charge of $5 during the week and $7 on weekends. Wednesdays are dedicated to Latin jazz; on Fridays and Saturdays there's live jazz near the bar and "disco-funk" on the dance floor.

Wett Bar
1320 Richards St.
☎662-7707
Deep jazz, funk, classic rock as well as the hits of the day. Excellent music.

Tour B: Chinatown and East Vancouver

Hot Jazz Society
2120 Main St.
☎873-4131
The Hot Jazz Society was one of the first places in Vancouver to offer good jazz. It's a veritable institution, where many of the big names in jazz perform. Call to find out who's playing.

Tour C: Downtown

Babalu
654 Nelson St.
at Granville St.
☎605-4343
is a lounge-style bar. It's the ideal spot to sip a cocktail while enjoying a little Frank Sinatra and a cigar. There is also dancing to jazzy rhythms. Cover charge of $3.

Chameleon Urban Lounge
every day
801 W. Georgia St.
☎669-0806
This excellent little downtown club is often packed on weekends, but it is calm during the week. Don't miss their trip-hop nights on Wednesdays, Afro-Cuban and Latin music on Thursdays, and Acid Jazz on Saturdays. Warning: get there early to avoid lineups. The cover charge is $5 on Fridays and Saturdays.

Railway Club
$6 members
$8 non-members
579 Dunsmuir St.
☎681-1625
Folk music or blues are presented in an oblong spot that brings to mind a railway car. A miniature electric train runs in a loop above customers' heads as they enjoy the live music.

Yale Hotel
1300 Granville St.
☎681-9253
The big names in blues regularly play at this, the blues mecca of Vancouver. Great ambience on the weekends. The cover charge varies depending on the performers.

Yaletown Brewing Co.
1111 Mainland St.
☎681-2739
The Yaletown Brewing Co. is a popular yuppie hangout in Yaletown and the ideal spot for an evening of brews with some friends.

Tour D: West End

DV8
595 Davie St.
☎682-4388
For 20- to 30-year olds. Evenings begin around 9:30pm.

Gay and Lesbian Bars

Celebrities
free admission
1022 Davie St.
☎689-3180
Celebrities is definitely the best-known gay bar in Vancouver. Straights also come here for the music. Drag queens make conspicuous appearances, especially on Wednesdays, during the female impersonators night. Packed on weekends.

Charlie's Lounge
455 Abbott St.
☎685-7777
Charlie's Lounge is a relaxed bar with an elegant gay clientele, located on the ground floor of an old hotel. Opens at 4pm on Mondays and Tuesdays and at 3pm from Wednesday to Saturday. Sundays, they serve brunch from 11am to 2pm. Musical improv sessions in the afternoon and retro dance music at night.

Denman Station
free admission
860 Denman St.
☎669-3448
Denman Station is a small, basement bar with a regular clientele. Thursdays are Electro Lush Lounge nights; Fridays, High Energy Dance Music; Saturdays, Miss Willie Taylor's All Star Show at 11pm; Sundays, karaoke.

Lotus Club
455 Abbott St.
☎685-7777
The Lotus Club is the only bar in Vancouver reserved exclusively for women. It's located in the same hotel as Charlie's Lounge and Chuck's Pub, on the ground floor.

Royal Hotel
1025 Granville St.
☎685-5335
A gay crowd throngs to a "modern" decor. Friday evenings are very popular, perhaps because of the live music. People wait in line as early as 5:30pm; Sunday evenings are a better idea.

Cultural Activities

Theatres

Art's Club Theatre *(1585 Johnston, ☎687-1644)* is a steadfast institution on the Vancouver theatre scene. Located on the waterfront on Granville Island, this theatre presents contemporary works with social themes. Audience members often get together in the theatre's bar after the plays.

The **Firehall Arts Centre** *(280 E. Cordova St., ☎689-0926)*, in the east-central part of the city, has a very good reputation and, like Art's Club Theatre, presents contemporary plays dealing with social themes. Worth a visit.

The **Ford Centre for the Performing Arts** *(777 Homer St., ☎280-2222)* is an immense, big-budget theatre that presents international mega-productions.

The **Queen Elizabeth Theatre** *(Hamilton St., at Georgia St., ☎665-3050)*, a large hall with 2,000 seats, presents musicals and variety shows, but is also the main performance space for the Vancouver Opera.

The **Vancouver Opera** *(845 Cambie St., ☎682-2871)* performs at the Queen Elizabeth Theatre (see above) because Vancouver is one of the major cities in the world that doesn't have an opera house. The address here is for the administrative office, which provides program information.

The old **Vogue Theatre** *(918 Granville, ☎331-7900)*, renovated not long ago, follows the trend in Vancouver of presenting all types of shows: theatre, comedy, music and even film. The programming varies.

Spectator Sports

The **Vancouver Canucks** *(General Motors Place, ☎899-GOAL)* are part of the National Hockey League. They play at GM Place Stadium from November to April.

Vancouver Grizzlies *(General Motors Place, ☎899-HOOP)* are one of the newest National Basketball Association teams.

The **B.C. Lions** *(B.C. Place Stadium, ☎280-4400)* are part of the Canadian Football League.

Casinos

If you're feeling lucky, try your hand at the **Royal Diamond Casino** (*750 Pacific Blvd. S., ☎685-2340*). Casinos in British Columbia are government owned and all the winnings are donated to charity. A good system!

At **Gateway Casinos** (*in front of the Radisson Hotel, Burnaby ☎436-2211; Royal Towers Hotel, New Westminster, ☎521-3262)* you can play blackjack, roulette or mini baccarat.

Calendar of Events

January

The **Polar Bear Swim** takes place every year on the morning of January 1. Hundreds of people actually choose to take a swim lasting a few minutes in the freezing waters of English Bay. If you don't feel brave enough to challenge that icy water yourself, you can always go there and watch or see it on television.

April

The **Vancouver Playhouse International Wine Festival** is an important festival where bottles of wine are auctioned and hundreds of wine growers gather to discuss their art and offer samples.

The Vancouver Sun Fun Run takes place on the third week of April when over 10,000 people participate in this celebration of sports and spring.

May

The **Vancouver International Marathon** *(☎872-2928)* starts at the Plaza of Nations, then goes through Stanley Park to North Vancouver, and back to Vancouver. Over 4,000 runners take part in this major sporting event on the first Sunday of May.

The **Vancouver International Children's Festival** *(Vanier Park, ☎687-7697)* takes place the last week of May under red and white tents. Children come from all over British Columbia for this big festival in the beautiful setting of Vanier Park, where 70,000 people gather every year.

June

Vancouver International Jazz Festival *(☎682-0706)*. Fans can come and satisfy their hunger for jazz at this distinguished festival. Artists perform throughout the city and the surrounding area.

Bard on the Beach *(Vanier Park, ☎737-0625 or 739-0559)* is an annual event in honour of Shakespeare. Plays are presented under a large tent, on the peninsula facing English Bay.

July

The **Benson & Hedges Symphony of Fire** *(English Bay, ☎738-4304)* is an international fireworks festival. A barge on English Bay, which serves as the base of operations, is the centre of attention. Dazzling show, guaranteed thrills.

August

The **Vancouver Folk Music Festival** *(☎602-9798)* has become a tradition in Vancouver. It takes place during the third week of August and features musicians from all over the world, from sunrise to sunset on Jericho Beach.

Abbotsford International Airshow *(Abbotsford, ☎852-9011)*. In Abbotsford, approximately 100km east of Vancouver, both young and old will be dazzled by F-16s, F-117 Stealths, and Migs. There are also are also old airplanes and clothing accessories. Don't forget your aviator glasses and sunscreen.

Vancouver International Comedy Festival *(☎683-0883)*. Every year on Granville Island comics provide several days of laughs.

The **Vancouver Fringe Festival** *(☎873-3646)* presents 10 days of theatre, including original pieces by contemporary writers.

At the **Greater Vancouver Open** *(Northview Golf and Country, Surry, ☎899-4641)*, the biggest names in golf compete on a splendid course.

September

Molson Indy Vancouver *(BC Place Stadium, False Creek, ☎684-4639, tickets ☎280-INDY)*. In the heart of downtown, a course is set up where Indy racing cars (the North American equivalent of Formula 1) compete in front of 100,000 enthusiastic spectators.

October

Vancouver International Film Festival *(☎685-0260)*. Vancouver, "Hollywood North," plays host to this increasingly significant festival which offers film buffs up to 150 films from all over the world.

December

The **VanDusen Garden's Festival of Lights** *(☎878-9274)* is another festival for the whole family. Throughout the Christmas season the VanDusen botanical garden is decorated with lights.

Shopping

Markets

Robson Market *(Robson St. at Cardero)* has it all and then some: vegetables; fresh fish, some of it cleaned out; stands with fruit salads; meats, sausages and ham; pastries and other baked goods; a counter for Alsatian and German specialties; flowers and plants; vitamins and natural products; natural medicine clinic; hair salon; small restaurants upstairs. The market is covered, but well lit.

Douglas Coupland

Vancouver can be proud of its star-author, Douglas Coupland, who, in 1991, at the age of 30, published his first novel, *Generation X*. His work coined a new catch-phrase that is now used by everyone from sociologists to ad agencies to describe this young, educated and underemployed generation.

Coupland's novel *Microserfs* (1995), is just as sociologically relevant, but this time it is the world of young computer whizzes that he describes, with sweeping generalizations about American popular culture that are both ironic and admiring. His observations interestingly parallel English-Canadian sentiment about the United States.

Life After God (1995) explores spirituality in a modern world and the impact of a generation raised without religion. *Girlfriend in a Coma* (1997) criticizes society's progress through a woman who wakes up from an 18-year coma to find out nothing has changed for the better.

Coupland's other works include *Polaroids From the Dead* (1996) and *Shampoo Planet* (1993). His most recent novel is *Miss Wyoming* (2000).

Granville Island Market *(9am to 6pm; Granville Island)* is Vancouver's best-known and most popular market. It is an immense commercial area surrounded by water with a fairground atmosphere. Good food, some of it prepared; fresh, good-quality vegetables, some of it organic; fresh fish and meat; wholesome breads; fast-food counters; pleasant shops selling jewellery, clothing and equipment for water sports and outdoor activities. Take a day to look, sample and wander. Parking is hard to find on the street but there are two indoor parking *(fee)* lots nearby.

Bookstores

Little Sisters Book and Art Emporium *(every day 10am to 11pm; 1238 Davie St., ☎669-1753 or 800-567-1662)* is the only gay bookshop in Western Canada. It offers gay literature as well as essays on homosexuality, feminism, etc. It is also a vast bazaar, with products that include humorous greeting cards. With the support of several Canadian literary figures, this bookshop has been fighting Canada Customs, which arbitrarily blocks the importation of certain publications. Books by recognized and respected authors such as Marcel Proust have been seized by Canada Customs, which has taken on the role of censor. Some of the same titles bound for regular bookshops have mysteriously escaped seizure by Canada Customs, leading to questions about discrimination.

Food

Kobayashi Shoten *(1518 Robson St., ☎683-1019)* is a Japanese store that sells groceries, take-out meals and gifts, as well as table settings and linens.

Rocky Mountain Chocolate Factory *(1017 Robson St., ☎688-4100)* is a divine little chocolate shop. You can savour bulk chocolate with nuts and fruits, or perhaps the bitter dark chocolate, for the real connoisseur.

The **Ten Ren Tea and Ginseng Company** *(550 Main St., ☎684-1566)* is without a doubt the best tea shop in Canada. Big jars hold an exceptional variety of teas from around the world.

Aboriginal Arts and Crafts

The **Inuit Gallery of Vancouver** *(345 Water St., ☎688-7323)* sells some magnificent pieces of Aboriginal art from Canada's Far North and the Queen Charlotte Islands.

Khot-La-Cha *(270 Whonoak St., North Vancouver, ☎987-3339)*. One block from Marine Drive and McGuire Street. Beautiful sculptures by First Nationls artists of the Salish Coast.

Hollywood North

The fact that the US dollar is stronger than the Canadian dollar has enabled Vancouver to become "Hollywood North." Hollywood producers have been flocking north to Vancouver, where they can shoot movies and television shows for half the cost of filming in Los Angeles or San Francisco.

The diversity of its cityscape has won Vancouver all sorts of honours. Over the years, it has masqueraded as Washington D.C., Chicago, Milwaukee and even Florida in various television series and films.

This interchangeability may be lucrative, but it has led some Vancouver residents to wonder when their city will star as itself in a movie.

Leona Lattimer *(1590 W. 2nd Ave., west of Granville Island, ☎732-4556)* is a lovely gallery where you can admire some fine Aboriginal art, or, if you like, purchase a piece. Quality jewellery and prints. Expensive.

Sporting Gear

Altus Mountain Gear *(137 W. Broadway, ☎876-5255)* carries everything for mountaineering: waterproof gear, clothing, tents, backpacks and more at cost price or for rent.

Mountain Equipment Co-op *(130 W. Broadway, ☎872-7858)* is a gigantic store that offers everything you need for your outdoor activities. You must be a member to make purchases; but membership only costs $5.

Ruddick's Fly Fishing *(1654 Duranleau St., Granville Island, ☎681-3747)* is a wonderful store for fly-fishing fans that even inspires newcomers to the sport. There are thousands of different flies for all sorts of fish. The owner will be glad to assist you. They also sell super-light canes, state-of-the-art fishing reels, souvenir clothing as well as fishing-related sculptures and gadgets.

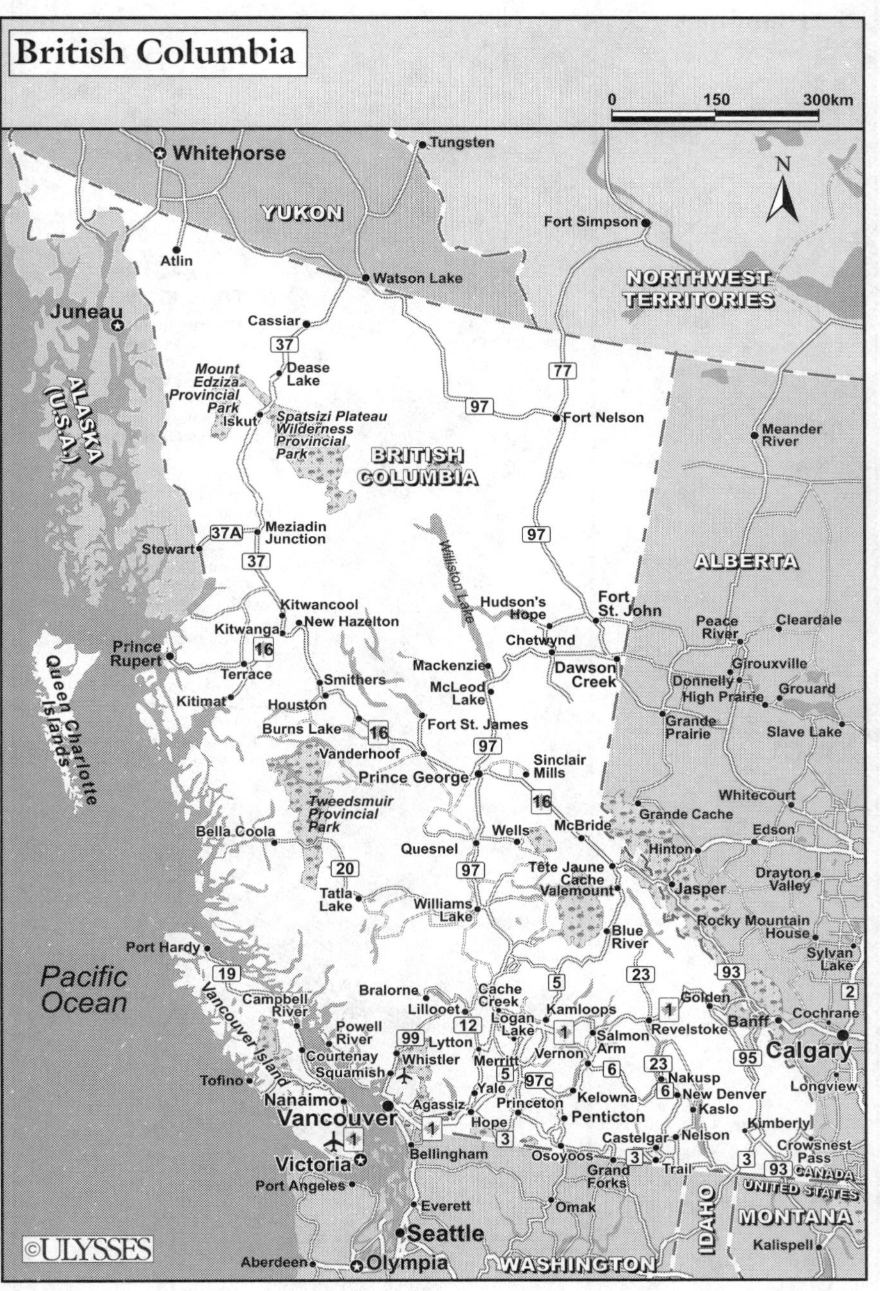
British Columbia
0
150
300km
N
Whitehorse
Tungsten
YUKON
Fort Simpson
Atlin
Watson Lake
NORTHWEST TERRITORIES
Juneau
Cassiar
37
Dease Lake
77
Mount Edziza Provincial Park
ALASKA (U.S.A.)
Iskut
Spatsizi Plateau Wilderness Provincial Park
97
Fort Nelson
Meander River
BRITISH COLUMBIA
Williston Lake
37A
Meziadin Junction
Stewart
37
97
ALBERTA
Kitwancool
Hudson's Hope
Fort St. John
Kitwanga
New Hazelton
Peace River
Cleardale
Prince Rupert
16
Chetwynd
Dawson Creek
Girouxville
Queen Charlotte Islands
Terrace
Smithers
Mackenzie
Donnelly
Grouard
Kitimat
Houston
McLeod Lake
High Prairie
Burns Lake
16
Fort St. James
Grande Prairie
Slave Lake
Vanderhoof
97
Sinclair Mills
Prince George
16
Whitecourt
Tweedsmuir Provincial Park
Grande Cache
Bella Coola
Wells
McBride
Edson
Quesnel
Hinton
20
97
Tête Jaune Cache
Drayton Valley
Valemount
Jasper
Tatla Lake
Williams Lake
Rocky Mountain House
Blue River
Port Hardy
Sylvan Lake
19
23
93
Pacific Ocean
5
Bralorne
Cache Creek
2
Vancouver Island
Campbell River
Lillooet
Kamloops
Golden
1
Cochrane
12
Logan Lake
Banff
Powell River
99
Lytton
1
Salmon Arm
Revelstoke
Calgary
Courtenay
Whistler
Vernon
95
23
Squamish
Merritt
6
Nakusp
Longview
Tofino
5
97c
Yale
6
New Denver
Nanaimo
Agassiz
Kelowna
Princeton
Kaslo
Vancouver
1
Penticton
Kimberly
Hope
3
Castelgar
Nelson
1
Crowsnest Pass
Bellingham
Victoria
Osoyoos
3
3
93
Grand Forks
Trail
CANADA
Port Angeles
UNITED STATES
IDAHO
Everett
Omak
MONTANA
Seattle
©ULYSSES
Kalispell
Aberdeen
Olympia
WASHINGTON

Victoria and Surroundings
ATTRACTIONS
Tour D: The Saanich Peninsula
1. Mount Douglas Park
2. Horticulture Centre of the Pacific
3. Dominion Astrophysical Observatory
4. Victoria Butterfly Gardens
5. Saanich Historical Artifacts Society
6. BC Aviation Museum
7. Fort Roder Hill & Fisgard Ligthouse
8. The Butchart Gardens
Tour E: From Victoria to the West Coast Trail
9. East Sooke Park
ACCOMMODATIONS
1. Guest Retreat B&B
2. Honoured Guest B&B
3. Oak Bay Beach Hotel
4. Travelodge Sidney
5. UVIC Housing and Conference Services
Honeymoon Bay
Lake Cowichan
North Cowichan
Duncan
Pacific Rim National Park (West Coast Trail Unit)
Port Renfrew
Strait of Juan de Fuca
Jordan River
Sooke
Metchosin
East Sooke Park
Swartz Bay
Sidney
Brentwood Bay
Saanich
Cordova Bay
Colwood
Victoria
Tsawwassen
Satellite Channel
Piers Island
Swartz Bay
Lands End Rd.
West Saanich Rd.
Tatlow Rd.
Wain Rd.
NORTH SAANICH
Patricia Bay
Mills Rd.
Victoria International Airport
McTavish Rd.
Yarrow Point
West Saanich
East Saanich Road
Central Saanich Rd.
Mt. Newton Rd.
Cordova Channel
James Island
Sidney Island
Brentwood Bay
Stellys Cross Rd.
Benvenuto Ave.
CENTRAL SAANICH
Martindale Rd.
Oldfield Rd
Willis Point Rd.
Mount Work Regional Park
Elk Lake
Elk/Beaver Lake Regional Park
Cordova Bay
West Saanich Rd.
Prospect Lake Rd.
Interurban Rd.
Hellmcken Rd
Royal Oak Dr.
Haro Strait
SAANICH
Quadra St.
HIGHLANDS
Burnside Rd.
Thetis Lake Park
McKenzie Ave.
University of Victoria
Arburtus St.
Tudor Ave.
LANGFORD
Cadboro Bay
Craigflower Rd.
Douglas St.
Cedar Hill
Shelbourne St.
Landsdowne Rd.
Hillside Ave.
Sooke Rd.
COLWOOD
Lagoon Rd.
Wishart Rd.
ESQUIMALT
Govern. St.
VICTORIA
Foul Bay Rd.
Beach Rd.
Oak Bay
OAK BAY
Chatham Islands
Discovery Island
Belleville
Fairfield Rd.
Dallas Rd.
McNeill Bay
See map of Victoria
©ULYSSES
0 2,5 5km

Victoria and Surroundings

Is Victoria ★★★ really more English than England, as people often say it is? Well, with high tea, lawn bowling and cricket as local pastimes, there is no denying its characteristic English flavour.

This is still a North American city, however, and along with all the English, it has welcomed large numbers of French Canadians, Chinese, Japanese, Scots, Irish, Germans and Americans.

Located at the southern tip of Vancouver Island, Victoria is the capital of the province and has a population of nearly 300,000 scattered across a large urban area. Its port looks out onto the Strait of Juan de Fuca, a natural border with Washington State. Victoria is set against a series of small mountains no higher than 300m in altitude, and its waterfront stretches several kilometres.

When Europeans began moving into the region in the mid-19th century, three Aboriginal groups, the Songhees, the Klallam and the Saanich, were already living here. In 1842, the Hudson's Bay Company established a fur-trading post near the Victoria Harbour. One year later, aided by the Aboriginal people, who were given a blanket for every 40 wooden stakes they cut, the company's adventurers built Fort Victoria alongside the seaport.

The fur trade attracted new workers, and with the gold rush of 1858, Victoria developed into a large town, welcoming thousands of miners on their way inland. The city flourished, and its port bustled with activity. In 1862, Victoria was officially incorporated; shortly thereafter, the fort was demolished, making way for real-estate development. The site is now known as Bastion Square, and the former warehouses of the fort have been transformed into commercial space.

For all those years, Victoria was a colony in its own right, just like British Columbia. The two were united in 1866, and it wasn't until a couple of years later that Victoria became the capital of British Columbia. The design of the parliament buildings was chosen by way of a competition. The winner was a 25-year-old architect named Francis Mawson Rattenbury, who left his mark all over the province. One of his most noteworthy projects was the prestigious Empress Hotel.

The downtown area rises up behind the port, whose waters are shared by ships, yachts and ferries. Like a railway station surrounded by fields, the port is the focal point; the squares, hotels, museums and parliament buildings are all located nearby. A stroll along the waterfront gives a good sense of how the city has preserved a human dimension in its squares and streets.

Victoria is the seat of the provincial government. Accordingly, the civil service occupies an important place in the local economy, as does tourism. This former colony's British heritage attracts many visitors in search of traditions like afternoon tea at the Empress Hotel; quite a few people come here to purchase tartans as well.

Like the Europeans and the Aboriginals, the Chinese played an important role in the city's development. They came here by the thousands to help build the railroad and settled in the northern part of town. The local Chinatown thus bears the stamp of authenticity, as it bears witness to a not so distant past. Victoria is also the home town of painter Emily Carr, who left her mark on the early 20th century with her scenes of native life on the west coast.

As the capital of an economically powerful province that is currently establishing itself as an economic powerhouse, Victoria has no intention of letting itself be outranked by the federal capital, Ottawa, when it comes to national politics. British Columbia enjoyed an economic boom in the '80s, and is no longer satisfied to be viewed merely as part of a Canadian region, but rather as an influential member of the Canadian federation. And this political power play is increasingly prominent as the international economy shifts toward Asia and places British Columbia in a strategic position.

To help you make the most of your visit to Victoria and the Saanich Peninsula, we have outlined five tours:

Tour A:
The Port and Old Town

Tour B:
The Victoria of Francis Rattenbury and Emily Carr ★★

Tour C:
The Waterfront ★

Tour D:
The Saanich Peninsula ★

Tour E:
From Victoria to the West Coast Trail ★★

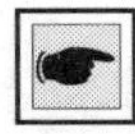

Finding Your Way Around

By Plane

Victoria International Airport (☎*953-7500*) is located north of Victoria on the Saanich Peninsula, a half-hour's drive from downtown on Hwy. 17.

Air Canada/Air BC Connector (☎*800-663-3721 or 360-9074*) offers 16 flights a day between Vancouver and Victoria airports, as well as 11 flights a day on a hydroplane between the ports of Victoria and Vancouver.

Canadian Airlines/Canadian Regional (☎*382-6111 or 800-363-7530*) offers 16 flights a day from Monday to Friday between Vancouver and Victoria airports, nine flights on Saturday and 11 flights on Sunday.

Helijet Airways (*$200-$275 return; Victoria* ☎*382-6222, Vancouver* ☎*604-273-1414 or 800-665-4354*) flies 37 times a day between the ports of Vancouver and Victoria.

Kenmore Air (☎*800-543-9595, or in Seattle, U.S.* ☎*425-486-1257*) shuttles back and forth between the ports Seattle, Washington and Victoria eight times a day in a hydroplane.

By Ferry

You can reach Victoria by car by taking a BC Ferry from Tsawwassen, located south of Vancouver on the coast. This ferry (*BC Ferry Corporation; in the summer, every day on the hour from 7am to 10pm; in the winter, every day every other hour from 7am to 9pm;* ☎*888-223-3779 in B.C. or 250-386-3431 from outside the province*) will drop you off at the Sydney terminal in Swartz Bay. From there, take Hwy. 17 South to Victoria (*see Tour D: The Saanich Peninsula, p 117*).

BC Ferries also offers transportation to Victoria from the east coast of Vancouver Island.

The ferry sets out from the Horseshoe Bay terminal, northwest of Vancouver, and takes passengers to Nanaimo. From there, follow the signs for the Trans-Canada Hwy. 1 South, which leads to Victoria, 113km away.

Visitors setting out from Seattle, Washington can take the seasonal ferry operated by **Victoria Line** (*May to Sep; Victoria* ☎*480-5555, or 800-668-1167*), which offers a chance to see the inland waters between Seattle and Victoria. Another option is to take the **Victoria Clipper** (*year-round; Victoria* ☎*382-8100, Seattle* ☎*206-448-5000 or 800-888-2535*), a sea ferry for pedestrians only, which takes passengers directly to the port of Victoria.

Black Ball Ferry
From Victoria to Port Angeles, U.S.A.
☎382-2202

The Clipper
Passengers from Victoria only to Seattle
☎382-8100

Scenic Gulf Island Ferry Tours Ltd.
2550 Beacon Ave., Sidney
☎655-4465

Victoria Star
From Bellingham, U.S.A. to Victoria
☎800-443-4552

By Car and By Scooter

Car Rentals

If you plan on renting a car, make the necessary arrangements once you arrive in Victoria; this will spare you the expense of bringing the car over on the ferry.

Avis Rent A Car
843 Douglas St.
☎386-8468

Budget Rent A Car
757 Douglas St.
☎953-5300

Roadside Assistance

Competition Towing
day or night
☎744-2844

Totem Towing
day or night
☎475-3211

Scooter Rentals

If you like to do things a little differently, why not explore Victoria on a little scooter (49 cc) from **Harbour Scooter Rentals** (*843 Douglas St., ☎384-2133*). Maps provided. Driver's license required.

By Bus

Airporter Bus (*☎386-2525*) transports passengers between Victoria International Airport and the downtown hotels.

Pacific Coach Lines (*☎385-4411 or 800-661-1725*) shuttles back and forth between Vancouver and Victoria eight times a day (16 times a day during summer).

Laidlaw Coach Lines (*$17.50 one way; ☎385-4411*) runs between Victoria and Nanaimo with stops in the major towns along the way. From Nanaimo, two other routes serve the north up to Part Hardy and the West Coast up to Tofino.

By Public Transportation

You can pick up bus schedules and a map of the public transportation system at the **Travel InfoCentre** (*812 Wharf St. ☎953-2033*).

Public transportation in the greater Victoria area is provided by **BC Transit** (*☎382-6161*).

By Taxi

Blue Bird Cabs
☎382-4235

Empire Taxi
☎382-8888

Empress Taxi
☎381-2222

Victoria Taxi
☎383-7111

Tours

Victoria Harbour Ferry Harbour Tours
☎480-0958
This company can take you to different places in the harbour (Mar to Oct).

Practical Information

Area Code: 250

Tourist Information

For any information regarding Victoria and its surroundings, contact:

The Victoria Travel Information Centre
every day 9am to nightfall
812 Wharf St., V8W 1T3
☎953-2033

Saanich Peninsula Chamber of Commerce
9768 3rd St., Sidney
☎656-0525

Emergencies

In case of serious emergency, dial **☎911**

Poison Centre
☎800-567-8911

Domestic Violence Hotline
☎386-6323

Air and Sea Rescue
☎800-567-5111

Victoria Police Station
850 Caledonia Ave.
☎*995-7654*

Victoria General Hospital
35 Helmcken Rd.
☎*727-4212*

Emergency Dental Service of British Columbia
☎*361-8901*

Money and Banking

Banks

American Express Canada
1203 Douglas St.
☎*385-8731*
☎*800-669-3636*

Bank of Nova Scotia
702 Yates St.
☎*953-5400*

Canadian Imperial Bank of Commerce
1175 Douglas St.
☎*356-4211*

Toronto Dominion Bank
1080 Douglas St.
☎*356-4000*

Royal Bank
1079 Douglas St.
☎*356-4500*

Currency Exchange

Currencies International
724 Douglas St.
☎*384-6631*

Custom House Currency Exchange
815 Wharf St.
☎*389-6007*

Money Mart
1720 Douglas St.
☎*386-3535*

Mail

Post Offices

Canada Post
Station B, 1625 Fort St.
☎*595-2552*

Downtown
905 Gordon St.
☎*381-6114*

Pharmacies

McGill & Orme
Mon to Sat 9am to 6pm, Sun and holidays noon to 4pm
649 Fort St.
☎*384-1195*

Shoppers Drug Mart
Mon to Fri 7am to 9pm, Sun 9am to 6pm
corner of Yates and Douglas
☎*381-4321 or 384-0544*

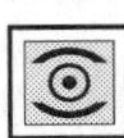

Exploring

Downtown Victoria is cramped, which can make parking somewhat difficult. There are a number of public lots where you can pay to park your car, including a very inexpensive one on View Street, between Douglas and Blanshard, at the edge of Old Town (on weekdays and holidays, the cost is$2 for the day).

Tour A: The Port and Old Town

Any tour of Victoria starts at the port, which was the main point of access into the city for decades. Back in the era of tall ships, the merchant marine operating on the Pacific Ocean used to stop here to pick up goods destined for England. Once the railway reached the coast, however, the merchandise was transported across Canada by train, thus reducing the amount of time required to reach the east side of the continent. From that point on, the merchant marine only provided a sea link to Asia.

Head to the **tourist office** (*812 Wharf St.,* ☎*953-2033*), where you can take in a general view of the port and the buildings alongside it, including the **Empress Hotel ★★** (see p 125) and the **Provincial Legislature Buildings ★** (see p 122). Start your tour by strolling northward along Government Street. You'll pass a series of stone buildings housing bookstores, cafes, antique shops and all sorts of other businesses. At View Street, turn left and walk down the little pedestrian street to **Bastion Square ★**.

Bastion Square marks the former site of Fort Victoria, constructed by the Hudson's Bay Company in 1843, with the help of hundreds of native people. Twenty years later, the fort was demolished to make way for the city. Today, the site is occupied by public buildings like the **Maritime Museum of British Columbia** (*$5; every day 9:30am to 4:30pm; 28 Bastion Sq., ☎385-4222*), which highlights great moments in the history of sailing, from the days when tall ships sidled up alongside one another in the harbour, up until the present time.

Walk down Bastion Square, turn right on Wharf Street, then head up the north side of Johnson Street. Go into **Market Square** ★, which is surrounded by shops facing onto the street. This place gets very lively during the jazz, blues and theatre festivals and on the Chinese New Year.

The Empress Hotel

Chinatown ★ (*west of Government Street, between Fisgard and Pandora*), is full of brightly coloured shops and its sidewalks are decorated with geometric patterns that form a Chinese character meaning "good fortune."
At one time, there were over 150 businesses in Chinatown as well as three schools, five temples, two churches and a hospital. On your way through this neighbourhood, you'll come across the Tong Ji Men arch, on Fisgard Street, a symbol of the spirit of cooperation between the Chinese and Canadian communities. **Fan Tan Alley** ★, which runs north-south (*south of Fisgard St.*), is supposedly the narrowest street in Victoria. People used to come here to buy opium until 1908, when the federal government banned the sale of the drug.

Craigdarroch Castle ★ (*$7.50; summer every day 9am to 7pm; winter every day 10am to 4:30pm; 1050 Joan Cr., ☎592-5323*) stands at the east end of the downtown area. It was built in 1890 for Robert Dunsmuir, who made a fortune in the coal-mining business.

He died before it was completed, but his widow and three children went on to live here. What makes this building interesting, aside from its dimensions, is its decorative woodwork and the view from the fifth floor of the tower. This residence is indicative of the opulent lifestyle enjoyed by the wealthy around the turn of the century.

Tour B: The Victoria of Francis Rattenbury and Emily Carr

Architect Francis Rattenbury and painter Emily Carr both left their mark on Victoria. Rattenbury designed the buildings that now symbolize the city, while Emily Carr immortalized the wilds of British Columbia.

The Empress Hotel ★★ (*behind the port of Victoria, ☎384-8111*) was built in 1905 for the Canadian Pacific railway company. It was designed by Francis Rattenbury in the Chateau style, just like the Chateau Frontenac in Québec City, only more modern and less romantic. As you enter through the main entrance and cross the lobby, let yourself be transported back to the 1920s, when influential people found their way into the guest books. Above all, make sure to stop by the Empress for afternoon tea (see p 130).

The **Crystal Garden**, by the same architect, is located behind the hotel. A big glass canopy supported by a visible metal structure, it originally housed a saltwater swimming pool and is now home to a variety of exotic birds and endangered animals.

At **Miniature World** (*$8; every day 8:30am to 9am in summer, 9am to 5pm in winter; in the Empress Hotel, 649 Humboldt St., ☎385-9731*), you'll see what patience and meticulousness can accomplish: an operational miniature sawmill and other fascinating creations, including two buildings dating back to the end of the 19th century. A sure hit with the kids.

Head south on Douglas Street, then turn right on Belleville to reach the **Royal British Columbia Museum ★★** (*$9.65; every day 9am to 5pm; 675 Belleville St., ☎800-661-5411 or 387-3701, message ☎387-3014*), where you can learn about the history of the city and the various peoples that have inhabited the province. The centrepieces of the collection are a reproduction of Captain Vancouver's ship and a Kwa-gulth First-Nation house. The museum also hosts some interesting temporary exhibitions.

The strange-looking white tower near the Provincial Legislature, at the corner of Belleville and Government Streets, is the largest **carillon** in Canada, with 62 bells. Its chimes can be heard every Sunday at 3pm from April to December.

Emily Carr House

The design for the **Provincial Legislature Buildings ★** (*free tours*) was chosen by way of a competition. The winner was architect Francis Rattenbury, who was just 25 years old at the time and who went on to design many other public and privately owned buildings.

If you like wax museums, make sure to visit the **Royal London Wax Museum** (*$8; every day 9am to 7:30pm; at the corner of Menzies and Belleville, ☎388-4461*), where you'll find Britain's entire royal family, the major explorers of Vancouver Island and the Far North, complete with accounts of their adventures, and much, much more!

Take Government Street south to Simcoe Street, and you will find yourself in the Carr family's neighbourhood. Built of wood, **Carr House ★** (*$5.35; mid-May to mid-Oct every day 10am to 5pm; 207 Government St., ☎383-5843*) was erected in 1864 for the family of Richard Carr. After the American gold rush, the Carrs, who had been living in California, returned to England then came back to North America to set up residence in Victoria. Mr. Carr made a fortune in real estate and owned many pieces of land, both developed and undeveloped, in this residential area. He died in 1888, having outlived his wife by two years. Emily was only 17 at the time. Shortly after, she went first to San Francisco, then London and finally to Paris to study art. She returned to British Columbia around 1910 and began teaching art to the children of Vancouver. She eventually went back to Victoria and followed in her father's footsteps, entering the real-estate business. She also began travelling more along the coast in order to paint, producing her greatest works in the 1930s.

A unique painter and a reclusive woman, Emily Carr is now recognized across Canada as a great artist who left her stamp on the art world. Be sure to visit the Vancouver Art Gallery (see p 73) to learn more about her art, since the main focus here is her private life. Carr House also distributes maps of the neighbourhood, which show where the family lived at various times.

One of these places was **Beacon Hill Park** ★ (*between Douglas and Cook Streets, facing the Juan de Fuca Strait*), a peaceful spot where Emily Carr spent many happy days drawing. A public park laid out in 1890, it features a number of trails leading through fields of wildflowers and landscaped sections. The view of the strait and the Olympic Mountains in the United States is positively magnificent from here. For a reminder of exactly where you are in relation to the rest of Canada, Km 0 of the Trans-Canada Highway lies at the south end of Douglas Street.

If you are getting around by car, by bicycle or by scooter (see p 112), take a ride down **Dallas Road**, which is surely the loveliest city tour in Victoria, offering an unimpeded view of the sea and the Olympic Mountains.

Both classical and contemporary works are on view at the **Art Gallery of Greater Victoria** (*donations welcome; Mon to Sat 10am to 5pm, Thu until 9pm, Sun 1pm to 5pm; 1040 Moss St.,* ☎*384-4101*), the city's museum of fine arts. Visitors will find pieces by Emily Carr and by contemporary local and Asian artists. A must for all art lovers. Contact the museum to find out about ongoing exhibitions and activities.

Government House (*1401 Rockland Ave.,* ☎*387-2080*) is another of Victoria's lovely attractions. The house is not open to the public, but its absolutely gorgeous 6ha garden may be visited. It is easy to see why the place has been nicknamed Garden City. There is no admission charge to visit the gardens, which are open every day.

Tour C: The Waterfront

The brand new **Oriental Discovery Museum** (*$6; every day 9:30am to 5pm; 631 Courtney St.,* ☎*388-6822*) presents exhibitions related to science and technology, as well as archaeological artifacts dating from the neolithic age.

Pedestrians and motorists alike will enjoy the marvellous panoramic views around Victoria. Start off your stroll along the waterfront at the **tourist office** (*812 Wharf St.*). Walk down to the piers to watch the street performers showing off. Farther along, near the Legislature, the **Pacific Undersea Gardens** (*$7; summer every day 10am to 7pm; winter every day 10am to 5pm; 490 Belleville St.,* ☎*382-5717*) highlight marine plant-life. A little farther still lies **Laurel Point Park**.

From the tourist office, head north on Wharf Street. Cross the Johnson Street Bridge, whose projecting seawall runs alongside the houses and the waterfront, offering a lovely general view of the buildings downtown. Farther along, past the Victoria Harbour, you will see the Strait of Juan de Fuca. Stop in at Spinnakers Pub and wet your whistle while taking in the panoramic view.

English Village and **Anne Hathaway's Cottage ★** (*$7.50; summer every day 9am to 7pm; winter every day 10am to 6:15pm during winter; 429 Lampson St., ☎388-4353*) lie west of downtown Victoria. Cross the Johnson Street Bridge, and after the sixth traffic light, turn left on Lampson Street. The Munro Bus, which you can catch at the corner of Douglas and Yates Streets, stops at the entrance. This little bit of England is a reconstruction of the birthplace of William Shakespeare and the home of Anne Hathaway, his wife. A stroll among these buildings will take you back in time. Try to make it for afternoon tea at the Old England Inn (see p 126).

Esquimalt is a small town known mainly for its naval military base and its **CFB Esquimalt Naval & Military Museum** (*Mon to Fri 10am to 3pm; ☎363-4312*), which has a large collection of military equipment and retraces the history of the base.

Tour D: The Saanich Peninsula

Victoria lies at the southern end of the Saanich Peninsula, which extends km to the north. The peninsula is first and foremost a suburb, as many people who work in Victoria live here. This region is an unavoidable part of any itinerary involving Vancouver Island and especially Victoria, since the big Swartz Bay Ferry Terminal is located in Sidney, a small town near the tip of the peninsula, a few kilometres from Victoria.

From downtown, drive south on Douglas Street and turn left on Dallas Road, which follows the shore. This road runs through a number of residential neighbourhoods, changes name a few times (at one point it becomes Beach Drive, then Cadboro Bay Road), and offers some lovely views along the way. You'll pass alongside Oak Bay and Cadboro Bay, which are lined with Tudor buildings and lush, well-tended vegetation. Once past Cadboro Bay, follow the shore line along Tudor Avenue. Take Arbutus, Ferndale, Barrie and Ash Roads to Mount Douglas Park.

At the entrance to **Mount Douglas Park ★★**, turn left on Cedar Hill Road, then right in order to reach the lookout, which offers a 360° view of the gulf islands, the Straits of Georgia and Juan de Fuca and the snow-capped peaks along the Canadian and U.S. coast. The colours of the sea and the mountains are most vibrant early in the morning and at the end of the day.

Upon leaving Mount Douglas Park, turn left onto Cordova Bay Road; it follows the shoreline until it becomes Royal Oak Drive, which intersects the Patricia Bay Highway (Hwy. 17) and then West Saanich Road (Hwy. 17A). These two highways access the east and west sides, respectively, of the Saanich Peninsula and then link in North Saanich by way of Wain Road. You can make this tour in a loop by reversing the order of one of the following two suggested routes, and you can take either tour from the ferry terminal in Swartz Bay by reversing its order.

West Saanich Road

The **Horticulture Centre of the Pacific** (*$5; every day Apr to Oct 8am to 8pm, Nov to Mar 8:30am to 4:30pm; 505 Quayle Rd., ☎479-6162*) is either a prelude or an encore to a visit to **Butchart Gardens** (see below). Attractions include a winter garden, the Takata Japanese garden and a collection of rhododendrons and dahlias.

If you like science and the stars, head over to the **Dominion Astrophysical Observatory** (*free admission; every day 9am to 4:30pm; on Little Saanich Mountain, 16km from Victoria, ☎363-0001*), which has one of the biggest telescopes in the world.

The amazing **Victoria Butterfly Gardens** (*$7.50; Mon to Fri 9:30am to 5:30am to 4pm; 1461 Benvenuto Ave., ☎652-3822*) are home to all sorts of butterflies, who flutter about freely in a tropical forest setting, accompanying you on your tour. An attractive souvenir shop and a restaurant are also found on the premises.

The Butchart Gardens ★★ (*$15.75 high season, $6 low season; every day 9am, summer until 10:30pm, winter until 5pm; Hwy. 17 N, 800 Benvenuto Ave., ☎652-4422*), which cover 26ha, were founded by the family of the same name in 1904. A wide array of flowers, shrubs and trees flourish in this unique space. Maps are available at the entrance. Fireworks light up the sky during July and August, and outdoor concerts are held here Monday to Saturday evenings from June to September.

Patricia Bay Highway

The **Saanich Historical Artifacts Society ★** (*every day, Sep to May 9am to noon, Jun to Aug 9am to 4pm; 7321 Lochside Dr., ☎652-5522*), located on the outskirts of Victoria, has one of the largest collections of steam engines, tractors and farming equipment in Canada. Of course, you have to be interested in that sort of thing. The museum is halfway between Sidney and Victoria and is easily accessible by Hwy. 17; head east on Island View Road then north on Lochside Drive and continue to the gate.

Sidney (*Visitor Information Centre, ☎656-3260*), a small town near the tip of the Saanich Peninsula, has attained a certain level of importance thanks to the presence of the **Swartz Bay Ferry Terminal**. Among the local attractions are the pretty **Sidney Museum ★** (*Mar to Jan, every day 9am to 4pm; 9801 Seaport Pl.*), which displays some magnificent whale skeletons and explains the biology and evolution of this animal.

The **BC Aviation Museum** (*every day, 10am to 7pm, at Victoria International Airport, the big white hangar near the control tower, ☎655-3300*) houses a fine collection of World War II airplanes, as well as some more recent models.

Located in the western part of the peninsula in an isolated area, the **Fort Rodd Hill & Fisgard Lighthouse** (*$3; 603 Fort Rodd Hill Rd, follow the Trans-Canada and take the Port Renfrew exit, 10km north of Victoria*) historic site will delight history buffs. You can walk along the property by the Strait of Georgia. Between 1878 and 1956, the fortifications first defended the British Empire and then independent Canada thereafter. Strategically placed, the artillery protected Victoria and Esquimalt, the gateway to Western Canada. As for the Fisgard lighthouse, located at the same place, it was the first lighthouse erected on the West Coast of Canada in the second half of the 19th century. It is still in operation.

Tour E: From Victoria to the West Coast Trail

Head north on Government Street, which turns into Hwy. 1A (Old Island Highway) and follow the signs for Sooke. At Colwood, take Hwy. 14, which becomes Sooke Road near Port Renfrew. You'll pass through the suburbs west of town when you get to Sooke, which lies about 30km from Victoria. At the 17 Mile House restaurant, turn left onto Gillespie Road. This will take you into **East Sooke Park** ★, where hiking trails lead through the wild vegetation by the sea. This is a perfect place for a family outing.

Head back to the 14, and turn left toward Port Renfrew. The highway runs alongside beaches and bays. The farther you get from Victoria, the more twists and turns there are in the road. The terrain is mountainous, and the views are spectacular. As you continue west on the 14, you'll notice a change in the landscape; forestry is still an important source of revenue for the province, and the large valleys in this region have been clear-cut.

Port Renfrew

Port Renfrew is a starting point for the **West Coast Trail** ★★★. This 75km trek is geared towards experienced, intrepid hikers prepared to face unstable weather conditions and widely varied terrain; in fact, it is considered one of the most difficult hiking trails in North America. For more information on the West Coast Trail, see the Vancouver Island and Gulf Islands chapter, p 156.

Parks and Beaches

Victoria is surrounded by a host of very different parks and beaches (city beaches, deserted beaches running alongside temperate rain forests, etc.). The west coast boasts numerous provincial parks, which all feature sandy beaches strewn with piles of driftwood. These parks offer nature lovers a breath of fresh air.

Tour C: The Waterfront

There are two beaches in Victoria where families can enjoy a day of sand-castle building and swimming in calm waters.

Willows Beach ★ (*public bathrooms, playground; in Oak Bay, at the corner of Estevan Avenue and Beach Drive*) lies alongside a chic residential neighbourhood near a marina and the Oak Bay Beach Hotel.

Cadboro Bay Beach ★ (*public bathrooms, playground; at the corner of Sinclair Road and Beach Drive*), a little farther east, is located in the University of Victoria neighbourhood and attracts a young crowd. It looks out onto a bay, with the Chatham Islands and Discovery Island in the distance. The ebb and flow of the tides has transformed the strand at **Beacon Hill Park** ★ (see p 116) into a pebble beach covered with pieces of driftwood.

The summit of **Mount Tolmie** ★★★ (*BC Parks, ☎391-2300*) offers sensational panoramic views of Victoria, Haro Strait, the ocean, and of magnificent Mount Baker and the Cascade Range in Washington State (USA).

Tour D: The Saanich Peninsula

Mount Douglas Park (*Hwy. 17, Royal Oak Dr. Exit; BC Parks, ☎391-2300*), which covers 10ha and offers access to the sea, is the perfect place for a picnic or a stroll (see p 117).

Tour E: From Victoria to the West Coast Trail

Goldstream Provincial Park ★★★ (*20min from Victoria by Hwy. 1; BC Parks, ☎391-2300*) is one of the major parks in the Victoria area. Picture 600-year-old Douglas firs lining hiking trails leading to Mount Finlayson and past magnificent waterfalls. In November, nature lovers come here to watch *coho*, *chinook* and *chum* salmon make their final voyage, spawn and die in Goldstream River. The fish are easy to see, as the water is crystal clear. Not to be missed.

An immense stretch of wilderness (1,422ha), **East Sooke Regional Park** (*information: Capital Regional District Parks, 490 Atkins Ave., Victoria, V9B 2Z8, ☎478-3344*) is sure to appeal to anyone who likes solitude and tranquillity. It is laced with over 50km of trails. At Anderson Cove, you'll find the starting point of a trail leading to Babbington Hill and Mount Macguire, whose summits offer a splendid view of the region. Eagles can be seen swirling about on thermal currents.

Follow the **Galloping Goose Regional Trail** for nearly 60km by bicycle, on horseback or on foot. A former railway line, it runs through some magnificent scenery. You'll spot geese, eagles and even vultures. The trail starts in the heart of Victoria and leads beyond Sooke, and can be picked up at numerous points in between. For more information, call ***☎478-3344***.

The **Juan de Fuca Marine Trail** (*information: BC Parks, South Vancouver Island District, 2930 Trans-Canada Hwy, Victoria, V9B 5T9, ☎391-2300*) stretches 47km, from the south end of Vancouver Island (from China Beach, west of the little village of Jordan River) to Botanical Beach, near Port Renfrew. This new trail, inaugurated in 1994 on the occasion of the Commonwealth Games, is geared toward experienced hikers, and, as a safety precaution, anyone planning to take it is advised to leave a detailed description of their itinerary with a friend before setting out.

Note that the northern part of this trail ends at Port Renfrew. Those who want to explore further can extend the hike on the 75km of the **West Coast Trail** ★★★ that leads to Bamfield. Together, the two paths add up to 120km of trails and require at least a 10-day expedition through the temperate rainforest of the West Coast.

On Hwy. 14, after Sooke, the waterfront is studded with beaches. **French Beach** ★, a stretch of pebbles and sand lined with logs, has picnicking facilities. It is also wheelchair accessible. A little farther west, still on the 14, lies **China Beach** ★★; to get there, you have to take a well laid-out trail down to the base of a cliff (about 15min). The beach is absolutely magnificent. It is not uncommon to spot a seal, a sea otter or even a grey whale or a killer whale swimming offshore. Just walk a few minutes in either direction to find yourself alone in a little bay. Surfers come here for the waves.

Botanical Beach ★★★, after Port Renfrew, is a veritable paradise for anyone interested in marine life. When the tide is out you'll discover all sorts of treasures: fish, starfish and various species of marine plant-life are left behind in little pools of water among the pebbles. To make the most of your visit to the beach, however, pick up a map of the tides from **Maps B.C.** (*Canadian Tide and Current Tables; 1802 Douglas St. Victoria, ☎387-1441*).

Pacific Rim National Park (*starting in Port Renfrew*) is a marvellous green space along the ocean front. It is divided into three sections: Long Beach, the Broken Group Islands and the West Coast Trail (see the Vancouver Island and Gulf Islands chapter, p 153).

Outdoor Activities

Cycling

Pacific Rim Mountain Bike Rentals, Sooke (*☎727-8858 or 646-2380*) is a friendly

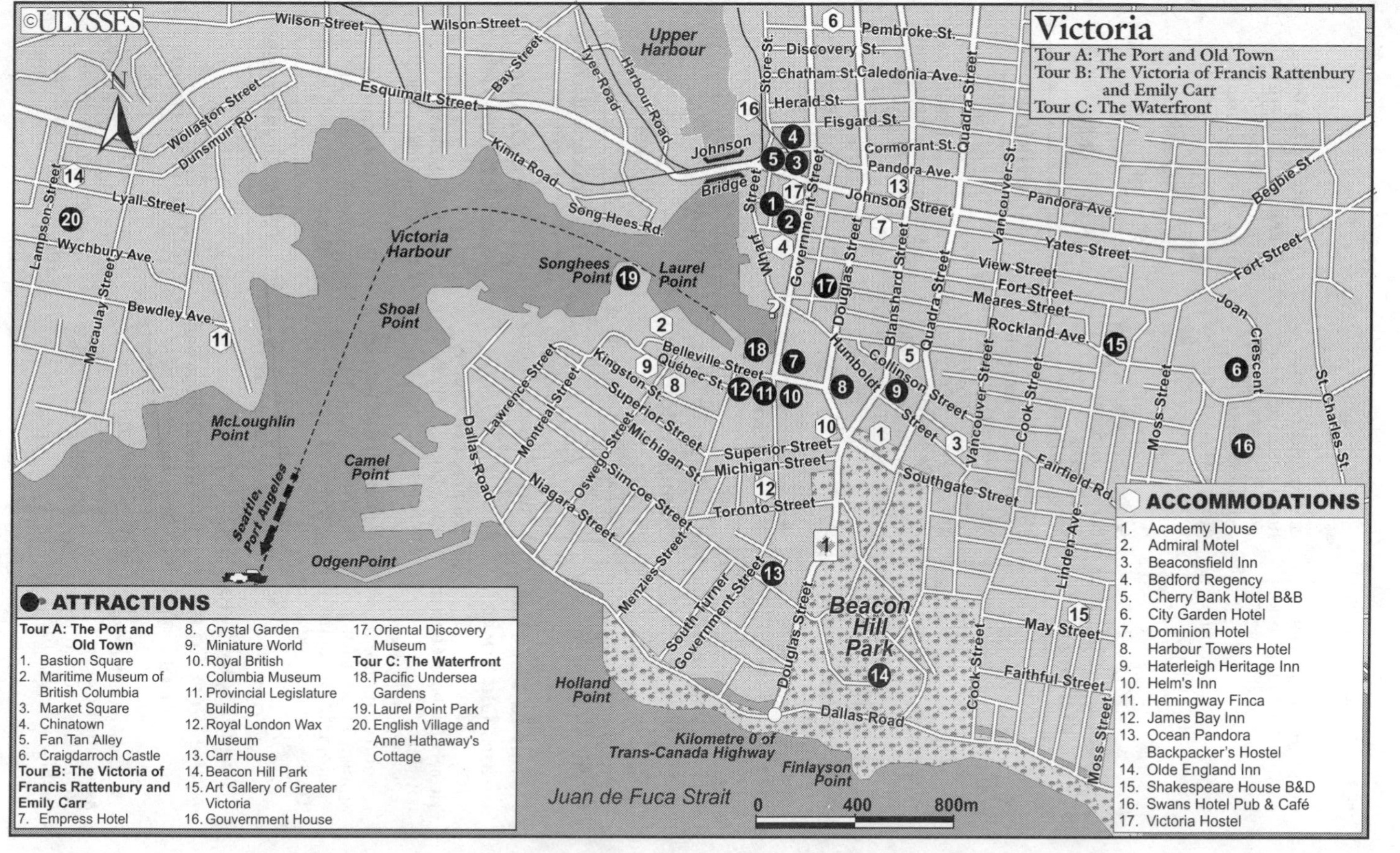
©ULYSSES
Victoria
Tour A: The Port and Old Town
Tour B: The Victoria of Francis Rattenbury and Emily Carr
Tour C: The Waterfront
ATTRACTIONS
Tour A: The Port and Old Town
1. Bastion Square
2. Maritime Museum of British Columbia
3. Market Square
4. Chinatown
5. Fan Tan Alley
6. Craigdarroch Castle
Tour B: The Victoria of Francis Rattenbury and Emily Carr
7. Empress Hotel
8. Crystal Garden
9. Miniature World
10. Royal British Columbia Museum
11. Provincial Legislature Building
12. Royal London Wax Museum
13. Carr House
14. Beacon Hill Park
15. Art Gallery of Greater Victoria
16. Gouvernment House
17. Oriental Discovery Museum
Tour C: The Waterfront
18. Pacific Undersea Gardens
19. Laurel Point Park
20. English Village and Anne Hathaway's Cottage
ACCOMMODATIONS
1. Academy House
2. Admiral Motel
3. Beaconsfield Inn
4. Bedford Regency
5. Cherry Bank Hotel B&B
6. City Garden Hotel
7. Dominion Hotel
8. Harbour Towers Hotel
9. Haterleigh Heritage Inn
10. Helm's Inn
11. Hemingway Finca
12. James Bay Inn
13. Ocean Pandora Backpacker's Hostel
14. Olde England Inn
15. Shakespeare House B&D
16. Swans Hotel Pub & Café
17. Victoria Hostel
Upper Harbour
Victoria Harbour
Songhees Point
Laurel Point
Shoal Point
McLoughlin Point
Camel Point
OdgenPoint
Holland Point
Finlayson Point
Beacon Hill Park
Juan de Fuca Strait
Kilometre 0 of Trans-Canada Highway
Seattle, Port Angeles
Wilson Street
Esquimalt Street
Bay Street
Tyee Road
Harbour Road
Wollaston Street
Dunsmuir Rd.
Kimta Road
Song-Hees Rd.
Johnson Bridge
Lampson Street
Lyall Street
Wychbury Ave.
Macaulay Street
Bewdley Ave.
Store St.
Wharf Street
Government Street
Douglas Street
Blanshard Street
Quadra Street
Vancouver St.
Cook Street
Moss Street
Linden Ave.
St. Charles St.
Pembroke St.
Discovery St.
Chatham St.
Caledonia Ave.
Herald St.
Fisgard St.
Cormorant St.
Pandora Ave.
Johnson Street
Yates Street
View Street
Fort Street
Meares Street
Rockland Ave.
Begbie St.
Joan Crescent
Belleville Street
Québec St.
Kingston St.
Superior Street
Michigan St.
Michigan Street
Toronto Street
Humboldt Street
Collinson Street
Southgate Street
Fairfield Rd.
May Street
Faithful Street
Dallas Road
Lawrence Street
Montreal Street
Oswego Street
Simcoe Street
Niagara Street
Menzies Street
South Turner
0 400 800m

outfit that rents out quality mountain bikes for $40 per day or $75 for two days. Special weekly rates. Guided tours ($15 per hour).

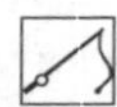

Fishing

As far as deep-sea fishing is concerned, salmon is king. There are five kinds of Pacific salmon: coho, chinook, sockeye, pink and chum. Given this variety, fishing is possible year round. Of course, you are likely to catch other kinds of fish, such as cod, halibut or snapper. The spawning season for coho, chum, sockeye and pink salmon lasts all summer, while chinook spawns from May to September and in winter in certain regions.

Tour A: The Port and Old Town

Victoria Harbour Charter (*50 Wharf St.*, ☎*381-5050*) hosts salmon-fishing excursions aboard a fully equipped 9m yacht. Thrills guaranteed.

Tour E: From Victoria to the West Coast Trail

The **Sooke Charter Boat Association** (*Sooke*, ☎*642-7783*) organizes fishing trips on the ocean and offers a hotel reservation service. The Sooke region is bounded by bays and coves where the rivers empty into the sea.

Sooke Charters
P.O. Box 66, Sooke,, V0S 1N0
☎642-3888
☎888-775-2659
Sooke Charters can provide you with all the necessary equipment, including bait. The rates are very affordable for this sport: $180 for three people (4hrs) or $200 for four.

Golf

Tour D: The Saanich Peninsula

Golf is the leisure activity on the Saanich Peninsula. Fans of the sport can try the following courses, listed in order of preference:

Ardmore Golf Course
930 Ardmore Dr., Sidney
☎656-4621

Cedar Hill Golf Course
1400 Derby, Saanich
☎595-3103

The Ball Return
10189 West Saanich Rd., Sidney
☎655-4419

The **Arbutus Ridge Golf Club** (*35min north of Victoria, Cobble Hill*, ☎*389-0070*) has a pretty 18-hole course and rents out equipment.

The **Cordova Bay Golf Course** (*5222 Cordova Bay Rd.*, ☎*658-4075*) also has an attractive 18-hole course with a driving range, a restaurant, a bar and a pro shop.

Hiking

Port Renfrew is one of two starting points for the stunning **West Coast Trail** ★★★ (the other is Bamfield). This is for experienced hikers only and requires a fair amount of preparation as well as prior bookings. For specific information see Vancouver Island and Gulf Islands chapter, p 156.

Horseback Riding

Tour D: The Saanich Peninsula

Woodgate Stables
8129 Derringer Rd., Saanichton
☎652-0287
Woodgate organizes pleasant outings just 20min north of Victoria.

Sea Kayaking

Tour C: The Waterfront

Sea kayaking is an interesting way to take in some lovely views of Victoria. **Ocean River**

Sports (*1437 Store St.,* ☎*381-4233*) arranges personalized excursions.

Scuba Diving

Tour D: The Saanich Peninsula

David Doubilet, a member of the Cousteau Society and a renowned photographer for *National Geographic*, describes Vancouver Island as "the best cold-water diving destination in the world." The entire coast is a maze of fjords and little islands. Veritable underwater gardens serve as a habitat for over 300 species of aquatic animals.

The Artificial Reef Society maintains some beautiful diving sites in **Sidney**, north of Victoria. The MacKenzie, a 110m destroyer, was sunk so that divers could explore it, and the same was done to the G.B. Church, a 57m boat. **Arrawac Marine** (*240 Meadowbrook Rd.,* ☎*479-5098*) organizes dives in the area.

Whale-Watching

Tour A: The Port and Old Town

At least 30 species of whales can be found in the waters around Victoria. Visitors can go whale-watching aboard an inflatable dinghy or a yacht. Here are two good outfits to try:

Orca Spirit Adventures (*in the port,* ☎*383-8411*) offers excursions aboard the Orca Spirit, an elegant and extremely comfortable 15m ship equipped with large observation platforms. Transportation from your hotel is available.

Sea King Adventures (*950 Wharf St.,* ☎*381-4173*) is a very professional company with an 8m boat that can comfortably accommodate 12 passengers. Reservations strongly recommended.

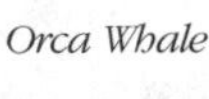

Orca Whale

Windsurfing

Tour C: The Waterfront

All you have to do is park your car on Dallas Road and plunge into the sea. The scenery is magnificent and the wind, perfect.

Accommodations

Tour A: The Port and Old Town

Ocean Pandora Backpacker's Hostel
$16-$20
K, sb
791 Pandora
☎385-1788
Ocean Pandora Backpacker's Hostel is one of the newest youth hostels to have sprung up in Victoria over the past few years. Around 100 beds are available in the dormitory and in the double rooms. You might smell the odour of synthetic material from the new mattresses. There's a little restaurant inside and Internet access is available.

Here are the addresses and phone numbers of some other youth hostels in Victoria:

Backpackers Hostel
$12
1608 Quadra
☎***386-4471***
⇄***386-5539***

The Cat's Meow Bed & Breakfast
$12-$17
1316 Grant
☎***595-8878***

Selkirk Guesthouse International
$14
934 Selkirk
☎389-1213

Beverly Lodge Hostel
$16
1729 Oak Bay
☎***598-7323***

The YHA Victoria Hostel
$16 members, $20 non-members, some private rooms
sb, K
516 Yates St.
☎***385-4511***
⇄***385-3232***
This stone and brick building with 108 beds is located in Old Town, right near the harbour. Members take precedence in youth hostels, so it can be difficult for non-members to get a bed, especially during the high season.

Dominion Hotel
$59-$124
tv, ℜ
759 Yates Street
☎***384-4136***
⇄***384-5342***
The elegant Dominion Hotel has welcomed visitors since 1876. The classic decor of its 101 rooms is sure to please. The pleasant restaurant-bar is located on the main floor.

Cherry Bank Hotel B&B
$65-$75, bkfst incl.
ℜ
825 Brudet Avenue
☎***385-5380***
The Cherry Bank Hotel B&B is situated in a residential area two streets from downtown. The unpretentious rooms are tastefully decorated in the same Victorian style as the building, which dates from 1893. Cherry Bank's Spare Rib House cooks up succulent steaks.

City Garden Hotel
$70-$90
≡, ⊛, ◷, *K, tv*
2852 Douglas Street
☎***388-0788***
☎***888-388-0787***
⇄***388-0787***
The City Garden Hotel is located on the outskirts of Victoria towards Nanaimo to the north. This new luxury hotel mainly attracts business travellers.

The Bedford Regency
$79-$165, bkfst
≡, ⊛, ℜ
1140 Government St., V8W 1Y2
☎***384-6835***
☎***800-665-6500***
⇄***386-8930***
The Bedford Regency is right downtown near the shops and the Inner Harbour. Each room has a goose-down duvet and some have a fireplace and a whirlpool bath. The facilities are new and the decor is classic and understated.

Academy House B&B
$95, bkfst incl.
865 Academy Close
☎***388-4329***
☎***877-388-4339***
⇄***388-5199***
Academy House B&B is a peaceful establishment located on the border of the wonderful Beacon Park. The high ceilings and small balconies add charm.

Swans Hotel Pub & Café
$119-$179
ℝ, ℜ, *tv*
506 Pandora Ave.
☎***361-3310***
☎***800-668-SWAN***
⇄***361-3491***
Without question, the undeniably charming Swans Hotel Pub & Café is one of the best places to stay in Victoria, especially if you're travelling in a group. The rooms are actually luxury apartments that can accommodate several people. Guests will find "real" works of art on the walls, plants, big-screen TVs and a pretty, inviting decor. The hotel, which dates back to the late 19th century, is located right in the heart of Old Town, steps away from Chinatown and the Inner Harbour. A fun pub that serves what locals claim to be the best beer in North America and an excellent restaurant known for its fresh oysters are on the ground floor.

Tour B: The Victoria of Francis Rattenbury and Emily Carr

The James Bay Inn
$56-$104
sb/pb, ℜ
270 Government St.
☎***384-7151***
☎***800-836-2649***
⇄***385-2311***
The James Bay Inn is a small hotel with 48 rooms, located a few minutes' walk from the Legislature and Beacon Hill Park. It was once a retirement home called St. Mary's Priory; painter Emily Carr spent the last part of her life here. The rooms are simply furnished with a bed, a television and a small desk.

Helm's Inn
$59-$99
ℜ, ℝ, *tv*, *K*, *P*
600 Douglas St.
☎***385-5767***
☎***800-665-4356***
⇄***385-2221***
All things considered, Helm's Inn is probably the best deal in Victoria. It is located within walking distance of downtown, the museums and the port and has spacious, elegantly decorated rooms and suites, all of them with fully equipped kitchens, as well as laundry facilities. A good, affordable choice.

The Admiral Motel
$79-$159
ℝ, *tv*, *P*
257 Belleville St.
☎/⇄***388-6267***
The Admiral Hotel is a quiet family establishment located right downtown, a stone's throw from the Empress Hotel and Inner Harbour. The rooms are very comfortable and the rates reasonable given the central location.

Harbour Towers Hotel
$115-$200
ℝ, *tv*, ℜ, ≈, *P*
345 Quebec St.
☎***385-2405***
☎***800-663-5896***
⇄***385-4453***
Without question, the Harbour Towers Hotel offers some of the prettiest possible views of Victoria and the sea. Complete comfort and impeccable service. A penthouse ($500 per night) with a fantastic view is also available for special occasions. Highly recommended.

Canadian Pacific Empress Hotel
$135-$305
≈, ⊛, ℜ, *tv*
721 Government St.
☎***384-8111***
☎***800-441-1414***
⇄***381-4334***
The Empress is located on the Inner Harbour, adjacent to the museums and the interesting public and commercial areas. Designed by architect Francis Rattenbury, this luxurious 475-room hotel offers a relaxing atmosphere and a Chateau-style setting. A new wing has been added to the original quintessentially Victorian building without detracting from its legendary charm. Visitors stop here for tea or simply to admire the ivy-covered facade.

Beaconsfield Inn
$200-$259 bkfst incl.
P
998 Humboldt St.
☎***384-4044***
☎***888-884-4044***
⇄***384-4052***
Located in the heart of Victoria, the Beaconsfield Inn, listed as a historic monument, combines luxury and sophistication. Guests can enjoy afternoon tea or a glass of sherry in the library and feast on a memorable breakfast. Expensive but British ambiance guaranteed.

The Haterleigh Heritage Inn
$202-$287 bkfst incl.
⊛, *P*
243 Kingston St.
☎***384-9995***
⇄***384-1935***
This old house, dating from 1901, has been lovingly restored with great attention to detail. A rich past lives on in its coloured glass windows and antique furnishings. The rooms are beautifully decorated and equipped with whirlpool baths and huge beds with goose-down comforters. Reputed to be the most romantic B&B in Victoria.

Tour C: The Waterfront

UVic Housing and Conference Services
$50 bkfst incl.
May 1 to Aug 31
sb, K
Sinclair and Finnerty Road
☎721-8396
Located on the University of Victoria campus, UVic's 999 rooms are open to visitors during the summer months. A number of these were built for the 1994 Commonwealth Games. The rates are based on triple occupancy, but single rooms are also available. The campus lies east of the downtown area on a hill, right near the Cadboro Bay Beach.

Hemmingway Finca
$75-$175, bkfst incl.
tv
1028 Bendley Ave. near Esquimalt
☎384-0862
⇄384-8113
The Hemmingway Finca is a luxury facility located on the other side of the bridge that spans Victoria's port. The refined antique décor is inspired by writer Ernest Hemmingway. Hunting and literary themes, central to the life of the American winner of the Nobel Prize, have been introduced into the furnishings of the premises.

Shakespeare House B&B
$65-$85 bkfst incl.
tv
1151 Oxford
☎388-5546
Situated between Beacon Park and the Straight of Juan de Fuca, Shakespeare House B&B was recently renovated and offers comfortable rooms. The classical English architecture of the building is interesting.

The Oak Bay Beach Hotel
$114-$185 bkfst incl.
ℜ, tv
1175 Beach Dr.
☎598-4556
☎800-668-7758
⇄598-6180
The Oak Bay Beach Hotel, which has 50 comfortably laid-out rooms, caters to visitors seeking English charm and a pleasant seaside atmosphere. Located on the waterfront in a residential neighbourhood, it offers an interesting view.

Tour D: The Saanich Peninsula

The Travelodge
$69-$145
tv
2280 Beacon Ave., Sidney
☎656-1176
☎800-578-7878
⇄656-7344
This member of the Travelodge chain offers lovely, comfortable and luxurious rooms at reasonable rates. The hotel is conveniently located a few minutes from Butchart Gardens, all the golf courses, the Swartz Bay BC Ferries terminal and Victoria International Airport.

The Olde England Inn
$75-$94
ℜ
429 Lampson St., V9A 5Y9
☎388-4353
⇄382-8311
The Olde England Inn is set amidst a replica of an English Village; a stay here really is like a trip back in time. There are period rooms with antiques and canopied beds or the more elaborate Royal Suites where the beds are draped in purple velvet and surmounted by a gold-gilt canopy. Anne Hathaway's thatched cottage is right near by, as are other English treasures like replicas of Shakespeare's birthplace and Dickens's Olde Curiosity Shop.

The Guest Retreat Bed & Breakfast
$80 bkfst incl.
tv, ℜ
2280 Amity Dr., Sidney
☎656-8073
⇄656-8027
This B&B is located steps away from the beach and has fully equipped apartments with private entrances and lots of closet space. The perfect place for an extended stay. Inquire about the weekly and monthly rates.

Honoured Guest Bed & Breakfast
$100-$180 bkfst incl.
⊛
8155 Lochside Dr., Saanichton
☎544-1333
⇄544-1330
The sumptuous Honoured Guest Bed &

Breakfast is located on the banks of the Cordova Channel, about 15km from Victoria via Hwy. 17. When the building was erected in 1994, the goal was to make the most of the landscape. The rooms have private entrances, some have access whirlpool baths and hot tubs, and all have sweeping views of the sea and Mount Baker.

Tour E: From Victoria to the West Coast Trail

Port Renfrew Hotel
$35
sb
at the end of Hwy. 14, Port Renfrew
☎647-5541
⇄647-5594
The Port Renfrew Hotel is located on the village pier, where hikers set out for the West Coast Trail. The rustic rooms are sure to please hikers longing for a dry place to sleep. There are laundry facilities on the premises, as well as a pub that serves hot meals (see p 131).

Sunny Shores Resort & Marina
$57
tv, ≈
5621 Sooke Rd., R.R. #1, Sooke
☎642-5731
⇄642-5737
Sunny Shores has modern rooms with cable television, as well as tent (15$) and RV sites (18$). Picnic tables, laundry facilities, large pool and miniature golf course. Open year round. Perfect for campers who like fishing. If you have a boat, you can moor it here.

Traveller's Inn on Douglas Street
$90 bkfst incl.
≡, K, tv, P
710 Queens Ave., Victoria
☎388-6641
☎370-1000
☎888-753-3774
⇄360-1190
This soberly decorated inn is a renovated building with 36 rooms. Basic services are available, but there are no telephones in the rooms.

The Seascape Inn Bed & Breakfast and Salmon Fishing Charters
$105
6435 Sooke Rd., Sooke
☎642-7677
The Seascpae Inn is a lovely place that looks out onto the port. The eggs Benedict are a wonderful way to start off the day, and the owner will even take you crab or salmon fishing if you like.

The Lighthouse Retreat Bed & Breakfast
$100 bkfst incl.
107 West Coast Rd., Sooke
☎646-2345
☎888-805-4448
Nestled in the magnificent West Coast forest, this B&B is unique as part of it is a lighthouse!

The Arbutus Beach Lodge
$74-$94
tv
5 Queesto Dr., Port Renfrew
☎647-5458
⇄647-5552The Arbutus Beach Lodge is a very pretty inn set on the beach, snuggled in the renowned West Coast forest. The surroundings are peaceful and the place is so comfortable that you'll feel like extending your stay. Whale-watching and fishing excursions are available upon request.

Arundel Manor Bed & Breakfast
$110-150 bkfst incl.
No smoking
980 Arundel Dr., Victoria
☎/⇄385-5442
You can enjoy a quiet, comfortable stay at the Arundel Manor Bed & Breakfast, a charming house built in 1912. Its three rooms are tastefully decorated, and on the side facing the water, the view is that much more striking. To get there, head north on Hwy. 1.

Sooke Harbour House
$270-360 bkfst and lunch incl.
♿
newspapers, bathrobes, no smoking
1528 Whiffen Spit Rd., Sooke, V0S 1N0
☎642-3421
⇄642-6988
Mr. and Mrs. Philip will give you a warm welcome at the Sooke Harbour House, their dream home. It might seem pricey, but rest assured that staying here will make your trip to Vancouver Is-

land a memorable one. The 13 rooms are all equipped with a fire-place and decorated with antiques and works of art. Breakfast is served in your room and lunch in the dining room (see p 135).

Restaurants

Tour A: The Port and Old Town

The Sally Café
$
1030 Fort
☎384-1899
The Sally Café makes scrumptious home-made fresh fruit muffins, as well as a variety of light fare to snack on at any time of day. They also serve breakfast. The place is famous for its melt-in-your-mouth cinnamon buns.

Paradiso di Stelle
$
Bastion Square near Wharf Street
For the best coffee in town, go to Paradiso di Stelle where the Italian tradition is reflected in your cup. The patio, which has a view of the port, is one of the loveliest in all of Victoria.

Alibaba
$
1011 Blanshard
☎385-6666
Alibaba pizza is a real treat. The generous portions are quarters of 30cm pizzas. The pesto pizza is a must!

Green Cuisine Vegetarian Restaurant
$
Marquet Square
560 Johnson
☎385-1809
Vegetarians should check out Green Cuisine Vegetarian Restaurant, which is 100% vegetarian (no animal or dairy products). From the salad bar, to home-made pastries, to organic coffee — there's something for everyone!

Yuen's Mountain Restaurant
$
866 Yates
☎382-8812
Yuen's Mountain Restaurant offers the ever popular deluxe Chinese all-you-can-eat buffet!

The California Wrap Bar
$
602 Broughton St.
☎382-9727
The California Wrap Bar is only open during the day. It's a great place to order and take out a wrap, a sandwich prepared with thinly rolled bread. The combinations are endless and they also serve delicious fresh juices. Expect to eat standing up since the bar is tiny and there's only one table and four stools on the sidewalk.

Garrick's Head Pub
$
Bastion Square, on View St.
☎384-6835
The sunny terrace at Garrick's Head Pub, located on a pedestrian street, is a pleasant place to get together over a local beer. The space may be limited inside, but there is a giant-screen TV for sports fans.

Java Coffeehouse
$
every day 10am to midnight, Fri and Sat to 1am
537 Johnson St.
☎381-2326
The Spacious Jave Coffeehouse has brick walls and high ceilings with exposed beams. Its established clientele is made up of both the young and the not so young. The coffee is excellent, the desserts (cheesecake, etc.) are tasty, and the lighting and paintings create a pleasant, relaxing atmosphere.

Handsome Swans Pub
$
506 Pandora Ave.
☎361-3310
The Handsome Swans Pub brews and serves the best beer in North America – at least, that's what they say here in Victoria. The also serve typical pub fare. A good place to meet other travellers. Live music Wednesdays and Sundays.

John's Place
$$
723 Pandora
☎389-0711
An eccentric urban mob is drawn to the warm decor of John's Place. The copious portions ensure satisfaction. This place is a must for eggs-Benedict

Victoria's Market Square, a charming little street full of colourful banners and...Victorian homes!
- *Walter Bibikow*

Whistler has an authentic mountain atmosphere, lively and geared towards the outdoors.
- *Derek Caron*

Dawn gently breaks the mist over Pacific Rim National Park
as the ocean washes over its dense forests and beaches. - *Sean O'Neill*

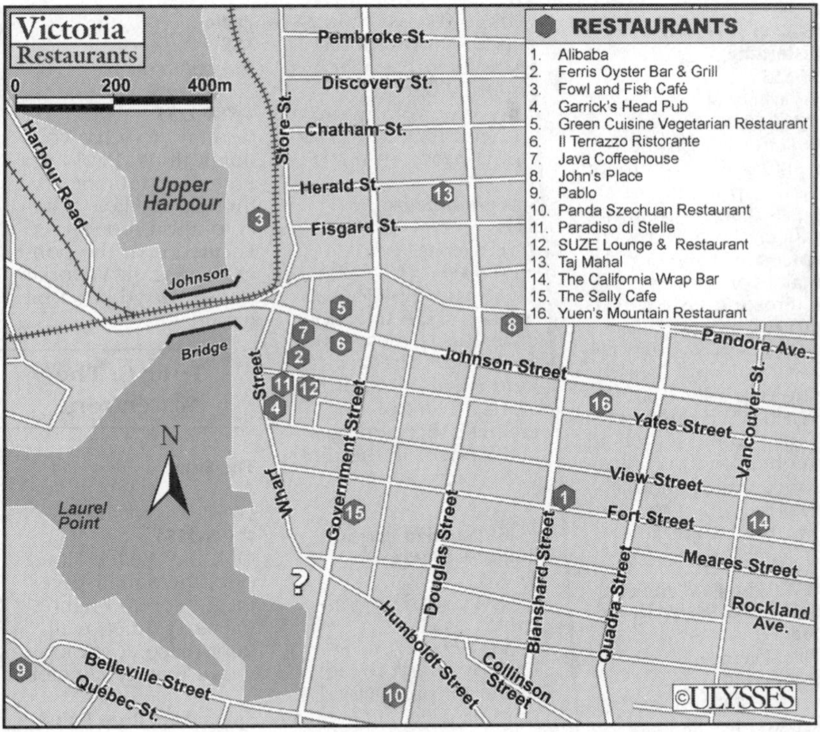

Victoria
Restaurants

RESTAURANTS

1. Alibaba
2. Ferris Oyster Bar & Grill
3. Fowl and Fish Café
4. Garrick's Head Pub
5. Green Cuisine Vegetarian Restaurant
6. Il Terrazzo Ristorante
7. Java Coffeehouse
8. John's Place
9. Pablo
10. Panda Szechuan Restaurant
11. Paradiso di Stelle
12. SUZE Lounge & Restaurant
13. Taj Mahal
14. The California Wrap Bar
15. The Sally Cafe
16. Yuen's Mountain Restaurant

©ULYSSES

lovers. As for cheesecake, let's just say that you won't be able to resist ordering a piece – even if you're already stuffed!

Ferris Oyster Bar & Grill
$$
536 Yates St.
☎360-1284
The pleasant Ferris Oyster Bar & Grill serves West Coast cuisine and excellent seafood. A good atmosphere for group dining.

Panda Szechuan Restaurant
$$
818 Douglas St.
☎388-0080
Panda is one of the best Chinese restaurants in Victoria. Authentic Chinese cuisine and impeccable service.

SUZE Lounge & Restaurant
$$
515 Yates St.
☎383-2829
Suze has a terrific atmosphere. The imaginative cuisine includes tasty pizza and pasta, good fish dishes and excellent home-made desserts. You can choose one of 18 kinds of martinis or order a Suze, the famous French apéritif for which the place is named. Highly recommended.

Taj Mahal
$$
679 Herald St.
☎383-4662
The Taj Mahal, an Indian restaurant, has an eye-catching exterior. Try the house specialties – lamb Biryani and Tandoori chicken. An excellent vegetarian menu is also available. Highly recommended.

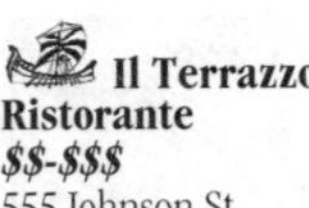

Il Terrazzo Ristorante
$$-$$$
555 Johnson St.
☎*361-0028*
Il Terazzo is an Italian restaurant with a menu made up mainly of pasta dishes. Creamy sauces flavoured with spices and sweet nuts make for some very interesting taste sensations. The clientele consists of young professionals and tourists. The one sour note is that the wine is kept on a mezzanine where all the heat in the room is concentrated, and is thus served at too warm a temperature.

The Fowl and Fish Café, Ale & Oyster House
$$$
1605 Store St.
☎*361-3150*
This restaurant is known for its tasty fresh oysters, but also serves some of the best West Coast cuisine in town, as well as traditional Spanish tapas and the locally-brewed Swans beer.

Tour B: The Victoria of Francis Rattenbury and Emily Carr

Empress Hotel's Bengal Lounge
$$
721 Government St.
☎*384-8111*
Recapturing the atmosphere of the British Empire of Queen Victoria, the beautiful Empress Hotel's Bengal Lounge serves a curry buffet featuring Indian specialties. The place is tastefully decorated with Eastern furniture, and guests have lots of elbow room.

Spare-Rib House
$$
824 Burdett Ave.
☎*385-5380*
The Spare-Rib House offers a wide selection of exquisite meats and fresh fish. The steak here is superb and the Honky Tonk piano creates a harmonious atmosphere in the dining room.

Canadian Pacific Empress Hotel
$$-$$$
behind the port, 721 Government St.
☎ *384-8111*
Tea-lovers get together in the Empress Hotel Canadian Pacific for tea with scones served with different kinds of jam. If you've got a big appetite, stop in for High Tea, which comes complete with cucumber and cream cheese sandwiches. This tradition supposedly originated during the reign of Queen Victoria, when the Duchess of Bedford, who tended to feel faint in the late afternoon, began fortifying herself with tea and little cakes and sandwiches. The old wood floors, comfortable furniture, giant teapots and courteous service make for an altogether satisfying experience.

Pablo
$$$
from 5pm on
225 Quebec St.
☎*388-4255*
Contrary to what you might think, Pablo is a French restaurant, though paella is available upon request. Located near the port in an elegant Victorian house. Good but a bit expensive.

Tour C: The Waterfront

The Snug
$
1175 Beach Dr.
☎*598-4556*
Oak Bay Beach Hotel's pub, the Snug, serves local beer and light meals. A quiet, well-kept place, it attracts a rather mature clientele.

Spinnakers Brew Pub & Restaurant
$
every day from 7am to 11pm
308 Catherine St.
☎*386-2739*
Spinnaker's serves beer and food in a laid-back setting, with the house specialties listed on big blackboards. The terrace is very well positioned, beckoning guests to kick back and relax. This place radiates a festive, convivial atmosphere.

The Olde England Inn
$
429 Lampson St.
☎388-4353
The restaurant adjoining the hotel of the same name, is a Tudor-style building furnished with antiques. It serves tea, complete with scones, crumpets and an assortment of jams. If you're looking for something more substantial, come for High Tea. Sit near the window facing the garden, so that you can enjoy the view of English Village; you'll think you're in England.

Tour D: The Saanich Peninsula

The Sidney Tea Room Restaurant
$$
9732 First St.
☎656-0490
The Sydney Tea Room serves delicious, sophisticated West Coast cuisine in a pleasant setting. A good choice.

Sorrento's Ristorante Italiano
$$
7120 Saanich Rd.
☎652-0055
Sorrento's is a very good restaurant in the Brentwood Shopping Centre, a stone's throw from Butchart Gardens. Pasta, pizza and Caesar salads.

Tour E: From Victoria to the West Coast Trail

17 Mile House
$
5126 Sooke Rd., Sooke
☎642-5942
Located right before the entrance to Sooke Harbour Park, the 17 Mile House serves light meals in a cozy setting. The thoroughly laid-back atmosphere here makes this just the place to quench your thirst after a day of walking along the waterfront in Sooke.

The Trail Cafe
$
Port Renfrew
☎647-5591
The Trail Cafe in Port Renfrew Hotel, serves breakfast, lunch and dinner. Stop in and listen to the hikers talking about their experiences on the West Coast Trail; you might pick up some advice and ideas.

Sooke Harbour House
$$$-$$$$
every day 3:30pm, dinner only
1528 Whiffen Spit Rd.
☎642-3421
The Sooke Harbour House has been praised to the skies by people from all over the world. The Philips's gourmet cuisine has seduced thousands of palates. The hosts settle for nothing but the best and are masters when it comes to preparing local produce. The dining room, set up inside a country house, offers a view of Sooke Harbour. Enjoy the classic ambiance as you take your seat and look over the menu. The dishes, prepared in the West Coast Style, reveal Japanese and French influences. Vegetarian dishes are available. See also p 127.

Entertainment

Bars and Nightclubs

Cues on View Billiard Room
708 View St.
☎480-7789
The Cues on View is a restaurant and an elegant pool room. The perfect place to kick off or wrap up an evening.

The Millennium
1601 Store St.
☎360-9098
This is an elegant jazz club where you can go dancing or enjoy a succulent dessert. Get ready for a good time!

Swans Pub
506 Pandora Ave.
☎361-3310
Swans Pub is a handsome place that serves the best beer in North America, or so they say in Victoria. A good place to meet other tourists. Reggae, rock and bluegrass Sunday to Thursday.

Steamer's Public House
570 Yates St.
☎*381-4340*
Steamer's is a good place to have a drink and kick up your heels to the tunes spun by the D.J. on Velvet Psychedelic Groove night (Sunday) or Kahuna Grande night (Thursday).

The Sticky Wicket Pub
919 Douglas St., Strathcona Hotel
☎*383-7137*
The Sticky Wicket Pub is located inside the Strathcona Hotel, just behind the Empress. This place attracts people of all ages and serves good beer. In nice weather, everyone heads up to the roof for some fun in the sun and a game of volleyball. At Legends Nightclub, also in the Strathcona, a clientele of all different ages dances to rock, R&B and jazz.

Planet Harpos
15 Bastion Sq.
☎*385-2626*
Planet Harpos, located in the heart of Old Town, has a hip, young atmosphere. Excellent D.J. Fluid night.

Uforia's
cover charge
1208 Wharf St.
☎*381-2331*
Uforia's attracts a fairly stylish crowd. People come here to party and kick up their heels on the dance floor.

Cultural Activities

Jazz

The **Victoria Jazz Society** (☎*388-4423*, ⇄*388-4407*) can provide you with information on local jazz and blues shows. The Victoria Jazz Festival takes place from late June to mid-July.

Theatre

The **Kaleidoscope Theatre** (*520 Herald St.*, ☎*383-8124*) puts on shows for young audiences.

The **McPherson Playhouse** (*3 Centennial Square*, ☎*386-6121*) presents plays and musicals.

All dance and classical music events are held at the **Royal Theatre** (*805 Broughton St.*, ☎*386-6121*).

Calendar of Events

January and February

Pacific Northwest Wine Festival (*Empress Hotel, Victoria*)

April

Annual TerrifVic Jazz Party (*Victoria*)

Boat Show (*Port Sidney Marina, Sidney*)

May

Fishing Tournament (*Port Sidney Marina, Sidney*)

Grand Banks Rendezvous: 200 boats meet in the port (*Port Sidney Marina, Sidney*)

June

Bayliner Rendezvous: 200 boats on display (*Port Sidney Marina, Sidney*)

Summer Fair (*every Sun; Saanich Historical Artifacts Grounds, Saanichton*)

Victoria Flying Club: Open House (*101-1352 Canso Rd., Sidney*)

July

All Sooke Day Logging Sports & Salmon BBQ (*Sooke*)

Crafts Fair (*Sancha Hall Annex, Sidney*)

Sidney Days Celebration: Pancake breakfast (*Sancha Hall, Sidney*)

Tribute to American Sailors (*Port Sidney Marina, Sidney*)

Victoria Shakespeare Festival (*Victoria*)

Victoria Jazzfest International (*Victoria*)

August

Centennial Days (*Centennial Park, Saanichton*)

Flower Fair (Sancha Hall, Sidney)

Fringe Theatre Festival (*Victoria*)

International Longboat Competition (*Sooke*)

First People's Festival (*Royal British Columbia Museum, Victoria*)

Saanich Fair (*Saanich*)

September

Annual Torque Masters Car Show (*Sancha Hall, Sidney*)

Antique Boat Show (*Port Sidney Marina, Sidney*)

Saanichton Fall Fair (*Saanich Peninsula*)

Sea Festival (*Port Sidney Marina, Sidney*)

October

Hallowe'en Bonfire & Fireworks (*Tulista Park, Sidney*)

Halloween Howl (*Panorama Leisure Centre*)

November

Christmas Bazaar (*Sancha Hall, Sidney*)

Crafts Fair at the New Saanich Fair Grounds (*1528 Stelly Rd., Brentwood Bay*)

December

Christmas Boat Parade (*Sidney Wharf, Tulista Park*)

Christmas Lights on Beacon Avenue (*Beacon Ave., Sidney*)

Shopping

Tour A: The Port and Old Town

The enormous **Eaton Centre** (*corner of Douglas and Fort Street, ☎381-4012*) has all sorts of boutiques, shops and restaurants. It is several-storeys high and includes an entire block of buildings.

The **Market Square** (*255 Johnson Street, ☎386-2441*) is smaller and more intimate than the Eaton Centre. The shops are smaller and a splendid interior courtyard invites shoppers to linger a while.

Sally's Antiques, Collectibles & Fine Olde Furniture Mall (*3108 Jacklin Rd., ☎474-6030*) is a lovely antique store that specializes in Victorian furniture.

The Used Items Emporium (*2951 Bridge St., ☎386-5112*) sells all sorts of second-hand items at reasonable prices. Even if you don't plan on buying anything, you're sure to leave with something.

With its stained-glass windows and 8m ceilings, **Munro's** (*1108 Government St., ☎382-2464*) is reputed to be the most beautiful bookstore in Canada. Good selection of Canadian, English and American books.

Hogarth's Sport & Ski (*2122A Government St., ☎480-1571*) is an excellent shop, especially for winter sports equipment and in-line skates. Good prices.

Below the Belt (*3174 Douglas St., ☎361-4308*) is a very hip, trendy clothing store, the best of its kind in Victoria.

The **Edinburgh Tartan Shop** (*921 Government St., ☎388-5275*) almost deserves to be called Victoria's Scottish embassy. Shetlands, kilts, coats, hats and 100% cashmere clothing. A local institution.

It is worth stopping in at **Rogers' Chocolates** (*913 Government St., ☎384-7021*) to see the shop's lovely early 20th century decor and pair of Art Nouveau lamps from Italy. Victoria Creams, available in a wide variety of flavours, are the specialty of the house.

Knives and Darts (*1306 Government St.*, ☎*383-2422*) sells an assortment of, well, knives and darts. Darts is very popular in the local pubs, and is taken quite seriously.

Tour B: The Victoria of Francis Rattenbury and Emily Carr

Hill's Indian Crafts (*1008 Government St.*, ☎*385-3911*) sells souvenirs in all different price ranges. The Aboriginal art is expensive. Wide choice of postcards.

The Antiquarian Print Room (*840 Fort St., 2nd floor*, ☎*380-1343*) is an antique shop that specializes in old books. Very interesting.

Vancouver Island and the Gulf Islands

Vast Vancouver Island stretches over 500km along the West Coast, with its southern tip facing the Olympic Mountains in Washington State (U.S.A.).

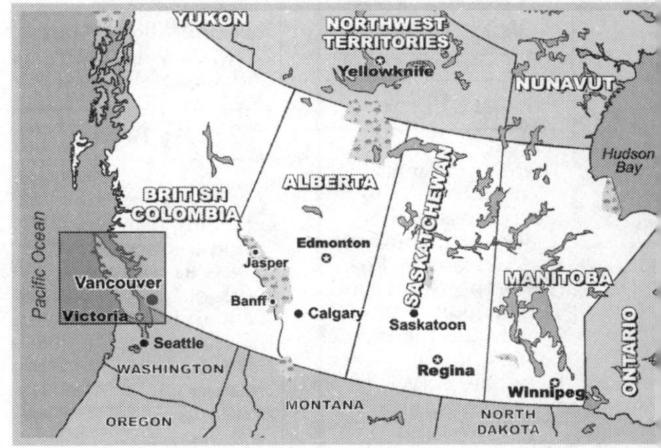

The island is split into two distinct regions by a chain of mountains, that divides the north from the south. The sea has sculpted the west side, creating big, deep fjords; the shoreline on the east side is much more continuous. Most of the towns and villages on the island lie either on the east coast or along the Strait of Georgia, where the Gulf Islands are located. There is another cluster of these islands in the Johnstone Strait, northeast of Vancouver Island.

The forest and fishing industries have provided several generations with a good source of income in this magnificent region. Thanks to the warm currents of the Pacific, the climate is mild all year round, enhancing the quality of life here.

Once isolated from the mainland, islanders now have access to efficient, modern means of transportation. A number of ferries connect the islands and the mainland every day. This chapter offers an overview of several islands worth exploring. During your trip, you might be lucky enough to spot a whale, a seal or a sea otter. The BC Ferries' captains have sharp eyes and will let you know if they see anything that might interest you.

To help you make the most of your visit to this part of British Columbia, we have outlined four tours:

Tour A:
From Victoria to Nanaimo and the Cowichan Valley ★★

Tour B:
From Nanaimo to Tofino ★★★

Tour C:
From Qualicum Beach to Port Hardy ★★

Tour D:
The Gulf Islands ★★★

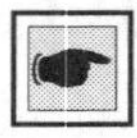

Finding Your Way Around

By Plane

There are regular flights from Vancouver to most towns in this region. Seaplanes transport passengers between the Gulf Islands. The majority of these islands and the municipalities on Vancouver Island are served by the following airlines:

Air Canada (*☎888-AIRCANADA or 800-776-3000, Vancouver ☎688-5515, Victoria ☎360-9074*). The AirBC affiliate of this company serves Victoria, Nanaimo, Campbell River, Comox and a number of other municipalities.

Baxter Aviation (*Nanaimo ☎754-1066, Vancouver ☎683-6525 or 800-661-5599*) has a fleet of seaplanes that fly between Vancouver and Nanaimo; it also serves other destinations on the island and on the Sunshine Coast.

Canadian Regional: ***☎(800) 665-1177***

Air Rainbow (*Campbell River, ☎888-287-8366 or 250-287-8371; www.air-rainbow.com*) mainly serves the northern part of Vancouver Island.

Hanna Air (*☎800-665-2359*) and **Harbour Air** (*☎604-278-3478 or 800-665-0212*) are small airlines (hydroplanes) that offer direct flights between Vancouver and **Mayne Island**.

By Boat

Visitors interested in travelling from one island to another have access to a vast network of ferries, that ply back and forth between the islands on a daily basis, and provide transportation to the coast.

BC Ferries carries passengers between Vancouver Island (Swartz Bay or Nanaimo) and the mainland (Horseshoe Bay or Tsawwassen), between Tsawwassen and the Gulf Islands (*reservations required for cars*), between Vancouver Island and the Gulf Islands, and between Quadra Island and Cortes Island. If you are travelling by car it is a good idea to make reservations in the summertime, or to arrive quite early, to avoid a wait. *For reservations and sailing times call ☎(888) 223-3779 in B.C., or (250) 386-3431 outside the province.*

If you're going from Port Hardy to the Queen Charlotte Islands or Prince Rupert, you can leave your car on the mainland.

BC Ferries provides service between Little River, on the coast east of Comox, and Powell River, on the Sunshine Coast.

BC Ferries also runs the **Tri-Island Ferry** (*Port McNeill, ☎956-4533*), which links Port McNeill to Sointula and Alert Bay.

Barkley Sound Service (*Box 188, Port Alberni, V9Y 7M7, ☎250-723-8313 or 800-663-7192*) crosses Barkley sound and links Port Alberni to Bamfield, north of the West Coast Trail, and Ucluelet, south of Long Beach.

By Bus

Island Coach Lines
700 Douglas St.,
Victoria V8W 2B3
☎(250)385-4411
☎388-5248
This company offers transportation from Nanaimo to Port Alberni, Ucluelet and Tofino, on the west coast of Vancouver Island.

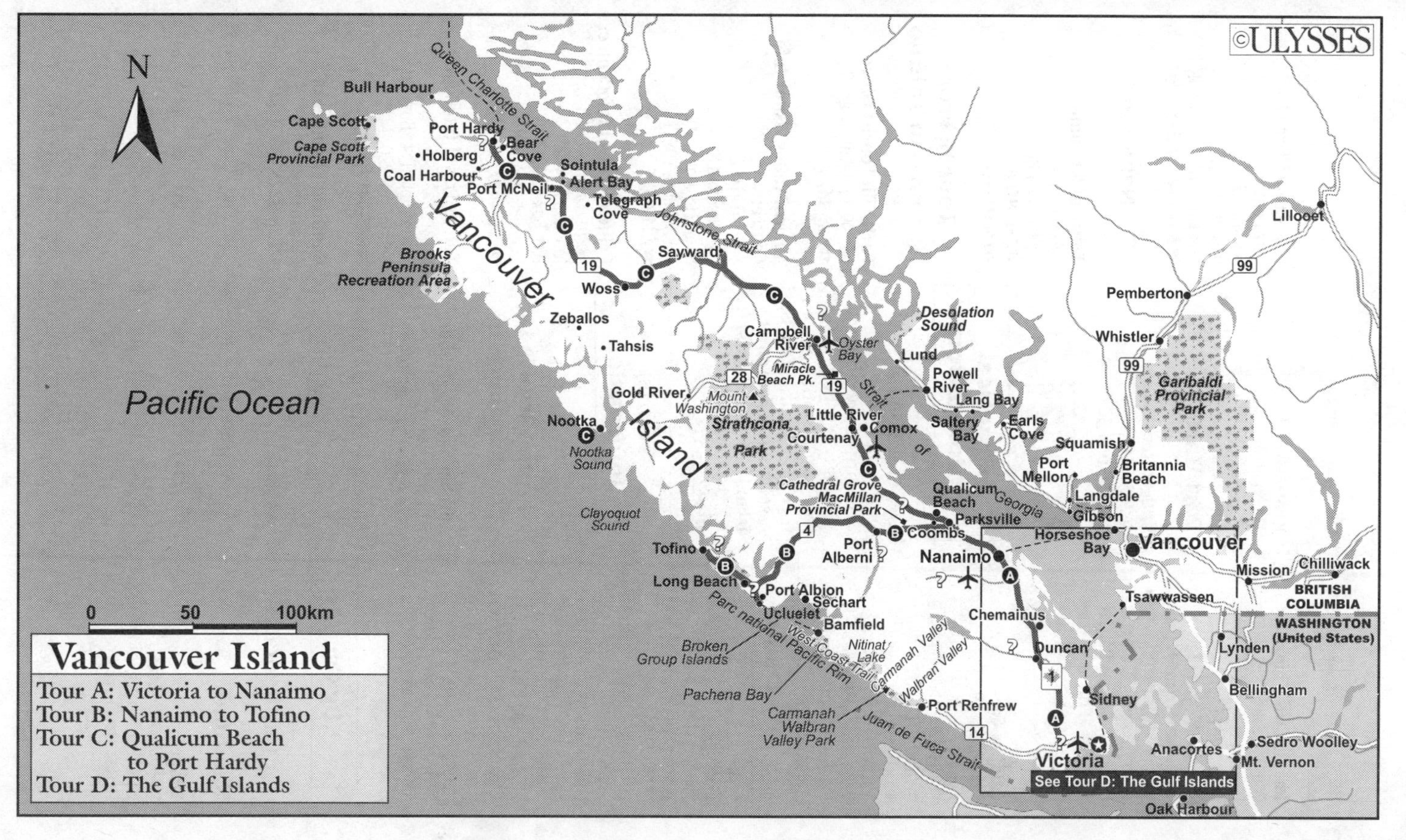

©ULYSSES
N
Vancouver Island
Tour A: Victoria to Nanaimo
Tour B: Nanaimo to Tofino
Tour C: Qualicum Beach to Port Hardy
Tour D: The Gulf Islands
0
50
100km
Pacific Ocean
Vancouver Island
Bull Harbour
Cape Scott
Cape Scott Provincial Park
Port Hardy
Bear Cove
Holberg
Coal Harbour
Port McNeil
Sointula
Alert Bay
Telegraph Cove
Queen Charlotte Strait
Johnstone Strait
Brooks Peninsula Recreation Area
Woss
Sayward
Zeballos
Tahsis
Gold River
Mount Washington
Nootka
Nootka Sound
Strathcona Park
Campbell River
Oyster Bay
Miracle Beach Pk.
Little River
Comox
Courtenay
Desolation Sound
Lund
Powell River
Lang Bay
Saltery Bay
Earls Cove
Strait of Georgia
Cathedral Grove
MacMillan Provincial Park
Qualicum Beach
Parksville
Coombs
Port Alberni
Clayoquot Sound
Tofino
Long Beach
Port Albion
Sechart
Ucluelet
Bamfield
Broken Group Islands
Parc national Pacific Rim
West Coast Trail
Nitinat Lake
Carmanah Valley
Walbran Valley
Pachena Bay
Carmanah Walbran Valley Park
Port Renfrew
Juan de Fuca Strait
Nanaimo
Chemainus
Duncan
Sidney
Victoria
See Tour D: The Gulf Islands
Squamish
Port Mellon
Britannia Beach
Langdale
Gibson
Horseshoe Bay
Vancouver
Tsawwassen
Mission
Chilliwack
BRITISH COLUMBIA
WASHINGTON (United States)
Lynden
Bellingham
Anacortes
Sedro Woolley
Mt. Vernon
Oak Harbour
Pemberton
Whistler
Garibaldi Provincial Park
Lillooet
99
19
28
4
14
1

Pacific Coach Lines
700 Douglas St.,
Victoria V8W 1B1
☎ ***385-4411***
Pacific Coach Lines operates from downtown Vancouver to downtown Victoria in conjunction with BC Ferries. These buses also serve the Gulf Islands.

Laidlaw Coach Lines
700 Douglas St.
Victoria
☎ ***385-441***
☎ ***(800) 318-0818***
Laidlaw services Victoria-Nanaimo, Nanaimo-Port Hardy and Nanaimo-Tofino.

By Train

E&N
Pandora Ave.
Victoria, V8W 3L5
☎ ***(800) 561-8630***
provides transportation along the east coast of the island. The major stops on this line are Victoria, Duncan, Nanaimo, Qualicum Beach and Courtenay. The train leaves Victoria at 8:15am from Monday to Saturday and at noon on Sunday.

By Car

Car Rentals

Nanaimo

Budget
☎ ***(800) 668-3233***
Budget will pick you up at the ferry terminal.

Rent-A-Wreck:
111 South Terminal Ave.
☎ ***753-6461***

Port Hardy

Budget Rent-A-Car:
☎ ***949-6442***
☎ ***(800) 668-3233***

Practical Information

Area Code: 250

To learn more about Vancouver Island before setting out on your trip, contact the **Tourism Association of Vancouver Island** (*302-45 Bastion Sq., Victoria, V8W 1J1,* ☎*382-3551*).

Tourist Information

Tour A: From Victoria to Nanaimo

Mill Bay Travel - Cobble Hill Info Centre
☎ ***743-3566 or 743-5099***

Duncan Travel InfoCentre:
year-round
381A Trans-Canada Hwy.,
Duncan, V9L 3R5
☎ ***746-4636***

Cowichan Lake:
Box 824, Lake Cowichan
☎ ***749-3244***

Chemainus Travel InfoCentre:
seasonal
9758 Willow St.
Box 1311 Chemainus, V0R 1K0
☎ ***246-3944 or 246-4701***

Nanaimo:

Tourism Nanaimo
Beban House
2290 Bowen Rd.
☎ ***756-0106***
☎ ***(800) 663-7337***

Tour B: From Nanaimo to Tolfino

ParksvilleTourist Office
Box 99, Parksville, V9P 2G3
☎ ***248-3613***

Alberni Valley Visitor Info Centre:
year-round
2533 Redford St. RR2,
Suite 215, Comp 10,
Port Alberni, V9Y 7L6
☎ ***724-6535***

Ucluelet Travel InfoCentre:
year-round
Junction Hwy. 4,
P.O. Box 428,
Ucluelet, V0R 3A0
☎ ***726-4641***

Tofino Travel InfoCentre:
seasonal
380 Campbell St., Box 476
Tofino, V0R 2Z0
☎ ***725-3414***

Bamfield Chamber of Commerce
☎ ***728-3228***

Tour C: From Qualicum Beach to Port Hardy

Qualicum Beach Travel InfoCentre:
year-round
2711 West Island Hwy.,
Qualicum Beach, V9K 2C4
☎***752-9532***

Campbell River Travel InfoCentre:
year-round
1235 Shopper's Row, Box 400,
Campbell River, V9W 5B6
☎***287-4636***
☎***(800) 463-4386***

Port McNeill Travel InfoCentre:
seasonal
1626 Beach Dr., Box 129
Port McNeill, V0N 2R0
☎***956-3131***

Port Hardy Travel InfoCentre:
year-round
7250 Market St., Box 249, Port Hardy, V0N 2P0
☎***949-7622***

Tour D: The Gulf Islands

Salt Spring Island Travel InfoCentre:
year-round
121 Lower Ganges Rd., Box 111,
Ganges, V8K 2T1
☎***537-5252***

Galiano Island Travel InfoCentre:
seasonal
Sturdies Bay, Box 73, Galiano,
V0N 1P0
☎***539-2233***

Gabriola Island Tourist Office
Box 249, V0R 1X0
☎***247-9332***

Saturna:
contact the Tourist Information Office of Vancouver Island (see above for address).

Quadra Island *and* **Cortes Island**:
contact the Campbell River Tourism Office (see above for address).

Exploring

Tour A: From Victoria to Nanaimo and the Cowichan Valley ★★

Head out of downtown Victoria on Douglas Street and take the Trans-Canada Highway 1 North toward Duncan and Nanaimo.

Travellers driving north from Victoria will have the chance to take in the beautiful region of **South Cowichan**, where lovely views of Saanich Islet and the strait that separates Vancouver Island from the mainland can be glimpsed all along the road. The **North Cowichan** area begins in the city of Maple Bay. This region opens right onto the ocean, and its towns are justifiably proud of their setting.

Mill Bay - Cobble Hill

This is your first stop in the region of South Cowichan, which boasts Mill Bay's large shopping emporium, the **Mill Bay Centre** (*Hwy 1, Mill Bay Rd. exit,* ☎*743-5099*), comprising some 40 shops, including grocery stores and clothing boutiques. Mill Bay Road, which later turns into Shawnigan-Mill Bay Road and then Shawnigan-Cobble Hill Road, will lead you to Cobble Hill, a region of parks and vineyards (see Cowichan Valley Wines section). Another attraction in Cobble Hill is **Quarry Regional Park** ★ (see p 152).

Shawnigan Lake

Approximately 10min on the road heading west from Mill Bay and Cobble Hill lies the lovely village of Shawnigan Lake. This small town's main attribute is, of course, the **lake** of the same name. It is the largest body of water in the region. The other major attraction here is the **Old Kinsol Trestle** ★★★ (*from Shawnigan Lake, take Glen Eagles Rd., turn right on Renfrew Rd. W., then continue on foot for 10min; information: South Cowichan Chamber of Commerce,* ☎*743-3566*), one of the longest wooden railway bridges in the world. Built in 1921, it was once used for the transport of copper ore.

Duncan

The **Native Heritage Centre** ★★ (*$10; May to Oct every day; in winter every day 9:30am to 5pm; 200 Cowichan Way, Box 20038, ☎746-8119, ⇌746-9854*), located in Duncan, was founded by the Cowichan First Nation in 1987. It has become a major tourist attraction over the last few years. The centre enables the Cowichan people to introduce others to their culture through interpretive activities and shows, as well as handicraft and art exhibitions. The tour is detailed and most interesting; a beautiful, well-made film, imbued with the spirit of the community, will enthral viewers.

Located near the Trans-Canada Highway and the Cowichan River, the centre is composed of several reconstructions of traditional structures, a restaurant, a café, a gallery and souvenir shop, and a historical interpretive centre that offers a totem-sculpture workshop. The art gallery sells only high quality hand-made articles, such as baskets, drums, jewellery, knitwear, original or limited edition prints, soapstone sculptures, dolls, blankets, books, as well as wood sculptures inspired by Salish, Nuu Cha Nulth (West Coast) and Kwagulth motifs.

The **Judy Hill Gallery** (*every day 9am to 6pm; 22 Station St., ☎746-6663, ⇌746-8113*) boasts the best Aboriginal art collection in the region. This art gallery represents close to 100 artists, all of whom are either painters, sculptors or weavers. Visitors will also find authentic "Cowichan" sweaters here.

The BC Forest Museum (*$10; every day Apr to Sep, closed in winter; 2892 Drinkwater, ☎715-1113*) offers rides on a steam locomotive and the chance to get acquainted with Vancouver Island's forest industry. Numerous activities are organized, as are fascinating demonstrations of bygone ways of woodcutting. Situated only 1km north of Duncan via the Trans-Canada Highway.

Maple Bay - Crofton

Located 10min from Duncan via Tzouhalem Road, Maple Bay is bordered by a lovely **bay** ★★. This is a paradise for yachting enthusiasts, canoeists and even divers, who can sound the depths Cousteau's team once explored.

A very pretty route leads to Crofton: from Maple Bay, take Herd Road to Osborne Bay Road. Crofton is especially known for being the point of departure of the ferry that travels to Salt Spring Island. Its main tourist attraction is the **Somenos Marsh Wildlife Refuge** ★ (see p 152), which shelters over 200 species of birds.

Lake Cowichan

Lake Cowichan is a small town built on the shores of the lake of the same name. Located 31km east of Duncan, it is easily reached via Hwy. 18. The lake is nicknamed *Kaatza*, which means "the big lake." Thirty kilometres long, it is one of the biggest lakes on the island.

The lovely **Kaatza Station Museum** (*summer every day 9am to 4pm; winter every day 1pm to 4pm; Saywell Park, on South Shore Rd., ☎749-6142*) explains the region's history and the remarkable influence the forest industry has had on the area. Visitors will also see a locomotive dating from 1928, which was once used to transport logs.

Fifty kilometres farther west, via a forest road, are **Carmanah Walbran Park** ★★★ and **Carmanah Pacific Provincial Park** ★★★ (*information at the Cowichan Lake tourist information centre, ☎749-3244*), magnificent wild expanses encompassing close to 17,000ha of ancient forests where certain trees stand almost 100m tall (see p 152).

Cowichan Valley Wines ★★★

Just south of the city of Duncan, on a **wine route** open to tourists, lie the vineyards whose wines are among the most renowned on Vancouver Island. Most properties are accessible from Hwy. 1, between Duncan and Victoria. Do not hesitate to pay wine growers a visit: they will be pleased to have you sample their nectars! The entrances are not always easy to find, so look out for particular roadsigns (often a bunch of grapes) that will indicate where to make a turn. Those travelling during the low season are advised to call ahead for an appointment.

The Cowichan Valley vineyards have slowly but surely acquired a good reputation. The region's mild climate, sandy beaches and peaceful bays, as well as the beauty of its rural landscapes, have attracted scores of poets and nature lovers. Wine growers from the world over increasingly covet this part of Vancouver Island, and many have managed to set themselves up here. A visit to the following five places is highly recommended: **Vigneti Zanatta, Cherry Point Vineyards, Blue Grouse Vineyards & Winery, Merridale Cider** and **Alderlea Vineyards**.

Vigneti Zanatta *(visits and wine tastings by appointment, Sat and Sun 1pm to 4pm; 5039 Marshall Rd., RR3, Duncan, ☎ 748-2338, ⇄ 748-5684).* The Zanatta family has been produ-cing wine for 40 years. Its vineyard stretches across the horizon, and it has aquired other parcels of land on the hillside over the years. After intensive studies in Italy, Loretta Zanatta developed a personal technique and bouquet. The result: wines made the Italian way, as simply as possible, which respect the flavour of the grape. The Zanatta family receives visitors by appointment, but those who arrive unannounced are also welcome to catch a glimpse of the splendid vineyards.

Cherry Point Vineyards *(every day 11:30am to 6pm; 840 Cherry Point Rd., RR3, Cobble Hill, ☎ 743-1272, ⇄ 743-1059).* Never has moraine been more welcoming! The 14ha (34 acres) of undulating hills that make up this property are reminiscent of an ancient glacial valley. Cherry Point's success certainly lies in the expertise of the proprietors, Wayne and Helena Ulrich. Since 1990, the couple has been dedicating all of its time and energy to the growth of its grapes in an effort to draw out their intricate flavours. The Ulrichs will be delighted to share their working philosophy with their guests. A new feature: you can spend the night on the property, as Cherry Point is also a Bed & Breakfast. You can savour a glass of white Pinot while gazing out your bedroom window during a wonderful stay at the farm. A pleasant, worthwhile experience.

Merridale Cider *(Mon to Sat 10:30am to 4:30pm; 1230 Merridale Rd., RR1, Cobble Hill, ☎ 743-4293)* makes its cider the traditional way. The owner, Al Piggott, grows his own apples in his 6ha (14 acres) orchard. It is, for that matter, the only orchard in Canada exclusively dedicated to the production of cider.

The **Blue Grouse Vineyards** *(by appointment; 4365 Blue Grouse Rd., RR7, Duncan, ☎ 743-3834, ⇄ 743-9305)* lie in the heart of Cowichan Valley. The owner, Hans Kiltz, offers interested parties a very informative tour of his vineyards. Friendly reception.

Alderlea Vineyards *(Thu to Sun 1pm to 5pm; 1751 Stamps Rd., RR1, ☎/⇄ 746-7122).* Some new cloned vines have been imported from France to increase the production of Pinot Gris, Pinot Noir and Maréchal Foch. After a number of experiments, Roger Dosman, the owner, now knows which grapes adapt best to the island's climate. Happy wine tasting!

Chemainus

Chemainus is a small town located about 20km north of Duncan. It owes its existence to the forest industry and probably would have sunk into oblivion had it not been for the ingenuity of its residents. The future looked bleak when the local sawmill shut down, but people here took control of the situation, reopening the facility and creating new jobs. Later, the town organized a big competition, calling upon various artists to cover the walls with murals illustrating the history of Chemainus. The 30 or so murals are worth the trip; it takes about an hour to see them all. The tourist office distributes a map containing a description of each one.

Nanaimo

Nanaimo is an important town because of its link to the coast, where ferries pick up hundreds of tourists headed for this region. It lies 35km from Vancouver, across the Strait of Georgia, and 1h 30min from Victoria by way of the Trans-Canada. Vacationers heading for the northern part of Vancouver Island or for Long Beach, to the west, pass through Nanaimo. This town is much more than just a stopover point, however; its seaport is graced with a pleasant promenade. Furthermore, visitors can easily catch a ferry to **Newcastle Island ★** and **Protection Island ★** to use the outdoor facilities and take in the view of Nanaimo. You can see all the local attractions, including old Nanaimo, on a walking tour.

Upon entering Nanaimo, Hwy. 1 becomes Nicol Street. Turn right on Comox Road and then immediately left on Arena Street, which will take you to Swy-A-Lana Park (you can leave your car there).

Go into the park and turn right when you reach the waterfront, where you'll find **Harbourside Walkway ★★**, a pleasant promenade lined with parks, historic sites and shops.

The Bastion ★(*Jul and Aug, every day 9am to 5pm*) was built by the Hudson's Bay Company in 1853 in order to protect the new trading post and the local residents. Its construction was supervised by two Quebecers, Jean-Baptiste Fortier and Leon Labine, both employees of the company. The Bastion never came under attack and was abandoned when the company left in 1862. It was later used as a prison, and has served as a gathering place and a museum since 1910.

The **ferry** (*summer, every day hourly from 9:10am to 11:10pm, Fri and Sat, last ferry midnight; winter, last ferry at 10:10pm, 11pm Fri and Sat; ☎753-8244*) for Protection Island departs from the end of Commercial Inlet. This little island is more or less a suburb of Nanaimo, with residents commuting to their jobs in town during the week. You can enjoy a refreshing beer and some excellent fish and chips at the island's floating pub (see p 169).

Nanaimo is renowned among scuba divers. The water is at its most beautiful between November and April (see p 161). Many people come here to go bungee jumping as well.

Tour B: From Nanaimo to Tofino

Take Terminal Avenue, head toward Parksville on Hwy. 19, then turn off toward Port Alberni on the 4.

Parksville

Parksville is a lovely little town that is resolutely tourism-oriented. Its magnificent **beach ★★★** boasts spectacular tides and will delight any visitor. In July, the **International Sandcastle Competition** (☎*954-3999*) takes place here.

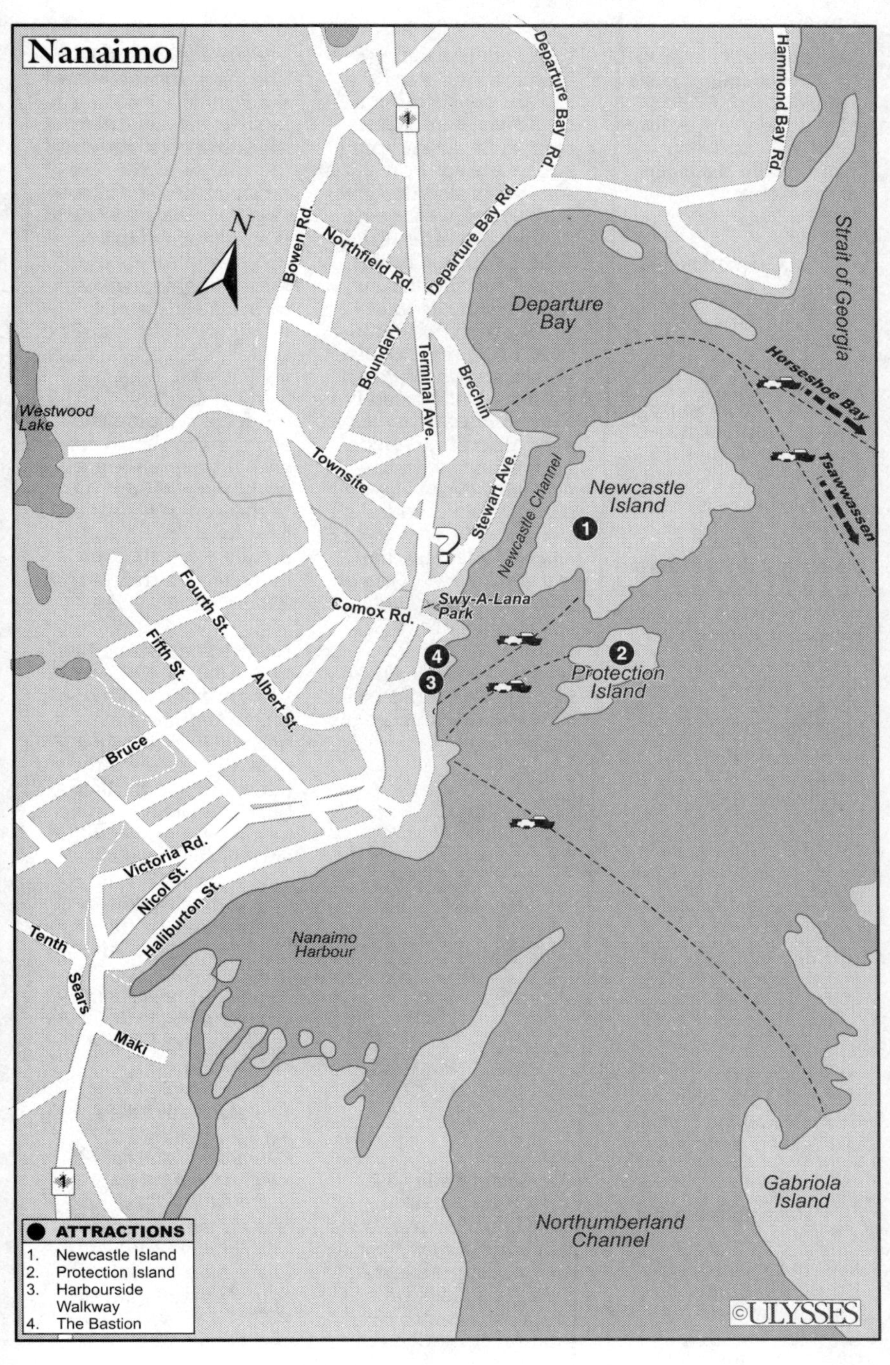
Nanaimo
N
Departure Bay Rd.
Hammond Bay Rd.
Departure Bay Rd.
Bowen Rd.
Northfield Rd.
Strait of Georgia
Departure Bay
Boundary
Terminal Ave.
Brechin
Horseshoe Bay
Westwood Lake
Townsite
Stewart Ave.
Newcastle Channel
Newcastle Island
Tsawwassen
Fourth St.
Comox Rd.
Swy-A-Lana Park
Fifth St.
Albert St.
Protection Island
Bruce
Victoria Rd.
Nicol St.
Halliburton St.
Tenth
Sears
Nanaimo Harbour
Maki
Gabriola Island
Northumberland Channel
ATTRACTIONS
1. Newcastle Island
2. Protection Island
3. Harbourside Walkway
4. The Bastion
©ULYSSES

Visitors can also stop by **Rhododendron Lake**, south of Parksville along Hwy. 19. A forest road will lead you toward a **wild rhododendron reserve** (☎*248-3613*).

Coombs

On your way west, stop in Coombs, a small community of 400 inhabitants whose **Old Country Market ★** piques the curiosity of passers-by. Built in 1975, this unusual place now lodges a family of goats!

Butterfly World of Vancouver Island ★★ (*mid-Mar to Oct 31 every day 10am to 5pm; 1 km west of Coombs via Hwy. 4; 1080 Winchester Rd.,* ☎*248-7026*). Come visit the foremost artificial butterfly habitat in Canada. A tropical forest has been laid out in a controlled environment in order to allow 80 species of butterflies to flutter about in total freedom. If passing through Coombs, Butterfly World is an absolute must.

The route to Port Alberni, passes through **Cathedral Grove MacMillan Provincial Park ★★★** (see p 153)

Port Alberni

Like many towns in British Columbia, Port Alberni owes its existence to the forest industry, fishing and trade. Its harbour is linked to the Pacific by a large canal, putting the town at an advantage as far as shipping is concerned. Port Alberni is also the gateway to the west coast of Vancouver Island. When you reach the top of the mountains surrounding Mount Arrowsmith, at an altitude of nearly 2,000m, you're almost at Port Alberni. Until recently, the range of activities in Port Alberni has been rather limited, but two new attractions have recently been added.

Alberni Valley Museum (*$4; Tue to Sun 10am to 5pm, Thu until 8pm; 4225 Wallace St.,* ☎*723-2182,* ⇄*723-1035*) has an assorted collection of exhibits on the history, culture and art of the region.

The **Steam Train** (*$3; weekends Jul and Aug, every hour between 11am and 4pm; corner Third Ave. and Argyle St.,* ☎*723-2182*) has rides on a restored two-stroke steam locomotive dating from 1929, which used to transport wood via Port Alberni. In the next few years, the town hopes to extend the ride, which is currently rather short.

Port Alberni is also renowned for its many salmon-fishing spots. Information can be obtained at the tourist office.

Salmon can be found in the local waters. They are born in the rivers, and after spending a good part of their life in the sea, return there to spawn, much to the delight of both commercial and amateur fishers.

Keep left as you enter Port Alberni. Take Port Alberni Highway to Third Avenue, turn left on Argyle Street and then right toward the harbour. The **Harbour Quay** is a pleasant place to have a cup of coffee and inquire about which boats can take you to Pacific Rim National Park for the day. In the middle of the public square, you'll see a fountain adorned with granite sculptures showing the life cycle of the salmon.

The **M.V. Lady Rose** (*$15-$40; year-round, Bamfield: Tue, Thu, Fri and Sat 8am, during summer, Tue, Thu, Sat 8am in winter; Ucluelet and Broken Group Islands: Mon, Wed, Fri 8am; Harbour Quay,* ☎*723-8313 or 800-663-7192*) offers year-round transportation between Port Alberni and Bamfield, at the north end of the West Coast Trail. During summer, the **Frances Barkley** carries passengers to and from Ucluelet and the Broken Group Islands, south of Long Beach. All sorts of discoveries await you on these trips; make sure to bring along a camera, a pair of binoculars and a raincoat.

On your way out of the port, turn left on Third Avenue and take Hwy. 4 in the direction of Tofino. This scenic road runs along a mountainside, passing through valleys and beside rivers. At the end, turn right toward Ucluelet.

★ Ucluelet

Located at the south end of Long Beach, Ucluelet is a charming town whose main street is lined with old wooden houses. In the past, the only way to get here was by boat. The local economy is based on fishing and tourism. Over 200 species of birds can be found around Ucluelet. Migrating grey whales swim in the coves and near the beaches here between the months of March to May, making whale-watching one of the main attractions on the west coast.

At the south end of the village, in **He Tin Kis Park ★★**, there is a wooden walkway leading through a small temperate rain forest beside Terrace Beach. This short walk will help you appreciate the beauty of this type of vegetation. The **Amphitrite Point Lighthouse ★** has stood on the shore since 1908. In those days, this area was known as the "cemetery of the Pacific" because so many ships had run up onto the reefs here. The wreckage of one tall ship still lies at the bottom of the sea near the point. The Canadian Coast Guard has a shipping checkpoint offshore (*guided tours available during summer*).

Back on Hwy. 4, on your way to Tofino, stop by at the Parks Canada office (*Easter to Oct; Hwy. 4; ☎726-4212*) to pick up a map of **Long Beach ★★**.

★ Tofino

Tofino, situated at the northwest end of Long Beach, is a lively town where the many visitors chat about sunsets and the outdoors. Spanish explorers Galiano and Valdes, who discovered this coast in the summer of 1792, named the place after Vincente Tofino, their hydrography professor.

Tofino has a population of just over 1000; during summer, this number quadruples. Vacationers come here to enjoy the sun and sand at Long Beach. The water is rather cold, however. Whale-watching and salmon fishing draw tourists as well.

This town is also an artists' colony. The local painters and sculptors draw much of their inspiration from the unspoiled landscape of the west coast. The **House of Himwitsa ★**(see p. ??) (*at the end of the main street, near the port*) displays works by Aboriginal artists.

From mid-March to mid-April, Tofino lives for the **Whale Festival**, a month in which the global grey-whale population passes through the region. Every year, close to 19,000 grey whales undertake a 16,000km migratory journey from the Baja peninsula, in Mexico, to the Bering and Chukchi Seas, off Alaska and Siberia. The huge mammals spend the whole summer here consuming the vast schools of krill that abound in these regions. Several festivities are organized in Tofino to mark the event. Contact the **See** for whale- watching companies p 160.

There is a day-trip to the only **Hot Springs** on Vancouver Island. The round trip only takes 2hrs and allows you to see some whales and white-headed eagles. You reach the hot springs after a long boat ride, which lets you off at the start of a 2km path through the woods. A 20min walk through the rain forest leads to the hot springs, which flow into the sea. You can jump from the boiling water into the refreshing sea-water. It's great for the circulation, but watch out for the strong ocean currents! Here are the names of a few companies that offer trips to the hot springs:

Chinook Charters (*$75; 450 Campbell, ☎725-3431 or 800-665-3646*)
Sea Trek (*$75 or $60/student; 441B Campbell, ☎725-4412*)

If you want to learn more about the rich (and increasingly rare) rain-forest ecosystem in this temperate region, take a look at the **Rainforest Interpretative Centre** (*free; 451 Main St., ☎725-2560*). **Friends of Clayoquot Sound** (*corner of Neil St. and First St., ☎725-4218*) is an organization that protects the forests and makes sure companies respect the governmental agreements; if companies do not respect these agreements, the group returns to block the logging roads. In a region where an ancient tree can fetch $100,000, it's an uphill battle. You can gain in-depth knowledge about the state of the forest and the organization's activities, and support their commendable efforts by buying a T-shirt or a poster.

Meares Island is one of the Clayoquot Sound islands that has a large area of old-growth forest, ancient trees that were here well before the arrival of the Europeans. To get there, simply go to the Fourth Street pier and look for the yellow boat called **Salty** (*$20 round-trip; ☎726-8321*). You can take a long walk on the island among these gigantic 1,000-year-old trees.

The lovely **Tonquin Beach** is a 20min walk from Tofino (*take First Street to the south, turn right on Arnet Road and then right again on Tonquin Road*). If you're not able to go all the way to Long Beach, Tonquin Beach will suffice. It's smaller, but very pretty.

★ Bamfield

Situated on the **Barkley Sound** fjord on Vancouver Island's west coast, **Bamfield** is a charming, rather remote little village that can be reached from **Port Alberni** or **Lake Cowichan** via a network of forest roads that are dusty in summer and muddy in winter. Equip yourselves with a good map, keep your headlights on and always give way to timber trucks, especially those behind you.

The region is a little paradise for outdoor activities and lovers of thousand-year-old forests. Bamfield is also one of the starting point of the famous **West Coast Trail ★★★**, which cuts through **Pacific Rim National Park ★★★**. This trail extends over the southeast coast of Barkley Sound, between the villages of **Bamfield** and **Port Renfrew**. This "Lifesaving Trail," a 77km-long path, was laid out at the turn of the century to help rescue shipwrecked sailors whose vessels frequently crashed against the coast's ominous reefs. These days, the trail attracts hikers from all over the world. Reservations are required and so is a good deal of preparation (see p 156).

Tour C: From Qualicum Beach to Port Hardy

This tour starts on the waterfront, whose beaches attract walkers and sand-castle builders. You are now in the central part of Vancouver Island, on the eastern shore. Families come here to enjoy the natural setting and the relatively warm waters of the Strait of Georgia. The beaches stretch all the way to Comox Valley. Inland, there are mountains measuring over 2,000m in altitude in Strathcona Provincial Park, which marks the division between the northern and southern parts of the island.

Qualicum Beach

Lured by the fine weather, many retirees settle in Qualicum Beach. This region gets more hours of sunshine than those farther south. Hwy. 19 is busy around Parksville and Qualicum Beach, whose main attraction is their series of beaches.

Denman Island & Hornby Island

To the delight of those who enjoy tranquillity, the tourists who flock to the gulf islands tend to ignore these two magnificent islands in the north.

Great care is taken to safeguard the quality of life on these two islands; the residents don't want rapid, destructive development to take place. This doesn't mean they are against tourists — on the contrary! The inhabitants of these islands enjoy living here and are more than willing to share the natural beauty with you.

Since most tourists head to Hornby to enjoy its magnificent beaches, Denman is the more peaceful of the two islands. Both islands have paved roads allowing beautiful trips by bike or on foot. Bike is definitely the best way to explore the harmonious wilderness of these islands. There are also some sheer cliffs that drop off into the sea, and the view is even more breathtaking when you follow the steep coast by sea kayak.

Comox Valley

With a population of 25,000, the Comox Valley is the third largest region on the island after Victoria and Nanaimo. It's also the only place in the province where the ski and golf seasons overlap, allowing you to practice these two sports within the same week if you're in the Okanagan Valley between April and May.

The towns of Cumberland, Comox and Courtenay are unique urban areas located between the glaciers of Strathcona Provincial Park and the east coast of the island. They are idyllic places for golfing and skiing, not to mention kayaking, fishing and mountain biking.

Campbell River

Campbell River is a choice destination for fans of salmon fishing. This sport can be enjoyed here year-round, and five varieties of salmon frequent the local waters. When you get to town, take the time to go to **The Museum at Campbell River ★** (*mid-May to Sep Mon to Sat 10am to 5pm, Sun noon to 5pm; winter Tue to Sun noon to 5pm; 470 Island Highway, opposite Sequoia Park, Fifth Ave., ☎287-3103*), which is interesting not only for its elegant architecture but also for its exhibits on Aboriginals and pioneers. Its collection includes a number of artifacts from Campbell River's early days. Furthermore, a significant part of the museum is devoted to Aboriginal engravings, sculpture and jewellery.

On your way into the centre of town, stop for a walk along **Discovery Pier ★** (*Government Wharf*), from which you can admire the Strait of Georgia and the Coast Mountains. At the end, turn right and walk down Shoppers Row, where you can purchase souvenirs, food or basic necessities. The Travel InfoCentre is located on this street as well.

As you leave town, head for Gold River on Hwy. 28. From mid-August to mid-October, you can see the salmon swimming upriver at the **Quinsam Salmon Hatchery ★** (*every day 8am to 4pm; Hwy. 28, ☎287-9564*) on the Campbell River.

Back on Hwy. 28, continue westward to Gold River and Nootka Sound.

Nootka Sound

The Spanish sailed these waters first, in 1774, though it was Captain James Cook who came ashore and claimed the land for England in 1778. You can explore this region, which is steeped in history, by taking a **boat tour** from Nootka harbour (☎*283-2325*).

Backtrack to Campbell River and head toward Port Hardy on Highland Hwy. 19.

Sayward

When you leave the highway at Sayward Junction, stop at the **Cable Cafe** ★ (☎*282-3433*). The exterior of this building is made of cables coiled on top of one another. Lumber companies once used these cables to transport wood to the train. More than 2km of cables cover the walls of this restaurant. The forest industry drives the economy of the little town of Sayward. Each July, on **World Championship Logger Sports Day**, lumberjacks come here to demonstrate their skill. This region is best explored by boat. Magnificent Johnstone Strait is scattered with lovely islands and teeming with marine animal life.

★★ Telegraph Cove

This little paradise set back from the eastern shore of Vancouver Island was once the end point of a telegraph line that ran along the coast, hence the name. Later, a wealthy family set up a sawmill on land they had purchased around the little bay. From that point on, time stopped; the little houses have been preserved, and the boardwalk alongside the bay is punctuated with commemorative plaques explaining the major stages in the village's history. Today, vacationers come here to go fishing, scuba diving and whale-watching. If you're lucky, you might catch a glimpse of a seal, an otter or even a whale from the boardwalk.

Be careful along the last kilometre of the road to Telegraph Cove. A local lumber company's trucks haul huge blocks of wood along this little secondary road, which leads to Beaver Cove. According to the highway code, these vehicles have the right of way.

Port McNeill

Farther north lies Port McNeill, a town of 2,500 inhabitants. It is the regional centre of three large lumber companies. **North Island Forest Tours** ★★ (*free; 5hr tour; Jun to early Sep, Mon to Fri; North Island Forestry Centre, Port McNeill,* ☎*956-3844*) will take you into the forest or along the local rivers so that you can see how trees are felled and how the giant trunks are handled. You must reserve a seat and bring along a snack.

Second only to the forest industry, boat touring is very important to the local economy. Visitors to this region can also enjoy wonderful fishing trips and whale-watching excursions in the strait. Native culture is well represented here, especially in **Sointula** and **Alert Bay**, on the neighbouring islands, which are served by ferries several times a day.

★★ Alert Bay

At the **U'mista Cultural Center** ★ (*$5; year-round Mon to Fri 9am to 5pm, noon to 5pm, and Sat and Sun during summer; Alert Bay,* ☎*974-5403*), you can learn about the Potlatch ("to give") ceremony through the history of the U'mista Aboriginal community. Missionaries tried to ban the ceremony; there was even a law forbidding members of the community from dancing, preparing objects for distribution or making public speeches. The ceremony was then held in secret and during bad weather, when the whites couldn't get to the island. A lovely collection of masks and jewellery adorns the walls. Don't miss the **Native Burial Grounds** and the **Memorial Totems** ★★, which testify to the richness of this art.

Port Hardy

Port Hardy, a town of fishers and forest workers, is located at the northeast end of Vancouver Island. There is a wealth of animal life in this region, both in the water and on the land. If you aren't interested in going fishing or whale-watching, treat yourself to a walk through the forest in Cape Scott Park. Visitors en route to Prince Rupert and the Queen Charlotte Islands board the ferry in Port Hardy (*$80 return*).

The **Copper Maker** ★ (*free admission; Mon to Sat 9am to 5pm; 114 Copper Way, Fort Rupert, on the outskirts of Port Hardy, ☎949-8491*) is an Aboriginal art gallery and studio, where you'll find totem poles several metres high, some in the process of being made, others waiting to be delivered to buyers. Take the time to watch the artists at work, and ask them to tell you about the symbolism behind their drawings and sculptures.

At the end of Hwy. 19, you'll find the town port, the starting point of a promenade along the waterfront. You can enjoy a pleasant stroll here while taking in the scenery and watching the boats on their way in and out of the harbour.

Tour D: The Gulf Islands

Each of these islands is a different place to commune with nature and enjoy a little seclusion, far from traffic jams. Time is measured here according to the arrival and departure of the ferries. A convivial atmosphere prevails on these little havens of peace, especially at the end of the day, when visitors and islanders mingle at the pub. Surprises await you on each trip — an island straight out of your dreams, perhaps, or the sight of a seal swimming under your kayak — moments that will become lifelong memories.

The Gulf Islands consist of some 200 islands scattered across the Strait of Georgia between the eastern shore of Vancouver Island and the west coast, near the San Juan Islands (U.S.A.).

★★

Gabriola Island

Only 20min or so by ferry from Nanaimo, Gabriola is an island where nature abounds. The best way to visit is to take a slow bike ride around the island. It's a peaceful haven where many Nanaimo residents have taken up permanent residence. For tourists seeking tranquillity and peaceful landscapes, it's an ideal place to spend a few days.

★

Salt Spring Island

Salt Spring is the largest and most populous of the Gulf Islands. Aboriginals used to come here during summer to catch shellfish, hunt fowl and gather plants. In 1859, the first Europeans settled on the island and began establishing farms and small businesses here. Today, many artists have chosen Salt Spring as their home and place of work. When they aren't practising their art on the street, they welcome the public into their studios. As Vancouver Island is just a short trip from Salt Spring, some residents work in Victoria. The town of Ganges is the commercial hub of the island. A promenade runs alongside its harbour, past a number of shops and through two marinas.

★★
Galiano Island

With just over a tenth of the population of Salt Spring, this island is a quiet, picturesque place. It was named after Dionisio Galiano, the Spanish explorer who first sailed these waters. About 30km long and over 2km wide, Galiano faces northwest on one end and southeast on the other. Its shores afford some lovely views and are dotted with shell beaches.

Galiano Planet Revival Festival of Music (☎*539-5778*) presents Aboriginal dance performances and a varied repertoire of folk, jazz and funk performed by local artists.

★
Mayne Island

Mayne Island, Galiano's neighbour to the south, is a quiet place inhabited mainly by retirees. The limited number of tourists makes for a peaceful atmosphere, while the relatively flat terrain is a cyclist's dream. In the mid-19th century, during the gold rush, miners heading from Victoria to the Fraser River used to stop here before crossing the Strait of Georgia, hence the name Miners Bay. The first Europeans to settle on the island grew apples here, and their vast orchards have survived to this day. A few local buildings bear witness to the arrival of the pioneers. The **St. Mary Magdalene** ★ (*Georgina Point Rd.*) church, built entirely of wood in 1897, merits a visit. Take the opportunity to see the stained-glass windows on Sunday, when the church is open for Mass.

The **Active Pass Lighthouse** ★ (*every day 1pm to 3pm; Georgina Point Rd.,* ☎*539-5286*) has been guiding sailors through these waters since 1885. The original structure, however, was replaced by a new tower in 1940, which was in turn replaced in 1969. The place is easy to get to and is indicated on most maps of the region.

★
Saturna Island

Saturna is possibly the most isolated and least accessible island of all the Gulf Islands, and its residents, who number around 300, are determined to keep it that way. Saturna has very limited facilities, and only two restaurants. Don't let this deter you. Nature lovers will be fascinated by the island's **unusual flora and fauna**, like, for example, the **giant mushrooms** that grow around **Mount Warburton**.

Saturna's annual **Canada Day** celebration (*Jul 1*) is a huge lamb roast. It's the island's biggest gathering of the year.

★
Pender Islands

North and South Pender are the second most populated islands after Salt Spring and are joined together by a wooden bridge. They are fairly well equipped for tourists. Visitors come primarily to cycle or to lounge on the beaches. **Mount Normand** has a good reputation among walkers. From the summit there's an exceptional view of the **San Juan Islands**. The laid-back, bohemian atmosphere is immediately apparent upon arriving, what with all the natural food stores and organic farms. Every Saturday, from May to October, the Driftwood Centre hosts a very colourful **farmer's market** where you'll find good fresh produce.

★★
Quadra Island

Quadra Island has about 4,000 residents. In the summer the number doubles with the influx of tourists drawn here by its exceptional reputation for salmon fishing. Quadra is covered almost entirely by forests. Locals are proud of the lack of crime on their island; politeness and a friendly smile are of the utmost importance. Quadra, like Cortes, is in the northern gulf and is one of the Discovery Islands. It can be reached by a ferry from Campbell River to

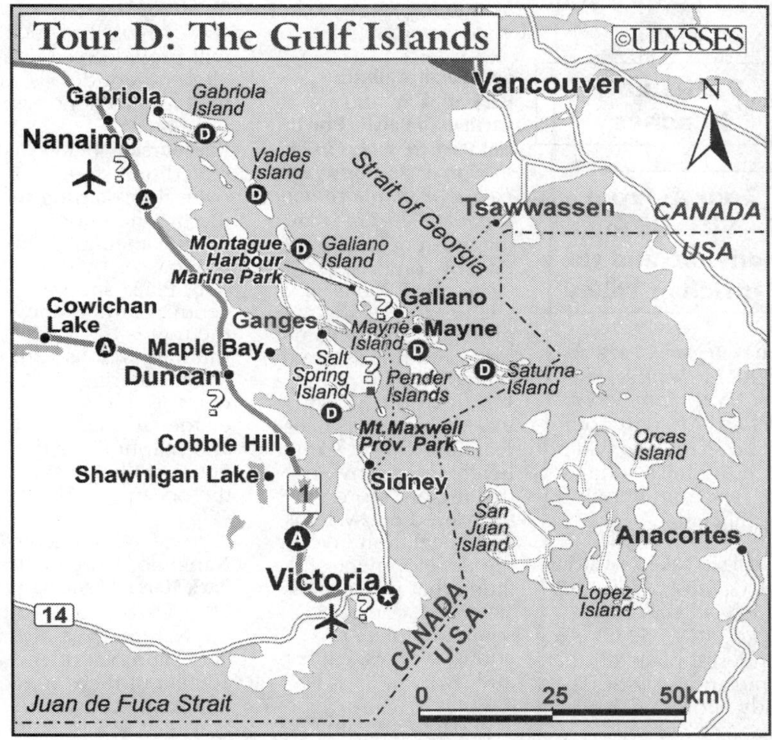

Quathiaski Cove in less than 10min. Once on the island be sure to visit the **Kwatkiutl Museum** (*every day 10am to 6pm; ☎285-3733*). This excellent museum of Aboriginal art presents relics that recount the lives of the island's first inhabitants. It is easily the most beautiful museum in the region. **Cape Mudge Lighthouse**, built in 1898, is nearby. Along the beach at the southern tip of the island, **petroglyphs**, drawn by Aboriginals 1000 years ago are revealed at low tide.

On the way to **Heriot Bay**, a small town in the northeast part of the island, you will come across the small BC Ferries terminal. This is where you catch the ferry to Cortes Island. Not far from the dock is the lovely little Rebecca Spit Marine Provincial Park.

★

Cortes Island

Cortes Island is located north of the Strait of Georgia, a few nautical miles from Desolation Sound and 45min from Quadra Island by ferry. The ferry ride alone, if the weather is nice, is worth the trip. Once on the island, you will soon realize that services for tourists are very limited. People come here to commune with nature: clear **lagoons** rich in aquatic life, deep **forests** and fine-sand **beaches**. It's a paradise for sea kayaking, cycling and all sorts of excursions. Cortes Island is approximately 25km long and 13km wide. The north end is wild and uninhabited. On the south end, you'll find restaurants, hotels and grocery stores.

Parks and Beaches

Tour A: From Victoria to Nanaimo and the Cowichan Valley

Quarry Regional Park ★ (*access by Empress Rd. from Shawnigan-Cobble Hill Rd.*). After an hour on the road, you will reach the hill's summit. The **view** from here is magnificent.

Shawnigan Lake Provincial Park (*south of Cobble Hill via Shawnigan-Cobble Hill Rd., ☎743-5332*) is a wonderful place for a picnic and a swim. The sandy shores of the lake are pleasantly shaded. A perfect getaway on a hot summer's day.

Somenos Marsh Wildlife Refuge ★ (*5min north of Duncan via the Trans-Canada Hwy., ☎246-2456*). Over 200 species of migratory birds flock here. A trail made of planks has been laid out in order to limit human impact on the marsh and to avoid disturbing the birds. Don't forget your camera and telephoto lens!

Lake Cowichan (*☎749-3244*), nicknamed Kaatza ("the big lake"), is ideal for sailing, sailboarding, swimming or any other water sport activity.

Carmanah Walbran Park ★★★ and **Carmanah Pacific Provincial Park ★★★** (*information at the Cowichan Lake tourism information centre, ☎749-3244*) are magnificent wild expanses comprising close to 17,000ha of ancient forests that are protected from chainsaws and flourish in the humid climate of the West Coast. The world's tallest spruces, reaching almost 95m in height, also grow in this region. Moreover, the varied ecosystems and vegetation favour the development of fauna that is every bit as varied, comprising squirrels, mice, raccoons, wolves, eagles and owls.

The parks are situated south of Bamfield, on Vancouver Island's west coast. The most direct route is through Cowichan Lake, but this means taking an unpaved, stony forest road. Make sure to check the condition of your tires before undertaking this 50km journey and bring a detailed map, for roadsigns are decidedly scarce.

Nanaimo offers kilometres of nature trails as well as great varieties of outdoor sites. For information concerning organized activities, drop by the first-rate **tourist office** (*Beban House, 2290 Bowen Rd., ☎756-0106 or 800-663-7337*), which will provide you with all pertinent details as well as excellent maps.

Harbourside Walkway is a paved trail stretching over 4km, starting from the marina in downtown Nanaimo. The trail passes by the Pioneer Plaza shopping centre. Farther along the trail is the Yacht Club, as well as various shops catering to sailors. It is a lovely promenade, at once urban and maritime, as the entire walkway skirts the ocean.

A stone's throw from Nanaimo, **Maffeo Sutton Park Morrell Sanctuary** (*☎756-0106*), owned by the Nature Trust of British Columbia, offers 1080ha of more rugged landscape. This park boasts at least 12km of well maintained trails that wind through a magnificent forest of Douglas firs surrounding beautiful Morrell Lake.

Newcastle Island Provincial Park (*picnic areas, campground, bicycle trails, swimming, hiking trail, fishing, restaurant, toilets; take the ferry, May to Oct, from Maffeo Sutton Park, Comox Rd., behind the Civic Arena, Nanaimo, ☎391-2300, 756-0106 or 800-663-7337*) is a 306ha island in the Nanaimo harbour. Its shore is studded with beaches, caverns and escarpments. The Coast Salish First Nation lived on this island before its coal-rich subsoil attracted miners here. A Japanese fishing community ran a saltery here for 30 years, up until 1941, during World War II, when the Canadian government placed the Japanese living and working on the coast into internment camps. The island later became a popular resort after being purchased by Canadian Pacific, which hosted big parties for its employees here. It has been public property since 1955.

Tour B: From Nanaimo to Tofino

Englishman River Falls Provincial Park (*heading west on Hwy. 4 to the intersection of Island Hwy. 19; the park's entrance is easily spotted;* ☎*248-3931*). This beautiful park lies 16km from the main roads: you will feel like you've reached the edge of the world. This is the perfect place for hiking and picnicking; it is also a fishing enthusiast's paradise as it boasts one of the best trout rivers on the island.

Little Qualicum Falls Provincial Park (*right near the village of Coombs,* ☎*248-3931*) is also a wonderful place for hiking and picnicking. The Little Qualicum River waterfalls create a stunning landscape. What is more, visitors can go swimming in real natural pools in the area surrounding Cameron Lake.

MacMillan Provincial Park - Cathedral Grove ★★★ (*east of Coombs, mid-way between Coombs and Port Alberni, along Hwy. 4,* ☎*248-3931*) is a wonderful, mystical place. The Douglas firs inhabiting this magnificent forest, some of which are over 800 years old, stand almost 80m tall. Hiking on the trails of Cathedral Grove will truly give you the impression of being back in the dinosaur age. It is also indicative of what the first European arrivals encountered on the West Coast. Cathedral Grove was considered a sacred place by Aboriginals. A must.

Located 6km east of **Bamfield**, **Pachena Bay ★★★** is a glorious beach in **Pacific Rim National Park**. This beautiful spot is one you will not soon forget. Camping on the beach is also permitted — and free! Seven day limit.

Pacific Rim National Park, Long Beach Section ★★★ (*Long Beach information centre, Hwy. 4,* ☎*726-4212*) This park is trimmed with kilometres of deserted beaches running alongside temperate rain forests. The beaches, hiking trails and various facilities are clearly indicated and easy to reach. The setting is enchanting, relaxing and stimulating at once, as well as being accessible year-round. The beaches are popular with surfing buffs, and **Live to Surf** (*1180 Pacific Rim Hwy., Tofino,* ☎*725-4464*) rents out surfboards and wetsuits.

Exploring the Tofino area by boat will enable you to uncover the hidden treasures of the neighbouring islands and bays. If you feel like walking about, you can check out the sulphur springs in the caves or the bears in the forest. **Sea Trek** (*441B Campbell St., Box 627, Tofino, V0R 2Z0,* ☎*725-4412 or 800-811-9155*) can arrange an excursion for you.

Tour C: From Qualicum Beach to Port Hardy

Qualicum Beach and **Parksville** are popular for their sandy beaches just off Hwy. 19.

Horne Lake Caves Provincial Park (☎*248-3931*) is, in fact, composed of four natural caves and offers a very different aspect of nature than one would expect to see on Vancouver Island. Situated on the western reach of Horne Lake, via Hwy. 19, just north of Qualicum Lake, the caves are open to the public. Visitors must, however, be in good physical condition, well equipped for spelunking and have previous experience. These visits are organized by **Riverbend Cave**.

Strathcona Park ★★ (*swimming, hiking, fishing and 161 campsites; 59km west of Campbell River on Hwy. 28,* ☎*954-4600*) is the oldest provincial park in British Columbia, and the largest on Vancouver Island. Its 210,000ha of forest and fresh water abound in natural treasures, including huge Douglas firs over 90m high. The highest peak on Vancouver Island is found here, the Golden Hinde, it measures 2,220m.

Helliwell Provincial Park (*Hornby Island*) is a little park where you can hike for a day (5km) among the large fir trees and the magnificent coast of Hornby Island. You can admire the crumbling rocks, which the sea has transformed into works of art through thousands of years of erosion.

The **Haig-Brown Kingfisher Creek Heritage Property ★** (*guided tours Jun 24 to Aug 31, 10am, 1pm and 3pm; 2250 Campbell River Rd., Campbell River,* ☎*286-6646*), located alongside the Campbell River, is worth a visit. It once belonged to celebrated Canadian author Roderick Haig-Brown, who fought all his life to protect wild animals and their habitat.

Miracle Beach Park ★ (*28km south of Campbell River, at the intersection of Miracle Beach Rd. and Hwy. 19,* ☎*954- 4600*) is the perfect place for families wishing to enjoy the beach while remaining close to all conveniences.

Cape Scott Provincial Park ★★ (*67km northwest of Port Hardy on Holberg Rd.; register at Port Hardy Chamber of Commerce,* ☎*949-7622; for all other information, BC Parks,* ☎*954-4600*) encompasses 15,070ha of temperate rain forest. Scott was a merchant from Bombay (India) who financed all sorts of commercial expeditions. Many ships have run aground on this coast, and a lighthouse was erected in 1960 in order to guide sailors safely along their way. Sandy beaches cover two-thirds of the 64km stretch of waterfront. On the hilly terrain farther inland, you'll find various species of giant trees, such as red cedars and pines. This remote part of Vancouver Island receives up to 500mm of rainfall annually, and is frequently hit by storms. It is best to visit during summertime.

Tour D: The Gulf Islands

Mount Maxwell Provincial Park ★ (*Salt Spring Island, from Fulford-Ganges Rd., take Cranberry Rd., then Mount Maxwell Rd. all the way to the end,* ☎*391-2300*) lies on a mountainside. The lookout is easily accessible, and the view of Vancouver Island and the islands to the south is worth the trip.

Montague Harbour Maritime Park ★★ (*on the west side of Galiano Island, 10km from the ferry terminal,* ☎*391-2300*) is a top-notch park featuring a lagoon, a shell beach and an equipped campground. The view of the sunset from the north beach will send you off into a reverie.

Bluffs Park ★ (*Galiano Island, take Bluff Dr. from Georgeson Bay Rd. or Burrill Rd.*) offers a view from above of aptly named Active Pass, where ferries heading for Swartz Bay (Victoria) and Tsawwassen (Vancouver) cross paths.

The **Bennet Bay beach** is a very pleasant spot, the best place on Mayne Island to take a walk.

Among the pleasant routes on the Pender Islands, the one that leads from **Mount Normand** to **Beaumont**

Provincial Park is undoubtedly the most interesting. Picnic tables and campsites are available in the park, around the beach, so visitors can spend the night.

Outdoor Activities

Bungee Jumping

Tour A: From Victoria to Nanaimo and the Cowichan Valley

If you're looking for some excitement, head to the **Bungy Zone** (*15min south of Nanaimo via Hwy. 1; turn right on Nanaimo River Rd.; Box 399, Station A, Nanaimo, V9R 5L3; ☎716-RUSH or 800-668-7771, www.bungyzone.com*). The spectacle of thrill-seekers leaping off a bridge over the Nanaimo River has become a local attraction. The first jump costs $100, but if you want more, you only have to pay $25 for each additional jump.

Mountain Biking

Tour B: From Nanaimo to Tofino

A path has recently been paved along the road that runs between Pacific Rim Park and Ucluelet. It's suitable for cross-country biking, but not mountain biking, since the road is made of asphalt. For bike rentals, inquire at **Raven Tours** (*☎726-7779*).

Although the region of Tofino only has a few mountain-bike paths, Long Beach is the ideal place to practice this sport. The compact sand on this endless beach insures good tire traction. **Tofino Kite & Bike Shop** (*441-A Campbell, ☎725-1221*) rents bikes.

Tour C: From Qualicum Beach to Port Hardy

Many mountain-bike enthusiasts travel to the Courtenay region, especially **Mount Washington** (*Howard Road, ☎338-1386*). Die-hard cyclists will love the Monster Mile Downhill and the Discovery Trail.

Hornby Island and Denman Island make wonderful bike trips. Several mountain-bike paths, especially on Hornby Island, disappear into the central massif of the island. The paths zigzag in the dense forest, and the varied topography of the terrain will delight even hard-to-please sports enthusiasts. Mountain-bike rentals: in Denman, **Scooter & Bike Rental**, *☎335-2293*; in Hornby, **Co-op** *☎335-1121*.

Golf

Tour C: From Qualicum Beach to Port Hardy

Located in the Comox Valley, **Crown Isle** (*$35-$60; 399 Clubhouse Dr., Courtenay, ☎703-5050 or 888-338-8439, ⇄703-5051, www.crown-isle.com*) is one of the most beautiful golf courses in the province. Its 18-hole course on its 326ha property has won it many prestigious international awards.

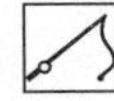

Fishing

Tour C: From Qualicum Beach to Port Hardy

You can fish at any time, day or night, on **Discovery Pier** (*$1 with valid fishing permit; rod rental 7am to 10pm, $2.50 per hour; 24hrs a *day; Government Wharf, Campbell River,* ☎*286-6199*), which stretches 150m. This is a popular place to go for a stroll.

Bailey's Charters (*$60 an hour; Box 124, Campbell River, V9W 5A7,* ☎*286-3474*) arranges guided salmon and trout fishing trips, which are a terrific way to explore the region's beautiful shoreline.

Calypso Fishing Charters (*384 Simms Rd., Campbell River,* ☎*923-2001,* ⇄*923-5121, cell phone 287-0542*) offers salmon-fishing excursions in the comfort of a fast boat equipped with a bathroom. Fuel and all fishing gear included. Reservations recommended. Rates: $55 for one or two people, $60 for three, all for a minimum of 4hrs.

Hook & Reel Charters (*16063 Bunny Rd., Campbell River,* ☎*287-4436,* ⇄*287-4360*) will take you salmon fishing in the Brown Bay area, 30min north of Campbell River via Hwy. 19.
Rates: *$45 to $65 for a minimum of 4hrs (taxes included).*

Tour D: The Gulf Islands

Discovery Charters (*Box 48, Quathiaski Cove, Quadra Island, V0P 1N0,* ☎*285-3146,* ⇄*285-3034*) is a respected establishment that offers salmon-fishing expeditions. After an exciting day at sea, you can take advantage of one of its many accommodation formulas. The little beach houses on the water are equipped with kitchenettes. Rates: from $69 to $150, depending on the formulas and fishing packages.

A-1 Charters (*Box 559 Heriot Bay, Quadra Island V0P 1H0,* ☎*285-3020*). Get away on a 7m yacht and visit the Discovery Islands while trying your luck at salmon fishing. You'll even see eagles flying around the boat. Rates: *$60 per hour.*

Hiking

Tour B: From Nanaimo to Tofino

At **Pacific Rim National Park, Long Beach section** ★★★ (*Long Beach information centre, Hwy. 4,* ☎*726-4212*), you can hike the **rain forest trail** ★★★ (*6.4km north of the information centre*), which runs through a temperate rain forest. Panels explaining the cycles of the forest and providing information on the animal species who live here have been set up along two trails. This park is steeped in history, and a number of trails provide a chronicle of bygone days. It is wise to ask park officials about the risk of encountering animals during your hike. Trails are occasionally closed when there are bears in the vicinity.

The **West Coast Trail** ★★★, part of Pacific Rim National Park (*Box 280, Ucluelet, BC, V0R 3A0*), skirts the southeast coast of **Barkley Sound** between the villages of **Bamfield** and **Port Renfrew**. The "Lifesaving Trail," as it has been nicknamed, is a 77km path that was laid out at the turn of the century to help rescue shipwrecked sailors. The trail roughly follows the path of a former telegraph line set up in 1890 along the rugged coastline: 66 ships have run aground in this area known as "Ship Graveyard of the Pacific." The landscape is characterized by sandy beaches and rocky headlands.

The trail runs through a shaded coastal forest where old plantings of spruces, western hemlock spruces and thujas predominate. Some of the tallest and largest trees (over 90m tall) in Canada stand along or near the trail.

Before your departure:
• Call or write to the park to request a brochure and read it carefully.
• Familiarize yourself with Vancouver Island's southern district and decide in advance

whether you will use Bamfield or Port Renfrew as a departure point.
• Choose your starting date, whether you will hike the whole trail or get off at Nitinat Lake, and how you will get to and from the trail.
• Take the time to study the route by reading one of the West Coast Trail guides:

The West Coast Trail & Nitinat Lakes, Sierra Club, Victoria

Blisters & Bliss, D. Foster & W. Aitken

Pacific Rim Explorer, Bruce Obee, Whitecap Books

It is important for interested hikers to know that the West Coast Trail can be dangerous: the course is arduous. Injuries and accidents are frequent. The trail is not meant for beginners, but rather, for physically fit and experienced hikers ready to tackle a rugged environment.

Visitors wishing to hike the trail must **reserve ahead of time**; an access permit is required. **Starting dates** are anytime from May 1 to September 30, the latest.

A non-refundable reservation deposit of $25 is required. Reservations can be made three months prior to your starting date by calling **Super Natural British Columbia** (*every day 6am to 6pm (Pacific Time); metropolitan Vancouver, ☎663-6000, Canada and United States, ☎800-663-6000*).

Groups can be no larger than 10 people, and are issued a permit, which must be put in a visible place on the leader's backpack. Hikers should be experienced and equipped for rainy weather. It is strongly recommended to bring along a portable gas stove and a first-aid kit. Equally important is a good pair of hiking boots; you don't want to be wearing ill-fitting footgear on this type of expedition, when you are completely on your own. Food and water will take up a lot of space in your backpack.

Meares Island, which stretches the width of Tofino, is a great place for a 2hr hike among the gigantic, ancient trees of the rain forest. Although the beginning of the path is easy, it becomes much more difficult when the wooden footbridges disappear into the dense greenery. Inquire about the condition of the path with Hugh, the captain of *Salty*, the boat that brings you to the island (*$20; ☎726-8361*).

Tour C: From Qualicum Beach to Port Hardy

Strathcona Provincial Park (*entrance west of Courtenay or Campbell River, ☎604-337-5121*) has a great variety of hiking paths. You can spend an afternoon or several days in the backcountry.

If your time is limited, take an hour to hike the 1km trail at **Paradise Meadows**, which leads to the parking lot of Mount Washington at Forbidden Plateau. Be sure to check the weather conditions before departing, since there can be snow even in July.

Mount Goeffrey Regional Nature Park is located in the middle of Hornby Island. Its paths climb up to the highest point on the island (1,000m), from where you can see an impressive panorama stretching all the way to the snow-capped peeks of Strathcona Park on Vancouver Island.

Cape Scott Provincial Park ★★ (*67km northwest of Port Hardy via Holberg Rd.; register at Port Hardy Chamber of Commerce, ☎949-7622; for all other information, BC Parks ☎954-4600*) encompasses 15,070ha of temperate rain forest. Hiking trails provide the only means of access to the cape, and it takes a good 8hrs to get there from the parking lot at San Josef Bay. You can, however, return to Port Hardy by boat (**AK Trips & Charters** *offers round-trip combination boat and van service; $115; Port Hardy, ☎949-7952*).

Tour D: The Gulf Islands

Llama Lakes Trekking (*Box 414, Quathiaski Cove, Quadra Island V0P 1N0, ☎285-2413, ≠285-2473*) offers guided hiking and camping trips. Food and camping equipment are supplied. If you don't have a vehicle, Llama Lakes Trekking will come and pick you up at the ferry dock in Quathiaski Cove or Heriot Bay, and take you to the trail. You can choose one-day to five-day hiking packages.

Sailing

Tour A: From Victoria to Nanaimo and the Cowichan Valley

Herizentm Sailing for Women (*36 Cutlass Lookout, Nanaimo, ☎741-1753*) is a very special sailing club catering exclusively to women. Also of note is that all the instructors here are women. Herizentm offers full training courses that include meals, refreshments and accommodations.

Courses:
Three-and-a-half days: *$720*
Four-and-a-half days: *$920*
Five-and-a-half days: *$1,120*

Plain Sailing (*3581 Country Club Dr., Nanaimo, ☎758-1827, summer ☎616-3375*) will take you sailing with a skipper around the Gulf Islands in July and August. Departures from Nanaimo. Price per person: $249 for three days for competent crew or daysailing skipper courses, $449 for both, or $50 per day for leisure cruises with skipper.

Tour C: From Nanaimo to Tofino

Mystic Oceans (*Vancouver, ☎604-730-7131, ≠604-730-7135, www.mysticoceans.bc.ca*) owns *White Raven*, an enormous steel sailboat measuring 32m. Originally built in 1920, it was completely restored in the 1990s. You can take different introductory sailing courses on board, ranging from three days ($285) to nine days ($1,450) of sailing. The experienced crew's thorough practical training is recognized worldwide. Information is available at the end of the pier on Fourth Street.

Tour D: The Gulf Islands

You can explore the shores of Galiano and the neighbouring islands aboard a superb 14m catamaran, thanks to **Canadian Gulf Islands Catamaran Cruises** (*$39; 4hr cruise, snack included; Montague Harbour, Galiano Island, ☎539-2930*). Depending on where you are — in a bay or farther offshore — you're sure to spot some land or sea creatures.

The **Sailing School on Salt Spring Island** (*422 Sky Valley Rd., Salt Spring Island, ☎537-2741*) offers Sail 'n' Stay packages.

Scuba Diving

Tour A: From Victoria to Nanaimo and the Cowichan Valley

Each year, hundreds of divers flock to the eastern shore of Vancouver Island, lured by the colourful underwater scenery and rich marine life. The Nanaimo region is a wonderful place for this type of sightseeing. **Sundown Diving Charters** (*22 Esplanade, Nanaimo, V9R 4Y7, ☎753-1880 or 888-773-3483, ≠753-6445*).

Emerald Coast Adventures (*Box 971, Stn "A", Nanaimo, V9R 5N2, ☎755-6946, ask for Bob or Janet*) will guide you on night dives to observe the marine life. Quite an experience.

Tour B: From Nanaimo to Tofino

The **Broken Group Archipelago** in **Pacific Rim National Park** (*information centre, ☎726-4212*) is a maze of islands, islets, reefs and crags, which lend themselves to interesting diving. All kinds of diving spots can be found here, from easy ones for beginners and others for more seasoned divers to still more challenging ones for experts.

Tour C: From Qualicum Beach to Port Hardy

Paradise Found Trekking (*$55; 3hrs; Jun 1 to Oct 15, ☎830-0662*) will take you where the salmon teem on the Campbell River. All the necessary equipment (mask, flippers and wet suit) is provided; all you have to do is let yourself be guided through the scores of salmon, some of which can measure up to 1m long.

Sun Fun Divers (*reservations required; 1697 Beach Dr., Port McNeill, V0N 2R0, ☎956-2243*) arranges scuba-diving trips in the Telegraph Cove, Alert Bay, Quatsino Narrows and Port McNeill regions. The water is clearest during the winter months.

Sea Kayaking

Tour A: From Victoria to Nanaimo and the Cowichan Valley

Wild Heart Adventures Sea Kayak Tours (*2774 Barnes, Nanaimo, ☎722-3683, www.island.net/wheart*) has been organizing first-rate expeditions all around Vancouver Island since 1990. The one-day or one-week expeditions offered by Wild Heart Adventures are safe, and you need not have experience to participate.

Tour B: From Nanaimo to Tofino

At **Tofino Sea Kayaking** (*320 Main St., Tofino, ☎725-4222 or ☎800-TOFINO-4*), all excursions begin with a class. Moreover, they are guided by pros who are highly experienced in sea-kayaking and qualified in lifesaving and first aid. Expeditions are organized in Lemmens, on Meares Island and Duffin Passage Islands. Those with enough experience to go solo can also rent a kayak here.

Tour D: The Gulf Islands

T'ai Li Lodge (*Cortes Bay, Cortes Island, ☎935-6749*) is a marine-adventure centre across from the park at Desolation Sound. You can learn to sail and sea kayak in fantastic surroundings with naturalist guides. A package with accommodation is also available.

Canadian Gulf Islands Catamaran Cruises (*$39; 4hr cruise, snack included; Montague Harbour, Galiano Island, ☎539-2930*) offer 2hr guided sea-kayak tours for $25.

The crew of **White Raven** (see p 163) organizes kayak excursions for $20. For about 2hrs, you sail off to explore the surrounding islands. The **White Raven**'s port of registry is at the pier on Fourth Street.

Even though you can reach the Broken Islands archipelago easily from Bamfield, kayak excursions from Ucluelet can also be arranged with **Majestic Ocean Kayaking** (*☎726-2868*).

Surfing

Tour B: From Nanaimo to Tofino and the Cowichan Valley

Pacific Rim National Park boasts a magnificent, 45km-long stretch of beach, known as **Long Beach**. Surfers will find unlimited waves, which provide a first-class "ride," cresting at 8m in winter! A surfer's dream. You too can devote yourself to this novel sport by renting equipment and taking courses.

A wetsuit is necessary because the water is very cold!

Here are a few good places in Tofino for rentals and information about necessary precautions:

Blue Planet Surf Company:
☎725-2182

Ocean Surf:
461 Cambell
☎725-3344

Live to Surf:
1180 Pacific Rim Hwy.
☎725-4464

Pacific Rim Adventures:
289 Cedar St.
☎725-2449

Whale-Watching

Tour B: From Nanaimo to Tofino

Island West Resort (*140 Bay St., ☎726-7515*) as well as **Quest Charters** (*Boat Basin, ☎726-7532*) are two of the companies that offer whale-watching excursions departing from Ucluelet.

Chinook Charters (*$50; 450 Campbell St., Box 501, Tofino, V0R 2Z0, ☎725-3431 or 800-665-3646*) will take you out to sea to observe grey whales at close range. The best time to go is in March and April, when there are large numbers of these sea mammals in the area.

Tour C: From Qualicum Beach to Port Hardy

Robson Bight Charters (*$70; Jun to Oct 9:30am; Sayward, ☎282-3833 or 800-658-0022*) arranges whale-watching tours in the Johnstone Strait. Each year, killer whales use this area as a sort of training ground for the new members of their families. A sight to remember.

Downhill Skiing

Tour C: From Qualicum Beach to Port Hardy

At the **Mount Washington Ski Resort** (*day pass $43; Howard Rd. or the Strathcona Pkwy., ☎338-1386, ⇄338-7295, www.mtwashington.bc.ca*), skiers can enjoy a 360° view encompassing the Coast Mountains and the dozens of islands at the mouth of the Strait of Georgia. The mountain, which is 1,609m high, receives heavy snowfall every year. The ski season starts in December.

Accommodations

Tour A: From Victoria to Nanaimo and the Cowichan Valley

Malahat

The Aerie Resort
$250-450, bkfst incl.
≡, ≈, ℜ, ⊛, ⌂
600 Ebedora Lane, Box 108, Malahat, V0R 2L0
☎743-7115
⇄743-4766
Part of the Relaix & Châteaux chain, The Aerie Resort lives up to its slogan "castle in the

mountains" with a beautiful, secluded location high atop the Malahat. The furnishings and little extras are lavish, to say the least: most of the standard rooms have a private patio or balcony, and for a little extra you can have a jacuzzi, fireplace, steam shower, four-poster bed or rich leather sleigh bed. There is an indoor and an outdoor pool, a tennis court and a European spa. Romantic, Gourmet and Pampering packages available.

Cowichan Bay

Inn at the Water Resort and Conference Centre
$75 to $105
tw, ℜ, ⌂, ≈, P
1681 Cowichan Bay Rd.
☎748-6222
☎(800) 663-7898
⇄748-7122
The Inn at the Water is a lovely hotel with 56 rooms, each offering a splendid view of the ocean and mountains. A bar and a restaurant also grace the hotel, as do an indoor swimming pool and liquor store. Seaplanes land right in front of the establishment.

Duncan

Altemieller's Bio Farm
$10
K
4895 Marchall Dr., RR1
☎*746-4117*
Altemieller's Bio Farm offers youth-hostel-style accommodation in the country a long ways from Duncan. The countryside here is the perfect place to unwind. Minimum comfort, but nevertheless a pleasant facility.

The Falcon Nest Motel
$50-$60
tw, P
5867 Trans-Canada Hwy.
☎748-8188
This is a small, rather antiquated but affordable motel. Moreover, it is conveniently located, just minutes from restaurants on the highway. The proprietor is charming.

The Village Green Inn
$64-$90
K, tw, ℜ, ⌂, ≈, P
141 Trans-Canada Hwy.
☎/⇄746-5126
☎(800) 665-3989
The Village Green Inn is the largest hotel in Duncan, providing 80 very comfortable rooms, with kitchenette upon request. The inn is located a short walking distance from downtown boutiques and the Cowichan Native Village. The inn also boasts a bar, a restaurant, a liquor store, a swimming pool and a tennis court.

Nanaimo

Nicol Street Hostel
$15
sb, K
65 Nicol St.
☎752-1188
⇄752-1185
The friendly, warm atmosphere at the Nicol Street Hostel makes up for its location on the noisy Trans-Canada Highway. Located a few blocks from the centre of town, the hostel offers its guests discounts at several restaurants in Nanaimo. The town of Nanaimo has two other youth hostels that are not as pleasant as this one.

Thompson's Hostel
$15
K
1660 Cedar Rd.
☎/⇄722-2251
Thompson's Hostel is the quietest of the two, and is located outside of the hustle and bustle of Nanaimo.

The Cambie International Hostel
$20 bkfst incl.
63 Victoria Cr.
☎754-5323
⇄754-5582
The Cambie International Hostel is located above a bar in the heart of downtown, which has its advantages and disadvantages, depending upon your personal preferences.

Carey House B&B
$35-$55 bkfst incl.
750 Arbutus Ave
☎752-3601
If you want to stay in a residential area in Nanaimo, try Carey House B&B. It's not expensive and reasonably comfortable. The place also serves good breakfasts.

Rocky Point Ocean View Bed & Breakfast
$65-$85 bkfst incl.
4903 Fillinger
☎/⇌751-1949
www.rockypoint.bc.ca
As its name suggests, the Rocky Point Ocean View Bed & Breakfast offers a wonderful view of the Strait of Georgia and, in clear weather, the mountains along the coast. The three rooms are a bit over-decorated, but the warm welcome more than compensates for this minor drawback.

The Best Western Dorchester Hotel
$75-$85
ℜ, tv
70 Church St.
☎754-6835
⇌754-2638
The Best Western Dorchester has 65 simply decorated, comfortable rooms that offer a lovely view of the port of Nanaimo. The layout is the same at the other Best Westerns in this region. A safe bet.

The Jingle Pot Bed & Breakfast
$75-$85 bkfst incl.
⌂, ≡, tv
4321 Jingle Pot Rd. V9T 5P4
☎758-5149
Run by a sailor named Captain Ivan, The Jingle Pot Bed & Breakfast has two rooms, which have been fitted out in a luxurious fashion to ensure that guests enjoy a pleasant stay. If you're planning on going boating, the captain can give you some good advice.

Whitehouse on Longloake B&B
$75-$89 bkfst incl.
231 Ferntree Pl.
☎756-1185
Located just 10min from the centre of town on the shore of Long Lake, Whitehouse on Longlake B&B has its own private beach. The ideal spot for families, this facility is close to many hiking and biking paths.

The Coast Bastion Inn
$89-$129
tv, ℜ, ⌂, ≈, P, ⊛
11 Bastion St.
☎753-6601
☎(800) 663-1144
⇌753-4155
This is a luxurious hotel whose 179 rooms all benefit from magnificent views of the region. Some are even equipped with whirpool baths. The hotel boasts a beauty salon, a chocolate shop, a restaurant and a pub.

Long Lake Inn
$95-$119
⊙, tv, P
4700 North Island Hwy
☎758-1144
☎(800) 565-1144
⇌758-5832
Enjoy a relaxing stay on the shores of Long Lake, north of Nanaimo. All rooms face the water, and guests have access to a private beach as well as a fitness centre. Only a stone's throw from BC Ferries' Departure Bay harbour.

Tour B: From Nanaimo to Tofino

Parksville

The Paradise Sea-Shell Motel and RV Park
$40 to $80
tv, P
411 West Island Hwy
Motel
☎248-6171
☎(800) 668-7352
RV park
☎248-6612
⇌248-9347
The Paradise Sea-Shell Motel and RV Park is located close to the big Parksville beach. Those with an RV can reserve a spot and benefit from the same amenities offered to motel guests: access to the beach and the colossal Paradise Adventure Mini-Golf (impossible to miss with its castle and giant shoe).

Port Alberni

Personal Touch Hostel
$15
K, sb
4908 Burde St.
☎723-2484
The Personal Touch Hostel is run by an Aboriginal family. The place isn't that pretty, but you can get a good night's sleep here and the prices are unbeatable.

Beaver Creek House B&B
$50-$55 bkfst incl.
7166 McKenzie Rd. RR1
☎724-5575
Located 6km from town on a peaceful property, Beaver Creek House

B&B offers standard comfort in a modern home.

The Coast Hospitality Inn
$150
tv, ℜ, ⌂, ≈, P
3835 Redford St.
☎728-8111
The Coast Hospitality Inn is located right in the middle of Port Alberni. The hotel boasts approximately 50 very comfortable and relatively luxurious rooms. It is particularly favoured by business people. There is a decent restaurant on the ground floor and a lively pub in the basement.

Ucluelet

The Ucluelet Campground
$21-$31
100 sites, toilets, showers,
🐕, ♿
260 Seaplane Base Rd.
☎726-4355
Located within walking distance of Ucluelet. Reservations required.

Ucluelet Hotel
$30-$40
sb
250 Main St.
☎726-4324
The Ucluelet Hotel is not the most charming hotel in the world, but it is reasonably priced and located in the heart of the town. Decent facility.

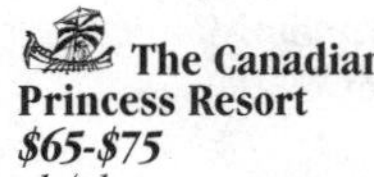 **The Canadian Princess Resort**
$65-$75
sb/pb
Peninsula Rd.
☎726-7771
☎(800) 663-7090
⇄726 7121
This is a ship that sailed the waters along the coast for nearly 40 years, and is now permanently moored at the Ucluelet pier. It has 26 rooms, which are small and don't have a lot of extras, but offer a pleasant nautical atmosphere.

Tofino

Tofino Guest House
$15 members
$20 non-members
K
241 Campbell St.
☎725-2288
There are numerous youth hostels in the Tofino region. The most recent addition is the Tofino Guest House, which opened in August 1999.

There are also some pleasant youth hostels outside Tofino on two neighbouring islands situated in a breathtaking natural setting.

Auberge on the Island
$18
K
Box 267, V0R 2C0
☎0+marine operator

Vargas Island Inn & Hostel
$18
K
Box 267, V0R 2Z0
☎725-3309

Both **Auberge On The Island** and **Vargas Island Inn & Hostel** offer dormitory-style accommodation in the middle of the magnificent temperate tropical forest.

White Raven
$25/person
K
Fourth Street Wharf
A unique way to spend the night is to sleep on a boat at the pier. The White Raven has its port of registry in Tofino every summer and it has eight cramped bunk beds. It's not spacious, but the crew is pleasant and the light rocking motion will gently put you to sleep.

Midori's Place Bed & Breakfast
$65 bkfst incl.
370 Gibson St.
☎725-2203
Located in the village, Midori's Place Bed & Breakfast has three comfortable, soberly decorated rooms. The amusing resident parrot enjoys repeating everything guests say.

The house is within walking distance of restaurants, shops and the village pier.

The Tin-Wis Best Western
$90-$140
tv, ℜ, ♿
1119 Pacific Rim Hwy.
☎***725-4445***
☎***(800) 528-1234***
⇄***725-4447***
The Tin-Wis Best Western is a large hotel run by Tla-O-Qui-Aht First Nations people. It offers all the comforts you would expect from a Best Western. The plants and wooden decorative elements blend harmoniously with the immediate surroundings, but the place is oversized (56 rooms).

Chesterman's Beach Bed & Breakfast
$125-$150 bkfst incl.
1345 Chesterman's Beach Rd.
☎/⇄***725-3726***
Picture a house on a beach lined with lush vegetation with the setting sun reflecting off the water; that's what awaits you at the heavenly Chesterman's Beach Bed & Breakfast. A simple walk on the beach every day is all you need to enjoy a satisfying vacation here. Three rooms are available.

The Wickaninnish Inn
$180-$300
tv, ℜ, ⌂, ≈, *P*
Osprey Lane at Chesterman Beach
Box 250
☎***725-3100***
⇄***725-3110***
The Wickaninnish Inn is a superb, high-class hotel set deep in the country, at the foot of an escarpment, with a fantastic view of Chesterman Beach. The rooms are comfortable and very well decorated. The hotel's restaurant, The Pointe (see p 170), is set up in a glassed-in, octogonal room offering a breathtaking 240-degree view of the sea.

Bamfield

The Bamfield Trails Motel Hook & Web Pub
$45-$65
tv, P
Frigate Rd.
☎***728-3231***
The Bamfield Trails Motel Hook & Web Pub is located right in the heart of the village, a few minutes from the port and services. The rooms are rather antiquated but relatively comfortable. A laundromat on the ground floor is at guests' disposal, as is a lively pub in summer.

The Bamfield Inn
$75
tv, ℜ, *P*
Bamfield Inlet
☎***728-3354***
⇄***728-3446***
The Bamfield Inn offers a lovely view of the port, boasts a good restaurant and organizes salmon-fishing and whale-watching excursions. There are washing machines on the premises.

Tide's Inn B&B
$80 bkfst incl.
22 South Bamfield Rd.
☎***728-3376***
Tide's Inn B&B is a wonderful facility located by the ocean. The rooms and breakfasts are impeccable. The friendly owners will lend you their kayaks, and you can also travel along the first few kilometres of the West Coast Trail nearby.

Tour C: From Qualicum Beach to Port Hardy

Qualicum Beach

The Quatna Manor Bed & Breakfast
$75-$90 bkfst incl.
sb/pb, no smoking
512 Quatna Rd.
☎***752-6685***
⇄***752-8385***
The Quatna Manor Bed & Breakfast is definitely a place to keep in mind. The friendly reception you will receive from hosts Bill and Betty will make your stay at their Tudor-style home that much more pleasant. A hearty breakfast is served in the dining room. Bill is retired from the air force. His job required a great deal of travelling, and his stories make for

memorable breakfast conversation.

Comox Valley (Comox-Cumberland Courtenay)

Comox Kale Hostel
$17
K, sb
4787 Lake Trail Rd.
☎***338-1914***
The Comox Kale Hostel is perfectly situated on a 4ha property about 12km west of Courtenay. With Strathcona Provincial Park nearby, this charming setting has many hiking and mountain-bike paths as well as some enchanting spots to go swimming. This B&B is obviously suitable for those who enjoy the great outdoors since it's a long way from civilization.

Alpine House B&B
$55 bkfst incl
sb
263 Alpine St., Comox
☎***339-6181***
☎***(877) 339-6181***
Alpine House B&B is situated directly in front of the hospital on a residential street in Comox. A great place for families, it has suites with several rooms.

Greystone Manor B&B
$80 bkfst incl.
4014 Haas Rd., RR6
☎***338-1422***
Built in 1918, Greystone Manor B&B offers incredible views of the enormous mountains along the Sunshine Coast. A gigantic English-style garden enhances the beauty of the premises. The rooms are attractively designed and your hosts will tell you about the attractions to visit in the valley.

Kingfisher Oceanside Resort & Spa
$90-$100
≈, ⊙, ⊛, ⌂, ℜ
4330 South Island Hwy., RR6
☎***338-1323***
☎***800-663-7929***
⇄***338-0058***
Kingfisher Oceanside Resort & Spa is located slightly south of Courtenay by the water's edge. It's a comfortable establishment that specializes in health retreats, offering a wide range of services (massages, mud baths, algae masks, sauna, and the like). It also has tennis courts, and guests can use the kayaks.

The Coast Westerly Hotel
$94-$112
tv, ℜ, ⌂, ≈, P
1590 Cliffe Ave. Courtenay
☎***338-7741***
☎***(800) 663-1144***
⇄***338-5442***
The Coast Westerly Hotel is situated right in the heart of Comox Valley, close to golf courses, beaches and the Mount Washington ski resort. The Coast Westerly Hotel is a vast establishment with 111 luxurious rooms, some of which offer beautiful views of the area.

Campbell River

Edgewater Motel
$45-$60
K, tv
4073 South Island Hwy. near Oyster Bay
☎/⇄***923-5421***
As its name suggests, the pretty little Edgewater Motel is located on the waterfront. The rooms are decent for the price, and you can prepare meals in them — a real plus if you're on a tight budget.

The Haig-Brown House
$65-$85 bkfst incl.
sb
2250 Campbell River Rd.
☎***286-6646***
⇄***286-6694***
The Haig-Brown House once belonged to Roderick Haig-Brown, renowned for both his writing and his efforts to protect the environment. Literary workshops are held on the estate, which is now a provincial heritage property. This spectacular place lies on the banks of the Campbell River. The rooms are simply decorated in old-fashioned style, and the walls of the study are lined with books. The dining room is bathed in natural light. The house and guest rooms are minded by Kevin Brown, who has a passion for both literature and the history of the Haig-Brown estate.

The Best Western Austrian Chalet
$77-$89
tv, ℜ, ⌂, ≈, *P*
462 South Island Hwy.
☎***923-4231***
☎***(800) 667-7207***
⇌***923-2840***
The Best Western Austrian Chalet is an attractive hotel overhanging Discovery Passage. It offers its guests a spectacular view of the ocean and mountains. Completely renovated in 1996, the Austrian Chalet has all the amenities, making it a first-class establishment.

Telegraph Cove

The Telegraph Cove Resorts
$23 for a campsite for two adults, water, electricity ; $89-$155 for a cabin for 2 to 8 people
K
☎***928-3131***
☎***(800) 200-4665***
⇌***928-3105***
The Telegraph Cove Resorts welcome visitors from May to October. The campground, equipped with basic facilities, is somewhat bare, but the view of the bay makes up for that. The cabins blend into the picturesque setting. The service is friendly, and you'll feel as if you're at some sort of summer camp. If you have to spend a few days in the northern part of the island, Telegraph Cove is a thoroughly pleasant place to visit.

Port Hardy

Mrs. P's Bed & Breakfast
$55 bkfst incl.
sb
8737 Telco St.
☎***949-9526***
Hosts Herma and Frank will give you a warm welcome at Mrs. P's Bed & Breakfast, which has two soberly decorated rooms in the basement. The place is located within walking distance of the harbour and a number of restaurants. Many travellers passing through town on their way to Prince Rupert arrive late and leave early, which would explain why local residents make so little fuss about renting rooms to visitors in need of a place to stay.

The North Shore Inn
$65-$85
tv, ℜ, *P*
7370 Market St.
☎***949-8500***
⇌***498-5160***
The North Shore Inn overlooks the ocean, as do all its rooms. The hotel is located right in the middle of Port Hardy and about 10min from the ferry terminal, whence guests can participate in fishing, scuba-diving and whale-watching excursions organized by the establishment. The hotel's restaurant, **Sign of the Steer Steak and Seafood House**, serves very good meat and seafood dishes (see p 171).

Glen Lyon Inn
$80-$90
tv, ℜ, *P*
6435 Hardy Bay Rd.
☎***949-7115***
⇌***949-7415***
Close to the BC Ferries terminal, the Glen Lyon Inn is a good hotel, offering rooms with a view of the ocean and excellent breakfasts. In fact, locals claim the Glen Lyon Inn serves the best breakfasts in town.

The Seagate Hotel
$90-$95
tv, ℜ
8600 Granville St.
☎***949-6348***
⇌***949-6347***
The Seagate Hotel is located a stone's throw from the town pier. All of the rooms are sparingly decorated, and the view makes those facing the port much more attractive.

The Gulf Islands are covered with **bed and breakfasts** of all types. Though these places are generally quite expensive, you are unlikely to hear any complaints from the guests.

Galiano Island

Montague Harbour (☎*539-2115*) offers campsites with lovely views of the coast.

For reservations at other bed & breakfasts on the island call **Galiano Getaways** (☎*539-5551*). They also offer adventure packages.

La Berengerie
$60 bkfst incl.
sb, ℜ
Montague Harbour Rd. Galiano
☎***539-5392***
At La Berengerie, which has four rooms, guests enjoy a relaxing atmosphere in the woods. Huguette Benger has been running the place since 1983. Originally from the South of France, Madame Benger came to Galiano on a vacation and decided to stay. Take the time to chat with her; she'll be delighted to tell you all about the island. Breakfast is served in a large dining room. La Berengerie is closed from November to March.

Sutil Lodge Bed & Breakfast
$65-$75 bkfst incl.
sb
Montague Harbour
☎***539-2930***
⇄***539-5390***
Located near the water, The extremely inviting Sutil Lodge Bed & Breakfast is a former fishing camp. Erected in the early 20th century, this large wooden building is surrounded by trees and faces the sea. The grounds and architecture of the lodge are reminiscent of a New England estate. Hosts Tom and Ann Hennessy arrange a number of boating trips.

Mount Galiano Eagle's Nest Bed & Breakfast
$75-$95 bkfst incl.
tv, P
2-720 Active Pass Dr.
☎***539-2567***
The Eagle's Nest is located right on one of the most beautiful waterfront properties of the Discovery Islands. The house is splendid and the view of the ocean is spectacular. If you haven't got a car, don't worry; they can pick you up at the ferry dock.

Salt Spring Island

Salt Spring Island Hostel
$10-$60
P
640 Cusheon Lake Rd.
☎***537-4149***
This is a youth hostel where you can choose between private rooms or the less expensive dormitory. The building is close to a lake, right in the forest.

The Seabreeze Inn
$49-$69
tv, P
1170 North End Rd.
☎***(800) 434-4112***
The Seabreeze Inn is a very comfortable, reasonably priced motel. Downtown Ganges is a 3min-drive away. The manager offers a wealth of information for tourists.

The Summerhill Guest House
$100-$125 bkfst incl.
209 Chu-An Dr.
☎***537-2727***
⇄***537-4301***
The Summerhill Guest House has been completely renovated. The interesting combination of landings and terraces lets in the sunlight and allows for some beautiful views of the Sansum Narrows. The breakfast is unusual and absolutely delicious. You'll feel right at home here.

The Beach House on Fulford Oceanside Bed and Breakfast
$110-$120 bkfst incl.
P
369 Isabella Point Rd.
☎***653-2040***
The Beach House is one of the rare bed and breakfasts on the beach at Salt Spring. In fact, from the French doors of your room, which also serve as a private entrance, it is just a few steps to the waterfront. The rooms offer impeccable comfort and original decor. Breakfasts too, have their own quality and charm. Keep this one in mind.

Mayne Island

Bayview Bed & Breakfast
$70-$90
P
764 Steward Dr.
☎***539-2924***
☎***(800) 376-2115***
⇄***539-2918***
Don and Linda Rose welcome you in the cosy comfort of their home and one of their three guest rooms.

Each has a terrace, a private entrance and its own original decor.

The Root Seller Inn
$80 bkfst incl.
children 6 and over
sb, no smoking
478 Village Bay Rd.
☎ ***539-2621***
⇄ ***539-2411***
The Root Seller Inn lies hidden behind the flowers and trees lovingly planted by charming Joan Drummond, who has been welcoming guests to the island for over 30 years. It all started at the Springwater Hotel in 1960, when she and her husband, having just arrived on the island, opened a hotel. Since 1983, Joan has been receiving guests in her home and showing them the island. The big wooden Cape Cod-style house, can accommodate eight people in three large rooms. It lies near Mariners Bay, so guests can contemplate the scenery and watch the ferries on their way through Active Pass from the blacony.

Oceanwood Country Inn
$110-$300
tv, ℜ, P
630 Dinner Bay Rd.
☎ ***539-5074***
⇄ ***539-3002***
This is another great spot on Mayne Island. This elegant English-style country inn offers pleasantly decorated rooms, each equipped with a fireplace. Visit the Fern Room and the Rose Room – they won't disappoint! The food is deliciously prepared. A stay at this exquisite establishment is sure to leave you with fond memories.

Pender Islands

Eatenton House Bed & Breakfast
$95-$135 bkfst incl.
P
4705 Scarff Rd.
R.R. 1
☎ ***629-8355***
Eatenton House Bed & Breakfast promises a rejuvenating stay in a totally natural setting. The cosy rooms have antique furniture and a fireplace. Noteworthy are the delicious breakfasts as well as the spectacular view of the mountains and ocean.

Saturna Island

The East Point Resort
$77-$104
P
187 East Point Rd.
☎ ***539-2975***
The East Point Resort provides natural surroundings with exclusive access to a smooth sandy beach. Visitors can choose from six small, luxurious and attractively decorated cottages.

Quadra Island

Whiskey Point Resort Motel
$79-$175
tv, P
725 Quathiaski Cove
☎ ***285-2424 or 285-2201***
The hotel is located just across from the ferry dock and dominates the whole bay of Quathiaski Cove. The rooms are very comfortable, well equipped for extended stays, and have kitchenettes. The manager is very friendly and will tell you about all the best places to visit. Show him your Ulysses guide – you're sure to be well received.

April Point Lodge & Fishing Resort
$99-$395
tv, P
903 April Point Rd.
☎ ***285-2222***
⇄ ***285-2411***
The April Point is a luxury establishment for lovers of salmon fishing, nature and gourmet food. If you feel like going for a ride, the hotel can lend you a bicycle.

Cortes Island

Gorge Harbour Marina Resort
$10-$55
tv, ℜ, P
Box 89 Whaletown, V0P 1Z0
follow signs from the ferry
☎ ***935-6433***
⇄ ***935-6402***
Cortes's big resort has approximately 40 RV sites, campsites as well as rustic, yet comfortable, rooms. Some

packages include breakfast. Services include a good restaurant, motor-boat rental, fishing expeditions, fishing permits, marine charts as well as camping equipment. This is a very calm and well maintained place where deer-sightings are not uncommon.

Hollyhock Seminars
prices vary depending on the packages
ℜ
from the Cortes ferry follow signs to Smelt Bay and Hollyhock; the road is winding, so be careful not to end up in Squirrel Cove; approximately 18km from the ferry;
☎935-6576
☎(800) 933-6339
⇄935-6424
Hollyhock Seminars is a "new age" retreat. You can choose to stay in either a tent or a room, both of which take advantage of the surrounding wilderness. Hollyhock offers a variety of relaxation packages that will allow you to re-energize.

Restaurants

Tour A: From Victoria to Nanaimo and the Cowichan Valley

Nanaimo

 **Dinghy Dock Pub**
$
11am to 11pm, midnight Fri and Sat
no. 8 Pirate's Plank Protection Island
☎753-2373
At this floating pub, which is attached to the Protection Island pier, you can enjoy a good local beer while observing the comings and goings in the Nanaimo harbour. The fish & chips are succulent. To get to the island, take the ferry from Commercial Inlet (*every hour from 9:10am to 11:10pm, midnight Fri and Sat*).

Javawocky Coffee House
$
8-90 Front St.
Pioneer Waterfront Plaza
☎753-1688
Located on the seawall, the Javawocky Coffee House serves a wide assortment of coffee and light meals and offers a view of the Nanaimo port and the crowd strolling about there.

Mambo Pizza
$
16 Victoria Cr.
☎753-6667
The pizza at Mambo Pizza's pizza is the antithesis of the frozen product. With a crust thinner than a plate, it's bursting with homemade flavour and freshness. Open until 1am

Wild Roots Café
$
299 Wallace St.
☎/⇄752-0200
The two glass facades of the Wild Roots Café make the place bright and cheery. It serves quality vegetarian food such as ratatouille, lasagne and delicious vegetarian hamburgers. The choice is yours!

Dar Lebanon
$$
closed Sun
347 Wesley St.
☎755-9150
Dar Lebanon is one of the best Lebanese restaurants in the region. The refined, affordable cuisine is served in a dining room tastefully furnished with Middle-Eastern imports. The vegetarian moussaka, a kind of stew covered with cheese, spinach and mushrooms, is particularly delightful.

Tour B: From Nanaimo to Tofino

Ucluelet

Matterson House
$
1682 Peninsula Rd.
☎***726-2200***
People come to the Matterson House, located on the main street, all day long in one of the oldest homes in Ucluelet. Don't hesitate to order salmon here; it's very fresh.

Blueberries Cafe & Cappuccino Bar
$$
1627B Peninsula Rd.
☎***726-7751***
Blueberries Cafe & Cappuccino Bar serves great dishes, such as chicken curry or scrumptious fettuccini with fresh seafood. And then there's the delectable blueberry deserts — with a cappuccino of course!

Long Beach

Wickaninnish Restaurant
$-$$
11am to 9:30pm
at the bottom of Wick Rd.
☎***726-7706***
Set on a big rock overlooking the beach, the Wickaninnish Restaurant offers a spectacular view of the Pacific Ocean. The menu is made up of seafood dishes. The pasta with smoked salmon is particularily tasty. Whatever you choose, your meal will be that much better accompanied by a glass of British Columbian white wine.

Tofino

The Blue Heron Restaurant
$
every day 11am to 10pm
634 Campbell St.
☎***725-3277***
The Blue Heron Restaurant is a spacious 165-seat restaurant enjoyed by families and tourists alike. The menu features regional specialties such as Fish 'n Chips. This restaurant offers unobstructed views of the port, Clayoquot Sound and Meares Island.

Breakers
$
131 First St.
☎***725-2558***
Breakers does the impossible: it serves up quality food in no time at all. On hot summer nights, there's often a long line waiting for the best ice cream cone in Tofino.

Common Load Bake Shop
$
180 First St.
☎***725-3915***
The Common Load Bake Shop offers a vast selection of breads and pastries freshly baked every morning. It also serves salads and a variety of sandwiches, served up in a log cabin with a warm atmosphere. Curry seems to be the favourite flavour here. Notice the collection of masks at the entrance.

The Rain Coast Café
$
101-120 Fourth St.
☎***725-2215***
The Rain Coast Café offers unique, alternative fare. The very colourful dishes pay homage to the world's various cuisines. Reservations recommended.

Surfside Pizza
$
Open until midnight
☎***725-2882***
The address is unnecessary as Surfside only delivers. A good place to order from should you suffer from hunger pangs in your hotel room.

The Loft Restaurant
$$
every day 11am to 10pm
346 Campbell St.
☎***725-4241***
The Loft Restaurant serves West Coast cuisine. Excellent seafood and pasta dishes.

The Pointe Restaurant
$$$
every day 7am to 10pm
at the Wickaninnish Inn, Osprey Lane at Chesterman Beach
☎***(800) 333-4604***
☎***725-3100***
This high-class restaurant is built against a crag and offers a superb view of Chesterman Beach. The Pointe Restaurant as well as the On-The-Rocks Bar are set up in a glass-walled, octogonal room with a stunning 240° view of the

ocean. The chef prepares excellent, quintessentially West Coast cuisine composed of farm and organic ingredients. An excellent choice.

Schooner Restaurant
$$$
331 Campbell St.
☎725-3444
The Schooner Restaurant is a classic. It serves seafood and British Columbian wines. An inviting place, it has been decorated to look like a ship's hold and deck. The soft lighting creates a relaxing comfortable atmosphere.

Tour C: From Qualicum Beach to Port Hardy

Comox Valley

The Bar None Cafe
$
244 Fourth St., Courtenay
☎334-3112
Vegetarian cuisine has no limits at the Bar None Cafe. Have a seat on the magnificent patio and taste one of its many sandwiches or simply a cappuccino (made from organic coffee beans of course!)

Orbitz Pizza
$
corner First St. and Fitzgerald Ave. Courtenay
☎338-7970
Orbitz Pizza makes the best pizza in the valley and serves it up in a hip decor.

Atlas Cafe
$$
250 Sixth St. Courtenay
☎338-9838
The Atlas Cafe serves up a variety of dishes from the four corners of the globe, such as Italy, Mexico, Greece and Japan. The refined cuisine here is delectable.

Campbell River

Hammond's Fish & Chips
$
Mon to Sat 11:30am to 7:30pm, Sun 4pm to 8pm
151 G Dogwood St.
☎286-0814
Hammond's Fish and Chips is a family-style restaurant that serves up fried cod and halibut. You won't go hungry here.

The Seasons Bistro
$
6:30am to 2pm and 5:30pm to 10pm
261 Island Hwy.
☎286-1131
The Seasons Bistro has an original menu featuring seafood pasta and pheasant with passionfruit. This place attracts both locals and tourists, and jazz lovers in particular.

Sayward

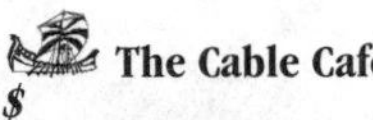 **The Cable Cafe**
$
☎282-3343
The Cable Cafe offers simple, quality meals at reasonable prices. This is a fun place, with walls made of coiled cables.

Port Hardy

The Seagate Hotel Restaurant
$
open at 6:30am
8600 Granville St.
☎949-6348
The Seagate Hotel Restaurant has a wide-ranging menu. While enjoying a view of the harbour, you will dine alongside local residents, including fishers fresh from a day at sea.

The Sign of the Steer Steak and Seafood House
$
every day 7am to 9:30pm
7370 Market St.
☎949-8500
The Sign of the Steer Steak and Seafood House is a good meat and seafood restaurant with a view of the sea, and the only establishment in town to feature live music shows in its Town & Country Show Pub Lounge. Very pleasant ambiance.

Tour D: The Gulf Islands

Galiano Island

La Berengerie
$$
open only in the evening
Montague Harbour Rd.
☎539-5392
La Berengerie has a four-course menu with a choice of fish or meat. The dining room, located on the ground floor of a bed and breakfast, is furnished with antiques. Candlelight makes the atmo-

sphere that much more inviting. Owner Huguette Benger prepares the delicious meals herself. During the day, her son's restaurant, **La Bohème**, serves vegetarian dishes on the terrace overlooking the garden.

Salt Spring Island

Vesuvius Inn Neighbourhood Pub
$
805 Vesuvius Bay Rd., Ganges
☎*537-2312*
Vesuvius has a fairly varied menu but specializes in West Coast cuisine. Try the Saturday and Sunday brunch, served until 3pm.

Alfresco Waterfront Restaurant
$$
Grace Point Sq. , Ganges
☎*537-5979*
Alfresco Waterfront Restaurant is an Italian restaurant with good soups, seafood and excellent duck and lamb dishes.

Seacourt Gourmet Restaurant
$$
108 Fulford St. , Ganges
The Seacourt is a very good restaurant that serves international cuisine with a spicy touch. The fish is excellent but the real musts are the authentic caesar salad and the succulent crepes suzette. These two dishes are prepared right in front of you. An excellent place.

House Piccolo
$$$
108 Hereford Ave., Ganges
☎*537-1844*
is an elegant restaurant whose menu features French, Italian and Scandinavian flavours. The cuisine is very sophisticated and very tasty. Be careful, the bill adds up quickly.

Quadra Island

Tsa-Kwa-Luten Lodge
$
May to Sep every day
Lighthouse, Quadra Island
☎*285-2042*
reservations recommended
The site is truly spectacular, providing an unobstructed view of Discovery Passage, and it's not unusual to see eagles flying over the restaurant. Regional specialties with a native influence are served here; try the excellent salmon hamburger. The wine list is extensive. In the summer, you can enjoy some barbecued salmon on the big outdoor terrace.

Heriot Bay Inn and Marina
$$
just across from the ferry terminal
☎*285-3322*
The restaurant has a very friendly atmosphere and a lovely view of the harbour. In the summer, you can eat on the terrace. The house specialties are seafood, steak and home-made pies. A good spot.

April Point Lodge & Fishing Resort
$$-$$$
903 April Point Rd.
☎*285-2222*
☎*888-334-3474*
For breakfast, lunch and dinner, the restaurant at this impressive resort serves meals that easily meet gourmets' high expectations. The wine list is equally impressive.

Cortes Island

The Old Floathouse Restaurant
$
summer every day 11am to 2pm and 6pm to 10pm
Whaletown
follow the signs from the ferry terminal Gorge Harbour Marina Resort
☎*935-6631*
in winter
☎*935-6433*
The Old Floathouse Restaurant is one of the rare good restaurants on the island. It also benefits from a superb location on a magnificent property.

Entertainment

Bars and Nightclubs

Tour D: The Gulf Islands

The Hummingbird Pub
$
every day until 12:30am
47 Sturdies Bay Rd. Galiano Island
☎*539-5472*
This is a friendly place where tourists and locals mingle over a good beer and a plate of fries.

Calendar of Events

January

Polar Bear Swim
Salt Spring Island
On January 1, hundreds of people rush into the ocean for an annual icy dip.

February

Orchid Show
Woodgrove Centre ☎*390-2721*

Chinese New Year
in the streets of Nanaimo
☎*753-1821*

March

Nanaimo Horticultural Society Show
Beban Park Social Centre
☎*756-5200*

St. Patrick's Day Parade
Harbour Park Mall
☎*754-3234*

Upper Island Music Festival
Beban Park Social Centre
☎*756-5200*

April

Arts & Crafts Show
Woodgrove Centre
☎*390-2721*

Antique Show
Woodgrove Centre
☎*390-2721*

May

Ballroom Dance Competitions
Beban Park Social Centre
☎*756-5200*

Fishing Derby
Silva Bay
☎*247-8807*

June

Nanaimo Jazz Festival
Nanaimo Art Gallery
☎*755-8790*

June to September

Fresh-food market on Saturdays, craft market on Sundays (*Salt Spring Island*)

July

Nanaimo Marine Festival
downtown
☎*753-7223*

International Bathtub Races
at the port of Nanaimo
☎*753-7223*

International Sandcastle Competition
Parksville Beach
☎*954-3999*

August

Fringe Theatre Festival
☎*753-8528*
Fulford Music Festival
Salt Spring Island

World Croquet Championship
☎*248-6171* or
Parksville Chamber of Commerce
☎*248-3613*

Kidfest
Parksville Community Park
☎*248-3252*

September

Vintage Car Rally
between Victoria and Nanaimo
☎*754-8141*
Crab Fest
Parksville Community Hall
☎*752-6263*

October

Oktoberfest
Beban Park Social Centre
☎*756-5200*

Wood Carving Show
Beban Park Social Centre
☎*756-5200*

November

Mozart's Requiem
Salt Spring Island
November 30 lighting of the Christmas trees

Shopping

Tour A: From Victoria to Nanaimo and the Cowichan Valley

Nanaimo

Nanaimo is truly a city of shopping centres. The shops here are really nothing special aside from their incredible variety. **Rutherford Mall** (*Mon to Wed 9:30am to 5:30pm, Thu and Fri 9:30am to 9pm, Sat 9:30am to 5:30pm, Sun 9:30am to 5pm; on North Island Hwy., close to Long Lake, at Rutherford Rd., ☎758-8111*) is a good example, with over 70 establishments, including department stores as well as clothing boutiques, jewellers, booksellers, restaurants, etc.

Tour B: From Nanaimo to Tofino

Ucluelet

The **Du Quaii Gallery** (*1971 Peninsula Rd., ☎726-7223*) exhibits Aboriginal art. It is worth the trip just to see the building, which looks like a Longhouse (a traditional Aboriginal cedar building).

Tofino

Eagle Aerie Gallery
350 Campbell St.
☎725-3235
The Eagle Aerie Gallery was built by the Aboriginal artist Roy Henry Vickers. The artist's world-renowned paintings, inspired from his life, are exhibited here. The smell of ancient wood emanates from the walls of the gallery. A must-see.

The House of Himwitsa (*300 Main St. ☎725-2017*) is an art gallery that displays drawings, paintings, sculptures and silver and gold jewellery. Ask about the legends referred to in these pieces and the symbolism employed by the artists.

Tofino Bakery (*455 Campbell St., ☎725-3228*) makes good bread and scrumptious pastries. An institution in Tofino.

Tour C: From Qualicum Beach to Port Hardy

Campbell River

The **Tyee Plaza** (*behind the Travel InfoCentre, ☎286-0418*) has a covered walkway and 24 stores and restaurants of all different sorts. If you are in a rush or looking for a shopping mall, this is the place to go.

Port Hardy

The **Copper Maker** (*every day; 112 Copper Way, Fort Rupert, ☎949-8491*) displays the works of a number of Aboriginal artists. Masks, pottery and symbolic jewellery can all be purchased here. These articles might seem expensive, but the prices are lower than in the bigger cities.

Tour D: The Gulf Islands

Salt Spring Island

Mouat's Home Hardware (*106 Fulford Rd., Ganges, Salt Spring Island, ☎537-5551*) is well stocked with all the necessary supplies for camping and outdoor activities.

The **Ganges Village Market** (*374 Lower Ganges Rd., Ganges, Salt Spring Island*) sells all kinds of groceries. There's also a bakery and a delicatessen.

Everlasting Summer (*194 MacLennan Dr., Salt Spring Island, ☎653-9418*) specializes in dried-flower bouquets and aromatic plant cultivation.

Don't miss the beautiful, romantic, rose garden where weddings are often held.

Pender Islands

Try **Southridge Farms Country Store** (*Pender Islands, ☎229-2051*) for organic fruits and vegetables.

Mayne Island

If you need supplies or equipment for camping or hiking, stop in at **Miners Trading Post** (*Mayne Island, ☎539-2214*), in the town of **Fernhill**. To get good organic fruits and vegetables, go to the **Mayne Open Market** (*Mayne Island, ☎539-5024*), called MOM by local residents.

You can also pick up venison or beef for a tasty barbecue at the **Arbutus Deer Farm** (*☎539-2301*).

Quadra Island

Heriot Bay Consignment Shop (*West Rd., not far from the ferry dock, Quadra Island, ☎285-3217*). You'll find absolutely everything at the Heriot Bay Consignment Shop and have a lot of fun in this second-hand store.

Southern British Columbia

This region, which borders on the United States, is characterized by a blend of the urban and the undeveloped.

The Vancouver area, for example, resembles a big American city, though it is set against a backdrop of green mountains and blue sea; here, you will find both wilderness and civilization.

The Okanagan Valley is home to countless orchards and some of the best wineries in the province. As one majestic landscape succeeds another, your eyes will be dazzled by the sea, the everlasting snows and the spring colours, which appear very early in this region.

Communing with nature is a memorable experience of any trip in southern British Columbia. The waters that wash the deserted beaches beckon you to relax and let your mind wander. Stately trees stand guard over tranquil areas untouched by the forestry industry. Dotted with national and provincial parks, which lie stretched across the loveliest parts of the province, this region has an extremely varied landscape, with everything from perpetual snows to desert valleys to rivers teeming with fish.

A trip to southern British Columbia offers a chance to explore towns and parks set between the sea and the sky and meet people from a wide range of cultures. We have outlined five tours through four large areas whose character and appearance range from one extreme to the other.

The tours are as follows:

Tour A:
The Sunshine Coast ★★

Tour B:
The Sea to Sky Highway – Fraser River Loop ★★

Tour C:
The Thompson River as Far as Revelstoke ★

Tour D:
Okanagan-Similkameen ★★★

Tour E:
Kootenay Country ★★

Finding Your Way Around

By Plane

A number of airlines serve the various parts of the province.

Air BC:
Kamloops, Kelowna, Penticton, Vernon, Powell River
in Vancouver
☎(604) 643-5600
☎(800) 663-3721

Canadian Regional:
Kamloops, Kelowna, Penticton
in Vancouver
☎(604) 279-6611
☎(800) 665-1177

Central Mountain Air:
Kamloops, Kelowna
☎(800) 663-3721
(*book through Air BC*).

By Car

Every highway in southern British Columbia is more spectacular than the last. One of these is the Trans-Canada (Hwy. 1), which runs east-west across mountains, rivers, canyons and desert valleys.

Hwy. 1, the Trans-Canada, provides an easy route eastward out of Vancouver, although the traffic is always fairly heavy. The road leads to Calgary, running along the Fraser River, the Thompson River and Lake Shuswap at different points along the way. Another option is to take Hwy. 7 (the continuation of Broadway Ave.) out of downtown Vancouver, along the north bank of the Fraser River. If you're pressed for time, you can take the newly opened Coquihalla Highway, which runs between Hope and Kamloops. This is a toll highway, the only one in the province; what's more, it is not as attractive as the others.

The spectacular Sea to Sky Highway (99) will take you up into northern British Columbia; simply cross the Lions Gate Bridge and follow the signs for Whistler and Squamish.

By Train

Once extremely busy, railway stations only see a few regular trains nowadays. The Canadian still crosses the Rockies, running along mountainsides and through numerous tunnels. From North Vancouver, you can take a train that skirts northward around Howe Sound, passing through Squamish and Whistler along the way and offering passengers a chance to contemplate the landscape.

BC Rail (*1311 W. First St., North Vancouver, ☎604-984-5246 or 800-663-8238*) serves the towns in the northern part of the province by way of the Whistler resort area.

Via Rail Canada
(*1150 Station St., Vancouver, ☎800-561-8630 in Western Canada*) serves the following towns: Port Coquitlam, Matsqui, Chilliwack, Hope, Boston Bar, Ashcroft, Kamloops North and several other communities in the northeastern part of the province.

By Bus

Greyhound Lines of Canada
Pacific Central Station, 1150 Station St., Vancouver
☎(604) 662-3222
☎(800) 661-8747

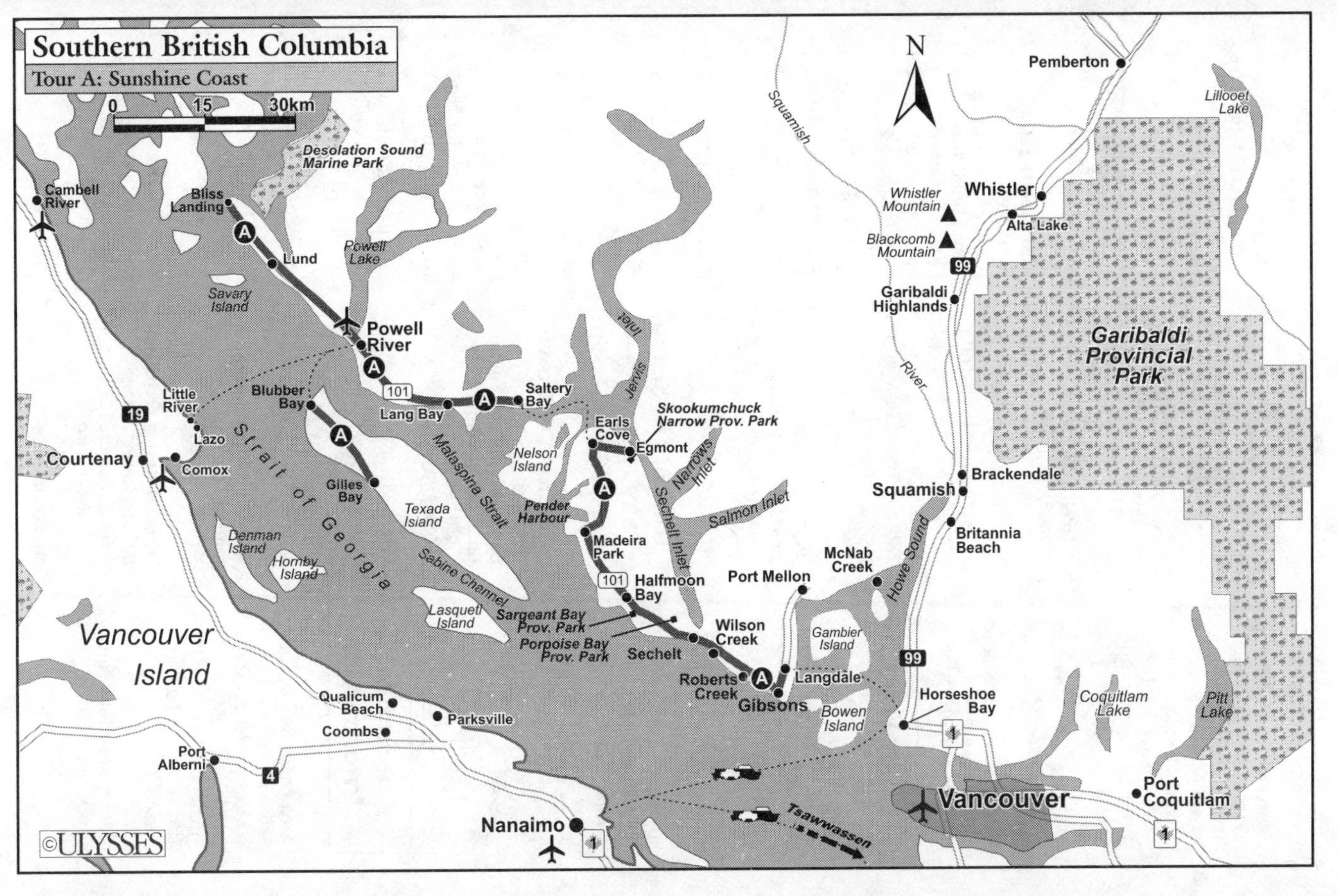
Southern British Columbia
Tour A: Sunshine Coast
0
15
30km
N
Desolation Sound Marine Park
Cambell River
Bliss Landing
Lund
Powell Lake
Savary Island
Powell River
Little River
Lazo
Courtenay
Comox
19
Blubber Bay
Gilles Bay
101
Lang Bay
Saltery Bay
Strait of Georgia
Malaspina Strait
Texada Island
Denman Island
Hornby Island
Sabine Channel
Lasqueti Island
Nelson Island
Pender Harbour
Earls Cove
Egmont
Skookumchuck Narrow Prov. Park
Jervis Inlet
Narrows Inlet
Sechelt Inlet
Salmon Inlet
Madeira Park
Halfmoon Bay
Sargeant Bay Prov. Park
Porpoise Bay Prov. Park
Sechelt
Wilson Creek
Roberts Creek
Gibsons
Langdale
Port Mellon
McNab Creek
Gambier Island
Bowen Island
Howe Sound
Horseshoe Bay
Vancouver Island
Qualicum Beach
Parksville
Coombs
Port Alberni
4
Nanaimo
1
Tsawwassen
Vancouver
Port Coquitlam
Coquitlam Lake
Pitt Lake
Squamish
Britannia Beach
Brackendale
Squamish River
Garibaldi Highlands
Whistler Mountain
Blackcomb Mountain
99
Whistler
Alta Lake
Pemberton
Lillooet Lake
Garibaldi Provincial Park
©ULYSSES

Maverick Coach Lines (Pacific Central Station, 1150 Station St., Vancouver ☎***604-662-8051***). Caters mainly to skiers going to Whistler for the day, but also serves other towns along Hwy. 99.

Whistler Transit System
☎***(604) 932-4020***

Powell River Bus Station
7245 Duncan St.
☎***(604) 485-5030***

By Ferry

To reach the Sunshine Coast, you must take a ferry from the coast or from Vancouver Island.

BC Ferries:
1112 Fort St.,
Victoria, V8V 4V2
Victoria:
☎***(250) 386-3431***
☎***(888) 223-3779***
from Saltery Bay:
☎***487-9333***
Powell River:
☎***485-2943***

Practical Information

Area Code: 604 in the Lower Mainland (*Vancouver and suburbs*), **250** in the rest of the province (*north of Whistler, east of Hope, the islands*)

In case of serious emergency, dial ☎911

Tourist Information

Tourism Association of Southwestern B.C.:
204-1755 West Broadway,
Vancouver, BC V6J 4S5
☎***(604) 739-9011***
☎***(800) 667-3306***

Tour A: The Sunshine Coast

Gibsons
Gibsons Travel InfoCentre:
668 Sunnycrest Rd.
☎***(604) 886-2325***

Powell River
Powell River Travel InfoCentre:
4690 Marine Ave.
☎***(604) 485-4701***

Tour B: The Sea to Sky Highway – Fraser River Loop

Squamish & Howe Sound
Squamish & Howe Sound Chamber of Commerce:
37950 Cleveland Ave.
☎***(604) 892-9244***

Whistler
Whistler Travel InfoCentre:
2097 Lake Placid Rd.
☎***(604) 932-5528***

Whistler Activity and Information Centre:
☎***(604) 932-2394***

Whistler Resort Accommodations Reservations:
☎***(604) 932-4222***
in Vancouver
☎***(604) 664-5625***
☎***(800) Whistler***

Lytton
Lytton Travel InfoCentre:
400 Fraser St.
☎***(250) 455-2523***

Hope
Hope Travel InfoCentre:
919 Water Ave.
☎***(604) 869-2021***

Harrison Hot Springs
Harrison Hot Springs Travel InfoCentre:
Open year-round
Hwy. 9, 499 Hot Springs Rd.
☎***(604) 796-3425***

Tour C: The Thompson River as Far as Revelstoke

Kamloops
High Country Tourism Association:
1-1490 Pearson Pl., BC V1S 1J9
☎***(250) 372-7770***
☎***(800) 567-2275***

Kamloops Travel InfoCentre:
1290 West Trans-Canada Hwy.
☎***(250) 374-3377***
All of the major **banks** are located on Victoria Street, near Third Ave.. The **post office** is at the corner of St. Paul St. and Third Ave..

For general information contact the **Kamloops Visitor Info Centre**
☎***(800) 662-1994***
☎***374-3377***

Revelstoke
Revelstoke Travel InfoCentre:
204 Campbell Ave.
☎***(250) 837-5345***
☎***(800) 487-1493***

Revelstoke City Hall
☎***837-2161***

Police
☎*837-5255*

Hospital
☎*837-2131*

Tour D: Okanagan-Similkameen

Okanagan-Similkameen Tourism Association:
1332 Water St., Kelowna, BC V1Y 9P4
☎*(250) 860-5999*

Hope:
(See Tour B above)

Princeton
Princeton Travel InfoCentre:
57 Hwy. 3E ☎*(250) 295-3103*

Osoyoos
Osoyoos Travel InfoCentre:
at the intersection of Hwys. 3 and 97
☎*(250) 495-7142*
☎*(888) 676-9667*

Penticton

Penticton Chamber of Commerce:
888 Westminster Ave.
☎*(250) 493-4055*
☎*(800) 663-5052*

Police:
☎*(250) 492-4300*

Penticton Regional Hospital:
☎*(250) 492-4000*

Kelowna
Kelowna Travel InfoCentre:
544 Harvey Ave.
☎*(250) 861-1515*

Hospital:
Kelowna General Hospital
2268 Pandosy St.
☎*(250) 862-4000*

Vernon
Vernon:
to the south, 701 Hwy. 97
☎*542-1415*
☎*(800) 665-0795*

Merritt
Merritt Travel InfoCentre:
at the intersection of Hwy. 5E and 97C
☎*(250) 378-2281*

Tour E: Kootenay Country

Kootenay Country Tourist Association:
610 Railway St., Nelson, BC V1L 1H4
☎*(250) 352-6033*

Nakusp and District Travel InfoCentre:
92 West Sixth Ave.
☎*(250) 265-4234*
☎*(800) 909-8819*

Nelson
Nelson & District Chamber of Commerce:
225 Hall St.
☎*(250) 352-3433*
☎*354-4636*

Hospital
☎*352-3111*

Ambulance
☎*352-2112*

Police
☎*352-2266*

Rossland
Rossland Tourist Information:
intersection of Hwy. 3B and Hwy. 22
☎*(250) 362-7722*

Internet

It is usually easy to connect to the Web at a terminal in one of the municipal libraries. In some cases, such as in the Okanagan Valley, there is a nominal fee of $2/hr.

Some Internet terminals have also been set up in a few youth hostels. The cost is $1/10min.

Exploring

British Columbia is exceptional in many respects, first of all because it has something to offer all manner of tourists, whether they're travelling by car or hiking. The southern part of the province is a large territory, which is flat in certain places and then suddenly very hilly in others. The construction of the railroad blazed a trail for the highways, each of which is more spectacular than the last.

Tour A: The Sunshine Coast

Most people get to the Sunshine Coast by boat. There are no roads linking Vancouver to these resort towns; the daily comings and goings are dictated by the ferry schedule. As a result, the mentality here is completely different. The towns that have grown up along this coast benefit from the sea and what it yields. The Sunshine

Coast runs along the Strait of Georgia, and is surrounded by Desolation Sound to the north, the Coast Mountains to the east and Howe Sound farther south.

Langdale

It takes 40min to reach Langdale, a small port city at the southern tip of the Sunshine Coast. Ferries shuttle back and forth several times a day, but you have to arrive at the Horseshoe Bay terminal at least an hour early for some weekend departures. **Horseshoe Bay** lies 20km northwest of Vancouver. With **BC Ferries** (*information: 7am to 10pm; **Vancouver**: ☎888-223-3779; **Victoria**: ☎250-386-3431*) You can save up to 15% on the price of your ticket if you return by way of Vancouver Island instead of opting for a round-trip. Ask for the Sunshine Coast Circlepac.

During the ferry ride, your notion of distance will change; the time required to get from point A to point B can no longer be measured in the same way. Let yourself be carried away; just sit back and contemplate the view between the sea and the mountains.

The Coast Salish First Nation were the first people to inhabit the coast. The Squamish and Sechelt lived in the present-day Gibsons region. Europeans first sailed these waters in the 1790s, but it wasn't until Captain Richards came here in 1859 and 1860 that a record was made of all the bays, coves, islands and sounds.

Gibsons

Visitors to Gibsons are sure to recognize the site of *The Beachcombers*, a Canadian Broadcasting Corporation (CBC) television series that was shot here for close to 20 years and broadcast in over 40 countries. On the way from Langdale to Gibsons, stop off at **Molly's Reach** (see p 229) to take a look at the photographs of the actors from the popular television show and to explore the little shops and restaurants along **Molly's Lane ★**. More recently Gibsons became Castle Rock for the film ***Needful Things***, based on a Steven King novel.

A visit to the **Sunshine Coast Maritime Museum ★** (*at the end of Molly's Lane, ☎886-4114*) is a must. You will be greeted by a charming woman who will inspire you with her passion for the local marine life.

The Sunshine Coast has been developed in a thin strip alongside the forest. The area abounds in plant and animal life — orchids and wild roses, deer and black bears. River otters and beavers can be found near the coast, while sea-lions and seals swim about farther offshore.

Sechelt

To get to **Sechelt**, take Hwy. 101 northward. The landscape is rather dreary, but its beauty is soon enhanced by the sea and the islands. Sechelt is an important administrative centre for the Aboriginal community. At the **House of Hewhiwus** (*5555 Hwy. 101, beside the tourist office*), you'll find a theatre, an art gallery and a souvenir shop. Members of the community can tell you about Aboriginal art, each piece of which is associated with a legend.

The Sunshine Coast is best explored aboard a boat on one of the neighbouring waterways. Turn right on Wharf Road and go to Government Wharf. **Sunshine Coast Tours ★** (*$55; Wed to Sun 9:30am to 2:30pm; ☎885-0351*) or **Tzoonie Gift House** (*5644 Cowrie St. Sechelt, ☎885-9802*) arranges outings on Sechelt Inlet, as far as the Skookumchuck Rapids, aimed at familiarizing visitors with the local

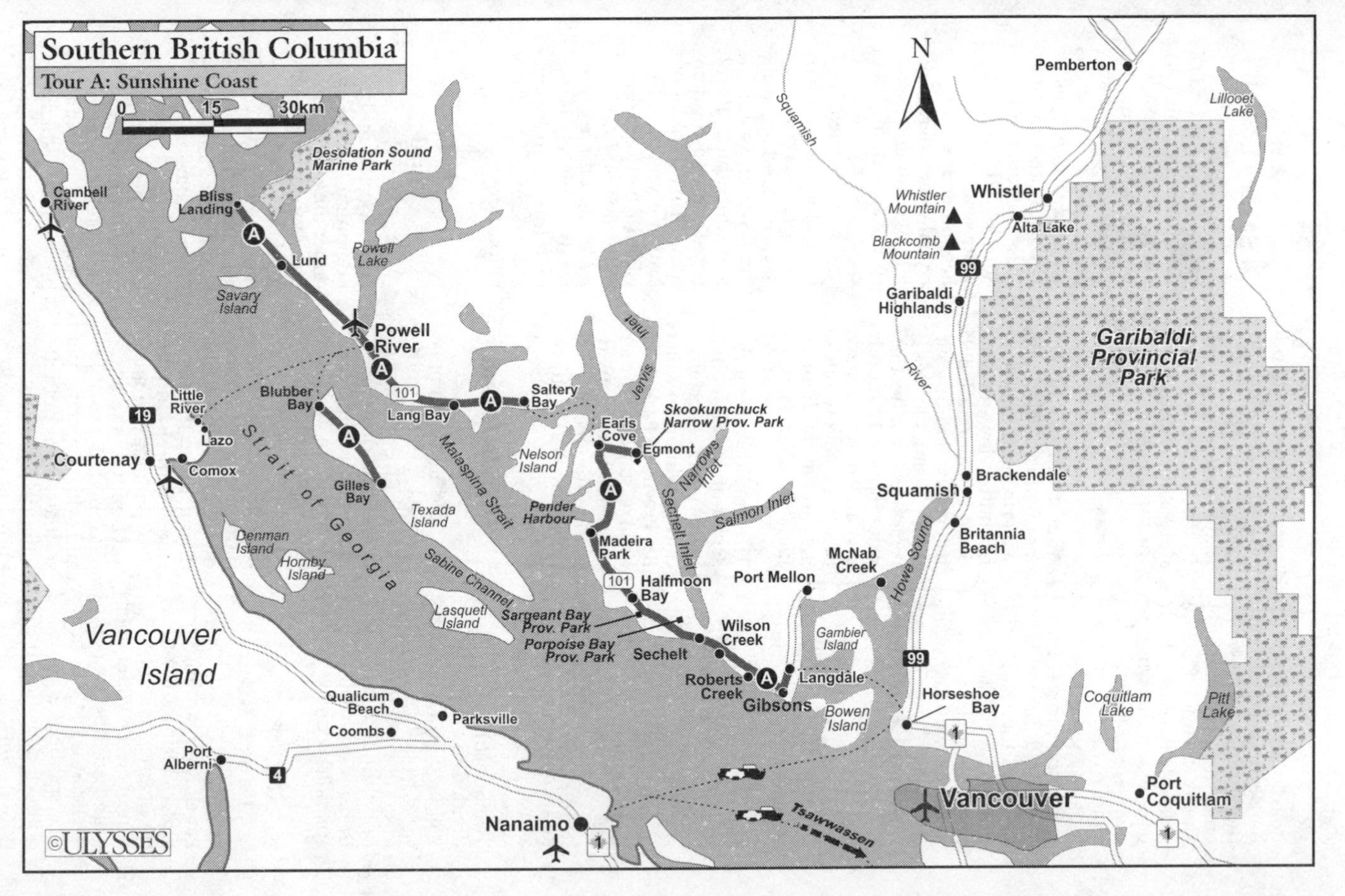

Southern British Columbia
Tour A: Sunshine Coast
0
15
30km
N
Pemberton
Squamish
Lillooet Lake
Desolation Sound Marine Park
Cambell River
Bliss Landing
Whistler Mountain
Whistler
Alta Lake
Blackcomb Mountain
99
Lund
Powell Lake
Savary Island
Garibaldi Highlands
Garibaldi Provincial Park
Powell River
Inlet
Jervis
River
Little River
Blubber Bay
101
Saltery Bay
Lang Bay
Skookumchuck Narrow Prov. Park
19
Earls Cove
Lazo
Egmont
Courtenay
Nelson Island
Narrows Inlet
Comox
Strait of Georgia
Malaspina Strait
Brackendale
Gilles Bay
Squamish
Texada Island
Pender Harbour
Salmon Inlet
Sechelt Inlet
Britannia Beach
Denman Island
Madeira Park
McNab Creek
Howe Sound
Hornby Island
Sabine Channel
101
Halfmoon Bay
Port Mellon
Lasqueti Island
Sargeant Bay Prov. Park
Wilson Creek
Gambier Island
Vancouver Island
Porpoise Bay Prov. Park
Sechelt
99
Roberts Creek
Langdale
Gibsons
Horseshoe Bay
Coquitlam Lake
Pitt Lake
Qualicum Beach
Parksville
Bowen Island
Coombs
1
Port Alberni
4
Port Coquitlam
Vancouver
Tsawwassen
Nanaimo
1
©ULYSSES
1

marine life. A salmon barbecue is served on the shore, and a you'll enjoy a ride on the Skookumchuck ("strong waters") Rapids at high tide, when the water is over 3m higher. If you simply want to take a look at the rapids, go to Egmont; to get there, keep right before Earls Cove on the road to Powell River. The parking lot is nearly 4km from the viewing area.

Pender Harbour

Still heading toward Earls Cove, you will pass alongside **Pender Harbour**, whose series of little islands is a fisher's dream come true. Easily accessible by both land and water, this place is popular with salmon fishers. **Lowe's Resort** (☎*883-2456*) arranges fishing, scuba-diving and sightseeing excursions.

The Sunshine Coast is divided in two. A ferry will take you from Earls Cove to Saltery Bay, offering yet another opportunity to take in British Columbia's splendid scenery.

★ Powell River

Powell River, an important waterfront town, boasts magnificent sunsets over Vancouver Island and the islands in the Strait of Georgia. The spotlight is on outdoor activities in this region, since the temperate climate is conducive to year-round fun and games. Forestry plays an important role in the local economy, but visitors come here for the lakes, the woods, the wildlife and the views.

After a walk in the mountains or along the waterfront, the most beautiful views of the Strait of Georgia will be forever etched in your mind. Visitors to this region enjoy a host of water sports 12 months a year. There are activities to suit every budget, and all of them are immediately accessible.

The limpid water lures scuba-diving buffs here every year, especially during winter. In **Saltery Bay Provincial Park ★**, a bronze statue of a mermaid lies hidden away among the ocean's treasures at a depth of 20m.

Texada Island

Located in the Strait of Georgia, not far from Powell River, Texada Island was once an important mining centre where, in 1880, iron was exploited. The island now attracts only nature lovers who explore it either on foot, by bicycle or by scuba diving. Since the services on the island are very limited, you are advised to come as equipped as possible and with a specific plan so that you're not left "stranded" without knowing what to do.

★★ Savary Island

Savary Island is one of the Northern Gulf Islands. It is accessible by taxi-boat from Powell River. The distance of the crossing is about 20km. It is nicknamed British Columbia's Hawaii and Pleasure Island, due to its **white sand beaches ★★★** and **crystal-clear water**, making swimming a pleasure. Large numbers of **eagles** visit the island and **seal** colonies frequent the shores. Activities practised on Savary Island are walking, cycling, swimming and sunbathing. It truly is *the* summer destination. Don't think about bringing your car; the island is very small (*8km long and 1km wide*), and there are no roads. A bicycle is therefore an indispensable means of transportation here.

★★ Lund

Lund, located at the beginning (or the end, depending on what direction you're heading in) of Hwy. 101, is the gateway to marvellous **Desolation Sound ★★**, a marine life sanctuary easily accessible by canoe or kayak. The town port is magnificent, with its old hotel, its adjoining shops and its wooden promenade, which skirts round the bay. Imagine a typical fishing village and your harbour will undoubtedly be filled with the fishing boats moored here. In terms of activities, there is much to choose from here, from fishing and whale-watching trips to snorkelling and kayaking.

You can take the ferry from Powell River to Vancouver Island or backtrack to Langdale and return to Vancouver by way of Horseshoe Bay.

Tour B: The Sea to Sky Highway Fraser River Loop

Magnificent panoramic views abound all along the coast. Whether you are travelling by car, by train or aboard a ferry, a succession of fjords, mountains, forests and scenic viewpoints will unfold before you. The Sea to Sky Highway is a winding road used by many visitors who come to Whistler for sporting vacations in both winter and summer. Forestry and tourism are the two mainsprings of this vast region's economy. Beautiful **Furry Creek** golf course, renowned throughout the province and even the country, attracts experienced golfers all summer. The challenge is to keep yourself from being distracted by the enchanting landscape. The first stop on the 99, coming from Vancouver, is Britannia Beach.

Britannia Beach

For nearly a century, **Britannia Beach** was an important mining town where thousands of tonnes of copper were extracted. It has been transformed into a giant museum where visitors can learn how the mines operated from the turn of the century to the early 1970s, when they shut down. A train ride through the tunnels will take you back to another era, while a guide explains and demonstrates the various drilling techniques that were used as the machinery became more and more advanced. The tour ends at the mill, where the ore was cleaned. The **B.C. Museum of Mining** ★ (*$10.50; May and Jun, Wed to Sun; Jul and Aug, every day; Sep and Oct, Wed to Sun, 10am to 4:30pm; ☎604-688-8735 or 896-2233*).

Hwy. 99 runs alongside Howe Sound to Squamish. For many years, the only means of getting to the town from the south was by boat; some communities still rely on ferries to reach the coast farther north.

Squamish

Located at the north end of Howe Sound, Squamish owes its existence to the forest industry, which still helps support the local economy. You can see the forestry workers in action in the woods, at the sawmill or in the sorting yard, where gigantic machines put blocks of wood in place. At the entrance from Squamish, you'll be intrigued by the big, black rock face, known as The Wall, that descends steeply to the edge of the road. If you like rock climbing, you can tackle it with a guide. The **Soo Coalition for Sustainable Forests** ★ (*4hr walk in the woods $30; dryland sort tour, $14 for two people; mill tour $14 for two people with own car, $24 without car; reservations required; ☎604- 892-9766*) is an organization that works toward preserving both the forest and the jobs related to the industry. It arranges tours of the forest and the lumber yard in order to educate the public on this subject.

The historic **Royal Hudson Steam Train** (*$45 round-trip; Jun to Sep, Wed to Sun; 10am departure from North Vancouver; 1311 W. First St.; it is also possible to come back by boat; for $78; ☎604-688-7246 or 800-663-8238*) runs between North Vancouver and Squamish, following the coastline and offering unimpeded views of the island and of the snow-capped peaks of the Coast Mountains.

Windsurfers come to Squamish, whose name means "mother of the wind," for the wind that sweeps down the sound and then shifts inland. Mountain-climbing is also becoming more popular in this region. The place to go is **Stawamus Chief Mountain**. The trails leading to this granite monolith will take you to places where you can watch the mountain climbers. For more information, contact the **Squamish & Howe Sound District Chamber of Commerce** (☎*892-9244*).

Hwy. 99 heads inland and runs alongside Garibaldi Park on its way through the valley that leads to Whistler.

Brackendale

Drawn by a mysterious force, every winter salmon make their way back from the Pacific Ocean to the Squamish and Cheakamus Rivers to spawn and die. Not far behind are the thousands of **bald eagles** that choose the small town of Brackendale as their winter residence. They feed on the decomposing salmon washed up along the river.

Only 65km north of Vancouver by the Sea to Sky Highway (Hwy. 99), the small Aboriginal community of Waiwecum, now called Brackendale, is actually a suburb of Squamish. It has recently been recognized as the most significant gathering site for bald eagles in the world, ahead of the Chilkat Bald Eagle Reserve in Alaska. Eagles are everywhere: on the trees, on the roofs of houses and along the road. This unique phenomenon draws over 2,000 amateur naturalists every weekend during the high season (December and January).

Every year, a census of the eagles is organized by the **Brackendale Art Gallery** that exhibits paintings and sculptures, some very fine work. Also in the summer, **Brennan Park Leisure Centre** ensures a good time for both young and old alike. There are also **five provincial parks**, all along the Sea to Sky Highway, that offer the chance to participate in all sorts of outdoor activities. Call ***☎(800) 689-9025*** for information. In 1986, only 537 eagles were registered, but nowadays it's not unusual to count over 3,700 along the Squamish River at Cheakamus and Mamquam.

For more information about the Brackendale eagles, contact the **Squamish & Howe Sound Visitor Info Centre** open all year, or the **Brackendale Art Gallery** (*noon to 10pm Sat, Sun and holidays; ☎898-3333*).

Some Advice: *This region is inhabited by many black and grizzly bears. Be very careful. Bears may sometimes seem peaceful and harmless but they can be very dangerous.*

★★ Whistler

Whistler has grown and become an important location not only for people who live there on a permanent basis, but also for the development of tourism. Besides the big hotels, more and more condominiums are being built and stores have multiplied. To allow visitors to get around more easily, a shuttle service around the village has been instituted. Of course, the shops are mostly geared towards tourists but many are also for residents; there are shopping centres and large grocery stores. This encourages people to buy condos as secondary residences and benefits Whistler's economy.

Whistler attracts skiers, golfers, hikers, sailors and snowboarders from all over the world. An impressive hotel complex graces the little village at the foot of Blackcomb and Whistler Mountains. Other amenities at this internationally renowned resort include restaurants, shops, sports facilities and a convention centre. Whistler is popular in summer and winter alike, and each

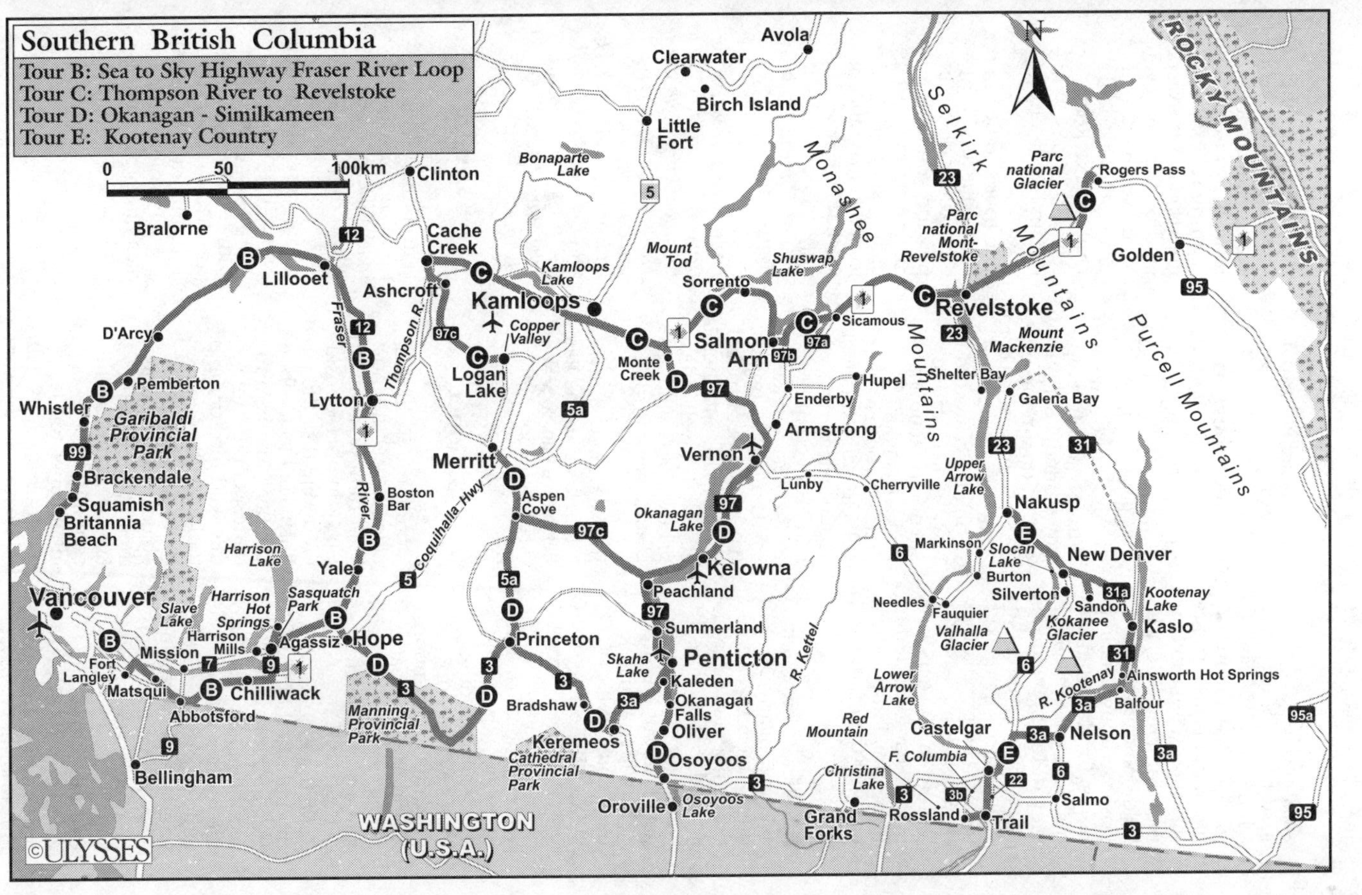
Southern British Columbia
Tour B: Sea to Sky Highway Fraser River Loop
Tour C: Thompson River to Revelstoke
Tour D: Okanagan - Similkameen
Tour E: Kootenay Country
0
50
100km
ROCKY MOUNTAINS
Selkirk Mountains
Monashee Mountains
Purcell Mountains
Avola
Clearwater
Birch Island
Little Fort
Bonaparte Lake
Clinton
Bralorne
Lillooet
Cache Creek
Ashcroft
Kamloops Lake
Kamloops
Mount Tod
Shuswap Lake
Sorrento
Salmon Arm
Sicamous
Revelstoke
Parc national Mont-Revelstoke
Parc national Glacier
Rogers Pass
Golden
D'Arcy
Pemberton
Whistler
Garibaldi Provincial Park
Brackendale
Squamish
Britannia Beach
Fraser River
Thompson R.
Lytton
Copper Valley
Logan Lake
Monte Creek
Enderby
Hupel
Armstrong
Mount Mackenzie
Shelter Bay
Galena Bay
Merritt
Boston Bar
Coquihalla Hwy
Aspen Cove
Vernon
Lunby
Cherryville
Upper Arrow Lake
Nakusp
Okanagan Lake
Kelowna
Harrison Lake
Yale
Markinson
Slocan Lake
Burton
New Denver
Vancouver
Slave Lake
Harrison Hot Springs
Harrison Mills
Sasquatch Park
Agassiz
Hope
Peachland
Summerland
Silverton
Sandon
Kootenay Lake
Needles
Fauquier
Valhalla Glacier
Kokanee Glacier
Kaslo
Fort Langley
Mission
Matsqui
Chilliwack
Abbotsford
Princeton
Skaha Lake
Penticton
Kaleden
Okanagan Falls
Oliver
R. Kettel
Lower Arrow Lake
Ainsworth Hot Springs
R. Kootenay
Balfour
Manning Provincial Park
Bradshaw
Keremeos
Cathedral Provincial Park
Osoyoos
Red Mountain
Castelgar
Nelson
F. Columbia
Christina Lake
Salmo
Bellingham
Oroville
Osoyoos Lake
Grand Forks
Rossland
Trail
WASHINGTON (U.S.A.)
©ULYSSES

season offers its own assortment of activities. In the early 1960s, a group of adventurers wanted this area to host the 1968 Winter Olympics and created Garibaldi Park for that purpose. Although their hopes for the Olympics did not come through, they did not give up on the idea of turning the valley into a huge ski resort. The population of Whistler increased tenfold in 20 years, and in the year 1993 alone over a million people enjoyed the outdoors here.

Whistler receives, on average, nearly 1000cm of snow each year, and the temperature hovers around -5°C during the winter months. For details about the host of activities available here, refer to the "Outdoor Activities" section (see p 210).

Whistler hosts all sorts of events throughout the year, including a men's World Cup downhill competition, World Cup acrobatic skiing, gay skiers' week and a jazz festival.

Take the time to walk through the hotel village at the foot of the mountains and soak up the festive, relaxed atmosphere. Everything has its price here, and enjoying yourself can be quite expensive.

Outside of the little village, at the edge of the Whistler area, lies Function Junction, a small-scale industrial centre.

Pemberton

The pretty little town of Pemberton is nestled in a hollow in impressive Mount Currie. This little farming area has rapidly gained a serious reputation among outdoor enthusiasts. There is an infinite number of hiking trails around the town which lead to small mountain lakes and spectacular glaciers. If you have a vehicle with sufficient ground clearance, you can also venture onto B.C. Forest Service roads. Rough campsites have been set up next to the road, and there's access to lovely little fishing spots with an abundance of trout.

In the winter, snowmobilers head to the **Pemberton Ice Cap ★★★** (see "Outdoor Activities", p 217).

Lillooet

During the Gold Rush, Lillooet was the most important place in British Columbia, considered Mile 0 of the Gold Rush Trail to Caribou Country. Miners and tradespeople came to this wild territory and took this dangerous route with the sole objective of making their fortune. Now Lillooet is a peaceful community of 2,000 inhabitants and is mostly known its natural beauty. In the summer, people come for the fishing and the camping. The dry, warm climate attracts tourists from neighbouring regions who are sometimes exasperated by the rain, even in the summer. You can reach Lillooet by Duffey Lake Road (Hwy. 99), past Whistler and Pemberton.

The tourist office in the town museum, beside the totem poles, can provide you with information on the best fishing spots and how to get to magnificent **Seton Lake★★★**. It is impossible to miss if you're coming from the north.

From Lillooet you can travel north on Hwy. 12 to the intersection with the Trans-Canada, which you can take south a few kilometres to Cache Creek and the road to Ashcroft (see p 190); or you can take Hwy. 12 south to Lytton.

Lytton

Lytton, the rafting centre of the province, marks the point at which the Thompson flows into the Fraser. Here again, the scenery is breathtaking. The valleys are desert-like, with low, dense vegetation. Those interested in running the rapids can rely solely on paddles or opt for motorized canoes.

Yale

Three major historical events contributed to the development of Yale: the growth of the fur trade, the gold rush and the construction of the railway. The town also marks the beginning of the Fraser Canyon, so buckle your seatbelts and keep your eyes wide open.

The **Alexandria Bridge** spans the Fraser at a striking point along the river that is only accessible by foot. The bridge is no longer part of the road system, but you can enjoy some splendid views of the Fraser from its promenade. A sign alongside the Trans-Canada Highway shows the way.

Hell's Gate ★ (*$10; ☎604-867-9277*) owes its name to Simon Fraser, the first European to navigate this river. For a while, even the salmon had trouble making their way through this gorge, which had narrowed as a result of major landslides. The current was so strong that the fish couldn't swim upriver to spawn. To solve the problem, a pass was cleared. A cablecar will take you down to the water's edge, 152m below.

Hope

Hope, located at the confluence of the Coquihalla, Fraser and Nicolum Rivers, marks the gateway to the Fraser Canyon. The Hudson's Bay Company established a fur-trading post named Fort Hope on this site in 1848; 10 years later, prospectors lured by the discovery of gold would stock up on supplies here.

The **Kettle Valley Railway** left a significant mark on the Hope region. Five tunnels known as the **Othello Tunnels** were bored through walls of granite so that trains could cross the Coquihalla canyon. Like other sections of this railroad, fallen debris and avalanches got the better of the tracks.

A visit to this magnificent linear park will give you an appreciation for the genius of those who built the railway and a chance to admire the majestic landscape looming up in front of it. Hollywood even picked this spot as a setting for the films *First Blood* and *Shoot to Kill*.

Take Wallace Street from downtown Hope, turn right on Sixth Ave., then left on Kawkawa Lake Road; after crossing a bridge and a set of railroad tracks, turn right on Othello Road. The entrance to the parking lot will be on your right. Don't forget to bring a camera.

A local chainsaw sculptor creates impressive pieces that delight visitors and residents alike. It all started when sculptor Pete Ryan transformed the trunk of a large tree in Memorial Park into an eagle with a salmon in its claws. Ever since, a number of his works, covering a variety of themes, have come to adorn downtown Hope.

If you'd like to take in a bird's-eye view of the region, go to the Hope airport and take a ride in a glider (see "Outdoor Activities", p 210).

From Hope travellers have several options. One is to hop on the Trans-Canada west and drive directly to Vancouver (150km). A more leisurely route, Hwy. 7 west, leads to Harrison Hot Springs and Mission, described below. Finally, travellers can push east through Manning Provincial Park (see p 193) to Princeton and Tour D (see p 193), in the beautiful Okanagan Valley, via Hwy. 3 east.

★

Harrison Hot Springs

The Harrison Hot Springs are located at the southern end of Harrison Lake. The Coast Salish First Nation used to come to here to soak in the warm mineral water, which supposedly has curative powers. Gold prospectors discovered the springs in 1858, when a storm on Lake Harrison forced them to return to shore and they happened to step into the warm water. The lake is surrounded by successive mountains peaks that stand out against the sky, making for a spectacular setting.

The indoor **Harrison Hot Springs Public Pool ★** (*$8.50; May to Nov, every day 8am to 9pm; Dec to Apr, Sun to Thu 8am to 9pm, Fri and Sat 8am to 10pm; at the intersection of Hot Springs Rd. and Lilloet Ave., ☎604-796-2244*) offers access to the springs. In addition to running the public pool, the Harrison Hotel has acquired rights to the springs. Every year in September and October, sandcastle enthusiasts flock to the beaches on Harrison Lake, with impressive results. The road, which runs alongside the lake, leads to Sasquatch Provincial Park (see p 208).

Mission *Xa:ytem* Long House Interpretive Centre (*3km east of Mission; donations welcomed, ☎820-9725*). This First Nations archaeological site was discovered in 1990. *Xa:ytem* (pronounced *HAY-tum*) is an Aboriginal word designating a boulder on a plateau on the Fraser River. According to geologists, the rock was deposited there by shifting glaciers. The Sto:lo First Nation, who have inhabited this region for more than 4,000 years, explain the boulder's presence by saying that it is what became of three chiefs who had committed a sin. Hundreds of relics have been found in this area, including tools and weapons made of stone. These articles are displayed in the centre, which has Sto:lo guides.

From Mission, take the bridge across the Fraser to Abotsford, then get on the Trans-Canada (Hwy. 1) to Langley.

Fort Langley

Fort Langley National Historic Site ★ (*$5; every day 10am to 5pm; Exit 66 North of the Trans-Canada, towards Fort Langley, at the intersection of Mavis and Royal Sts.; ☎888-4424*). Fort Langley was erected in 1827, 4km downriver from its present location, on the south bank of the Fraser. It was moved in 1839, only to be ravaged by fire the following year. The Hudson's Bay Company used the fort to store furs that were to be shipped out to Europe.

On November 19, 1858, British Columbia's status was officially proclaimed here, marking the end of the Hudson's Bay Company's control over the territory. Of the 16 buildings that once stood inside the palisade, only the warehouse remains. Erected around 1840, it is the oldest European-style structure on the west side of the Rockies. Six other buildings, as well as the palisade itself, have been reconstructed in order to acquaint the public with that era.

Tour C: The Thompson River as far as Revelstoke

Ashcroft

Ashcroft lies a few kilometres east of Hwy. 1. In 1860, gold prospectors heading north set out from here. You can go back to the Trans-Canada 1 East and make your way to Kamloops, passing through Cache Creek on the way in order to skirt Kamloops Lake and see the ginseng fields (see below). We recommend taking Hwy. 97C to Logan Lake and the Copper Valley mine. As you make your way through a magnificent desert valley, you'll see the Sundance Guest Ranch (see p 222 for details on staying there), which looks out over the Thompson River. Ever since the 1950s, this ranch has been sending visitors off on horseback rides across thousands of hectares of fields. Like most ranches in the region, it was once the home of stockbreeders.

Copper Valley ★★ (*May to Sep Mon to Fri 9:30am and 12:30pm, Sat and Sun 9:30am, 12:30pm and 3:30pm; tours last 2hrs 30min;* ☎*250-523-2443*). Copper Valley is one of the largest open-cut copper mines in the world. The industrial machinery and the equipment used to transport the ore are completely outsized. Though you can't tour the mine, you'll notice its lunar landscape from the highway.

Continue driving east. When you reach the Coquihalla Highway (5), head for Kamloops.

Kamloops

Kamloops (pop. 68,500), the capital of inland British Columbia, is a major stopover point. The local economy is driven chiefly by the forestry and tourism industries, with mining and stockbreeding playing subsidiary roles.

The Kamloops area offers many interesting vacation opportunities. The stunning natural surroundings and favourable climate cater to outdoor enthusiasts. Stroll about the city; it has great restaurants, nightclubs, movie theatres, tourist centres with information on golf, skiing, fishing and many other seasonal outdoor activities.

Culture also plays an important role in Kamloops. The **Kamloops Symphony Orchestra**, the **Western Canada Theatre Company** and the **Kamloops Museum and Art Gallery** are all very active.

West of Kamloops, ginseng crops lie hidden in fields beneath big pieces of black cloth. Large farms produce this root, which is highly coveted by Asians for the health benefits it is supposed to procure. The variety grown here, known as American ginseng, was discovered in eastern Canada several hundred years ago by Aboriginal people, who made potions with it. At the **Sunmore Company** (*925 McGill Place,* ☎*250-374-3017*), you can drop in and learn about ginseng farming in North America and how local methods differ from those employed in Asia.

Another activity that underlines the importance of the rivers in British Columbia is a cruise aboard the *Wanda-Sue*, which sails along the Thompson River through bare mountains. Aboriginals, trappers, gold prospectors, lumberjacks and railway workers all travelled by boat before the railway lines and roads were laid here. The ***Wanda-Sue*** ★ sets out from the Old Kamloops Yacht Club (*$11.50; Apr to Sep; the trip lasts two hours; 1140 River St., near Tenth Ave.,* ☎*250-374-7447*).

Leave Kamloops and head towards Revelstoke on the Trans-Canada, which runs alongside the water, beaches, mountains and golf courses. The towns of Sorrento and Salmon Arm look out onto vast Shuswap Lake, which is popular with water-sports fans, due to the pleasant temperature of its waters. One way of exploring the lake is to rent a houseboat from **Waterway Houseboat Vacations** (*reservations required; 9am to 5pm; Sicamous,* ☎*250-836-2505 or 800-663-4022,* ⇄*250-836-4848*). The boats are well equipped and as comfortable as hotel rooms.

Seewepeme Museum & Heritage Park (*$6; Jun to Aug Mon to Fri 8:30am to 8pm. Sep to May Mon to Fri 8:30am to 4:30pm; 335 Yellowhead Hwy.,* ☎*828-9801*, ⇄372-1127, museum@secwepemc.org) is located on the Kamloops Aboriginal reserve east of town (take the Jasper exit on the Trans-Canada Hwy.).

This museum gives you an opportunity to discover the culture of the Shuswaps, Kamloops's Aboriginal people. There is also an interesting museum, and an exhibit has been set up outside on a 4.8ha area along the Thompson River. It allows visitors to understand this people's way of life. Entire villages have been recreated, and the Sushwaps' hunting, fishing and agricultural methods are presented. Costumed animators recreate the Aboriginal spirit of the region.

The Trans-Canada continues its route across valleys and mountains; gorges become narrower and narrower and the heart of the Rockies appears on the horizon. The vegetation is much more luxuriant here, with small blue-grey shrubs giving way to mighty trees.

★★ Revelstoke

The history of Revelstoke is closely linked to the construction of the transcontinental railway. Many Italians came here to apply their expertise in building tunnels. To this day, the town's 9,000 residents rely mainly on the railroad for their income. Tourism and the production of electricity also play important roles in the economy of this magnificent town.

Revelstoke is a century-old town that has managed to retain its charm. Numerous Queen Anne, Victorian, Art Deco and neoclassical buildings here bear witness to days gone by. Pick up a copy of the **Heritage Walking & Driving Tour** ★ at the Revelstoke Museum (see below) or at the **Travel InfoCentre** (*204 Campbell Ave.,* ☎*250-837-5345*).

The **Revelstoke Railway Museum** ★ (*$7; Jul and Aug every day 9am to 8pm; Dec to Mar by appt.; call ahead for spring and autumn hours; 719 Track St.,* ☎*250-837-6060*) focuses on the construction of the railway across the Rockies and the history of Revelstoke. The exhibit features old objects, photos from the local archives and most importantly a 1940s locomotive and a company director's personal railway car, built in 1929.

At the **Revelstoke Dam** ★ (*free admission; May to Jun 9am to 5pm; Jun to Sep 8am to 8pm; Sep and Oct 9am to 5pm; closed Nov to May although group visits are permitted during the low season; take Hwy. 23 North,* ☎*250-837-6211*), you can learn about the production of hydroelectricity and visit a number of rooms, as well as the dam itself, an impressive concrete structure.

Hiking enthusiasts will be thrilled by all the outdoor excursions to be enjoyed in this area (p 212).

Revelstoke is a crossroads between the Rockies and the Kootenays, to the south. If you plan on continuing east to Alberta, stay on the Trans-Canada to Golden, Field and Lake Louise (see The Rocky Mountains, p 303). We recommend driving down into the Kootenays, which are lesser known than the Rockies, but equally fascinating. Before heading south, however, continue until you reach **Rogers Pass** ★★, named after the engineer who discovered it in 1881. This valley was originally supposed to serve as a passage between the east and the west, but after a number of catastrophes, during which avalanches claimed the lives of hundreds of people, the Canadian Pacific railway company decided to build a tunnel instead. At the **Rogers Pass Centre** ★ (☎*250-814-5233*), located an hour from Revelstoke in Glacier National Park, visitors can learn about the epic history of the railway. A trail that runs along the former tracks will take you past the ruins of a railway station destroyed in an avalanche.

Back in Revelstoke, cross the town bridge and head toward Shelter Bay on Hwy. 23 South in order to take the free ferry (every day 5pm to 12:30am) and continue southward to Nakusp (p 203). Get your camera ready during the trip across Upper Arrow Lake (25min), because you're in for some splendid views of the Kootenays.

Tour D: Okanagan-Similkameen

This tour starts off in Hope. See p 189.

All sorts of natural treasures await discovery in this part of British Columbia. With its stretches of water and blanket of fruit trees, the Okanagan Valley, which runs north-south, is one of the most beautiful areas in the province. Okanagan wines have won a number of prizes; the orchards feed a good portion of the country, and the lakes and mountains are a dream come true for sporty types. The climate is conducive to a wide variety of activities: the winters, mild in town and snowy in the mountains, can be enjoyed by all. In the spring, the fruit trees are in bloom, while in summer and fall, a day of fruit-picking is often followed by a dip in one of the many lakes.

Head east on Hwy. 3 to Princeton.

Located 45min from Hope, **Manning Provincial Park ★★** attracts hundreds of visitors each season. Twice the size of Cathedral Park, it covers 60,000ha of wilderness, where you'll find all sorts of treasures (see Parks and Beaches, p 209, and Hiking, p 213).

Princeton

Princeton is situated not far from the Cascade Mountains, where the Tulameen and Similkameen Rivers converge. Founded in 1883 by a cowboy who discovered gold, this **Granite City** has experienced its share of Gold Rush fever. The 2,000 miners and prospectors left behind some traces from those bygone days, some of which are still around today. Although there's no gold you will find salloons and old-style shops. With its two rivers, Princeton is a favourable spot for sports such as **kayaking**, **canoeing** and **rafting**. Its many lakes are visited by a wide variety of birds. Cycling is also a pleasant way of discovering the surrounding area and performing some spectacular feats at nearby **Kettle Valley**.

American researchers come to the **Princeton Museum and Archives ★** (*Jul and Aug, every day 9am to 6pm; Sep to Jun, Mon to Fri 1pm to 5pm; Margaret Stoneberg, curator, ☎295-7588, home ☎295-3362*) to study its impressive collection of fossils. You'll get caught up in curator Margaret Stoneberg's enthusiasm as she tells you about the pieces and how they bear witness to the region's history. Due to underfunding, the fossils pile up without being properly displayed, but it is nevertheless amazing to see how much the museum holds.

The **Maverick Cattle Drives Ltd.** (*$125, reservations required; lunch, morning and afternoon outings, cattle driving; ☎250-295-6243 or 295-3753*) welcomes visitors who want to experience life on a ranch. You'll find yourself on the back of a horse, riding in the warm summer breeze across fields of wheat, taking in the view of the nearby glaciers. This wonderful experience also involves carrying out a number of tasks on the ranch.

At the end of the day, all the cowboys get together at the saloon.

As you continue eastward on Hwy. 3, you will be leaving the vast Okanagan-Similkameen region and heading into the southwestern part of the province, back to the confluence of the Fraser and Coquihalla Rivers.

Keremeos

Keremeos is the **kingdom of fruit**. This is why this small town, abundantly stocked with mini-markets is nicknamed the "fruit-stand capital of the world." All along the road, shops compete for the freshest fruit, the best display of farm products and to have the best decor. The apple pyramids are delightful, as are the gigantic ones made with pumkins around Hallowe'en.

In Keremeos, history is recounted at the **Grist Mill ★** (*May to Oct; R.R. 1, Upper Bench Rd., ☎250-499-2888*), founded in 1877 to produce flour for local Aboriginal people, cowboys and miners. The water mill, equipment and original buildings have been restored and are now part of British Columbia's heritage.

Cathedral Provincial Park ★★ covers 33,000ha of mountains, lakes, valleys, wildlife and flowers. It is criss-crossed by trails that everyone can enjoy, since most cover fairly level terrain and are suitable for a variety of fitness levels. Furthermore, almost all of the bears in this region were driven off by the cowboys decades ago. A mountaintop inn accommodates visitors wishing to stay in the park (see "Parks and Beaches", p 210, and "Hiking", p 213).

At the park exit, get back on Hwy. 3, which will take you to Osoyoos.

Osoyoos

Osoyoos lies at the bottom of the valley, flanked on one side by Osoyoos Lake and on the other by verdant slopes decked with vineyards and orchards. It is located a few kilometres from the U.S. border, in an arid climate more reminiscent of an American desert, or even southern Italy, than a Canadian town. The main attraction here is the exceptionally warm lake, where you can enjoy a variety of water sports during summer.

On your way into town on Hwy. 3 from the east, take a look at **Spotted Lake ★**. A natural phenomenon causes white rings to form on the surface of this lake, whose waters contain high levels of mineral salts. The lake is located on private property, so you can only look at it from the road.

Osoyoos's main street is crowded with lousy motels, which detract from the beauty of the setting. The public parks on the west side are worth visiting, however, especially at the end of the day when the sun lights up the valley.

A tiny desert north of Osoyoos, the **Vest Pocket Desert ★★★**, is an amazing sight in this part of Canada. In fact it's the only one in the country. The unique wildlife and vegetation here bear witness to nature's endless store of surprises.

Without irrigation, this valley would still be a desert and the orchards and vineyards would not have been able to thrive and bear fruit each year; let yourself be carried away across this colourful sea of ripe fruit.

This mini-desert is part of the same desert that begins in Baja California, Mexico and the state of Chihuahua before crossing the western United States.

In 1999, the **Desert Centre** (*$4; 3km north of Osoyoos, ☎495-2470, mail@desert.org*) opened its doors to heighten awareness about the fragility of this particular ecosystem. Footbridges cross a 2km trail along the rattlesnake's habitat. The explanations of the biologist-guide will teach you about the complexity of life in this world without water. It is fascinating to learn how desert animals and vegetation can survive here.

★★★ The Wine Route

How can you visit the Okanagan Valley without a tour of the wine route? The Okanagan-Similkameen region offers a memorable opportunity to discover a completely original wine route. The landscape in particular is unique; the hills and valleys aren't the colour and shape that you would expect when touring vineyards. Vines flourish in this climate and everything possible has been done to make the most of the region, and the results of these efforts have been fruitful.

Two aspects of wine-producing distinguish the region. The newer one, which is being developped in the Similkameen Valley, is associated with farm cultivation and expansion of the fertile soil. The other, more traditional aspect in the large Okanagan Valley is related to a proud heritage of wine growing since the 1800s. This valley has similar characteristics to German wine-producing areas that are renowned for the quality of their wines. The presence of three lakes (Skaha to the south, Kalamalka to the north, and Okanagan in between) creates a climate that is perfectly suited to producing great wines.

British Columbia puts considerable effort into promoting the quality of its wines. It was toward the end of the 1970s when a decision was made to exploit the wine in the area. Through the perseverance of the government and wine growers, the **Chardonnay**, **Pinot Noir**, **Merlot** and **Gewurztraminer**, to name a few, all established undeniable reputations. In 1990, the need was felt to create quality standards, and, as a result, the Vintners Quality Alliance started putting its mark on bottles, "**VQA,**" to certify high-quality wine from British Columbia.

Of course, festivals are organized throughout the warm months. The **Annual Spring Okanagan Wine Festival** takes place during the first five days in May. There are scores of outings, picnics, meals well doused in the fruit of the vine, and dances, not to mention educational wine-tasting sessions for beginners.

The other big wine event is the **Annual Fall Okanagan Wine Festival**, which takes place during the first half of October every year. Some 28 estates participate in it and, as well as sampling all sorts of red and white wines, you can try other delicacies, such as roast pigeon, baked salmon and chocolate specialties, all presented and prepared with great care.
Advance reservations are recommended. **Wine Festival Passports** are issued and holders are eligible for a prize draw. For information call ☎***(800) 972-5151***.

The clearly indicated wine route offers pleasant trips from estate to estate among farms and orchards, revealing first-class views of Okanagan Lake at every turn.

This mouth-watering trail of vineyard discovery goes from Osoyoos to Vernon; each vies to offer the best reception and most elegant presentation to attract people. Wines are available to sample. Medals, international awards and anything attesting to a wine's quality cover the walls of shops. Even if it costs five dollars to try a few drops of Ice Wine, a specialty of the region made from grapes that are picked frozen at the beginning of winter, curious wine-lovers are happy to oblige.

The list of estates and shops is long and interesting. Over the short distance of 200km, there are more than 25 establishments, with new ones opening to the public. Some are active throughout the year, but a few are

Vineyards Open to the Public

The letters and numbers in the following vineyard addresses are a local reference system – if you ask for directions, area residents will understand "RR 1, S58, C10," for example. In any case the wine route is well charted and every winery is clearly marked by a sign on the main road. Telephone before your tour for exact directions and to be sure that the vineyards of interest to you are open.

Oliver

Tinhorn Creek Vineyard: RR 1, S58, C10 (Road 7), H0H 1T0, ☎498-3743
Vincor International: Box 1650, Hwy. 97, V0H 1T0, ☎498-4981
Gehringer Brothers Estate Winery: RR 1, S23, C4, (Road 8), V0H 1T0, ☎498-3537
Domaine Combret: P.O.Box 1170, V0H 1T0, ☎498-8878
Gersighel Wineberg: RR 1, S40, C20, (29690 Hwy. 97), V0H 1T0
Okanagan Vineyards Winery: Route 11, RR 1, S24, C5, V0H 1T0, ☎(604) 498-6663

Okanagan Falls

Blue Mountain Vineyards & Cellars: RR 1, S3, C4, (Allendale Road), V0H 1R0, ☎497-8244
Hawthorn Mountain Vineyards (former Lecomte Estate Winery): Box 480, Green Lake Road, ☎497-8267
Wild Goose Vineyards & Winery: RR 1, S3, C11, Sun Valley Way, V0H 1R0, ☎497-8919

Penticton

Poplar Grove: 1060 Poplar Grove Rd., V2A 6J6, ☎492-2352
Hillside Cellars: 1350 Naramata Rd., V2A 6J6, ☎493-4424

Naramata

Kettle Valley Winery: 2988 Hayman Rd., V0H 1N0, ☎496-5898
Lake Breeze Vineyards: Sammet Rd., Box 9, V0H 1N0, ☎496-5659
Lang Vineyards: RR 1, S11, C55, 2493 Gammon Road, V0H 1N0, ☎496-5987

Summerland

Sumac Ridge Estate Winery: 17403 Hwy. 97, Box 307, V0H 1Z0, ☎494-0451
Scherzinger Vineyards: 7311 Fiske Rd., V0H 1Z0, ☎494-8815

Peachland

Hainle Vineyards Estate Winery: 5355 Trepanier Bench Rd., RR 2, S27A, C6, V0H 1X0, ☎ 767-2525 or 1-800-767-3109

Kelowna

Calona Vineyards: 11 Richter St., V1Y 2K6, ☎ 762-9144 or 800-663-5086
House of Roses Vineyards: 2770 Garner Rd., RR 5, V1X 4K4, ☎ (604) 765-0802
Quails Gate Estate Winery: 3303 Boucherie Rd., V1Z 2H3, ☎ (604) 769-4451 or 800-420-WINE
Summerhill Estate Winery: 4870 Chute Lake Rd., V1Y 7R3, ☎ (604) 764-8000 or 800-667-3538
Cedarcreek Estate Winery: 5445 Lakeshore Rd., V1Y 7R3, ☎ (604) 764-8866

Vernon

Bella Vista Vineyards: 3111 Agnew Rd., V1T 5J8, ☎ 558-0770

Region's Best-Known Wines

White Wines

Auxerrois: Reminiscent of Alsatian wine, slightly fruity.
Bacchus: Another wine similar to Alsatian wine, but drier.
Chardonnay: Very popular. Neither too dry nor too sweet. Served as an aperitif or with meals.
Chasselas: This wine takes its inspiration from the Swiss Alps and has an aroma of apples and lemons.
Gewurztraminer: With a slightly spicy aftertaste, this wine, as its homonym in Alsatian indicates, is served with fish and seafood.
Reisling: The climate is favourable to the cultivation of this grape which is quite dry and has a flowery, honey-like aroma.
Pinot Blanc: This white wine has become famous in British Columbia. It's taste, which is both dry and fruity, and its rich body make it worthy of its ancestor born in France in the 14th century.

Red Wines

Cabernet Sauvignon: Classified in the Bordeaux category, it has good body and is fragrant.
Chancellor: A fruity wine whose flavour has hints of strawberries and cherries.
Merlot: Another wine in the Bordeaux family – sweet, with a rich berry flavour.
Pinot Noir: A spicy, smooth wine with a plum and black-cherry flavour.

open to visitors only during the tourist season. Call ahead before planning a wine-tasting trip.

For more information on the wine route, touring the vineyards and the wine festivals, contact the **B.C. Wine Information Centre** (*888 Westminster Ave., Penticton, ☎250-490-2006 or 800-663-5052*) or the Okanagan-Similkameen Tourism Association.

The wine route runs through the vast Okanagan region. North of Osoyoos and south of Oliver, you'll come across the **Domaine Combret ★** (*32057-131st Rd. 13, Oliver, ☎250-498-8878, ≠498-8879*). In 1995, the *Office International de la Vigne et du Vin*, based in Burgundy, France, awarded this French-owned vineyard the highest international distinction for its Chardonnay. Its Reisling also won a prize in 1995. You must call beforehand for a tour of the premises, as the wine growers spend a good part of the day outside among the vines during the grape-picking season. Originally from the south of France, the Combrets come from a long line of vinters. Robert Combret first visited the Okanagan Valley in the 1950s. He returned in the early 1990s. His son Olivier runs the family business now. Stop by and enjoy a sample some of his wine.

Take Hwy. 97 toward Penticton. Alternatively, you can continue east on Hwy. 3 to Grand Forks *(see p 206).*

Kaleden

Tucked away atop a mountain near **Kaleden** is the **Dominion Radio Astrophysical Observatory ★** (*Jul and Aug, Sun 2pm to 5pm, ☎250-493-7505*), run by the Canadian Research Council. If you're looking for a star, this place can help you find it.

Penticton

Penticton lies between Okanagan Lake, to the north, and Skaha Lake, to the south. The town has nearly 30,000 inhabitants and boasts a dry, temperate climate. Tourism is the mainspring of Penticton's economy. The area's First Nations named the site *Pen-tak-tin*, meaning "the place where you stay forever." A beach lined with trees and a pedestrian walkway run along the north end of town. The dry landscape, outlined by the curves of the sandy shoreline, contrasts with the vineyards and orchards. People come to Penticton for the outdoor activities, fine dining and local *joie de vivre*.

Take Main Street to Lakeshore Drive, turn left and stop in front of the **SS Sicamous** (*$4; summer, every day 9am to 9pm; winter, Mon to Fri 7am to 3pm*), a survivor of a bygone era. This paddle-boat was once the principal means of transportation on Okanagan Lake. Built in Ontario in 1914 and assembled here, it was in service for over 20 years before being hauled up onto the beach.

Penticton hosts a major sporting event, the **World Cup Ironman Triathlon**, a swimming, cycling and running race. Athletes from all over the world take part in the Ironman, and many of them live in Penticton while awaiting the next competition. They train here, and it is not uncommon to see them working in the fields. The triathlon takes place in August, at the beginning of the fruit-picking season. For further information contact the **Ironman Office** (*☎250-490-8787*) or see Mike Barrett, the owner of the **Hog's Breath Coffee Co.** (*202 Main St., ☎493-7800*), who has competed in numerous triathlons. Athletes often congregate at this café.

A visit to an orchard is a must, especially in the heart of summer, during the fruit-picking season. Not only is the fruit plentiful, but more

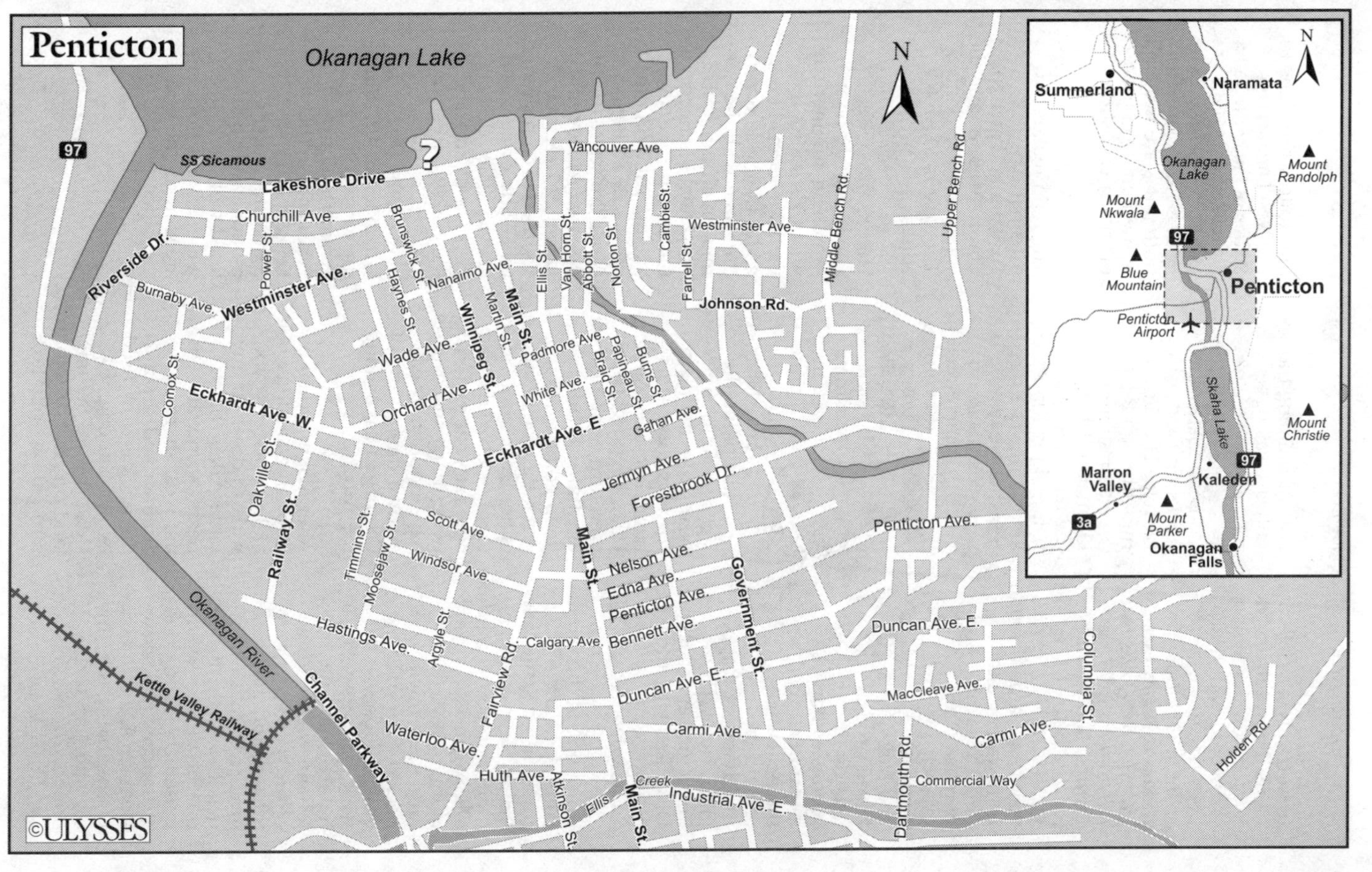

Penticton
Okanagan Lake
97
SS Sicamous
Lakeshore Drive
Churchill Ave.
Riverside Dr.
Burnaby Ave.
Westminster Ave.
Power St.
Brunswick St.
Haynes St.
Nanaimo Ave.
Wade Ave.
Winnipeg St.
Martin St.
Main St.
Comox St.
Eckhardt Ave. W.
Orchard Ave.
Padmore Ave.
White Ave.
Braid St.
Papineau St.
Burns St.
Gahan Ave.
Eckhardt Ave. E
Ellis St.
Van Horn St.
Abbott St.
Norton St.
Vancouver Ave.
CambieSt.
Farrell St.
Westminster Ave.
Johnson Rd.
Middle Bench Rd.
Upper Bench Rd.
Oakville St.
Railway St.
Jermyn Ave.
Forestbrook Dr.
Scott Ave.
Windsor Ave.
Timmins St.
Moosejaw St.
Argyle St.
Hastings Ave.
Calgary Ave.
Fairview Rd.
Nelson Ave.
Edna Ave.
Penticton Ave.
Bennett Ave.
Government St.
Penticton Ave.
Duncan Ave. E.
Duncan Ave. E.
MacCleave Ave.
Columbia St.
Carmi Ave.
Carmi Ave.
Holden Rd.
Commercial Way
Dartmouth Rd.
Waterloo Ave.
Huth Ave.
Atkinson St.
Ellis
Creek
Industrial Ave. E.
Main St.
Okanagan River
Channel Parkway
Kettle Valley Railway
©ULYSSES
N
Summerland
Naramata
Okanagan Lake
Mount Randolph
Mount Nkwala
97
Blue Mountain
Penticton
Penticton Airport
Skaha Lake
Mount Christie
97
Marron Valley
Kaleden
Mount Parker
3a
Okanagan Falls

importantly it's delicious. From July to late September, the region is covered with fruit trees bursting with scent and colour. The **Dickinson Family Farm** (*turn left onto Jones Flat Rd. from Hwy. 97 North, then right onto Bentley Rd. 19208, ☎250-494-0300*) invites visitors to stroll through its rows of fruit trees. You can purchase fruit (apples, pears, etc.) and fruit-based products on the premises. For a real treat, try the peach butter and the freshly pressed apple juice. Head out of Penticton on Lakeshore Drive and take the 97 North toward Summerland.

An outing in the mountains along the former route of the **Kettle Valley Railway ★★** offers another perspective of the Okanagan Valley. Laid at the turn of the century, these tracks connected Nelson, in the east, to Hope, in the west, thus providing a link between the hinterland, where tonnes of ore were being extracted, and the coast. Mother Nature was a major obstacle throughout the railway's short existence; fallen debris, avalanches and snowstorms made the tracks impossible to use, and the line was abandoned. The $20 million cost of building the railway was never recovered.

You can follow the tracks on foot or by bicycle. The railway runs through Penticton on either shore of Okanagan Lake, and the terrain is relatively flat, making for a pleasant outing. The directions, however, are not very clear. Start on Main Street, in downtown Penticton, and follow the signs for Naramata Road, then turn right onto MacMillan. At this point, the signs seem to disappear. Take the main road; as soon as its name becomes Chute Lake, keep right and then turn right again on Smethurst Road and keep going until you reach the end. You can either leave your car in town or drive the first 6km (at your own risk); pedestrians and cyclists have priority. You'll enjoy a direct view of Okanagan Lake along the way.

After 4.8km, you'll pass through a small tunnel. Make noise as you walk to drive off any rattlesnakes, black bears or cougars. On the west shore, in Summerland, a part of the track is now used by a steam engine. Head toward Summerland on Hwy. 97 North, turn left on Solly Road and follow the signs for the **West Summerland Station of the Kettle Valley Steam Railway** (*May to Oct; ☎250-494-8422, ≠494-8452*). Maps for both areas are available at the Penticton tourist office on Lakeshore Drive.

The train makes two trips per day, at 10:30am and at 1:30pm Thu to Mon, during the summer season only. The cost is $11 for adults.

Here is the perfect family activity on a scorching summer day when it's so hot that the lake seems like it could boil: ride down the canal with the current on an innertube. The canal connects Okanagan Lake and Skoaha Lake on the other side of Penticton. **Coyote Cruises** (*$10/inner tube and return transportation; 215 Riverside Dr., ☎492-2115*) rents inner tubes and organizes the activity. The "descent" lasts about 2hrs and is incredibly refreshing!

Stay on the 97 North, which leads through the towns of **Summerland** and **Peachland** on the way to **Kelowna**. This stretch of road runs along a mountainside, and is lined with orchards, wineries and stopping areas from one end to the other.

★ Kelowna

Kelowna, one of the most important towns in inland British Columbia, has a population of 90,000. Its economy is driven by fruit farming, wine-making and, as of more recently, a few light industries as well. Tourism is also important to Kelowna, and the town has a lot to offer its many visitors.

The beautiful sandy beaches that border Okanagan Lake draw more and more tourists every year. You can lounge under a beautiful summer sky, organize a family picnic, or simply admire the scenery.

Kelowna is the heart and mind of the Okanagan Valley. It was here that a French Oblate by the name of Father Charles Pandosy set up the first Catholic mission in the hinterland of British Columbia in 1859. He introduced apple and grape growing into the Okanagan Valley and was thus largely responsible for its becoming a major fruit-producing region.

The **Father Pandosy Mission** (*May to early Oct, every day; on Benvoulin Rd., at the corner of Casorso Rd., ☎250-860-8369*), which has been listed as a provincial historic site since 1983, includes a church and a number of farm buildings.

The statue of the monster **Ogopogo**, whose native name is Nha-a-itk, has drawn international media attention to Kelowna. Aboriginals were so dependent on Okanagan Lake and wanted to take such good care of it that they were afraid to anger Ogopogo, the lake god. He is said to look like a snake and some have even spotted him. Both Canadian and Japanese television programs have featured the subject on mystery shows.

Located on the shores of Okanagan Lake, Kelowna boasts several waterfront parks. One of these is **Knox Mountain Park**, where you'll find a magnificent viewing area. You might even catch a glimpse of Ogopogo. To get to the park, take Ellis Street north out of downtown.

Like Penticton, Kelowna is located along the **Kettle Valley Railway**; again, though, you have to know where you're going, since there are no signs to follow between the downtown area and the top of the valley. After strolling along Bernard Street and the beaches on Okanagan Lake for a little while, get back in your car and take South Pandosy Street, turn left (eastward) on KLO Road, which becomes McCulloch, and then right on June Springs Road. Free parking is available at the end of the road.

It takes about 20min to reach the first metal bridge, which stretches across the **Myra Canyon ★★**. If you enjoy walking, you'll love this excursion. The local **Chamber of Commerce** (*544 Harvey Ave., ☎861-1515*) or the **Okanagan-Similkameen Tourism Association** (*1332 Water St., ☎860-5999*) can help you plan outings that take several days. Cyclists can pedal about to their heart's content; the more adventurous can spend a day riding to Penticton.

Almost all the wine produced in British Columbia comes from the Okanagan region (see The Wine Route, p 195). Over the past few years, local wines have won a number of international prizes. There are three vineyards along Lakeshore Road, south of Kelowna, including the **Cedar Creek Winery** (*5445 Lakeshore Rd., ☎250-764-8866, ⇄250-764-2603*), which, like its competitors in the region, produces much more white wine than red. It is located on a pretty hill surrounded by vines and looking out onto Okanagan Lake. A free tour of the premises will give you a chance to sample some of the wines; the chardonnay is particularly noteworthy. You can also purchase a few bottles while you're there.

As far as culture is concerned, the visual arts are of great importance in Kelowna as can be seen by the large number of galleries.

The **Art Gallery** (☎ *762-4544*) presents local artists and encourages work by students in the region, but also plays host to international exhibitions. The **Geert Maas Sculpture Gardens and Gallery** (☎*860-2533*) exhibits bronze sculptures that are worth the trip. Maas is an artist and sculptor who has provided works to collectors from 20 countries. He meets people by appointment, but the gallery is open from May to October. And if you're really a sculpture enthusiast, the **Bronze Rooster Gallery** (☎*868-2533*) has many of these, as well as paintings by Canadian artists.

The tour wouldn't be complete without a stop at the **Turtle Island Gallery** (☎ *717-8235*), which has an impressive collection of works by local First Nations artists. Music and theatre also share in the prestige: **The Sunshine Theatre** (☎ *763-4025*), Kelowna's community theatre, regularly presents interesting plays and the **Okanagan Symphony Orchestra** (☎ *763-7544*) offers a complete and highly diverse season of programming every year.

Vernon

Get back on the 97 North and continue on to Vernon, which is set amidst three lakes. The town started out modestly in the 1860s, when Cornelius O'Keefe established a ranch here. The northern part of Vernon is an important stockbreeding area. Stop by the **Historic O'Keefe Ranch** (*every day May to Oct; 12km north of Vernon on Hwy. 97,* ☎*250-542-7868*), where you'll find the original ranch house, wooden church and ranching equipment. Forestry and agriculture play greater economic roles here than in Kelowna and Penticton, where tourism is more important.

Hwy. 97 North intersects the Trans-Canada at Monte Creek, east of Kamloops (see Tour C, p 191). You can also reach the 1 from the 97A, which leads to Sicamous, west of Revelstoke (see Tour C, p 192). Otherwise, backtrack to Kelowna and take Hwy. 97C to Merritt.

Merritt

Merritt lies in a region with over 150 lakes, surrounded by mountains and pastures where tens of thousands of heads of cattle can be seen grazing. If you'd like to step back in time to the days when cowboys met here to talk and live it up, head downtown to the **Coldwater Hotel**, built in 1908, or over to the **Quilchena Hotel**, located 23km northeast of Merritt on the 5A.

From Merritt, either take Hwy. 5 either north to Kamploops (see Tour C, p 191) or south to Princeton (see p 193). Another option is to take Hwy. 8 northwest to Spences Bridge, where you can get on the Trans-Canada (Hwy. 1) south to Lytton (see Tour B, p 188).

Tour E: Kootenay Country

This tour can be picked up from Revelstoke (see Tour C, p 192), or from Osoyoos (see Tour D, p 194), in which case its order must be reversed.

Located off the beaten tourist track, this region is a gold mine for visitors with a taste for mountains, lakes, history and chance encounters. Once again, the landscape is one of the major attractions; this is British Columbia, after all! Because this region is under-appreciated, it remains virtually unspoiled, making it that much more interesting to explore.

Located in the southeast part of the province, the Kootenays are a series of mountains (the Rockies, the

Purcells, the Selkirks and the Monashees) stretching from the north to the south. The great Columbia River runs through this region, creating the vast body of water known as Arrow Lake on its way. Natural resources such as forests and mines have played a major role in the region's development. A number of towns bear witness to the different stages in the Kootenays' history.

Nakusp

Before setting off across the Kootenays, you might want to stop at Nakusp's **Leland Hotel** (*Fourth Ave.*), located on the shores of Arrow Lake. You can sit on the terrace and have a bite to eat while taking in the scenery. During the mining boom, hundreds of prospectors flooded into Nakusp and other places like it throughout these mountains.

However, if these sulphurous springs are your cup of tea, then you will be interested to know that there are two of them on the road that heads north to the pier of the Galeano Bay ferry. You can also camp at these two places for about $20.

The **Nakusp Hot Springs** (*$5.50; 12km north of Nakusp, ☎265-4528, ⇌265-3788, www.nakusp.com*) are nestled in the rolling valley behind Nakusp, quite a distance from Upper Aroow Lake. The old, round building adds a certain charm to the facility, which is somewhat overridden with tourists.

The **Halcyon Hot Springs** (*$6; 32km north of Nakusp, ☎265-3554 or 888-689-4699, ⇌265-3887, www.halcyon-hotsprings.com*) directly face Upper Arrow Lake and offer an endless view of the snow-capped peaks on the opposite shore. Relax while admiring the incredible panorama.

New Denver

New Denver was the gateway to silver country at the turn of the century, when there was an abundant supply of the metal in this region. The history of that era is presented at the **Silvery Slocan Museum** (*Jul to Sep, every day 10am to 4pm; at the corner of Sixth St. and Marine Dr., ☎250-358-2201*). When Canada declared war on Japan during the Second World War, Japanese residents of British Columbia were interned in camps in a number of towns in this region, including New Denver and Sandon. To learn more about their experience, stop in at the **Nikkei Internment Memorial Centre** (*$4; May to Oct, every day 9:30am to 5pm; by appt. during winter; 306 Josephine St., ☎250-358-7288*).

Take Hwy. 31A in the direction of Kaslo, and stop at Sandon, the former capital of Canada's silver mines.

★★ Sandon

At the turn of the century, 5,000 people lived and worked in Sandon. By 1930, the price of silver had dropped and the mine had been exhausted, prompting an exodus from the town. During World War II, Sandon became an internment centre for Japanese who had been living on the coast. Shortly after the war, it became a ghost town once again, and a number of buildings were destroyed by fire and floods. Today, visitors can admire what remains of a number of old buildings, as well as the first hydroelectric power plant constructed in the Canadian West, which still produces electricity.

A 12km road, negotiable with an all-purpose vehicle, leads from Sandon to the Idaho Lookout, where you can take in a view of the Kokanee and Valhalla glaciers.

Get back on Hwy. 31A and continue on to Kaslo.

Kaslo

Kaslo was built on the hills on the west shore of Kootenay Lake during the heyday of silver mining. A walk along the waterfront and a visit to the town hall will give you a glimpse of how beautiful the setting is. At the beginning of the century, people used to come here by paddle-boat. For nearly 60 years, up until 1957, the *SS Moyie* shuttled passengers back and forth across Kootenay Lake for Canadian Pacific. The boat has since been transformed into a museum.

At **Ainsworth Hot Springs ★** (*$6; swimsuit and towel rentals available; ☎229-4212*), which is located in an enchanting setting along the shore to the south, bathers can alternate between very cold and very warm water. The swimming pool overlooks Kootenay Lake and the valley which is brilliant at sunset. The U-shaped cave studded with stalactites, the humidity and the almost total absence of light will transport you to another world. The temperature rises as you near the springs at the back of the cave, reaching as high as 40°C.

Take Hwy. 31 south. At Balfour, take Hwy. 3A to Nelson.

★★ Nelson

Make sure to park your car as soon as possible and explore this magnificent town on foot. Located at the southern end of the West Arm of Kootenay Lake, Nelson lies on the west flank of the Selkirk Mountains. In 1887, during the silver boom, miners set up camp here, working together to build hotels, homes and public facilities. Numerous buildings now bear witness to the town's prosperous past. Nelson has managed to continue its economic growth today, thanks to light industry, tourism and the civil service.

The Travel InfoCentre distributes two small pamphlets that will guide you through over 350 historic buildings. The town's elegant architecture makes walking about here a real pleasure. Classical, Queen Anne and Victorian buildings proudly line the streets. The stained-glass windows of the **Nelson Congregational Church ★** (*at the corner of Stanley and Silica Streets*), the Chateau-style **town hall ★** (*502 Vernon St.*), the group of buildings on **Baker Street** and above all the Italian-style **fire station ★** (*919 Ward St.*) are eloquent reminders of the opulence of the silver mining era.

Its lovely architecture is not the only thing that sets Nelson apart from other inland towns in British Columbia. You will also find a number of art galleries here, many of which are integrated into restaurants, so you can contemplate works of art while looking over the menu. This setup is known as the **Artwalk**, which enables artists to exhibit their work in participating businesses each year. For further information, contact the **West Kootenay Regional Arts Council** (*☎250-352-2402*).

Nelson was also chosen as the location for the American film *Roxanne*, starring Steve Martin. While strolling through town, you will come across the places where various scenes were shot, most notably the fire station overlooking town. For details, contact the Travel InfoCentre.

The **Nelson Brewing Company ★** (*512 Latimer St., by appointment ☎352-3582*) was founded in 1893, and still produces beer for the local market. The company has occupied the same Victorian building since 1899.

Old **Streetcar no. 23** of the **Nelson Electric Tramway Company** (*$3; May 22 to Labour Day, every day noon to 6pm; Labour Day to Oct Sat and Sun*) has been put back into service and carries passengers 1km through Lakeside Park, near the town bridge.

At the intersection of Ward and Vernon Streets, head for Hwy. 3A, which will take you to Castlegar.

Castlegar

Castlegar, which lies at the confluence of the Columbia and Kootenay Rivers, has no downtown area. While crossing the bridge in the direction of the airport, you'll see a suspended bridge built by the Doukhobors; turn left for a closer look.

Back on the highway, go uphill, then turn right to reach the **Doukhobor Museum ★** (*$3; May to Sep every day 9am to 5pm,* ☎*250-365-6622*). Fleeing persecution in Russia, the Doukhobors emigrated to Canada in 1898. They wanted to live according to their own rules rather than those of the State; for example, they were against participation in any war. They established communities on the prairies and farmed the land, adhering to their traditional way of life and gradually developing towns and setting up industries. One group, led by Piotr Verigin, left the prairies for British Columbia and took up residence in the Castlegar area. After the economic crisis of 1929 and the death of Verigin, the community diminished, but their descendants have taken up the task of telling visitors about their ancestors.

After exiting the museum, turn right and take Hwy. 3 in the direction of Grand Forks, then turn onto the 3B in order to reach Rossland. You can take the 22 there as well, but the 3 and the 3B are worth the detour.

★ Rossland

Rossland is a picturesque little turn-of-the-century town that thrived during the gold rush and has managed to retain its charm. Located inside the crater of a former volcano, at an altitude of 1,023m above sea level, it attracts skiers and people who simply enjoy being in the mountains. Nancy Greene Provincial Park, named after the 1968 Olympic champion, a native of Rossland, boasts several majestic peaks. Red Mountain, renowned for its high-quality powder, is a world-class resort. Skier Kerrin Lee-Gartner, who won the gold medal in the 1992 Olympic Games, is also from Rossland.

All of the gold was mined from this region long before these Olympic skiers arrived. In 1890, a prospector discovered a large vein of gold here. The news spread, and hundreds of adventurers came to try their luck, resulting in a gold rush. Numerous hotels, offices and theatres were built, and Rossland flourished. Then came the crash of 1929, which hit the town hard; that same year, a major fire destroyed part of the downtown area.

Rossland was on the decline; the famous **Le Roi** mine closed down, and the future did not look bright. Visitors can learn about the history of the gold rush at the **Le Roi mine ★** and the **Rossland Historical Museum** (*$10 for mine tour and museum, $5 for museum; mid-May to mid-Sep, every day 9am to 5pm; at the intersection of the 3B and the 22; take Columbia Ave. east of the downtown area,* ☎*250-362-7722*), which features an audiovisual presentation and a collection of objects from that era. The **Ski Hall of Fame**, located in the same building, highlights the careers of Nancy Greene and Kerrin Lee-Gartner.

Trail

The neighbouring town of Trail came to Rossland's rescue in a way. This large mining town has been transforming the ore from Rossland's mines since 1896. Cominco, a large metallurgical company, employs a sizeable portion of the local population to this day.

Rossland's yellow gold has been replaced by the "white gold" on the slopes, which attracts thousands of skiers here every year. (See Red Mountain, p 216).

Get back on Hwy. 3 and head for Grand Forks. This pleasant road runs alongside Christina Lake on its way across the southern part of the Mona-shee Mountains.

Grand Forks

Grand Forks lies at the confluence of the Kettle and North Fork Rivers. Numerous artifacts have been found here, indicating that Aboriginal people once lived in this area. The first Europeans to come to this valley regularly were trappers working for the Hudson's Bay Company. The region later developed around the mining industry, but a drop in the price of copper in 1919 thwarted the community's growth. Thanks to farming and forestry, Grand Forks is once again a thriving town.

Keep heading west on Hwy. 3.

Starting in Grand Forks, the landscape becomes desert-like again. The road leads through some lovely valleys, but the real highlight of the trip comes when you enter the **Okanagan** valley from the east. The town of Osoyoos (see p 194) and Osoyoos Lake are visible several hundred metres below.

Parks

Porpoise Bay Provincial Park (*British Columbia Provincial Parks,* ☎*689-9025*), northeast of Sechelt, is a sylvan park that offers nature interpretation programs with naturalists. One of the most pleasant sand beaches in the area is at Porpoise Bay. You can go for a swim under the watchful eye of a lifeguard. It's a perfect spot for the family.

Divers will be pleased to learn about the **HMCS Chaudiere**, a warship that was sunk at Kunechin Point in order to create an artificial reef. The park has 84 campsites. Reservations are accepted (☎*800-689-9025*); during the summer they are recommended. Payment is made in cash upon arrival.

Sargeant Bay Provincial Park (*British Columbia Provincial Parks* ☎*689-9025*) is located 7km west of Sechelt, on the Sunshine Coast. The area offers infinite sailing and kayaking possibilities. Sargeant Bay is famous for its rich marine life. You can get to the park by car on Hwy. 101, or by boat. A picnic area has been set up at the entrance to the park.

The **Skookumchuck Rapids of Skookumchuck Narrows Provincial Park ★★★** (☎*885-0662*) are definitely one of the Sunshine Coast's most spectacular features. When the tides change, the sea water rushes into the Skookumchuck Narrows Canyon as if it were a great funnel. Skookumchuck is a Chinook word that means "powerful water." The significance of the word is clear when you see the rapids with your own eyes. To get there, go north on Hwy. 101 past Sechelt and Pender Harbour to the Egmont exit, 1km from the ferry terminal at Earl's Cove. Continue on Egmont Road until you reach the parking lot of Skookumchuck Narrows Provincial Park.

From here, a trail will lead you to the rapids. Bring a raincoat and good shoes, since it will take 30min to reach the site. These are considered to be among the **biggest rapids in the world**. If you're lucky, you'll see some kayakers literally surfing the waves.

Saltery Bay Provincial Park (*north of the Saltery Bay terminal, 42 campsites, beaches, scuba diving,* ♿*; B.C. Parks, Garibaldi/Sunshine Coast District,* ☎*604-898-3678*) is an outstanding place to go scuba diving; a bronze mermaid awaits you underwater, and you have a good chance of spotting a killer whale, a seal or a sea-lion.

Shelter Point Regional Park (*Powell River Regional District, 5776 Marine Ave., Powell River,* ☎*486-7228*) is located on the southwest coast of Texada Island, approximately 20km from the Blubber Bay ferries. There's a campground here, with washrooms and showers, and a shelter where you can prepare food. This is a place for isolation, fishing and communion with nature. Dogs are allowed in the park.

Jedediah Island Marine Provincial Park (*British Columbia Provincial Parks,* ☎*689-9025*) is an island between Lasqueti Island and Texada Island, in the Strait of Georgia. The island was acquired by coastal residents in 1995, who made it into a park. There are thousand-year-old trees and major bird colonies. This magnificent wild area is only accessible by boat.

Desolation Sound Marine Park ★★ (*north of Lund, accessible by boat; campsites, hiking, kayaking, swimming, fishing, scuba diving, potable water, toilets; B.C. Parks at Tenedos Bay, Sechelt Area Supervisor,* ☎*604-885-9019*) is popular with ocean lovers, who come here to observe the animal life inhabiting these warm waters. More and more people are coming here to go sea kayaking, something even novices can enjoy.

Tour B: The Sea to Sky Highway Fraser River Loop

Alice Lake, Brandywine Falls, Garibaldi, Porteau Cove and Shannon Falls are the provincial parks located around Squamish. Here, you can camp, fish, swim, kayak, canoe, climb, walk or even do some mountain-biking. Call ☎*(800) 689-9025* for information.

Shannon Falls Provincial Park (*British Columbia Provincial Parks,* ☎*689-9025*), along Hwy. 99 toward Squamish, is the site of one of the most impressive waterfalls in Canada. It's practically impossible to see the origin of the falls since they're so incredibly high. The pure clear water of Shannon Creek was once used by Carling O'Keefe breweries, until they gave the land to the provincial government. The park has trails all around the falls and picnic areas.

Porteau Cove Provincial Park (*British Columbia Provincial Parks,* ☎*689-9025*) is located some 20km north of Horseshoe Bay, on the east coast of Howe Sound, between Gambier and Bowen Island. The waters contain a number of sunken shipwrecks to the delight of the many scuba divers that come here. One example is an old minesweeper from World War II.

Stawamus Chief Provincial Park (*British Columbia Provincial Parks,* ☎*689-9025*) is located almost right after Shannon Falls Provincial Park, in the direction of Squamish on Hwy. 99 (Sea to Sky). The park is renowned for its rock-climbing and hiking. The view from the summit of The Chief is truly magnificent. The park is open all year and has 15 campsites. Reservations are not accepted.

Alice Lake Provincial Park (*British Columbia Provincial Parks,* ☎*689-9025, to reserve a campsite:* ☎*800-689-9025*) is 13km north of Squamish around the lake of the same name (Alice Lake) and has 88 campsites. It's a very popular park, especially in the middle of summer when the weather is really hot. Tourists and children flock to the beach to cool off. There are showers and many hiking trails.

Brandywine Falls Provincial Park (*British Columbia Provincial Parks, ☎689-9025*) is a small park, with 15 campsites, 47km north of Squamish. The many waterfalls and vertiginous peaks make this area a photographer's paradise. Daisy Lake and the splendid mountains of Garibaldi Park are not far from here.

Vast **Garibaldi Provincial Park ★★** (*information Garibaldi/Sunshine District, Brackendale; 10km north of Squamish, ☎604-898-3678*), which covers 195,000ha, is extremely popular with hikers during summertime. Hwy. 99 runs along the west side of the park, offering access to the various trails.

In the Whistler valley, near the village, there are five lakes where you can go swimming, windsurfing, canoeing and sailing. Here are two of them:

At little **Alpha Lake** (*at the traffic like at Whistler Creekside, turn left on Lake Placid Rd. and continue until you reach the beach*), you can enjoy a picnic, rent a canoe or play tennis or volleyball.

Alta Lake (*north of Whistler Creekside on Hwy. 99; turn left on Alta Vista Rd. and right on Alpine Crescent, then keep left until the end of the road to reach Lakeside Park*) attracts windsurfers. Sailboard rentals are available here, along with canoes and kayaks.

Joffre Lakes Provincial Park (*Pemberton Chamber of Commerce, ☎894-6175*) is located about 20km from Pemberton. It's a superb mountain park where you'll find three turquoise lakes and vertiginous summits covered by an enormous glacier. The trail is in good condition but be prepared to climb the steeper slopes. Watch out for mosquitoes in July.

Birkenhead Lake Provincial Park (*British Columbia Provincial Parks, ☎689-9025*) is 55km northeast of Pemberton, reached by an access road at D'Arcy. The park is equipped with campsites and a boat-launching ramp. Deer, moose and bears are not rare sights in this lovely mountain park. The lake offers great trout fishing too. The park is open from May to September.

The **Sasquatch Provincial Park** (*beach, playground, boat-launching ramp; Cultus Lake, ☎604-824-2300 or 796-3107*) lies tucked away in the mountains by Harrison Lake. You can camp, and beaches have been laid out so that visitors can spend a pleasant day here enjoying one of the lakes. According to a Coast Salish Aboriginal legend, the Sasquatch is half-man, half-beast and lives in the woods. To this day, some Aboriginals claim to have seen the creature around Harrison Lake.

Kilby Provincial Park (*British Columbia Provincial Parks, ☎689-9025, campsite reservations: ☎800-689-9025*) is a lovely park on the banks of the Fraser River, only 29km northwest of Chilliwack. It is known for being peaceful and for the abundance of birds of prey such as eagles and owls. You can plan a picnic or spend a few days at one of the 38 campsites.

Don't miss the **General Store Museum**. This grocery store from the beginning of the 1900s will make you feel like you're back in pioneer days. The park is open all year.

Chilliwack Lake Provincial Park (*British Columbia Provincial Parks, ☎689-9025, campsite reservations: ☎800-689-9025*) is located 64km southeast of Chilliwack. It can be reached by a well-maintained gravel road that is accessible from the Trans-Canada Highway (Hwy. 1). This park offers many services and activities: large beaches, campsites, etc. It is mostly frequented by people who live in the area. So, expect many families, children and Jet Skis. It is open from May to October.

Cultus Lake Provincial Park (*British Columbia Provincial Parks, ☎689-9025, campsite reservations: ☎800-689-9025*) is 656ha in size and is located 13km south of Chilliwack on the Trans-Canada Highway. There are four campgrounds with showers, washrooms, and firewood. Due to its proximity to the Fraser Valley's urban centres, this park is literally stormed by campers when the weather is nice, and, therefore, its campgrounds, Fraser Creek (80 sites); Delta Grove (58 sites); Entrance Bay (52 sites) and Maple Bay (106 sites) are almost always full on weekends.

Golden Ears Provincial Park (*British Columbia Provincial Parks, ☎689-9025, campsite reservations: ☎800-689-9025*) is located in the coastal mountain chain, not far from the small town of Maple Ridge, only 41 kilometres east of Vancouver by Hwy. 7 from Haney or Albion. There are two campgrounds near Alouette Lake with washrooms and showers. The first, Alouette, has 205 campsites and the other, Gold Creek, has 138.

Fishing and hiking are the activities of choice. The park is unusual in that it allows horseback riding. You can go for a ride by contacting the ranches at the park's entrance.

Tour C: The Thompson River as Far as Revelstoke

There are five municipal parks in the Kamloops area where various tournaments and competitions are held. You can go for a walk and catch a football or softball game, a cricket or tennis match or a golf tournament. Some parks are more children-oriented. **Prince Charles Park** (*☎800-662-1994*) has facilities for disabled people.

Kamloops Wildlife Park (*☎800-662-1994 or 573-3242*) is a zoo where both young and old can observe animals in their natural habitat. You'll see bears, of course, but also Siberian tigers and wolves.

You can explore the woods on scores of paths in **Mount Revelstoke ★★** and **Glacier ★★ National Parks** (*for maps, information and regulations, contact Parks Canada in Revelstoke, ☎250-837-7500*). The level of difficulty varies; some trails run past centuries-old trees or lead to the tops of mountains, affording splendid panoramic views.

Tour D: Okanagan-Similkameen

Manning Provincial Park ★★ (*tourist information: summer, every day 8:30am to 4:30pm; winter, Mon to Fri 8:30am to 4:30pm; ☎250-840-8836*) is located on the boundary of the southwestern part of the province and the huge Okanagan-Similkameen region. It lies 225km from Vancouver, making it a popular getaway for city-dwellers in search of vast green spaces.

Cathedral Provincial Park ★★ (*No dogs, no mountain bikes; for detailed maps and information, contact the BC Parks District Manager; Box 399, Summerland, B.C. V0H 1Z0, ☎250-494-6500*) is located 30km southwest of Keremeos, in the southern part of the province, right alongside the U.S. border. There are two distinct kinds of vegetation here — the temperate forest and the plant growth characteristic of the arid Okanagan region. At low altitudes, Douglas firs dominate the landscape, giving way to spruce and heather higher up. Deer, mountain goats and wild sheep sometimes venture out near the turquoise-coloured lakes.

Knox Mountain Park lies north of Kelowna and offers a beautiful view of Okanagan Lake, whose waters are supposedly inhabited by a monster named Ogopogo. To get there from downtown, head north on Ellis Street.

Kalamalka Provincial Park (*a few kilometres south of Vernon,* ☎*800-689-9025*) is a pretty wooded area with a beach and the perfect spot to spend an afternoon or a day. *National Geographic* ranks Kalamalka Lake as one of the 10 most beautiful lakes in the world — and as soon as you see its turquoise blue water, you will know why. Kalamalka means "many colours" in the Aboriginal language. People come here to stroll on its many hiking trails, go mountain biking or simply relax by the water's edge. Don't forget your bathing suit!

Tour E: Kootenay Country

Kokanee Glacier Provincial Park ★★ (*contact the BC Parks Kootenay District Area Office for maps; Nelson,* ☎*250-825-3500*) has about 10 hiking trails of average difficulty, which require a total of about 4hrs of walking. The park, which looks out over two lakes (Kootenay and Slocan), is accessible from a number of different places.

This is also the park where Michel Trudeau, youngest son of former Canadian Prime Minister, Pierre Trudeau, drowned during a skiing excursion on November 13, 1998.

Michel Trudeau, an experienced skier and guide, was swept 40m into Lake Kootenay by an avalanche.

Outdoor Activities

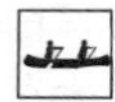

Canoeing

Tour A: The Sunshine Coast

A canoe trip is a must, especially if you're dying to discover a series of lakes and are up for portaging. The **Powell Forest Canoe Route** ★, a tour of eight lakes, takes four days. For more information, contact the **Sunshine Coast Forest District Office** (*7077 Duncan St., Powell River, B.C., V8A 1W1,* ☎*604-485-0700*).

Flying

Tour B: The Sea to Sky Highway – Fraser River Loop

Gliding enthusiasts have claimed the sky over Hope as their flying space. A westerly wind sweeps down the Fraser River Valley and up the big mountains around

Hope, enabling the aircraft to stay in the air for hours. For $60, you can accompany a pilot aboard an engineless plane. At Exit 165 on Hwy. 1, west of Hope, follow the sign for the airport; turn left at Old Yale, just before the viaduct, and continue until you reach the red and white building of the **Vancouver Soaring Association** (☎*604-521-5501*).

Birdwatching

Tour D: Okanagan-Similkameen

If you like birds, don't miss Vaseaux Lake at the **Federal Migratory Bird Sanctuary**, 10km south of Okanagan Falls on Rte. 97. Don't forget your binoculars.

Fishing

Tour C: Thompson River as far as Revelstroke

Kamloops is nicknamed "fly fishing capital of the world." With its 200 lakes less than an hour's drive away, you don't have to go far to reel in a prize catch. Some of the most popular lakes are Roche Lake, Jeune Lake, Crystal Lake and Tunkwa Lake. For tourists guides, licences or any other information, contact **Gordons Honey's** (*SS2, Camp 40, Kamloops,* ☎*828-1286, gordon_honey@bc.sympatico.ca*). For a daily report (**Fishing Report Hotline**), ☎*374-2929 extension 3320.*

Tour D: Okanagan-Similkameen

All around Merritt, the **Nicola Valley** offers an abundance of **lakes**, around 150, true to the local proverb (a lake a day as long as you stay) and is a paradise for fishing. Information is available at the many shops that sell mandatory fishing permits.

Golf

Tour B: The Sea to Sky Highway – Fraser River Loop

Furry Creek Golf & Country Club (*Box 1000, Lions Bay, V0N 2E0; Pro Shop:* ☎*922-9461; Club House:* ☎*922-9576*). Located on the east shore of Howe Sound, Furry Creek is 48km north of Vancouver by Hwy. 99 (Sea to Sky Highway) and 66km south of Whistler. The landscape is fabulous. With the sea and mountains having such a hypnotizing effect, golfers have a hard time concentrating. The restaurant serves West Coast meals and has glass walls through which you can see magnificent views of the surrounding greenery.

People come to Whistler Valley from May to October to play golf in spectacular surroundings. The greens fees vary greatly from one club to the next. At the **Whistler Golf Club** (*$75-$100; May to Oct; take the Village Gate Blvd., turn right at Whistler Way and go under the 99,* ☎*604-932-4544*) you'll discover a magnificent, winding golf course set against the steep cliffs of the mountains. The **Pemberton Valley Golf and Country Club** (*$45; May to Oct;* ☎*604-894-5122*), in Pemberton, 23km north of Whistler, is just as beautiful as the clubs in Whistler but much less expensive.

Tour C: The Thompson River as Far as Revelstoke

Kamloops has at least six 18-hole, and a few nine-hole golf courses:

Aberdeen Hills Golf Links is an 18-hole course with a magnificent view of the city and the hills (*1185 Links Way, Kamloops,* ☎*828-1149*). **Rivershore Golf Club** is an 18-hole course developed by Robert Trent Jones, Sr. located alongside the Thompson River. It goes without saying that the view is exceptional (*South*

Thompson River, Kamloops, ☎573-4622).

Tour D: Okanagan-Similkameen

The Okanagan Valley has been called a **Golf Mecca** for the quality of its courses and tournaments. Pleasant temperatures, views of the vineyards, as well as some worthwhile **Stay & Golf** packages, all serve to encourage ever-increasing numbers of golfers.

There are about 40 golf courses in the province's hinterland, most located near the towns of **Penticton**, **Kelowna** and **Vernon**. The terrain varies greatly depending on whether you're playing in the north, amidst wooded mountains, or in the desert-like south, which is scattered with little blueish shrubs.

Gallaghers Canyon Golf & Country Club. This 18-hole course designed by Bill Robinson and the Furbers is sure to please golfers seeking a challenge. As the name indicates, it is built in a forest hollow along Gallaghers Canyon; it goes without saying that the view is spectacular.

There are other prestigious golf courses in this region; for complete complementary information about the establishments or rates contact the **Okanagan Similkameen Tourism Association** (*1322 Water St., Kelowna, V1Y 9P4, ☎861-7493*).

Hiking

Tour A: The Sunshine Coast

Inland Lake Park, located 12km north of Powell River, has been specially designed to enable people in wheelchairs to enjoy nature. The lake is 13km in circumference. Campsites have been laid out, and a few log houses are reserved for people with limited mobility. The picnic tables and swimming docks have been built with wheelchair-users in mind. The premier of British Columbia awarded the forest ministry a medal for the layout of this park.

Tour B: The Sea to Sky Highway – Fraser River Loop

Except for the built-up area around Whistler, **Garibaldi Provincial Park** (*information Garibaldi/Sunshine District, Brackendale; 10km north of Squamish, ☎604-898-3678*) is a huge stretch of untouched wilderness. Hiking here is a magical experience, especially when you reach Garibaldi Lake, whose turquoise waters contrast with the blue of the glacier in the background. The trails cover long distances, so you have to bring along food, as well as clothing for different temperatures.

A series of hiking trails runs all the way up **Whistler Mountain** (*☎604-932-3434*) and **Blackcomb Mountain** (*☎604-932-3141*). From atop Whistler, you can see Black Tusk, a black sugar-loaf 2315m high.

Tour C: The Thompson River as Far as Revelstoke

There are opportunities for all sorts of walks and hikes for all levels around Kamloops. Excursions can last from 1 to 7hrs. The hike up **Mount Peter and Paul** follows a somewhat difficult route but the view from the summit is ample reward for the 7hrs of walking. You have to call the Indian Band Office (*☎828-9700*) to get authorization to go through the Aboriginal reserve. The **Paul Lake Provincial Park** trail takes you to Paul Lake Road. It's an easy and pleasant walk that takes between 1.5 and 2hrs.

At **Mount Revelstoke National Park★★** (*$4; permit required for entry into the park; outside Revelstoke, east of the bridge on the Trans-Canada, InfoLine ☎250-837-7500*), you have to drive 24km up to the summit of the mountain, where you'll find a trail and a number of picnic areas.

There are a number of trails in **Glacier National Park** (*east of Revelstoke; for maps, information and regulations, contact Parks Canada in Revelstoke, ☎250-837-7500*), which enable you to view flourishing plant and animal life up close. There are varying levels of difficulty; some trails run past centuries-old trees or climb to the tops of mountains, offering views of the neighbouring peaks.

Tour D: Okanagan-Similkameen

Manning Provincial Park (*tourist information, summer, every day 8:30am to 4:30pm; winter, Mon to Fri 8:30am to 4:30pm; ☎250-840-8836*) is located on the boundary of the south-western part of the province and the huge Oka-nagan-Similkameen region. It is popular with Vancouverites in search of vast green spaces. The magnificent mountains and valleys are criss-crossed by hiking trails.

The entrance to **Cathedral Provincial Park** (*for detailed maps and information,* **BC Parks District Manager**, *Box 399, Summerland, B.C. V0H 1Z0, ☎250-494-6500; no dogs, no mountain bikes*) is located near Keremeos, on Hwy. 3. Some of the trails here extend more than 15km, and require a day of hiking, on average. At the summit, the trails are shorter and crisscross hilly terrain teeming with plant and animal life. You can ride to the top in an all-purpose vehicle; to reserve a seat, call the **Cathedral Lakes Lodge** (*☎888-255-4453*).

For a hike that takes only an hour but is incredibly beautiful, go to **Kalamalka Provincial Park**, a few kilometres from Vernon. The short trail leads right up to a little hill that steeply drops off into wonderful Kalamalka Lake.

Tour E: Kootenay Country

Kokanee Glacier Provincial Park (*for maps, contact the BC Parks Kootenay District Area Office, Nelson, ☎250-825-3500*) has about 10 hiking trails of average difficulty, for a total of about 4hrs of walking. The Woodbury Creek Trail, which takes less than 2hrs to cover, leads to Sunset Lake via Ainsworth Hot Springs.

Mountain Biking

Tour E: Kootenay Country

Rossland, in Kootenay Country, is the self-proclaimed mountain-bike capital of British Columbia – with good reason, it would seem. Long trails of varying levels of difficulty make this place accessible to anyone with an interest in the sport. Former railway lines, cross-country trails and wood-cutting paths all converge near the centre of town. The terrain is far from flat; this is a very mountainous region. You can pick up a map of the trails at the local **Visitor InfoCentre** (*☎250-326-7722*) or at any of the bike rental centres.

Mountain Climbing

Tour B: The Sea to Sky Highway – Fraser River Loop

Mountain climbing is becoming more popular in the Sea to Sky region. The place to go is **Stawamus Chief Mountain**. The trails leading to this granite monolith also lead to spots where you can watch the mountain climbers. For more information, contact the **Squamish & Howe Sound District Chamber of Commerce** (*☎892-9244*).

Tour D: Okanagan-Similkameen

The Penticton region is renowned among North American mountain climbers for its wide assortment of rock walls. Many of these surfaces measure a single rope's length, and the level of difficulty can vary greatly. For further information, contact Ray Keetch of **Ray's Sports Den** (*101-399 Main St., no. 100, Penticton, V2A 5B7, ☎250-493-1216*).

For climbing and hiking enthusiasts, **Wild Horse Canyon**, at the end of Lakeshore Road, approximately 16km southwest of Kelowna, offers extraordinary views of the surrounding area. The same is true of **Gallaghers Canyon**, which is more easily accessible, just next to the golf course.

River Rafting

Tour B: The Sea to Sky Highway–Fraser River Loop

Hundreds of adventurers come to the gorges of the Fraser and Thompson Rivers each year to brave the tumultuous waters in small groups. A number of packages are available to visitors wishing to travel downriver on inflatable rafts, including those offered by **Kumsheen Raft Adventures** (*Lytton ☎250-455-2296, ⇄455-2297*).

Scuba Diving

Tour A: The Sunshine Coast

Porpoise Bay Charters (*7629 Inlet Dr., Sechelt, ☎885-5950*) will fill your tanks if you are a certified diver, if not, you can join their team which goes to **Porpoise Bay Provincial Park** to dive around the ***HMCS Chaudiere***, a warship that was sunk at Kunechin Point to create a natural reef.

Skiing

Tour B: The Sea to Sky Highway – Fraser River Loop

The Whistler ski resort is considered one of the best in North America, with an annual snowfall of 9m and a 1,600m vertical drop. There are two mountains to choose from: **Whistler Mountain** and **Blackcomb Mountain** (*hotel reservations, ☎604-932-4222; from Vancouver, ☎685-3650; from the U.S., ☎800-634-9622*). The skiing here is extraordinary, and the facilities ultra-modern – but mind your budget! You will understand why prices are so high upon seeing hordes of Japanese and American tourists monopolize the hotels and intermediate ski runs.

Whistler and Blackcomb Mountains together make up the largest skiing area in Canada. These world-class, twin ski playgrounds are blessed with heavy snowfalls and boast enough hotels to house a city's entire population.

This top-of- the-range ski metropolis also offers the possibility of gliding through pristine powder and, weather permitting, you will find yourself swooshing through an incredibly beautiful alpine landscape.

Whistler Mountain (*$51; from Vancouver, Hwy. 99 heading north for 130km, information ☎932-3434, ski conditions ☎932-4191*) is the elder of the two resorts. Experts, powderhounds and skijumpers will all flock to Peak Chair, the chair lift that leads to the top of Whistler Mountain. From its summit, diehard skiers and snowboarders have access to a ski area composed of blue (intermediate) and expert (black-diamond and double-diamond) trails, covered in deep fleecy snow.

Blackcomb Mountain (*$48; in Whistler; from Vancouver, Hwy. 99 heading north for 130km; 4545 Blackcomb Way, Whistler, B.C., V0N 1B4; information ☎932-3141, ski conditions ☎932-4211*) is the "stalwart" skiing mecca of ski buffs in North America. For years now, a fierce debate has been waged by skiers over which of the two mountains (Whistler or Blackcomb) is the best. One thing is certain, Blackcomb wins first place for its vertical drop of 1,609m. Check out the glacier at Blackcomb – it is truly magnificent!

If you're looking for a thrill, you can hop aboard a helicopter and set off for vast stretches of virgin powder. Contact **Whistler Heli-Skiing Ltd.** (*$450, three rides up, lunch, guide; ☎604-932-4105, ⇄938-1225*).

Mountain Heli Sports (*4340 Sundial Cr., Whistler, ☎604- 932-2070*) is a very versatile agency, offering not only flights over mountains and Vancouver, but heli-skiing as well.

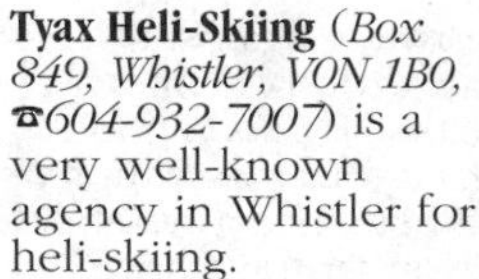

Tyax Heli-Skiing (*Box 849, Whistler, V0N 1B0, ☎604-932-7007*) is a very well-known agency in Whistler for heli-skiing.

Tour C: The Thompson River as Far as Revelstoke

Albeit smaller than Whistler, the **Sun Peaks** (*day pass $44; 45min north of Kamloops, on Todd Mountain; ☎250-578-7222*) resort has recently undergone major renovations and now offers new equipment and accommodations.

Olympic champion Nancy Greene welcomes visitors to **Sun Peaks Resort** where they offer complete ski programs. (*45min NE of Kamloops, 3150 Creekside Way, ste. 50, Sun Peaks, B.C., V0E 1Z1, ☎800-807-3257*).

Located 6km south of downtown on Airport Way, **Mount Mackenzie Ski** (*Revelstoke ☎250-837-5268*) is a family resort renowned for its high-quality powder. It is also fully equipped with ski lifts, dining facilities, a ski school and an equipment rental centre.

Mount Revelstoke National Park (*☎250-837-7500*) (see Parks, p 209, or Hiking, p 212) covers an immense stretch of virgin snow set against a backdrop of white peaks. This is a good place for cross-country skiing, since a number of longer trails have been laid out with shelters.

The immense skiing area at **Glacier National Park** (*☎837-7500*) (see "Parks", p 209) is perfect for those in search of adventure and quality powder. Because of the steep slopes and risk of avalanches, visitors are required to obtain a permit in order to ski here.

Heli-skiing and cat-skiing are available in this region; they attract a large number of skiers in search of unexplored terrain, far from ski lifts and artificial snow. This region receives record snowfall; in fact, Environment Canada has set up a centre here in order to measure the levels of precipitation. A number of outfits, including **Cat Powder Skiing Inc**. (*☎837-9489*) and **Selkirk Tangiers Heli-Skiing Ltd.** (*☎800- 663-7080 or 837-5378*), offer package deals.

Tour D: Okanagan-Similkameen

The Okanagan valley is one of the places where you can ski in the morning and play golf in the afternoon. For skiing, **Silver Star** (*$41; ☎542-0224 or 800-663-4431, ⇄558-6090, www.silverstarmtn.com*) is a mountain situated less than 30min from Vernon. It offers 84 runs and gets more than 6m of snow annually.

You can go downhill skiing all over this region. The major resorts are the **Apex Resort**, near Penticton, **Big White Ski Resort** and the **Silver Star Mountain Resort** near Kelowna.

Skiing in the Okanagan, which already has a good reputation, is now enjoying a new boom with the creation of **Big White Ski Resort** (*☎800- 663-2772*). The Schumann family has invested $45 million in the site, which was already very attractive and deemed acceptable for fine skiing. With 5 to 6m of snow falling here every year, the powder on these slopes doesn't need to be made artificially.

Everyone in the family appreciates winter skiing and snowboarding. Two hours from Kelowna and 1hr from Penticton, **Mont Baldy** has been offering affordable skiing on pleasant powder-covered slopes for 25 years.

Tour E: Kootenay Country

Kokanee Glacier is a provincial park located 21km northeast of Nelson on Hwy. 3A. The road is gravel for 16 of the 21km and is not maintained in winter, when the only way to reach the park is on cross-country skis or by helicopter. Visitors are strongly advised to obtain specialized equipment for this type of excursion. The Slocan Chief Cabin can accommodate up to 12 people, but you have to make reservations through the **BC Parks Kootenay District Area Office** (*Nelson, ☎250-825-3500*).

Ski Whitewater lies a few minutes south of Nelson on Hwy. 6. This resort is the perfect place to spend a day skiing, whether you're an expert or just starting out.

Red Mountain, located 5min from Rossland, is one of the main centres of economic activity in this region. In the past, miners used to work the mountain; today, it is a playground for skiiers. Granite Mountain, renowned for its deep, fluffy powder, is also part of this resort. Opposite Red Mountain, **BlackJack Cross Country Trails** consists of 50km of cross-country ski trails of all different levels of difficulty. **Red Mountain Resorts Inc**. (*☎362-7384, ski conditions ☎362- 5500, reservations ☎800-663-0105*).

Snowmobiling

Tour B: The Sea to Sky Highway – Fraser River Loop

The **Pemberton Ice Cap** has the biggest snowmobiling site in British Columbia. It's in an extraordinary alpine zone among the glaciers and sharp peaks of the coastal chain. The season begins early in December and ends at the end of May. It's important to be informed about the snow conditions before heading out to the mountains. Avalanches occur very frequently. It's also important to travel in groups and to have adequate survival equipment with you. For excursions and information, contact **Mountain Echo** (☎*894-5316*).

Windsurfing

Tour B: The Sea to Sky Highway – Fraser River Loop

Windsurfers come to **Squamish** for the constant winds that sweep down the sound and then head inland. For information, contact the **Squamish & Howe Sound District Chamber of Commerce** (☎*604-892-9244*).

Alta Lake (*north of Whistler Creekside on Hwy. 99; turn left on Alta Vista Rd. and right on Alpine Crescent, then keep left until the end of the road to reach Lakeside Park*) attracts windsurfers. This little lake is located in an enchanting setting, which offers lovely panoramic views of Whistler and Blackcomb.

Tour E: Kootenay Country

Lakeside Park, to the right of the bridge on the way into Nelson, offers access to Kootenay Lake. During summer, you can swim and windsurf here to your heart's content.

Accommodations

Tour A: The Sunshine Coast

Gibsons

Bonniebrook Lodge & RV Campground
$16-$19 for camping and $79-$115 for rooms
≈, tv, P
9.4km west on Gower Point Rd. follow directions from Hwy. 101
☎***886-2887***
⇄***886-8853***
Bonniebrook is a calm, pleasant place with easy access to the water.

Langdale Heights RV Resort
$19
2170 Port Mellon Hwy.
☎***886-2182***
⇄***886-2182***
Langdale Heights is located just 4.5km from the Langdale ferry terminal. It offers RV connections, even for telephones and cable TV! There are also spots for campers with tents. The unusual thing about Langdale Heights is that it has a magnificent nine-hole golf course, which is free for clients.

The Maritimer Bed & Breakfast
$80 bkfst incl.
tv, children 12 and over, no smoking
521 S. Fletcher Rd.
☎***(604) 886-0664***
Run by Gerry and Noreen Tretick, The Maritimer Bed and Breakfast overlooks the town and the marina. The charming scenery, friendly hosts and cozy atmosphere are sure to please. A private suite in the attic includes a sundeck. On the ground floor, there is a large room decorated with antique furniture and works of art by Noreen; a beautiful quilt graces one of the walls. Breakfast, served on the terrace, which looks right out onto the bay, includes a shrimp omelette; this is the seashore, after all.

Sechelt

Bella Beach Inn
$62-$69
ℝ, tv, P
from Vancouver, take the Horseshoe Bay ferry to Langdale continue north on Hwy. 101 to Davies Bay
☎885-7191
or for reservations
☎800-665-1925
⇌885-3794

This spot is considered one of the most beautiful places to stay on the Sunshine Coast. You can enjoy magnificent sunsets right from your window. The rooms are very pretty and extremely comfortable, and visitors have almost immediate access to the beach. The hotel has a seafood restaurant.

Four Winds Bed & Breakfast
$100-$120 bkfst incl.
P
5482 Hill Rd.
☎885-3144
⇌885-3182

Four Winds Bed & Breakfast is on the water's edge and offers a superb from all the rooms there are superb views of the Strait of Georgia. The rooms are decorated in a cosy manner. Breakfasts are succulent and afternoon tea is charming. You'll also have the chance to relax with the help of a professional massage therapist or in the outdoor whirlpool.

Powell River

Willingdon Beach Municipal Campsite
$14-$20
parking
4845 Marine Ave
☎485-2242

Here is a campsite in a lovely park not far from the water. The sites are well maintained and showers are free. It's right near a kindergarten.

Oceanside Campground & Cabins
$14-$50 for cabins
$14-$18 for campsites
$69-$89
P
8063 Hwy. 101
☎485-2435
or for reservations
☎888-889-2435

This is an excellent spot for families. The campsites overlook the sea and are not far from downtown Powell River. There's a big playground for children and a water park with slides. Recreational vehicles are accepted and it's open all year.

Beacon Bed & Breakfast
$95-$125 bkfst incl.
♿, no smoking, ⊛, children 12 and over
3750 Marine Ave.
☎(604) 485-5563
⇌485-9450

Your hosts, Shirley and Roger Randall, will make you feel right at home. What's more, they will take great pleasure in telling you all about their part of the country. The Beacon faces west and looks out onto the sea, so you can enjoy the sunset while taking a bath, no less! The simply laid-out rooms each have fully equipped bathrooms. Breakfast includes a special treat: blueberry pancakes.

The Coast Town Centre Hotel
$95-$115
ℜ, 🐕, P, ⊛, tv
4660 Joyce Ave.
☎(604) 485-3000
☎(800) 663-1144
⇌485-3031

The Coast Town Centre is near Town Centre Mall, a large shopping centre in the heart of Powell River. The rooms are impeccable and spacious, and the hotel is equipped with a fitness centre. They also organize salmon-fishing excursions.

The Beach Gardens Resort & Marina
$99
tv, ≈, ⌂, ℝ, P, ℜ, 🐕
7074 Westminster Ave.
☎(604) 485-6267
☎(800) 663-7070
⇌485-2343

All the rooms are on the water's edge and offer spectacular views of the coast. At the restaurant you can savour some of their excellent West Coast cuisine. An indoor pool and a fitness centre top off the list of facilities. Afterwards, you can go for a drink in the Canoe Room pub. The resort also has a liquor store.

Texada Island

The Retreat
$72-$76 for rooms
$19 for campsites
ℝ, *tv, P*
Gillies Bay
☎486-7360
The Retreat is in a very isolated area right near Shelter Point Regional Park. The Retreat offers fantastic views of the Strait of Georgia and Vancouver Island from its balconies. There are seven units with kitchens for extended visits and seven RV sites.

Savary Island

Savary Island Summer House
$250 bkfst incl.
P
Vancouver Blvd.
☎483-4758
⇄925-3536
is a bed and breakfast in a huge log house, and the breakfasts are great. If you want, they'll prepare a picnic for you too. The rooms are pleasant and attractively decorated. Don't miss the chance to relax next to the big fireplace in their spacious living room.

Lund

Lund Hotel
$69-$85
tv, ℜ
at the end of Hwy. 101
☎483-2400
A relaxing atmosphere prevails at the century-old Lund Hotel, which opens onto the bay. The peaceful location and view of the boats coming and going more than compensate for the motel-style rooms.

Tour B: The Sea to Sky Highway – Fraser River Loop

Whistler

The village of Whistler is scattered with restaurants, hotels, apartments and bed & breakfasts. There is a reservation service to help you take your pick.

Whistler Resort
☎(604) 932-4222
Vancouver
☎(604) 664-5625
outside British Columbia
☎(800) 944-7853

Whistler YHA
$18 members
$22 non-members
5678 Alta Lake Rd.
Whistler, V0N 1B0
☎(604) 932-5492
Whistler YHA has 32 beds and a fun vacation ambiance.

Shoestring Lodge
$50-$65 for a room
$21 for a shared room
tv, ℜ, *P*
1km north of the village
to the right on Nancy Greene Dr.
☎(604) 932-3338
⇄932-8347
The Shoestring Lodge is one of the least expensive places to stay in Whistler. Its low rates make it very popular, so reservations are imperative. The rooms include beds, televisions and small bathrooms; the decor is as neutral as can be. The youthful atmosphere will make you feel as if you're at a university summer camp where the students just want to have fun, and that's pretty much what this place is. The pub is known for its excellent evening entertainment (see p 235).

Stancliff House B&B
$75-$85 bkfst incl
tv, ⊛
3333 Panorama Ridge
☎932-2393
Stancliff House B&B is one of the most reasonably priced B&Bs. The view of the surrounding mountains is beautiful and the breakfasts are excellent. The home is near the centre of Whistler, but away from the hustle and bustle.

Holiday Inn
$79-$159
ℝ, *tv,* ⌂, ℜ, *P*
Whistler Village Centre
☎800-HOLIDAY
☎800-229-3188
☎604-938-0876
www.whistlerhi.com
The Holiday Inn is located right near the two mountains. Every room has a fireplace and a kitchenette; some have balconies. All the comforts of a well-equipped hotel are offered, including a very sophisticated fitness centre.

Chalet Beau Sejour
summer $80
winter $105 bkfst incl.
⊛, shuttle, no smoking
7414 Ambassador Cr.
White Gold Estate
☎(604) 938-4966
⇄938-6296
The Chalet Beau Sejour, run by Sue and Hal, is a big, inviting house set on a mountainside. You can take in a lovely view of the valley and the mountains while eating the copious breakfast Sue loves to prepare. A tour guide, she knows the region like the back of her hand; don't hesitate to ask her what to see and do.

Affordable Holiday Homes in Whistler
$99 for a suite during the high season
tv, ⊛, P
2021 Karen Cr.
☎(800) 882-6991
Affordable Holiday Homes in Whistler rents five-bedroom, four-bathroom condominiums and studios. Some are 5min from the village, at the foot of the lifts. Prices depend on the season and the size. An unbeatable price for Whistler.

Listel Whistler Hotel
$99-$199
♿, 🐕, tv, ≈, ⊛, ⌂, ℜ
4121 Village Green
☎(604) 932-1133
Vancouver
☎(604) 688-5634
☎(800) 663-5472
⇄(604) 932-8383
The Listel Whistler Hotel is located in the heart of the village, so you don't have to look far to find some place to eat or entertain yourself. The simple layout of the rooms makes for a comfortable stay.

Tantalus Lodge
$99-$379
=, K
4200 Whistler Way
☎(604) 932-4146
☎(800) 268-1133
⇄932-2405
www.deltahotels.com
Tantalus Lodge is situated near golfing and not far from the slopes. Its 76 condominiums are spacious and fully equipped. Tennis and volleyball courts extend the range of the town's activities.

Canadian Pacific Chateau Whistler Resort
$129-$529
⏲, 🐕, ♿, tv, ≈, ⊛, ⌂, ℜ
4599 Chateau Blvd.
☎(604) 938-8000
☎(800) 606-8244
☎(800) 441-1414
⇄938-2099
The luxurious Canadian Pacific Chateau Whistler Resort lies at the foot of the slopes of Blackcomb Mountain. It resembles a smaller version of Whistler Village, fully equipped to meet all your dining and entertainment needs and to ensure that your stay is a relaxing one.

Westbrook Whistler
$149-$300
ℝ, tv, ⌂, ℜ, P
4340 Sundial Cr.
at the foot of the lifts
☎(800) 661-2321
☎(604) 932-2321
The Westbrook Whistler has attractive rooms, some with kitchenettes, and beautiful suites with fireplaces. The staff even organizes receptions for newlyweds. Golf packages are available.

Blackcomb Lodge
$150-$250
≈, K, tv
4220 Gateway Dr.
right in the heart of Whistler Village
☎(800) 667-2857
☎(604) 664-5639
The Blackcomb Lodge is a luxury complex whose suites are equipped with all the possible comforts, such as whirlpools and saunas. Some have balconies. Throughout the year, various packages are offered: skiing in the winter and golf in the summer. The reception is flawless. The establishment is also home to a excellent restaurant, Ristorante Araxi (see p 231).

Pan Pacific Lodge
$195-$630
≡, tv, =, ⊛
4320 Sundial Cr.
☎(604) 905-2999
☎(888) 905-9995
⇄905-2995
www.panpac.com
Pan Pacific Lodge is inspired by the old hotels of the Rockies, and the establishment blends in well with the countryside. Built in the

middle of town at the foot of the gondolas that go to the summits of Whistler and Blackcomb, it is difficult to find a better situated or a more luxurious hotel.

Pemberton

Hitching Post Motel
$57
K
Portage Rd., Mount Currie
30min north of Whistler on Hwy. 99
☎(604) 894-6276
Hitching Post Motel offers rooms with kitchenettes in a calm spot with beautiful views of Mount Currie.

Chris's Corner Bed & Breakfast
$65-$85
tv
7406 Larch St.
☎894-6787
⇄894-2026
Chris's Corner Bed & Breakfast is a lovely house decorated in Nordic style. Each of the three rooms has its own character. The living room has everything you might need for an extended stay: parlour games, TV and VCR. Visitors can also relax on the large outdoor terrace, where there's a magnificent view of the mountains.

Log House Bed & Breakfast
$70-$100
$25 per extra person
tv, pb
1357 Elmwood Dr.
☎(800) 894-6000
Log House Bed & Breakfast is close to everything, is non-smoking and has four attractive, spacious rooms with all the comforts you could ask for, including a TV and a whirlpool.

Rainbow Valley Inn Bed & Breakfast
$79 sb
$99 pb
bkfst incl.
1964 Sea to Sky Hwy.
at the foot of Mount Currie
follow Whistler Rd. to Pemberton and turn right at the Petro Canada station
go for 5km farther, the inn is on the right
☎(604) 894-3300
The Rainbow Valley Inn Bed & Breakfast has three rooms and is close to all the activities at Mount Currie. Skiing, snowmobiling, walking, horseback riding, golf and rafting are sure to keep you occupied. There's a TV and a VCR in the spacious living room to keep you entertained on cool nights.

Lillooet

Cayoosh Creek Campground
Apr 15 to Oct 15
Hwy. 99
☎256-4180
Cayoosh Creek Campground has been set up along a 500m stretch of the Fraser River. The campground offers showers, a beach and a volleyball court, all right near downtown. Warning: there's not much shade.

4 Pines Motel
$38-$100
ℝ, tv
108 Eighth Ave., Box 35
☎256-4247
⇄256-4120
4 Pines Motel is located in downtown Lillooet, across from the tourist office. The rooms are well equipped with air conditioning, kitchenettes and satellite television.

Jay-Gee Motel
$42-$85
ℝ, tv, ℜ
Bouvette Rd.
turn left on Main St. then right on Mountain View Rd.
☎256-7525
Jay-Gee Motel has many facilities and is very comfortable. Some rooms have kitchenettes. There's a small restaurant in the motel.

Hope

Manning Provincial Park
four campsites
and wilderness camping
sb
☎(250) 840-8836
Manning Provincial Park lies on the boundary of the southwestern part of the province and the huge Okanagan-Similkameen region, 225km from Vancouver. City-dwellers come here by the thousands to enjoy all sorts of sports, the most popular being hiking and mountain biking and cross-country skiing in the winter. During summer, you can drive up to Cascade Lookout to take in the view.

Simon's On Fraser
$75-$100 bkfst incl.
690 Fraser St.
☎***(604) 869-2562***
Simon's On Fraser, a pretty little house adjacent to Memorial Park, has simply decorated, cozy rooms. The house, which is adorned with woodwork, has been completely renovated and repainted in bright colours.

Harrison Hot Springs

Sasquatch Provincial Park
$10 for four people
177 wooded lots
beach, playground, boat-launching ramp
cash only
Cultus Lake
☎***(604) 824-2300***
☎***796-3107***
At Sasquatch Provincial Park, you choose your own campsite and a park employee passes by to collect payment. Hidden in the mountains near Harrison Lake, this park has three campgrounds, which welcome nature lovers every year. According to a Coast Salish legend, the Sasquatch is half-man, half-beast and lives in the woods. To this day, some Aboriginal people claim to have seen the creature around Harrison Lake.

Bigfoot Campgrounds
$16-$20 for two
electricity included
670 Hot Springs Rd.
☎***(604) 696-9767***
Bigfoot Campgrounds is a large, 5ha park that offers all the comforts and has a grocery store, minigolf and video games.

Glenco Motel & RV Park
$16-$18 camping
$50-$60 hotel
K, ≡, tv
259 Hot Springs Rd., downtown
☎***(604) 796-2574***
Glenco Motel & RV Park offers motel accommodations and campsites.

Harrison Heritage House and Kottage
$60-$130 bkfst incl.
no smoking
312 Lillooet Ave.
☎***(604) 796-9552***
Jo-Anne and Dennis Sandve will give you a warm welcome at their pretty house, located one street away from the beach and the public pool. Jo-Anne makes her own preserves. Certain rooms have whirlpools and fireplaces.

Harrison Hot Springs Hotel
$114-$200
♿, ≈, ℜ, ⌂
100 Esplanade
☎***(604) 796-2244***
☎***(800) 663-2266***
⇄***796-3682***
The Harrison Hot Springs Hotel offers the benefits of the lake and the mountain. It is also the only hotel with access to the mineral springs; it's a fun place where visitors get a sense of well-being. Outdoor heated pools, golf, dancing, children's playground and more.

Little House on the Lake
$175 bkfst incl.
⊛, no smoking
no children under 16
6305 Rockwell Dr.
☎/⇄***(604) 796-2186***
☎***(800) 939-1116***
The Little House on the Lake is a superb loghouse set on the east shore of the lake. This is an extremely comfortable place to relax and enjoy water sports like sailing and kayaking.

Tour C: The Thompson River as Far as Revelstoke

Ashcroft

Sundance Guest Ranch
$80-$185 per person
fb, horseback riding twice a day (cowboy boots required, rentals available)
≈, tennis, tv
Highland Valley Rd.
Box 489, V0K 1A0
☎***(250) 453-2422***
Run by former clients, the Sundance Guest Ranch will take you back to a bygone era when cowboys roamed freely on horseback across as yet unexplored regions. The cost covers a stay of at least one day. Guests have access to a living room, where they can bring their drinks; there is a separate living room just for children.

Kamloops

Kamloops Hostel
$15 members
$19 non-members
K, sb
7 West Seymore
☎828-7991
⇄828-4224
The Kamloops Hostel, the town's youth hostel, just opened in the old Provincial Law Courts building, which dates from 1909. The dining room is located in the courtroom where the original witness stands and seats for the judge and jury have all been preserved.

Acadian Motor Inn
$40-$60
1390 Columbia
☎374-5581
⇄374-5596
Acadian Motor Inn is not the most conveniently located facility if you don't have a car. On the other hand, it offers excellent value for your money.

Casa Marquis Motor Inn
$52-$62
≈, K, tv
530 Columbia
☎(800) 665-3343
Casa Marquis Motor Inn, is a reasonably priced motel that meets all the needs of travellers.

Joyce's Bed & Breakfast
$60 bkfst incl.
≡, sb, P, no smoking
49 W. Nicola St.
☎(250) 374-1417
☎(800) 215-1417
Located steps away from the centre of town, Joyce's Bed & Breakfast is a turn-of-the-century house with big balconies that offer a view of the surrounding scenery. You've got to be a cat-lover to stay here, since the house has three feline residents. Although you'll find little to inspire you indoors, the armchairs on the huge balcony beckon travel-weary visitors to relax and enjoy the view of Kamloops. The three rooms are decent, and given the price, it's worth making an effort.

Best Western Kamloops Towne Lodge
$89-$138
≈, ⊛, ⌂, ⊙, ℜ, ♿
1250 Rogers Way
☎(250) 828-6660
in western North America
☎(800) 665-6674
⇄828-6698
Located right near the Trans-Canada Highway on the way into town, the Best Western Kamloops Towne Lodge is a very comfortable, classic-style hotel that offers some splendid views of Kamloops and the Thompson River. You can also enjoy the scenery from one of the nearby motels, which vary only in price.

Sun Peaks Resort
$90-$169
ℜ
45min NE of Kamloops
3150 Creekside Way, Ste. 50
Sun Peaks., V0E 1Z1
☎(800) 807-3257
⇄(250) 578-7843
Sun Peaks Resort is open all year and provides all the comforts. In the winter you can ski with Olympic champion Nancy Greene, but there are also a number of other activities, like swimming in the outdoor heated pool, snowmobile excursions, or the Christmas torch run. Families are welcome and young children can stay at the hotel and ski for free. There are plenty of summer activities, including golf and mountain biking. The complex also has a variety of dining establishments.

Salmon Arm

Bastion R.V. Park & Campground
$17 for two people
P, tv
3967 Sunnybrae Canoe Point Rd.
Shuswap Lake, 6km from the Trans-Canada Hwy.
☎835-4419
Bastion RV Park & Campground, has shaded or sunny sites and all the usual services for family camping. Monthly rents are possible during the winter, credit cards are not accepted, and small animals have to be kept on a leash. Call in advance to reserve or for information on when they're open during the different seasons.

Best Western Villager West Motor Inn
$70-$95
K, ⊛, ≈, ℜ
61-10th St. SW
☎(800)528-1234
☎832-9793
Best Western Villager West Motor Inn has rooms for non-smokers, a heated indoor pool, a whirlpool and a restau-

rant. They also organize cruises on the lake.

Revelstoke

Revelstoke Youth Hostel
$15-$19
K, sb
400 Second St. W.
☎837-4050
⇄837-6410
www.hostels.bc.ca
The Revelstoke Youth Hostel was completely renovated a short while ago. It is now a cheery and very comfortable facility, conveniently located in the centre of town. Free Internet access. Ski-accommodation packages starting from only $20/day!

Piano Keep Bed & Breakfast
$80-$100 bkfst incl.
no smoking, ≡
815 MacKenzie Ave.
☎/⇄(250) 837-2120
The Piano Keep Bed & Breakfast is an imposing Edwardian house set in the midst of a garden. Host Vern Enyedy welcomes his guests in a charming setting featuring pianos from different eras. Both a collector and a music lover, Vern will demonstrate his musical skill.

Best Western Wayside Inn
$89-$109
≡, ♞, ♿, *tv*, ≈, ⊛, ⌂, ℜ
1901 Laforme Blvd.
☎(250) 837-6161
in B.C. and Alberta
☎(800) 663-5307
☎(800) 528-1234
⇄837-5460
The Best Western Wayside Inn, on the north side of the Trans-Canada, is not only close to everything, but offers the added attraction of a pastoral setting with views of Revelstoke and the Columbia River.

Tour D: Okanagan-Similkameen

Cathedral Provincial Park

Cathedral Lakes Lodge
$99-$199
for reservations
☎(888) 255-4453
administration
☎(250) 226-7560
⇄226-7528
S4C8 Slocan Park, V0G 2E0
Cathedral Lakes Lodge has 10 rooms and 6 small cottages. The road to the top of the mountain is only open to the lodge's all-terrain vehicle, so you have to leave your car on Ashnola River Road in the lodge's base camp. If you go by foot, it will take you more than 6hrs to reach the lodge. Do not forget to reserve your seat in the vehicle. Turn left 4.8km west of Keremeos, cross over the covered bridge and drive along Ashnola River Road for 20.8km. If you plan on taking the bus, you have to call the lodge ahead of time to make arrangements for someone to pick you up. All this might seem complicated, but once you reach the top, you're sure to be enchanted by the mountain goats, marmots and flowers, not to mention glaciers stretching as far as the eye can see. Canoes and rowboats are available and the logge has a fireplace and a bar.

Southwest of Penticton

Olde Osprey Inn, Bed & Breakfast
$75-$100 bkfst incl.
sb, ♞, *no smoking*
Sheep Creek Rd.
☎/⇄(250) 497-7134
This magnificent log house was built by George Mullen, who astutely chose a site on a mountainside with an unimpeded view of Yellow Lake and the surrounding area. Joy Whitley, for her part, makes sure your stay is as comfortable as possible. She is a painter, and some of her work is on display here. Joy's daughter, furthermore, is a musician. This amiable family knows how to put their guests at

ease. The occasional osprey flies by, at which point everything comes to a halt as all eyes turn skyward.

Osoyoos

Cabana Beach Campground
$21-$27
May 1 to Sep 30
2231 Lakeshore Dr.
☎495-7705
Cabana Beach Campground has facilities for recreational vehicles and all the necessary services as well as access to the beach. Animals are not allowed from July 1 to August 15.

Avalon Motel
$40-$55 bkfst incl.
≈, ☎, ℑ, tv
Rte. 3
☎800-264-5999
☎495-6334
The Avalon Motel is a quiet 12 unit motel in town, close to restaurants, the museum, shops and beaches.

Bella Vista Resort Motel
$40-$70
K, ≈, tv
close to Route 3
☎888-495-6751
The Bella Vista Resort Motel has 14 rooms in a calm setting that is well-suited to families. Free coffee is served, and there are picnic areas with tables and barbecues. It also has its own private sandy beach.

Holiday Inn Sunspree Resort
$89-$220 depending on the season
K, ≈, ⊙, tv
Rte. 3
☎495-7223
The Holiday Inn Sunspree Resort is a luxury establishment that offers seaside condominiums. Open since May 1997, it has a private beach, indoor pool, gym, conference rooms, restaurant, golf packages and more. There are also large suites for families.

Lake Osoyoos Guest House
$105 bkfst incl.
waterfront, K, cash only
5809 Oleander Dr.
☎(250) 495-3297
☎(800) 671-8711
⇄495-5310
At the Lake Osoyoos Guest House, Sofia Grasso cooks up breakfast in her huge kitchen while guests sip freshly squeezed juice at the edge of Osoyoos Lake. Guests have use of a pedalboat to enjoy the lake and the changing colours of the valley as the day wears on.

Penticton

Penticton YHA
$15 members
$19 non-members
464 Ellis St., Penticton, V2A 4M2
☎(250) 492-3992
Penticton YHA has room for 52 people in dormitory and double rooms. Kitchen and lounge.

5000 Motel
$31-$69
K, ≈, tv, P
1742 Main St., downtown
☎493-5000
The 5000 Motel is conveniently located near everything.

Club Paradise Motel
$40-$75
K, ≡, tv, ⊛
1000 Lakeshore
☎493-8400
Club Paradise Motel offers good value for your money. The suites with balconies and barbecues are particularly inviting. The property faces the street that leads to the beach.

The Riordan House, Bed & Breakfast
$55-$75 bkfst incl.
sb
children 13 and older
no smoking
689 Winnipeg St.
☎/⇄(250) 493-5997
The Riordan House Bed & Breakfast is an Arts & Crafts style house built in 1920. Its owners, John and Donna Ortiz, have decorated it with antiques. Their little dog, Dust, will give you a loud welcome, but his bark is bigger than his bite.

Slumber Lodge
$58-$108
⌂, ≡, tv
274 Lakeshore
☎492-4008
☎(800) 663-2831
⇄492-7578
The recently renovated Slumber Lodge also faces the lakeshore. Clean and modern facility.

Spanish Villa Resort
$58-$108
≡, tv
890 Lakeshore
☎/⇄492-2922
☎(800) 552-9199
The Spanish Villa Resort is a good choice for families who want to be near the beach while enjoying a small, fully equipped apartment.

Penticton Inn
$72-$169
K, ≡, tv
333 Main St., downtown not far from the beach
☎(800) 666-2221
☎492-3600
The Penticton Inn has 126 rooms, each with its own character, for family vacations, honeymoons or business trips. Jacuzzies in some rooms, health club with saunas, restaurant, golf and ski packages.

Tiki Shores Condominium Beach Resort
$89
⊛, ⌂, tv, ℜ, ♿, no smoking
914 Lakeshore Dr.
☎(250) 492-8769
⇄492-8160
This motel is located steps away from the beach on Okanagan Lake, near the tourist office and a number of restaurants.

Summerland

The Illahie Beach
$16-$20
170 campsites, free showers, laundry, pay phone, convenience store, beach
north of Penticton on Hwy. 97
☎494-0800
The Illahie Beach campground welcomes vacationers from April to October. The beaches and views of the Okanagan Valley make for a heavenly setting.

Peachland

Castle Haymour
$99-$249
6239 Rte. 97 S.
☎767-3124
The Castle Haymour has suites with whirlpools and offers panoramic views of Okanagan Lake. Honeymoon packages are available; you can have breakfast served to you in bed. Romantic ambience.

Kelowna

Kelowna Samesun Motel Hostel
$15 members, $19 non-members
K
245 Harvey
☎/⇄763-9814
Kelowna's youth hostel, the Kelowna Samesun Motel Hostel, is located in the centre of town and can accommodate 24 people in its dormitories.

Chinook Motel
$45-$65
≡, K, tv
1864 Gordon Dr.
☎763-3657
☎(888) 493-8893
⇄868-8893
The Chinook Motel is ideally located near everything, including the beach and the town centre. The facility offers typical motel comfort with no surprises.

Crawford View Bed & Breakfast
$45-$68 bkfst incl.
≈, tennis, pb
810 Crawford Rd.
☎(250) 764-1140
⇄764-2892
The Crawford View Bed & Breakfast overlooks the valley and Okanagan Lake. You will be enchanted by your hosts, Fred and Gaby Geismayr, as well as by the beautiful surroundings. The recently built wooden house is surrounded by an apple orchard, a tennis court and a swimming pool. At the end of September, the Geismayrs are busy picking apples, but all the activity simply adds to the charm of the place.

Travellers Choice Motor Inn
$54-$79
≈, ⊛, K
1780 Gordon Dr.
☎(800) 665-2610
Travellers Choice Motor Inn is a comfortable motel located in a calm area with an indoor pool and a whirlpool.

Okanagan University
$55
3180 College Way
☎***470-6055***
⇄***470-6051***
In summer, you can rent a room or an apartment with up to four rooms at Okanagan University.

Holiday Park Resort
$59-$85
S1-415 Commonwealth Rd.
north of the city
☎***(800) 752-9678***
☎***766-4255***
Holiday Park Resort offers comfort and luxury in a lovely natural setting on the waterfront. Health, golf and wine festival packages are offered at reasonable prices.

Lake Okanagan Resort
$75-$200
ℜ
2751 Westside Rd.
☎***(800) 663-3273***
☎***769-3511***
www.lakeokanagan.com
Lake Okanagan Resort is located right on the lake and offers a complete luxury service to ensure a pleasant vacation. Golf, skiing, swimming, tennis, hiking and horseback riding are all offered. Families can take advantage of rooms, condos or cottages and there are even activities for kids. After a wonderful day outdoors you can sample one of their fine dinners to music.

Hotel Eldorado
$89-$165
tv
500 Cook Rd.
☎/⇄***765-2779***
Hotel Eldorado is located north of Kelowna at the exit for Old Vernon Road. It is quieter than other establishments since it is located a ways from the centre of town. The rooms are tastefully decorated, and the smell of freshly baked bread will put a smile on your face in the morning.

The Grand Okanagan
$119-$265
ℜ
1310 Water St.
☎***(800) 465-4651***
☎***763-4500***
www.grandokanagan.com
The motto of The Grand Okanagan is "Simply Grand," which is a sign of what awaits: a luxurious stay on the waterfront, elegant rooms and exquisite cuisine. Staff members are courteous and the many activities are all associated with the exceptional natural setting and take place around the lake, beaches, golf courses and vineyards. There are also many dining options throughout the region.

Vernon

Dutch's Tent & Trailer Court
$15-$22
15408 Kalamalka Rd.
☎***545-1023***
Dutch's Tent & Trailer Court rents campsites near a little creek only 5min from Vernon's main beach.

Lodged Inn/Vernon Hostel
$15
3201 Pleasant Valley Rd.
☎***549-3742***
☎***(888) 737-9427***
lodgeinn@bc.sympatico.ca
Located in an old home dating from 1894, Lodged Inn/Vernon Hostel is one of the loveliest youth hostels around. You really feel at home here, and the centre of town is only minutes away. The owner, who loves the great outdoors (climbing, mountain biking, canoeing, skiing, etc.), will give you some great tips.

Richmond House B&B
$65-$75 bkfst
⊛
4008 Pleasant Valley Rd.
☎/⇄***549-1767***
Richmond House B&B is an old Victorian-style home that has been completely restored. Its modern jacuzzi blends well with the antique furniture in the other rooms and the tasty breakfast leaves no one hungry.

Merritt

A.P. Guest Ranch
$65-$120
ℜ
Rte. 5A
☎***378-6520***
The A.P. Guest Ranch, where both the landscape and the decor are Old West style, has a bed & breakfast and cottages. Offered are all the activities of a ranch

in addition to horse rides on trails with exclusive views, fishing, snowmobile excursions and skiing. Quite an experience. The restaurant is open in the evenings.

Quilchena Hotel
$79-$98
sb/pb, ℜ
Apr to Oct
23 km northeast of Merritt on Hwy. 5A
☎(250) 378-2611
⇄378-6091
The historic Quilchena Hotel, located by the shore of a lake, harkens back to the days when cowboys relaxed around the dinner table. The place is furnished with antiques. Fishing and bikes for rent.

Tour E: Kootenay Country

Ainsworth Hot Springs

Ainsworth Hot Springs Resort
$66-$86
♿, ≈, *tv*, ℜ, *no smoking*, ⌂, in the caves, naturally warm water and ice-cold ≈
Hwy. 31
☎(250) 229-4212
☎(800) 668-1171
⇄229-5600
The Ainsworth Hot Springs Resort is part of the facilities surrounding the caves. Guests have free access to the caves, and can get passes for friends.

Nelson

City Tourist Park
$13-$16
no charge for children under 14
90 High St.
☎(250) 352-7618
off-season *☎352-6075*
The City Tourist Park is a 33-sites campground located in downtown Nelson, within walking distance of the major local attractions and restaurants. At the end of the day, head over to neighbouring Gyro Park to take in the view of the town and Kootenay Lake.

Dancing Bear Inn
$17 members
$20 non-members
171 Baker St., V1L 4H1
☎(250) 352-7573
Dancing Bear Inn is the local YHA hostel with common kitchen, lounge. Open year-round.

Inn the Garden Bed & Breakfast
$60-$70 bkfst incl.
sb/pb, adults only, P, no smoking
408 Victoria St.
☎(250) 352-3226
⇄352-3284
This charming Victorian house, renovated by owners Lynda Stevens and Jerry Van Veen, lies steps away from the main street. They also have a 3-bedroom cottage. The couple's warm welcome will make your stay in Nelson that much more pleasant. Ask them to tell you about the town's architectural heritage: it is one of their passions.

The Heritage Inn
$69-$89 bkfst incl.
tv, ℜ, ♿
422 Vernon St.
☎(250) 352-5331
⇄352-5214
The Heritage Inn was established in 1898, when the Hume brothers decided to build a grand hotel. Over the years, the building has been modified with each new owner. In 1980, major renovations breathed new life into the old place. The library is worth visiting; with its woodwork and fireplace, it has all the elements necessary to create a pleasant atmosphere. The walls of the rooms and corridors are covered with photographs capturing the highlights of Nelson's history.

Rossland

Mountain Shadow Hostel
$17 members
$21 non-members
2125 Columbia Ave.
V0G 1Y0
☎(250) 362-7160
Mountain Shadow Hostel, a YHA hostel, has a great location and friendly staff. Kitchen, tv lounge, dorm and double rooms.

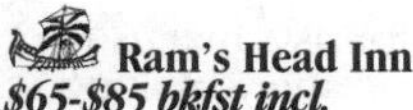 **Ram's Head Inn**
$65-$85 bkfst incl.
⊛, ⌂, *no smoking*
at the foot of the slopes
on Red Mountain Rd.
Box 636, V0G 1Y0
☎***(250) 362-9577***
⇄***362-5681***

An inviting house owned by Tauna and Greg Butler, the Ram's Head Inn feels like a home away from home. The fireplace, woodwork, simple decor and pleasant smells wafting out of the kitchen create a pleasant, informal atmosphere.

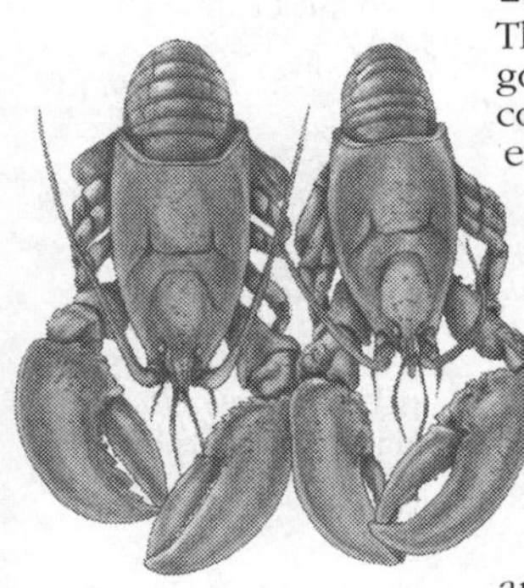

Hotel Uplander
$86-$96
≡, *K, tv*, ⊙, ⊛, ℜ
1919 Columbia
☎/⇄***362-7375***

The Hotel Uplander is a luxurious property situated right in the centre of town. A shuttle service brings you to the Red Mountain ski slopes. The hotel offers ski and golf packages depending on the season. A comfortable, quality establishment.

Restaurants

Tour A: The Sunshine Coast

Gibsons

Daily Roast
$
Mon to Fri 5am to 10pm
Sat 6:30am to 10pm
Sun 9am to 5pm
5547 Wharf Rd.
☎***885-4345***

The Daily Roast is a good café with the best coffee in the area; the expresso is excellent. It also sells cookies and homemade muffins.

Lighthouse Pub
$
every day
just after Porpoise Bay Rd.
on the waterfront
☎***885-4949***

Great hamburgers and good beer. Friendly, lively atmosphere. During your meal, you can watch hydroplanes taking off. A liquor store is integrated into the pub.

Molly's Reach Restaurant
$
every day
647 School Rd.
☎***886-9710***

Gibsons became famous throughout the world as the setting for *The Beachcombers*, a Canadian Broadcasting Corporation (CBC) television series. The show was produced for close to 20 years and broadcast in over 40 countries. Molly's Reach Restaurant is the place where all the characters met; itappeared in every episode. The walls of the restaurant are decorated with photos from the series. The environment is always lively and enjoyable and the food id good. If you go to Gibsons you must to go to Molly's Reach.

Sechelt

Mother Earth Café
$
every day
on Cowrie St.
close to the Cenotaph
☎***885-7626***

Mother Earth Café serves natural homemade food. Very good for your health: pasta, soups and a salad counter.

Poseidon Restaurant
$$
every day
Davis Bay, on Hwy. 101
☎***885-6046***

The Poseidon Restaurant is a good Greek restaurant that also serves pasta, steak and seafood.

Powell River

Beach Gardens Resort Hotel
$$-$$$
7074 Westminster Ave.
☎***(604) 485-6267***
☎***(800) 663-7070***

The dining room at the Beach Gardens Resort Hotel looks out onto the Malaspina Strait. The menu lists divine seafood dishes flavoured with Okanagan wines.

Tour B: The Sea to Sky Highway – Fraser River Loop

Britannia Beach

The Cookhouse
$
☎***896-0010***
The Cookhouse serves soup, sandwiches, hamburgers and fries with a homemade taste.

Squamish

Klahanie Restaurant
$
Hwy. 9, across from Shannon Falls
☎***892-5312***
Klahanie Restaurant serves home-made food.

Loggers Inn Restaurant
$
38139 Cleveland Ave.
☎***892-3733***
Loggers Inn Restaurant, has two specialties: fresh fish and steak.

Lotus Gardens
$
38180 Cleveland Ave.
☎***892-5853***
Lotus Gardens is a Chinese restaurant with a long, detailed menu, with many different chicken, pork, fish and vegetable dishes. You can also get your meal to take out.

Midway Restaurant
$-$$
40330 Tantalus Way
in the Best Western
☎***898-4874***
Midway Restaurant offers home-style food in a friendly, lively environment.

Squamish Valley Golf & Country Club
$-$$
2458 Mamquam Rd.
☎***898-9521*** and ***898-9691***
Squamish Valley Golf & Country Club's restaurant serves breakfast, lunch and supper and offers daily specials. The staff is friendly and it's open all year, as is their Sport Bar & Grill.

Whistler

Black's Pub & Restaurant
$
below Whistler and Blackcomb Mountains
☎***932-6408*** or ***932-6945***
Black's Pub & Restaurant serves breakfast, lunch and dinner for the whole family in a friendly atmosphere. The views are exceptional and it has one of the best beer selections in Whistler.

Città Bistro
$
every day 11am to 1am
Whistler Village Square
☎***(604) 932-4177***
Located in the heart of the village, Città Bistro has an elaborate menu with selections ranging from salads to pita pizzas. This is the perfect place to sample one of the local beers. In both winter and summer, a pleasant mix of locals and tourists makes for an extremely inviting atmosphere.

Pika's
$
Dec to Apr, 7:30am to 3:30pm
at the top of the Whistler Village Gondola
☎***(604) 932-3434***
If you want to be among the first to ski the slopes in the morning, head to Pika's for breakfast; it is worth getting up early the day after a storm.

Hard Rock Café
$-$$
Sun to Thu 11:30am to midnight
Fri and Sat to 1am
in the village of Whistler
near Blackcomb Way
☎***(604) 938-9922***
The Hard Rock Café has a lively clientele and a menu featuring salads and hamburgers.

Zeuski's
$-$$
Town Plaza
☎***932-6009***
Zeuski's is a Greek restaurant. Tzatziki, hummus and souvlaki are served and the prices are very reasonable for Whistler.

Thai One On
$$
every day, dinner
in the Le Chamois hotel
at the foot of the Blackcomb Mountain slopes
☎***(604) 932-4822***
As may be gathered by its name, Thai One On serves Thai food, with its wonderful blend of coconut milk and hot peppers.

Ristorante Araxi
$$-$$$
Whistler Village
☎938-3337
Ristorante Araxi is the Italian restaurant of choice on the Pacific coast. It specializes in pasta, pizza, veal and chicken but salmon is also served. The wine cellar is renowned as are the head chef and pastry chef.

Monk's Grill
$$-$$$
4555 Blackcomb Way
at the foot of Blackcomb
☎932-9677
Monk's Grill is great for an après-ski dinner. On the menu are oysters, shrimp, filet mignon, loin of lamb and salmon.

Trattoria di Umberto
$$-$$$
near Blackcomb Way
on the ground floor
of the Mountainside Lodge
☎(604) 932-5858
At the Trattoria di Umberto, you'll find pasta dishes and a homey atmosphere.

Pemberton

The Pony Expresso
$
1426 Portage Rd.
☎894-5700
At The Pony Expresso, the fine coffee is complemented with fresh bagels.

Spirit Circle Art Craft & Tea Co.
$
on Lillooet Hwy.
as you're leaving Pemberton
☎894-6336
The Spirit Circle Art Craft & Tea Co. is a tearoom-shop-restaurant where you can get the best-ever veggie-burgers. There's also a wide variety of teas and of Aboriginal craft work. An excellent spot.

Willy G's
$-$$
10-1359 Aster Rd.
☎(604) 894-6411
Willy G's has a reputation for preparing fine food. On the menu are steak, fish and pasta.

Harrison Hot Springs

Black Forest Restaurant
$-$$
180 Esplanade Ave.
☎796-9343
The Black Forest Restaurant is an Alsatian-style restaurant with flowery windows. The food, including schnitzel, Chateaubriand and fresh pasta, has a European flavour. They also serve B.C. salmon. The wine list is extensive. It's open year round in the evening, but only in the summer for breakfast.

Kitami
$$
318 Hot Springs Rd.
☎796-2728
Kitami is a Japanese restaurant that invites you to enjoy a meal in one of their Tatami Rooms or at the sushi bar.

Harrison Hot Spring Hotel
$$-$$$
100 Esplanade
☎800-663-2266
The restaurant at the Harrison Hot Spring Hotel offers dinners that are a gastronomical delight accompanied by music and dancing. They serve meats and fish.

Tour C: The Thompson River as Far as Revelstoke

Kamloops

Internet Café
$
462 Victoria
☎828-7889
Internet Café, whose motto is "the world is at your fingertips invites you to check your messages, play the lottery or surf the Internet while enjoying a salad or hamburger. The atmosphere is friendly and, if needed, the staff will help you on the computer.

Bagel Street Cafe
$
428 Victoria St.
☎372-9322
Bagel Street Cafe offers a variety of bagels and coffees. Try the sun-dried tomato bagel with Swiss cheese, spinach and artichoke hearts.

Earl's
$-$$
800-1210 Summit Dr.
☎*372-3275*
Earl's serves a fine variety of tasty salads as well as many original meat and fish dishes, all made with fresh ingredients.

The Keg
$-$$
1430 Summit Dr.
☎*828-2666*
The Keg, another chain restaurant, is a safe bet for steak lovers. Very good service.

Grass Roots Tea House
$$
May to Sep
lunch 11:30am to 2:30pm
tea 2pm to 4pm
dinner 6:30pm (one service, reserve by 2pm)
reservations required during winter
262 Lorne St.
☎*(250) 374-9890*
Located in Riverside Park, the Grass Roots Tea House is a charming place surrounded by trees, where you can enjoy a cup of ginseng tea. Reservations are required for dinner, and the menu varies depending on what day of the week it is.

Déjà Vu
$$$
Tue to Sat 5pm to 10pm
172 Battle St.
☎*374-3227*
Déjà Vu serves West Coast and French cuisine featuring an imaginative blend of fruit and seafood.

Revelstoke

Frontier Restaurant
$
daily 5am to midnight
near the tourist office
at the intersection of the Trans-Canada Hwy. and the 23
☎*(250) 837-5119*
At the Frontier Restaurant, you can put away a big breakfast in a typically western setting.

Black Forest
$$-$$$
5min west of Revelstoke
on the Trans-Canada
☎*(250) 837-3495*
The Black Forest is a Bavarian-style restaurant that serves Canadian and European cuisine. Top billing on the menu goes to cheese and fish. The setting and view of Mount Albert are enchanting.

Tour D: Okanagan-Similkameen

Penticton

Great Canadian Bagel
$
2210 Main St.
Lougheed Super Centre
beside Zellers
☎*490-9796*
The Great Canadian Bagel is the place for good, fresh, wonderful-smelling bagels that you can enliven with your choice of toppings and trimmings.

Hog's Breath Coffee Co.
$
every day
202 Main St.
☎*(250) 493-7800*
The Hog's Breath is the perfect place to start off your day with a good cup of coffee, and even more importantly, some peach muffins (in season): you'll love them! If you're looking for outdoors destinations, the owner, Mike Barrett, will gladly offer some suggestions.

Johnny Appleseeds Juice Bar & Cafe
$
3018 30th Ave.
☎*542-7712*
Johnny Appleseeds Juice Bar & Cafe serves excellent fresh juice concoctions, such as the Eye Opener, which combines orange, pineapple and apple juice. Coffee and delicious light fare are also served.

The Pasta Factory
$-$$
75 Front St.
☎*493-5666*
The Pasta Factory offers a lively, pleasant family atmosphere with good pasta and service. Reservations recommended.

Salty's Beach House
$-$$
1000 Lakeshore Dr.
☎*(250) 493-5001*
Seafood fans will find their favourite foods at Salty's Beach House. Make sure to come here at lunchtime so you can enjoy the view of Okanagan Lake from the terrace. The pirate-

ship decor gives the place a festive atmosphere.

Earl's
$$
1848 Main St.
☎493-7455
The quality is always consistent and this chain. You'll enjoy having your meal on the terrace.

Hang Chow Restaurant
$$
3102 30th Ave.
☎545-9195
The Chinese buffet at Hang Chow Restaurant is a good choice when you're famished.

Lost Moose Lodge
$$
8min. from the centre of Penticton
Beaverdell Rd.
☎490-0526
Lost Moose Lodge offers music, spectacular views and good barbecued food. It was restaurant of the year in 1996.

Niko's Taverna
$$
2334 30th Ave.
☎542-4300
Niko's Taverna is a plainly decorated Greek restaurant that serves up generous portions. The oven-baked vegetarian casserole with feta cheese is scrumptious.

Theo's Restaurant
$$-$$$
687 Main St.
☎(250) 492-4019
Fine Greek cuisine and a relaxed atmosphere make for a pleasant meal at this extremely popular spot.

Granny Bogners Restaurant
$$$
302 Eckhardt Ave. W.
☎(250) 493-2711
This magnificent Tudor house was built in 1912 for a local doctor. In 1976, Hans and Angela Strobel converted it into a restaurant, where they serve fine French cuisine made with local produce.

Kelowna

P.J.'s Allstar Café
$
Orchard Park Mall
☎861-5354
P.J.'s Allstar Café serves *fajitas*, chicken and burgers in a lively, friendly and relaxed atmosphere. Reasonable prices.

Joey Tomato's Kitchen
$-$$
every day
300-2475 Hwy. 97 N
at the intersection of Hwy. 33
☎(250) 860-8999
Joey Tomato's Kitchen is located near a large boulevard in a neighbourhood of shopping malls. The people who run this place have created a pleasant atmosphere. The terrace, with its plants, parasols and little Italian car, will keep your attention. The dining room is also extremely attractive – a large space brightened up by cans of food and bottles of oil, making you feel as if you're, well, in Joey's kitchen. And the pasta! Make sure to try the fettucine with salmon and tomatoes: it's a real treat.

The Yamas Taverna
$-$$
1630 Ellis St.
downtown
☎763-5823
The Yamas Taverna is a Greek restaurant *par excellence*. White and blue, and abundantly flowered, this restaurant assures clients an excellent evening with a Meditteranean flavour. Voted as "Best New Restaurant" and "Best Meal for the Money," you won't be disappointed, especially on Saturday nights when they feature belly dancing.

Perkins
$$
2170 Harvey
☎717-1500
Perkins is a family restaurant that serves pancakes, club sandwiches and steaks all day long.

Red Robin
$$
2334 30th Ave.
☎762-9700
Red Robin's speciality is enormous, tasty hamburgers as well as a variety of exotic drinks. Relaxed, laid-back atmosphere.

La Bussola Restaurant
$$-$$$
234 Leon Ave.
right near City Park
☎763-3110
La Bussola Restaurant is famous for the quality of its food and the

pleasant, intimate setting. For 23 years Franco and Lauretta have been welcoming clients and delighting them with their Italian food. Reservations are recommended.

Christopher's
$$-$$$
242 Lawrence Ave.
right near city Park
☎861-3464
Christopher's is one of the best restaurants in Kelowna. It was chosen as the "Best Steak & Seafood" restaurant in 1996. Open every day, it serves a very good lunch buffet; the ambience is elegant and the service is very friendly. Reservations recommended.

Mekong
$$$
1030 Harvey
☎763-2238
Mekong serves refined Chinese and Szechwan cuisine in its luxurious dining room.

Merritt

Coldwater Hotel
$-$$
restaurant Sun to Thu
7:30am to 9pm
saloon to 2am
at the corner of Quilchena and Voght
☎(250) 378-5711
Both the restaurant and the saloon in the Coldwater Hotel have always been popular with local cowboys. The food is somewhat heavy, but the prices are right. The rooms can be rented by the month or by the year.

Best Western
$$
4025 Walters St.
☎378-4253
Best Western offers service inside or on the terrace. Elegant country-style atmosphere. Sunday brunch and prime ribs on Fridays.

Tour E: Kootenay Country

Nelson

El Zocalo Mexican Café
$$
802 Baker St.
☎(250) 352-7223
The successful El Zocalo Mexican Café occupies a Mexican-style building and features live Mexican music. Guests enjoy delicious, traditional Mexican cuisine in a fiesta-like atmosphere.

All Seasons Café
$$-$$$
every day
lunch 11:30am to 2:30pm
dinner 5pm to 10pm
Sun brunch 10am to 3pm
closed for lunch in winter
620 Herridge Lane, behind Baker St.
☎(250) 352-0101
The All Seasons Café is not to be missed. It lies hidden beneath the trees, so its terrace is bathed in shade. The soups might surprise you a bit – apple and broccoli (in season) is one example. The menu is determined by the season and what's available in the area, with lots of space accorded to the fine wines of British Columbia. The friendly, efficient service, elegant decor and quality cuisine make for an altogether satisfying meal. The walls are adorned with works of art.

Rossland

Many quaint cafes line Columbia Street in the heart of Rossland. The population doubles in December when the slopes open, giving the town a festive, ski-vacation-like atmosphere. Sunshine Cafe and Bean There offer light fare and hearty breakfasts.

Bean There
$
2040 Columbia
☎362-5273

Sunshine Cafe
$
2120 Columbia
☎362-7630

Flying Steamshovel Inn
$$
Washington St., corner Second Ave.
Flying Steamshovel Inn has a Western-style decor and a saloon-like atmosphere. The menu includes big, fat sandwiches, pasta, salads and, of course, a good selection of beer on tap.

Mountain Gypsy Cafe
$$
2167 Washington St.
☎362-3342
Mountain Gypsy Cafe offers a unique variety of eclectic dishes, from couscous to chicken.

The prices are very reasonable.

Olive Oyl's
$$-$$$
2067 Columbia
☎263-5322
Olive Oyl's cuisine is best described as contemporary or fusion cuisine, combining several different culinary trends. Its offerings include pasta, pizza and enormous brunches, all meticulously prepared and presented.

Entertainment

Bars and Nightclubs

Boot Pub
Whistler
1km north of the village on the right, on Nancy Greene Dr.
☎932-3338
At the Boot Pub, located in the Shoestring Lodge hotel, live musicians play R&B to an enthusiastic clientele.

Tommy Africa's
Gateway Dr., Whistler
☎932-6090
Young reggae fans get together at Tommy Africa's. Line-ups are common due to its popularity.

Cinnamon Bear Bar
4050 Whistler Way, Whistler
in the Delta Hotel
☎932-1982
The relaxed atmosphere at the Cinnamon Bear Bar attracts sporty types of all ages.

Calendar of Events

January 1

The **Polar Bear Swim** is an old tradition; every year hundreds of Gibsons residents plunge into the icy water of Davis Bay.

May

Okanagan Wine Festival
☎800-972-5151
The four-day **Okanagan Wine Festival**, held each May and October, is not to be missed. Eighty organized events offer the opportunity for many pleasant wine-tasting experiences.

Beer also plays a role in this prolific region, and **Fest of Ale** *(call the wine festival organization for the exact date)* honours the area's many microbreweries.

June

Summer Festival
Lion's Park, Sechelt
☎883-9746

July

Merritt Mountain Music Festival
From July 17 to 20, be prepared to have a good time at the **Merritt Mountain Music Festival**, attended by over 70,000 fans. The program includes, in addition to the concerts, games for kids, helicopter rides, dancing, bingo, delicious wonderful-smelling pancake breakfasts served by the Merritt Lions Club and much more.

August

Peach Festival
It's now been 50 years since the first **Peach Festival**, held at the beginning of every August. Families in the area are invited to come and enjoy a pancake breakfast, wonderful fruits and vegetables, peaches among them of course and, to top it all off, a fireworks display.

Gibsons Landing Jazz Festival
Gibsons

Festival of the Written Arts
Rockwood
☎885-9613

September

Oyster & Wine Festival
St. Bart's, Sechelt
☎886-2400 or ***886-9677***

Sechelt Fall Festival
Hackett Park and downtown Sechelt
☎885-0662

Pender Harbour Jazz Festival
Lowe's Resort
Sechelt
☎883-9266

October

Okanagan Wine Festival
☎800-972-5151
See listing for May.

Kelowna's famous **Wine Festivals** *(☎861-6654)* are held every spring and fall and the **BC Wine Label Awards** are held in October at the **Wine Museum** (*☎250-868-0441*).

December

Lighted Boat Parade for Christmas
Gibsons Harbour
☎886-8500

Shopping

Tour B: The Sea to Sky Highway – Fraser River Loop

Squamish

Vertical Reality Sports Store *(38154 Second Ave., ☎892-8248)* sells and rents mountain bikes, offers guided tours, gives advice on rock-climbing and will even take you there.

Whistler

Outside the little village, at the edge of the Whistler region, lies Function Junction, a small industrial area of sorts. You won't find just any industries here, however!

Whistler Brewery *(free admission; Alpha Lake Rd., Function Junction, south of Whistler Creekside, ☎932-6185).* This microbrewery distributes its products locally, and they are extremely popular. You just might learn the recipe for their beer while touring the facilities.

Blackcomb Cold Beer & Wine Store *(across from The Chateau Whistler Inn, ☎932-9795)* has a large selection of B.C. wines. Helpful and courteous staff.

The Wright Choice Catering *(12-1370 Alpha Lake Rd., ☎905-0444)* will make supper for you. Every day you can pick up something different such as *focaccia*, pizza, grilled vegetables and chicken. They also prepare complete picnics, ready to take out.

Little Mountain Bakery *(7-1212 Alpha Lake Rd., Function Junction, ☎932-4220)* sells bread, pastries and sweets.

Whistler Flowers Bouquet *(Market Place, ☎932-2599)* has a wonderful selection of fresh flowers and bouquets for special occasions. You can also have flowers sent anywhere in the world.

All Seasons SPA *(Chateau Whistler Resort, ☎938-2086)* will help you relax and recuperate in grand style.

Whistler-in-Colour *(Tyndalle Stone Lodge 121, 4338 Main St., ☎905-4238)* is a large store specializing in perfume and cosmetics.

Kelty Expedition Gear *(Function Junction, ☎932-6381)* sells and rents anything you might need for outdoor activities as well as guitars to liven up an evening around the bonfire.

Whistler Sailing *(Lakeside & Wayside Parks Alta Lake, ☎932-7245)* has all the necessities for sailing and water sports.

Adele-Campbell *(close to the entrance of the Delta Whistler Resort, ☎938-0887)* exhibits works by renowned artists from B.C. and throughout Canada.

The Plaza Galleries *(22-4314 Main St., ☎938-6233)* present works by artists in the region.

The Grove Gallery *(Delta Whistler Resort, ☎932-3517)* offers landscapes of Whistler and the mountains.

Whistler Inuit Gallery *(Canadian Pacific Chateau, ☎938-3366)* exhibits its very attractive wood, bone, marble and bronze pieces by Aboriginal sculptors.

Harrison Hot Springs

Curiosities *(160 Lillooet Ave., ☎796-9431)*, as the name suggests, sells souvenirs, toys for children, T-shirts and other vacation clothing.

A Question of Balance *(880 Hot Springs Rd., ☎796-9622)* is an art gallery created by Canadian craftspeople. The knitting, sewing, ceramics and blown glass are beautiful and interesting.

Harrison Watersports *(6069 Rockwell Dr., behind the Rivtow Office, on Harrison Lake, ☎604-796-3513 or 795-6775)* rents Jet Skis and organizes rides.

Crafts & Things Market *(☎796-2084)*. From March to November, Harrison Hot Springs hosts a number of markets; call for dates and times.

Tour C: The Thompson River as Far as Revelstoke

Kamloops

Farmer's Markets *(Saturdays, 200 block-St Paul St.; Wed at the corner of Third Ave. and Victoria St.)*. Delightful food markets are organized from May to October.

Tour D: Okanagan-Similkameen

Kelowna

The **Far West Factory Outlet** *(230-2469 Rte. 97, ☎860-9010)* sells comfortable, light clothing by major name brands.

Valhalla Pure Outfitters *(453 Bernard Ave., downtown, ☎763-9696)* is a popular local manufacturer that specializes in clothing.

Mosaïc Books *(1420 St. Paul St., downtown, ☎736-4418)* carries a good selection of maps for excursions and books.

VIA Rail: Discover Canada By Train!

In this part of North America where the highway is king, the train is often overlooked as a different and enjoyable way of exploring Canada. What better way to contemplate the spectacular and unique Western Canadian scenery than through huge picture windows while comfortably seated in your wide reclining chair?

The Routes

Experience the romance of the rails and the spectacular scenery in the comfort and elegance of the restored Art-Deco surroundings of Via's longhaul trains.

An exciting way of seeing the country is aboard the **Canadian**, which departs from Toronto and travels all the way to Vancouver running through Ontario's forests, the central Prairies and the mountains of the West. The **Skeena** offers just as spectacular a route, departing from Jasper in the Rockies and traversing the mountains travelling along the magnificent Skeena River all the way to Prince Rupert. Finally, the **Malahat** makes daily trips on Vancouver Island, between Victoria and Courtenay, serving up magnificent views along the way.

Economy or First Class?

In economy class, cars have comfortable seats with wide corridors. If you prefer something more luxurious, go first class, called Silver & Blue Class aboard the **Canadian**. This includes sleeping cars and exclusive access to the Park Car and to many dome cars to fully enjoy the stunning views. Also included are all meals, taken in the refined ambiance of dining cars.

The **Skeena**'s prestigious Totem Class service includes meal service at your seat and exclusive use of the Park Car. You have access to one of the panoramic domes on the upper deck and to the congenial Bullet Lounge downstairs where you can exchange travel stories with holidaymakers from all over the world.

Save with ***VIA!***

VIA offers several types of savings:

Up to 40% off on travel outside peak periods and tourist season, on certain days of the week and on advance bookings (five days), depending on the destination;

Student rebates (24 years and under with presentation of ISIC card, 40% year-round on advance booking except during Christmas period);

A 10% discount for people aged 60 and over, on certain days during off-peak travel times up to 50%, depending on the destination;

Special rates for children (2 to 15 years, half-price; free for 2 years and under, accompanied by an adult)

Special Tickets

With the **CANRAILPASS**, you can travel throughout Canada on one ticket. The ticket allows 12 days of unlimited travel in a 30-day period for $616 in high season and $390 in low season (Jan 1 to May 31 and Oct 16 to Dec 31).

The **North America Rail Pass**, valid on all VIA and Amtrak trains, is available in economy class for a 30-day period for $675 during off-peak periods and $965 during peak periods.

For further information, call your travel agent or closest VIA office, or visit the website at: www.viarail.ca

Northern British Columbia

British Columbia has long been renowned for its exceptional and varied range of outdoor activities.

If you have a taste for adventure and exploring, or if you simply love nature, you will be repeatedly delighted and surprised by the unspoiled, little known northern part of the province.

Eighty percent of this territory is studded with mountains, many of which are perpetually covered with snow or glaciers. The lakes, which collect the runoff from the glaciers, are almost iridescent, while the forests are among the most renowned in the world. These enchanting surroundings offer endless possibilities for outdoor activities — just let your imagination run wild.

Two distinct regions make up northern British Columbia, the North by Northwest and the Peace River-Alaska Highway regions; together, they account for 50% of the province's total area. Despite their isolated location, a number of towns are fully equipped to welcome tourists with campgrounds, hotels and restaurants that offer amenities comparable to those found in big cities.

Only three major roads lead through these vast northern spaces. The Stewart-Cassiar Highway (Hwy. 37), to the west, passes through the heart of the North by Northwest region. The Alaska Highway, in the east, starts at Dawson Creek. And finally, the Yellowhead Highway (Hwy. 16) runs along the southern part of these two regions, all the way to the shores of the Pacific, where visitors can set out for the Queen Charlotte Islands.

The starting point of any visit to northern British Columbia is the city of Prince George. From there north, the summer days grow noticeably longer. This phenomenon becomes more and more evident the farther north you go. The summertime sky never darkens completely, and depending on where you find yourself, you might even see the midnight sun. Near the province's border with the Yukon, along the 60th parallel, the summer sky always has a trace of light even in the dead of night, and the northern lights, or aurora borealis, are a common sight during the long winter months.

Summer is characterized by long sunny days with temperatures often higher than in the south. The winters are long. In the northwest, where the snowfall is very heavy, the weather is relatively mild, despite sub-zero Celsius temperatures. In the northeast, the climate is continental, with less snow and severe, dry cold.

Contrary to popular belief, the cost of living in the country is by no means less expensive than in big cities. Farming and stockbreeding are not carried out on a major scale in northern British Columbia, nor are any raw materials processed here; as a result, food, fuel, hotels, etc. are all 50% to 100% more expensive, depending on where you are. As far as telephone calls are concerned, keep in mind that phone booths are quite rare, and can only be found near parks and in towns and villages.

A trip to northern British Columbia offers a chance to take in some of the most beautiful scenery in Canada. To help you make the most of your trip, we have outlined seven tours:

Tour A:
The Gold Rush Trail and the Cariboo Mountains ★★

Tour B:
To the Alaska Highway ★★

Tour C:
The Hudson's Hope Route ★★

Tour D:
The Alaska Highway ★★★

Tour E:
The Stewart-Cassiar Highway ★★★

Tour F:
To Stewart, BC and Hyder, AK ★★★;

Tour G:
The Yellowhead Highway ★★★

Tour H: The Queen Charlotte Islands (Haida Gwaii) ★★★.

Finding Your Way Around

By Car

Tour A: The Gold Rush Trail and the Cariboo Mountains

This tour forms a straight line between Prince George and William's Lake, a distance of about 200km. Starting at Quesnel, the halfway point, the Cariboo Mountains are about a 100km jaunt to the east.

This region sprung up over 100 years ago. Before heading off into the remote regions, gold diggers stopped in the towns of the Fraser

River Plateau (William's Lake and Quesnel) to stock up on provisions and gear for the tough job ahead.

Hwy. 97 heads southward between Prince George and William's Lake. At the halfway point, just a few kilometres north of Quesnel, Hwy. 26 branches off to the east towards the old mining towns of Bowron Lake Provincial Park – a paradise for canoeists.

Tour B: To the Alaska Highway

Hwy. 97 leads from Prince George to Dawson Creek, Km/mile 0 of the Alaska Highway. The region has developed mostly around the lumber and hydroelectric industries. It is quite common to come across bears and moose here, particularly in the provincial parks, which have well laid-out campsites. Halfway through the tour, you will reach the turnoff for Hwy. 39, which leads to Mackenzie, another 29km away. Since the 39 is a dead-end, you'll have to backtrack to pick up the 97 again. Crossing Pine Pass, you'll see the first foothills of the Rockies and discover how truly immense the forest is. About 100km past Powder King, the ski resort, lies the town of Chetwynd. From there, you can reach Tumbler Ridge, but you will have to double back to the 97 again to complete the tour.

Tour C: The Hudson's Hope Route

Another way of getting to the Alaska Highway from Prince George is to take the 29 North, which leads to the village of Hudson's Hope and intersects with the Alaska Highway at Km 86.

Tour D: The Alaska Highway

This tour covers the part of the Alaska Highway that runs through British Columbia. It starts at Km/mile 0, in Dawson Creek, and leads to the town of Watson Lake, a little over a 1,000km away, just over the province's border with the Yukon. The first town you will pass through is Fort St. John, followed by Fort Nelson and the Stone Mountain, Muncho Lake and Liard Hot Springs Provincial Parks.

When the Alaska Highway was first being laid, distances were gauged in miles. Since Canada adopted the metric system in the 1970s, the Canadian portion of this legendary highway has been officially measured in terms of kilometres as well. Even today, however, it is not uncommon to come across road maps and government brochures with distances still labelled in miles. Furthermore, in deference to tradition (and American influence), the entire road is studded with commemorative milestones showing no metric equivalents.

Visitors can combine Tours C and D into a single big loop, since the Stewart-Cassiar Highway and the Alaska Highway intersect at Junction 37, at mile 649 of the Alaska Highway, not far from Watson Lake.

Road Conditions

Dawson Creek:
☎ ***(800) 663-4997***

Fort Nelson:
☎ ***774-7447 or 774-6956***

Tour E: The Stewart-Cassiar Highway

Visitors usually take this tour from south to north, starting at Kitwanga. On the left, 169km from Kitwanga, Hwy. 37A branches off toward Stewart and Hyder, Alaska (see "Tour E," below). You will head north on Hwy. 37 for the entire tour, which covers a little under 600km. The road passes numerous little towns along the way, including Tatoffa, Iskut, Dease Lake, Good Hope Lake and Upper Liard (Yukon). Once you've arrived at Dease Lake, it is worth

Some Advice Before Taking the Stewart Cassiar and Alaska Highways

Most of the northern highways in British Columbia are paved. Some portions of the Stewart Cassiar Highway and the Alaska Highway however, are gravel. Flat tires are common so it is important to check your spare tire. Bring along an anti-flat spray as tire-repair shops are relatively uncommon. Ensure that your vehicle is in good working order before heading out. A tow to the nearest town and waiting around for parts from Vancouver will cost you a lot of time and money.

Fill up your gas tank whenever you can since gas stations are rare. Take a 25-litre jerry can just to be sure.

Don't forget to buckle up and keep your headlights on at all times for better visibility on the sometimes dusty, long straight stretches.

The Weather and the Highway

You've probably figured out that winters are cold in this part of the province, but not many people know that the summers in northern B.C. are sunny and often very hot. The temperature can fall below -50°C in January, but can easily reach 35°C in July.

Choosing the right clothes for the seasons is essential. In summer: cotton is the material of choice and a basic wardrobe consists of shorts, long-sleeve shirts, T-shirts, sweaters and sturdy shoes. Sandals are good to have if you're driving for long periods. If you will be stopping in the mountains bring a windbreaker, a hat and sunscreen. The effects of the sun can be easy to forget in this northern region, but they are just as harmful as anywhere else. Be aware that it can also snow, even during the summer, and, although snowfalls tend to be brief, it's better to be prepared.

During the winter it's best to dress in layers; this provides the best insulation, rather than wearing a big coat. Don't forget gloves, a hat, good boots and blankets. A breakdown or flat can turn out to be a survival test ending in tragedy if you're not prepared. Happy travelling!

taking the time to visit Telegraph Creek, 129km away; a well-marked, well-maintained dirt road leads there. Like Tour C, Tour D ends at Watson Lake, in the Yukon. You can combine Tours C and D into one big loop, since the Stewart-Cassiar and Alaska Highways intersect at Junction 37, at mile 649 of the Alaska Highway, near Watson Lake.

Tour F: To Stewart, BC and Hyder, AK

This tour starts at Meziadin Junction, along the Stewart-Cassiar Highway (see Tour D, above); turn right onto Hwy. 37 A, commonly known as

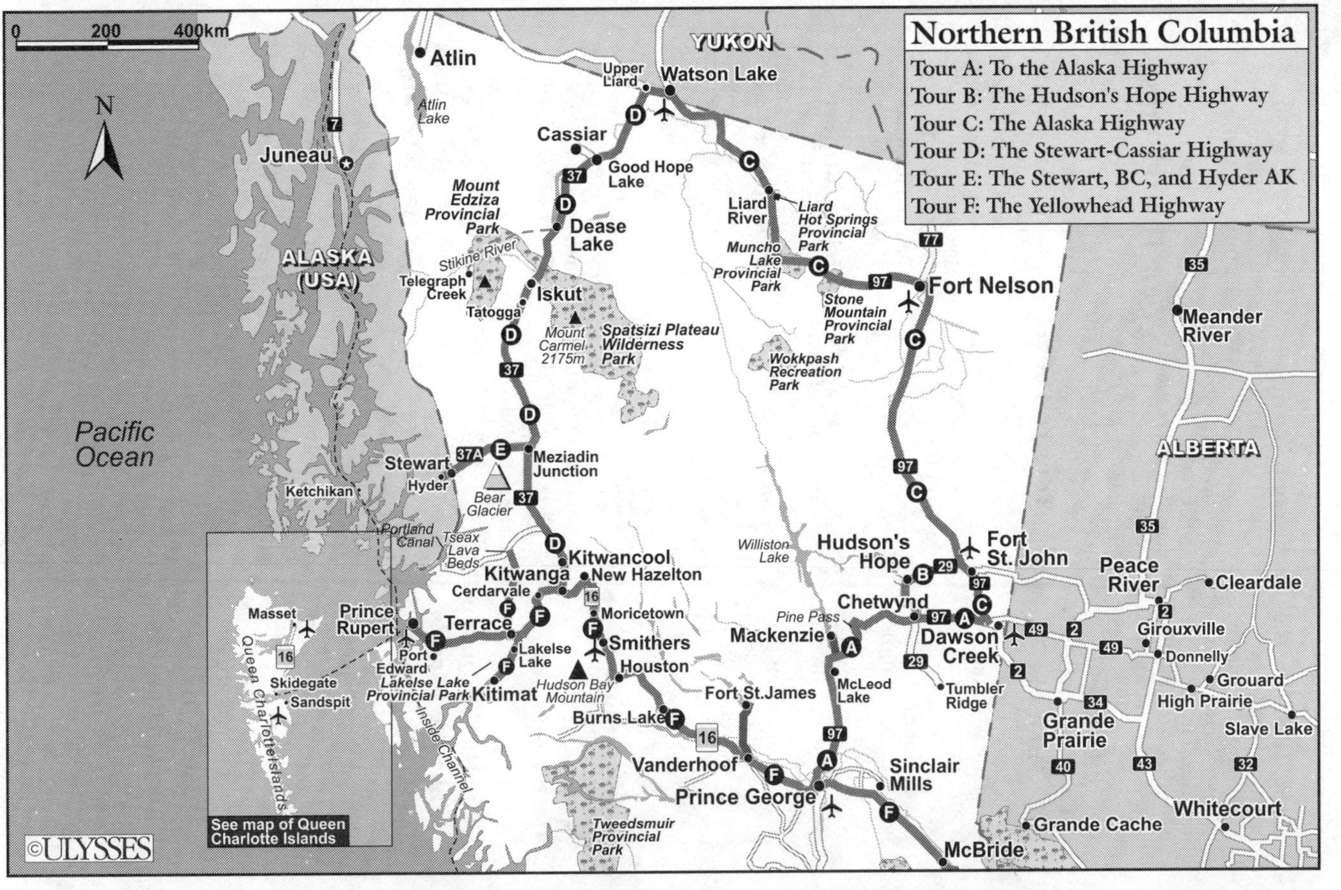

Northern British Columbia
Tour A: To the Alaska Highway
Tour B: The Hudson's Hope Highway
Tour C: The Alaska Highway
Tour D: The Stewart-Cassiar Highway
Tour E: The Stewart, BC, and Hyder AK
Tour F: The Yellowhead Highway
0 200 400km
N
Pacific Ocean
ALASKA (USA)
YUKON
ALBERTA
Atlin
Atlin Lake
Juneau
Upper Liard
Watson Lake
Cassiar
Good Hope Lake
Mount Edziza Provincial Park
Dease Lake
Stikine River
Telegraph Creek
Tatogga
Iskut
Mount Carmel 2175m
Spatsizi Plateau Wilderness Park
Liard River
Liard Hot Springs Provincial Park
Muncho Lake Provincial Park
Stone Mountain Provincial Park
Wokkpash Recreation Park
Fort Nelson
Meander River
Stewart
Hyder
Meziadin Junction
Bear Glacier
Ketchikan
Portland Canal
Tseax Lava Beds
Kitwancool
Kitwanga
New Hazelton
Cerdarvale
Moricetown
Smithers
Terrace
Lakelse Lake
Prince Rupert
Port Edward
Lakelse Lake Provincial Park
Kitimat
Hudson Bay Mountain
Houston
Burns Lake
Fort St.James
Vanderhoof
Prince George
Tweedsmuir Provincial Park
Inside Channel
Masset
Skidegate
Sandspit
Queen Charlotte Islands
See map of Queen Charlotte Islands
Williston Lake
Hudson's Hope
Chetwynd
Pine Pass
Mackenzie
McLeod Lake
Fort St. John
Dawson Creek
Tumbler Ridge
Sinclair Mills
McBride
Peace River
Cleardale
Girouxville
Donnelly
Grouard
High Prairie
Slave Lake
Grande Prairie
Grande Cache
Whitecourt
©ULYSSES

Glacier Highway. The town of Stewart lies 65km away, while the village of Hyder, Alaska lies 2km farther, on the road that runs alongside the Portland Canal.

Tour G: The Yellowhead Highway

This tour will take you from the town of McBride, in eastern British Columbia, to Prince Rupert, on the coast, about 1,000km away. The Yellowhead Highway runs through an impressive variety of landscapes (mountains, plains and plateaux), as well as several sizeable towns, including Prince George, Smithers, Terrace and Prince Rupert.

Road conditions

Prince Rupert:
☎(800) 663-4997

Tour H: The Queen Charlotte Islands (Haida Gwaii)

All the local villages are linked by a single 120km road, Hwy. 16.

By Plane

Tour B: To the Alaska Highway

Prince George

The airport is located a few kilometres east of downtown and is accessible by way of the Yellowhead Bridge to the north and the Simon Fraser Bridge to the south(*☎963-2400*). The airport is served by **Air B.C.** (*☎561-2905*), **Canadian International** (*☎563-0521*) and **Central Mountain** (*☎361-2063 or 800-663-3721*).

Tour D: The Alaska Highway

Dawson Creek

Dawson Creek Municipal Airport, south of town, accessible by way of Hwy. 2. It is served daily by **Air B.C.** and **Central Mountain Air** (*both companies ☎782-1720*); regional flights are offered by **Kenn Borek Air** (*☎782-5623*).

Fort Saint John

The airport (*☎787-7170*) is 10km from town, on the road to Cecil Lake, along 100th Ave. It is served by **Canadian Regional** (*☎787-7781*) and **Central Mountain Air** (*☎785-6100*).

Fort Nelson

The airport (*☎774-2069*) is 10km from downtown via Airport Rd. Served by **Canadian Regional** (*☎774-3111*) and **Central Mountain Air** (*☎774-3789*).

Watson Lake

The airport is 13km from downtown; take the Campbell Highway north. It is served by **Alkan Air** (*in Whitehorse ☎867-668-2107*), the Yukon's main airline, and **Central Mountain Air** (*☎867-536-7999*) as well as a number of other companies.

Tour G: The Yellowhead Highway

Smithers

The airport is on Hwy. 16, 10km west of Smithers (*☎847-3664*). It is served by **Central Mountain Air** (*☎800-663-3721*) and **Canadian Regional** (*☎800-665-1177*).

Prince Rupert

The airport is on Digby Island; transportation is provided by a small municipal ferry (*$11 one-way*) at the end of Hwy. 16, at the southwest end of Prince Rupert. The airport is served by **Air B.C.** (*☎624-4554*) and **Canadian Regional** (*☎624-9181*).

Tour G: The Queen Charlotte Islands (Haida Gwaii)

There is an airport in Masset, on the northern part of Graham Island, and another in Sandspit, on Moresby Island. Both are clearly indicated. These airports are served by **Thunderbird Air** (*☎231-8933 or 800-898-0177*) and **Canadian Regional** (*☎800-665-1177*).

By Bus

Tour A: The Gold Rush Trail and The Cariboo Mountains

Quesnel
Greyhound
365 Kinchant St.
☎*992-2231*

William's Lake
Greyhound
215 Donald Rd.
☎398-7733

Tour B: To the Alaska Highway

Prince George
Greyhound
at the corner of 12th and Victoria Sts.
☎*564-5454*

Tour D: The Alaska Highway

Dawson Creek
Greyhound
1201 Alaska Ave.
☎*782-3131*

Fort Saint John
Greyhound
10355 101st Ave.
☎*785-6695*

Fort Nelson
Greyhound
at the corner of West 51st and Liard St.
☎*774-6322*

Watson Lake (Yukon)
Greyhound
at the corner of the Campbell and Alaska Highways
☎*(867) 536-2606*

Tour E: The Stewart-Cassiar Highway

Stewart
Seaport Limousine
516 Railway St.
☎*636-2622*

Tour G: The Yellowhead Highway

Smithers
Greyhound
on Hwy. 16, a couple of blocks from the Travel InfoCentre
☎*847-2204*

Prince Rupert
Greyhound
at the corner of Third Ave. and Sixth St.
☎*624-5090*

By Train

Tour G: The Yellowhead Highway

Smithers
The train station is on Railway Ave., not far from downtown (☎*800-561-8630*) Tickets must be purchased through a travel agent: **Mackenzie Travel** (☎*847-2979*); **Uniglobe Priority Travel** (☎*847-4314*).

Prince Rupert
Via Rail
on Waterfront Ave.
☎*627-7589*

By Ferry

Tour G: The Yellowhead Highway

Prince Rupert
BC Ferries
west end of Second Ave. (Hwy. 16) in Fairview
☎*624-9627*
☎*(888) 223-3779 (throughout British Columbia)*

Tour H: The Queen Charlotte Islands (Haida Gwaii)

To get to this archipelago, you must take either a plane or a ferry to Graham Island, the largest and most populous of the 150 islands. **BC Ferries**: (☎*888-223-3779 from within B.C.*, ☎*250-386-3431 from outside the province*), reservations are strongly recommended, especially during summer. A small ferry shuttles back and forth between Skidegate Landing, on Graham Island, and Alliford Bay, on Moresby Island, the second largest of the Queen Charlotte Islands.

Practical Information

Area Code: All telephone numbers in this chapter use the **250** area code unless otherwise indicated, including Hyder, Alaska; the only exception is Watson Lake, in the Yukon, where the area code is **867**.

Tourist Information

British Columbia Tourism
☎(800) 663-6000
⇄387-1590

Tour A: The Gold Rush Trail and the Cariboo Mountains

Quesnel
Mon to Sat 9am to 6pm
405 Barlow St.
☎992-8716
visitorinto@cityquesnel.bc.ca

William's Lake
Mon to Sat 9am to 6pm
1148 South Broadway St.
☎392-5025

Tour B: To the Alaska Highway

Prince George
Mon to Sat 8:30am to 5pm
1198 Victoria St., Prince George
☎562-3700
☎(800) 668-7646
⇄563-5584

Mackenzie
The tourist office is only open in the summer (*at the intersection of Hwy. 39 and 97, 29km from downtown ☎750-4497*); during the rest of the year, you can obtain information from the **Chamber of Commerce** (*86 Centennial St., ☎997-5459*).

Chetwynd
North Access Rd., which follows the highway
☎788-3345

Dawson Creek
summer, every day 8am to 7pm; winter, Tue to Sat 9am to noon and 1pm to 5pm
900 Alaska Ave.
☎782-9595

Tour C: The Hudson's Hope Route

Hudson's Hope
summer only
opposite the museum and the church
☎783-9154
☎783-9901(*off-season*)

Tour D: The Alaska Highway

Fort St. John
9923 96th Ave., just across from a 50m derrick
☎785-3033

Fort Nelson
summer, every day 8am to 8pm
west end of the downtown area, inside the recreation centre
☎774-6400 or 774-2541

Watson Lake (Yukon)
summer, every day
at the junction of the Alaska and Campbell Highways
☎(867) 536-7469

Tour E: The Stewart-Cassiar Highway

Dease Lake
Hwy. 37
☎771-3900

Kitwanga
summer, everyday
Valley Rd.
☎849-5760

Telegraph Creek
☎235-3196

Tour F: To Stewart, BC and Hyder, AK

Stewart
222 Fifth Ave.
☎636-9224

Hyder
in the Hyder Community Building on Main St.
☎636-9148

Tour G: The Yellowhead Highway

Prince Rupert
First Ave., at McBride Ave., adjoining the Museum of Northern British Columbia
☎624-5637
☎(800) 667-1994

McBride
summer, every day 9am to 5pm
in a railway car (the sculpture of a family of grizzlies at the entrance makes it easy to spot)
☎569-2229

Vanderhoof
downtown on Burrard St.
☎567-2124

Fort St. James
in the Chamber of Commerce
☎996-7063

Houston
Along the highway; you'll spot the fishing pole from far away.
☎845-7640.

Smithers
at the intersection of Hwy. 16 and Main St.
☎847-5072

Hazelton
intersection of Hwy. 16 and 62
☎842-6071
☎842-6571(*Sep to Apr*)

Kitimat
2109 Forest Ave., Box 214, V8C 2G7
☎632-6294
☎(800) 664-6554

Terrace
every day 9am to 8pm during summer, Mon to Fri 9am to 4:30pm during winter
4511 Keith Ave.
☎635-2063
☎(800) 499-1637

Tour H: The Queen Charlotte Islands (Haida Gwaii)

Queen Charlotte City
Visitor InfoCentre
a few hundred metres before the village of Queen Charlotte City
☎559-4742

Masset
open in summer only
in a small trailer on the south edge of the village
☎626-3300

Exploring

Tour A: The Gold Rush Trail and the Cariboo Mountains

This tour extends from the north to the south between Prince George and William's Lake. Some typical tourist attractions are found east of Quesnel via Hwy. 26. For those who want to explore a little deeper, we suggest going farther south of William's Lake to discover the splender of Well's Gray Provincial Park. Another option is to take the bumpy road that heads west from William's Lake. It leads to Bella Coola and the only seaport between Prince Rupert and Vancouver Island. This much longer, rougher trip will delight those who like to stray from the beaten path. As for breathtaking scenery, your only problem will be deciding which one of the infinite number of places to chose from.

★★★

Quesnel

Located 188km south of Prince George, it takes a little more than 30min to reach Quesnel. Its tree-lined streets and flowers, as well as its location at the confluence of two rivers, make it the most beautiful town in the region.

Like many other towns in the area, Quesnel lived through the 19th-century Gold Rush. Gold diggers stocked up on foodstuffs and survival gear in Quesnel before heading off to look for those famous nuggets in the distant valleys, which is how Quesnel got its nickname "Gold Pan City."

Today, the forest industry has replaced the mining industry as the economic engine for the region. More than 2,000 families rely on it for their livelihood.

Quesnel is a departure point for various excursions. If you only have a few days to spend in this region, concentrate on Quesnel and choose among the wide range of activities it has to offer: canoeing, rafting, a visit to a reconstructed mining town or a paper mill. During the third week of July, Billy Barker Days celebrates the historical heritage of the town. The theme, of course, is based on the Gold Rush. There are activities for the entire family.

Quesnel & District Museum (*$2; 405 Barlow St., ☎992-9580*) also houses the tourist information centre, which makes for a practical and pleasurable visit. The permanent collection exhibits every-day items that the pioneers used in the fields, mines and in the home more than a century ago.

Pinnacles Park (*on the outskirts of the west side of town; follow the directions*) is a spectacular – and free – tourist attraction. A 20min walk through the evergreen forest leads to a group of sandy hills called "hoodoos." They are unusual earth-tone vertical formations whose origin dates back some 12 million years when they were formed by the erosion of several layers of volcanic ash. Today, only the strongest layers remain intact. They proudly thrust up into the sky.

Quesnel has three pulp and paper mills that can be visited by calling beforehand.

Quesnel River Pulp
1000 Finning Rd.
☎992-8919

Cariboo Pulp & Paper
☎992-0200

West Fraser Mills
☎992-9244

Barkerville ★★★ (*$5.50; 125km east of Quesnel*) sprung up out of nowhere in 1862 when Billy Barker discovered gold in William's Creek. During the eight years that followed, 100,000 people came here to try their luck, making Barkerville the largest town west of Chicago and north of San Francisco.

Unfortunately, the reserves were completely exhausted. Today, the town is a protected historic site where more than 125 buildings have been restored to their original frontier-town look. The result is striking: saloon, hotel, post office, printer and blacksmith. Everything here is a perfect illusion. Illusion you say? There are even a few gold prospectors that still pan the bottom of the river that flows through the region.

Just 30km from Barkervile, the **Bowron Lake Provincial Park ★★★** is famous for one particular activity: canoeing (see p?). As soon as you see all the boats mounted on the cars flocking to Quesnel, you realize that the mountains are a world-renowned attraction for vacationers.

Wells Gray Provincial Park (*via 100 Mile House on Clearwater, ☎851-3000, ⇄828-4633*) is the second largest park in the province. There is a great range of possible activities, such as canoeing, hiking or fishing (one-day or week-long excursions). The park is also famous for its many mesmerizing waterfalls.

Tour B: To the Alaska Highway

This tour starts in the town of Prince George. You can reach Km/mile 0 of the Alaska Highway, in Dawson Creek, by taking Hwy. 97, which crosses the Rocky Mountains. The itinerary suggested below leads through pleasant wooded areas strewn with lakes.

★★ Prince George

Prince George (*pop. 70,000*) considers itself the capital of northern British Columbia. As any map will tell you, however, it actually lies in the centre of the province. Its geographic location has enabled it to become a hub not only for the railway, but also for road transport, since it lies at the intersection of Hwy. 16, which runs the width of the province, and Hwy. 97, which runs the length.

Prince George is 800km north of Vancouver, about an hour's flight or a 10hr drive along the Trans-Canada and Hwy. 97 North. The town's history is linked to two rivers, the Nechako and the Fraser. By the beginning of 19th century, trappers and *coureurs des bois* were using these waterways to

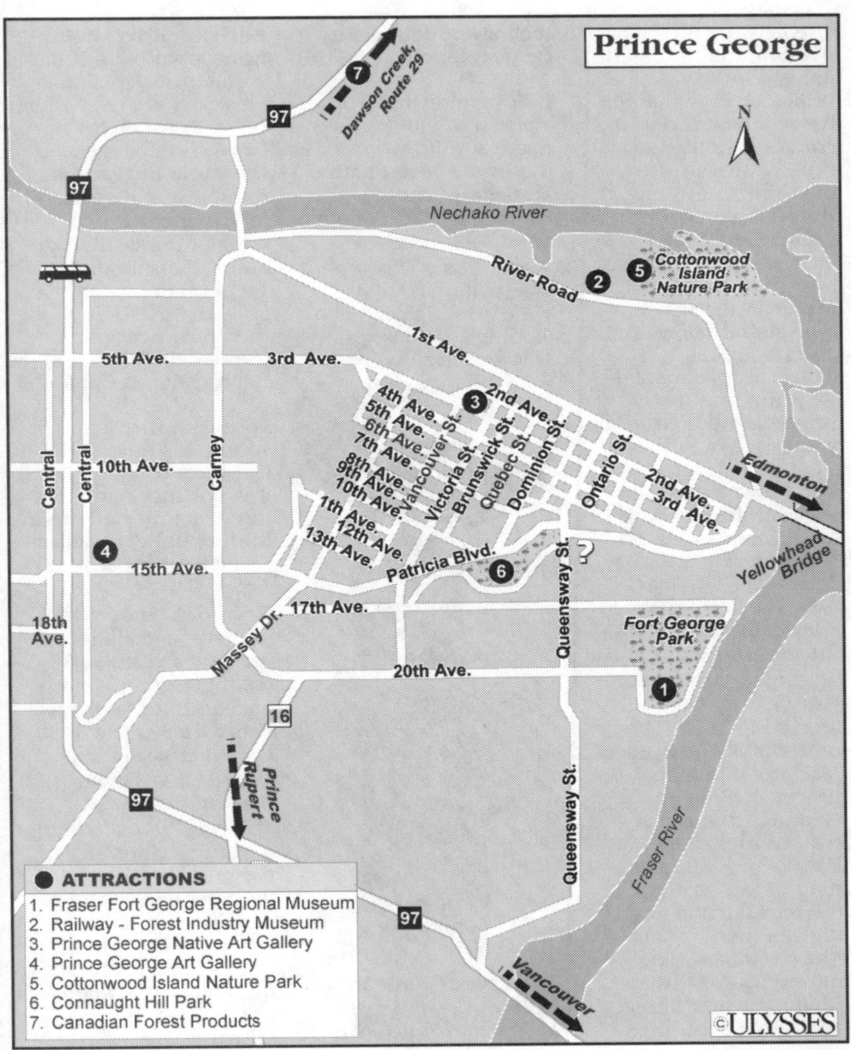

reach the vast territories of the north. Before long, they saw that the region was rich in wolves, minks, musk-rats, foxes, etc. Fur-trading posts thus began to spring up along the banks of the two rivers.

In 1807, the first building, Fort George, was erected. In 1821, it was taken over by the Hudson's Bay Company. In 1908, when the Grand Trunk Pacific Railway (GTR) was constructed, Fort George was slated to become an important distribution centre for the transcontinental railroad. All of these major changes led to a considerable growth in population, and it became necessary to develop a second residential area, known as South Fort George.

The GTR finally began operating in the region in 1914. A second area, Prince George, had to be developed to accommodate the flood of new arrivals. Now the third largest city in British Columbia, Prince George derives most of its income from forestry. It is home to no fewer than 15 sawmills and three pulp and paper mills. The climate is continental — warm and dry in the summer and cold in the winter.

The **Fraser Fort George Regional Museum ★★** (*$6.50; mid-May to mid-Sep, every day 10am to 5pm; mid-Sep to mid-May, Tue to Sun noon to 5pm; at the end of 20th Ave., ☎562-1612*) stands on the very site where Fort George was erected in 1807. The museum is an excellent place to learn about the history of Prince George, from the arrival of Alexander Mackenzie and the beginning of the fur trade to the introduction and development of the forest industry. The museum's Northwood Gallery, a sure hit with young children, presents an exhibit on the region's flora and fauna. Along the Fraser River lies the **Railway & Forest Industry Museum ★★** (*$4.50; mid-May to mid-Sep, every day 10am to 6pm; River Rd, ☎563-7351*), which will take you back in time to the days when the railroad was new and modern woodcutting techniques had yet to be developed.

If you enjoy and appreciate Aboriginal art, make sure to stop at the **Prince George Native Art Gallery** (*Tue to Fri 9am to 5pm, Sat 10am to 4pm; 1600 Third Ave., ☎562-7385*). This private gallery displays a wide array of art, including carvings, prints and jewellery.

The **Prince George Art Gallery** (*Mon to Sat 10am to 5pm and Sun 1pm to 5pm; 2820 15th Ave., ☎563-6447*) is a municipal art gallery, which presents the work of local artists with styles ranging from abstract to impressionist.

For a short walk or a picnic, head to the **Cottonwood Island Nature Park ★★**, which covers 33ha along the Nechako River, right near downtown. It has an interesting wildlife-observation area, where you can watch foxes, beavers and eagles. **Connaught Hill Park ★**, located in the centre of town, offers a 360° view of Prince George and its surroundings. To get there, take Queensway southward, then turn right on Connaught Drive and right again on Caine.

Forestry is the mainspring of Prince George's economy, so it is not surprising that three factories are open to the public. **Canadian Forest Products ★★** (*PG Pulpmill Road, ☎563-0161*) offers free tours of its facilities. A bus takes visitors to cutting and replanting areas. At the **Northwood Pulp & Timber and North Central Plywoods ★★** (*mid-May to Sep; reservations recommended, ☎562-3700*), everything is very modern, from the greenhouse where the next generation of trees is nurtured to the sawmill where the trunks are cut up. The third factory, owned by Northwood, is supposedly the "greenest" in Canada. It produces pulp and paper, as well as construction materials. Visitors will learn how paper, chipboard and plywood are made. As the tour involves a long walk, partly on uneven terrain, it is recommended to wear closed, flat shoes and pants.

Mackenzie

A small, ultra-modern community, Mackenzie is a typical boom town. It was built in 1966, following the construction of the Peace River dam. Less than a year after the first stone was laid, hundreds of workers arrived in the area, which was completely undeveloped at the time. Today, with a population of 5,700, Mackenzie has become a village of superlatives, boasting the largest artificial lake on the continent, **Williston Lake**, a byproduct of the dam, as well as the **world's biggest tree-chipper**, which was used to clear a passage through the forest back when the town was founded.

Chetwynd

This little town was once known as Little Prairie, but its name was changed in honour of Railway Minister Ralph Chetwynd, who pioneered rail transport in northern British Columbia. Today, Chetwynd is a prosperous working-class town. It was constructed to the north of one of the largest coal deposits in the world. Natural gas and the forest industry have further strengthened the local economy. A simple walk down the street reveals how important forestry is here; Chetwynd is the self-proclaimed **world capital of chainsaw sculpture**, and carved animals adorn the tops of buildings all over town.

Dawson Creek

Dawson Creek was named after Dr. George Dawson, a geologist who, in 1879, discovered that the surrounding plains were ideal for agriculture. He might have thought that Dawson Creek would become a farming capital, but he probably never suspected that oil and natural gas would be discovered here.

The other major turning-point in Dawson Creek's history took place in 1942, when the town became Km/mile 0 of the Alaska Highway. Today, nearly 30,000 tourists from all over the world come to Dawson Creek to start their journey northward.

The **Station Museum ★** and the **Dawson Creek Art Gallery★** are part of the **Northern Alberta Railway Park (NAR) ★★**. You can't miss the NAR, with its immense grain elevator, which was renovated in 1931 and stands at the corner of Alaska Avenue and Eighth St..

The **Station Museum ★** (*Jun to Sep, every day 8am to 7pm; winter, Tue to Sat 9am to noon and 1pm to 5pm*) traces the history of the Alaska Highway, as well as that of the area's first inhabitants. The collection on display includes the largest mammoth tusk ever found in the Canadian West, as well as a number of dinosaur bones.

Inside the grain elevator, the **Dawson Creek Art Gallery** (*winter, Tue to Sat 10am to noon and 1pm to 5pm; rest of the year, every day 9am to 6pm;* ☎ *782-2601*) displays handicrafts and works by local artists; it also hosts travelling exhibitions.

Right beside the NAR Park, you'll spot a sign — surely the most photographed one in the province — indicating the starting point of the Alaska Highway. The legendary **Mile 0 Post**, also worth a picture, is located downtown.

If you'd like to sample the local produce, stop at the **Dawson Creek Farmer's Market** (*Sat 8am to 3pm*), which is held near the NAR Park, just behind the sign for the Alaska Highway.

Tour C: The Hudson's Hope Route

This tour is an alternate route from Prince George to Dawson Creek. Simply take Hwy. 29 from Chetwynd.

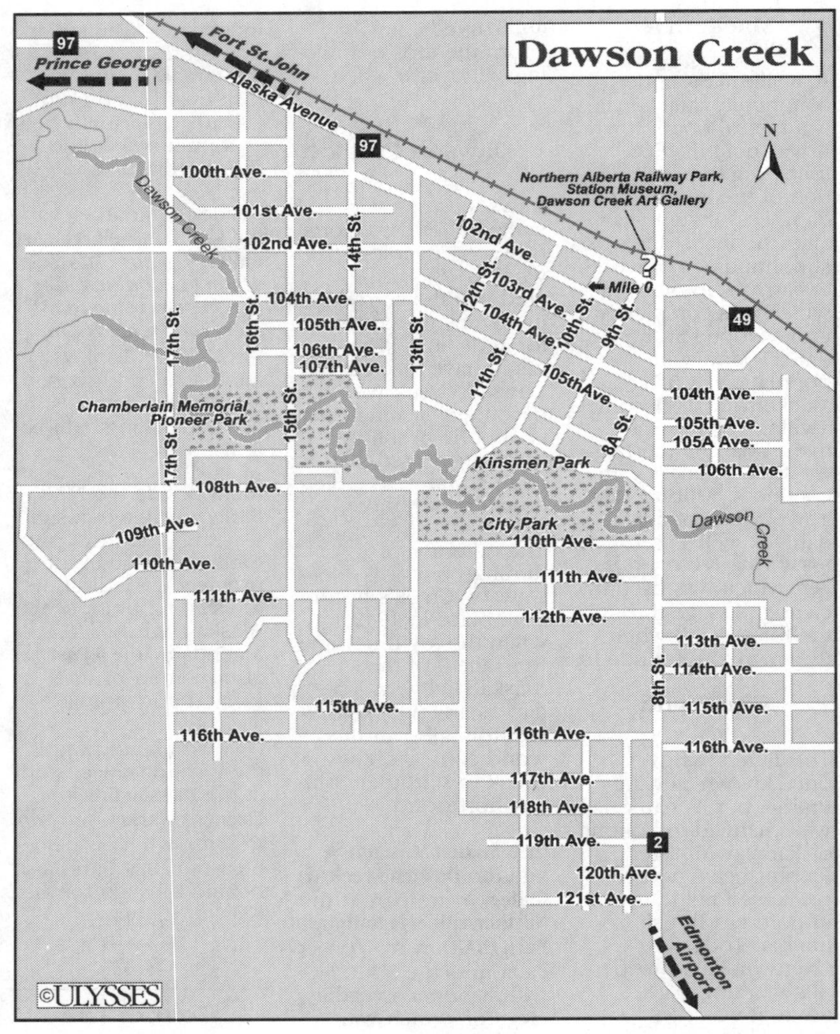

Hudson's Hope

This area was first explored in 1793 by Alexander Mackenzie. In 1805, a fur-trading post was set up here. Nowadays, Hudson's Hope is known mainly for its hydroelectric complexes, one of which was built in the 1960s (WAC Bennett), the other slightly more recently (Peace Canyon).

The tourist office is located right near **St. Peter's United Church ★**, a charming old wooden building. Also nearby is the **Hudson's Hope Museum**, which displays fossils, some of dinosaurs, and various artifacts from the area.

Of course, the major points of interest in Hudson's Hope are the **WAC Bennett ★★** (*late May to early Oct, every* *day 8am to 4pm; phone for reservations in winter; about 20km west of Hudson's Hope, ☎783-5211)* and **Peace Canyon ★★** *(late May to Aug, every day 8am to 4pm; Sep and Oct, Mon to Fri 8am to 4pm; phone for reservations in winter; 7km south of Hudson's Hope, ☎783-9943)* hydroelectric facilities. Free tours are available at both. The WAC Bennett dam is the largest structure in the world, a hodgepodge of stone and concrete that fills in a natural valley. Its reservoir, Williston Lake, is the largest artificial lake on the planet!

Tour D: The Alaska Highway

This tour starts at Km/mile 0 of the highway, in Dawson Creek (see Tour A, p 251), and ends at kilometre 1011/mile 632, in Watson Lake, in the Yukon. The entire road is paved and well-maintained. Before setting out, though, make sure that your car's engine and tires are in good condition, since there aren't very many repair shops along the way. A lot of roadwork is carried out during summer, and the resulting dust makes driving conditions more difficult. You are therefore better off leaving your lights on at all times. In summer as in winter, it is always wise to check the road conditions before setting out by calling ***☎(800) 663-4997***.

The Alaska Highway started out as a war measure. The Americans, who initiated the project, wanted to create a communication route that permit the transport of military equipment, provisions and troops by land to Alaska. Construction started in March 1942, in the village of Dawson Creek, which had only 600 inhabitants at the time. Within a few weeks, over 10,000 people, mostly military workers, had flooded into the area.

Over 11,000 American soldiers and engineers, 6,000 civilian workers and 7,000 machines and tractors of all manner were required to clear a passage through thousands of kilometres of wilderness. The cost of this gargantuan project, which stretched 2,436km and included 133 bridges, came to $140 million (Canadian). Even today, the building of the Alaska Highway is viewed as a feat of engineering on a par with the Panamá Canal. The Canadian section was given to Canada by the United States in 1946 and remained under military supervision until 1964.

Today, this extraordinary highway is a vital social and economic link for all northern towns. It also offers tourists from all over the world unhoped-for access to the majestic landscapes of this region.

★

Fort St. John

kilometre 75.6/mile 47

Fort St. John is the largest community on the British-Columbian section of the Alaska Highway. A prosperous, modern little town of about 14,000, it has a highly diversified economy. Agriculture plays a significant role here, as there are 800 farms in the area, but petroleum and natural gas are the main sources of income. It is not without good reason that Fort St. John calls itself the energy capital of British Columbia.

In keeping with this oil community's industrial calling, the tourist office is located near a 50m-high derrick, just steps away from the downtown area. In the same building, the **Fort St. John-North Peace Museum ★** *($2; Jul and Aug every day 9am to 6pm; rest of the year Mon to Sat 9am to 5pm; at the corner of 93rd Ave. and 100th St., ☎787-0430)* deals with the history and prehistoric past of the Fort St. John region, with a collection of nearly 6,000 objects, including some fossils and bones. The **Peace Gallery North** *(Mon to Thu 10am to 5pm, Fri 10am to 6pm, Sat 11am to 5pm; in the cultural centre, ☎787-0993)* ex

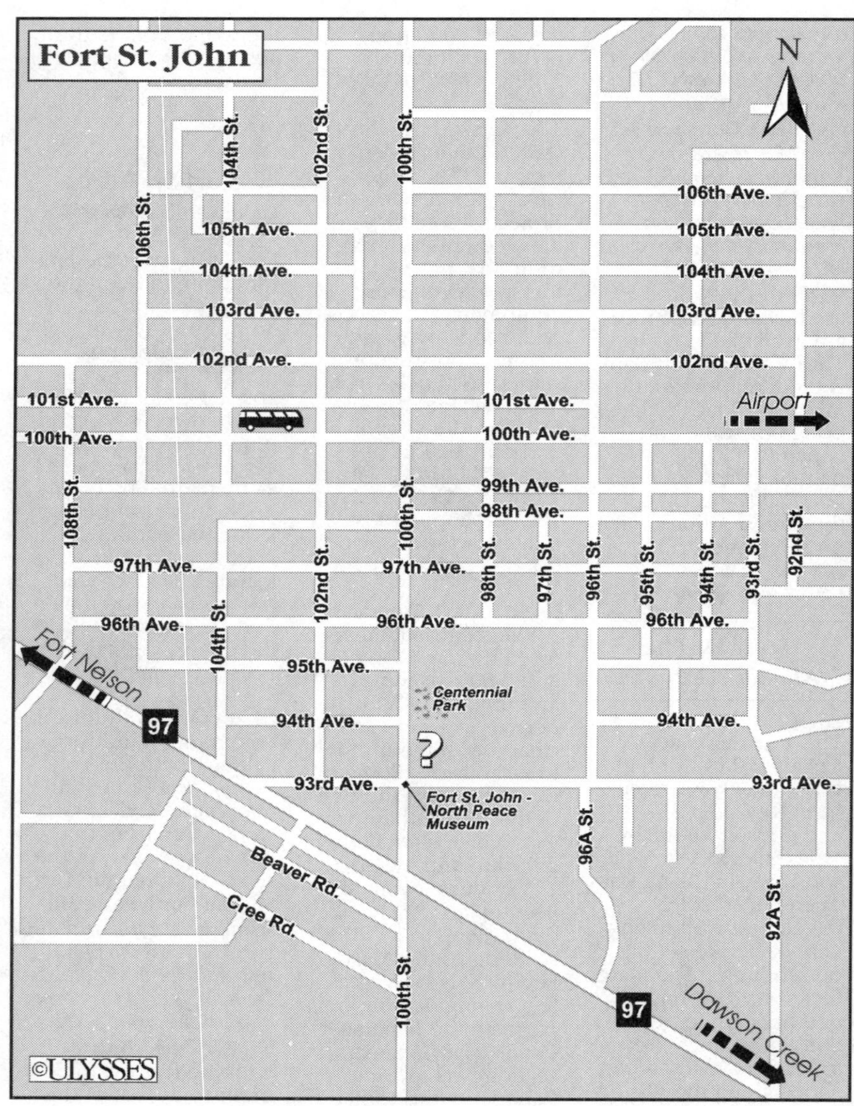

hibits a large number of works by local artists.

The Honey Place ★ (*summer, Mon to Sat 9am to 5:30pm; winter, Tue to Sat 10am to 5pm; tours, Jul and Sep by appointment only; kilometre 67.2/mile 42 of the Alaska Highway,* ☎*785-4808*) arranges guided tours of the world's largest glassed-in hive, offering visitors a chance to observe, first-hand, the marvellous spectacle of bees making honey.

Fort Nelson

kilometre 454.3/mile 283

This small industrial town has fewer than 4,000 inhabitants. Its history has been linked to the fur trade since 1805. In 1922, the town was connected to Fort St. John by the Godsell Trail, thus ending its isolation. In those years, Fort Nelson was home to only 200 Aboriginals and a handful of whites. Later, after the Alaska Highway was constructed, the town grew considerably when service stations, hotels and restaurants set up business here. It officially became a municipality in 1987.

History lovers will enjoy a visit to the **Fort Nelson Heritage Museum** ★ (*$3; mid-May to Sep, every day 8:30am to 7:30pm; opposite the tourist office, downtown, ☎774-3536*).

★★★

Stone Mountain Provincial Park

kilometre 627/mile 392

The entrance to **Stone Mountain Provincial Park** (*BC Parks, ☎787-3407*) is located at the highest point on the Alaska Highway, at an altitude of 1,267m. It covers 25,691ha of rocky peaks, geological formations and lakes, and is home to the largest variety of animal life in northern British Columbia. There are large numbers of moose here, as well as deer, beavers, black bears, grizzlies and wolves, not to mention the hundreds of caribou, which can often be seen near the road. Visitors unaccustomed to walking in the mountains in northern latitudes are advised not to venture too high. The climatic conditions can change rapidly, and the temperature can drop more than 10° in a few hours. It snows quite often on these peaks, even in the middle of summer.

★★

Wokkpash Recreation Area

The **Wokkpash Recreation Area** is a provincial park connected to Stone Mountain (*BC Parks, ☎787-3407*). Only accessible by foot or on horseback, this 37,800ha stretch of wilderness is not a place for inexperienced hikers. Simply getting there is an expedition. The most well-known trail leads from MacDonald Creek to Wokkpash Valley, covering a distance of 70km on foot or 50km by four-wheel-drive vehicle, with a 1,200m change in altitude. It requires at least seven days of walking. Beware of flash floods on rainy days.

★★

Muncho Lake Provincial Park

kilometre 729/mile 456

Muncho Lake (*BC Parks, ☎787-3407*) is one of the loveliest provincial parks in Canada and definitely one of the highlights on the British Columbian portion of the Alaska Highway. It encompasses 88,416ha of bare, jagged mountains around magnificent Muncho Lake, which stretches 12km. Like all parks in the region, it owes its existence to the Alaska Highway. Large numbers of beavers, black bears, grizzlies, wolves and mountain goats make their home here, while the magnificent plant-life includes a variety of orchids. There are almost no trails in the park, so the best way to explore it is along the Alaska Highway.

★★

Liard Hot Springs Provincial Park

kilometre 764.7/mile 477.7

Liard Hot Springs Provincial Park (*BC Parks, ☎787-3407*) is the most popular place for travellers to stop. Here, you can relax in natural pools fed by 49°C hot springs. The microclimate created by the high temperature of the water, which remains constant in summer and winter alike, has enabled a unique assortment of plants to thrive here. Giant ferns and a profusion of carnivorous plants give the area a slightly tropical look.

★★★

Watson Lake (Yukon)

kilometre 1021/mile 612.9

The Alaska Highway tour comes to an end at Watson Lake, in the Yukon. Around 1897, an Englishman by the name of Frank Watson set out from Edmonton to lead the adventurous life of a gold-digger in Dawson City. After passing through regions that hadn't even been mapped yet, he ended up on the banks of the Liard River. He decided to stop his travels there and take up residence on the shores of the lake that now bears his name. The construction of a military airport in 1941 and the laying of the Alaska Highway the following year enabled Watson Lake to develop into a real town. It is now a transportation, communication and supply hub for the neighbouring communities, as well as for the mining and forest industries.

A visit to the **Alaska Highway Interpretive Centre** ★★ (*at the intersection of the Alaska and Campbell Highways; mid-May to mid-Sep every day 8am to 8pm;* ☎*867-536-7469*) is a must for anyone interested in the history of the Alaska Highway. The epic story of the famous highway comes to life through a slide show and photographs. The **Alaska Highway Signpost Forest** ★★★ is far and away the main attraction in Watson Lake. It is a collection of over 37,450 signs from the world over, placed on the posts by the tourists themselves. Some of them are highly original. You can create your own sign when planning your trip, or have one made for you on the spot for a few dollars.

Tour E: The Stewart-Cassiar Highway

This tour usually starts in Kitwanga (43km south of Hazelton on Hwy. 16, see Tour G, p ?), but travellers who have taken the Alaska Highway can set out from Watson Lake instead. You can actually combine Tours D and E into one big loop, as the two highways intersect at **Junction 37**, at kilometre 1038/mile 649 of the Alaska Highway, a few kilometres from Watson Lake.

Completed in 1972, the Stewart-Cassiar Highway (37) meets all highway standards and can thus be used at any time of the year. Three large sections of the road are unpaved, however, and get dusty in dry, hot weather and muddy in the rain, making driving conditions difficult from time to time. For this reason, the Ministry of Transportation recommends keeping your lights on at all times. Although you are better off driving this road with a car with high ground clearance or with an all-terrain four-wheel-drive vehicle, you can get by with a conventional automobile.

The Stewart-Cassiar Highway is the trucking route used to bring supplies to communities in the northern part of the province and beyond. While the trip is a bit shorter than the Alaska Highway, the scenery is equally magnificent.

★

Kitwanga

Kitwanga, which has just under 1,500 inhabitants, is the first community you'll come across on your way south. Known mainly for its historic past, it is home to **Kitwanga Fort National Historic Site** ★ and Battle Hill, setting of a battle between Aboriginals over 200 years ago. The site is open year-round and is located near the video club that doubles as the local tourist office.

If you'd like to see some beautiful **totem poles** ★, make a quick stop at the **Gitwangak**

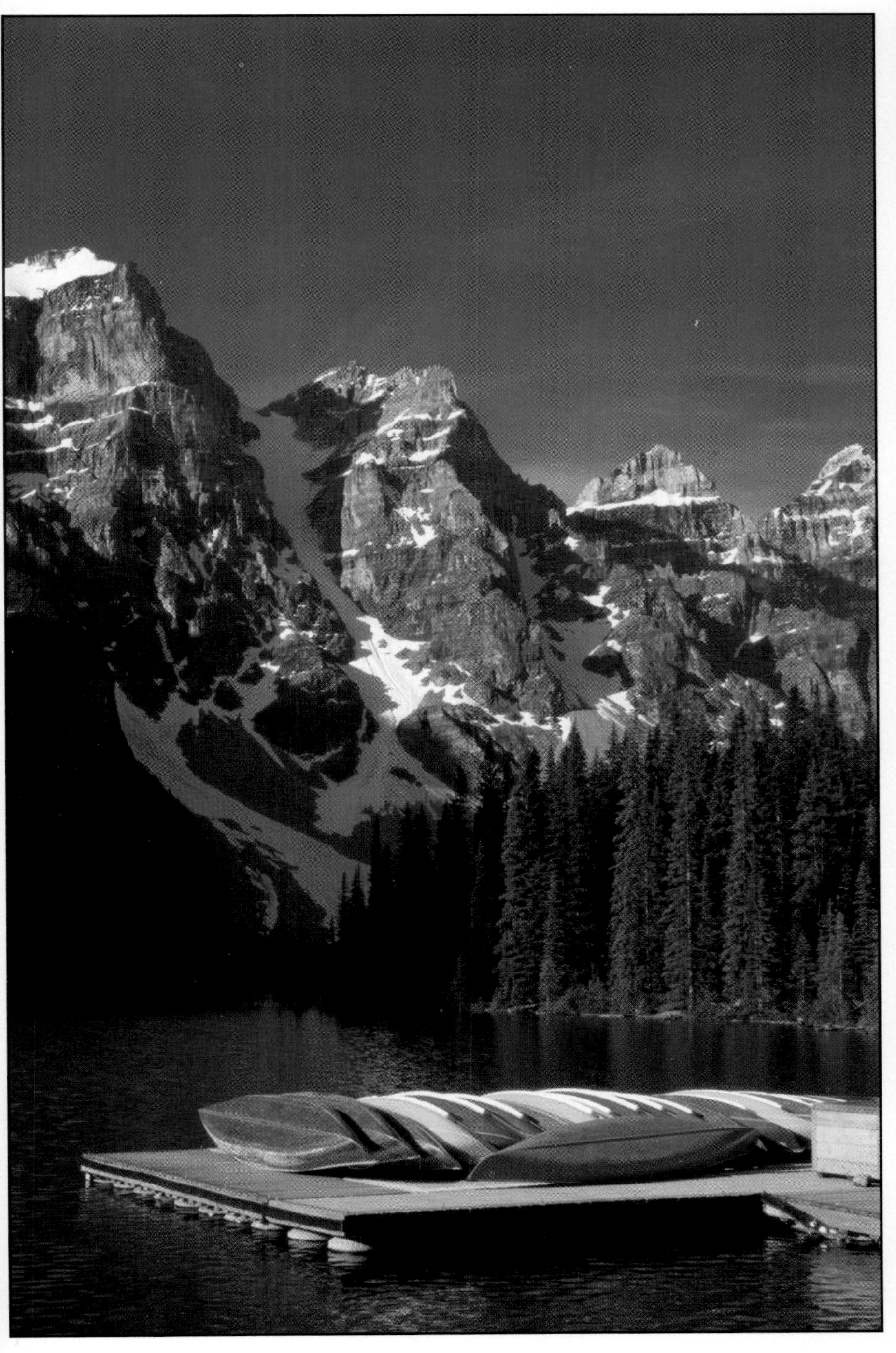

Isn't it tempting to hop in one of these canoes
and explore the waterways of the Rockies? - *Tibor Bognar*

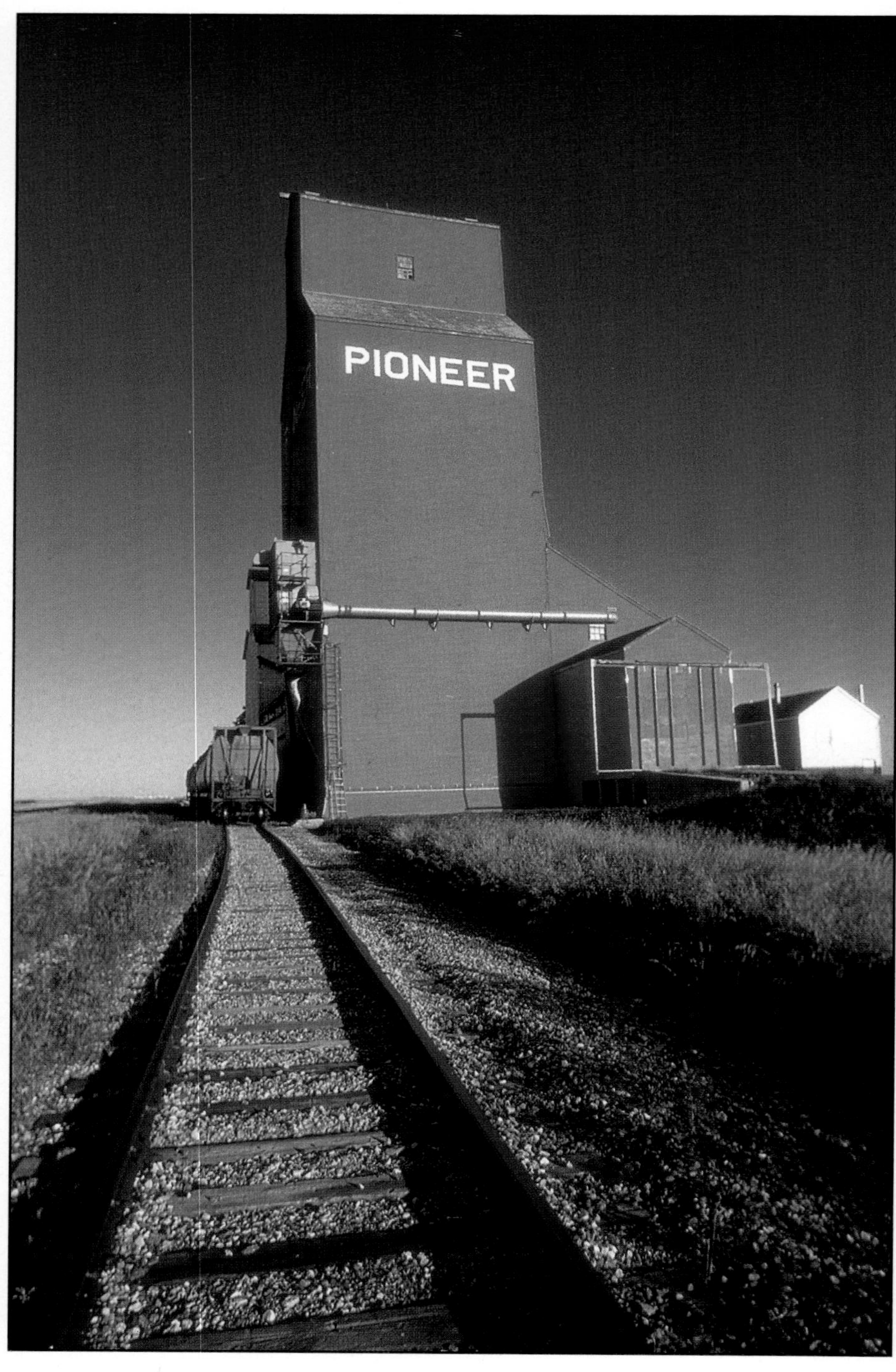

Grain silos and railroads are part of the classic Prairie landscape.
- *Walter Bibikow*

Indian Reserve (*shortly before the village of Kitwanga, just after the intersection of Hwy. 16 and 37*); a whole series of them is lined up opposite **St. Paul's Anglican Church** ★, built in 1893.

★ Kitwancool

This little Gitksan village is known chiefly for its **totem poles** ★. The oldest one, **Hole-in-the-Ice**, dates back nearly 140 years.

Meziadin Junction

Meziadin Junction, located 170km from Kitwanga, is the starting point for the excursion to **Stewart, BC and Hyder, AK** ★★★. See Tour E, p ?.

★★ Spatsizi Plateau Wilderness Park

The Spatsizi Plateau Wilderness Park is only for real adventurers (*on Tattoga Lake, not far from Iskut, on Hwy. 37, 361km north of the intersection of Hwy. 16 and 37, in Kitwanga. Take Ealue Lake Road for 22km. Cross the Klappan River to the BC Rail dirt road, which leads 114km to the southwest end of the park. Never set out on an excursion here without calling BC Parks beforehand, ☎847-7320*). The plateau stretches across 656,785ha of wilderness, and is accessible by foot, by boat or by hydroplane.

Spatsizi means "red goat" in the language of the Tahltan First Nation. The name was inspired by the scarlet-coloured mountains, whose soil is rich in iron oxide. The park is in fact located on a plateau, at a nearly steady altitude of about 1,800m. The highest peak in the park is Mount Will (2,500m), in the Skeena Mountain chain.

This region's dry, continental climate is characterized by cold winters with only light snowfall and summers with an average temperature of 20°C and little rainfall. These weather conditions have enabled a large number of animals, including caribou, grizzlies, beavers, and nearly 140 bird species, to make their home here.

Iskut

Iskut is a small community of 300 people, mostly Aboriginal. In the heart of the reserve, you will find a service centre — that is, a gas station, a post office and a grocery store (*Iskut Lake Co-op, ☎234-3241*). Iskut's most distinguishing feature is its surrounding **countryside** ★★, which is positively magnificent, especially when it is decked out in autumn colours. In the fall, it is not uncommon to see wolves crossing the highway at nightfall.

★★ Mount Edziza Provincial Park

Mount Edziza Provincial Park covers 230,000ha in the northwest part of the province, west of the Iskut River and south of the Stikine River. It is most notable for its volcanic sites, the most spectacular in all of Canada.

Mount Edziza (2,787m), the highest peak in the park, is a perfect example of a volcanic formation. The eruption that created this impressive basalt cone occurred nearly four million years ago. The lava from Mount Edziza flowed almost 65km. Afterward, numerous little eruptions took place, creating about 30 more cones, including the perfectly symmetrical Eve cone.

Like many parks in northern British Columbia, Mount Edziza Provincial Park is very hard to reach and offers no services. Only experienced, well-equipped hikers can get there safely. Although the temperature can climb as high as 30°C during summer, it can snow at any time of the year here. (*To plan a trip, call BC Parks, ☎771-4591, at Dease Lake, or 847-7320*).

Dease Lake

With 750 inhabitants, Dease Lake is the largest community on the Stewart-Cassiar Highway (Hwy. 37). It is the self-proclaimed jade capital of the world, due to the large number of quarries around the village. Lovely handcrafted sculptures are available in the many shops along the highway. Dease Lake is also an important industrial centre and a hub for government services.

Above all, this is a place to enjoy outdoor activities. Vast **Dease Lake ★★**, 47km long, is ideal for trout and pike fishing, as well as being the point of departure for plane and horseback rides in Mount Edziza Provincial Park and the Spatsizi Plateau Wilderness Park.

★★★ Telegraph Creek

It is worth going to Telegraph Creek, if only for the pleasure of driving there. Laid in 1922, the winding road leads through some splendid scenery. The village at the end beckons visitors back in time to the pioneer era.

To get there, go to the end of Boulder St., Dease Lake's main street. The road that leads to Telegraph Creek, 119km away, is well maintained but rather narrow, making it extremely ill-suited to large vehicles and trailers. All along the way, you'll enjoy **unforgettable views ★★** of Tuya River, the Grand Canyon of the Stikine, the Tahltan-Stikine lava beds, etc. The village itself, a small community of 450 people, makes a striking first impression. While its **period buildings ★** give it a quaint look, it is fully equipped to accommodate the needs of tourists (gas station, repair shop, restaurant, hotel, etc.). For information about tourist activities in the area, head to the **Stikine RiverSong** (*café, inn, grocery store and information office; ☎235-3196*).

Good Hope Lake

This little Aboriginal village (pop. 100) is of interest mainly for its magnificent **crystal-clear lake ★★★**.

Tour F: To Stewart, BC and Hyder, AK

This tour starts at Meziadin Junction (see p 257), along the Stewart-Cassiar Highway. Head west on Hwy. 37A, aptly nicknamed Glacier Highway. You will notice a major change in the scenery along the way. The mountains, with their snow- and glacier-capped peaks, look more and more imposing the closer you get.

Exactly 23km from Meziadin Junction, around a bend in the road, you will be greeted by the spectacular sight of **Bear Glacier ★★★**, which rises in all its azure-coloured splendour out of the milky waters of Strohn Lake at the same level as the road! Nineteen kilometres farther, you'll reach Stewart, a frontier town located just twokm from the little village of Hyder, Alaska. Both communities lie at the end of the 145km-long **Portland Canal ★★★**, the fourth deepest fjord in the world. In addition to forming a natural border between Canada and the United States, this narrow stretch of water gives Stewart direct access to the sea, making this little town of 1000 people the most northerly ice-free port in Canada.

The setting is simply magnificent. The town is surrounded on all sides by towering, glacier-studded mountains. In the summer, the mild temperature is governed by the occasionally damp Pacific climate, while heavy snowfall is common in the winter (over 20m total).

Stewart

Stewart boasts a large number of period buildings, such as the **Fire Hall** (1910), located on Fourth St., and the **Stone Storehouse**, on the Canadian-U.S. border. The latter was erected by the U.S. army in 1896 and originally served as a prison.

★★ Hyder, Alaska

Hyder (pop. 70) considers itself the most friendly ghost town in Alaska. This little community is known mainly for its three pubs, open 23hrs a day, and its duty-free shops. Keep in mind that although there is no customs office between the two countries here, the border still exists, and ignorance of the law is no excuse. It is best to respect all regulations concerning limits on tax-free merchandise. The tourist office and the **museum** ★★, which exhibits documents related to Hyder's history, are located in the **Hyder Community Building** (*Main St., ☎636-9148*).

Fifteen minutes past Hyder lies **Fish Creek** ★★★, the most important spawning area for **pink salmon** in all of Alaska (Jul to Sep). Dozens of **black bears** and **grizzlies** come here to feast on the fish, which are easy to catch after their long, exhausting journey.

Salmon

A platform has been set up so that tourists can observe this gripping spectacle. Caution: Keep a good distance from the bears. Don't be fooled by their friendly, clumsy appearance; they are unpredictable by nature, and can run as fast as 55km/h!

The same road leads to **Salmon Glacier** ★★★, the world's fifth largest glacier. The road is very narrow in places, making it unsuitable for large vehicles. Watch out for ruts and large rocks. The road is closed from November to June. For a worry-free trip, call **Seaport Limousine** (*guided minibus tours; ☎636-2622*).

In clear weather, the view of the glacier is breathtaking.

Tour G: The Yellowhead Highway

The Yellowhead is an impressive highway that starts in Winnipeg, Manitoba, runs through Saskatchewan and Alberta, and ends at Prince Rupert. This tour covers the part between McBride, in eastern British Columbia and Prince Rupert, about 1000km away in the westernmost part of the province. The incredibly varied scenery along the way includes high mountains, canyons, valleys and dense forests. This tour provides an excellent overview of the geology and topography of British Columbia.

McBride

This little working-class community of 719 people is sustained by the forest industry. It lies in a pleasant setting at the foot of the Rockies, on the banks of the Fraser River. Information about the area is available at the **tourist office** (*in a railway car, easily recognizable by the sculpture of a family of grizzlies at the entrance; late*

May to early Sep every day 9am to 5pm; ☎569-3366). We recommend walking up to the **Tear Mountain overlook ★★★**, which offers an unimpeded view of the region.

★★ Prince George

See Tour A: To the Alaska Highway, p 248.

Vanderhoof

Vanderhoof is a small farming community with a population of just over 4,000. The town is surrounded by lakes renowned for trout fishing.

Fort St. James

Fort St. James, a little town of 2,000 inhabitants, lies about 60km from Vanderhoof via Hwy. 27. Its main claim to fame is **Fort St. James National Historic Park ★★** (*$4; every day mid-May to Sep 9am to 5pm; ☎996-7191*), an authentic trading post established by the Hudson's Bay Company in 1896. Actors in period dress recreate the atmosphere of bygone days.

Burns Lake

There's no doubt that Burns Lake is a perfect place for **fishing**. The carved wooden fish at the entrance to town is a clear indication of what kind of atmosphere you'll find here. The local mottos are "3,000 Miles of Fishing" and "The Land of a Thousand Lakes." Fishers flock here for the lake trout, salmon and pike. However, knowing where exactly to cast your line can prove quite difficult if you're not familiar with the region, given the maze of dirt roads. Your best bet is to call the **Chamber of Commerce** before setting out (*☎692-3773 or 692-3751*).

Burns Lake Museum (*Hwy. 16 West, Burns Lake, ☎692-3773, ⇄692-3493*) is a small historical museum that relates the origins of Burns Lake and the pioneering spirit of the first settlers. There's also a collection of old tools and equipment that belonged to the area's first lumberjacks.

Houston

Houston, like Burns Lake, has clearly identified its summertime vocation: **fishing**. Not just any fishing, though; Houston is the self-proclaimed world steelhead capital. This famous sea trout is among the noblest of fish. Fishing buffs will be encouraged by the sight of the world's largest fly rod (20m) at the entrance of the tourist office, which also distributes a guide to the good fishing spots.

★★ Smithers

Smithers is a pretty, pleasant town with unique **architecture ★★**. The mountain setting, dominated by glacier-capped **Hudson Bay Mountain ★★★**, is splendid. Since its reconstruction in 1979, the town has taken on the look of a Swiss village. For this reason, many Europeans, lured by the local atmosphere and way of life, are among the town's 5000 residents. The **Ski Smithers ★★** (*153m vertical drop, 18 runs*) ski area, which looks out over the valley, has powdery conditions from November on. A few metres away from the tourist office, the **Bulkley Valley Museum ★★** (*summer every day 10am to 5pm; winter Mon to Sat 10am to 5pm; in the Central Park Building at the corner of Main and Hwy. 16, ☎847-5322*) exhibits objects used by the pioneers and photographs from the local archives. The Central Park Building also houses the **Smithers Art Gallery** (*☎847-3898*). Another interesting place to visit is **Driftwood Canyon Provincial Park ★★**, a major fossil site in this region. The tourist office can provide you with a map so you don't lose your way. On the weekend preceding Labour Day weekend, Smithers hosts the **Bulkley Valley Fall**

Fair ★★★, one of the largest agricultural fairs in British Columbia.

★★ Moricetown Canyon and Falls

Along the Bulkley River, 40km west of Smithers on Aboriginal land, there is a fishing area known as **Moricetown Canyon**, which has been frequented by Aboriginals for centuries. Today, the Aboriginal people still use the same fishing methods as their ancestors. Using long poles with hooks on them, they catch onto the salmon, then trap them in nets as they swim upstream. This is a very popular place to take pictures.

★★ Hazelton

Hazelton is the largest of three villages, the other two being South Hazelton and New Hazelton. Inhabited mainly by Aboriginal people (pop. 8,000), these three communities date back to the late 19th century, when the Hudson's Bay Company established a fur-trading post in the area (1868). The main attraction here is the **'Ksan Historical Village and Museum ★★★** (*$3, tours $10; Apr to Sep every day 9am to 6pm; call for winter schedule; 7km from Hwy. 16, just after Hazelton, ☎842-5544*), a replica of a Gitksan village, where visitors can watch artists at work.

Terrace

Terrace is one of the larger towns on the Yellowhead Highway (Hwy. 16). It lies on the banks of the magnificent Skeena River, the second largest river in the province after the Fraser, and is surrounded by the Coast Mountains.

Terrace is typical of a community dedicated to work, in that little effort has been put into making the town pretty and inviting. The surrounding **scenery★★★**, on the other hand, is splendid.

Check out the **Heritage Park Museum ★★** (*summer every day 10am to 6pm; Kerby St., ☎635-4546*) which deals with the history of the pioneers. There are a number of period buildings here, including a hotel, a barn, a theatre and six log cabins. Most date from 1910.

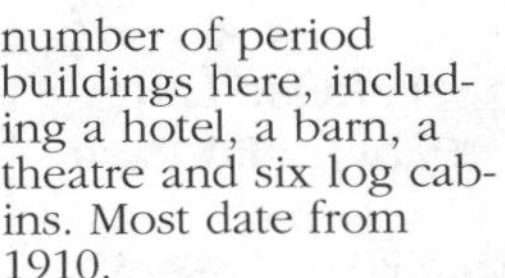

★★★ Tseax Lava Beds

Off Hwy. 16 and north of Terrace on Kalum Lake Drive, are the **Tseax Lava Beds**, the only natural site of its kind in Canada. Here, you'll find a number of **volcanic craters** and a stretch of lava 3km wide and 18km long. According to experts, the last eruptions took place about 350 years ago, which, on a geological scale, equates to a few minutes. Turquoise-coloured water has reappeared on the surface, adding a bit of colour to this lunar landscape. Right beside the lava beds is the **Nisga'a Memorial Lava Bed Park**, founded in memory of the 2,000 Nisga'a people who perished during the last eruption. With a little luck, you'll spot a Kermodei bear. The sight of one of these creatures, which belong to the same family as the black bear, but have a pure white coat, can make for a truly unforgettable visit.

★★
Lakelse Lake Provincial Park

Located on Hwy. 37 halfway between Terrace and Kitimat, **Lakelse Lake Provincial Park** is the perfect spot for those looking to relax. On the shores of the magnificent lake for which the park is named, you'll find a splendid **sandy beach** ★★. A number of picnic areas have been laid out here, along with hiking trails and a campground.

Kitimat

Visitors interested in both industry and nature will find a combination of the two in the little town of Kitimat (pop. 11,300), less than an hour from Terrace. Kitimat is an industrial town in the true sense of the term. It was established in the mid-1950s to accommodate workers from the **Alcan** (☎*639-8259*) aluminum factory, the **Eurocan Pulp** (☎*639-3597*) paper mill and the **Methanex** (☎*639-9292*) petrochemical plant, which together employed over two thirds of the population. All three companies offer free guided tours of their facilities, but reservations are required. Those interested in local history can stop at the **Centennial Museum** (*Mon to Fri 10am to 5pm, Sat noon to 5pm; 293 City Centre,* ☎*632-7022*), which exhibits Aboriginal artifacts found in the area. Although the surrounding mountains make Kitimat seem landlocked, the town is actually a port with direct access to the Pacific by way of the **Douglas Channel** ★★★. Salmon pass through this natural fjord on their way to the ocean's tributaries, making Kitimat a popular fishing spot.

★★★
From Terrace to Prince Rupert

The 132km stretch of highway between Terrace and Prince Rupert is undoubtedly one of the loveliest in Canada. The road follows the magnificent **Skeena River** ★★★ almost curve for curve as it peacefully weaves its way between the **Coast Mountains** ★★★. On fine days, the **scenery** ★★★ is extraordinary. Rest and picnic areas have been laid out all along the way.

★★★
Prince Rupert

The landscape changes radically near Prince Rupert. Huge hills covered with vegetation typical of the Pacific coast (large cedars, spruce trees) stretch as far as the eye can see. There is water everywhere, and although you will feel surrounded by lakes, what you see is actually the ocean creeping inland. A look at a map reveals that there are thousands of islands and fjords in this region. In fact, the town of Prince Rupert itself is located on an island, Kaien Island, 140km south of Ketchikan (Alaska). Prince Rupert is the most northerly point serviced by BC Ferries, and an important terminal for ferries from Alaska (Alaska Marine Highway).

The **scenery** ★★ is quite simply superb; mountains blanketed by dense forest encircle the town, and a splendid **natural harbour** ★★, the second largest in the Canadian West, will remind you that you have reached the coast. The history of Prince Rupert dates back to 1905, when engineers from the Grand Trunk Pacific Railway (GTPR), the transcontinental railroad, came here to look into the possibility of ending the line here. Over 19,000km of possible routes were studied before it was decided that the railroad would in fact run alongside the Skeena River. Charles Hays, president of the GTPR, held a contest to christen the new terminus. The name Prince Rupert was chosen from nearly 12,000 entries, in honour of the explorer and first head of the Hudson's Bay Company, a cousin of Charles II of England.

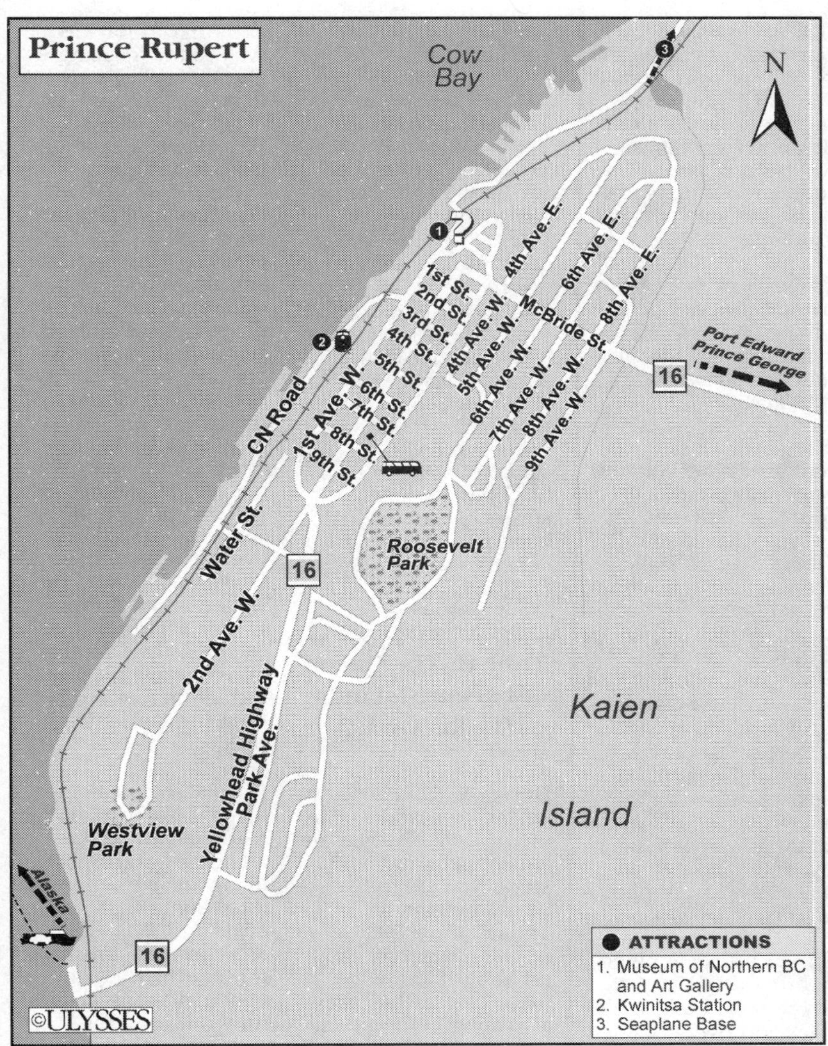

Today, Prince Rupert (pop. 20,000) is a lovely, prosperous community unlike any other town in northern British Columbia. You won't find any concrete or garish neon signs here; instead, you will be greeted by opulent-looking **Victorian architecture ★★**, large, pleasant streets, lovely shops and numerous restaurants reflecting a cosmopolitan atmosphere.

The tourist office, which offers direct access into the interesting **Museum of Northern British Columbia ★★** (*summer Mon to Sat 9am to 9pm, Sun 9am to 5pm; rest of the year Mon to Fri 9am to 5pm;* ☎*624-3207*). This museum displays various artifacts, as well as magnificent works of art and jewellery, which serve as proof that Aboriginal people have been living in this region for over 5,000 years. The gift shop, located inside the museum, features a vast selection of books on indigenous art, as well as displaying crafts and paintings.

Boat trips ★★ to **archeological sites** can be arranged at the tourist office. Space is limited and reservations are required.

The small seaside **Kwinitsa Station** (*summer only*) was built in 1911. It is one of 400 identical stations along the Grand Trunk Pacific Railway, the transcontinental line from Winnipeg to Prince Rupert. If you head north on Sixth Ave., you will see signs for the **Seaplane Base** ★★, one of the largest of its kind in Canada. The continuous spectacle of the aircraft taking off and landing has something hypnotic about it, and makes for lovely photographs.

The picturesque neighbourhood of **Cow Bay** ★★★, built on piles and overlooking a pretty sailing harbour, is a must-see. All sorts of shops, cafes and restaurants are clustered together in a colourful seaside setting. The **Seafest** takes place on the second weekend in June. Paraders march through the streets at 11am on Saturday, and sporting activities are held all weekend.

About 15km from Prince Rupert, in the little village of Port Edward, you will find the **North Pacific Cannery Village Museum** ★★ (*May to Sep every day 10am to 7pm; 1889 Skeena Dr.,* ☎*628-3538*), a former salmon canning factory built over 100 years ago. During summer, actor David Boyce puts on a show that traces the history of the Skeena River and salmon fishing, which has been the mainspring of the regional economy for over a century now.

Tour H: The Queen Charlotte Islands (Haida Gwaii)

However you choose to get to the islands, once there you'll discover an atmosphere and landscape that are truly beyond compare. Though the 5,000 islanders are very modest about their little piece of paradise, they actually go out of their way to attract and welcome visitors from the world over. The archipelago consists of 150 islands of various sizes. Almost all of the urban areas are located on the largest one, **Graham Island**, to the north. **Moresby Island** is the second most populous. Here, you'll find two villages, Sandspit and Alliford Bay, as well as the amazing Gwaii Haanas National Park.

The Queen Charlotte Islands lie about 770km, as the crow flies, from Vancouver. Because they are located so far west, the sun rises and sets at different times here than on the mainland. Although the islands are known for their wet climate, the more populated eastern coasts receive only slightly more rainfall than Vancouver (1,250mm). The precipitation on the western coasts, however, reaches record levels (4,500mm). The jagged relief of the Queen Charlotte and San Christoval Mountains has always protected the east coast from the westerly storms.

Despite the weather, the Haidas, who already inhabited the archipelago, established living areas on the west coast some 10,000 years ago. The Haidas are known to this day for their high-quality handicrafts and beautiful works of art.

Because the islands are so isolated, services are limited here. There are only two automated-teller machines on the archipelago, one in Masset and the other in Queen Charlotte City.

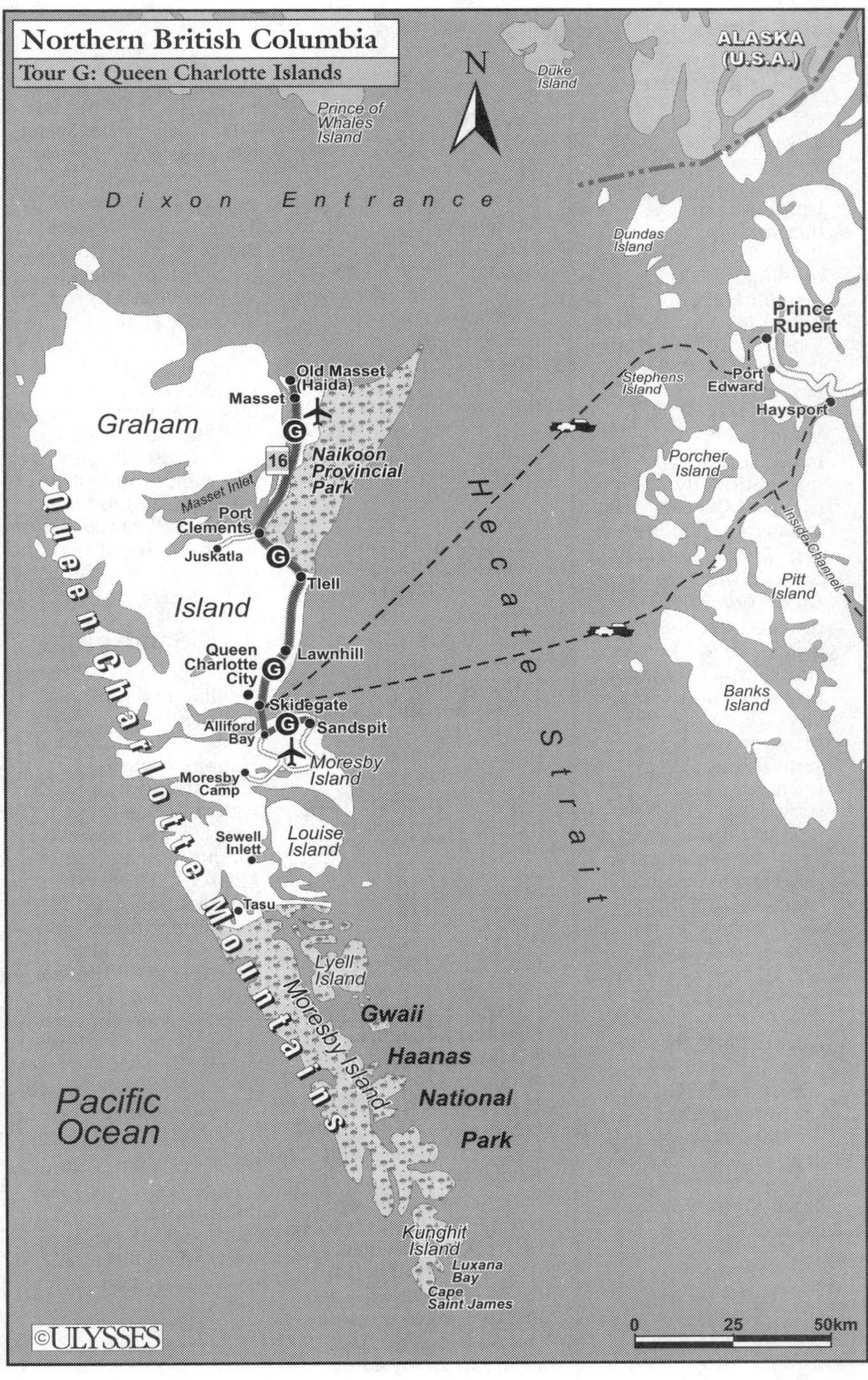

Northern British Columbia
Tour G: Queen Charlotte Islands
N
ALASKA (U.S.A.)
Duke Island
Prince of Whales Island
Dixon Entrance
Dundas Island
Prince Rupert
Port Edward
Haysport
Stephens Island
Old Masset (Haida)
Masset
Graham
16
Naikoon Provincial Park
Masset Inlet
Port Clements
Juskatla
Tlell
Island
Queen Charlotte City
Lawnhill
Skidegate
Alliford Bay
Sandspit
Moresby Island
Moresby Camp
Sewell Inlett
Louise Island
Tasu
Hecate Strait
Porcher Island
Inside Channel
Pitt Island
Banks Island
Queen Charlotte Mountains
Lyell Island
Moresby Island
Gwaii Haanas National Park
Pacific Ocean
Kunghit Island
Luxana Bay
Cape Saint James
0 25 50km
©ULYSSES

Skidegate

This is the first place you'll see if you take the ferry to the Queen Charlotte Islands, since the landing stage is located at the edge of the village. Skidegate is a small Haida community of 470 inhabitants, located on the beach in the heart of **Roonay Bay ★★★**.

While you're here, make sure to visit the internationally renowned **Queen Charlotte Islands Museum ★★★** (*Tue to Fri 10am to 5pm, Sat and Sun 1pm to 5pm, closed Mon; ☎559-4643*), devoted exclusively to articles made by the Haidas over the ages, up until the present day. All modes of expression are represented here: everything from totem poles, sculptures and drawings to fabrics and basketry, not to mention jewellery made with precious metals. The shop boasts an impressive but pricely selection of books and quality souvenirs.

Balance Rock, the area's most unusual sight, lies 1km away in the opposite direction (north). As its name indicates, it is a boulder balanced on a pretty pebbly **beach ★★**. You can't miss it.

★★ Queen Charlotte City

Located 4km south of Skidegate, Queen Charlotte City is a pleasant coastal village with 1,100 inhabitants. The atmosphere is very relaxed here, and the streets are filled with young people during the summer season. This is the jumping-off point for sea-kayak expeditions.

Right before Queen Charlotte City, on your way from Skidegate, you'll see **Joy's Island Jewellers**, a souvenir shop that doubles as the archipelago's official **tourist office**. There is not much to do in town. The islands' greatest attractions are the sea, the forest, the fauna (there are eagles everywhere) and the coasts, where you will discover traces of the Haida Nation.

As far as organized tours are concerned, the best-known company is definitely **Queen Charlotte Adventures** (*on the way into town, ☎559-8990 or 800-668-4288, ≠ 559-8983*), which will take you to the **Gwaii Haanas National Park ★★★** (*☎559-8818 or 637-5362*) by motorboat, since the area cannot be reached by land. This park, located at the southern tip of the archipelago, is home to many unusual sights, each more remarkable than the last. First, there is **Hot Springs Island ★★★**, a paradise for anyone who enjoys a good soak. Then there's **Laskeek Bay ★★★**, frequented by dolphins and whales. **Ninstints★★★**, a former Haida village on the tip of the island of Sgan Gwaii, is a UNESCO World Heritage Site. Here, you will find the largest collection of totem poles and Aboriginal-built structures in the Queen Charlotte Islands. There is something unreal and mystical about the location itself.

Sandspit

A village of lumberjacks, Sandspit (pop. 740), like Gwaii Haanas National Park, is located on Moresby Island. It has the second largest airport on the archipelago, after Masset's. The ferry shuttles back and forth between Queen Charlotte City and Moresby Island several times a day. The fare is inexpensive, and the crossing only takes a few minutes.

Tlell

This pretty little rural village (pop. 150) lies 43km north of Skidegate along the lovely **Tlell River**, which is popular with fishing buffs.

Port Clements

Port Clements is a community of 450 people, most of whom derive their income from fishing or the forest industry. The big draw here used to be the incredible **Golden Spruce ★★★**, at least until the 300-year-old, 50m-high tree was deliberately destroyed in January of 1997. A malefactor armed with a chainsaw committed this senseless act as a protest against what he called "university-trained professionals". He was arrested and claimed he meant no disrespect to the Haida. The fact remains, however, that a piece of Haida legend and culture, not to mention a biological treasure, is no more. The Golden Spruce was the only tree known to exhibit the golden pigmentation instead of the typical green foliage, the result of a mysterious genetic mutation.

Masset

Masset is the most important town on the Queen Charlotte Islands, with a population of 1,400 people. Since 1971, life here has been shaped to some extent by the local Canadian Forces base. Along with Queen Charlotte City and Sandspit, Masset is one of the few towns on the archipelago with a **tourist office**. It has all of the services one would expect to find in a large town, including an airport, restaurants, an auto-repair shop, a hospital, etc.

Old Masset

Old Masset, also known as Haida, is a Haida village of 630 inhabitants, which faces onto peaceful **Masset Sound**. It is best to go straight to the local tourist office, where you can learn the addresses of the resident artists. You'll find many works of art at **Haida Arts and Jewellery**, a shop with traditional architecture (*every day 11am to 5pm during summer*). The two totem poles at its entrance make it easy to spot.

★★★ Naikoon Provincial Park

Naikoon is one of the islands' treasures. You can get there from the highway in Masset, or through Tlell, where the park headquarters are located (*BC Parks, ☎557-4390*). The former option, through McIntyre Bay, is the most spectacular. The road runs along **South Beach ★★**, an extraordinary 15km stretch of sand, through a dense, damp and mossy forest. It ends at Agate Beach, where the park campground is located. **Agate Beach ★★** lies at the foot of **Tow Hill ★★**, a 109m-high rock that is home to a number of bald eagles. The **view ★★★** from the top is phenomenal (30min on foot). After Tow Hill, the beach continues, becoming **North Beach ★★★** for 10km. The park is also known for its lengthy hiking trails, which can be a real adventure. A good example is the one at **East Beach ★★★**, which covers 89km along an endless beach, through forests and across tidewaters.

Outdoor Activities

Birdwatching

These vast northern spaces abound with birds. Most notably, the Queen Charlotte Islands are home to the largest concentration of peregrine falcons in North America. Great herons and bald eagles, furthermore, are as common a sight around local villages as pigeons are in the big cities to the south.

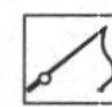

Fishing

Northern British Columbia is a fishing paradise, for trout as well as the king of fish, salmon. The latter can be caught either in the region's rivers or in the sea. Don't forget to obtain a permit beforehand.

There are a number of well-known spots, like **Burns Lake**, whose town slogans say it all: "3,000 Miles of Fishing" and "The Land of a Thousand Lakes." The **Chamber of Commerce** (*☎692-3773 or 692-3751*) is a mine of information for fishing buffs.

As in Burns Lake, life in **Houston** centres around fishing during the summer – and not just any kind of fishing; the town is the self-proclaimed steelhead capital of the world. The **tourist office** (*☎845-7640*) can show you where you have the best chances of catching this famous sea trout.

Around **Smithers**, the Bulkhead River is teeming with steelhead and salmon. **Kitimat** is also renowned for fishing, for it is here that salmon swim up the Douglas Channel, a natural fjord, to the ocean's tributaries. A wealth of information is available at the **tourist office** (*2109 Forest Ave., ☎632-6294 or 800-664-6554*).

The Queen Charlotte archipelago is ideal for deep-sea fishing, as it is home to the Chinook salmon, aptly nicknamed the "King" because of its size (up to 40 kg). For further information, contact **Queen Charlotte Adventures** (*☎559-8990 or 800-668-4288*).

Tour A: The Gold Rush Trail and the Cariboo Mountains

The region of Quesnel (Tour A) conceals many idyllic spots for fly-fishing. Fishpot Lake, 125km west of Quesnel, is one of these places. For more information, go to the tourist information office.

Hiking

Hiking is far and away the top activity in northern British Columbia. It enables visitors to appreciate the region's enchanting, unspoiled wilderness at close range. There are so many provincial and national parks here that even the most demanding outdoor enthusiast will have a hard time choosing between them. Those not to be missed include Stone Mountain, Wokkpash Recreation Area, Muncho Lake, Liard Hot Springs, the Spatsizi Plateau Wilderness Park, Mount Edziza and the Tseax Lava Beds.

Tour A: Gold Rush Trail and the Cariboo Mountains

At **Barkerville**, a network of trails follows the paths taken by the gold diggers. The wilderness is still relatively untouched and the flora and fauna are breathtaking. There are old cabins, once inhabited by gold diggers, along the path. The proposed tours take one day, but it is also possible to camp overnight and return the next day. A trail pass is available at the information office at the entrance to the historic town of Barkerville.

★★★ Tweedsmuir Provincial Park

Tweedsmuir is the largest park in British Columbia. The best way to get here is via Hwy. 20, which meets the West Coast at William's Lake. After driving 360km, you finally arrive at this paradise of lakes, greenery and mountains. This heaven on earth can be explored by foot, thanks to a network of trails. Excursions can range from a few hours up to a month.

One of the most impressive attractions has to be **Hunlen Falls**. Fed by Turner Lake, this waterfall is 260m high (more than four times the height of Niagara Falls). A 16.4km path leads to a great observation point. Set aside an entire day for this trip. The hilly terrain offers a 2,000m climb for experienced hikers. To get there, follow the directions along Hwy. 20.

Alexander Mackenzie Trail is a 420km trip. It follows the last leg of the journey that Alexander Mackenzie made over several months in 1793 before he became the first Englishman to view the West Coast of North America from this latitude. The 80km section (five to seven days) that crosses Tweedsmuir Park probably offers the most impressive panoramic views. Those interested in making the entire trip, which begins near Quesnel and ends at Bella Coola, can obtain more information from the **Alexander Mackenzie Trail Association** (*Box 425, Station A, Kelowna, BC, V1Y 7P1*)

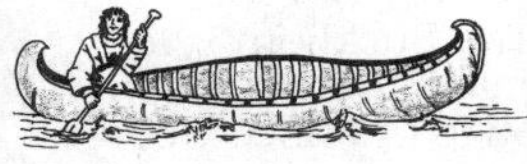

Rafting

Tour A: The Gold Rush Trail and the Cariboo Mountains

Big Canyon Rafting (*$70; 1347 Moffat Dr., ☎992-RAFT*) offers rides of several hours on the tumultuous Quesnel River.

Canoeing

Tour A: The Gold Rush Trail and the Cariboo Mountains

A canoe trip through six connected lakes between Kidney Lake and Turner Lake can be made in **Tweedsmuir Provincial Park**. The six short portages offer breathtaking views. Several beaches are scattered along the 15km journey. Canoe rentals available on site (*☎398-4414*).

You can have one of the most beautiful canoe trips in the world at **Bowron Lake Provincial Park**. There are some 115km of lakes, rivers and short portages, all framed by 2,500m mountains. It's a memorable experience that you'll want to repeat – even before your first day has ended. All camping equipment and canoe rentals are available at **Becker's.** Stock up on supplies at Quesnel before leaving, and plan seven days for this epic journey among the moose and eagles.

Kayaking

Gwaii Haanas National Park offers some excellent sea kayaking. Excursions are organized by **Queen Charlotte Adventures** (*Queen Charlotte City, ☎559-8990 or 800-668-4288, ⇄559-8983*) and by **Moresby Explorers** (*Sandspit, ☎/⇄ 637-2215 or 800-806-7633*).

Winter Activities

During winter, snow takes over the landscape. Cross-country skiing and snowshoeing can be enjoyed just about everywhere. As for downhill skiing, **Ski Smithers** (*☎250-847-2058*) on **Hudson Bay Mountain** has a 533m vertical drop and 18 runs, offers powdery conditions beginning in November. It is the largest ski area in the northern part of the province. **Powder King**, a smaller resort located between Prince George and Dawson Creek, boasts excellent snow coverage.

Accommodations

Tour A: The Gold Rush Trail and the Cariboo Mountains

Quesnel

Gold Pan Motel
$38-$48
≡, *tv*, ℝ
855 Front St.
☎992-2107
☎(800) 295-4334
⇄992-1125
The Gold Pan Motel is located in the middle of Quesnel. It has the comfort typical of a mid-priced facility.

Cascade Inn
$42-$64
≡, *tv*, ℝ, ≈, ⊛
383 St. Laurent Ave.
☎992-5575
☎(800) 663-1581
⇄992-2254
There are other motels in the mid-price range. The Cascade Inn is peaceful. Suites with kitchenettes are available for an additional $5.

Anne & Randy Schneider's
$60 bkfst incl.
5065 Parkland Rd., Bjornson Site, 15km north of town, RR8
☎992-7905
rschneider@universe.com
Anne & Randy Schneider's bed and breakfast is suitable for those looking for a quiet retreat by a lake. You can even use the canoe that rests peacefully on the shore. Cosy rooms and cordial hospitality.

Barkerville

Many camping grounds are located near the historic town of Barkerville. More than 160 campsites are available. For reservations, call ☎(800) 689-9025. The prices range between $10 and $22.

Barkerville's two bed and breakfasts are the only lodging available in the town. Be sure to reserve well in advance. The turn-of-the century ambience is wonderfully recreated at both of these B&Bs. The decor is splendid and the staff is courteous. The St. George deserves honourable mention.

Kelly House
$75-$95 bkfst incl.
☎994-3328
⇄997-3312
bcity@goldcity.com

St. George
$100 bkfst incl.
☎/⇄994-0008
www.cariboo.net.com/stgeorge

For less expensive alternatives, a group of mid-range hotels are located in the town next to Wells.

White Cap Motor Inn
$10/camping or $60/room
K, *tv*, ⊛
Ski Hill Rd.
☎994-3489
☎(800) 377-2028
⇄994-3426
The White Cap Motor Inn offers decent, though haphazardly decorated, rooms. The Swiss staff speaks German and is very welcoming.

Bowron Lake

The accommodations here include campsites ($10-$20), cabins ($15) and luxurious cottages ($50-$150).

Becker's Lodge
☎992-8864
☎(800) 808-4761
⇄992-8893
www.beckers.bc.ca
Becker's Lodge has magnificent log cabins. The wealthy German owner also has a chain of bakeries in Europe. With his firm handshake, cowboy hat and theatrical personality, everyone who meets Lother agrees: he is definitely a colourful character! The facilities that he built are beautiful and blend nicely with the countryside. The luxurious cottages are cosy and exquisitely designed.

Tour B: To the Alaska Highway

Prince George

The Buckhorn Bed & Breakfast
$50 bkfst incl.
🐕, ♿
14900 Buckhorn Place
☎(888) 933-8555
☎/⇄963-8884
The Buckhorn is located at the southern edge of Prince George, 1km east of Hwy. 97 and 13km south of the Fraser Bridge. A charming Victorian house, it

has two bedrooms, each with a queen-size bed, a single bed and an adjoining bathroom.

Best Western
$60-$70
≡, ≈, ⌂, ⊙
910 Victoria St.
☎*563-1267*
☎*(800) 528-1234*
⇄*563-9904*
The Best Western provides accommodations in the heart of Prince George. Its 53 rooms are clean and pleasant.

Connaught Motor Inn
$60-$70
≈, ℝ, *tv*, 🐕
1550 Victoria
☎*(800) 663-6620*
☎/⇄*562-4441*
Located downtown, the Connaught Motor Inn is right near all sorts of shops and services. It is a large, comfortable motel with a swimming pool and 98 rooms, each equipped with cable television and a refrigerator.

Westhaven Cottage
$70
23357 Fyfe Rd.
☎*964-0180*
South of Prince George, is a heavenly place called the Westhaven Cottage Set in the heart of nature, this charming cottage offers a splendid view of the lake. Guests have access to a private beach and hiking and cross-country ski trails.

The Manor House
$135
⊛, *K*
8384 Toombs Dr.
☎*562-9255*
⇄*562-8255*
"Elegant" is the word that best describes the Manor House, located northwest of town on the banks of the Nechako River. This immense place lives up to its name. The luxurious rooms are equipped with a gas fireplace, a bathroom, a kitchenette, a private entrance (in some cases) and an outdoor whirlpool bath.

Coast Inn of the North
$155
ℜ, 🐕, ♿, ≈, ⊙, ⌂
770 Brunswick
☎*563-0121*
☎*(800) 663-1144*
⇄*563-1948*
If you like urban comfort, try the Coast Inn of the North, also located downtown. A modern, 152-room hotel, it boasts a swimming pool, sauna, workout room, nightclub, pub, shop, etc.

Mackenzie

Alexander Mackenzie Hotel
$69-$72
🐕, K
403 Mackenzie Blvd.
☎*997-3266*
⇄*997-4675*
As far as accommodations in Mackenzie are concerned, the 99-room Alexander Mackenzie Hotel is hard to beat. This modern, luxurious place is like an oasis in the midst of the region's vast stretches of wilderness. It is located right in the centre of town, just a few steps away from Williston Lake, and includes a shopping centre with 37 stores. The rooms are spacious and some have a kitchenette.

Chetwynd

Country Squire Inn
$44-$52
⌂, ℝ, *tv*
5317 South Access Rd.
☎*788-2276*
⇄*788-3018*
Similar to the Stagecoach in style, the Country Squire Inn is a full-comfort modern hotel, complete with refrigerators in every room, satellite television, a laundry, an ice machine, a sauna and a whirlpool.

The Stagecoach Inn
$64-$74
⌂, *K*, ℝ, ℜ, *tv*
5413 South Access
☎*788-9666*
Chetwynd's main street is studded with quality motels. The Stagecoach Inn is situated in the heart of the village, close to all the local services. It has a restaurant, a sauna and 55 rooms, some with a kitchen. The modern, spacious rooms are equipped with a television with a movie channel.

Dawson Creek

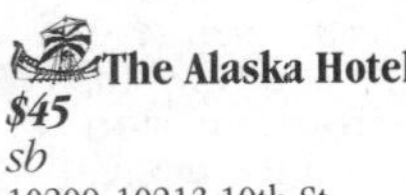

The Alaska Hotel
$45
sb
10209-10213 10th St.
☎782-7998
⇄782-6277
The Alaska Hotel is the symbol of Dawson Creek just as the Eiffel Tower is that of Paris. It would be hard to miss this white building with green trim, built in 1928, with "Alaska" written in capital letters on its facade. The rooms have not lost their old-fashioned charm, and the bathrooms for some are on the landing. On the ground floor, the best pub in town features live country, rock and blues music every weekend.

Trail Inn
$69-$79
tv, ⌂, *P*
1748 Alaska Ave.
☎782-8595
☎(800) 663-2749
⇄782-9657
The Trail Inn is located at the intersection of the Alaska Highway and Hart Highway, just after the Pioneer Village. It's a very comfortable hotel and rooms are equipped with mini refrigerators. Guests have access to a sauna.

George Dawson Inn
$75-$81
tv, ℜ
11705 Eighth St.
☎782-9151
☎(800) 663-2745
⇄782-1617
Somewhat different in style, the George Dawson Inn is a large modern hotel with 80 spacious, well-equipped rooms. Luxury suites are also available. The inn has a tavern and a restaurant as well.

Tour C: The Hudson's Hope Route

Hudson's Hope

The Sportsman's Inn
$44-$67
ℜ, *K*
10501 Cartier Ave.
☎783-5523
⇄783-5511
The Sportsman's Inn is well-suited to long stays, as 37 of its 50 rooms are equipped with kitchenettes. The hotel also includes a bar and a restaurant. All sorts of information of interest to fishing buffs is provided free of charge.

Tour D: The Alaska Highway

Fort St. John

The Pioneer Inn
$100-$115
🐕, ♿, ≈, ⊛, ⌂, ℜ, *tv*
9830 100th Ave.
☎787-0521
⇄787-2648
The Pioneer Inn, located in the centre of town, just 8km from the airport, is the last luxury hotel on the British-Columbian portion of the Alaska Highway. It has a bar, a restaurant, an indoor pool, a sauna and a whirlpool. The large, well-equipped rooms have cable television with sports and movie channels.

Mile 72 Alaska Highway

Shepherd's Inn
$40-$55
ℜ, *P*
Mile 73 Alaska Hwy.
☎827-3676
The Shepherd's Inn is located 45km north of Fort St. John. You'll find comfortable, rustic rooms here, as well as a small restaurant that serves home-made meals.

Pink Mountain

Mai's Kitchen
$35-$55
Mile 147 of the Alaska Hwy.
☎772-3215
Mai's is a peaceful place to spend the night. The rooms are rustic and you can sam-

ple some of their home-made bread. There is a service station here as well.

Fort Nelson

Coach House Inn
$50
♞, ⊛, ≡, ≈, ⌂, ℜ
4711 50th Ave. S.
☎774-3911
⇄774-3730
With its almost "city-style" level of comfort, the Coach House Inn is far and away the best hotel in Fort Nelson. It is located in the centre of town, on the west service road of the Alaska Highway, and offers 68 spacious, air-conditioned rooms, some of which are reserved for non-smokers. Guests enjoy the use of a swimming pool, a sauna, a bar and two restaurants. Special rates are available for seniors, members of the military and business travellers.

Muncho Lake Provincial Park

J & H Wilderness Resort
$58
May to Sep
♞
Mile 463 of the Alaska Hwy.
☎776-3453
⇄776-3454
The J & H Wilderness Resort is the ultimate northern motel. Its eight little rustic-style rooms lie just steps away from magnificent Muncho Lake. The rooms have no telephone or television, but nothing beats the feeling of spending the night in such heavenly surroundings.

Northern Rockies Lodge
$78
♞, ♿
Mile 462 of the Alaska Hwy.
☎776-3481
⇄776-3482
The Northern Rockies Lodge is becoming better known in Europe than in Canada. The owners, a brush pilot named Urs and his wife Marianne, attract many visitors from Germany, their native country. It is not uncommon to find charter buses parked in front of this 40-unit hotel, located just a stone's throw from the lake. Some of the rooms are motel-style, others cottage-style.

Liard Hot Springs Provincial Park

The Trapper Ray
$70
♞, ♿, ℜ
Km 801/mile 497 of the Alaska Hwy.
☎/⇄776-7349
Located on the Alaska Highway, just opposite the entrance to Liard Hot Springs Provincial Park, the Trapper Ray is a brand new establishment built in the purest northern style. An immense, two-storey log "cabin," it has 12 rooms, a restaurant, a souvenir shop and a gas station.

Watson Lake (Yukon)

Big Horn Hotel
$85
♞, ♿, ⊛, *K*
on the west side of the Alaska Hwy., downtown
☎(867)536-2020
⇄(867) 536-2021
With its trailer-style architecture, the Big Horn Hotel is not exactly attractive from the outside. Nevertheless, the place has 29 spacious, luxurious and comfortable rooms (some equipped with a kitchenette and a whirlpool), whose elaborate decor is worth a look. The rates, moreover, are reasonable for the area.

Watson Lake Hotel
$98
♞, ℜ
downtown, right near the Signpost Forest, on the east side of the Alaska Hwy.
☎(867) 536-2724
⇄(867) 536-7781
The Watson Lake Hotel is the best known place to stay in town. Watson Lake's oldest hotel, it has typical Yukon architecture, with massive beams and log walls. The 48 rooms are extremely comfortable. There is a coffee shop, a restaurant and a bar.

Belvedere Motor Hotel
$99
♞
on the west side of the Alaska Hwy., downtown
☎(867) 536-7712
⇄(867) 536-7563
The Belvedere Motor Hotel is located right near the Big Horn Ho-

tel & Tavern, to which it bears certain similarities. Unlike its competitor, however, it also offers rooms with a waterbed and houses a travel agency, a magazine and souvenir shop and a hairdressing salon.

Tour E: The Stewart-Cassiar Highway

Meziadin Junction

Meziadin Lake Provincial Park
Meziadin Junction
☎*847-7320*
Meziadin Lake Provincial Park has 46 campsites for tents and motorhomes, a picnic area and a beach. It's a pleasant spot if you like fishing.

Iskut

Trappers Souvenirs
$30
7km north of Iskut; radiomobile 2M3 520 Mehaus Channel
Trappers Souvenirs is a souvenir shop that rents out a log cabin at a modest price.

Red Goat Lodge
$17 members, $20 non-members
3.2km south of Iskut
☎/⇌*234-3261*
The Red Goat Lodge is the local YHA hostel. It looks out onto pretty Eddontenajon Lake. It lies adjacent to a campground, which is truly first-rate, considering its isolated location here in the wild. Dormitory rooms are all that is available for the moment. This is a popular place, so it is wise to make reservations. Kitchen, coin laundry, tv lounge, canoes.

Dease Lake

The Northway Motor Inn
$72
K, ℜ, tv
downtown on Boulder Ave.
☎*771-5341*
⇌*771-5342*
The Northway Motor Inn has 44 spacious, comfortable units, most of which have a kitchen equipped with a dishwasher. Monthly rates are available as well. A restaurant and a coffee shop lie a short walk away.

Telegraph Creek

Stikine Riversong
$55
on Stikine Ave.
☎*235-3196*
⇌*235-3194*
stikine.riversong@kermode.net
Set up inside an historic building, the Stikine Riversong is a cafe, an eight-room inn and a grocery store rolled into one. The rooms are somewhat basic but nonetheless very pleasant. This is the only place of its kind in Telegraph Creek, so it is wise to make reservations in order to avoid any unpleasant surprises.

Tour F: To Stewart, BC and Hyder, AK

Stewart

The King Edward Hotel & Motel
$70-90
ℜ, K
right in the centre of the village, at the corner of Fifth and Columbia St.
☎*636-2244*
⇌*636-9160*
The King Edward Hotel & Motel is the best hotel in Stewart. It has 50 comfortable, well-equipped units, some with a complete kitchen for longer stays. There is also a cafeteria on the premises.

Hyder, Alaska

The Sealaska Inn
$50 CAN
ℜ
on Premier Ave.
☎*250-636-2486*
⇌*636-9003*
The Sealaska Inn is a pleasant place located over a pub. The atmosphere is lively, and can get noisy, especially on weekends, so you might have a hard time falling asleep some nights.

Tour G: The Yellowhead Highway

Vanderhoof

The Grand Trunk Inn
$50-$60
ℜ, K
2351 Church St.
☎***567-3188***
⇌***567-3056***
The Grand Trunk Inn lies in the centre of town, one block north of Hwy. 16. It is one of the larger hotels in Vanderhoof, with 32 units, some of which include a kitchen. The rooms are simple but comfortable. A hairdressing salon, a pub and a restaurant are all located on the premises.

Fort St. James

The Stuart Lodge
$60-$65
K, tv
Stone Bay Rd.
☎/⇌***996-7917***
roesster@mail.wdcomputer.com
The Stuart Lodge is set on 24ha of land on the shores of Stuart Lake, 5km north of Fort St. James. In addition to offering a view of the lake, its six charming little cottages are fully equipped, complete with a barbecue and a television. Small motorboats are also available for rent.

Smithers

Berg's Valley Tours Bed & Breakfast
$55 bkfst incl.
no smoking
3924 13th Ave.
☎***847-5925***
⇌***847-5945***
Berg's Valley Tours Bed & Breakfast is perfect for active types, as the owners, David and Beverley, offer guided hikes in the mountains, including a trip in an all-terrain vehicle and a snack, as well as skiing packages and guided driving tours of the region.

Lakeside Art Gallery Bed & Breakfast
$75-95
5km west of Smithers, 1km west of the airport, along Hwy. 16
☎/⇌***847-9174***
☎***888-606-0011***
In Smithers, make sure to stop at the Lakeside Art Gallery Bed & Breakfast. This big white house on the shores of Kathlyn Lake offers an almost unreal view of glacier-capped Hudson Bay Mountain. The place has four rooms, all elegantly decorated. Small boats and canoes are available so that visitors can enjoy an outing on the lake. The friendly owner, Charlie, can show you where the good salmon-fishing spots are. This is probably the best place to stay on the Yellowhead Highway.

Hazelton

Ksan Campground
near the Ksan Historic Indian Village Museum
☎***842-5544***
The Ksan Campground is an extremely well-equipped and well-maintained campground. It can accommodate large motorhomes. There are trails around the site for walks. A small tourist shop has been set up at the campground.

Terrace

Lakelse Lake Lodge
$55
on Hwy. 37, halfway between Terrace and Kitimat
☎/⇌***798-9541***
This lodge resembles a European-style guesthouse. The friendly owner, Emmanuel, a Frenchman from the Basque Country, serves good, light dishes. He enjoys chatting with his guests, and can tell you where to go for some "miraculous" trout fishing.

Mount Layton Hotsprings Resort
$64-$72
tv, ℜ
22km south of Terrace via Hwy. 37
☎***798-2214***
☎***(800) 663-3862***
⇌***798-2478***
With its water slides and swimming pools filled by natural hot springs, the Mount Layton Hotsprings Resort, located just 15min from Terrace, is a fantastic place to stay during summertime.

Its 22 rooms are comfortable and well-equipped.

Coast Inn of the West
$115-$135
, ℜ, tv
4620 Lakelse Ave.
☎638-8141
⇌638-8999
A big hotel for a big town, the Coast Inn of the West is impeccable but expensive. It has 58 luxurious rooms with nothing lacking. A number of floors are reserved for non-smokers.

Kitimat

Aluminium City Motel
$49
tv, , K, ℝ
633 Dadook Cres.
☎639-9323
⇌639-2096
The Aluminium City Motel is located just a few minutes' walk from the salmon river, making it the perfect place for fishing buffs. Its parking lot was designed to accommodate pickup trucks pulling boat trailers. All 48 units are equipped with a refrigerator, and some have a kitchenette as well. Special rates are available for families who plan on spending an extended period of time here.

City Centre Motel
$52
♿, *K*
480 City Centre
☎632-4848
☎(800) 663-3391
⇌632-5300
The City Centre Motel is right in the centre of town, near all the local services. The comfortable, spacious rooms are equipped with a kitchenette. This is definitely one of the best deals in town.

Prince Rupert

Crest Motor Hotel
$139
tv, , , , ℜ
222 First Ave. W
☎624-6771
⇌627-7666
The Crest Motor Hotel boasts the best view in town, since it is located alongside a cliff overlooking the port. The rooms are worthy of the finest luxury hotel, and the service is impeccable. You really get your money's worth here. The Crest also has two excellent restaurants. All of these things combined make it one of the finest hotels in the North by Northwest region.

Tour H: The Queen Charlotte Islands (HaidaGwaii)

Queen Charlotte City

Spruce Point Lodge
$65
, tv
609 Sixth Ave.
☎/⇌559-8234
The pretty Spruce Point Lodge has very simple, yet very comfortable, rooms, each with a bathroom, a television, and its own private entrance. There is a common terrace with a view of magnificent Hecate Strait. Mary, the owner, keeps up to date on everything that's going on in the region, and knows a lot about the various companies that organize outdoor activities and adventures.

The Sea Raven
$70
tv, K, , ℜ, ℝ
3301 Third Ave.
☎559-4423
⇌559-8617
www.searaven.com
The Sea Raven is a comfortable, modern hotel. Some of the rooms offer a view of the sea. The restaurant adjoining the hotel is excellent.

Sandspit

Moresby Island Guest House
$55-$60
tv, P
385 Alliford Bay Rd.
☎637-5300
⇌637-5300
www.bbcanada.com
The Moresby Island Guest House is located on magnificent Shingle Bay, close to the airport, shops, restaurants and beaches. The 10 rooms are clean and comfortable and big enough for families. There is a common kitchen that can be used to prepare breakfast.

Seaport Bed & Breakfast
$40 bkfst incl.
K
371 Alliford Bay Rd.
☎***637-5698***
⇄***637-5697***
Just a stone's throw away from the airport, the Seaport Bed & Breakfast has two cottages, actually trailers, with a view of the bay. Each one is equipped with a kitchenette. Smoking is not permitted in the rooms, and credit cards are not accepted, but you won't find better value for your money on Moresby Island.

Sandspit Inn
$93-$105
tv, P
Airport Rd.
☎***637-5334***
⇄***637-5334***
The Sandspit Inn is a modern 35-unit hotel that offers rooms with a kitchen for an extra $12. It is located right near the Sandspit airport and has a large business clientele.

Tlell

Pezuta Lodging & Hostel
$20-$35
Hwy. 16
☎***557-4250***
⇄***557-4260***
The Pezuta is a very rustic inn, perfect for backpackers exploring the islands. You can choose between a private room or a shared room. Friendly atmosphere in the summer. You'll meet some interesting people from all over the world. Pezuta is open all year.

Tlell River House
$75
tv, ℜ
Beitush Rd.
☎***557-4211***
☎***(800) 667-8906***
⇄***557-4622***
This inn is hidden away in the woods, in a pleasant setting alongside the Tlell River and Hecate Strait. The rooms are simple and comfortable, and the restaurant serves quality food.

Port Clements

Golden Spruce Motel
$50-$58
K
2 Grouse St.
☎***557-4325***
⇄***557-4502***
The Golden Spruce is one of the few hotels in the Port Clements area. It has 12 very simple units, some of which are equipped with a kitchenette. There is also a coin laundry on the premises.

Masset

The Alaska View Lodge
$70 sb, $80 pb bkfst incl.
at the entrance of Naikoon Provincial Park, midway between Masset and Tow Hill
☎***626-3333***
☎***(800) 661-0019***
The Alaska View Lodge boasts a privileged site at the edge of the renowned Pacific forest, alongside South Beach, a magnificent 10km stretch of sand. The owners, Eliane, from Paris, and her husband Charly, from Bern (Switzerland), have created an "Old World" atmosphere for their guests. The Alaska View Lodge is an excellent choice for visitors looking to step out of their element into truly heavenly surroundings.

Singing Surf Inn
$78
tv, ℜ
1504 Old Beach Rd.
☎***626-3318***
⇄***626-5204***
Located on the way into town, the Singing Surf Inn is a veritable institution in Masset. The comfortable rooms are equipped with satellite television, and some offer a view of the port. The hotel also has a souvenir shop, a bar and a restaurant.

Naikoon Provincial Park

At **Naikoon Provincial Park** (*B.C. Parks,* ☎*557-4390*) there are two campgrounds: one at **Agate Beach** with 43 sites, west of Tow Hill, and the other at **Misty Meadows**, with around 30 sites. They both have washrooms, drinking water and firewood. They are often full during the summer but don't worry, wilderness camping is allowed in the park. There are three shelters to protect against bad weather, where you can also do a bit of cooking. They are at **Cape Ball, Ocanda** and **Fife Point**. There are no stores around the park, the closest supplies are in Masset, 30km away.

Restaurants

Tour A: The Gold Rush Trail and the Cariboo Mountains

Quesnel

Granville's Coffee
$
383 Reid St.
☎992-3667
Granville's Coffee is a cute little place to stop for an expertly prepared coffee. The decor is brightened up by wood panelling and jute coffee bags covering the ceiling. They serve delectable sandwiches as well as scrumptious desserts.

Mr Mikes
$$
450 Reid St.
☎992-7742
With its fireplace, sitting imposingly in the middle of the dining room, Mr Mikes resembles a chalet. The hamburgers are great and the service is impeccable.

Savata's
$$$
240 Reid St.
☎992-9453
Savata's cooks up steaks to perfection according to the customer's taste. The antique furnishings and the subdued lighting give this place a privileged status in Quesnel. Don't miss the salad bar – it offers a great selection.

Tour B: To the Alaska Highway

Prince George

Cariboo Steak & Seafood
$$
1165 Fifth Ave.
☎564-1220
If you're tired of gobbling down hamburgers, try the Cariboo Steak & Seafood, which serves very good steak and has a large all-you-can-eat buffet at lunchtime.

The Keg
$$
582 George St.
☎563-1768
Another excellent place for steak is The Keg, a member of the well-known chain. In fact, steak is the specialty of the house, and is prepared in a number of ways. You can have yours served with seafood if you like.

Niner's Diner
$$
508 George St.
☎562-1299
One of Prince George's trendiest spots, Niner's Diner has a 1950s decor and serves very generous portions. The menu includes gigantic salads, delicious burgers and gargantuan pasta dishes. Line-ups are common at lunchtime.

Mackenzie

The Alexander Mackenzie Hotel
$$
403 Mackenzie Blvd.
☎997-6549
The Alexander Mackenzie is *the* place to eat in town. The menu lists a variety of hamburgers, as well as chicken and a good choice of salads.

Chetwynd

Stagecoach Inn
$
5413 South Access
☎788-9666
In the heart of the village, the Stagecoach Inn has a small, family-style restaurant. You won't find gourmet cuisine here, but the food is of good quality.

The Swiss Inn Restaurant
$$
downtown on Hwy. 97, 800m east of the traffic light
☎788-2566
The Swiss Inn Restaurant serves Swiss German-style cuisine. The menu lists dishes like schnitzel, as well as typical North American fare, such as pizza, steak and seafood.

Dawson Creek

The Dynasty
$
1009 102nd St.
☎782-3138
The all-you-can-eat lunch buffet at the Dynasty features good Chinese food, as well as traditional meat and

seafood dishes. The atmosphere is very homey.

The Alaska Restaurant
$$
10209 10th St.
☎782-7040
The Alaska Restaurant, a green building dating back to 1928, with the word "Alaska" written in orange letters on its facade, is easy to spot from a distance. The "gold rush" decor is pleasant, and the food, high-quality. The impressive wine list is especially noteworthy.

Tour C: The Hudson's Hope Route

Hudson's Hope

The Sportsman's Inn
$
10501 Cartier Ave.
☎783-5523
The restaurant of the Sportsman's Inn is without a doubt the best place to eat in Hudson's Hope. This is a family-style place with a traditional menu.

Tour D: The Alaska Highway

Fort St. John

Boston Pizza
$
9824 100th St.
☎787-0455
As indicated by its name, Boston Pizza serves a wide selection of pizza. The menu also lists spicy ribs, pasta dishes, steaks and sandwiches.

The Pioneer Inn
$$
9830 100th Ave.
☎787-0521
The restaurant at the Pioneer Inn, located downtown, has a varied menu and serves generous portions.

Fort Nelson

Coach House Inn
$$
4711 50th Ave. S
☎774-3911
The restaurant at the Coach House Inn, a traditional stopping place for travellers on the Alaska Highway, is always very busy during summer. It serves a variety of dishes and even has a special menu for children. An all-you-can-eat buffet is sometimes served at dinnertime.

Muncho Lake Provincial Park

J & H Wilderness Resort
$
Mile 463 of the Alaska Hwy.
☎776-3453
At the restaurant of the J & H Wilderness Resort, the Club steak is so thick that only those with hearty appetites will be able to finish it.

The Northern Rockies Lodge
$$
Mile 462 of the Alaska Hwy.
☎776-3481
The Northern Rockies Lodge serves hamburgers, as well as German dishes. You won't go wrong ordering the sausages and sauerkraut. Close your eyes and let your imagination transport you to Alsace or Germany. German beer is available on tap here – of course!

Liard Hot Springs Provincial Park

The Trapper Ray
$
Km 801/mile 497 of the Alaska Hwy.
☎776-7349
The Trapper Ray, just opposite the entrance to the park, serves tasty, copious breakfasts.

Watson Lake (Yukon)

Junction 37 Service
$$
Km 1043/mile 649 of the Alaska Hwy.
This service station also has a decent restaurant. This is hardly gourmet cuisine, but a meal here is sure to satisfy even the heartiest appetite.

Watson Lake Hotel
$$$
Km 1021/mile 635 of the Alaska Hwy., downtown on the east side of the Hwy., right near the Signpost Forest
☎(867) 536-7718
The Watson Lake Hotel has two restaurants. One serves relatively standard fare, like sandwiches, and occasionally has a salad bar, while the other offers a fixed-price menu featuring more elaborate cuisine. In both cases, there's something for everyone. Rather pricey.

Tour E: The Stewart-Cassiar Highway

Iskut

Tenajohn Motel
$
in the centre of the village, along Hwy. 37
☎234-3141
The restaurant of the Tenajohn Motel sometimes serves unexpected dishes at dinnertime, depending on the choice of ingredients delivered that week.

Dease Lake

Northway
$
on Boulder Ave., downtown
☎771-5341
With its big green roof, Northway is the easiest restaurant to find in town. The menu lists soups and sandwiches.

Telegraph Creek

The Stikine Riversong
$$
on Stikine Ave.
☎235-3196
Located in an historic building, this a small bistro (as well as an inn and a grocery store) is only open during summer. It has a good reputation, and is the one place in Telegraph Creek where you can enjoy a good meal.

Tour F: To Stewart, BC and Hyder, AK

Stewart

King Edward Restaurant
$
at the corner of Fifth and Columbia Sts., in the heart of the village
☎636-2244
The King Edward is a perpetually busy cafeteria, where truckers, miners and tourists start arriving early for breakfast.

Hyder, Alaska

Sealaska Inn
$$
on Premier Ave.
☎250-636-9001
The restaurant of the Sealaska Inn is proud of its fish and chips, which are actually pretty good. The hamburgers are also worth a try.

Tour G: The Yellowhead Highway

Prince George

See Tour A: To the Alaska Highway, p 278.

Smithers

Smitty's Family Restaurant
$$
downtown on Hwy. 16
☎847-3357
Smitty's has special menus for children and seniors. The sandwiches are very thick, and the desserts will satisfy even the biggest appetites.

The Aspen
$$$
west of town on Hwy. 16, inside the Aspen Motor Inn
☎847-4551
The Aspen, which serves good, fresh seafood, is highly reputed in Smithers.

Terrace

White Spot
$-$$
4620 Lakelse Ave.
☎638-7977
The White Spot is located in the same building as the Coast Inn of the West. It is one of a chain of restaurants in the province, known for their sandwiches, salads and burgers.

Lakelse Lake Lodge
$$$
on Hwy. 37, halfway between Terrace and Kitimat
☎798-9541
The owner, Emmanuel, a Frenchman from the Basque Country, prepares light dishes using local game, trout and salmon. The atmosphere is pleasant and convivial.

Kitimat

The Chalet Restaurant
$$
852 Tsimshian
☎632-2662
The Chalet offers a varied menu, in keeping with Kitimat's cosmopolitan character. It serves generous breakfasts in the morning.

Prince Rupert

The Breakers Pub
$$
117 George Hill's Way
☎624-5990
The Breakers Pub, located in the pretty neighbourhood of Cow Bay, serves excellent fish and chips and well prepared fish dishes on a lovely terrace with a view of the port. This is a very pleasant place to spend the afternoon. A wide choice of draft beer is also available.

Smile's Seafood Café
$$
in the heart of the Cow Bay area
☎624-3072
Smile's is the most highly reputed place in town for seafood and fish, with good reason. The portions are generous, and the prices relatively modest.

The Crest Motor Hotel
$$$
222 First Ave.
☎624-6771
The Crest Motor Hotel has two good restaurants. The first, something like a snack-bar, serves tasty sandwiches, while the other, more classic in style, prepares delicious and very elaborate dishes.

Tour H: The Queen Charlotte Islands (Haida Gwaii)

Queen Charlotte City

Sea Raven Restaurant
$$
3301 Third Ave.
☎559-4423
The Sea Raven is a very good seafood restaurant with a varied menu. The daily special is always well-prepared.

The Oceana
$$$
Third Ave.
☎559-8683
The Oceana is a top-notch Chinese restaurant with a pretty view of the strait. The dishes are well-prepared and served in generous portions.

Tlell

The Tlell River House
$$$
Beltush Rd.
☎557-4211
The Tlell River House serves gourmet dishes in the purest country-style European tradition. It is one of the finest restaurants on the island. Watch out, though: the prices add up quickly!

Masset

The Singing Surf Inn Restaurant
$
1504 Old Beach Rd.
☎626-3318
The Singing Surf Inn restaurant is an institution in Masset. You won't find gourmet cuisine here, but the setting and the view are pleasant.

Cafe Gallery
$$
Collison Ave.
☎ 626-3672
At the Cafe Gallery, located downtown, you can admire paintings by Aboriginal artists while eating. There's nothing too exciting on the menu, with the exception, perhaps, of the Reuben sandwich. It's best with strong mustard.

Entertainment

Bars and Danceclubs

Wide open spaces are, of course, a big part of travelling in Northern British Columbia. Nevertheless, after a long day of exploring, there is nothing like relaxing to some music with a nice cold drink, at least for some anyhow. The bar situation is limited at best, depending of course on where you end up; danceclubs are nonexistant.

There are, however, friendly local bars, usually attached to a hotel or restaurant. Those attached to hotels are often called lounges, and are the gathering spots of local townspeople. It is not uncommon to find yourself in a discussion with a gold-digger, trapper or fisher at these places.

Dawson Creek

Alaska Hotel
10209 10th St.
☎782-7998
The best pub in town, where rock, country and blues are played all weekend long, is located in the lobby of the Alaska Hotel.

Watson Lake (Yukon)

1940s Canteen Show
every day at 8pm, Jun to Aug
behind the signpost forest
☎(867) 536-7781
The musical revue 1940s Canteen Show takes you back to the days of the construction of the Alaska Highway.

Cultural Activities

Prince George

Prince George is the cultural capital of the north. It has its own symphony orchestra and many theatre companies. Shows are only presented in the winter. When the weather is nice people tend to prefer outdoor activities.

Prince George Symphony Orchestra
performance season from Sep to May
☎562-0800
Call for program information.

The Prince George Theatre Workshop
(*performance season from Sep to May; ☎964-9092*) has been active in Prince George for 30 years. It offers comedy, drama and classic theatre productions.

Theatre NorthWest
(*118-101 North Tabor Blvd., Prince George, ☎563-6969*) is a professional theatre company offering quality plays with both Canadian and international performers. Contact the company for program details.

Calendar of Events

January

The **Prince George Iceman** (*Prince George, ☎564-1552*), is a series of events including an 8km cross-country ski run, over 10km on foot, then 5km of ice skating and finally, an 800m swim.

February

Mardi Gras of Winter (*Prince George, ☎564-3737*) is an important winter celebration with over a hundred organized events.

March

Prince George Music Festival features all the big names in the Prince George music scene. Organ, brass, string instruments and singing.

May

Northern Children's Festival (*Prince George, ☎562-4882*) is an impressive event devoted to childhood. Thousands of families head to Fort George Park for performances by international artists. Entrance is free.

Fishing Contest (*Third week, Chetwynd*)

Mile 0 Celebration (*Third week, Dawson Creek*)

June

The **Prince George Rodeo** (*Exhibition Grounds, Prince George*) is really worth the trip, particularly if you've never been to a rodeo. You can also attend an air show put on by parachutists, as well as square-dancing and country-music shows.

Hudson's Hope Rodeo (*First week, Hudson's Hope*)

Children's Festival (*Second week, Mackenzie*)

Doe River Rodeo (*Third week, Dawson Creek*)

July

Mackenzie, Pouce Coupe, Hudson's Hope, Fort St. John, Fort Nelson host Canada Day celebrations on the First.

The Prince George Airshow (*Prince George, ☎561-0071*) presents both modern and old military planes, and many skillful acrobatic performances.

August

International Food Festival (*Prince George, ☎563-4096*). At this festival you can sample specialties from all over the world. Delicious!

Prince George Exhibition (*Prince George, ☎563-4096*) is a big event in this city. It's an agricultural and food fair also touching on the home and gardening. The lumberjack show is always a big hit with kids.

Dekah'l Pow-Wow *(Prince George)* is a festival of Aboriginal dance that respects ancestral traditions down to the smallest details.

If you are so inclined, you can participate in the **Prince George Triathlon** (*Prince George, ☎561-7633*), a competition that consists of a 1.5km swim, a 40km bicycle race and a 10km run.

Peace Rafting Race (*Second week, Taylor*)

Rodeo, Fall Fair Stampede (*Second week, Dawson Creek*)

Rodeo (*Second week, Fort Nelson*)

October

Oktoberfest is an important tradition in Prince George's German community. You can dance to the sounds of "oom-pah-pah" music or just enjoy the beer.

Shopping

Dawson Creek

Make sure to stop at the **Dawson Creek Farmer's Market** *(Sat 8am to 3pm)* to sample the local produce. It is located near the NAR Park, right behind the sign for the Alaska Highway.

From May 1 to October 4 there are **farmer's markets** every Saturday in Chetwynd and Fort St. John.

Tlell

Sitka Studio (*at the end of Richardson Rd., ☎557-4241*) is a small art gallery open every day. It also has books.

Old Masset

Haida Arts and Jewellery (*every day 11am to 5pm*), with its traditional architecture and two totem poles marking the entrance, offers a fine selection of art.

Geological Terms for Mountain Terrain

Suspended valley: A valley whose floor is higher than that of the valley towards which it leads.

Glacial cirque: a crescent-shaped basin formed in a mountainous region by the erosive action of ice. When two cirques meet they form a ridge.

Crevasse: a deep crack or fissure in the top layer of a glacier. Transversal crevasses fracture the ice from one side to the other and are commonly seen when the glacier covers a steep uphill section of a mountain. Marginal crevasses are found on the edge of glaciers and result from friction with the mountainside. Longitudinal crevasses are found at the extremities of the glacier.

Sérac: series of crevasses where the glacier overhangs a cliff or covers a steep slope. As the glacier continues to advance, the crevasses at the base of the cliff will close up while others will open farther up.

Ogive: The colour of a glacier is not uniform, but actually contains stripes of white and grey. The lighter and paler areas are called ogives and result from the crevasses of a sérac which, when they open in summer, gather dust and silt and, when they open in winter, collect snow and air pockets.

Moraine: glacial deposits (mix of silt, sand, gravel and rock debris carried by a glacier). As the glacier retreats, it deposits masses of rocky debris at its sides. These are called lateral moraines when the debris comes from the neighbouring faces and frontal moraine when the deposits are at the end of the glacier.

Névé or firn: mass of hardened, porous snow that attaches to the glacier.

Glacial trough: A U-shaped valley carved out by a glacier.

Icecap: A convex-shaped, thick mass of ice that covers an area of land. Several glaciers can branch off from one icecap, as is the case in the Columbia Icefields.

Alpine glacier: smaller glaciers located in high-altitude valleys that resemble long tongues of ice and do not originate from icecaps. The Angel Glacier on Mount Edith Cavell is a good example.

Glacial nest: small glaciers that form on rocky cliffs and appear suspended.

The Rocky Mountains

In Canada, the term "Rockies" designates a chain of high Pacific mountains reaching elevations of between 3,000 and 4,000m.

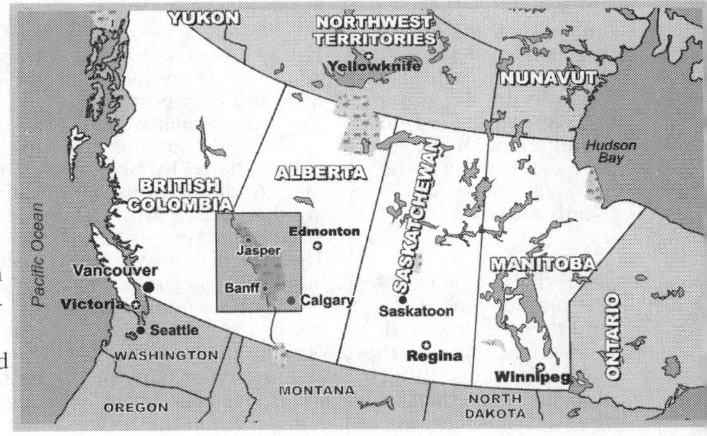

These mountains consist of crystalline and metamorphous rock that has been thrust upwards by collision between the Pacific tectonic plate and the North American continental plate, and then later carved out and eroded by glaciers.

The mountain chain runs east-west along the border between Alberta and British Columbia, and covers the Yukon territory. This vast region, which stretches more than 22,000km², is known the world over for its natural beauty and welcomes some six million visitors each year. Exceptional mountain scenery, wild rivers sure to thrill white-water rafting enthusiasts, still lakes whose waters vary from emerald green to turquoise blue, parks abounding in all sorts of wildlife, world-renowned ski centres and quality resort hotels all come together to make for an unforgettable vacation.

Geography

The history of the Rockies begins about 600 million years ago, when a deep sea covered the area where the mountains now stand. Bit by bit, layers of sediment, including clay shale, silt-laden rocks, sand and conglomerates from the erosion of the Canadian Shield to the east, accumulated at the bottom of this sea. These sedimentary layers were up to 20km deep in some places, and under the pressure of their own weight they crystallized to form a rocky platform. This explains the presence of marine fossils like shells and seaweed in many cliff faces; the Burgess Shale in Yoho National Park, declared a UNESCO World Heritage Site in 1981, is one of the most important fossil sites in the world with the fossilized remains of some 140 species.

About 160 million years ago, following a shift of the tectonic plates, the earth's forces began to exert a tremendous amount of pressure on the sedimentary rock, compressing, folding and pushing it upward until it finally broke apart. The western chains emerged first (Yoho and Kootenay National Parks) and then the principal chains (the highest including the immense ice fields and Mount Robson, the highest point in the Rockies at 3,954m) straddling the Continental Divide, the line that separates the drainage basins of North America.

A few million years later, the chains next to the prairies emerged, and then, after a final terrestrial upheaval, the rolling foothills of the Rockies. The effect of the earth's forces on this ancient platform of sedimentary rock are evident everywhere. The rippling of the rock can be seen on mountain faces; when the movement has resulted in the rock forming an "*A*" geologists refer to it as "anticlinal", and when it forms a "*U*", as "synclinal."

Of course, the Rocky Mountains were further shaped by other forces, the next step was the extreme erosion caused by constant battering by wind, rain, snow and ice, and by freezing and thawing.

Initially, water was the most important factor in the transformation of the Rockies' strata. One need only consider the fact that 7,500km^3 of water fall on Earth each year, to imagine the enormous destructive potential of the waterways that would result from that much rain. A constant flow of water can erode even the hardest rock, acting just like sandpaper.

The grains of sand broken loose from the rock and transported by the torrential waters of mountain streams scrape the rocky bottom, gradually polishing the surface and infiltrating crevices. These slowly grow until huge pieces of rock break off or enormous cavities are hollowed out like those in the Maligne River Canyon, which are called "potholes." When the rock is of a more crumbly variety, or even water soluble like limestone, the rain and snow easily carve out deep fissures. The mountains finally lost their primitive look thanks to this slow but unrelenting erosion, as the water eventually worked its way through several layers of rock, forming deep V-shaped valleys.

Glaciers

About two million years ago, during the first ice age, a huge, moving ice field covered more than one-fifth of the surface of the earth, through which only the highest summits of the Rockies emerged. The ice receded and advanced over this region three times.

The glaciers and their runoff radically changed the landscape of the Rockies, breaking off the upper portions of the rock along the edges, and reshaping the rock over which they advanced. Contrary to the water, which bored deep into the earth, the glaciers altered the mountains in depth and width, creating huge U-shaped valleys known as "glacial troughs." The icefields region is an excellent example, with its wide, steep-sided valleys. The bigger the glacier the more destructive it was to the mountain and the deeper and wider the valley it created.

In the icefield region, visitors will see what are termed "suspended valleys," which result from the erosion caused by a small glacier that attaches itself to a larger mass of ice. The valley left behind by the smaller glacier is not nearly as deep as the one left by the larger glacier, and appears to be suspended once the ice has melted; an example is the Maligne Valley, which is suspended 120m above the Athabasca Valley.

Flora

The forests of the Rocky Mountains are essentially made up of **lodgepole pine**. Aboriginal people used these trees to build tipis because they grow very straight, are fairly tall and have little foliage. Ironically, forest fires guarantee the trees' survival. Heat causes the resin in the pine cones to melt slowly, releasing the seeds that are held within. The seeds are then dispersed by the wind, and the forest essentially rises from its own ashes. If such fires were completely eliminated, the lodgepole pines would get old and the forest would be taken over by other vegetation and die, which would in turn force out the moose. From time to time, therefore, Parks Canada sets controlled fires, and the burnt-out trunks of lodgepole pine are a common sight along the roads.

The **aspen** is the most common broad-leaved tree in the forests of the Rocky Mountains. Its trunk is white and its leaves round. The slightest breeze makes the leaves tremble, and for this is it often called a trembling aspen.

The **Englemann spruce** is found at high altitudes, near the tree line. It is the first tree to grow at these altitudes on the gravel of ancient moraines. This tree has a long lifespan; some near the Athabasca glacier are more than 700 years old. It generally has a twisted trunk due to strong winds that sweep across the mountainsides. In valleys, the spruce can measure up to 20m.

The **Douglas fir**, found north of Jasper, grows in forests at the bottom of the valleys of the Rockies.

The wildflower season does not last very long in alpine regions. The flowering time, production of seeds and reproduction are a veritable race against the clock during the few short weeks of summer. Their perennial nature, however, helps them to survive. In fact, perennial plants store everything they need for new shoots, leaves and flowers in their roots and rhizomes or in the previous year's bulb.

Before the snow has even melted, they are ready to emerge from the earth. The secret of alpine zone flowers lies in the fact that they remain dormant all winter and then take full advantage of the humidity and strong sunshine of summer.

The **western anemone** is a common sight in mountainous zones. Though it is not common to see it in bloom, it is easy to spot in summer, when its stem has a downy covering. Towards the end of summer, the seeds, with their long, feather-like appendages, are carried off by the wind, assuring the reproduction of the flower.

Heather has also adapted well to the rigours of the alpine zone. Its hardy leaves help it to store energy and spare it from having to produce new leaves every year. Among the many types of heather common to this region are **pink heather**, which has little red flowers, **yellow heather** with white flowers and yellow sepals, and **purple heather** with white, bell-shaped flowers and reddish-brown sepals. Purple heather resembles a cushiony sponge and grows at the tree line on mountain slopes long ago abandoned by glaciers.

This **Indian paintbrush** varies from pale yellow to vibrant red. Flower is easy to spot since it is actually its leaves that are coloured, while the flower lies tucked among the upper folds of the stem.

The **bluebell** is a tiny blue flower that grows close to the ground in gravel or sand near water.

Fauna

The **black bear** is the smallest bear in North America. As its name suggests, it is usually black, although there are some with dark brown fur. Its head is quite high and the line between its shoulders and its hindquarters is much straighter than on a grizzly. The male weighs between 170 and 350kg and can grow to up to 168 centimetres long and 97cm at the withers. The female is one-third smaller. These bears are found in dense forests at lower altitudes and in clearings. They are mammals and feed on roots, wild berries and leaves.

The **grizzly**'s colouring varies between black and blond and its fur often appears to be greying, hence its name.

Larger and heavier than its cousin the black bear, the grizzly measures 110cm at the withers, and up to twom when standing on its hind legs. Its average weight is about 200 kilograms, though some have been known to weigh up to 450 kilograms. The grizzly can be distinguished from the black bear by the large hump at its shoulders. This hump is actually the muscle mass of its imposing front paws. Its hindquarters are also lower than its shoulders, and it carries its head fairly low. Despite these differences, it is often difficult to tell a young grizzly from a black bear. Take extreme caution if you encounter a bear, as these animals are unpredictable and can be very dangerous.

Cougars (also called pumas or mountains lions) are the largest of the Felidae, or cat family, that inhabit the Rockies and Kananaskis Country, where about 100 have been counted. These large cats weigh from 72 to 103kg (45kg for females), and when hungry can attack pet dogs and even humans. Unfortunately, these nocturnal felines are rarely be seen.

Lynxes are also members of the cat family, but are much smaller than pumas, weighing about 11kg. Their bob tails and pointed ears topped with little tufts of longer fur make them easy to identify. Also nocturnal, they are hard to spot.

Cervidae: The Rockies are a veritable paradise for cervidae, which can be seen in great numbers. It is not uncommon to spot **moose**, huge mammals that can weigh up to 500kg and whose characteristic antlers are large and impressive. **Mule-deer**, **white-tailed deer**, **mountain caribou** and **moose** can often be spotted along the highways.

Bighorn sheep are not cervidae, but rather horned ungulates, or hoofed animals. The difference between these two families is that ungulates do not lose their horns every year, but rather keep them for their whole life. Bighorn sheep are easy to identify thanks to their curved horns. They are a common sight along the road. They are quite tame and will readily approach people in the hopes of being fed. Under no circumstances should you give them any food since they will quickly develop the bad habit of approaching people and thus run the risk of being killed by the many cars that travel park roads.**Mountain goats** also belong to the horned ungulate family. Their numbers are low, and they are rarely spotted, except in alpine areas. They are recognizable by their long white fur and two small, black pointed horns. They are very timid and will not tolerate being approached.

Wolves, **coyotes** and **foxes** can also be seen in the parks, especially in the forests of Kananaskis Country.

The **bald eagle**, **golden eagle**, **great-horned owl** and several **falcon** species are among the birds of prey found in the Rockies.

Ptarmigans resemble chickens. Their colouring changes with seasons, varying between a white-speckled brown in the summer to snowy white in the winter. **Grouse** are also common.

Two other noteworthy, though sometimes annoying, birds are the **grey jay** and **Clark's nutcracker**, who won't hesitate to swipe the food right off your plate the minute you decide to have a picnic in the forest.

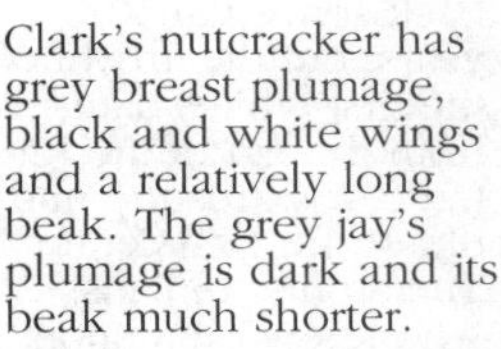

Clark's nutcracker has grey breast plumage, black and white wings and a relatively long beak. The grey jay's plumage is dark and its beak much shorter.

Two types of pesky insects abound during certain seasons in the Rockies. First the **mosquito**, of which there are no less than 28 different species, all equally exasperating to human beings. Arm yourself for an encounter with these critters, either with insect repellent or mosquito netting. Between the months of April and June, another insect, the **Anderson tick**, makes life in the Rockies more of an adventure. These should be avoided but not to the point of panic (on the rare occasions when it is carrying Rocky Mountain fever it can cause death). The tick is found in the dry grassy parts of the Rockies. Regularly check your clothes and yourself if you are walking in these areas in the spring. If you find one, slowly remove it (burning it does not work) and see a doctor at the first sign of headache, numbness or pain.

History

The presence of human beings in this area goes back some 11,000 years, but the arrival of the first whites dates from the era of the fur trade, towards the middle of the 18th century. The Stoney Indians, who knew the region well, served as guides to these new arrivals, showing them mountain passes that would play an important role in the fur trade.

No less than 80° of longitude separate the most easterly point of Newfoundland and the Queen Charlotte Islands in the west. This immense territory, however, had only about four million inhabitants by 1850. To overcome the threat posed by the American giant to the south, which was richer and more populous, and following political and economic crises in 1837 under the government of William Mackenzie, a desire emerged to establish a more efficient political organization. Canadian Confederation became a reality with the 1867 vote on the British North America Act.

This new Canadian state, which went from colony to British Dominion, consisted originally of four provinces, Ontario, Québec, Nova Scotia and New Brunswick, all located in the east. Therefore, when the United States purchased Alaska from Russia for $7 million in March 1867, British Columbia found itself in a precarious position, hemmed in on two sides by the United States. Furthermore, British Columbia was cut off geographically from the Canadian Confederation. When delegates from this province wanted to get to Ottawa they first had to travel to San Francisco by boat and then take the new transcontinental train line through Chicago to Toronto.

Before Canada could be united, therefore, British Columbia demanded an end to this isolation and the construction of a road connecting the province with the rest of the Confederation. To its great surprise, the Macdonald government offered even more, the construction of a railway! Linking the Maritime provinces in the east to Victoria was indeed a prodigious feat and certainly an unprecedented technological and financial challenge for such a young and sparsely populated country.

Transportation creates commerce, and such a vast nation clearly could not grow and prosper without relying on modern modes of communication. It had to establish commercial stability despite the harsh realities of winter, which slowed and occasionally immobilized ground and maritime transportation, thereby isolating entire regions of this huge country.

The economy of the Rocky Mountains took off following the construction of the railway, as prospectors, alpinists, geologists and all sorts of visitors joined the railway agents, participating in some of the most memorable moments in the region's history.

Economy

"If we can't export the scenery, we'll import the tourists!" This statement by William C. Van Horne, vice-president of the Canadian Pacific Railway, pretty well sums up the situation. The economy of the Canadian Rockies, in the five national parks of Alberta and British Columbia, relies almost solely on tourism. The preservation of these areas is assured by their status as national parks, which also guarantees the complete absence of any type of development, be it mining or forestry. In fact, coal, copper, lead and silver mines (see Silver City, p 303) as well as ochre deposits (see Paint Pots, p 316) were abandoned and villages were moved in order to return the mountains to their original state and to stop human industry from marring all this natural beauty.

Finding Your Way Around

Getting to the Rockies

Very reasonable fees are charged to gain access to the national parks of the Canadian Rockies, and these must be paid at the entrance gate of each park *($5 for one day, $35 per year).*

Up until recently the fees only applied to cars entering the parks, but from now on every person mus
t pay an individual fee. This allows Parks Canada to earn extra revenue from travellers arriving by foot, bike, train or bus, which contributes to maintaining park facilities.

Parks Canada also charges travellers wishing to practise certain activities (excursions of more than one day, rock-climbing, interpretive activities...) and for the use of certain facilities, like hot springs.

A complete list of the fees for each year is available at park entrance, at the parks' information centres (see addresses and telephone numbers below) or by calling *☎800-651-7959.*

By Plane

Most people fly into the airports in Calgary, Edmonton or Vancouver and then drive to the national and provincial parks.

By Bus

Tour A: Banff National Park

The **Bus Station** *(☎ 403-762-6767 or 800-661-8747)*, located on the way into Banff on Mount Norquay Road, at the corner of Gopher Road, is used by **Greyhound** *(☎800-661-8747)* and **Brewster Transportation and Tours** *(☎ 403-762-6735)*. This latter company takes care of local transportation and organizes trips to the icefields and Jasper.

Tour C: Jasper National Park

The **Greyhound Bus Station** *(☎ 403-852-3926)* is located right in the middle of Jasper, on Connaught Drive. **Heritage Cabs** *(☎ 403-852-5558)* serves the area.

By Train

Tour A: Banff National Park

The **Rocky Mountaineer Train Station** is right next to the bus station on Railway Drive.

Taxis are available for the trip downtown

Legion Taxi
☎(403)762-3353

Mountain Taxi
☎(403)762-3351

Taxi Taxi
☎(403)762-3111

Banff Taxi and Tours
☎(403)762-4444

Tour C: Jasper National Park

Via
☎800-561-8630
The train station is located next to the Greyhound bus terminal.

By Car

Because of the hemmed-in location of the Rockies, driving is the most practical means of transportation here. The roads throughout this mountainous region are generally in good condition considering the winds, snow and ice that quickly deteriorate infrastructure. Driving along these winding roads does, however, require extra attention and caution, especially in winter. Be sure to stop regularly to rest and, of course, to admire the spectacular scenery.

It is important to check road conditions before heading off in the winter, as heavy snowfalls often lead to road closures. Furthermore, your car should also be equipped with snow tires, studded tires or in some cases chains. Generally, however, the major arteries are open year-round, while secondary roads are often used as cross-country ski trails in the winter.

For information on road conditions in Banff call:

Environment Canada *(☎ 403-762-2088)* or **The Banff Warden's Office** *(☎ 403-762-1450)*

In Jasper, call: **The Weather Service** *(☎ 403- 852-3185)* or **The Alberta Motor Association** *(Jun to Aug, ☎ 403-852-4444; year-round, ☎(800)222-4357)*, which you can also call for roadside assistance.

For Yoho National Park, call the **tourist office**: ***summer:*** *☎ 250-343-5324* ***winter:*** *☎ 250-343-6432*

For Kootenay National Park, the **park office** *(☎ 250-347-9615)*. This kind of information is also available at the entrance gates of the national parks and in all local offices of Parks Canada.

This chapter is divided into five tours:

Tour A: Banff National Park ★★★

Tour B: The Icefields Parkway ★★★

Tour C: Jasper National Park ★★★

Tour D: Yoho and Kootenay National Parks ★★

Tour E: Kananaskis Country ★★

Tour A: Banff National Park

Banff National Park is the most well-known and visited of Canadian parks. It is incredibly beautiful, but its renown also makes it one of the busiest parks, overrun with visitors from all over the world. Its main town, Banff, has grown as a result of tourism and is home to a large number of shops, hotels and restaurants of all different types.

This tour starts in the small town of Canmore, located only about 20km from the entrance to the park, then leads to Banff on the Trans-Canada Highway or on the Bow Valley Parkway (Hwy 1A), which runs parallel to the former. The tour weaves its way around Banff town site and ends up in the village of Lake Louise, known the world over for its exquisite, shimmering, emerald-green lake.

Tour B: The Icefields Parkway

This tour starts in the village of Lake Louise and snakes its way through Banff National Park on Hwy. 93. It allows you to discover some of the highest summits of the Canadian Rockies before ending up in the immense Columbia Icefield. Stunning landscapes line the whole route, and by stopping at the various lookout points along the way you'll find yourself journeying through the geological history of these mountains and valleys and reliving the experiences of the adventurers who discovered this region. The focal point of this tour is the Athabasca Glacier, at the entrance to Jasper National Park. With the proper equipment and an understanding of safety techniques for hiking on ice, adventurers can set off from the Columbia Icefields information centre to conquer the Athabasca, Dome and Stutfield glaciers.

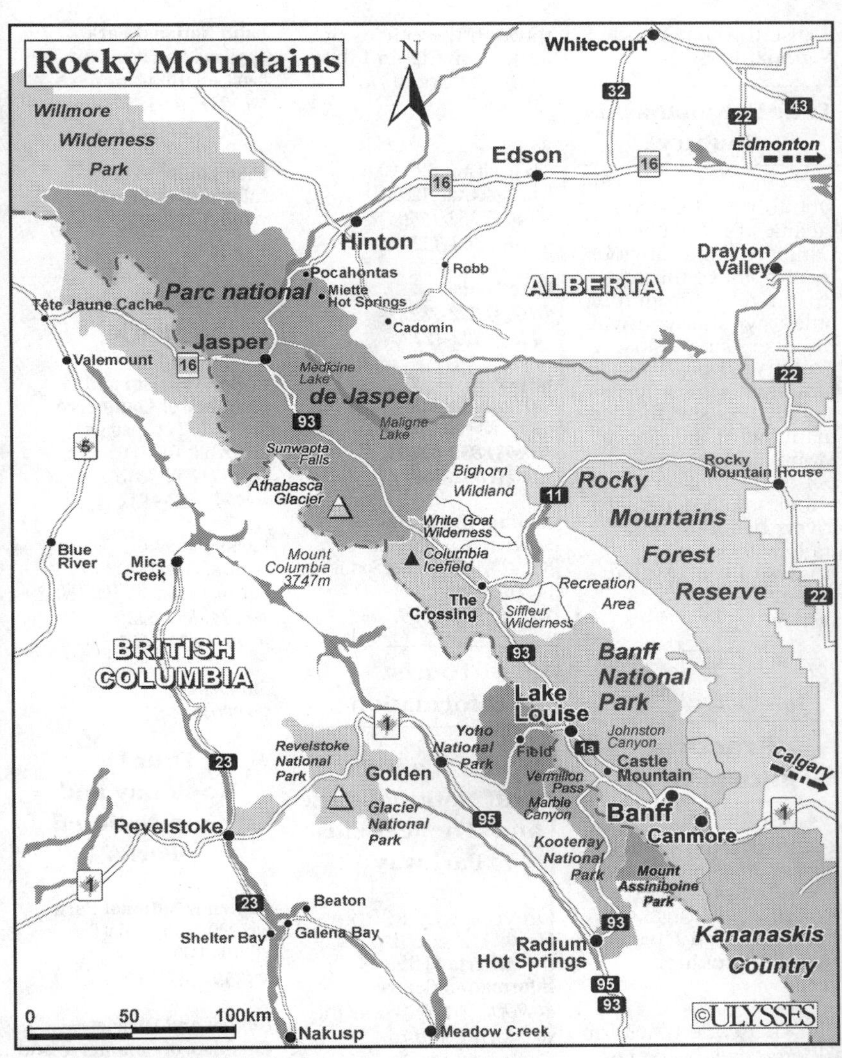

Tour C: Jasper National Park

This tour explores the surroundings of Jasper, the central point of the national park of the same name, before heading northeast on Hwy. 16 to the small town of Hinton, located about 30km from the entrance to Jasper National Park.

Tour D: Kootenay and Yoho National Parks

Sometimes referred to as the Golden Triangle, this tour starts out from Castle Mountain in Banff National Park, then heads down Hwy. 93, which passes through Kootenay National Park to Radium Hot Springs. The tour then heads back up the valley of the Columbia River towards Golden and then on to Lake

Louise through Yoho National Park.

Tour E: Kananaskis Country

Due to its extensive facilities for travellers, Canmore is the obvious focal point of this tour. It is therefore from this little town that you will discover Kananaskis Country. Though its mountainous scenery is slightly less spectacular than that of the Rocky Mountain national parks, this region nevertheless offers nature lovers beautiful hiking trails without the hordes of tourists that invade Banff and Jasper.

Practical Information

The parks in the Rocky Mountains straddle two Canadian provinces, Alberta and British Columbia, which have two different area codes.

The area code is **403** for Alberta, except for Jasper, which is **780**, and **250** for British Columbia.

Parks Canada Offices

Information about the different parks and regions is available through the offices of Parks Canada and the tourist information offices.

Banff
224 Banff Ave., Box 900
Banff, Alberta, T0L 0C0
☎ ***(403) 762-1550***
⇄ ***(403) 762-3229***

Lake Louise
☎ ***(403) 522-2822***
⇄ ***(403) 522-1212***

Jasper
500 Connaught Drive, Box 10
Jasper, Alberta, T0E 1E0
☎ ***(403) 852-6220***
⇄ ***(403) 852-5601***

Radium Hot Springs
Kootenay National Park
Box 220, Radium Hot Springs
BC, V0A 1M0
☎ ***(250) 347-9615***

Tourist Information

Tour A and B: Banff National Park and The Icefields Parkway

On your way in from Hwy. 1A, you'll pass the **Alberta Visitor Information Centre** *(☎800- 661-8888)* at the western edge of Canmore, at Dead Mans Flats.

Banff Visitor Centre
224 Banff Ave., Box 900
Banff, AB, T0L 0C0
☎ ***(403) 762-8421***
☎ ***(403) 762-0270***
⇄ ***(403) 762-8163***

Banff National Park
224 Banff Ave., Box 900
Banff, AB, T0L 0C0
☎ ***(403) 762-1550***
⇄ ***(403) 762-1551***

Lake Louise Visitor Information Centre
☎ ***(403) 522-3833***

Tour C: Jasper National Park

Jasper Tourism and Chamber of Commerce
Box 98, 632 Connaught Dr.
Jasper, AB, T0E 1E0
☎ ***(403) 852-3858***
⇄ ***(403) 852-4932***

Parks Canada
500 Connaught Dr.
Box 10, Jasper, AB, T0E 1E0
☎ ***(403) 852-6220***
⇄ ***(403) 852-5601***

Ski Jasper
☎ ***(800)473-8135***

Tour D: Kootenay and Yoho National Parks

Kootenay National Park
Box 220, Radium Hot Springs
BC, V0A 1M0
☎ ***(250) 347-9615***

Golden and District Chamber of Commerce and Travel Information Centre
located in the centre of town
☎ ***(250)344-7125***

Field
every day 9am to 6pm
at the entrance to town
☎ ***(250) 343-6324***

Respect the Mountain!

As a hiker, it is important to realize your role in preserving and respecting the fragility of the ecosystem and to comprehend your impact on your surroundings. Here are a few guidelines:

First of all, stay on the trails, even if they are covered in snow or mud, in order to protect the ground vegetation and avoid widening the trail.

Unless you're heading off on a long trek, wear lightweight hiking boots as they do less damage to vegetation. When in a group in alpine regions, spread out and walk on rocks as much as possible to avoid damaging vegetation.

It is just as important to protect waterways, bodies of water and the ground water when in mountainous regions. When digging back-country latrines, place them at least 30m from all water sources, and cover everything (paper included) with earth.

Never clean yourself in lakes or streams.

At campsites, only dispose of waste water in designated areas.

The water in mountain regions is not always potable and therefore should be boiled for at least 10min before drinking.

Never leave any garbage behind. Garbage bags are provided at Parks Canada offices.

Certain types of flowers are endangered, so do not pick anything.

Leave everything as you find it. This way those that follow can enjoy the beauty of nature as you did.

For safety reasons, always keep your dog on a leash, or leave it at home. Dogs that roam free have a tendency to wander off and chase wild animals. They have even been known to chase down bears and then take refuge with their masters.

Finally, if you are exploring the Rockies on horseback, remember that only trails set aside for these animals may be followed.

Tour E: Kananaskis Country

Kananaskis Country Head Office
Suite 100, 3115 12th St. NE
Calgary, AB, T2E 7J2
☎(403) 297-3362

Tourism Canmore Kananaskis
801 Eighth St., Canmore
T1W 2B3
☎678-1295
⇌678-1296
www.canmorekananaskis.com

Bow Valley Provincial Park Office
Located near the town of Seeby
☎(403) 673-3663

Peter Lougheed Provincial Park Visitor Information Centre
Located 3.6 km from Kananaskis Trail (Hwy 40)
☎(403) 591-6344

Barrier Lake Information Centre
☎(403) 673-3985

Elbow Valley Information Centre
☎(403) 949-4261

Internet

Tour A: Banff

Surprisingly, at the beginning 1999, there was only one Internet café. **Cyber Web Café** *($8/hr, every day 10am to midnight; 215 Banff Ave., basement of Sundance Mall, ☎762-9226).*

Tour B: Jasper

The two places in Jasper where you can connect to the Internet are across from each other. **Soft Rock Internet Cafe** *(622 Connaught, ☎852-5850)* also offers light snacks. **More Than Mail** *(624 Connaught ☎852-3151)* is a store that also offers fax, telephone and postal services.

Exploring and Parks

Tour A: Banff National Park

The history of the **Canadian Pacific** railway is inextricably linked to that of the national parks of the Rocky Mountains. In November of 1883, three workmen abandoned the railway construction site in the Bow Valley and headed towards Banff in search of gold. When they reached Sulphur Mountain, however, brothers William and Tom McCardell and Frank McCabe discovered sulphur hot springs instead. They took a concession in order to turn a profit with the springs, but were unable to counter the various land rights disputes that followed. The series of events drew the attention of the federal government, which sent out an agent to control the concession. The renown of these hot springs had already spread from railway workers to the vice-president of Canadian Pacific, who came here in 1885 and declared that the springs were certainly worth a million dollars. Realizing the enormous economic potential of the Sulphur Mountain hot springs, which were already known as **Cave and Basin**, the federal government quickly purchased the rights to the concession from the three workers and consolidated its property rights on the site by creating a nature reserve the same year.

Two years later, in 1887, the reserve became the first national park in Canada and was named Rockies Park, and then Banff National Park. In those days there was no need to protect the still abundant wildlife, and the mindset of government was not yet preoccupied with the preservation of natural areas. On the contrary, the government's main concern was to find an economically exploitable site with which to replenish the state coffers, in need of a boost after the construction of the railroad. To complement the springs which were already in vogue with wealthy

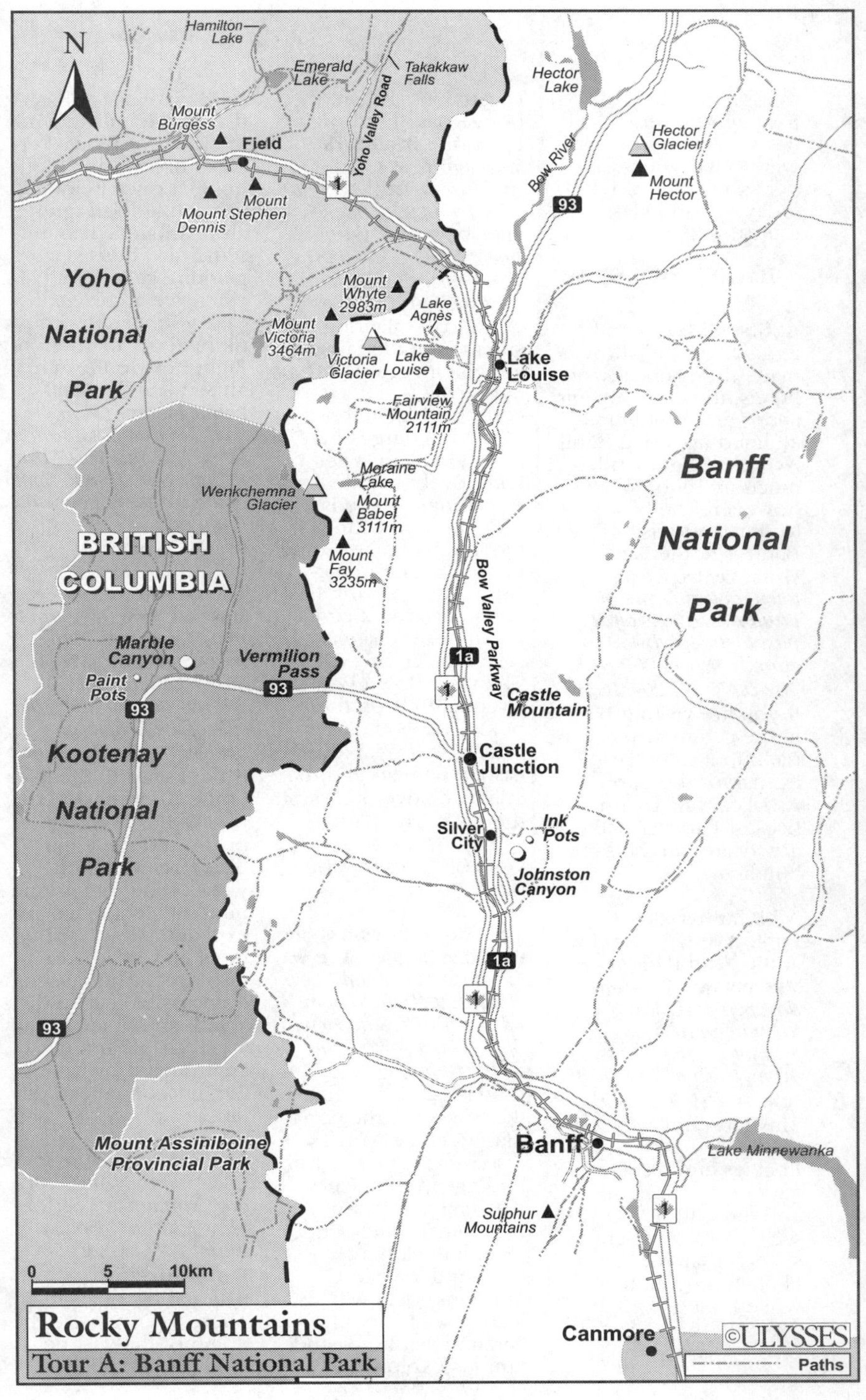
N
Hamilton Lake
Emerald Lake
Takakkaw Falls
Yoho Valley Road
Mount Burgess
Field
1
Mount Dennis
Mount Stephen
Hector Lake
Bow River
Hector Glacier
Mount Hector
93
Yoho National Park
Mount Whyte 2983m
Lake Agnes
Mount Victoria 3464m
Victoria Glacier
Lake Louise
Lake Louise
Fairview Mountain 2111m
Moraine Lake
Wenkchemna Glacier
Mount Babel 3111m
Mount Fay 3235m
Banff National Park
BRITISH COLUMBIA
Bow Valley Parkway
Marble Canyon
Paint Pots
Vermilion Pass
93
1a
Castle Mountain
Kootenay National Park
Castle Junction
Silver City
Ink Pots
Johnston Canyon
1a
1
93
Mount Assiniboine Provincial Park
Banff
Lake Minnewanka
Sulphur Mountains
0 5 10km
Rocky Mountains
Tour A: Banff National Park
Canmore
©ULYSSES
Paths

tourists in search of spa treatments, tourist facilities and luxury hotels were built. Thus was born the town of Banff, today a world-class tourist mecca.

Banff Town Site

At first glance, Banff looks like a small town made up essentially of hotels, motels, souvenir shops and restaurants all lined up along Banff Avenue. The town has much more to offer, however. The best spot to start your visit of Banff is at the **Banff Visitor Centre** *(downtown, at the corner of Banff Ave. and Wolf St., next to the Presbyterian church, ☎ 403-762-8421, 762-0270, ⇄ 726-8163).* If you are visiting Banff in the summer, you can pick up a calendar of events for the Banff Arts Festival. The offices of Parks Canada are located in the same building.

A bit farther along Banff Avenue, stop in at the **Natural History Museum** ★ *($3; every day; Sep and May 10am to 8pm; Jul and Aug 10am to 10pm; Oct to Apr 10am to 6pm; 112 Banff Ave., ☎ 403-762-1558).* This museum retraces the history of the Rockies and displays various rocks, fossils and dinosaur tracks, as well as several plant species that you're likely to encounter while hiking.

Located just before the bridge over the Bow River, the **Banff Park Museum** ★★ *($2.25; mid-Jun to Aug, every day 10am to 6pm; winter, 1pm to 5pm; 92 Banff Ave., ☎ 403-762-1558)* is the oldest natural-history museum in Western Canada. During the summer, guided tours are given regularly at 3pm (call ahead to confirm). The interior of the building is in pure Victorian style, with lovely wooden mouldings. There is a collection of stuffed, mounted animals, some of which date from 1860. The museum has been declared a national historic site.

The view down Banff Avenue ends on the other side of the bridge, at the famous **Cascade Gardens** and the administrative offices of the park. The park itself offers a wonderful view of Cascade Mountain.

The **Whyte Museum of the Canadian Rockies** ★★★ *($4; mid-May to Mid-Oct, every day 10am to 6pm; winter, Tue to Sun 1pm to 5pm, Thu 1pm to 9pm; 111 Bear St., ☎ 403-762-2291)* relates the history of the Canadian Rockies. You'll discover archaeological findings from ancient Kootenay and Stoney Aboriginal settlements, including clothing, tools and jewellery. Museum-goers will also learn the history of certain local heros and famous explorers like Bill Peyto, as well as that of the railway and the town of Banff. Personal objects and clothing that once belonged to notable local figures are exhibited. The museum also houses a painting gallery and extensive archives, in case you want to know more about the region. Right next to the Whyte Museum is the **Banff Public Library** *(Mon, Wed, Fri and Sat 11am to 6pm, Tue and Thu 11am to 9pm, Sun 1pm to 5pm; at the corner of Bear and Buffalo Sts., ☎ 403-762-2661).*

The **Luxton Museum** ★★ *($6; Jun to mid-Oct 9am to 7pm, mid-Oct to Dec, Wed to Sun 10am to 3pm; 1 Birch Ave., on the other side of the Bow River Bridge, ☎ 403-762-2388)* is dedicated to the lives of the Aboriginal peoples of the northern plains and the Canadian Rockies. Their ways of life, rituals and hunting techniques are explained, and various tools they used are displayed. The museum is accessible to the disabled, and guided tours are available but must be arranged by calling the museum ahead of time.

Cave and Basin ★★★ *($2.25; Jun to Aug, every day 9am to 6pm; Sep to May 9:30am to 5pm; at the end of Cave Ave., ☎ 403-762-1556)* is a national historic site. These springs were the origin of the vast network of Canadian

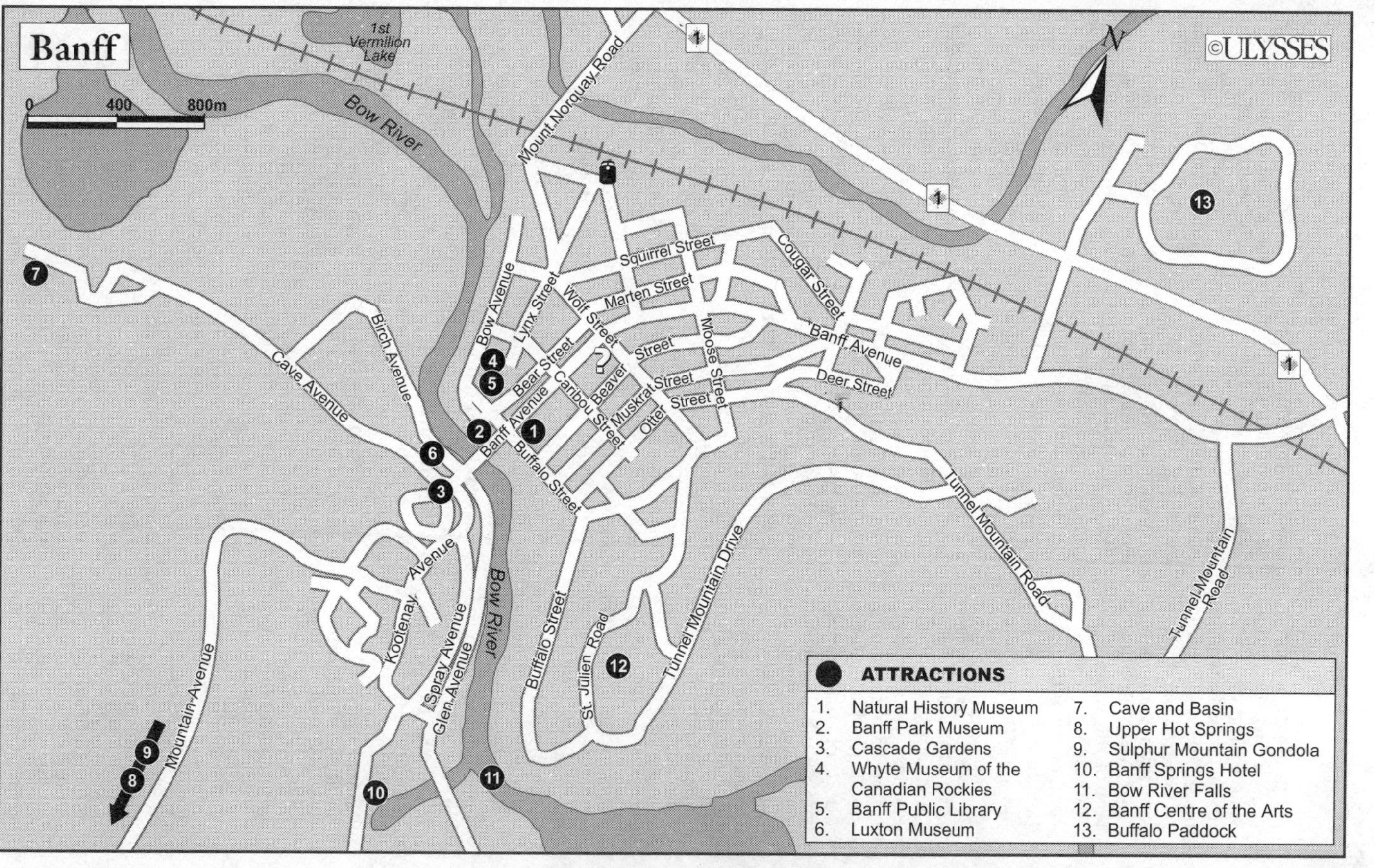

Banff
©ULYSSES
0
400
800m
N
1st Vermilion Lake
Bow River
Mount Norquay Road
Squirrel Street
Marten Street
Cougar Street
Wolf Street
Lynx Street
Bow Avenue
Bear Street
Caribou Street
Beaver Street
Muskrat Street
Otter Street
Moose Street
Banff Avenue
Deer Street
Buffalo Street
Birch Avenue
Cave Avenue
Kootenay Avenue
Spray Avenue
Glen Avenue
Mountain Avenue
St. Julien Road
Tunnel Mountain Drive
Tunnel Mountain Road
ATTRACTIONS
1. Natural History Museum
2. Banff Park Museum
3. Cascade Gardens
4. Whyte Museum of the Canadian Rockies
5. Banff Public Library
6. Luxton Museum
7. Cave and Basin
8. Upper Hot Springs
9. Sulphur Mountain Gondola
10. Banff Springs Hotel
11. Bow River Falls
12. Banff Centre of the Arts
13. Buffalo Paddock

national parks (see p 296). However, despite extremely costly renovations to the basins in 1984, the pool has been closed for security reasons since 1992. The sulphur content of the water actually deteriorates the cement, and the pool's paving is badly damaged in some places.

You can still visit the cave into which three Canadian Pacific workers descended in search of the springs, and smell the distinctive odour of sulphurous gas, caused by bacteria that oxydize the sulphates in the water before it spurts out of the earth. The original basin is still there, but swimming is no longer permitted.

If you watch the water, you'll see the sulphur gas bubbling to the surface, while at the bottom of the basin you can see depressions appearing in the sand caused by this same gas (this is most obvious in the centre of the basin). In the theatre you can take in a short film on Banff National Park and the history of the hot springs and their purchase by the government for only $900.

You'll learn that the McCardell brothers and Frank McCabe were not actually the first to discover the springs, – Assiniboine Aboriginal people were already familiar with their therapeutic powers. European explorers had also already spoken of them. However, the three Canadian Pacific workers, knowing a good thing when they saw it, were the first to try to gain exclusive rights over the springs and the government simply followed suit.

If you want to experience the sensation of Sulphur Mountain's waters (how rapturous it is to soak in them after a long day of hiking!), head up Mountain Avenue, at the foot of the mountain, to the hot spring facilities of **Upper Hot Spring ★★★** *($7 for access to the pool; $32 for the whirlpool thermal baths and basins; bathing suit and towel rentals available; every day 10am to 10pm, call ahead to verify schedule and fees; up from Mountain Ave., ☎ 403-762-1515)*. The establishment includes a hot-water bath (40°C) for soaking and a warm pool (27°C) for swimming. If you have at least an hour and are at least 17 years old, then by all means try out the thermal baths. This is a Turkish bath which consists of immersion in hot water followed by aromatherapy treatment. You then lay out on a bed and are ensconced in sheets and blankets. The soothing effect is truly divine.

Aboriginal people and early visitors alike believed in the curative powers of sulphurous waters, which were thought to improve one's health and even to cure skin problems. Though the water's curative powers are contested these days, there is no denying their calming effect on body and soul.

If you don't have the energy to hike up to the top of the mountain, you can take the **Sulphur Mountain Gondola** *($14; open until sundown; at the end of Mountain Ave., at the far end edge of the Upper Hot Springs parking lot, ☎ 403-762-2523)*. The panoramic view of Banff, Mount Rundle, the Bow Valley, the Aylmer and the Cascade Mountains is superb. The gondola starts out at an altitude of 1,583m and climbs to 2,281m. Be sure to bring along warm clothes, as it can be cold at the summit.

The **Banff Springs Hotel ★★★** is also worth a look. After visiting the springs at Cave and Basin, William Cornelius Van Horne, vice-president of the Canadian Pacific railway company, decided to have a sumptuous hotel built to accommodate the tourists who would soon be flocking to the hot springs. Construction began in 1887, and the hotel opened its doors in June 1888. Although the cost of the project had already reached $250,000, the railway company launched a

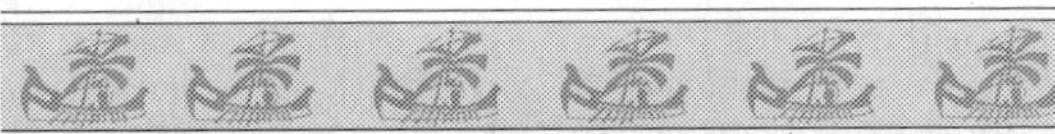

Why is the Water Hot?

By penetrating into fissures in the rock, water makes its way under the western slope of Sulphur Mountain, absorbing calcium, sulphur and other minerals along the way.

At a certain depth, the heat of the earth's centre warms the water as it is being forced up by pressure through a fault in the northeastern slope of the mountain.
As the water flows up to the surface, the calcium settles around the source in pale-coloured layers that eventually harden into rock, called "tufa".

These formations can be seen on the mountainside, at the small exterior spring 20m from the entrance to the facilities.

promotional campaign to attract wealthy visitors from all over the world. By the beginning of the century, Banff had become so well known that the Banff Springs Hotel was one of the busiest hotels in North America. More space was needed, so a new wing was built in 1903. It was separated from the original building by a small wooden bridge in case of fire. A year later a tower was built at the end of each wing. Even though this immense hotel welcomed 22,000 guests in 1911, the facilities again proved too small for the forever increasing demand. Construction was thus begun on a central tower.

The building was finally completed as it stands today in 1928. The Tudor style interior layout, as well as the tapestries, paintings and furniture in the common rooms, are all original. If you decide to stay at the Banff Springs Hotel (see p 336) you may run into the ghost of Sam McAuley, the bellboy who helps guests who have lost their keys, or that of the unlucky young bride who died the day of her wedding when she fell down the stairs and who supposedly haunts the corridors of the hotel. Heading downhill from the Banff Springs Hotel, you can stop a while at a pretty lookout point over **Bow River Falls**.

The **Banff Centre of the Arts** *(between St. Julien Rd. and Tunnel Mountain Dr., ☎403-762-6300 or 762-6281)* was created in 1933. More commonly known as the Banff Centre since 1978, this renowned cultural centre hosts the **Banff Festival of the Arts** in the month of August. The festival attracts numerous artists and involves presentations of dance, opera, jazz and theatre. The centre also offers courses in classical and jazz ballet, theatre, music, photography and pottery. Finally, each year the centre organizes an international mountain film festival.

There is a sports centre inside the complex as well.

Around Banff

The **Buffalo Paddock ★★** *(free admission; May to Oct; head towards Lake Minnewanka, then take the Trans-Canada towards Lake Louise; the entrance lies 1km farther, on the right)* provides an interesting opportunity, if you're lucky, to admire these majestic creatures up close. It is important, however, to stay in your car, even if you want to take photographs, as these animals can be very unpredictable and the slightest provocation may cause them to charge.

This paddock was originally built by a group of wealthy Banff residents, who were planning to make it into a zoo. Since the whole idea of a zoo is not in keeping with the spirit of national parks, the plains bison were sent off by train to be liberated in Wood Buffalo National Park, in northern Alberta and the southwest part of the Northwest Territories. They were replaced by wood buffalo who had migrated into the area and had to be protected from diseases that were killing off their species.

The **Banff Mount Norquay Ski Hill** was the first one created in Banff National Park. This 2,522m mountain was named in honour of John Norquay, the premier of Manitoba. In the winter, a cable-car carries passengers to the summit to admire the magnificent scenery of the Bow River Valley, as well as of the town of Banff.

By following the Lake Minnewanka road, you'll soon come upon the vestiges of the former mining town of **Bankhead ★**. The disappearance of this small town is linked to the creation of Banff National Park. In fact, Bankhead, a product of the coal-mining activity in the area, had to be completely dismantled because all forms of mining and forestry development are prohibited in national parks. Today a trail leads around the few remaining foundations and slag heaps, visible in the distance. Back on the road, 200m higher up on the right, are the remains of the church steps. The pleasant **Upper Bankhead** site, a bit farther along on the left, has been equipped with picnic tables and small firepits.

Twenty-two kilometres long and 2km wide, **Lake Minnewanka ★★** is now the biggest lake in Banff National Park, but this expanse of water is not completely natural. Its name means "lake of the water spirit." These days it is one of the few lakes in the park where motor boats are permitted. Originally, the area was occupied by Stoney Indian encampments. Because of the difficulties involved with diving in alpine waters and the scattering of vestiges that can be seen here, this lake is popular with scuba-divers. Guided walks are given Tuesdays, Thursdays and Saturdays at 2pm. Besides taking a guided boat-tour with **Cruise and Tour Devil's Gap** *($26; Lake Minnewanka Boat Tours, Box 2189, Dept B, Banff, ☎ 403-762-3473, ⇄ 762-2800)*, you can fish on the lake if you first obtain the appropriate permit from Parks Canada, and skating is possible in the winter. A 16-km hiking trail leads to the far end of the lake. At the **Aylmer Lookout Viewpoint** you will probably spot some of the mountain goats that frequent the area.

★★ Bow Valley Parkway

To get from Banff to Lake Louise, take the Bow Valley Parkway (Hwy.1A), which is a much more picturesque route than the Trans-Canada. About 140 million years ago, mountains emerged from an ancient sea as a result of pressure from the earth's strata. Flowing from the mountains, the Bow

River was born, littering the plains to the east with sediment. Forty million years later, the foothills rose from the plains and threatened to prevent the river from following its course. However, even when rocks got in its path, the river managed to continue its route, sweeping away the rocky debris. This continual erosion resulted in the formation of a steep-sided, V-shaped valley.

At the beginning of the ice age, about a million years ago, the riverbed of the Bow was taken over by moving ice. The glacier transformed the steep sides of the valley, which took on the shape of a *U*. As the last glacier receded, it left behind the debris it had been carrying, and the meltwater formed a torrential river which tumbled down the valley. Meltwater no longer feeds the Bow, which can barely make it through the debris left behind by the glaciers. Weaving its way along the mountains, the Bow Valley Parkway affords some exquisite views of the Bow River. It is important to heed the warning and drive slowly as animals often approach the road at sunrise and sunset.

A stop at beautiful **Johnston Canyon ★★★**, located on the right-hand side about 20km beyond Banff, is a must. A small dirt trail has been cleared through the canyon, where you can behold the devastating effect even a small torrent of water can have on all kinds of rock. The first waterfall, called the Upper Falls, is only 1.1km along the trail, and the path there is easy, though a bit slippery in spots. The second, called the Lower Falls lies another 1.6km farther. This canyon is a veritable bird sanctuary, you might spot some dippers, who live in the canyon year-round and like to dive into the icy waters in search of insect larvae.

Black swifts build their nests in the shady hollows of the canyon. They arrive in mid-June and stay until the beginning of fall, long enough to raise their young before heading back south to the warmth of the tropics. Beyond both these falls, you can see what are called the "shimmering walls." A sign explains the phenomenon, which results from the combination of several varieties of algae saturated with minerals. When the sun hits the wall the effect is spectacular. The second waterfalls are the highest in the canyon. The trail continues for another three kilometres to the **Ink Pots**, formed by seven cold springs, in different shades of blue and green. The Ink Pots trail is 5.8km long.

The abandoned town of **Silver City** lies farther up the Bow Valley Parkway, on the left. Silver, copper and lead were discovered in the area in 1883. Prospectors arrived two years later, but the mineral deposits were quickly exhausted and ultimately the town was abandoned. In its glory days, this little city had some 175 buildings and several hotels, but just vestiges of these remain.

★★★ Lake Louise

Jewel of the Canadian Rockies, Lake Louise is known the world over thanks to its small, still, emerald-green lake. Few natural sites in Canada can boast as much success: this little place welcomes and average of about six million visitors a year!

The public's fancy with this spot is nothing new, and visitors today owe its rediscovery (not discovery, since this area was already well known to Aboriginal people) to Tom Wilson, a railway surveyor for Canadian Pacific. In 1882, while working near the Pipestone River, Tom Wilson heard the rumbling of an avalanche coming from the Victoria Glacier. He proceeded to ask a Stoney Aboriginal man named Nimrod to lead him to the "Lake of the Little Fishes", which is what the local Aboriginal people called the lake. Struck by the colour of the water, Tom Wilson renamed the lake "Emerald Lake." Well aware of how beautiful the site was, the railway company erected a first building on the shores of the lake and at the foot of the glacier in 1890. This construction was completely destroyed by fire and rebuilt in 1909; it could accommodate about 500 people. At the time, rooms at the Chateau Lake Louise were rented for $4. To transport the numerous visitors already eager to view the scenery, construction of a railway line was undertaken. Up until 1926, when a road was finished, all of the tourists arrived by train at the Laggan station, located 6km from the lake. From there, guests of the Chateau Lake Louise were brought to the hotel in a horse-drawn trolley.

Today, you can reach the lake by car, but finding a place to park here can be a real challenge. Stroll quietly around the lake or climb the mountain along the network of little trails radiating out from the lake's shore for a magnificent view of the Victoria Glacier, the lake and the glacial valley. Reaching **Lake Agnes** requires extra effort, but the **view ★★★** of **Victoria** (3,464m), **White** (2,983m), **Fairview** (2,111m), **Babel** (3,111m) and **Fay** (3,235m) **Mountains** is well worth the exertion.

If you aren't up to such a climb, you can always take the **Lake Louise Gondola**, which is open from 9am to 9pm and transports you to an altitude of 2,089m in just 10 minutes.

Though the present-day **Chateau Lake Louise ★★** has nothing to do with the original construction, it remains an attraction in itself. This vast Canadian Pacific Hotel can accommodate 700 visitors. Besides restaurants, the hotel houses a small shopping arcade with boutiques selling all kinds of souvenirs.

In the centre of the village of Lake Louise, the Samson Mall houses the **tourist information office** *(☎ 403-522-3833)* and the offices of Parks Canada. Souvenir shops, photo shops, bookstores and a few cafés and restaurants, all busy with visitors, are located next door. Be careful, as prices tend to be a bit high; you are better off bringing along lots of film so that you won't have to stock up here.

★★★ Moraine Lake

When heading to Lake Louise, you will come to a turnoff for Moraine Lake on the left. This narrow, winding road weaves its way along the mountain for about 10km before reaching Moraine Lake, which was immortalized on the old Canadian $20 bill. Though much smaller than Lake Louise, Moraine Lake is no less spectacular. Inaccessible in the winter, the lake often remains frozen until the month of June. Don't arrive unprepared for the cool temperatures, even in the summer. Bring a sweater and a wind-breaker if you plan to stroll along the shores. The valley of Moraine Lake, known as the "valley of the 10 peaks", was created by the **Wenkchemna Glacier**, which is still melting. The 10 summits were originally known by the Assiniboine words for the numbers one to 10, but many have since been renamed, and only the appellation Wenkchemna remains. The Moraine Lake Lodge, on the shore of the lake, has a restaurant and a small café (see p 351) where you can warm up.

★ Canmore

Canmore is a paradise for lovers of the great outdoors. It has the greatest concentration of Canadian mountaineers who have participated in expeditions to the Himalayas. Canmore has a unique training ground and it

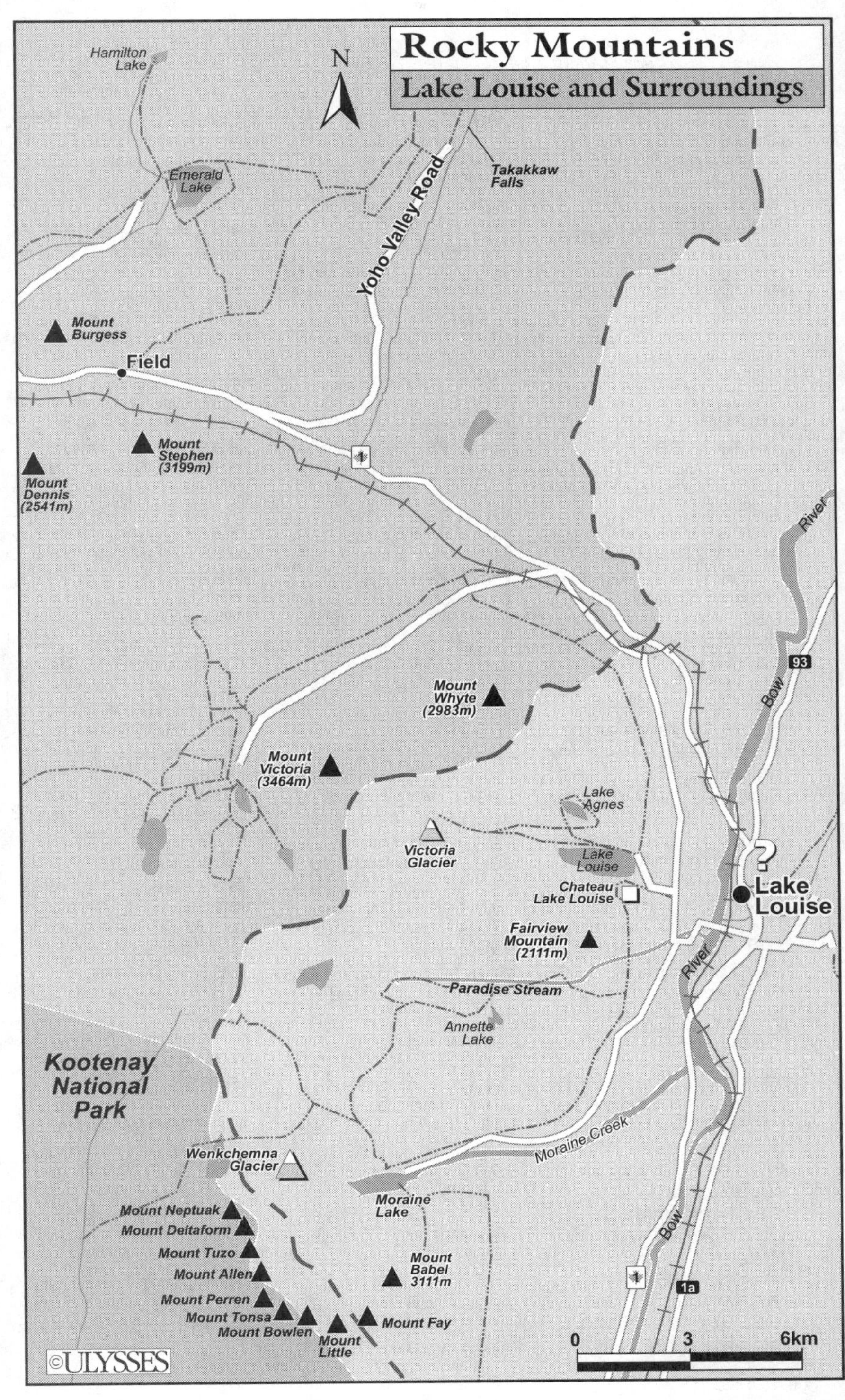

Rocky Mountains
Lake Louise and Surroundings
N
Hamilton Lake
Emerald Lake
Yoho Valley Road
Takakkaw Falls
Mount Burgess
Field
Mount Stephen (3199m)
Mount Dennis (2541m)
River
Bow
93
Mount Whyte (2983m)
Mount Victoria (3464m)
Lake Agnes
Victoria Glacier
Lake Louise
Chateau Lake Louise
Lake Louise
Fairview Mountain (2111m)
Paradise Stream
Annette Lake
River
Kootenay National Park
Moraine Creek
Wenkchemna Glacier
Moraine Lake
Mount Neptuak
Mount Deltaform
Mount Tuzo
Mount Allen
Mount Perren
Mount Tonsa
Mount Bowlen
Mount Little
Mount Fay
Mount Babel 3111m
Bow
1a
0
3
6km
©ULYSSES

is also the place for fly-fishing enthusiasts. An idyllic spot for mountain biking, Canmore hosts the mountain-biking World Cup every year. Due to its enchanting location and its recreational activities, it's one of the most rapidly developing towns in the country.

The name Canmore comes from the Gaelic *Ceann mor*, which means "big head." The name was given as a nickname to the Scottish king Malcolm III, son of Duncan I, who became king in 1054 and established his place in history by killing the usurper Macbeth.

After searching for the most practical route for the railway to the west, Canadian Pacific chose to go through the Bow Valley. It was decided that the supply station for the project would be placed at the entrance to the Rockies, and thus was born the town of Canmore. Mineral deposits found here later were mined until July 13th, 1979.

This quiet little town of about 6,000 experienced its finest hour during the 1988 Winter Olympics. The cross-country, nordic combined and biathlon events were held here, along with the disabled cross-country skiing demonstration event. Since the games, the facilities at the **Canmore Nordic Centre** *(every day; from the centre of town head up Main St., turn right on 8th Ave. and right to cross the Bow River. Turn left and head up Rundle Dr., then turn left again on Sister Dr. Take Spray Lake Rd. to the right and continue straight. The parking lot of the centre is located farther up on the right,* ☎ *403-678-2400)* have been used for other international events like the World Cup of Skiing in 1995. In summer the cross-country trails become walking and mountain biking trails. Dogs are permitted between April 11th and October 30th if they are on a leash. Bears are common in the region in the summer, so be extra careful.

By continuing beyond the Canmore Nordic Centre, you'll come upon two small lakes called **Grassi Lakes**. To reach them, head up Three Sisters Drive and turn right on Spray Lakes Road. Turn left at the turn-off near the artificial lake called the Reservoir, then left again on the first small dirt road. The starting point for a hiking trail begins a bit farther along. The lakes are named after Lawrence Grassi, an Italian immigrant who worked for the Canadian Pacific railway company and cleared the trail to the lakes. A short walk climbs quickly up to Grassi Falls and then on to the crystal-clear lakes. A great view of Canmore and the Bow Valley can be had from this spot. Good walking shoes are necessary. The Canmore area is also well known for its dog-sled races.

Marvellously well situated at the entrance to Banff National Park and at the gateway to Kananaskis Country, Canmore welcomes many visitors each year, but it is often easier to find accommodations here than in Banff. Nevertheless, it is a good idea to reserve your room well in advance.

The main attraction of this small town, besides the Canmore Nordic Centre, is its exceptional location and the many outdoor activities possible here. Besides skiing, dog-sled races, ice-climbing, heli-skiing, snowmobile trips and ice fishing in the winter, summer activities include parasailing, hang-gliding, hiking, mountain biking, rock-climbing, canoeing, and the list goes on... All sorts of useful addresses can be found in the Outdoor Activities section of this chapter (see p 320).

The **Canmore Centennial Museum** *(free admission; every day, noon to 4pm; Jul and Aug, Mon to Fri 9am to 5pm; 801 7th Ave.,* ☎ *403-678-2462)* is a tiny little museum that retraces the town's mining history. It also has a section on the 1988 Winter Olympics.

The **Canmore Recreation Centre** *(every day 6am to 10pm; 1900 8th Ave., ☎ 403-678-5597, ⇄ 678-6661)* organizes all sorts of summer activities for children. The facilities include a municipal pool, a sports centre and an exercise centre.

Tour B: The Icefields Parkway

The route through the icefields follows Hwy. 93 from Lake Louise for 230km to the Continental Divide, which is covered by glaciers, before ending up in Jasper. This wide, well-paved road is one of the busiest in the Rockies during the summer, with a speed limit of 90km per hour. It runs through some incredibly majestic scenery.

The **Hector Lake ★★** lookout on the left, 17km from Lake Louise, offers a great view of both the lake and Mount Hector. The lake is fed by meltwater from the Balfour Glacier and the Waputik Icefields.

One kilometre before **Mosquito Creek**, you can clearly see the Crowfoot Glacier from the road. Photographs reproduced on information panels by the road show just how much the glacier has melted in recent years. A bit farther along you can stop to take in the magnificent view of Bow Lake, and then visit little **Num-Ti-Jah Lodge** ("Num-Ti-Jah" is an aboriginal name that means "pine marten"), built in 1922 by a mountain guide named Jimmy Simpson. At the time, there was no road leading this far, and all the building materials had to be hauled in on horseback. One of Simpson's descendants has since converted the place into a hotel and cleared a road for guests. Since all the tour buses stop here, the administration of the Num-Ti-Jah Lodge (see p 341) has decided in an effort to protect the privacy of its clientele, that only people with reservations for the night should be permitted to enter the building. It is therefore preferable to limit your tour to the outside of the chalet; otherwise you may receive a rather gruff welcome.

Bow Summit ★★ (2,609m) lies at the highest point of the Icefields Parkway and on the continental divide for the waters of the Bow and Mistayac rivers. At this point the vegetation changes drastically, giving way almost completely to subalpine plant-life. By the side of the road, there is a rest area that overlooks **Peyto Lake** (pronounced Pee-Toh). You can take a hike through an area of alpine vegetation, and if the weather is right, you can admire a lovely little lake. Western anemones *(Anemone Occidentalis)* line the trail, as do various types of heather and very pretty Indian paintbrush. Bring a good sweater and a jacket for this walk to protect yourself from the wind and the cool temperatures at this altitude. Originally from the region of Kent in England, Bill Peyto is one of the most well-known local characters.

During your trip through Banff National Park, you will certainly encounter his image, complete with cocked hat, pipe and piercing gaze. Peyto arrived in Canada at the age of 18, and settled in the Rockies where he became one of the most celebrated trappers, prospectors and mountain guides. He enjoyed stopping off at Bow Summit to admire the little lake down below, which was named in his memory. Curiously, the colour of this lake varies considerably depending on the season. With the first signs of spring it brightens to a marvellous metallic blue, which becomes paler and pale as more and more sediment mixes with the water.

At the intersection of Hwys. 93 and 11, called **The Crossing**, you'll find a few souvenir shops, a hotel and some restaurants. Make sure your gas tank is full since there are no other gas stations before Jasper. This region was once inhabited by the Kootenay Aboriginal people forced to the western slopes by Aboriginal people armed with guns, thanks to white merchants from the southeastern Rockies. Fearing that the Kootenay would eventually arm themselves, the Peigans blocked the way of white explorers who were attempting to cross the pass, and thus kept their enemies completely isolated.

About 30km farther along, at the **Weeping Wall** lookout, you can see several waterfalls cascading over the cliffs of **Mount Cirrus** as the ice melts. In the winter, the falls freeze, forming a spectacular wall of ice, to the delight of ice-climbers.

The **Castleguard Cave** is located 117km from Jasper. A network of underwater caves, the longest in Canada, extends over 20km under the Columbia Icefield. Because of frequent flooding and the inherent dangers of spelunking, you must have authorization from Parks Canada to enter the caves.

The **Parker Ridge ★★** trail, just 3km farther, makes for a wonderful outing. About 2.5km long, it leads up to the ridge, where, if you're lucky, you may spot some mountain goats. It also offers a great view of the Saskatchewan Glacier. Both the vegetation and the temperature change as you pass from the subalpine to the alpine zone. Warm clothing and a pair of gloves are a good idea.

At the **Sunwapta Pass** you can admire the grandiose scenery which marks the dividing line between Banff and Jasper National Parks. At 2,035m, this is the highest pass along the Icefields Parkway, after Bow Summit.

The **Athabasca Glacier ★★★** and the **Columbia Icefield** are the focal points of the icefields tour. At the Athabasca Glacier, information panels show the impressive retreat of the glacier over the years. Those who wish to explore the ice on foot should beware of crevasses, which can be up to 40m deep. There are 30,000 on the Athabasca Glacier, some hidden under thin layes of snow or ice. Those without sufficient experience climbing on glaciers or lacking the proper equipment are better off with a ticket aboard the **Snowcoach Tour** *($30; May to mid-Oct, every day; tickets sold at the Brewster counter, near the tourist information centre, ☎ 403-852-3332).* These specially equipped buses take people out onto the glacier. Once there, passengers can get off the bus to explore specific areas, that are considered safe by the staff of **Brewster Transportation**. The Brewster Transportation company was created in 1900 by two Banff businessmen, brothers Jim and Bill Brewster. The company has continuously contributed to the expansion of tourism in the Banff National Park area, even building a few hotels. Today the prosperous enterprise offers millions of travellers the opportunity to get around the national parks and more importantly, to explore the magnificent Athabasca Glacier up close.

The **Stutfield Glacier ★★** lookout provides a view of one of the six huge glaciers fed by the Columbia Icefield, which continues one kilometre into the valley.

About 3km farther, on the west side, are several avalanche corridors, some of which come right up to the road. Generally, however, park rangers trigger avalanches before the thick layers of snow become dangerous.

Fifty-five kilometres before Jasper, the **Sunwapta Falls ★★★** and canyon provide a good example of how water can work away at limestone. The countryside offers some typical examples of suspended

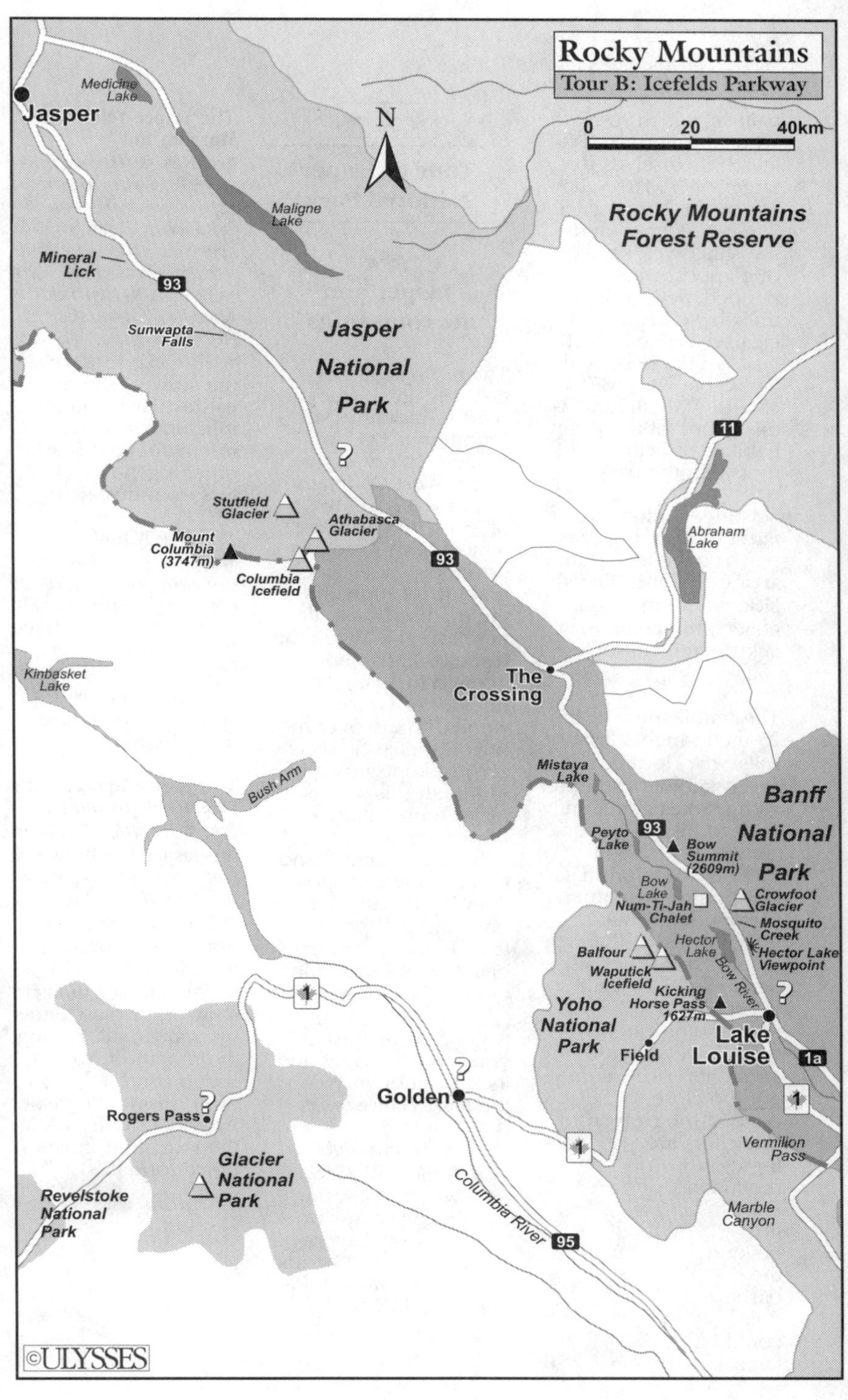

Rocky Mountains
Tour B: Icefelds Parkway
0
20
40km
N
Medicine Lake
Jasper
Maligne Lake
Rocky Mountains Forest Reserve
Mineral Lick
93
Sunwapta Falls
Jasper National Park
11
Stutfield Glacier
Athabasca Glacier
Mount Columbia (3747m)
Columbia Icefield
Abraham Lake
Kinbasket Lake
The Crossing
Bush Arm
Mistaya Lake
Banff National Park
Peyto Lake
Bow Summit (2609m)
Bow Lake
Num-Ti-Jah Chalet
Crowfoot Glacier
Mosquito Creek
Hector Lake
Hector Lake Viewpoint
Balfour
Waputick Icefield
Bow River
Kicking Horse Pass 1627m
Yoho National Park
Lake Louise
Field
1a
1
Golden
Rogers Pass
Vermilion Pass
Glacier National Park
Revelstoke National Park
Columbia River
Marble Canyon
95

valleys, which result when smaller glaciers attach themselves to larger ones. The valley left by the larger glacier is much deeper, and the shallower, smaller one appears suspended. Several hiking trails have been cleared, one of which leads to the base of the Sunwapta Falls. Be careful while hiking as this is one of the prime habitats of bears and moose in the park.

Seventeen kilometres farther, heading to Jasper, you'll come to an area called the **Mineral Lick**, where mountain goats often come to lick the mineral-rich soil.

The trail leading to the 25-metre-high **Athabasca Falls ★★**, located seven kilometres farther along, takes about an hour to hike. The concrete structure built there is an unfortunate addition to the natural surroundings, but heavy traffic in the area would have otherwise destroyed the fragile vegetation. Furthermore, some careless types have suffered accidents because they got too close to the edge of the canyon. Travellers are therefore reminded not to go beyond the barriers; doing so could be fatal.

Tour C: Jasper National Park

★★ Jasper and Surroundings

The town of Jasper takes its name from an old fur-trading post, founded in 1811 by William Henry of the North West Company. Jasper is a small town of just 4,000 residents which owes its tourist development to its geographic location and the train station built here in 1911. When the Icefields Parkway was opened in 1940, the number of visitors who wanted to discover the region's majestic scenery just kept growing. Although this area is a major tourist draw, Jasper remains a decidedly more tranquil and less commercial spot than Banff. This doesn't prevent hotel prices from being just as exorbitant as elsewhere in the Rockies, however.

A good place to start your visit of Jasper and its surroundings is at the **tourist office** *(every day 8am to 7pm; 500 Connaught Dr., ☎ 780-852-3858)*, where you can pick up maps of the region. The offices of Parks Canada are in the same building *(☎ 780-852-6176)*.

The **Jasper-Yellowhead Museum and Archives ★** *(free admission; mid-May to early Sep, every day 10am to 9pm; early Sep to mid-Oct, every day 10am to 5pm; winter, Thu to Sun 10am to 5pm; 400 Pyramid Lake Rd., facing the Aquatic Centre, ☎ 780-852-3013)* tells the story of the region's earliest First Nations inhabitants, as well as mountain guides and other legendary characters from this area.

The **Den Wildlife Museum ★** *($5; every day 9am to 10pm; at the corner of Connaught Dr. and Miette St., inside the Whistler Inn, ☎ 780-852-3361)* exhibits a collection of stuffed and mounted animals from the region.

The **Jasper Aquatic Centre** *($5; 401 Pyramid Lake Rd., ☎ 780-852-3663)* and the **Jasper Activity Centre** *(on Pyramid Ave., near the Aquatic Centre, ☎ 780-852-3381)* are both open to visitors who want to go for a swim, take a sauna or shower, or play tennis or racquetball. During the month of August, a rodeo contest is organized inside the Jasper Activity Centre (ask at the tourist information office for dates).

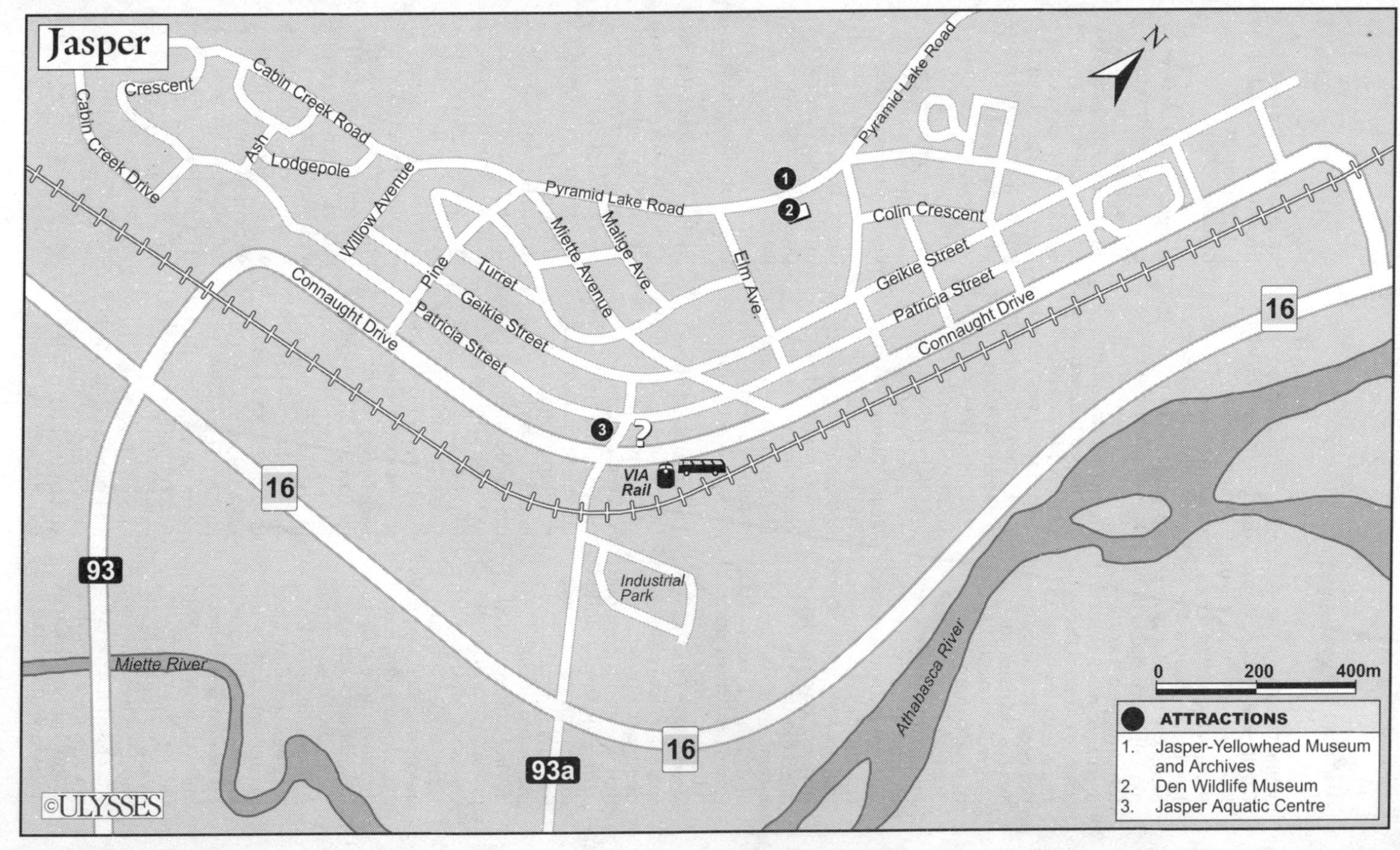
Jasper
N
Crescent
Cabin Creek Road
Cabin Creek Drive
Ash
Lodgepole
Willow Avenue
Pyramid Lake Road
Pyramid Lake Road
1
2
Colin Crescent
Miette Avenue
Malige Ave.
Elm Ave.
Turret
Pine
Geikie Street
Geikie Street
Patricia Street
Patricia Street
Connaught Drive
Connaught Drive
3
?
VIA Rail
16
16
16
93
93a
Industrial Park
Miette River
Athabasca River
0
200
400m
ATTRACTIONS
1. Jasper-Yellowhead Museum and Archives
2. Den Wildlife Museum
3. Jasper Aquatic Centre
©ULYSSES

Mount Edith Cavell ★★★ is 3,363m high. To get there, take the southern exit for Jasper and follow the signs for the Marmot ski hill. Turn right, then left, and you'll come to a narrow road, which leads to one of the most lofty summits in the area. The road snakes through the forest for about 20km before coming to a parking lot. Several hiking trails have been cleared to allow visitors to enjoy a better view of this majestic mountain, as well as its suspended glacier, the **Angel Glacier**. The mountain is named after Edith Louisa Cavell, a British nurse who became known in World War I for her refusal to leave her post near Brussels so that she could continue caring for the wounded in two camps. Arrested for spying by the Germans and accused of having helped Allied prisoners escape, she was shot on October 12th, 1915. To commemorate this woman's exceptional courage, the government of Canada decided to name the most impressive mountain in the Athabasca Valley after the martyred nurse. Previous to this, Mount Edith Cavell had been known by many other names. Native people called it "the white ghost", while travellers who used it as a reference point called it "the mountain of the Great Crossing", then "the Duke", "Mount Fitzhugh" and finally "Mount Geikie." No name had stuck, however, until the government decided to call it Mount Edith Cavell.

In just a few minutes, the **Jasper Tramway** ★★ *($16; mid-Apr to late Oct; take the southern exit for Jasper and follow the signs for Mount Whistler, ☎780-852-3093)* whisks you up some 2,277m and deposits you on the northern face of **Mount Whistler**. You'll find a restaurant and souvenir shop at the arrival point, while a small trail covers the last fewm up to the summit (2,470m). The view is outstanding.

The road to Maligne Lake follows the valley of the river of the same name for 46km. Because of the tight curves of this winding road and the many animals which cross it, the speed limit is 60km per hour. Before reaching the lake, the road passes by one of the most beautiful resorts in Canada, the **Jasper Park Lodge**, run by Canadian Pacific. You can have a picnic, go boating or take a swim in one of the two pretty little lakes, **Agnes** and **Edith**, right next to this facility. Ten thousand years ago, as the glacier was retreating from this valley, two immense blocks of ice broke free and remained in place amidst the moraines and other debris left by the glaciers. As they melted they formed these two small lakes. Lake Agnes has a beach.

Maligne Canyon ★★★ lies at the beginning of Maligne Road. Hiking trails have been cleared so that visitors may admire this spectacular narrow gorge abounding with cascades, fossils and potholes sculpted by the turbulent waters. Several bridges span the canyon. The first offers a view of the falls; the second, of the effect of ice on rock; and the third, of the deepest point (51m) of the gorge.

Dominated by the Maligne and Colin chains, **Medicine Lake** ★ looks like any other lake in the summer, but come October it disappears completely. In the spring, you'll find nothing but a tiny stream flowing slowly along the muddy lake-bottom. The depth of this lake can vary 20m over one year, a phenomenon aboriginal people attributed to a reprimand by a medicine man. It is actually due to the presence of an underwater river which has worked its way through the limestone and reappears in the Maligne River. When the glaciers melt in the summer, the underground network of rivers becomes insufficient to drain the water, which thus rises to the surface and forms a lake. The bottom of

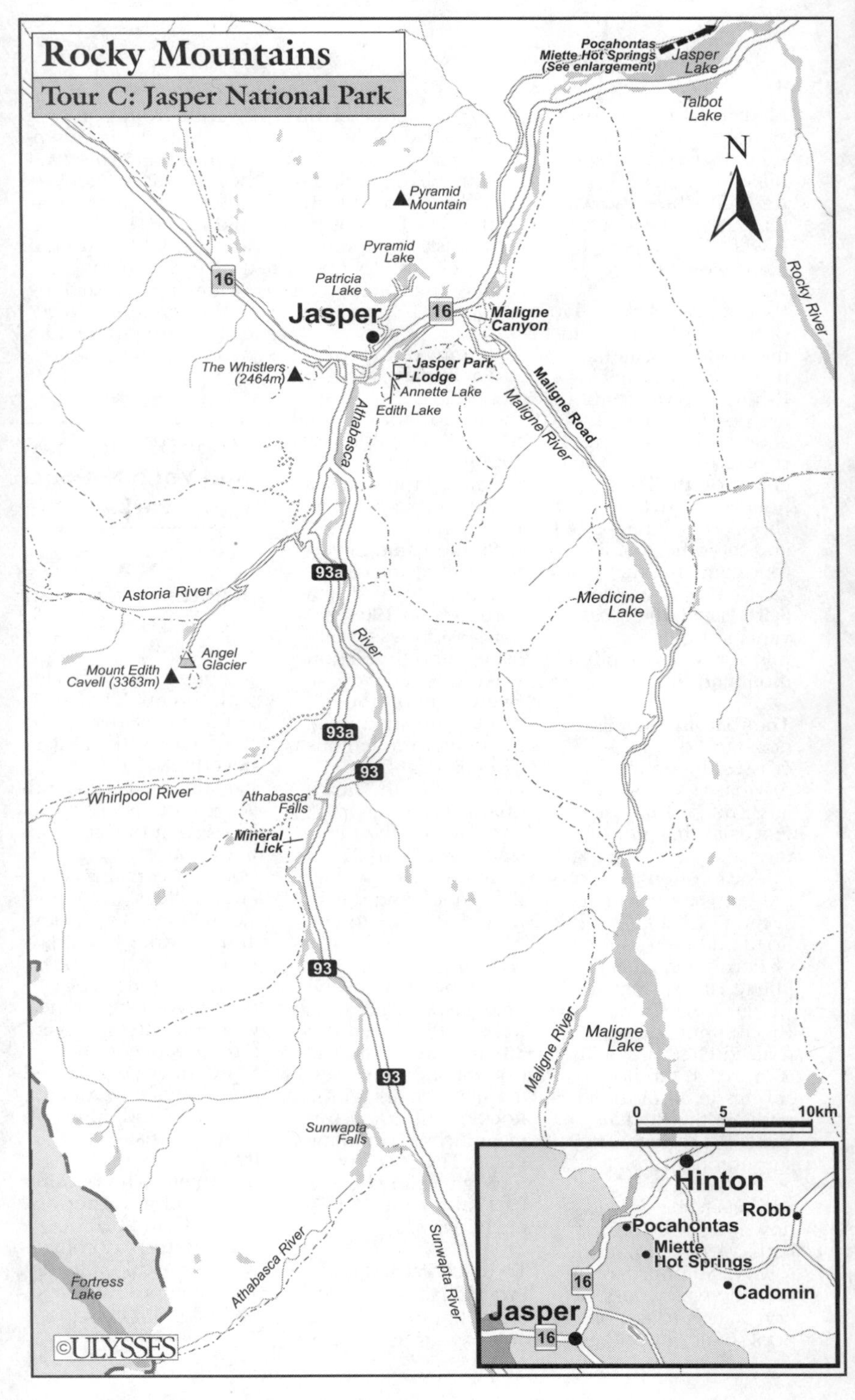

Rocky Mountains
Tour C: Jasper National Park
Pocahontas
Miette Hot Springs
(See enlargement)
Jasper Lake
Talbot Lake
N
Rocky River
Pyramid Mountain
Pyramid Lake
Patricia Lake
16
Jasper
16
Maligne Canyon
The Whistlers (2464m)
Jasper Park Lodge
Annette Lake
Edith Lake
Athabasca
Maligne Road
Maligne River
93a
Astoria River
Medicine Lake
River
Angel Glacier
Mount Edith Cavell (3363m)
93a
93
Whirlpool River
Athabasca Falls
Mineral Lick
93
93
Maligne River
Maligne Lake
0
5
10km
Sunwapta Falls
Hinton
Robb
Pocahontas
Miette Hot Springs
16
Cadomin
Jasper
16
Athabasca River
Sunwapta River
Fortress Lake
©ULYSSES

Medicine Lake consists of dolines (shallow, funnel-shaped holes) filled with gravel, through which the water flows. The short lower trail offers a good view of these.

Maligne Lake ★★ is one of the prettiest lakes in the Rockies. Water activities like boating, fishing and canoeing are possible here, and a short trail runs along part of the shore. The chalet on the shore houses a souvenir shop, a restaurant-café and the offices of a tour company that organizes trips to little **Spirit Island**, the ideal vantage point for admiring the surrounding mountain tops.

The road that heads north to Edmonton crosses the entire Athabasca Valley. A large herd of moose grazes in this part of the valley, and the animals can often be spotted between the intersection of Maligne Road and the old town of Pocahontas, near Miette Hot Springs.

By continuing on the road to Hinton, you'll soon reach the hottest springs in all of the parks in the Rockies, **Miette Hot Springs**. The sulphurous water gushes forth at 57°C and has to be cooled down to 39°C for the baths. A paved path follows Sulphur Stream past the water purification station to the old pool, built out of logs in 1938; the trail finally ends at one of three hot springs beside the stream. Several hiking trails have been cleared in the area for those who wish to explore the back country and admire the splendid scenery.

The ruins of the town of **Pocahontas**, abandoned in 1921, lie at the turnoff for the road to Miette Hot Springs. Bit by bit, nature has reclaimed the remains of the buildings. Pocahontas was originally the name of Native American princess. When coal was discovered here in 1908, a concession was established, and the region was exploited extensively. Full of hope, residents named the town after the famous Virginia coal basin, Pocahontas, the headquarters of the company. When the mines shut down in 1921, many buildings were dismantled and transported to other towns.

Hwy. 16, the Yellowhead Highway, links Jasper with Mount Robson Provincial Park, 26km away in British Columbia. It traverses the main chains of the Rockies, affording some magnificent panoramic vistas. The road runs through Yellowhead Pass, along the Continental Divide.

To reach **Patricia** and **Pyramid** lakes, located only 7km from Jasper, you have to take Cedar Avenue from Connaught Drive in downtown Jasper. This road becomes Pyramid Avenue and leads to Pyramid Lake. This is an ideal spot for a walk or a picnic. You can go swimming or canoeing in the lake; motorized canoes are permitted here as well.

Tour D: Kootenay and Yoho National Parks

★★ Kootenay National Park

Although less popular with the public than Banff and Jasper, Kootenay National Park nevertheless boasts beautiful, majestic landscapes and is just as interesting to visit as its more touristy neighbours. It contains two large valleys, the humid Vermillion River Valley and the drier Kootenay River Valley; the contrast is striking. The park owes its existence to a bold attempt to lay a road between the Windermere region and the province of Alberta. In 1905, Randolphe Bruce, a businessman from the town of Invermere who became lieutenant governor of British Columbia, decided to turn a profit with the local orchards. To accomplish this end, he had to be able to transport produce to

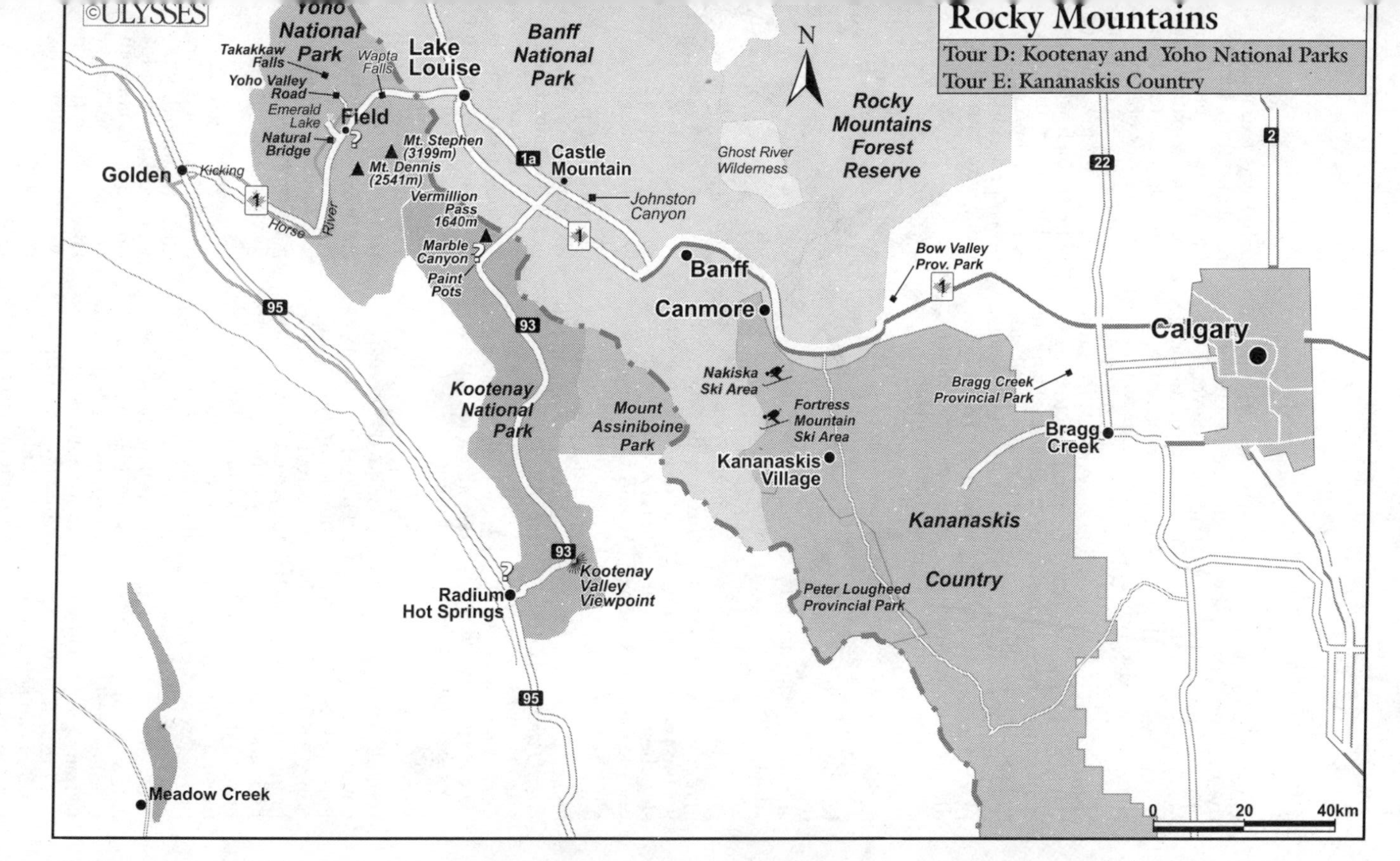
Rocky Mountains
Tour D: Kootenay and Yoho National Parks
Tour E: Kananaskis Country
©ULYSSES
N
Yoho National Park
Takakkaw Falls
Yoho Valley Road
Emerald Lake
Natural Bridge
Wapta Falls
Field
Lake Louise
Mt. Stephen (3199m)
Mt. Dennis (2541m)
Golden
Kicking Horse River
Banff National Park
1a
Castle Mountain
Johnston Canyon
Vermillion Pass 1640m
Marble Canyon
Paint Pots
Ghost River Wilderness
Rocky Mountains Forest Reserve
Banff
Canmore
Bow Valley Prov. Park
Calgary
2
22
1
95
93
Kootenay National Park
Mount Assiniboine Park
Nakiska Ski Area
Fortress Mountain Ski Area
Kananaskis Village
Bragg Creek Provincial Park
Bragg Creek
Kananaskis Country
Peter Lougheed Provincial Park
Kootenay Valley Viewpoint
Radium Hot Springs
Meadow Creek
0
20
40km

other parts of the country, hence the necessity of laying a road between isolated Windermere and the cities to the east. Bruce was so influential that construction began in 1911. A number of obstacles presented themselves, and the audacious project soon proved too costly for the province to finance alone. The 22km of road, born of a bitter struggle between man and nature, ended up leading nowhere, and the enterprise was abandoned. Refusing to admit defeat, Bruce turned to the federal government, which agreed to help in return for the property alongside the road; thus was born Kootenay National Park in 1922.

To reach Kootenay National Park from Banff, take the Trans-Canada to Castle Mountain Junction. Hwy. 93, on the left, runs the entire length of the park.

Vermillion Pass, at the entrance of Kootenay Park, marks the Continental Divide; from this point on, rivers in Banff Park and points east flow to the east, while those in Kootenay Park flow west and empty into the Pacific.

A few kilometres farther lies **Marble Canyon ★★**, along with a tourist office where visitors can see a short film on the history of the park. Marble Canyon is very narrow, but you'll find a lovely waterfall at the end of the trail there. Several bridges span the gorge, and the erosion caused by torrential waters makes for some amazing scenery. Five hundred metres to the right, past the canyon, you'll find a trail leading to the famous **Paint Pots ★★**. These ochre deposits are created by subterranean springs which cause iron oxide to rise to the surface. Aboriginal people used this substance as paint. They would clean the ochre, mix it with water, and mould it into little loaves, which they would bake in a fire. They would then ground it into a fine powder and mix it with fish oil. They could use the final product to paint their bodies or decorate their tipis and clothing.

According to the Aboriginals, a great animal spirit and a thunder spirit lived in the streams. Sometimes they would hear a melody coming from here, other times battle songs; in their minds, this meant that the spirits were speaking to them. For them, the ochre was the symbol of spirits, legends and important customs, while the first whites to come here saw it as an opportunity to make money. At the beginning of the century, the ochre was extracted by hand and then sent to Calgary to be used as a coloring for paint. You can still see a few remnants of this era, including machines, tools and even a few piles of ochre, which were left behind when the area was made into a national park and all work here came to a halt.

One of the best places in the park for elk- and moose-watching is the **Animal Lick**, a mineral-rich salt marsh. The best time to go is early in the morning or at dusk. Viewing areas have been laid out along the road so that you can admire the scenery. The view is particularly lovely from the **Kootenay Valley Viewpoint ★★**, located at the park exit.

Upon arriving at Radium Hot Springs, right after the tunnel, you will see a parking lot on your left. You can get out of your car and take a look at the limestone cliffs, which have been stained red by iron oxide.

Radium Hot Springs

This little town, located at the entrance to the park, is surprisingly mundane. You can, however, take a dip in the pool at the **Radium Hot Pools** ★★ *($5; at the entrance of Kootenay Park, ☎ 250-347-9485)*, whose warm waters are apparently renowned for their therapeutic virtues. Whether or not you believe these claims, which have yet to be backed by any medical evidence, a soak in these 45°C non-sulphurous waters is definitely very relaxing.

South of Radium Hot Springs, Hwy. 95 continues south through the British Columbia Rockies meeting up with Hwy. 3 from Crowsnest Pass. This alternative route is one way of getting to Southern Alberta .

Invermere

Invermere is a service town for the surrounding cottage country, where Albertans and British Columbians escape to on weekends. Picturesque **Windermere Lake** ★, really of widening of Columbia River, is popular with boaters.

The **Windermere Valley Pioneer Museum** *(free admission; summer, every day, ☎ 250-342-9769)*, with its collection of memorabilia, is yet another place to immerse yourself in those pioneer days.

Eighteen kilometres west of Invermere is **Panorama Resort**, ski hill and hotel with a variety of lodging options.

Fairmont Hot Springs

This tiny town exists almost exclusively as a tourist centre for the hot springs. There is golf, skiing and great scenery. The hot springs, located at the resort of the same name are free if you are staying at the resort and $8 otherwise.

Continue south for about 100km to Fort Steele.

Fort Steele

The **Fort Steele Heritage Town** ★ *($7.50; south of Fort Steele on Hwy 93/95; every day 9:30 to 5:30pm, ☎ 250-426-7352)* is one of the better boomtown-style attractions in Western Canada. The restored and reconstructed buildings are made that much more authentic by the incredible setting. The old steam train or a horse-drawn wagon will toot you about. Call ahead for details on the musical variety shows at the **Wild Horse Theatre** *(☎ 250-426-6923)*.

Continuing east of Hwy. 3 towards the Alberta border, there is good downhill skiing in ***Fernie****.*

Alternatively, continue your tour north from Radium Hot Springs by heading up Hwy. 95, which runs along the floor of the Columbia River Valley, to the little town of ***Golden****. The scenery along this road is quite pretty, with the foothills of the Rockies on one side and the Purcell Mountains on the other. From Golden the Trans-Canada Highway continues on to Revelstoke), about 150 kilometres west of the edge of the Rocky Mountain parks.*

★★

Yoho National Park

As in all the other parks in the Rockies, you must pay an entrance fee *($5 for one day, $35 a year)* if you wish to stay here. This fee does not apply if you are simply passing through the park.

About 5km from the park entrance, on the right, you'll find a trail leading to **Wapta Falls**, on the **Kicking Horse River**, thus named when adventurer James Hector suffered the painful misfortune of being kicked in the chest by his horse here in 1858. The river is a very popular place to go rafting. The falls are 30m high, and the trail leading to them is fairly short and easy.

A little farther along, you'll find another trail leading to the **Hoodoos**, natural rock formations created by erosion. The trail, which starts at the Hoodoo Creek campground, is very steep but only 3.2km long and offers an excellent view of the Hoodoos.

A small road offers access to the **Natural Bridge**, sculpted by the torrential waters of Kicking Horse River. There were falls here before, but the water, full of sand and gravel, acted like sandpaper, gradually wearing its way into the rock and creating the formation we see now. This spot also offers a splendid view of **Mount Stephen** (3,199m) and **Mount Dennis** (2,541m).

Hiking to **Emerald Lake ★★** has become a tradition here in Yoho National Park. A short trail (5.2km) takes you around the lake. You can then visit the **Hamilton Falls**. Picnic areas have been laid out near the lake. Thanks to a small canoe-rental outfit, you can also enjoy some time on the water. There is a small souvenir shop beside the boat-launching ramp.

The park's tourist office is located in Field, 33km east of the park entrance. During summer, visitors can learn more about the Yoho Valley by taking part in any number of interpretive activities. There are 400km of hiking trails leading through the valley deep into the heart of the region. Maps of these trails, as well as of those reserved for mountain bikes, are available at the **tourist office** *(Jul and Aug, every day 8:30am to 7pm; rest of year 9am to 7pm; on the way into town, ☎250-343-6783)* in **Field**.

You can also purchase a topographical map of the park for $13. If you plan on staying more than a day here, you must register at the Parks Canada office, located in the same place. You can climb some of the mountains, but a special permit is required to scale Mount Stephen because fossils have been discovered in the area you must pass through to reach the top.

You can buy some provisions at the little **Siding General Store** *(every day 8am to 8pm, in summer 7am to 9pm; on Stephen Ave., beside the post office)* in Field.

You must be accompanied by a guide to visit the **Burgess Shale ★★★**. In 1886, a paleontologist discovered several large trilobite beds on Mount Stephen, near Field. Since the Rockies were once covered by an ocean, all of these fossils were beautifully preserved by a thick layer of marine sediment. The invaluable fossil beds on Mount Burgess, beside Mount Stephen, were pushed to the surface by the geological upheavals that led to the emergence of the Rockies. You'll need to set aside an entire day to visit the Burgess Shale, since the trip there and back is a 20km hike.

To enlist the services of a guide, contact the park offices *(☎ 250-343-6783)* or the **Yoho Burgess Shale Foundation** *(☎ 250-343-6480 or in summer 800-343-3006)* several days in advance.

A few kilometres past Field, **Yoho Valley Road** branches off to the left, toward **Takakaw Falls**. On the way, you can stop at the **Upper Spiral Tunnel Viewpoint** ★★ to admire the advanced technology the engineers working for the railway company had to employ in order to lay a dependable line across this hilly terrain. The small road twists and turns for 13km, leading to a wonderful scenic viewpoint from which you can contemplate the Yoho and Kicking Horse Rivers. It comes to a dead end at the **Takakaw Falls** ★★ (254m), which are among the highest falls in Canada.

Tour E: Kananaskis Country

When Captain John Palliser led a British scientific expedition here from 1857 and 1860, the numerous lakes and rivers he found led him to christen the region Kananaskis, which means "gathering of the waters." Located 90km from Calgary, this region covers more than 4,000 square kilometres, including the **Bow Valley**, **Bragg Creek** and **Peter Lougheed** provincial parks. Because of its proximity to Calgary, its beautiful scenery and the huge variety of outdoor activities that can be enjoyed here, it soon became one of the most popular destinations in the province, first with Albertans and then with visitors from all over the world.

No matter what season it is, Kananaskis Country has a great deal to offer. During summer, it is a veritable paradise for outdoor enthusiasts, who can play both golf and tennis here, or go horseback riding, mountain biking, kayaking, river rafting, fishing or hiking. With its 250km of paved roads and 460km of marked trails, this region is easier to explore than any other in Alberta. In winter, the trails are used for cross-country skiing and snowmobiling. Visitors can also go downhill skiing at Fortress Mountain or at Nakiska, speed down the toboggan runs, go skating on one of the region's many lakes or try dogsledding. Maps pertaining to these activities are available at the **Barrier Lake Information Centre** *(summer, every day 8:30am to 6pm, except Fri 8:30am to 7pm; autumn, Mon to Thu 9am to 4pm, Fri to Sun 9am to 6pm; winter every day 9am to 4pm; on Hwy 40 near Barrier Lake, ☎ 403-673-3985)*, where you'll also find the torch from the Calgary Olympics. It was carried all over Canada for three months, and then used to light the Olympic flame in Calgary on February 13, 1988. Eight events (downhill, slalom and giant slalom) were held in the Kananaskis region, on Mount Allan, in Nakiska.

The **Nakiska Ski Resort** *(near Kananaskis Village, ☎ 403-591-7777)* was designed specifically for the Olympic Games, at the same time as the Kananaskis Village hotel complex. It boasts top-notch, modern facilities and excellent runs.

Kananaskis Village consists mainly of a central square surrounded by three luxurious hotels. It was designed to be the leading resort in this region. Its construction was funded by the Alberta Heritage Savings Trust and a number of private investors. The village was officially opened on December 20, 1987. It has a post office, located beside the **tourist information centre** *(summer, every day 9am to 9pm; winter, Mon to Fri 9am to 5pm)*, as well as a sauna and a hot tub *($2; every day 9am to 8:30pm)*, both of which are open to the general public. The Kananaskis Hotel houses a shopping arcade complete with souvenir and clothing shops, cafés and restaurants.

The **Kananaskis Golf Club** leaves absolutely nothing to be desired. Its fabulous 36-hole course stretches along the narrow Kananaskis River valley at the foot of **Mount Lorette** and **Mount Kidd**.

The **Fortress Mountain Ski Resort** *(turn right at Fortress Junction, ☎ 403-229-3637 or 591-7108)* is less popular than Nakiska, but nevertheless has some good runs. Furthermore, snowfall is heavy here on the Continental Divide, at the edge of Peter Lougheed Provincial Park.

The tourist office in **Peter Lougheed Provincial Park** *(near the two Kananaskis Lakes)* features an interactive presentation that provides all sorts of information on local flora, fauna, geography, geology and climatic phenomena. Mount Lougheed and the park were named after two well-known members of the Lougheed family. Born in Ontario, the honorable Sir James Lougheed (1854-1925) became a very prominent lawyer in both his home province and in Alberta, particularly in Calgary, where he was Canadian Pacific's legal advisor. He was named to the senate in 1889, led the Conservative Party from 1906 to 1921 and finally became a minister. The park owes its existence to his grandson, the honorable Peter Lougheed (1928-), who was elected Premier of Alberta on August 30, 1971. You can pick up a listing of the numerous interpretive programs offered here at the tourist office.

Right near the tourist office, you'll find **William Watson Lodge**, a centre for the disabled and the elderly which offers a view of **Lower Kananaskis Lake**. At the end of the road leading to **Upper Kananaskis Lake**, turn left and drive a few kilometres farther to **Interlakes**, where you can take in a magnificent view.

The **Smithdorien Trail**, a gravel road stretching 64km, leads back to Canmore. Although parts of it have been deeply rutted by rain and snow, the road is wide and you'll have it almost all to yourself. There are no service stations along the way. This is a beautiful area that seems completely cut off from the rest of the world. The road comes to an end at Grassi Falls in Canmore.

Outdoor Activities

The Canadian Rockies, which cover an area of over 22,000 square kilometres, are a paradise for anyone who appreciates mountain landscapes and clean air, enjoys having lots of space to roam and takes pleasure in outdoor activities like hiking, mountain climbing, horseback riding, canoeing, river rafting, golf and cross-country and downhill skiing. Because this region has been set aside as a series of national parks, it has not been marred by the unbridled construction of ski resorts and chalets, which do not always blend harmoniously with the landscape. Consequently, although the Rockies welcome six million visitors annually, you don't have to go far off the beaten track to enjoy some quiet moments that will remain with you forever.

Climate

The cool winds that characterize the Rockies might make you forget the dangers of the sun, which in mountain regions, are very real. Be sure to prepare yourself with a good sunscreen, a hat and sunglasses. When hiking in the mountains the combination of the physical exertion, the sun and the changing weather conditions can often lead to hypothermia, which can ultimately be fatal. The best way to avoid these problems is to dress properly.

Clothing

An excursion in the mountains requires careful planning. Whether you plan on visiting the Rockies in winter or summer, it is important to always bring along warm and comfortable clothing.

During the winter, do not forget to bring along warm long underwear that allows your skin to breathe, natural wool or synthetic fleece sweaters, a few good pairs of socks, a jacket and pants that are windproof, gloves, a scarf and a hat. If you plan on doing any cross-country skiing, remember that it is always better to wear layers instead of one heavy jacket which will prove too warm when you make the least exertion, but not warm enough when you stop to rest. A small backpack is a good idea to for carrying some food, an extra sweater and a pair of socks in case your feet get wet. Never stop to rest in wet clothes, bring along a change of clothes instead.

The same precautions should be taken in summer. Temperatures are much lower at higher altitudes, and the smallest wind can significantly lower temperatures. Furthermore, climatic changes occur quickly in the mountains. Be sure to dress properly when heading out on an excursion, a good sweater and windbreaker are a good idea, even in summer. An ear warmer and gloves might also come in handy. Rain is common, so bring along a water-resistant jacket. Finally, with proper footwear, including a good pair of socks and a solid pair of hiking boots, you'll be ready to tackle the most spectacular trails of the region.

Hiking

Hiking is probably the most popular outdoor activity in the region's national parks, which are crisscrossed by rails suitable for everyone from novices to experts. Environment Canada's park service puts out free brochures on some of the wonderful hiking trips to be enjoyed in the Rockies; these are available at the tourist information offices in Banff, Lake Louise and Jasper. You can pick up a map of the hiking trails in Kootenay National Park for one dollar at the Parks Canada offices located at each entrance of the park. Keep in mind that if you plan on spending several days in the heart of one of these parks, you must register with Parks Canada, specifying your itinerary and the length of your stay.

Tour A: Banff National Park

Banff

The relatively easy **Cave and Basin Trail** (6.8km) leads to the historic site of the same name, offering some lovely views of the Bow River along the way. It starts at Banff Centre, on St. Julian Road. Follow the Bow River trail to the falls and walk alongside the water. Go over the Banff Avenue bridge and turn right on Cave Avenue. The trail leads to the parking lot of the Cave and Basin hot springs. Return the way you came.

The **Stoney Squaw** trail is definitely worth a visit. The excursion departs from the parking lot at Mount-Norquay Ski Centre. The path climbs 1,880m and the 5km course takes about 2hrs to complete. The path is relatively easy to hike and it offers magnificent views of Mount Cascade.

Those looking for a challenge will enjoy the 6km of steep hills leading up to the summit of **Mount Rundle** (3,000m). The trail zigzags in the valley before arriving at the end of the forest and then continuing up the mountain. For quite a ways, the passage is barely wider than a fewm, with sheer cliffs on both sides. The view of Spray River and Mount Sulphur is arresting. Be sure to bring warm clothing as winter snowstorms can rage even in June. The trail begins after the bridge that crosses Spray River near the golf club. Follow the edge of the woods on the right-hand side after the bridge. Plan for at least 6hrs of hiking, and make sure you have good knees!

The continuation of the Cave and Basin trail, the **Sundance Canyon Trail** (13.6km), is even easier. Go past the Cave and Basin building and head back down toward the Bow River. The well-marked trail runs alongside Sundance Creek, climbing up to the canyon and then making a loop, giving you a chance to see a little more of the landscape.

The **Sulphur Mountain Trail** is a little more difficult than the two mentioned above because it involves a significant change in altitude. It starts near the base station of the Sulphur Mountain Gondola, then winds its way up the mountain, offering a magnificent, panoramic view of the Bow River valley.

The trail leading to the **Vermilion Lakes** starts at the Banff Centre, although there are all sorts of other ways to get there. Follow the Tunnel Mountain Trail, which leads to the Bow River falls. Take Buffalo Street, then, a little farther along on the left, the trail that runs along the river. Cross the Banff Avenue bridge, then walk along the banks of the Bow River. You will come to the canoe rental service on Bow Avenue. The first of the three Vermilion Lakes lies just over the railroad tracks.

Continue your tour along Vermilion Lakes Drive. The area around these swampy lakes is wonderful for bird-watching. This hike is a bit long, but very easy. You can also reach the Vermilion Lakes by canoe, starting from the Bow River.

This guide would not be complete if it didn't mention the hiking trail that leads to the summit of **Cascade Mountain**. The departure is from the parking lot at Mount Norquay Ski Center on the other side of the Trans-Canada Highway. This 18km trail is even more exhausting than that of Mount Rundle. On the other hand, it has the most beautiful panoramic view of Banff and Bow Valley. The snow always melts late in the year on the shady side of Cascade Mountain. For this reason, the trail only opens, at the earliest, at the beginning of July.

If you would like to take part in a longer excursion organized by professionals, you can contact one of the following outfitters: **White Mountain Adventures** *(Box 2294, Canmore, Alberta, T0L 0M0, ☎ 403-678-4099 or 800-408-0005)* and **Time Travel's Nature Photography & Hiking Excursions** *(☎ 403-678-3336)*. Reservations required.

Lake Louise

To reach **Lake Agnes and the Big Beehives**, start out at the Chateau Lake Louise and walk along the lakeside promenade. On the right, you will see a little trail leading up the mountain through the forest. This will take you to Mirror Lake (2.7km) and Agnes Lake (3.6km). When you get to Agnes Lake, which lies 365m higher than Lake Louise, you will find a small café set up inside a cabin, where you can regain your strength over a cup of tea or hot chocolate before continuing your ascent to the Big Beehives. The trail runs alongside little Agnes Lake then climbs steeply for 140m to the Little Beehives. The Big Beehives lie another 30m uphill. Your efforts will be richly rewarded by a superb view of Lake Louise and its valley.

You can also set out on an excursion to the **Plain of the Six Glaciers** from the Chateau Lake Louise. Walk along the lakeside promenade and, instead of taking the trail that branches off toward Agnes Lake, keep following the shoreline. The trail runs near some moraines (masses of rocks deposited by glaciers), then comes to an end 5.5km from the starting point near a small cabin where you can have a light meal or a hot drink. From there, you can climb 1.3km farther to the magnificent viewpoint at Abbot Pass and Death Trap.

Immediately to the left after the parking lot at Moraine Lake is a trail leading to the **Consolation Lakes**. This trail, which is only three kilometres long and requires little effort, affords some magnificent panoramic views of the Temple Mountains and the Ten Peaks. Visitors are advised to wear good walking shoes for this outing, since the trail is scattered with moraines and large rocks.

For a view of Moraine Lake and the Ten Peaks, which are depicted on the old Canadian $20 bill, take the **Moraine Lakeshore Trail**, a short path that leads all the way to the far end of the lake.

Pika

Tour C: Jasper National Park

The **Old Fort trail** is easy to climb and is suitable for all ages and fitness levels. The trail takes about an hour to complete. You can admire the mountain peaks in the area, the zigzagging Athabasca River and the small town of Jasper. To get there, take Hwy. 93A to south of Jasper and then turn left after Hwy. 16.

Mount Edith Cavell

The **Path of the Glacier Trail** (1.5 km) starts near the parking lot at Mount Edith Cavell and leads to a small lake formed by the run-off from the glacier. You can admire the glacier suspended above you and ponder the dramatic impact glaciers have had on the vegetation and topography of these mountain valleys.

To reach the **Cavell Meadow Trail and Peak** from the parking lot at Mount Edith Cavell, walk up the trail on the left, which will take you opposite the Angel Glacier. You won't have to look hard to spot marmots and pikas along the way. Upon reaching the forest, the trail climbs steeply up to a clear-cut zone. You can already see the Angel Glacier from here; in fact, it appears to be very close. You can keep going to Cavell Meadow Park, since the trail winds its way farther and farther up. The last 500m are the most demanding, but your efforts will be richly rewarded by a magnificent view.

Maligne Lake

The **Maligne Lake Trail** is a short lakeside trail that starts at the second parking lot near the chalet, where you can purchase drinks and souvenirs. Only 3.2km and easy enough to be enjoyed by the most inexperienced hiker, it leads to the Schäffer Viewpoint, which was named after Mary Schäffer, the first woman to explore the valley. After the viewpoint, the trail leads into the forest, where you'll find "potholes" created by the glaciers, then heads back to the chalet.

The trail to **Mona and Lorraine Lakes** is also short, relatively easy and extremely pleasant. It leads through a forest of lodgepole pine to the two charming little lakes.

Patricia Lake

To reach the trail that skirts **Patricia Lake**, take the road to Pyramid Lake as far as the parking lot for the stables. This short (4.8 km), easy hike makes for a charming excursion. The trail starts out by climbing gently through the forest, then heads back down to the south shore of the lake. It then winds its way down to a small valley frequented by deer, moose and beavers, as well as by a large number of birds. It is best to come here in the early morning or late afternoon, when the temperature is cool and the animals come out of the forest to feed in the fields and quench their thirst at watering holes. Trivia buffs might be interested to know that Patricia Lake was named after the daughter of the Duke of Connaught, Canada's Governor General from 1911 to 1914.

Mountain Biking

Mountain bikes are permitted on certain trails. Always keep in mind that there might be people or bears around each bend. We also recommend limiting your speed on downhill stretches.

Tour A: Banff National Park

You won't have any trouble renting a bicycle in Banff, since you can do so at a number of hotels. Just the same, here are a few places you can try: **Bactrax** *(from $5/hr or $16/day; every day 8am to 8pm; Ptarmigan Inn, 339 Banff Ave.,* ☎ *403-762-8177)*; **Cycling the Rockies** *($50;* ☎ *403-678-6770)* organizes mountain-bike trips in the Banff area (each package includes a bicycle, a helmet, transportation to the point of departure, refreshments and the services of a guide).

Tour C: Jasper National Park

The Jasper area is criss-crossed by bike trails.

A 9km trail leads from the parking lot opposite the Jasper Aquatic Centre to **Mina Lake and Riley Lake**. The pitch is fairly steep until you reach the firebreak road leading to Cabin Lake. Cross this road and continue to Mina Lake. Three and a half kilometres farther along, another trail branches off toward Riley Lake. To return to Jasper, take Pyramid Lake Road.

The **Saturday Night Lake Loop** starts at the Cabin Creek West parking lot and climbs gently for 24.6km, offering a view of the Miette and Athabasca Valleys. Past Caledonia Lake, it winds through the forest to the High Lakes, where the grade becomes steeper. It then leads to Saturday Night Lake and Cabin Lake. From there, follow the firebreak road to Pyramid Lake Road, which will take you back to Jasper.

The **Athabasca River Trail** (25km) starts at the Old Fort Point parking lot, near Jasper Park Lodge. For the first 10km of the trail after the lodge's golf course, you will have to climb some fairly steep slopes, especially as you approach the Maligne Canyon. Bicycles are forbidden between the first and fifth bridges of the canyon trail, so you have to take Maligne Road for this part of the trip. After the fifth bridge, turn left and ride alongside the Athabasca River on trail 7. If you don't want to go back the way you came, take Hwy. 16.

Like the Athabasca River Trail, the **Valley of the Five Lakes Trail** and the **Wabasso Lake Trail** both start at the Old Fort Point parking lot. Trails 1, 1A and 9 begin here. The trip, which covers 11.2km, is quite easy up until the first lake in the valley, although a few spots are a bit rocky. At the first lake, the trail splits in two; take the path on the left, since it offers the best view of the lakes. The two trails merge into one again near a pond at the turnoff for Wabasso Lake. Pick up Hwy. 93, unless you want to go to Wabasso Lake, in which case you have to take trail 9 (19.3 km), to the left of the pond.

Head back to Jasper on the Icefields Parkway.

You have to drive to the parking lot at Celestine Lake, which marks the beginning of the trail (48 km). A gravel road leads to the **Snake Indian Falls**, 22km away. About 1km farther, the road turns into a small trail that leads to Rock Lake.

Tour E: The Kananaskis Region

In summer, **Canmore Nordic Center**'s ski slopes turn into mountain-bike trails. The **Banff Trail** is a 40km path that goes right up to the Banff Springs golf course before returning to Canmore.

The **Georgetown Trail** is relatively flat and joins the Bow River near Georgetown, formerly a mining town.

Mountain Bike Rentals

Freewheel Cycle rents out quality mountain bikes. You can also have repairs done here *(618 Patricia St., Jasper, ☎ 780-852-3898).*

At **On-Line Sport & Tackle** you'll find bikes, helmets and maps of bike paths *($18 per day; 600 Patricia St., Jasper, ☎ 780-852-3630).*

Trail Sports
Canmore Nordic Center
☎780-678-6764

Motorcycling

Tour C: Jasper National Park

Some people dream about touring the Rockies by motorcycle. **SMV Motorcycle Tours & Rentals** *(site 54, Industrial Park, Box 2404, Jasper, T0E 1E0, ☎/≠ 780-852-5752, or ☎888-852-BIKE)* rents out a variety of bikes, ranging from small-engined vehicles (50cc) to the powerful Harley Electraglide and BMW K 100 S. Rates range from $15 to $75 an hour and there are daily and weekly rates as well.

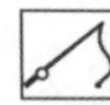

Fishing

Fishing permits are required in all Canadian national parks. You can obtain one at any of the parks' administrative or tourist information offices, from park rangers and at some boat-rental outfits. Visitors under the age of 16 do not need permits if they are accompanied by a permit-holder. The waters are teeming with rainbow and brown trout, char and pike. There are a number of rules to follow. You can obtain a copy of the regulations concerning sport fishing in the region's national parks through any Parks Canada office. Fishing is permitted year-round in the Bow River, but is only legal during very specific periods on some lakes. For more information on these dates, contact Parks Canada.

Tour A: Banff National Park

Banff Fishing Unlimited
Box 216
Canmore, T0L 0M0
☎(403)762-4936
⇄678-8895
Banff Fishing Unlimited rents out equipment and provides professional guides, who can direct you to the best spots.

Monod Sports
Box 310
Banff, T0L 0C0
☎(403)762-4571
⇄762-3565
Monod Sports specializes in fly fishing; guided excursions include equipment

Minnewanka Tour
every day 9am to 9pm
on the landing stage
at the entrance to Minewanka Lake
Box 2189
Banff, T0L 0C0
☎(403)762-3473

Mountain Fly Fishers
Box 909, Railway Ave
Canmore, T1W 1P3
☎(403)678-9522
☎(800)450-9664
⇄678-2183
Mountain Fly Fishers arranges fly-fishing trips that last several days. Prices vary according to the length of the trip.

Tour C: Jasper National Park

Maligne Tours
from $145 per person
626 Connaught Dr., Jasper
☎(780)852-3370
⇄780-852-3370
Maligne Tours offers guided fishing trips, with meals and equipment included. Reservations required.

On-Line Sport & Tackle
$119 for half a day
$149 for a full day
600 Patricia St., Box 730
Jasper, T0E 1E0
☎(780)852-3630
⇄(780)4245

Rafting

The rivers running through the Rockies have a lot to offer thrill-seekers. Whether it's your first time out or you already have some rafting experience, you'll find all sorts of interesting challenges here.

The most popular places to go rafting in the Banff area are **Kicking Horse River** and **Lower Canyon**. A few words of advice: wear a bathing suit and closed running shoes that you don't mind getting wet, dress very warmly (heavy wool and a windbreaker) and bring along a towel and a change of clothes for the end of the day.

Tours A and D: Banff, Kootenay and Yoho National Parks

Hydra River Guides
$75 plus tax
209 Bear St., Box 778
Banff, T0L 0C0
☎(403)760-9154
☎(800)684-888
⇄760-3196
Hydra River Guides offers day trips in Upper Canyon on Kicking Horse River.

Wild Water Adventures
full- and half-day packages
$109 and $67 respectively
Lake Louise and Banff
☎(403)522-2211
☎(800)-647-4444

Rocky Mountain Raft Tours
Box 1771
Banff, T0L 0C0
☎(403)762-3632

Glacier Raft Company
$85 per day
$49 for half a day
Banff, Alberta
☎(403)762-4347
Golden, BC
☎(250)344-6521
The Glacier Raft Company organizes trips down the Kicking Horse River. There is a special rate *($99, tax included)* for the **Kicking Horse Challenge**, which is a slightly wilder ride than the others.

Wet'n'Wild Adventure
$74 and up
Golden, BC
☎**(250)344-6546**
☎**800-668-9119**
⇄**344-7650**
Wet'n'Wild Adventure offers trips from Golden, Lake Louise and Banff. A half-day on the Kicking Horse River will cost about $60. Those wishing to spend several days on the water can take advantage of some interesting package deals ranging in price from $150 to $200 per person. A minimum number of passengers is required, however.

Alpine Rafting Company
$30-$80
Box 1272
Golden, BC, V0A 1H0
☎**(250)344-6778**
☎**(800)663-7080**
The Alpine Rafting Company has a variety of packages for novice and experienced rafters down the Kicking Horse River.

Kootenay River Runners
$75-$300
Box 81, Edgewater
BC, V0A 1E0
☎**(250)347-9210**
☎**(800)-599-4399**
108 Banff Ave., Banff
☎**(403)762-5385**
The Kootenay River Runners also have a branch in Banff, at the corner of Caribou and Bear Streets.

Rocky Mountain Rafting
$49 and up
Box 1767, Golden
BC, V0A 1H0
☎**(250)344-6979**
☎**(800)808-RAFT**
Rocky Mountain Rafting, located in the Best Western, arranges trips down the Kicking Horse River.

Tour C: Jasper National Park

Whitewater Rafting
Box 362
Jasper, T0E 1E0
☎**(780)852-RAFT**
☎**(800)557-RAFT**
⇄**(780)852-3623**
Whitewater Rafting has a counter in **Jasper Park Lodge** *(☎ 780-852-3301)*, and another at the **Avalanche Esso** gas station *(702 Connaught Dr., ☎ 780-852-4FUN)*. This company organizes trips down the Athabasca, Maligne and Sunwapta Rivers.

Maligne River Adventures
$59 and up
626 Connaught Dr.
Box 280, Jasper
T0E 1E0
☎**(780)852-3370**
⇄**(780)3405**
Maligne River Adventures, in addition to other excursions, offers an interesting three-day trip down the Kakwa River for $450 *(May and Jun)*. Some experience is required, since these are class IV rapids, and are thus rather difficult to negotiate.

Two outfitters offer trips for novices and children who would like to try rafting on slower moving rapids: **Jasper Raft Tours** *($39, children $20; Box 398, Jasper, T0E 1E0, ☎ 780-852-3613, ⇄ 780-852-3923)* and **Mount Robson Adventure Holidays** *($40 and up; children $15 and up Box 687, Valemount, BC, Mount Robson Provincial Park, V0E 2Z0, ☎ 250-566-4368, ⇄250-566-4351)*, which also has a branch in Jasper *(604 Connaught Dr.)*.

Horseback Riding

Horseback riding is a pleasant way to explore the more remote parts of the parks in the Rockies. A number of trails have been set aside for riders and their mounts. If you would like to ride your own horse, you must inform the agents at one of the Parks Canada offices and obtain a map of the bridle paths.

Tour A: Banff National Park

Warner Guiding and Outfitting *(Box 2280, Banff, T0L 0C0, ☎403-762-4551, ⇄ 762-8130)* offers short, easy rides of 1, 2, or 3hrs, as well as real expeditions. Three days of riding in Mystic Valley will cost about $500, and a six-day wildlife interpretation trip, $1,100. In all, there are over 15 excursions to choose from, with something for everyone, whether you're a camping buff or prefer staying in lodges. All of these outings, of course, are led by professional guides who can tell you anything you might like to know about the flora, fauna and geological characteristics of the areas you will be riding through. Warner Guiding and Outfitting also organizes expeditions in collaboration with Parks Canada.

Brewster Lake Louise Stables is located right beside the Chateau Lake Louise *($25/hr, $100/day; Box 964, Banff, T0L 0C0, ☎ 403-762-5454 or 522-3511 ext. 1142, ⇄ 762-3953).*

Tour C: Jasper National Park

Maligne Tours *($55/person; 626 Connaught Dr., Jasper, T0E 1E0, ☎ 780-852-3370, or Jasper Park Lodge, ☎ 780-852-4779)* organizes 3.5hr rides to the top of the Bald Hills every morning and afternoon (10am and 2pm). These outings give visitors a chance to admire a variety of magnificent landscapes and take in a splendid view of the glaciers.

Pyramid Stables *(near Patricia Lake, 4km from Jasper heading toward Pyramid Lake, ☎ 780-852-3562)* arranges short pony rides for small children and longer outings for adults.

Skyline Trail Rides *(from $25; Jasper Park Lodge, Jasper, T0E 1E0, ☎ 780-852-4215, 852-3301 ext. 6189, or 888-852-7787).*

Tour D: Kootenay and Yoho National Parks

Longhorn Stables is located right at the edge of Radium, on the way to Golden *($20/hr, $35/2hrs, $110/day; Box 387, Radium Hot Springs, BC, V0A 1M0, ☎ 250-347-9755 or 347-6453).*

Paragliding

This activity is forbidden in the national parks in the Rockies but is permitted in Kananaskis Country. **Glenn Derouin** *(113B 15th St., Canmore, AB, T1W 1M1, ☎ 403-678-4973, ⇄ 678-4973)* offers one-day courses *($150)* and tandem flights *($100)* appropriate for beginners, as well as other packages.

Golf

Tour A: Banff National Park

Canmore Golf & Curling Club
$25/ 9 holes
$38/18
☎(403)678-5959
Equipment can be rented on the premises *($40).*

Banff Springs Hotel
☎(403)762-6801
The Banff Springs Hotel has a magnificent 18-hole course set in enchantingly beautiful surroundings.

Tour C: Jasper National Park

Jasper Park Lodge
☎(780)852-3301
There is a lovely golf course near the Jasper Park Lodge. Reservations can be made at the front desk of the lodge.

Tour D: Kootenay and Yoho National Parks

The Columbia River Valley is a veritable paradise for golfers, with more courses than you can count. We have only indicated a few below; for a more exhaustive list, pick up the golfing brochure at the tourist office in Radium Hot Springs.

Golden Golf & Country Club
$37/18 holes
Box 1615, Golden
BC, V0A 1H0
☎(250)344-2700
⇌344-2922
The magnificent golf course at the Golden Golf & Country Club is surrounded by grandiose landscapes. It lies alongside the Trans-Canada Highway, near the Columbia River, between the Rockies and the Purcell Mountains.

Way-Lyn Ranch Golf Course
Hwy. 95A, S.S.3, site 19-4
Cranbrook, BC, V1C 6H3
☎(250)427-2825
The nine-hole Way-Lyn Ranch Golf Course is located between the towns of Cranbrook and Kimberley.

Trickle Creek
$42/18 holes
Box 190
Kimberley BC, V1A 2Y6
☎(250)427-5171
☎(888)874-2553
⇌427-3878
Trickle Creek is an 18-hole golf course. Reservations recommended.

The golf course at the **Springs at Radium Golf Resort** *(Box 310, Radium Hot Springs, BC, V0A 1M0, ☎ 250-347-9311 or (800)667-6444, ⇌ 347-6299)* and the **Springs Golf Course** *(Box 430, Radium Hot Springs, BC, V0A 1M0, ☎ 250-347-6200, ⇌ 347-6210)* are two of the loveliest golf courses in British Columbia.

Tour E: Kananaskis Country

Kananaskis Country Golf Course
Kananaskis Village
Box 1710
☎591-7154
⇌591-7072
Kananaskis Country Golf Course has two excellent 18-hole golf courses located south of the Trans-Canada Highway via Hwy. 40.

Silvertip
$105
1000 Silvertip Trail, Canmore
☎877-5444
Silvertip was built in 1998 on the sunny side of the Bow River valley. Each hole of this adventurous golf course snakes up and down the mountainside, with great views of the countryside. Experts, get out your clubs!

Downhill Skiing

It is impossible to look at the Rockies without imagining the hours of pleasure you'll have tearing down the endless slopes. Able to satisfy the most demanding skiers, the resorts here offer a variety of beautifully maintained trails covering all levels of difficulty and excellent skiing conditions. The ski season generally starts around October and can continue into May.

Tour A: Banff National Park

Banff Mount Norquay
$39 full-day pass
on Norquay Rd.
Box 219, Banff, AB, T0L 0C0
☎(403)762-4421
Banff Mount Norquay was one of the first ski resorts in North America. It takes just 10min to drive here from downtown Banff. For ski conditions, call ☎ (403)762-4421. The resort has both a ski school and a rental shop.

Sunshine Village
$47 full-day
8km west of Banff
Box 1510
Banff, AB, T0L 0C0
☎(403)760-6500
☎(800)661-1676
Sunshine Village is a beautiful ski resort located at an altitude of 2,700m on the Continental Divide between the provinces of Alberta and British Columbia. Located above the tree line, this resort is endowed with lots of sun. Dial ☎ (403)277-SNOW for ski conditions. Ski rentals available.

Lake Louise
$51 per day
Box 5
Lake Louise, AB
T0L 1E0
☎(403)522-3555
Lake Louise has the largest ski resort in Canada, covering four mountainsides and offering skiers over 50 different runs. Both downhill and cross-country equipment are available for rent here.

For ski conditions, call ☎ *(403)244-6665.*

Tour C: Jasper National Park

Marmot Basin
$42 full day
take Hwy. 93 toward Banff
then turn right on 93A
Box 1300
Jasper, AB, T0E 1E0
☎(780)852-3816
☎(780)488-5909 for ski conditions

Marmot Basin is located about 20min by car from downtown Jasper. Ski rentals available.

Tour D: Kootenay and Yoho National Parks

Kimberley Ski Resort
$35 full day
Box 40, Kimberley, BC
V1A 2Y5
☎(250)427-4881
☎(800)667-0871

The Kimberley Ski Resort is the only real attraction in Kimberley, an amazing little Bavarian village. It has some decent trails that are perfect for family skiing.

Whitetooth
$32 per day
Box 1925, Golden, BC
V0A 1H0
☎(250)344-6114

Whitetooth is relatively small, but getting bigger every year. It has a few good, well-maintained runs.

Panorama Resort Ski Hill
$45
Box 2797, Panorama, BC
V0A 1T0
☎(250)342-6941

Panorama Resort Ski Hill boasts a vertical rise of 1,300m with glade and bowl skiing in the Purcell Mountains.

Fernie Snow Valley
Ski Area Rd.
☎(250)423-4655

Fernie Snow Valley has a vertical rise 600m. The town is small, but the ski hill is modern and well serviced.

Tour E: Kananaskis Country

Nakiska
$40 day
Box 1988
Kananaskis Village, AB
T0L 2H0
☎(403)591-7777
☎229-3288
for ski conditions

Nakiska hosted the men's and women's downhill, slalom and combination events during the 1988 Winter Olympics. Built specifically for that purpose, along with Kananaskis Village, this resort boasts excellent, modern infrastructure and top-notch trails. Downhill and cross-country equipment are both available for rent here .

Fortress Mountain
$55 day
take Hwy. 40
past Kananaskis Village
and turn right at Fortress Junction, Suite 505
1550 Eighth St. SW, Calgary, AB
T2R 1K1
☎(403)256-8473
☎244-6665
☎244-4909
for ski conditions

Fortress Mountain, located on the Continental Divide, at the edge of Peter Lougheed Provincial Park, is less popular than Nakiska but nevertheless has some very interesting runs.

Cross-Country Skiing

There are countless cross-country trails in the parks of the Rockies, whose tourist information offices distribute maps of the major trails around the towns of Banff and Jasper and the village of Lake Louise.

Canmore Nordic Centre
1988 Olympic Way, ste. 100
Canmore, AB, T1W 2T6
☎***(403)678-2400***
⇌***678-5696***
The Canmore Nordic Centre, which hosted the cross-country events of the 1988 Winter Olympics, deserves special mention for its magnificent network of trails.

Heli-Skiing

Heli-skiing is an extraordinary experience for top-notch skiers longing for untouched stretches of powder. The calmness and immensity of the surroundings are striking and you can take in panoramic views that could once be enjoyed only by mountain climbers. Prices for this type of excursion vary greatly, depending on where the helicopter takes you. We therefore recommend shopping around a bit.

Assiniboine Heli Tours
Box 2430
Canmore, AB, T0L 0M0
☎***(403)678-5459***
⇌***678-3075***
Assiniboine Heli Tours organizes group outings to the peaks around Banff, Lake Louise and Whistler, as well as the Purcell, Selkirk and Chilcotin Mountains.

Canadian Mountain Holidays
Box. 1660
Banff, AB, T0L 0C0
☎***(800)661-0252***
☎***(403)762-7100***
⇌***762-5879***
Canadian Mountain Holidays has been in operation for 30 years, and the quality of the service leaves nothing to be desired. You can choose from a wide variety of excursions ranging from one to several days in length. Professional guides escort visitors to Mount Revelstoke, Valemount, the Monashees and the Cariboos .

Selkirk Tangiers Helicopter Skiing
Jan to mid-Apr
Box 1409
Golden, BC, V0A 1H0
☎***(800)663-7080***
☎***(403)762-5627***
for Alberta
☎***(250)344-5016***
for British Columbia
Selkirk Tangiers Helicopter Skiing offers day- and week-long excursions in the Selkirk and Monashee Mountains.

R.K. Heli-ski Panorama
Dec to Apr
reservation counters
in the Banff Spring Hotel
and the Chateau Lake Louise
and in downtown Banff
at R&R Sports
☎***(250)342-3889***
☎***(800)661-6060***
⇌***(250)342-3466***
R.K. Heli-ski Panorama arranges guided excursions for intermediate and advanced skiers in the Purcell Mountains in British Columbia.

Mountain Climbing

Tour A: Banff National Park

Yamnuska
200, 58-103 Bow Valley Trail
Canmore
☎***678-4164***
⇌***678-4450***
www.yamnuska.com
Yamnuska is both the name of the climbing school and the name of the first mountain you see as you leave Calgary. The school offers a range of climbing courses, from glacier climbing, to mountain survival-training, to anything that has to do with mountaineering in general, whether by foot, skis or snow board. It's the most renowned school of its kind in the country, and its professionalism is impeccable.

Alpine Club of Canada
Indian Flats Road
4.5km east of Canmore
☎*678-3200*
⇄*678-3224*
The Alpine Club of Canada is also for mountain lovers since it has a wide range of expeditions, from the first great climb, to an easy afternoon climb. The possibilities are endless, and the prices accommodate all budgets. One of the most interesting excursions involves spending the night in one of many huts belonging to the association.

Tour C: Jasper National Park

Peter Amann of the **Mountain Guiding and Schools** offers mountaineering lessons for novices and experienced climbers alike *(from $150 for 2 days; Box 1495, Jasper, AB, T0E 1E0, ☎/⇄780-852-3237, mann@incentre.net)*.

Dog Sledding

Tour A: Banff National Park

Kingmik Expeditions Dog Sled Tours
Box 227
Lake Louise, AB, T0L 1E0
☎*(403)522-3525*
⇄*(250)344-5298*
⇄*(250)344-5282*
Kingmik Expeditions Dog Sled Tours has a variety of packages ranging from half-hour tours to five-day expeditions.

Snowy Owl Sled Dog Tours
Box 8039
Canmore, AB, T1W 2T8
☎*(403)678-4369*
⇄*678-6702*
Snowy Owl Sled Dog Tours specializes in dogsledding and ice-fishing trips.

Snowmobiling

Tour A: Banff National Park

The guides at **Challenge Enterprises Snowmobile Tours** *(909 Railway Ave., Box 8127, Canmore, AB, T1W 2T8, ☎ 403-678-2628 or 800-892-3429, ⇄ 678-2183)* are all instructors. Some tours last several days and offer a chance to explore some of the region's back country. Nights are spent in back-country cabins.

Tour D: Kootenay and Yoho National Parks

The **Golden Snowmobile Club** *(Box 167, Golden, BC, V0A 1H0; Chamber of Commerce, ☎ 250-344-7125)* arranges outings in the Golden area. You will be supplied with a map of the various trails.

Accommodations

Tour A: Banff National Park

Banff

Banff is a tourist town whose population doubles in summer, when, needless to say, the prices also double. The prices in brackets therefore show the variations between low and high seasons.

A list of private homes that receive paying guests is provided at the tourist information office located at 224 Banff Ave. You may obtain this list by writing to the following address:

Banff-Lake Louise Tourist Office
Box 900
Banff, AB, T0L 0C0
☎*(403) 762-8421*
⇄*(403) 762-8163*

It is impossible to reserve a campsite in advance in the park, which has a policy of first come, first served, unless you are leading a fairly large group, in which case you should contact the Parks Canada offices in Banff.

Campsites generally cost between $13 and $16, according to the location and the facilities at the site. We advise you to arrive early to choose your spot. In the high season, the Banff campgrounds are literally overrun with hordes of tourists. It is forbidden to pitch your tent outside the area set aside for this purpose. Camping at unauthorized sites is strictly prohibited, for reasons of safety and also to preserve the natural environment of the park.

Tunnel Mountain Trailer Campground
on Tunnel Mountain Rd.
near the Banff Youth Hostel
Tunnel mountain Trailer Campground has more than 300 spaces set up exclusively for trailers. Electricity, showers, toilets and telephones on site.

Tunnel Mountain 1 and 2
on Tunnel Mountain Rd
near the Banff Youth Hostel
Tunnel Mountain 1 and 2 has about 840 spaces for trailers and for tents.Toilets, showers and and telephones are available.

Two Jack Lake Campgrounds
$13-$16
take the road going
to Lake Minnewanka
then head toward Two Jack Lake
☎(403)762-1759
The two Two Jack Lake Campgrounds are located on either side of the road that runs alongside Two Jack Lake. There are showers at the campground near the water. The other campground, deeper in the forest, offers a more basic level of comfort. It is easier to find spaces at these two campgrounds than at those in Banff. Toilets and telephones on site.

Johnston Canyon Campground
$16
on Hwy. 1A
toward Lake Louise
a little before the
Castle Mountain crossroads
☎(403)762-1581
Set in the forest, the Johnston Canyon Campground is much less busy than the other campgrounds. Set up for trailers and tents, it offers about 100 places and is equipped with toilets, showers and telephones.

YWCA
$19-$60 per person
102 Spray Ave.
☎(403)762-3560
☎(800)813-4138
⇄762-2606
YMCA offers a very basic level of comfort. You must bring your own sleeping-bag if you want to sleep in a dormitory.

Otherwise, for about $60, you can rent a private room with a bathroom. Very near the centre of town.

Banff International Youth Hostel
$20 members
$29 non-members
Tunnel Mountain Rd.
Box 1358, Banff, AB
TOL 0C0
☎(403)762-4122
in Calgary ☎237-8282
Banff International Youth Hostel remains the cheapest solution, but it is often full. It is essential to reserve well in advance or else to arrive early. This friendly youth hostel is only about a 20min walk from the centre of town. It offers a warm welcome, and the desk staff will be pleased to help you organize river rafting and other outdoor activities.

Norquay's Timberline Inn
$64-$143 for rooms
$160-$285 for cabins
just before the entrance to Banff
north of the Trans-Canada Hwy.
and near Mount Norquay
Box 69, Banff, AB, TOL 0C0
☎(403)762-2281
⇄762-8331
Norquay's Timberline Inn offers views of Mount Norquay from its lower-priced rooms, and views of the valley and city of Banff from the others. Though the higher-priced rooms have prettier views, they unfortunately also overlook the Trans-Canada.

There are two very peaceful cabins available on the Mount Norquay side in the middle of the forest, one for six people and the other for four. This establishment plans to renovate its rooms completely in 2000-2001.

Red Carpet Inn
$65-$150
≡, ⊛, tv
425 Banff Ave.
☎762-4184
☎(800)563-4609
⇄762-4694
Recently renovated, the Red Carpet Inn offers simply decorated, lovely rooms. Enjoy a good night's sleep on the soft mattresses.

Holiday Lodge
$67 bkfst incl.
311 Marten St.
Box 904, Banff, AB, T0L 0C0
☎(403)762-3648
⇄762-8813
Holiday Lodge has five clean, relatively comfortable rooms and two cabins. This old restored house, located in the centre of town, offers good, copious breakfasts.

Homestead Inn
$70-$130
tv
217 Lynx St.
☎762-4471
☎(800)661-1021
⇄762-8877
The Homestead Inn is located in the heart of Banff, but not on busy Banff Avenue, which is an advantage in itself. Tastefully decorated rooms and large beds.

King Edward Hotel
$75-$150
tv
137 Banff Ave.
☎462-2202
☎(800)344-4232
⇄762-0876
The King Edward Hotel is one of the largest buildings in town. It had a complete facelift a while ago, but it has kept its old-world charm. The attentive staff makes for a pleasant stay.

Park Avenue Bed & Breakfast
$75 bkfst incl.
no credit cards
135B Park Ave., Box 783
Banff, AB, T0L 0C0
☎(403)762-2025
Park Avenue Bed & Breakfast rents two rooms exclusively to non-smokers.

Inns of Banff, Swiss Village and Rundle Manor
$80-$215
tv
600 Banff Ave.
Box 1077, Banff
AB, T0L 0C0
☎(403)762-4581
☎(800)661-1272
⇄762-2434
These three hotels are really one big hotel, with a common reservation service. Depending on your budget, you have the choice of three distinct buildings. Inns of Banff, the most luxurious, has 180 very spacious rooms, each facing a small terrace. The Swiss Village has a little more character and fits the setting much better. The rooms, however are a bit expensive at $150 and are less comfortable. Finally, Rundle Manor is the most rustic of the three but lacks charm. The Rundle's units have small kitchens, living rooms and one or two separate bedrooms. This is a safe bet for family travellers. Guests at the Rundle Manor and Swiss Village have access to the facilities of the Inns of Banff.

Banff Voyager Inn
$85-$140
⊛, tv, ⌂, ≈, ℜ
555 Banff Ave.
Box 1540, Banff, AB
T0L 0C0
☎(403)762-3301
☎(800)879-1991
⇄762-4131
Banff Voyager Inn has comfortable rooms, some with mountain views.

Bow View Motor Lodge
$90-$150
♿, ⊛, tv, ≈, ℜ
228 Bow Ave., Box 339
Banff, AB, T0L 0C0
☎(403)762-2261
☎(800)661-1565
⇄762-8093
The Bow View Motor Lodge has the immense advantage of being located next to the Bow River and far from noisy Banff Avenue. Only a five minute walk from the centre of town, this charming hotel provides comfortable rooms; those facing the river have balconies. The restaurant, pretty and peaceful, welcomes guests for breakfast.

Rundle Stone Lodge
$95-$190
♿, *tv*, ≈, ⊛
537 Banff Ave., Box 489
Banff, AB, T0L 0C0
☎(403)762-2201
☎(800)661-8630
⇄762-4501
Rundle Stone Lodge occupies a handsome building along Banff's main street. In the part of the building located along Banff Avenue, the rooms are attractive and spacious, each with a balcony. Some also have whirlpool baths. The hotel offers its guests a covered, heated parking area in the winter. Rooms for disabled travellers are available on the ground floor.

Tannanhof Pension
$95-$165 bkfst incl.
🐕
121 Cave Ave., Box 1914
Banff, AB, T0L 0C0
☎(403)762-4636
⇄760-2484
Tannanhof Pension has eight rooms and two suites located in a lovely, big house. Some rooms have cable television and private baths, while others share a bathroom. Each of the two suites has a bathroom with tub and shower, a fireplace and a sofa-bed for two extra people. Breakfast is German-style with a choice of four dishes.

Traveller's Inn
$95-$195
♿, , *tv*, ⌂, ⊛
401 Banff Ave., Box 1017
Banff, AB, T0L 0C0
☎(403)762-4401
☎(800)661-0227
⇄762-5905
Most rooms at the hotel have small balconies that offer fine mountain views. Rooms are simply decorated, big and cosy. The hotel has a small restaurant that serves breakfast, as well as heated underground parking, an advantage in the winter. During the ski season, guests have the use of lockers for skis and boots, as well as a small store for the rental and repair of winter sports equipment.

Caribou Lodge
$100-$190
♿, ⊛, *tv*, ℜ, ⌂, ⊘
521 Banff Ave., Box 279
Banff, AB, T0L 0C0
☎(403)762-5887
☎(800)563-8764
⇄762-5918
Caribou Lodge is another Banff Avenue hotel offering comfortable, spacious rooms. A rustic western decor of varnished wood characterizes the reception area and guest rooms.

Ptarmigan Inn
$100-$200
⊛, ⌂, ≡, ℜ, *tv*
337 Banff Ave
☎762-2207
☎800-661-8310
⇄762-3577
The Ptarmigan Inn reopened its doors in February 1999 after several million dollars' worth of renovations, which have made the place more attractive. The natural wood in particular adds charm to its 134 rooms.

Douglas Fir Resort & Chalets
$120-$200
=, ⊛, ⌂, ≡, *K*, *tv*
525 Tunnel Mountain Road
☎762-5591 or 800-661-9267
⇄762-8774
www.douglasfir.com
The recently renovated Douglas Fir Resort & Chalets has 133 rooms and fully equipped cottages (fridge, stove, fireplace, etc) that are ideal for families. Their pleasant layout makes them feel like apartments. The resort offers an incredible view of Mount Rundle and you can take advantage of the squash courts, pool and indoor waterslides.

High Country Inn
$125
⌂, *tv*, ≈, ⊛
419 Banff Ave., Box 700
Banff, AB, T0L 0C0
☎(403)762-2236
☎(800)661-1244
⇄762-5084
Located on Banff's main drag, this inn has comfortable, spacious rooms with balconies. Furnishings are very ordinary, however, and detract from the beauty of the setting.

Banff Rocky Mountain Resort
$150-$230
tv, ⊛, ≈, ⊘
at the entrance to the town along Banff Ave.
Box 100, Banff, AB, T0L 0C0
☎(403)762-5531
☎(800)661-9563
⇄(403)762-5166

Banff Rocky Mountain Resort is an ideal spot if you are travelling as a family in Banff National Park. The delightful little chalets are warm and very well equipped. On the ground floor is a bathroom with shower, a very functional kitchen facing a living room and dining room with a fireplace while upstairs are two bedrooms and another bathroom. These apartments also have small private terraces. Near the main building are picnic and barbecue areas as well as lounge chairs where you can lie in the sun.

Brewster's Mountain Lodge
$200-$400
⊛, △, *tv*
208 Caribou St.
Box 2286, T0L 0C0
☎(403)762-5454
☎(800)691-5085
⇄(403)762-3953

Brewster's Mountain Lodge features spacious rooms with a mountain decor including cosy log furniture. It is centrally located and a good place to organize your trip from as they offer many touring options.

Tunnel Mountain Chalets
$220-$280 per chalet
⊛, △, ≈, *tv*, *K*
intersection of Tunnel Mountain Rd.
and Tunnel Mountain Dr.
Box 1137, T0L 0C0
☎(403)762-4515
☎(800)661-1859
⇄(403)762-5183

Tunnel Mountain Chalets offers fully-equipped cottages and condo-style units with kitchens, fireplaces and patios. This is a great option for families and for those looking to save some money by preparing their own meals. The interiors are standard, but clean and very comfortable. The larger units can slepp up to eight people.

Rimrock Resort Hotel
$225-$1,200
⊛, ≡, ℜ, ≈, △, *tv*
100 Mountain Ave.
Box 1110, T0L 0C0
☎(403)762-3365
☎(800)661-1587
⇄(403)762-4132

From afar, the Rimrock Resort Hotel stands out majestically from the mountainside much like the Banff Springs does. The rooms are equally well appointed though more modern. The various categories of rooms are based on the views they offer, the best view is of the Bow and Spray Valleys ($335). The hotel is right across the street from the Upper Hot Springs.

Banff Springs Hotel
$240-$520
⊛, ⊘, ≈, △, ♿, 🐕, *tv*, ℜ, ≈, *bar*
Spray Ave., Box 960
Banff, AB, T0L 0C0
☎(403)762-2211
☎(800)441-1414
⇄762-4447

Banff Springs Hotel is the biggest hotel in Banff. Overlooking the town, this five-star hotel, part of the Canadian Pacific chain, offers 770 luxurious rooms in an atmosphere reminiscent of an old Scottish castle. The hotel was designed by architect Price, to whom is also credited Windsor Station in Montréal and the Château Frontenac in Quebec City. Besides typical turn-of-the-century chateau style, old-fashioned furnishings and superb views from every window, the hotel offers its guests bowling, tennis courts, a pool, a sauna, a large whirlpool bath, and a massage room. You can also stroll and shop in the more than 50 shops in the hotel. Golfers will be delighted to find a superb 27-hole course, designed by architect Stanley Thompson, on the grounds.

Mount Royal Hotel
$250
tv, bar, ⊛, ⊙, ℜ
138 Banff Ave., Box 550
Banff, AB, T0L 0C0
☎(403)762-3331
☎(800)267-3035
⇄762-8938
Mount Royal Hotel, right in the centre of town not far from the tourist information centre, rents comfortable rooms.

Between Banff and Lake Louise

Johnston Canyon Resort
$98-$240
from Banff, take the Trans-Canada Hwy. to the Bow Valley exit then take Hwy. 1A the Bow Valley Parkway
Box 875, Banff, AB, T0L 0C0
☎(403)762-2971
⇄762-0868
Johnston Canyon Resort constitutes a group of small log cabins right in the middle of the forest. The absolute calm is suitable for retreats. Some cabins offer a basic level of comfort, while others are fully equipped and have kitchens, sitting rooms and fireplaces. The biggest cabin can accommodate four people comfortably. A small grocery store, offering a basic range of products, is part of this tourism complex.

Near Silver City

Castle Mountain Campground
$13
on your right, just after Silver City
☎(403)762-1550
⇄762-3880
No reservation is required to spend the night here. You have to register yourself at the campground entrance, by placing your payment in one of the envelopes provided and dropping it into the payment box.

Castle Mountain Youth Hostel
$20/ members
$24/ non-members
27 km from Banff on Hwy 1A at the Castle Junction crossroads across from Castle Mountain Village
for reservations, call the Banff reservations office
☎(403)762-4122
⇄762-3441
Castle Mountain Youth Hostel occupies a small building with two dormitories and a common room set around a big fireplace. The atmosphere is very pleasant, and the manager, who is from Québec, will be happy to advise you on hikes in the area.

Castle Mountain Village
$190-$210
tv, K
Box 178, Lake Louise, AB
T0L 1E0
☎(403)522-2783
☎762-3868
Castle Mountain Village is a superb collection of 19 small log cabins located at Castle Junction on Hwy. 1A. Each cabin can accommodate four people, and some can house up to eight. A small grocery store provides everyday products. The interiors of the cabins are very comfortable and seem intended to make you feel at ease. Kitchens are fully equipped and include microwave ovens and dishwashers. The main bathrooms have whirlpool baths. A roaring fire in the fireplace and the VCRs provided in the newer cabins constitute the perfect remedy for those cold mountain evenings. A very good choice.

Lake Louise

Lake Louise Campground
$18
showers
leaving the Trans-Canada Hwy. turn left at the main Lake Louise crossroads and continue straight
then cross the railroad and turn left on Fairview;
the campground is at the end of the road
As everywhere in Lake Louise, there are few places available, making it important to arrive early. The Bow River cuts through the campground.

Canadian Alpine Centre
$21-$31 per person
♿, ⌂, *sb*
on Village Rd., Box 115
Lake Louise, AB, T0L 1E0
☎(403)522-2200
⇄522-2253
The Canadian Alpine Centre is a youth hostel offering rooms with two, four or six beds. Although fairly expen-

sive, it is much more comfortable than other youth hostels. Guests have access to a laundry room, a common kitchen, a library, and the little **Bill Peyto's Café**. The hostel is equipped to receive disabled travellers. A piece of advice: reserve well in advance.

Mountaineer Lodge
$100-$240
⌂, ♿, *tv*, ⊛
Box 150, Lake Louise, AB
T0L 1E0
☎(403)522-3844
⇄522-3902
Located in the village of Lake Louise, the Mountaineer Lodge has 78 rather simply furnished rooms.

Skoki Lodge
$131 per person fb
open mid-Dec to Apr and Jun to Sep
⌂, *outhouse*
reached by an 11km trail (hike, ride, or ski) from the Lake Louise ski slopes
Box 5, Lake Louise, AB
T0L 1E0
☎(403)522-3555
All meals are included in the price of the room.

Paradise Lodge & Bungalows
$135-$230
K, ♿, *tv*, ℝ
on your right, just after the Lake Moraine cutoff
Box 7, Lake Louise, AB, T0L 1E0
☎(403)522-3595
⇄522-3987
Paradise Lodge & Bungalows is a complex with 21 small log bungalows and 24 luxury suites. It should be noted that rooms do not have telephones.

Lake Louise Inn
$143-$264
*, *tv*, ≈, ℜ
210 Village Rd., Box 209
Lake Louise, AB, T0L 1E0
☎(403)522-3791
☎(800)661-9237
⇄522-2018
Lake Louise Inn is located in the village of Lake Louise. The hotel offers very comfortable, warmly decorated rooms.

Deer Lodge
$160-$210
ℜ, ⊛
near the lake
on the right before reaching the Chateau Lake Louise
Box 100
Lake Louise, AB, T0L 1E0
☎(403)522-3747
⇄522-3883
Deer Lodge is a very handsome and comfortable hotel. Rooms are spacious and tastefully decorated. The atmosphere is very pleasant.

Moraine Lake Lodge
$320-$395
♿, ℜ
Box 70
Lake Louise, AB, T0L 1E0
☎(403)522-3733
⇄522-3719
Jun to Sep
☎(250)985-7456
Oct to May
⇄(250)985-7479
Moraine Lake Lodge is located at the edge of Lake Moraine. Rooms do not have phones or televisions. The setting is magnificent but packed with tourists at all times, detracting from its tranquillity.

Chateau Lake Louise
$329-$490
♿, *tv*, ≈, ℜ, ⌂
Lake Louise, AB, T0L 1E0
☎(403)522-3511
⇄522-3834
Chateau Lake Louise is one of the best-known hotels in the region. Built originally in 1890, the hotel burned to the ground in 1892 and was rebuilt the following year. Another fire devastated parts of it in 1924. Since then, it has been expanded and embellished almost continuously. Today, this vast hotel, which belongs to the Canadian Pacific chain, has 511 rooms with space for more than 1,300 guests, and a staff of nearly 725 to look after your every need. Perched by the turquoise waters of Lake Louise, facing the Victoria Glacier, the hotel boasts a divine setting.

Post Hotel
$350-$520
tv, ≈, ℜ
Box 69, Lake Louise, AB
T0L 1E0
☎(403)522-3989
☎(800)661-1586
⇄522-3966
The magnificent Post Hotel is part of the Relais et Châteaux chain. Everything at this elegant establishment, from the rooms to the grounds, is tastefully and carefully laid out. The restaurant is exquisite and the staff, friendly. If you can afford the extra cost, then this is the best place in Lake Louise.

Canmore

Two campgrounds have been set up for trailers and tents less than 10km from Canmore on the way from Calgary. The **Bow River Campground** and the **Three Sisters Campground** each charge about $10 per site.

Restwell Trailer Park
$18
across Hwy 1A and the railway line near Policeman Creek
☎(403)678-5111
Restwell Trailer Park has 247 spaces for trailers and tents. Electricity, toilets, showers and water are available.

Alpine Club of Canada
$20-$35
4.5km east of Canmore on Hwy. 1A
☎678-3200
⇄678-3224
The Alpine Club of Canada offers an interesting alternative for nature lovers who want to sleep "in the great outdoors." This association has huts, not only near Canmore, but also in several areas of the Rocky Mountains. You can even combine hiking tours with accommodation in these huts.

Rundle Mountain Motel & Gasthaus
$63-$108
tv, ≈
1723 Mountain Ave.
Canmore, AB, T1W 1L7
☎(403)678-5322
☎(800)661-1610
⇄678-5813
Rundle Mountain Motel & Gasthaus is a motel modelled on Savoy-style chalets. It has 51 rooms that are in keeping with this type of establishment.

Ambleside Lodge
$65-$105
non-smokers only
123A Rundle Dr.
Canmore, AB, T1W 2L6
☎(403)678-3976
⇄678-3916
Ambleside Lodge welcomes you to a large and handsome residence in the style of a Savoyard chalet just a few minutes from the centre of town. The big, friendly common room is graced with a beautiful fireplace. Some rooms have private baths.

Cougar Canyon B&B
$65-$90
3 Canyon Rd., Box 3515
Canmore, AB, T0L 0M0
☎(403)678-6636
⇄(250)3293
Cougar Canyon B&B has two second-floor guest rooms each with an *en suite* full bath. One of the rooms has a queen-size bed, the other two twin beds. A loft adjoins these rooms and features panoramic views, a fireplace, a television, a VCR, and a small library. Guests join hosts for breakfast in a main-floor dining room with a double-sided fireplace which is very cozy in winter. Full breakfasts start with fresh-squeezed orange juice and include home baking. There are hiking trails at the back door, and four world-class golf courses and five ski hills are within a 1hr drive; cross-country skiing and mountain biking can be enjoyed across town at Canmore Nordic Centre. English and German spoken.

Best Western Green Gables Inn
$79-$139
≈, ℜ, *tv*, ⊙, ⊛
1602 Secnd Ave. (Hwy. 1A)
Canmore, AB, T1W 1M8
☎(403)678-5488
☎(800)661-2133
⇄678-2670
To reach the Best Western Green Gables Inn take the Canmore exit from the highway and follow Hwy. 1A. This Best Western hotel has plenty of charm, and the rooms are particularly spacious and tastefully decorated in very warm tones.

Lady MacDonald Country Inn
$80-$175
♿, *tv*
Bow Valley Trail, Box 2128
Canmore, AB, T0L 0M0
☎(403)678-3665
☎(800)567-3919
⇄678-9714
Lady MacDonald Country Inn is a magnificent little inn established in a very pretty house.

Eleven elegantly decorated rooms are placed at guests' disposal. Some rooms have been specially equipped to receive disabled travellers; others are spread over two floors to welcome families of four. The superb "Three Sisters Room" offers a magnificent view of the Rundle Range and Three Sisters mountains, as well as a fireplace and a whirlpool bath.

Georgetown Inn
$89-$169 bkfst incl.
♿, tv, ℜ
1101 Bow Valley Trail
Canmore, AB, T1W 1N4
☎(403)678-3439
⇄678-6909
Georgetown Inn has resolutely gone for an old-fashioned British ambiance. Rooms are comfortable, and some are equipped with whirlpool baths. Breakfast, which you can take in the Three Sisters dining room, is included in the price of your room. The fireplace, the old books and the reproductions hung on the walls give this place a warm atmosphere.

Rocky Mountain Ski Lodge
$100-$220
K, tv
1711 Mountain Ave., Box 8070
Canmore, AB, T1W 2T8
☎(403)678-5445
☎(800)665-6111
⇄678-6484
Rocky Mountain Ski Lodge faces a pleasant little garden. Rooms are clean and spacious. Units with living-rooms, fireplaces, and fully equipped kitchens start at $120.

The Creek House
$195 or
$2,100- $2,800/week for 4 people
701 Mallard Alley
☎678-2463
☎(888)678-6100
⇄678-8721
www.creekhouse.com
The Creek House is one of the most beautiful places to spend the night in Canmore and all of the Rockies. Gail and Greg bought and completely renovated this old house on the edge of the Bow River, from where you can see Cascade Mountain (3,000m). The decor in the rooms is impeccable. An artist made some magnificent murals, such as the one in the stairwell. At the end of 1999, Greg added the final touch — a rooftop jacuzzi!

Tour B: The Icefields Parkway

Between Lake Louise and the Icefields Parkway

Honeymoon Lake Campground
$10
$3 extra for a wood fire
51km south of Jasper and
52km north of the
Columbia Icefield interpretive centre
With the Sunwapta falls close by, this campground promises you a fine view of the Athabasca Valley.

Jonas Creek Campground
$10
$3 extra for a wood fire
77km south of Jasper and
9km north of the
Beauty Creek Youth Hostel

Mount Kerkeslin Campground
$10
$3 extra for a wood fire
Mount Kerkeslin Campground is located 35km south of Jasper.

Rampart Creek Youth Hostel
$10/ members
$14/ non-members
closed Oct to Dec
near the campground
of the same name on Hwy. 93
☎(403)762-4122
Banff reservations centre:
☎(403)237-8282
Rampart Creek Youth Hostel comes off as a little rustic, but it is very well situated for hikers and cyclists visiting the glaciers.

Wilcox Creek Campground
Columbia Icefield Campground
$10
$3 extra for a wood fire
a few kilometres from the Columbia Icefield
These two campgrounds are equipped with the basics. You have to register yourself.

Waterfowl Lake Campground
$13
$3 extra for a wood fire
above Lake Mistaya
just after the Mount Chephren lookout
As everywhere in the parks, it is first come,

first served. Reservations onlu for groups. If that is the case, call the Parks Canada offices in Banff.

Athabasca Falls Youth Hostel
$15/ members
$19/non-members
32 km south of Jasper
☎(403)852-3215
In keeping with the rustic decor, this hostel has no running water, but it does have electricity and a kitchen. It is situated next to Athabasca Falls. Cyclists and hikers will appreciate this hostel's great location.

Beauty Creek Youth Hostel
$15/ members
$19/non-members
Sep to May people can pick up the key at the Jasper International Youth Hostel
$50 deposit
87km from Jasper and
17km north of the
Columbia Icefield interpretation centre
☎(403)852-3215
A day's pedalling from Jasper, this is a good spot for cyclists. The level of comfort is basic, but the atmosphere is pleasant. Moreover, you can take a side trip to beautiful Stanley Falls, located close by.

Hilda Creek Youth Hostel
$15/ members
$19/non-members
closed Oct to Dec
just before the entrance
to Jasper National Park
☎(403)762-4122
or the Calgary reservations centre
☎(403)237-8282
This is a genuine mountain refuge, with no running water or electricity. This spot is heartily recommended for hikers, because of its proximity to the finest hiking areas around the Athabasca Glacier. Information is available here, and the staff will be happy to indicate the must-sees. The welcome is friendly, and the scenery will take your breath away.

Mosquito Creek Youth Hostel
$15/members
$19/non-members
⌂
on Hwy. 93
a few kilometres after Lake Hector
to reserve, call the Banff Youth Hostel
☎(403)237-8282
☎762-4122
Mosquito Creek Youth Hostel offers a very basic level of comfort, with no running water or electricity. There is however a wood-fired sauna. Lodging is in mixed dormitories.

Rampart Creek Campground
$15 members
$19 non-members
$3 extra for a wood fire
a few kilometres from the intersection of Hwys. 11 and 93
The entrance to the campground is unguarded. You must register yourself, and leave the payment for your stay in an envelope.

The Crossing
$95
⌂, ℜ, *tv*, ⊛
at the crossroads of Hwys. 93 and 11, 80km from Lake Louise
Box 333, Lake Louise, AB
T0L 1E0
☎(403)761-7000
⇄761-7006
The Crossing is a good place to stop along the Icefields Parkway.

Num-Ti-Jah Lodge
$125-$180
pb
on the shore of Bow Lake
about 35 km from Lake Louise
☎(403)522-2167
⇄522-2425
Num-Ti-Jah Lodge was built by Jimmy Simpson, a famous mountain guide and trapper from the region. Jimmy Simpson's two daughters also have a place in the history of the Rockies. Peg and Mary became world-class figure skaters in their time and made numerous tours of Canada and the United States.

The name Num-Ti-Jah comes from a Stoney Indian word for pine marten. The spot is popular with tourists, because Bow Lake is one of the most beautiful lakes in the region.

Columbia Icefield Chalet
$160-$200
open May to mid-Oct
ℜ, ♿, *pb*
Box 1140, Banff, T0L 0C0
Icefields Parkway at the foot of the Athabasca Glacier
☎(403)852-6550
⇄(403)852-6568
off-season
☎/⇄ (403)762-6735
The Columbia Icefield Chalet, with its terrifc location, boasts equally terrific views. If you can afford the extra $25 opt for the glacier-view rooms. All rooms are fairly standard, with queen-sized beds and large bathrooms. You are staying here for the setting, after all.

Tour C: Jasper National Park

Jasper

Jasper Home Accommodation Association
$30-$60
Box 758, Jasper, T0E 1E0
www.visit-jasper.com/JHAA.html
The Jasper Home Accommodation Association is a group of private homes, each offering up to three bedrooms. The prices and inspections are regulated by Parks Canada, which insures certain quality standards. A good, reasonably priced alternative for those who want more than an anonymous hotel room.

Skyline Accommodation
$30-$50
sb
726 Patricia St., Box 2616
Jasper, AB, T0E 1E0
☎(403)852-5035
Roger and Judy Smolnicky have renovated their big house to create three spacious guest rooms. The shared bath is very clean.

Private Accommodation at the Knauers'
$60 bkfst incl.
sb/pb, tv
708 Patricia St., Box 4
Jasper, AB, T0E 1E0
☎(403)852-4916
⇄852-1143
Private Accommodation at the Knauers' has three fairly large rooms with their own private entrance. Two of the rooms are next to a big, attractive bathroom, while the other has its own facilities. There is a refrigerator at the entrance for guests. This spot is for non-smokers, and pets are not admitted. Continental breakfast is served in the rooms.

Patricia Lake Bungalows
$65-$140
summer only
tv, K, ⊛
5km north by Patricia Lake Road
☎852-3560
⇄952-4060
patlake@telusplanet.net
The Patricia Lake Bungalows are located in an idyllic setting in the mountains facing a pretty lake. The discreetly decorated individual bungalows are all cosy, and the kitchenettes make you feel at home. Just a stone's throw from outdoor activity areas.

Whistler Inn
$70-$268
tv, ℜ, ⌂
Box 250, Jasper, AB, T0E 1E0
☎ (403)852-3361
☎(800)282-9919
⇄852-4993
Renovations and upgrades have transformed the old Pyramid Hotel into the Whistler Inn. There is a steam room and an outdoor, rooftop hot tub. Each of the rooms, whose decor is standard but very tasteful, offers a view of the surroundings. Parking and ski lockers.

Maligne Lodge
$75-$164
≈, 🐕, ♿, ℜ, ⌂, ⊛
on Connaught Dr.
leaving Jasper toward Banff
Box 757, Jasper, AB, T0E 1E0
☎(403)852-3143
☎(800)661-1315
⇄852-4789
Maligne Lodge offers 98 very comfortable rooms and suites, some of

them with fireplaces and whirlpool baths.

Tonquin Inn
$79-$169
🐕, ♿, tv, ≈, △, K, ℜ
on Connaught Dr.
at the entrance to Jasper coming from Icefields Parkway
Box 658, Jasper, AB, T0E 1E0
☎(403)852-4987
☎(800)661-1315
⇄852-4413
The newer wing is laid out around the pool, providing all rooms with direct access to it. The rooms in the old wing are less attractive and resemble motel rooms, though they do provide an adequate level of comfort. We suggest, nevertheless, that you request a room in the new wing when reserving your room.

Astoria Hotel
$80-$139
ℜ, tv
404 Connaught Dr.
☎852-3351
☎(800) 661-7343
⇄852-5472
The Astoria Hotel has the character and charm of a small European hotel. The attractively designed building faces the busiest street in Jasper in the centre of town. Built in 1920, it's one the oldest building in Jasper.

Athabasca Hotel
$85-$135
sb/pb, ℜ, bar, tv
Box 1420, Jasper, AB
T0E 1E0
☎(403)852-3386
☎(800)563-9859
⇄852-4955
Athabasca Hotel is located right in the centre of Jasper, facing the Via Rail station and the Brewster and Greyhound bus terminal. Decorated in old English style, the rooms are appealing, but not very big. The least expensive are near a central bathroom, but the others have their own facilities. Neither flashy nor luxurious, this hotel is quite adequate, and the rooms are pleasant. This is the cheapest place to stay in Jasper, so you'll have to reserve in advance. The hotel does not have an elevator.

Marmot Lodge
$85-$170
♿, 🐕, tv, ≈, ℜ, K, ⊛
on Connaught Dr.
at the Jasper exit, toward Edmonton
Box 1200, Jasper, AB, T0E 1E0
☎(403)852-4471
☎(800)661-6521
⇄852-3280
Marmot Lodge offers very attractive rooms at what are considered reasonable prices in Jasper. The rooms are decorated in bright colours and old photographs hang on the walls, for a change from the normal decor. A terrace with tables has been set up in front of the pool, and this is a good spot for sunbathing. The decor, the friendly staff and the scenery all contribute to making this hotel a very pleasant place. It provides the best quality-to-price ratio in town.

Jasper Inn
$96-$400
tv, ℜ, ≈, K, ⊛, ℝ
98 Geikie St., Box 879
Jasper, AB, T0E 1E0
☎(403)852-4461
☎(800)661-1933
⇄852-5916
Jasper Inn offers spacious, attractive, comfortable rooms, some of them equipped with kitchenettes.

Amethyst Lodge
$119-$189
tv, ≡, ⊛
200 Connaught Dr.
☎852-3394
☎(888)8JASPER
⇄852-5198
Amethyst Lodge is a luxurious hotel whose exterior is not aesthetically pleasing, but its rooms are spacious and comfortable. Good location.

Lobstick Lodge
$119-$189
≡, ⊛, △, ℜ
96 Geikie St.
☎852-4431
☎(888)8JASPER
⇄852-4142
Lobstick Lodge is located some distance from town, but it's a fine, quality hotel.

Chateau Jasper
$128-$290
♿, ≈, ℜ
Box 1418, Jasper, AB, T0E 1E0
☎(403)852-5644
☎(800)661-9323
⇄852-4860
Chateau Jasper offers comfortable, very attractive rooms.

Tekkara Lodge
$139
K, ℑ
summer only
1km south of Jasper
☎852-3058
⇌852-4636
Tekkara Lodge is located in an idyllic spot near the banks of the Miette and Athabasca Rivers. The furnishing is luxurious and spacious, and includes a fireplace and a kitchenette. Open your window and let yourself be lulled by the streams that flow down the glaciers in front of your door.

Jasper Park Lodge
$169-$419
♿, ≈, ℜ, ℝ, tv, ⊙, ⊛, ⌂
Box 40, Jasper, AB, T0E 1E0
☎(403)852-3301
☎(800)441-1414
⇌852-5107
Jasper Park Lodge is beyond a doubt the most beautiful hotel complex in the whole Jasper area. Now part of the Canadian Pacific chain, the Jasper Park Lodge has attractive, spacious, comfortable rooms. It was built in 1921 by the Grand Trunk Railway Company to compete with Canadian Pacific's Banff Springs Hotel. The staff is very professional, attentive and friendly. A whole range of activities is organized for guests. These include horseback riding and river rafting. You will also find one of the finest golf courses in Canada, several tennis courts, a big pool, a sports centre, and canoes, sailboards and bicycles for rent in the summer, plus ski equipment in the winter. Several hiking trails crisscross the site, among them a very pleasant 3.8km trail alongside Lake Beauvert. Whether you're staying in a room in the main building or in a small chalet, you are assured of comfort and tranquillity.

Each year Jasper Park Lodge organizes theme events, and hotel guests are invited to participate. Some weekends may be dedicated to the mountains and relaxation, with yoga and aerobics classes as well as water gymnastics and visits to the sauna; while another weekend may be set aside for wine tastings of Beaujolais Nouveau; other activities are organized for New Year's. Ask for the activities leaflet for more information.

Sawridge Hotel
$169-$229
♿, tv, ≈, ℜ, ⊛, ⌂, laundry
82 Connaught Dr., Box 2080
Jasper, AB, T0E 1E0
☎(403)852-5111
☎(800)661-6427
⇌852-5942
Sawridge Hotel offers big, warmly decorated rooms.

Outside Jasper

Wapiti Campground
$14-$18
open Jun 9 to Sep 11
4 km from Jasper
Wapiti Campground has 366 sites for trailers and tents. Water, electricity and toilets are available.

Whistler Campground
$15-$22
open May 5 to Oct 10
2.5km south of Jasper
take Hwy. 93 then turn on the road leading to the Whistler Mountain ski lift, taking the first left for the campground
Whistler Campground, with its 781 sites, has facilities for both trailers and tents. Water, showers and electricity are available. You can also find firewood on the site. The maximum stay at the campsite is 15 days. To reserve, call the Parks Canada office in Jasper (see p 294).

Jasper's three youth hostels are located outside the town.

Jasper International Youth Hostel
$15/ members
$20/ non-members
7km west of Jasper taking the Skytram road
☎(403)852-3215
Jasper International Youth Hostel is quite a comfortable establishment. It is a few minutes' walk from the summer gondola that goes to the top of Whistler Mountain, where there is a superb view over the Athabasca Valley. Reserve well in advance.

Maligne Canyon Youth Hostel
$15/members
$19/non-members
closed Wed in winter
11km east of Jasper
on the Maligne Lake road
☎(403)852-3215
Maligne Canyon Youth Hostel comes across as the ideal spot for anyone who likes hiking and other outdoor activities. The Skyline hiking trail begins right near the hostel, leading experienced hikers through Alpine scenery. The hike takes two or three days, but the superb view over the Jasper valley is a good reward for your efforts. Also located near the hostel, the Maligne River canyon offers some fine rapids and waterfalls photo opportunities. Do not hesitate to talk with the manager of the hostel: he is an expert on local fauna and conducts research for Jasper National Park.

Mount Edith Cavell Youth Hostel
$15/members
$19/non-members
26km south of Jasper
take Hwy. 93A and then
go 13km up the curvy road
leading to Mount Edith Cavell
☎(403)852-3215
Mount Edith Cavell Youth Hostel constitutes a genuine high mountain refuge, without water or electricity. It is built on one of the most beautiful mountains in the area, Mount Edith Cavell. Take warm clothing and a good sleeping bag, for you are in a high mountain area, and the temperatures are unpredictable. If you enjoy tranquillity and beautiful walks, you are in paradise here.

Becker's Chalets
$75-$150 per cabin
♿, *tv, K,* ℜ
on Icefields Parkway
5 km south of Jasper
Box 579, Jasper, AB, T0E 1E0
☎(403)852-3779
⇄852-7202
Becker's Chalets, also located along the Athabasca River, are comfortable and well equipped. You will also find a laundromat.

Pine Bungalow Cabins
$75-$100
♿, *K*
on Hwy. 16
near the Jasper golf course
Box 7, Jasper, AB, T0E 1E0
☎(403)852-3491
⇄852-3432
Pine Bungalow Cabins fit the category of a motel. The cabins are fully equipped, and some even have fireplaces, but furnishings are very modest and in rather poor taste. All the same, it is one of Jasper's cheapest places to stay.

Jasper House
$80-$168
tv, K, ℜ
a few kilometres south of Jasper
on Icefields Parkway
at the foot of Mount Whistler
Box 817, Jasper, AB, T0E 1E0
☎(403)852-4535
⇄852-5335
Jasper House consists of a group of little chalet-style log houses built along the Athabasca River. Comfortable and quiet, the rooms are big and well equipped.

Pyramid Lake Resort
$89-$189
summer only
♿, *tv,* ℜ
on the shore of Pyramid Lake
5 km from Jasper
take Pyramid Lake Rd.
to Jasper and follow the signs
to Lake Patricia and Pyramid Lake
Box 388, Jasper, AB, T0E 1E0
☎(403)852-4900
☎852-3536
⇄852-7007
Pyramid Lake Resort offers simple but comfortable rooms facing Pyramid Lake, where you can enjoy your favourite nautical activities. Rentals of motorboats, canoes, and water-skis are available at the hotel.

Alpine Village
$100-$200 per cabin
tv, K, ℝ, ⊛
2km south of Jasper
near the cutoff for Mount Whistler
Box 610, Jasper, AB, T0E 1E0
☎(403)852-3285
Alpine Village is an attractive group of comfortable little wood cabins. Facing the Athabasca River, the spot is calm and peaceful. If possible, ask for one of the cabins facing the river directly: these are the most pleasant. Reserve far in advance, as early as January for the summer.

Miette Hot Springs

Miette Hot Spring Bungalows
$5-$80
K, ℜ
next to the Miette Hot Springs
Jasper East, Box 907, Jasper, AB, T0E 1E0
☎(403)866-3750
☎866-3760, in the off-season
☎852-4039
⇄866-2214

Miette Hot Spring Bungalows offers accommodations in bungalows and a motel. The motel rooms are rather ordinary, but those in the bungalows offer good quality.

Pocahontas Bungalows
$75-$110 per cabin
🐕, *K*
on Hwy. 16, near Punchbowl Falls
Box 820, Jasper, AB, T0E 1E0
☎(403)866-3732
☎(800)843-3372
⇄866-3777

Pocahontas Bungalows is a small group of cabins located at the entrance to Jasper National Park, on the road leading to Miette Hot Springs. The least expensive cabins do not have kitchenettes.

Outside Hinton

Suite Dreams B&B
$75-$100 bkfst incl
tv, ≡

When you arrive at the junction with the 40N, turn right toward the south, then immediately left onto William's Road. Located a few kilometres before Hinton, **Suite Dreams B&B** is a superb Victorian-style home that has three magnificently decorated bedrooms. Reserve early during the summer season.

Overlander Mountain Lodge
$100-$150
ℜ
2km to the left after leaving Jasper National Park toward Hinton
Box 6118, Hinton, AB, T7V 1X5
☎(403)866-2330
⇄866-2332

The Overlander Mountain Lodge has several charming cabins. This establishment is rendered more pleasant because it is set in a much calmer area than the outskirts of Jasper, and the surrounding scenery is truly exquisite. This place stands out from the majority of motel-style establishments in this town. Reservations should be made far in advance, as Hinton is a common alternative to lodging in Jasper.

Tour D: Kootenay and Yoho National Parks

From Castle Junction to Radium Hot Springs

Kootenay Park Lodge
$74-$92 per cabin
mid-May to late Sep
🐕, ℜ, ℝ
on Hwy. 93 heading south
42km from Castle Junction
Box 1390, Banff, AB, T0L 0C0
☎(403)762-9196
in the off-season, phone Calgary
☎/⇄ (403)283-7482

Kootenay Park Lodge rents 10 small log cabins clinging to the steep slopes of the mountains of Kootenay National Park. On site you will find a small store offering sandwiches and everyday items. The restaurant is open only from 8am to 10am, 12 to 2pm and 6pm to 8:30pm.

Storm Mountain Lodge
$125 per cabin
ℜ
after Castle Mountain Junction go toward Radium Hot Springs at your right from the Continental Divide between Alberta and British Columbia
Box 670, Banff, AB, T0L 0C0
☎(403)762-4155

Storm Mountain Lodge comprises 12 small cabins at the eastern entrance of Kootenay National Park. The level of comfort is basic, but the setting is enchanting.

The small restaurant closes very early.

Radium Hot Springs

Surprisingly, accommodations in Radium Hot Springs consist essentially of very ordinary motel rooms. All along the town's main drag you will find motel fronts that rival each other in ugliness. The region is popular with visitors, however, so here are a few suggestions.

Redstreak
$16-$21
☎250-347-9615
Located a short distance from the road before you arrive in Radium, Redstreak has 242 campsites and is the least expensive campground in the area. Toilets and showers on site.

Canyon Camp
$22
🐕, ☎
Box 279, Radium Springs
BC, V0A 1M0
☎(250)347-9564
⇄347-9501
Canyon Camp is an attractive campground with many spaces for trailers and tents along Sinclair Creek. The spots shaded by numerous trees confer a pleasing atmosphere on this campground. Toilets, showers and telephones on site.

Misty River Lodge
$55-$75
🐕, ≡, *tv, K*
5036 Hwy 93, Box 363
Radium Hot Springs, BC,
V0A 1M0
☎(250)347-9912
⇄347-9397
Misty River Lodge is the only exception to the "ugly-motel" rule in Radium Hot Springs. The rooms offer a decent level of comfort. The bathrooms are spacious and very clean. Without a doubt, the best motel in town.

Crystal Springs Motel
$48-$60
♿, *tv*, ⊛
Box 218, Radium Hot Springs,
BC, V0A 1M0
☎(250)347-9759
☎(800)347-9759
⇄ 347-9736

Crescent Motel
$75
tv
Box 116
Radium Hot Springs, BC,
V0A 1M0
☎250-347-9570

Both the Crystal Springs Motel and the Crescent Motel have typical motel-style rooms, although the Crescent is definitely not the friendliest place in town.

Motel Tyrol
$60-$70
⌂, ≈, ⊛
Box 312, Radium Hot Springs
BC, V0A 1M0
☎(250)347-9402
Motel Tyrol offers adequate, modestly furnished rooms. The terrace by the pool is pleasant.

The Chalet
$95
♿, ◷, ⌂, *tv*, ⊛
Box 456, Radium Hot Springs
BC, V0A 1M0
☎(250)347-9305
⇄347-9306
The Chalet offers several rooms with balconies, modestly furnished but comfortable. Perched above the little town of Radium Hot Springs, this big Savoy chalet-style house offers an interesting view of the valley below.

Radium Hot Springs Lodge
$100-$125
tv, ℜ, ≈, ⌂
facing the Radium Hot Springs thermal pool
Box 70, Radium Hot Springs,
BC, V0A 1M0,
☎(250)347-9341
☎(888)222-9341
⇄347-9342
Radium Hot Springs Lodge has large, extremely ordinary, though modestly furnished, rooms. Its restaurant tries to be chic but serves over-priced food of average quality. All the same, the hotel is well located and can be considered among the few good spots in Radium Hot Springs.

Fairmont Hot Springs

Fairmont Hot Springs Resort
$139
&, ≈, ℜ, *tv*, ℝ, ⊛, △, ℜ
on Hwy. 93-95
near the Fairmont ski hills
Box 10, Fairmont Hot Springs
BC, V0B 1L0
☎***(250)345-6311***
☎***(800)663-4979***
⇌***345-6616***

Fairmont Hot Springs Resort is a magnificent hotel complex, wonderfully laid out, offering special spa, ski and golf packages. Hotel guests can also take advantage of tennis courts and a two superb 18-hole golf course. Guests have unlimited access to the hot springs. This establishment also has a vast adjacent campground *($15-$35)*.

Invermere

Delphine Lodge
$60-$80 bkfst incl.
pb/sb, 🐕
Main St., Wilmer, V0A 1K0
☎ ***(250)342-6851***

The Delphine Lodge is actually in Wilmer, 5km from Invermere. Though the rooms are a bit small, they and the lodge are packed with lovely antiques and rustic furniture. Handmade quilts, pretty garden, a fireplace and various of special little touches make this historic inn (1890s) a cosy favourite. Non-smoking. Only small pets (check ahead).

Panorama Resort
$130-175
≈, ℜ, △, ⊛, *K*
18 km west of Invermere
Box 2797, V0A 1T0
☎***(250)342-6941***
☎***(800)663-2929***
⇌***(250)3442-3395***

Panorama Resort offers standard, pleasant hotel rooms, as well as equipped condo-style units, which are particularly handy if you are here to ski, downhill or cross-country. Besides skiing, tennis, horseback riding and golf are offered. Pleasant family atmosphere.

Fernie

Raging Elk Fernie Youth Hostel
$15 members
$16 non-members
Box 580, Fernie, V0B 1M0
☎***(250)423-6811***

Raging Elk Fernie Youth Hostel is the local YHA hostel. Rates include a pancake breakfast. There are two, four and six-bed rooms. Common kitchen, tv room and coin-laundry.

Yoho National Park

Monarch and **Kicking Horse Campsites**
$12-$17
☎***(205)343-6783***

Monarch and Kicking Horse are located a few kilometres east of Field. *toilets, showers at Kicking Horse*

Emerald Lake Lodge
$165-$275
Box 10, Field, V0A 1G0
☎***343-6321***
☎***(800)663-6336***
⇌***343-6724***

Emerald Lake Lodge, in Yoho National Park, was built by Canadian Pacific in the 1890s and today is an exquisite mountain hideaway. The central lodge, built of hand-hewn timber, is the hub of activity, while guests stay in any of 24 cabins. Each room features a fieldstone fireplace, willow-branch chairs, a down duvet, a private balcony and terrific lake views. Just 40km from Lake Louise.

Golden and Surroundings

Golden Municipal Campground
$15
🐕
1407 S. Ninth St., Box 350
Golden, BC, V0A 1H0
☎***(250)344-5412***

Golden Municipal Campground has 70 spaces for tents and trailers. The campground is situated next to tennis courts and a pool and has toilets and showers.

Whispering Spruce Campground and RV Park
$15
open Apr 15 to Oct 15
🐕, ☎
1422 Golden View Rd.
Box 233, Golden, BC, V0A 1H0
☎***(250)344-6680***

Whispering Spruce Campground and R.V. Park has 130 spaces for tents and trailers. Arrive early to reserve your place. Laundromat, showers and telephones on site.

Columbia Valley Lodge
$55-$75 bkfst incl.
on Hwy 95 a few kilometres south of Golden, Box 2669A
Golden, BC, V0A 1H0
☎/⇄ (250)348-2508
Columbia Valley Lodge has 12 rustic rooms. It resembles a mountain refuge with a basic level of comfort, but it is nonetheless completely adequate. This is a good stopping point for cyclists travelling around the area.

McLaren Lodge
$70 bkfst incl.
above Hwy. 95 leaving Golden toward Yoho National Park
Box 2586, Golden, BC
V0A 1H0
☎(250)344-6133
⇄344-7650
McLaren Lodge is a good spot in Golden for nature-lovers. The owners of this little hotel organize river-rafting excursions. Rooms are rather small and have a pleasant old-fashioned air. This spot has the best quality-to-price ratio in Golden.

Golden Rim Motor Inn
$80-$85
ℜ, *tv*
Box 371, Golden, BC, V0A 1H0
☎(250)344-5996
Golden Rim Motor Inn has ordinary motel-style rooms.

Prestige Inn
$110
*, ♿, *K*, ⊛, *tv*, ≈, ℜ, ⊙
1049 Trans-Canada Hwy
Box 9, Golden, BC, V0A 1H0
☎(250)344-7990
⇄344-7902
Prestige Inn is Golden's best hotel. Rooms are quite spacious, and bathrooms are well equipped.

Tour E: Kananaskis Country

Eau Claire Campground
$14
just north of Fortress Junction near the Fortress Mountain
☎(403)591-7226
Eau Claire Campground is a small campground situated right in the forest. Dress warmly, as the nights are cool in this spot.

Kananaskis Interlakes Campgrounds
$15
leaving Upper Kananaskis Lake go left and follow the road a few kilometres to Interlakes
☎(403)591-7226
Kananaskis Interlakes Campgrounds offers a superb vista over the lakes and forest. There is a no-reservations, first-come, first-served policy here.

Mount Kidd RV Park
$19-$30
*, ♿, ⌂
on Hwy. 40, a few kilometres south of Kananaskis Village
☎(403)591-7700
Mount Kidd RV Park has a surprising set-up. Located at the edge of the river in a forested area, it is definitely the most pleasant campground in the region. Guests also have the use of tennis courts or can head off on any of the many hiking trails in the area. Be sure to reserve ahead (groups especially) at this popular spot. Toilets, showers and laundromat on site.

Kananaskis Village

Ribbon Creek Youth Hostel
$15/ members
$19/ non-members
along the road leading to the central square of Kananaskis Village T0L 2H0
☎(403)762-4122
Ribbon Creek Youth Hostel is a pleasant little hostel that is almost always crowded. Do not wait to the last minute to reserve, or you will be disappointed. The common room, in front of the fireplace, is a pleasant spot to recover from the day's activities.

Best Western Kananaskis Inn
$160-$180
♿, *tv*, *K*, ⌂, ⊛, ≈, ℜ
on the town square of Kananaskis Village, T0L 2H0
☎(403)591-7500
☎(800)528-1234
⇄591-7633
Kananaskis Inn Best Western has 95 comfortable, pleasantly furnished rooms. The atmosphere at this hotel is quite agreeable, and the staff are friendly. However, the lobby is often besieged by visitors searching for souvenir shops or tea rooms.

The Canadian Pacific Lodge at Kananaskis & Kananaskis Hotel
$285
tv, ℜ, ≈, ⌂, ⊛, ⊙
on the Kananaskis Village town square, T0L 2H0
☎(403)591-7711
☎(800)441-1414
⇄591-7770
The Lodge at Kananaskis & The Kananaskis Hotel, along with the Hotel Kananaskis, are part of the Canadian Pacific hotel chain. The lodge has 250 spacious, intimate rooms of great comfort, and advance reservations are recommended year-round. The hotel itself offers 70 comfortable rooms and is very pleasant thanks to the friendly staff.

Restaurants

Tour A: Banff National Park

Banff

The restaurant at the Caribou Lodge (see p 335), **The Keg**, serves American breakfasts and buffet-style food.

The Cake Company
$
every day
218 Bear St.
☎762-2230
The Cake Company is a little tea room that is ideal for a hot drink and a delicious slice of home-made cake.

Joe BTFSPLK's
$
221 Banff Ave.
facing the tourist information centre
☎(403)762-5529
Joe BTFSPLK's (pronounced bi-tif'-spliks) is a small restaurant with 1950s decor and good hamburgers. You'll learn that Joe BTFSPLK was a strange comic book character who walked around with a cloud above his head causing disasters wherever he went. It seems the only way today to avoid annoyances (such as spending too much money) may be to come to this little restaurant, very popular with locals for the burgers, fries, salads, chicken fingers and milkshakes. The restaurant also serves breakfasts for under $6.

Rose and Crown
$
every day 11am to 2am
upstairs at 202 Banff Ave.
☎(403)762-2121
Rose and Crown prepares light meals consisting essentially of hamburgers, chicken wings and *nachos*. In the evening, the spot becomes a bar with musicians.

Silver Dragon Restaurant
$
every day 11:30am to 11pm
211 Banff Ave.
☎(403)762-3939
Silver Dragon Restaurant offers adequate Chinese cuisine. Delivery available.

Athena Pizza
$$
every day
112 Banff Ave.
☎762-4022 or **762-2022**
Athena Pizza cooks up pizzas in its oven after topping them with a ton of ingredients. Tasty pizza made to order.

Balkan Restaurant
$$
every day 11am to 11pm
120 Banff Ave.
☎(403)762-3454
Balkan Restaurant is Banff's Greek restaurant. The blue and white decor with fake vines and grape clusters, recalls the Mediterranean. The main dishes are good, although they are unimaginative and often show North American influences. The staff seems overworked and is not always very pleasant.

Grizzly House
$$
every day 11:30am to midnight
207 Banff Ave.
☎(403)762-4055
Grizzly House specializes in big, tender, juicy steaks. The western decor is a bit corny, but your attention will quickly be diverted by your delicious meal.

Korean Restaurant
$$
every day from 11:30am to 10pm
upstairs at Cascade Plaza
317 Banff Ave.
☎(403)762-8862
For anyone who has never tried Korean cuisine, here is a good

chance to discover fine, deliciously prepared food. The staff will be happy to advise you in your selections.

Magpie & Stump
$$
203 Cariboo St.
☎***762-4067***
Magpie & Stump serves Mexican dishes accompanied with refried beans, Spanish rice, salads, sour cream and salsa. Its classy decor gives it a distinguished ambience.

Sukiyaki House
$$
every day
upstairs at 211 Banff Ave.
☎***(403)762-2002***
Sukiyaki House offers excellent Japanese cuisine at affordable prices. The sushi is perfect, and the staff is very courteous. The impersonal decor, however, leaves a bit to be desired.

Ticino
$$
5:30pm to 10:30pm
415 Banff Ave.
☎***(403)762-3848***
Ticino serves pretty good Italian cuisine as well as fondues. The decor is very ordinary, and the music tends to be too loud.

Caboose
$$$
every day 5pm to 10pm
corner of Elk St. and Lynx St.
☎***(403)762-3622***
☎***762-2102***
Caboose is one of Banff's better eateries. The fish dishes, trout or salmon, are excellent, or you may prefer the lobster with steak, American style, or perhaps the crab. This is a favourite with regular visitors.

Le Beaujolais
$$$$
every day
212 Buffalo St.
☎***(403)762-2712***
Le Beaujolais prepares excellent French cuisine. The dining room is very elegant and the staff is highly attentive. British Columbia salmon, baked with Pernod, is a true delicacy. The best food in Banff.

Lake Louise

Beeline Chicken & Pizza
$
every day
in Samson Mall
in the centre of Lake Louise village
☎***(403)522-2006***
Beeline Chicken & Pizza prepares good hamburgers as well as pizzas, nachos and burritos.

Lake Louise Grill & Bar
$
every day
in Samson Mall
in the centre of Lake Louise village
☎***(403)522-3879***
Lake Louise Grill & Bar serves Chinese food and traditional American cuisine in lacklustre fashion.

Moraine Lake Lodge
$$
every day
at the edge of Morraine Lake
☎***(403)522-3733***
The Moraine Lake Lodge has a restaurant where you can enjoy good meals while contemplating the superb view over the lake and the Ten Peaks which stretch before your eyes.

Deer Lodge Restaurant
$$$
every day
near the lake on the right before the Chateau Lake Louise
☎***(403)522-3747***
Deer Lodge Restaurant is an attractive restaurant with a somewhat rustic decor. The food is excellent.

Edelweiss Dining Room
$$$
every day
Chateau Lake Louise
☎***(403)522-3511***
The Edelweiss Dining Room offers delicious French cuisine in very elegant surroundings with a view over the lake. Reservations are recommended.

Post Hotel
$$$
at the edge of the Pipestone River near the youth hostel
☎***(403)522-3989***
Post Hotel houses an excellent restaurant recognized by the Relais et Châteaux association. Reservations are necessary, because this is one of the best dining rooms in Lake Louise. The setting is enchanting.

Canmore

Boston Pizza
$
every day from 11am
1704 Bow Valley Trail
☎**(403)678-3300**
Boston Pizza falls into the fast-food category. This restaurant serves a wide variety of pizzas, nachos and big sandwiches.

The Kabin
$
every day
1712 Hwy. 1A
☎**(403)678-4878**
The Kabin offers copious breakfasts, as well as lunches and suppers, in a restored old wooden house. In warm weather, you can eat on the terrace.

Nutter's
$
every day
900 Railway Ave.
☎**(403)678-3335**
Nutter's is the best spot to find the fixings for sandwiches or other snacks for your backcountry hikes. You will find a large selection of energizing or natural foods to take out, or you can eat in at the small tables near the windows.

Santa Lucia
$
closed Sun
714 8th St.
☎**(403)678-3414**
Santa Lucia is a small Italian restaurant with a family atmosphere. The *gnocchis* are excellent. Delivery available.

Chez François
$$
adjacent to the Best Western Green Gables Inn
Hwy 1A
☎**(403)678-6111**
Chez François is probably the best place to eat in Canmore. The chef, who comes from Québec, offers excellent French cuisine and a warm atmosphere in his restaurant.

Peppermill
$$
726 Ninth St.
☎**(403)678-2292**
Peppermill is a good little 12-table restaurant with a traditional menu. The house specialty is pepper steak. The Swiss chef will happily serve a delicious *fendant du Valais* (Swiss white wine). Reservations are recommended.

Sinclairs
$$
every day
637 Eighth St.
☎**(403)678-5370**
Sinclairs offers good food in a warm ambiance enhanced by a fireplace. Reservations are recommended in high season, because the restaurant is often full. The restaurant also offers an excellent selection of teas, a rarity around here.

Tour B: The Icefields Parkway

This tour crosses a sparsely populated area, and restaurants are few and far between. There are nonetheless a few little cafés that serve light meals.

The Crossing
$-$$
every day
at the junction of Hwys. 93 and 11
80 km from Lake Louise
☎**(403)761-7000**
The Crossing houses a fairly large cafeteria with light meals where just about every traveller seems to stop. As a result, it is very crowded, with long line-ups.

Num-Ti-Jah Lodge
$-$$
every day
at the edge of Bow Lake
about 35km from Lake Louise
☎**(403)522-2167**
The café at the Num-Ti-Jah Lodge serves sandwiches, muffins and cakes. You can warm up in this little café with tea or other hot beverages. This spot is popular with tourists and is often crowded.

Tour C: Jasper National Park

Jasper

Bear's Paw Bakery
$
Cedar Ave.
near Connaught Dr.
☎**780-852-3233**
Bear's Paw Bakery makes buns and other treats at the crack of dawn. It also serves good coffee and juice. A good place for breakfast or a snack after hiking.

Coco's Café
$
every day
608 Patricia St.
☎(780)852-4550
Coco's Café is a little spot that serves bagels, sandwiches and cheesecake.

Miss Italia Ristorante
$
every day
610 Patricia St.
upstairs at the Centre Mall
☎(780)852-4002
Miss Italia Ristorante offers decent Italian cooking. The staff is friendly and attentive.

Smitty's Restaurant
$
near the tourist information centre
☎(780)852-3111
Smitty's Restaurant is a rather unattractive family restaurant, but it serves hearty pancake breakfasts and simple meals throughout the day.

Soft Rock Internet Cafe
$
633 Connaught Dr.
☎780-852-5850
The Soft Rock Internet Cafe is much more than simply a place to send a few E-mails. It serves up enormous breakfasts all day long.

Spooner's Coffee Bar
$
every day
610 Patricia St.
☎780-852-4046
Light meals and freshly squeezed juices are served at Spooner's Coffee Bar. The café has a good selection of teas. The view over the nearby mountains and the young atmosphere combine to make this a very pleasant spot.

The Jasper Marketplace
$-$$
627 Patricia St.
☎780-852-9676
The Jasper Marketplace is a pleasant place to have a snack any time of day. Healthy, quality food.

Amethyst Dining Room
$$
every day
in the Amethyst Lodge
200 Connaught Dr.
☎780-852-3394
The Amethyst Dining Room has been fully renovated and now offers its traditional menu in a pleasant atmosphere.

Cantonese Restaurant
$$
every day
across from the bus terminal on Connaught Dr.
☎780-852-3559
Cantonese Restaurant serves Szechwan and Cantonese dishes in a typically Chinese decor.

Jasper Inn Restaurant
$$
every day
Jasper Inn, 98 Geikie St.
☎780-852-3232
Jasper Inn Restaurant serves up excellent fish and seafood. This is a very popular spot.

Jasper Pizza Place
$$
402 Connaught Drive
☎780-852-3225
Jasper Pizza Place serves up a good selection of pizzas cooked in a conventional oven. Many original combinations are offered: spinach and feta cheese, Mexican with jalapeños…

L&W Restaurant
$$
corner Hazel Ave. and Patricia St.
☎780-852-4441
The L&W Restaurant is a family-style restaurant that serves steaks, spaghetti and other dishes in a beautiful dining room filled with plants.

Tokyo Tom's Restaurant
$$
every day
410 Connaught Dr.
☎780-852-3780
Tokyo Tom's Restaurant serves tasty Japanese food. The sukiyaki is excellent, but the gloomy decor is not.

Beauvallon Dining Room
$$$
every day
Charlton's Chateau Jasper
96 Geikie St.
☎780-852-5644
Beauvallon Dining Room prepares excellent French cuisine and is one of Jasper's finest dining establishments.

Beauvert Dining Room
$$$
every day
in Jasper Park Lodge
at the northern approach to Jasper
☎780-852-3301
Beauvert Dining Room is a rather fancy restaurant. The French cuisine on offer is excellent. One of the best restaurants in Jasper.

Outside Jasper

Pyramid Lake Resort
$
summer only, every day
at the edge of Pyramid Lake
5 km from Jasper
take Pyramid Lake Rd. to Jasper and follow the signs to Lake Patricia and Pyramid Lake
☎*(780)852-4900*
The restaurant at the Pyramid Lake Resort serves simple meals. The cuisine is good and unpretentious.

Alpine Village
$$
every day
2km south of Jasper
near the Mount Whistler cutoff
☎*780-852-3285*
The restaurant at the Alpine Village does not have a particularly pleasant decor, but the food is acceptable nonetheless.

Becker's Chalet Restaurant
$$
every day
on Icefield Parkway
5km south of Jasper
☎*780-852-3535*
Becker's Chalet Restaurant, located at the edge of the Athabasca River, serves perfectly decent traditional cooking. Unfortunately, the decor is rather impersonal.

Hinton and Surroundings

Athens Corner Restaurant
$
every day
in the Hill Shopping Centre
☎*780-865-3956*
Athens Corner Restaurant offers tried-and-true Canadian dishes as well as Greek and Italian items, all at reasonable prices.

Greentree Café
$
every day 5:30am to 11pm
in the Greentree Motor Lodge
☎*780-865-3321*
Greentree Café prepares delicious and copious breakfasts at unbeatable prices.

Ranchers
$
every day
in the Hill Shopping Centre
☎*780-865-4116*
Ranchers prepares all sorts of pizzas. This spot is generally quite busy.

Fireside Dining Room
$$
every day
in the Greentree Motor Lodge
☎*780-865-3321*
Fireside Dining Room is the best and most attractive restaurant in Hinton.

Overlander Mountain Lodge
$$$
every day
in the Overlander Mountain Lodge
2 km past the toll booths leaving Jasper National Park heading toward Hinton
head left toward the hotel
☎*780-866-2330*
The Overlander Mountain Lodge's attractive restaurant serves excellent food. The menu changes daily, but if you have the opportunity, give in to temptation and savour the rainbow trout stuffed with crab and shrimp and covered with *béarnaise* sauce.

Tour D: Kootenay and Yoho National Parks

Kootenay Park Lodge Restaurant
$
mid-May to late Sep
every day 8am to 10am
noon to 2pm and 6pm to 8:30pm
on Hwy. 93 heading south
42km from Castle Junction
☎*(403)762-9196*
Kootenay Park Lodge Restaurant offers light meals in simple surroundings. Isolated amidst grandiose scenery, you may want to finish your meal with a stroll through the surrounding countryside.

Storm Mountain Lodge Restaurant
$$
every day 7am to 10:30am
noon to 2pm and 5:30pm to 7:30pm
after Castle Mountain Junction head toward Radium Hot Springs watching for the restaurant on your right
☎*(403)762-4155*
Storm Mountain Lodge Restaurant closes very early. The braised salmon and the clams are excellent.The Lodge was recently renovated.

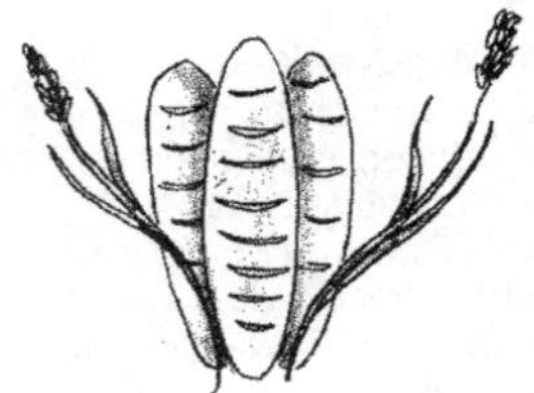

Radium Hot Springs and Surroundings

Husky House Restaurant
$
every day 7am to 10:30pm
next to the gas station at the junction with Hwy. 93
☎(250)347-9811
Husky House Restaurant offers simple meals at affordable prices.

Silver Garden Restaurant
$
every day
4935 Hwy. 93
☎(250)347-9848
Silver Garden Restaurant offers excellent Chinese food.

Fairmont Hot Springs Resort
$$
every day
on Hwy. 93-95 near the Fairmont ski hill
☎(250)345-6311
The restaurant at the Fairmont Hot Springs Resort will satisfy the most demanding customers. Its healthy food is excellent, and the decor is pleasant.

Radium Hot Springs Lodge
$$
every day
across from the Radium Hot Springs thermal pool
☎(250)347-9342
Some say Radium Hot Springs Lodge has the best dining room in Radium Hot Springs. This restaurant, however, seems a tad put-on and serves food that unfortunately is not worth what they charge for it and its staff is not very courteous.

Yoho National Park

Emerald Lake Lodge
$$$$
Box 10 Field
☎343-6321
Emerald Lake Lodge boasts one of the finest dining rooms in the Canadian Rockies. It serves Rocky Mountain Cuisine, a blend of the fine meals once served in CPR dining cars, the hearty fare once enjoyed by mountain guides and local ingredients like berries and wild game. The exceptional surroundings are sure to make your meal memorable.

Golden

As you cross the city, you will pass several fast-food restaurants.

Golden Rim Motor Inn
$
every day
1416 Golden View Rd.
☎(250)344-5056
Golden Rim Motor Inn houses a gloomy little restaurant which prepares simple, traditional items.

Golden Village Inn
$$
every day
on the Trans-Canada Hwy at the entrance to Golden
☎(250)344-5996
There is a restaurant in the Golden Village Inn. The building, perched on a hill, is relatively uncrowded, and the food is adequate.

Prestige Inn
$$
every day
1049 Trans-Canada Hwy
☎(250)344-7661
The restaurant at the Prestige Inn encompasses the best of traditional cuisine in Golden.

Tour E: Kananaskis Country

Chief Chiniki
$
every day
on Hwy 21, at Morley
☎(403)881-3748
Chief Chiniki offers typical North American dishes at reasonable prices. The staff is very friendly and attentive.

Obsessions
$
every day
in Kananaskis Village
Obsessions is a little bar reserved for non-smokers where light meals are served.

Kananaskis Inn Restaurant
$$
in the Kananaskis Inn in the centre of the village
☎(403)591-7500
The Kananaskis Inn Restaurant has a simple but warm decor. The menu is interesting, and the food is quite good.

Mount Engadine Lodge
$$
Spray Lakes Rd.
☎(403)678-2880
Mount Engadine Lodge offers an interesting *table d'hôte*. The European-style cuisine is delicious.

L'Escapade
$$$
in the Hotel Kananaskis
☎(403)591-7711
L'Escapade is the French restaurant located in the Hotel Kananaskis. Prettily decorated with red carpeting, comfortable armchairs and bay windows, this spot exudes warmth, all the better to linger over the excellent cuisine.

Entertainment

Tour A: Banff National Park

Banff

The primarily tourism-driven existence of the small town of Banff has lead to the opening of several establishments aimed at entertaining visitors. There is something here for everyone.

Banff Springs Hotel
Spray Ave.
☎(403)762-6860
The Banff Springs Hotel has a number of entertainment options, depending on what you're looking for. Dancing is possible in the Rob Roy room. Those in search of something more soothing can spend the evening in the Rundle Lounge where live classical piano music is presented.

Out of Bounds Bar & Grill
137 Banff Ave.
☎(403)762-8434
Out of Bounds Bar & Grill is a hopping night club that occasionally showcases live bands.

Rose and Crown
202 Banff Ave.
☎(403)762-2121
The Rose and Crown combines the western motif with classic English pub decor. There is a dance floor, and live bands often play here. You can also try your hand at a game of darts or pool.

Wild Bill's Legendary Saloon
upstairs at 201 Banff Ave.
☎(403)762-0333
If you prefer kicking up your heels in a real "western" setting, pull on your jeans and cowboy boots, grab your Stetson and saddle up for Wild Bill's Legendary Saloon. With a bit of luck, a friendly cowboy may just show you how to dance the two-step.

The Barbary Coast
upstairs at 119 Banff Ave.
☎(403)762-4616
The Barbary Coast presents rock and blues bands just about every night. This is a pleasant, friendly spot.

King Eddy's Billiards
upstairs at 137 Banff Ave.
☎(403)762-4629
Pool fans hang out at King Eddy's Billiards.

The Buffalo Paddock Lounge and Pub
124 Banff Ave.
☎(403)762-3331
The Buffalo Paddock Lounge and Pub is a huge, slightly noisy bar in the basement of the Mount Royal Hotel.

Bumper's Loft Lounge
603 Banff Ave.
☎(403)762-2622
Bumper's Loft Lounge often shows short skiing films and plays traditional and folk music.

Lake Louise

Nights out are considerable more laid back in the town of Lake Louise. There are, however, two favourites that are sure to please night owls.

The charming little **Charlie Two's Pub** is located in the **Lake Louise Inn** (*Village Rd.*, *☎(403)522-3791*). This is a pleasant spot to have a drink and listen to some music. Simple dishes are also served.

Glacier Saloon
Chateau Lake Louise
☎(403)522-3511
The Glacier Saloon generally attracts a young, dancing crowd.

Tour C: Jasper National Park

Jasper

There are two good spots for those in search of the latest tunes. They are **Pete's on Patricia** (*upstairs at 614 Patricia St., ☎780-852-6262*) and the **Atha-B Pub** (*Athabasca Hotel, 510 Patricia St., ☎780-852-3386*), each of which has a dance floor, the latest music and a bar. **Tent City** (*in the basement of the Jasper Park Lodge, ☎780-852-3301*) is a good choice for sports fans.

Nick's Bar
Juniper St. between Connaught Dr. and Geikie St.
☎(780)852-4966
Nick's Bar shows acrobatic skiing movies on a large screen – the stuff of dreams for those who wish they could tear down the slopes on two skis. A few light dishes are also served here. A pianist provides the musical entertainment some evenings.

Those in search of an English-style pub have two choices: the **Whistler Inn** (*105 Miette Ave., ☎780-852-3361*) is great for a pint and a game of darts or pool (a warm fireplace makes for a cozy atmosphere), while **Champs** (*Sawridge Hotel, 82 Connaught Dr., ☎780-852-5111*) offers a similar type of diversion with dart boards and pool tables.

Buckles Saloon
at the west end of Connaught Dr.
☎780-852-7074
Country-music fans can do some two-stepping at Buckles Saloon. The decor is in keeping with Canada's wild west. You can dine on beer, hamburgers and sandwiches.

Bonhomme Lounge
Chateau Jasper
96 Geikie St.
☎780-852-5644
For a more relaxing ambience, you may prefer a fine liqueur and the classical harp music at the Bonhomme Lounge.

Shopping

Tour A: Banff National Park

Banff

Banff's main drag is lined with souvenir shops, sports stores and clothing stores of all kinds. When it comes to shopping, the landscape is dotted with jewellery, souvenirs, essentials, sporting goods and T-shirts.

The **Hudson's Bay Company** (*125 Banff Ave., ☎(403)762-5525*) is owned by the oldest clothing manufacturer in Canada, established in 1670, and still sells clothes, along with souvenirs, cosmetics and much more.

The Shirt Company (*200 Banff Ave., ☎(403)762-2624*), as its name suggest, sells T-shirts for all tastes and sizes.

Monod Sports (*129 Banff Ave., ☎403-762-4571*) is the place for all of your outdoor needs. You'll find a good selection of hiking boots, all sorts of camping accessories as well as clothing.

Known throughout Canada for their quality leather goods, **Roots Canada** (*134 Banff Ave., ☎403-762-3260*) sells shoes, purses, handbags and beautiful leather jackets, as well as comfortable clothing.

Orca Canada (*121 Banff Ave., ☎403-762-2888*) jewellers is good place for gift ideas. Many pieces found here, and in other jewellers in the region, contain "ammolite," a fossilized rock found in Alberta. Though it can be expensive, it does make a typically Albertan gift.

A Bit of Banff (*120 Banff Ave., ☎403-762-4996*) sells every kind of souvenir imaginable from postcards to posters, picture books on the Rockies, and Aboriginal masks and soapstone carvings. Be careful, however, as these carvings tend to be overpriced here.

The **Luxton Museum Shop** *(Luxton Museum, 1 Birch Ave., ☎403-762-2388)* is a small souvenir shop that sells First Nations artwork as well as books on the subject.

The **Chocolaterie Bernard Callebaut** *(Charles Reid Mall, 127 Banff Ave.)* is a favourite of Belgian-chocolate lovers. The truffles are excellent.

The **Wine Store** *(in the basement of 302 Caribou St., ☎403-762-3528)* is the place *par excellence* for a good bottle of wine.

Lake Louise and Surroundings

Moraine Lake Trading *(Moraine Lake Lodge, ☎403-522-3733)* is a small boutique where you'll find pieces of artwork made by Aboriginal artists.

Woodruff and Blum Booksellers *(Samson Mall, Lake Louise, ☎403-522-3842, ⇄ 522-2536)* has an excellent selection of both souvenir photography books and practical books on hiking trails in the region, rock-climbing, fishing and canoeing. It also sells postcards, compact discs, posters and topographical maps.

Tour C: Jasper National Park

Jasper

Maligne Lake Books *(Beauvert Promenade, Jasper Park Lodge, ☎780-852-4779)* sells beautiful books of photography, newspapers and novels.

Exposures Keith Allen Photography *(Building 54, Stan Wright Industrial Park, ☎780-852-5325)* does custom framing and has a large stock of black-and-white and colour photographs of the area dating from the 1940s on, including unedited shots of Marilyn Monroe from the making of *River of No Return*, which was filmed in Jasper.

Besides photo-developing services, **Film Lab** *(Beauvert Promenade, Jasper Park Lodge, ☎780-852-4099)* also offers professional photography services.

Jasper Originals *(Beauvert Promenade, Jasper Park Lodge, ☎780-852-5378)* sells interesting pieces of art in the form of paintings, sculptures, pottery and jewellery that make lovely souvenirs.

Jasper Camera and Gifts *(412 Connaught Dr., ☎780-852-3165)* has a good selection of books on the Rockies. You will also find Crabtree & Evelyn products here. The shop sells binoculars, so that you can observe the wildlife up-close when adventuring in the mountains, and also develops film.

The Liquor Hut *(Patricia St. and Hazel Ave., ☎780-852-3152)* stocks a fine selection of wines and spirits.

Outside Jasper

The **Sunwapta Falls Resort Gift Shop** *(53km south of Jasper, on the Icefields Parkway, ☎780-852-4852)* sells Aboriginal artwork like blankets, moccasins and soapstone carvings. The jewellery section of the boutique includes jade, lapis-lazuli and "ammolite" pieces.

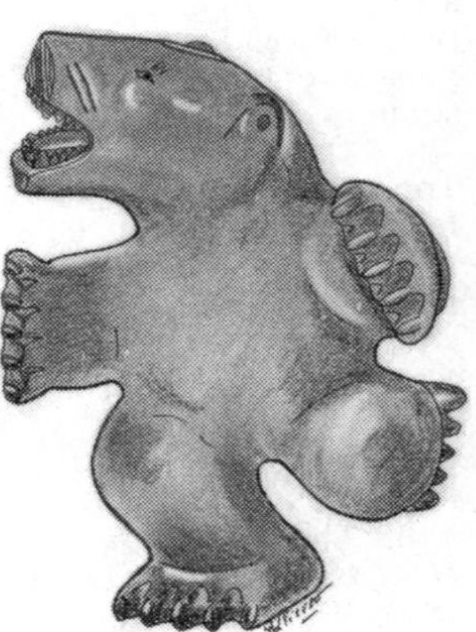

Calgary

Calgary is a thriving metropolis of concrete and steel, and a western city through and through.

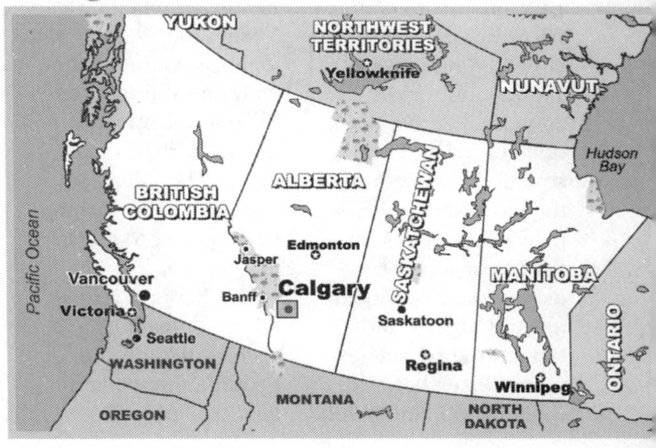

Set against the Rocky Mountains to the west and prairie ranchlands to the east, this young, prosperous city flourished during the oil booms of the 1940's, 1950's and 1970's but its nickname, Cowtown, tells a different story. Before the oil, there were cowboys and gentlemen, and Calgary originally grew thanks to a handful of wealthy ranching families.

The area now known as Calgary first attracted the attention of hunters and traders after the disappearance of the buffalo in the 1860s. Whisky traders arrived from the United States, generally causing havoc with their illicit trade. This brought the North West Mounted Police, and in 1875, after building Fort Macleod, they headed north and built a fort at the confluence of the Bow and Elbow Rivers. It was named Calgary, which in Gaelic means "clear, running water." The first settlers came with the railroad, when the Canadian Pacific Railway decided the line would cross the mountains at Kicking Horse Pass. The station was built in 1883 and the town site laid out; just nine years later, Calgary was incorporated as a city. Tragically, a fire razed most of it in 1886, prompting city planners to draw up a by-law stipulating that all new buildings had to be constructed of sandstone. Calgary thus took on a grand look of permanence that is still very much in evidence today.

Next came ranching. Over-grazed lands in the United States and an open grazing policy north of the border drew many ranchers to the fertile plains around Calgary. Wealthy English and American investors soon bought up land near Calgary, and once again Calgary boomed. The beginning of the 20th century was a time of population growth and expansion, only slightly jarred by World War I. Oil was the next big ticket. Crude oil was discovered in Turner Valley in 1914 and Calgary was on its way to becoming a modern city. Starting in the 1950's, and for the next 30 years, the population soared and construction boomed. As the global energy crisis pushed oil prices up, world corporations moved their headquarters to Calgary, and though the oil was extracted elsewhere, the deals were made here.

Thitry years ago, Robert Kroetsch, an Alberta storyteller, novelist, poet and critic, called Calgary a city that dreams of cattle, oil, money and women. Cattle, money and oil are still top concerns of many of the local residents, and as the city matures, issues like the arts, culture and the environment have also gained importance. Quality of life is a top priority here: urban parks, cycling paths and a glacier-fed river make the outdoors very accessible. Calgary is also the only Child Friendly city in North America, which means that children rate all the sights, restaurants, etc. The city gives much to its residents, and the residents give back. In 1988, they were both rewarded when Calgary hosted the Winter Olympic Games. After suffering through the drop in oil prices, the city flourished once again. The Olympics contributed something very special to the heritage of this friendly city; a heritage that is felt by Calgarians and visitors alike in the genuinely warm attitude that prevails.

Finding Your Way Around

By Car

The majority of Calgary's streets are numbered, and the city is divided into four quadrants, NE, NW, SE and SW. This may seem extremely unimaginative on the part of city-planners, but it makes it easy for just about anyone to find their way around. Avenues run east-west and streets run north-south. **Centre Street** divides the city between east and west, while the Bow River is the dividing line between north and south. The Trans-Canada Highway runs through the city, where it is known as 16th Ave. N. Many of the major arteries through the city have much more imaginative names; not only are they not numbered but they are called trails, an appellation that reflects their original use. These are **Macleod Trail**, which runs south from downtown (ultimately leading to Fort Macleod, hence its name); **Deerfoot Trail** which runs north-south through the city and is part of Highway 2; and **Crowchild Trail** which heads northwest and joins **Bow Trail** before becoming Highway 1A.

Calgary's "Motel Village" is located along 16th Ave. NW between 18th St. NW and 22nd St. NW.

Car Rentals

National Car Rental
Airport
☎ ***(403) 221-1692***
Northeast
2335 78th Ave. NE
☎ ***(403) 250-1396***
Southeast
114 Fifth Ave. SE
☎ ***(403) 263-6386***

Budget
Airport
☎ ***(403) 226-1550***
Downtown
140 Sixth Ave. SE
☎ ***(403) 226-0000***
☎ ***(800) 267-0505***

Avis
Airport
☎*(403) 221-1700*
Downtown
211 Sixth Ave. SW
☎*(403) 269-6166*
☎*(800) TRY-AVIS*

Thrifty
Airport
☎*(403) 221-1961*
Downtown
123 Fifth Ave. SE
☎*(403)262-4400*
☎*(800) 367-2277*

Discount
Airport
☎*(403) 299-1222*
Downtown
240 Ninth Ave. SW
☎*(403) 299-1224*

Hertz
Airport
☎*(403) 221-1300*
Downtown
Bay Store, 227 Sixth Ave. SW
☎*(403) 221-1679*

Dollar
Airport
☎*(403) 221-1888*

By Plane

Calgary International Airport is located northeast of downtown Calgary. It is Canada's fourth-largest airport and houses a whole slew of facilities and services. It features restaurants, an information centre, hotel courtesy phones, major car rental counters, currency exchange and a bus tour operator.

Air Canada, Canadian Airlines International, American Airlines, Delta Airlines, Northwest Airlines, United Airlines and K.L.M. all have regular flights to the airport. Regional companies (Air B.C. and Canadian Regional) also serve Calgary International.

There is a shuttle from the Calgary airport to the major downtown hotels; the **Airporter** (☎*403-531-3909*) charges $8.50 one-way and 15$ return, while a taxi will run about $25.

By Train

Via does not service Calgary. The train passes through Edmonton, there is a bus connection between the two cities.

The only rail service from Calgary is offered by **Great Canadian Railtour Company Ltd. - Rocky Mountain Railtours**. See p ? for more information.

By Bus

Calgary Greyhound Bus Depot
877 Greyhound Way SW, off 16th St.
☎*(403) 265-9111*
☎*(800) 661-8747*
Services: restaurant, lockers, tourist information.

Brewster Transportation and Tours offers coach service from Calgary to Banff departing from Calgary International Airport. For information call ☎*(403) 221-8242* or *(800) 661-1152*, or visit their web site at *www.brewster.ca*.

Public Transit

Public transit in Calgary consists of an extensive bus network and a light-rail transit system known as the **C-Train**. There are three C-Train routes: the Anderson C-Train follows Macleod Trail south to Anderson Road., the Whitehorn C-Train heads northeast out of the city and the Brentwood C-Train runs along Seventh Avenue and then heads northwest. The C-Train is free in the downtown core. You can transfer from a bus to a C-Train, tickets are $1.60 for a single trip or $5.50 for a day pass. For bus information call **Calgary Transit** at ☎*262-1000*; you can tell them where you are and where you want to go and they'll gladly explain how to do it.

By Foot

A system of interconnected enclosed walkways links many of Calgary's downtown sights, shops and hotels. Known as the **+15**, it is located 15 feet above the ground. The malls along Seventh Avenue SW are all connected as are the Calgary Tower, Glenbow Museum and Palliser Hotel.

Practical Information

The area code for Calgary is 403.

Information on everything from road conditions to movie listings to provincial parks is available from the **Talking Yellow Pages**. In Calgary call ☎*521-5222*. A series of recorded messages is accessible by dialling specific codes. The codes are listed in the front of the yellow pages phone book; Telephone booths usually have a telephone book.

Tourist Information

Calgary Tower Centre Tourist Information:
Centre St. and Ninth Ave. SW
Mid-May to early Sep, every day 8:30am to 5pm; winter, Mon to Fri 8:30am to 5pm, Sat and Sun 9:30am to 5pm
☎263-8510
☎800-661-1678

B&B Association of Calgary
☎543-3900
≠543-3901

Internet

There's no shortage of Internet cafés in Calgary. The cost is usually $10/hr to connect to the web. **Wired** (*$$; 1032 17th Ave. SW, between Ninth and Tenth Streets SW ☎244-7070, root@wired-café.com*) is conveniently located close to downtown.

ATTRACTIONS

Tour A: Downtown
1. Calgary Tower
2. Glenbow Museum
3. Olympic Plaza
4. City Hall
5. Stephen Avenue Mall
6. Devonian Gardens
7. Energeum
8. The Calgary Science Centre
9. Mewata Armoury

Tour B: Along the Bow River
10. Eau Claire Market
11. Prince's Island Park
12. Crescent Road Viewpoint
13. Chinese Cultural Centre
14. Fort Calgary
15. Deane House
16. Calgary Zoo, Botanic Gardens and Prehistoric Park

Tour C: Southeast and Southwest
17. Stampede Park
18. Saddledome
19. Grain Academy

ACCOMMODATIONS

1. Best Western Suites Calgary Centre
2. Calgary International Youth Hostel
3. Calgary Marriott Hotel
4. Inglewood Bed & Breakfast
5. Lord Nelson Inn
6. Plaza Regis Hotel
7. Prince Royal Inn
8. Sandman Hotel
9. St-Louis Hotel
10. The Palliser

RESTAURANTS

1. 1886 Café
2. Barley Mill
3. Buchanan's
4. Caesar's Steakhouse
5. Cajun Charlie's
6. CJ'S Pizza Place
7. Drinwaters Grill
8. Galaxie Diner
9. Good Earth Café
10. Heartland Café
11. Hy's
12. Joey Tomato's
13. Deane House Restaurant
14. Mescalero
15. Mongolie Grill
16. Nellie's Kitchen
17. Owl's Nest
18. Passage to India
19. Pongo
20. River Café
21. Sam's Original Deli and Restaurant
22. Silver Dragon
23. Teatro
24. The King & I Thai Restaurant
25. Wicked Wedge Pizza Co.

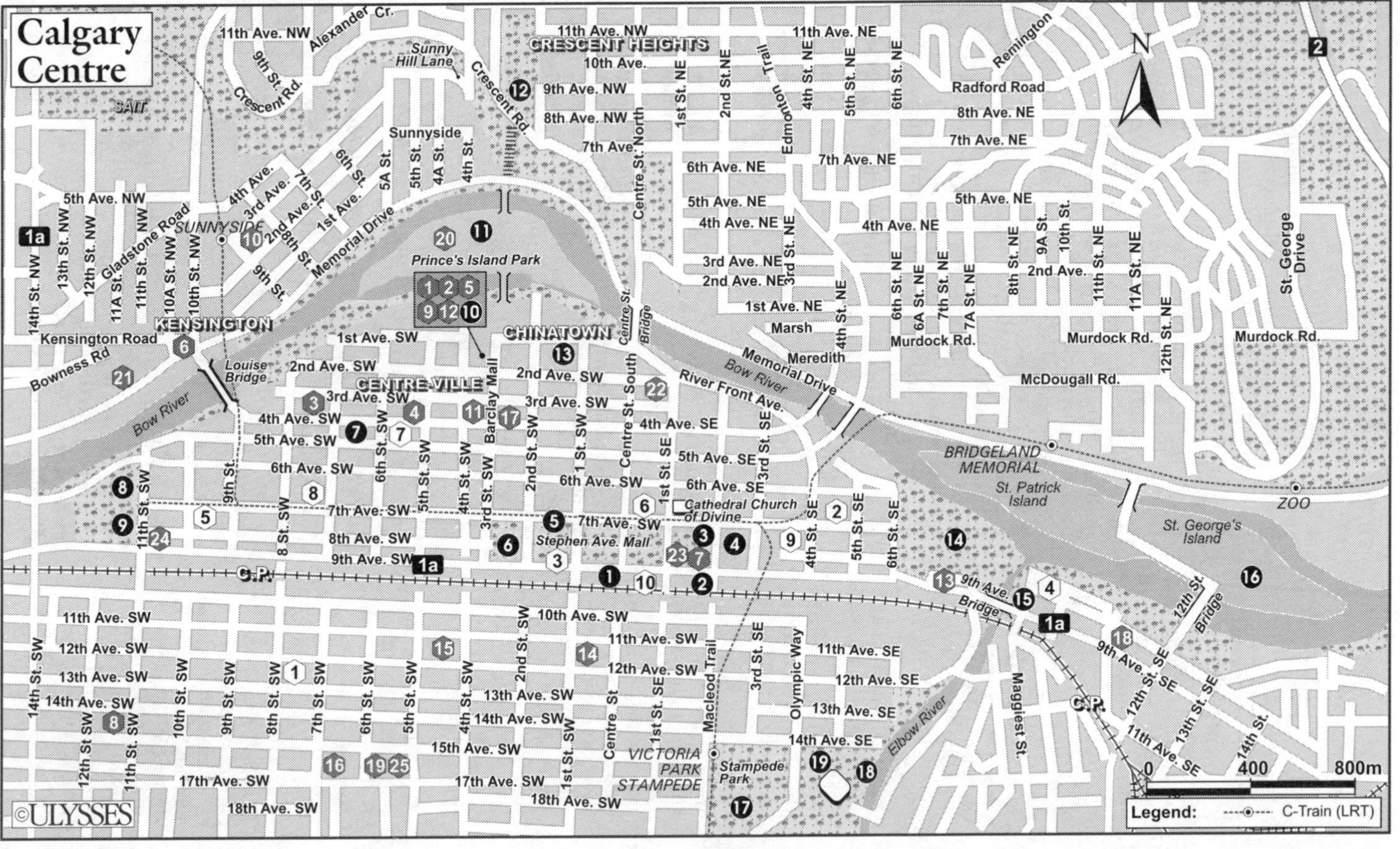
Calgary Centre
CRESCENT HEIGHTS
SUNNYSIDE
KENSINGTON
CHINATOWN
CENTRE-VILLE
Prince's Island Park
Bow River
Elbow River
BRIDGELAND MEMORIAL
St. Patrick Island
St. George's Island
ZOO
VICTORIA PARK STAMPEDE
Stampede Park
Stephen Ave. Mall
Cathedral Church of Divine
Barclay Mall
Louise Bridge
Centre St. Bridge
12th St. Bridge
9th Ave. Bridge
Memorial Drive
River Front Ave.
Kensington Road
Bowness Rd
Gladstone Road
Crescent Rd.
Edmonton Trail
Macleod Trail
Olympic Way
Murdock Rd.
McDougall Rd.
St. George Drive
Radford Road
Remington
Alexander Cr.
Sunny Hill Lane
Maggiest St.
Marsh
Meredith
SAIT
C.P.
N
0
400
800m
Legend:
C-Train (LRT)
©ULYSSES

Exploring

Tour A: Downtown

We recommend starting your tour of Calgary at the 190m, 762-step, 55-storey **Calgary Tower** ★★ (*$6.15; every day, summer 7:30am to 11pm, winter 8am to 10pm; Ninth Ave, corner of Centre St SW,* ☎*266-7171*). The city's most famous landmark not only offers a breathtaking view of the city, including the ski-jump towers at Canada Olympic Park, the Saddledome and the Canadian Rockies through high-power telescopes, but also houses the city's tourist information centre, a revolving restaurant and a bar. Photographers should take note that the specially tinted windows on the observation deck make for great photos.

Across the street, at the corner of First Street SE, is the stunning **Glenbow Museum** ★★★ (*$8; Mon to Wed 9am to 5pm, Thu and Fri 9am to 9pm; 130 Ninth Ave. SE,* ☎*268-4100*). Three floors of permanent and travelling exhibits chronicle the exciting history of Western Canada. The displays include contemporary and Aboriginal art, and an overview of the various stages of the settling of the West, from the First Nations to the first pioneers, the fur trade, the North West Mounted Police, ranching, oil and agriculture. Photographs, costumes and everyday items bring to life the hardships and extraordinary obstacles faced by settlers. There is also an extensive exhibit on the Aboriginal peoples of the whole country. Check out the genuine teepee and the sparkling minerals, both part of the province's diverse history. A great permanent exhibit documents the stories of warriors throughout the ages. The museum also hosts travelling exhibitions. Free gallery tours are offered once or twice weekly. Great museum shop and café.

The **Cathedral Church of the Redeemer** (*every day 11:30 to 1:30; 604 First Street SE,* ☎*269-1905*) brings calm and serenity to the feverish pace of the business district on Seventh Avenue SE (the C-Train street). The Victorian-style church, which was built in 1905, has an array of stained glass windows. Silence and reflection reign here.

Exit onto Eighth Ave. SE and head to the Olympic Plaza and City Hall.

Built for the medal presentation ceremonies of the '88 Winter Olympics, the **Olympic Plaza** ★★★ (*205 Eighth Ave. SE*) is a fine example of Calgary's potential realized. This lovely square features a large wading pool (used as a skating rink in winter) surrounded by pillars and columns in an arrangement reminiscent of a Greek temple. The park is now the site of concerts and special events, and is frequented by street performers throughout the year; it is also a popular lunch spot with office workers. Each pillar in the Legacy Wall commemorates a medal winner, and the paving bricks are inscribed with the names of people who supported the Olympics by purchasing bricks for $19.88 each!

Across from the Olympic Plaza is **City Hall** (Second St. SE, corner of Macleod Tr.), one of few surviving examples of the monumental civic halls that went up during the Prairies boom. It was built in 1911 and still houses a few offices.

At this point head west along Stephen Ave.

The **Stephen Avenue Mall** (*Eighth Ave between First St. SE and Sixth St. SW*) is an excellent example not only of Calgary's potential, but also of the contrasts that characterize this cowtown metropolis — the mall is part vibrant pedestrian meeting place, part wasteland and unsavoury hangout. It has fountains, benches, cobblestone, restaurants and shops, but also more than its share of boarded-up storefronts and cheap souvenir and T-shirt shops. The beautiful sandstone buildings that line the Avenue are certainly a testament to better and different times, as are the businesses they house, including an old-fashioned shoe hospital and several western outfitters. One of these buildings is the **Alberta Hotel**, a busy place in pre-prohibition days. Other buildings house trendy cafés and art galleries, as the street once again becomes a meeting place for lawyers, doctors and the who's who of Calgary, just as it was at the beginning of the century.

West of First Street SW, you might opt for the **+15 walkway system**, which provides an aseptic alternative to the street below. Purists may scoff at the city's system of interconnected walkways that can take you just about anywhere you want to go, but it is a wonderful alternative to the underground passages found in many large cities. And you certainly won't scoff on cold winter days, when the +15 provides warm, bright and welcome relief!

Among the city's stately buildings along the walkway is the **Hudson's Bay Company** department store, at the corner of First Street SW. Across First Street is **A+B Sound** at 140 Eighth Ave., a music store housed in the gorgeously restored former Bank of Montreal building.

Interconnected malls line the street west of First Street SW, including the Scotia Centre, TD Square, Bankers Hall, Eaton Centre and Holt Renfrew. Though this type of commercialism might not appeal to everyone, hidden within TD Square is a unique attraction — Alberta's largest indoor garden, **Devonian Gardens ★★** (*free admission, donations accepted; every day 9am to 9pm; 317 Seventh Ave. SW, between Second and Third Sts. SW, Level 4, TD Square, ☎268-3888*). For a tranquil break from shopping, head upstairs, where 1ha of greenery and blossoms await. Stroll along garden paths high above the concrete and steel and enjoy the art exhibitions and performances that are often presented here.

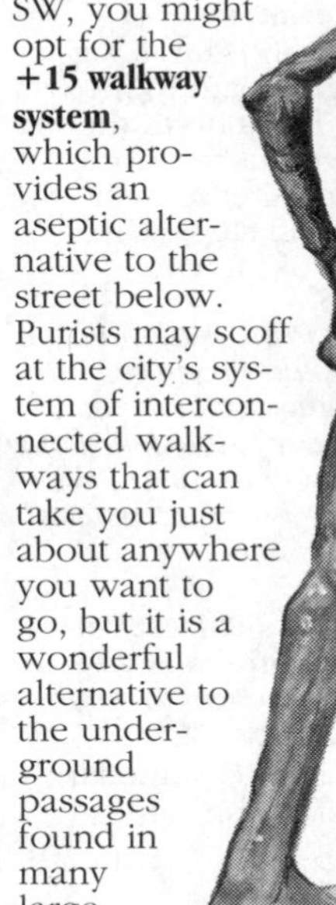

Public Sculpture in Calgary

Head west on foot along Eighth Ave SW. If you are tired you can take the LRT free of charge all along Seventh Ave SW, although the walk is easy and more interesting. Head up Fifth St. SW to the Energeum.

At the **Energeum ★**(*free admission; summer, Sun to Fri 10:30am to 4:30 pm; rest of year, Mon to Fri 10:30am to 4:30pm; Energy Resources Building, 640 Fifth Ave. SW, ☎297-4293*) you can learn all about Alberta's number one resource, energy. Whether it is oil, natural gas, oil sands, coal or hydroelectricity, everything from pipelines to rigs to oil sands plants is explained through hands-on exhibits and computer games.

Across the street is the Renaissance Revival **McDougall Centre**, a government building that was declared a historic site in 1982.

Return to Seventh Ave. SW and take the LRT to the end, then walk a block to the Science Centre.

The peculiar looking concrete building on 11th Street SW is **The Calgary Science Centre** ★★★ (*$9; every day 10am to 4pm; 701 11th St. SW, ☎221-3700*), a wonderful museum that children will love. Hands-on displays and multimedia machines cover a whole slew of interesting topics. The museum boasts a planetarium, an observatory, a science hall and two theatres that showcase mystery plays and special-effects shows. The recently completed 220-seat domed theatre features an exceptional sound system, all the better to explore the wonders of the scientific world.

South on 11th Street SW is the **Mewata Armoury**, a historic site that is now home to the King's Own Calgary Regiment and the Calgary Highlanders. For more information on Calgary's international military history, visit the Museum of the Regiments (see p 370).

Tour B: Along the Bow

Starting in trendy Kensington, this tour includes a lovely stroll along the Bow River.

Kensington is a hip area that is hard to pin down. To get a true sense of the alternative attitude that pervades the coffee shops, bookstores and boutiques, explore Kensington Road between 10th and 14th Streets NW.

From Kensington, cross the Louise Bridge and take the pathway along the Bow River to the Eau Claire Market.

The recently built **Eau Claire Market** ★★ (*Mon to Wed 10am to 6pm, Thu and Fri 10am to 9pm, Sat 10am to 6pm, Sun 10am to 5pm; next to the Bow River and Prince's Island Park, ☎264-6450*) is part of a general initiative in Calgary to keep people downtown after hours. The large warehouse-like building houses specialty food shops selling fresh fruit, vegetables, fish, meats, bagels and baked goods; neat gift shops with local and imported arts and crafts; clothing stores; a great bookstore; fast-food and fine restaurants; a movie theatre and a 300-seat **IMAX** (*☎974-4600*) theatre.

The area around the market has seen a considerable amount of development recently, including the construction of the market itself and of a beautiful new YMCA, plus the renovation of several buildings into restaurants and bars. It has become quite an appealing area to explore.

Take the Second Street Bridge to **Prince's Island Park** ★, a picturesque green space with jogging paths and picnic tables. You'll also find the lovely River Café (see p 378), which serves a delicious weekend brunch. Continue across the island and over the next bridge to the north side of the Bow. A long stairway leads up to the **Crescent Road Viewpoint** ★ atop McHugh Bluff, a zig-zagging path to the left also leads up to the viewpoint for those who prefer to avoid the 160-odd steps. Great view of the city.

Cross Prince's Island once again and continue walking east along the pathway to the stone lions of the Centre Street Bridge. Calgary's Chinatown lies to the south.

Calgary's **Chinese Cultural Centre** ★★ (*$2; every day 9am to 9pm; 197 First St. SW, ☎262-5071*) is the largest of its kind in Canada.

Craftsmen were brought in from China to design the building, whose central dome is patterned after the Temple of Heaven in Beijing. The highlight of the intricate tile-work is a glistening golden dragon. The centre houses a gift shop, a museum, a gallery and a restaurant.

Calgary's small **Chinatown** lies around Centre Street. Although it only has about 2,000 residents, the street names written in Chinese characters and the sidewalk stands selling durian, ginseng, lychees and tangerines all help to create a wonderful feeling of stepping into another world. The markets and restaurants here are run by descendants of Chinese immigrants who came west to work on the railroads in the 1880s.

Though the pathway continues along the Bow all the way to Fort Calgary, it is a long walk and not necessarily very safe. From Chinatown walk down to Seventh Ave. and take bus #1 or #411 to the fort.

Fort Calgary ★★★ (*$5; May to mid-Oct every day 9am to 5pm; 750 Ninth Ave. SE, ☎290-1875*) was built as part of the March West, which brought the North West Mounted Police to the Canadian west to stop the whisky trade. "F" Troop arrived at the confluence of the Bow and Elbow rivers in 1875, and chose to set up camp here either because it was the only spot with clean water or because it was halfway between Fort Macleod and Fort Saskatchewan. Nothing remains of the original Fort Calgary — the structures and outline of the foundations on the site today are part of an ongoing project of excavation and discovery undertaken mostly by volunteers. In fact, the fort will never be completely rebuilt as that would interfere with archaeological work underway. An excellent interpretive centre includes great hands-on displays (the signs actually say "please touch"), woodworking demonstrations and the chance to try on the famous, scarlet Mountie uniform. Friendly guides in period costume provide tours.

Polar Bear

Right on the other side of the Elbow River, across the Ninth Avenue Bridge is **Deane House** (*Wed to Sun 11am to 2pm, 806 Ninth Ave. SE, ☎269-7747*), the last remaining house from the garrison. It was built in 1906 for Richard Burton Deane, the Fort Post Commander at Fort Calgary who was later in charge of the jail in Regina where Louis Riel was held. The house originally stood next to the fort, across the river from its present location, and has been moved three times. Used in the past as a boarding house and as an artist's co-op, it has been restored and is now one of the city's better tea houses (see p 378).

Take the Whitehorn C-train from downtown northeast to the Calgary Zoo north entrance, or walk across the 12th St. Bridge to St. George's Island and the south entrance.

The **Calgary Zoo, Botanical Gardens and Prehistoric Park ★★** (*$9.50 summer, $8 winter; May to Sep, every day 9am to 6pm; Sep to May, every day 9am to 4pm; St. George's Island, 1300 Zoo Rd. NE, ☎232-9300 or 232-9372*) is the second largest zoo in Canada. It opened in 1920 and is known for its realistic re-creations of natural habitats, now home to over 300 species of animals and 10,000 plants and trees. Exhibits are organized by continent and include tropical birds, Siberian tigers, snow leopards and polar bears, as well as animals indigenous to this area. The Prehistoric Park recreates the world of dinosaurs with 27 full-size replicas set amidst plants and rock formations from prehistoric Alberta.

Beyond these two riverside attractions is an area known as **Inglewood**. Interesting shops, especially antique shops, line Ninth Avenue SE just beyond the Elbow River.

Tour C: Southeast and Southwest

This tour explores Calgary immediately south of downtown, which for the purposes of this guide, we will delineate by the CPR tracks between Ninth and 10th Avenues.

The Southeast is Calgary's industrial area, but it is also home to the largest urban park in Canada, Fish Creek Provincial Park (the park also stretches into the Southwest, see p 373), not to mention the site of the "Greatest Outdoor Show on Earth," the Calgary Stampede. At the intersection of Ninth Avenue SE and the Bow, lies the Inglewood Bird Sanctuary, a good spot for strolling and bird-watching (see p 373).

The Southwest is home to the city's more attractive neighbourhoods, most of them overlooking the Elbow River. In Mount Royal, for example, the lots and houses are much bigger than elsewhere in the city. The earliest settlement in this area was the Mission District, established by Catholic missionaries in the 1870s and known as Rouleauville at the time.

From downtown take the Anderson C-Train south to the Victoria Park/Stampede stop.

Unless you're in town during the Stampede, **Stampede Park** (*14th Ave. and Olympic Way SE*) has a limited appeal. The park is best known as the site of the famous Calgary Stampede, which takes place every year in July. Known simply as "The Week" by Calgarians, it is also called the "Greatest Outdoor Show on Earth." If you are around at this time of year, get out your Stetson, hitch up your horse and get ready for a rompin' good time, Ya-hoo! See the Entertainment section, p 382.

The Stampede grounds are used year-round for a variety of activities. The aptly named **Saddledome** has the world's largest cable-suspended roof and is a giant testimony to the city's cowboy roots. Apparently, there was some controversy over its name, though it is hard to imagine what else they could have called it! It is home to the city's National Hockey League team, the Calgary Flames, and is also used for concerts, conventions and sporting events. The figure skating and ice-hockey events of the 1988 Olympics were held here. Tours are available (*☎777-1375*). Also on the park grounds is the **Grain Academy** ★ (*free admission; year-round Mon to Fri 10am to 4pm; Apr to Sep, Mon to Sat noon to 4pm; on the +15 level of the Round-Up Centre, ☎263-4594*), which traces the history of grain farming and features a working railway and grain elevator. Finally, thoroughbred and harness racing take place on the grounds year-round and there is also a casino.

After exploring the Stampede grounds make your way west along 17th Avenue on foot or by catching bus #5 or #7 at First Street. Once at the corner of 17th Avenue SW and Fourth Street SW, a detour is called for.

Saddledome

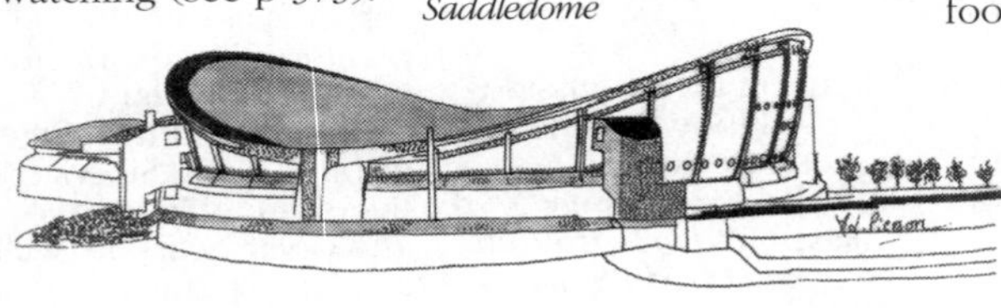

The Rodeo

Rodeos are business in Alberta. In some schools, cowboy skills are part of the sports program and are on a par with football and hockey.

There are essentially six official events in a rodeo. In the **bare-back-riding**, **saddle-bronc-riding**, and **bull-riding** events, the cowboy must stay on the bucking animal for eight seconds to even qualify, at which point he is given a score based on style, rhythm and control. In bare-back and saddle-bronc riding, the animal is a horse, and in all three cases a cinch is placed around the animal's hind quarters which causes him to buck. The bull-riding event is of course the most exciting, with the bulls weighing in at around 820kg.

In the **calf-roping** event the cowboy must lasso the calf from his horse, race to the animal and tie three of its legs. This is a timed event, and the time includes a final six seconds during which the calf must remain tied.

Big cowboys are the usual participants in the **steer-wrestling** event where the cowboy slides off his horse onto the steer, grabs its horns, twists them and throws the steer to the ground. Again the fastest time wins.

The **barrel-racing** event is the only one for cowgirls. Riders must circle three barrels in a clover-leaf pattern, and there is a five-second penalty for knocking one over. The fastest time wins.

Other entertaining events and rodeo clowns keep the crowd happy in between the official events. One of the most amusing crowd-pleasers is **mutton bus-ting**, where young cowpokes are strap-ped to sheep and sent flying around the corral.

Whether you continue west or decide to head north, the cafés, boutiques and galleries lining these two streets will draw you in.

Continue along 17th Avenue by car or on bus #94 to 24th Street and the Naval Museum.

Believe it or not, Canada's second-largest naval museum, the **Naval Museum of Alberta** (*free admission; Tue to Fri 1pm to 5pm, Sat and Sun 10am to 6pm; 1820 24th St. SW, ☎242-0002*) is over 1,000km from the ocean. It salutes Canadian sailors, especially those from the prairie provinces. The story of the Royal Canadian Navy unfolds from 1910 through photographs, uniforms, and models, as well as actual fighter planes.

To reach the Museum of the Regiments, take Crowchild Trail south or bus #63.

The **Museum of the Regiments** (*donation; Thu to Tue 10am to 4pm; 4520 Crowchild Trail SW, ☎974-2850*), Canada's second largest military museum, was opened by Queen Elizabeth in 1990. It honours four regiments: Lord Strathcona's Horse Regiment, Princess Patricia's Canadian Light Infantry, the King's own Calgary Regiment and the Calgary Highlanders. Uniforms, medals, photographs and maps of famous battles are displayed. Sound effects like staccato machine-gun fire and the rumble of far-off bombs create an eerie atmosphere as you tour the museum. Vintage tanks and carriers can be viewed on the spotless grounds of the impressive building that houses the museum.

To reach Heritage Park continue south on Crowchild, then take Glenmore Trail, turn right on 14th Street SW. Heritage Drive leads into the park.

Heritage Park Historical Village ★★ (*$11, May to Sep every day, Sep to Oct weekends and holidays only; 1900 Heritage Dr. SW, ☎259-1900*) is a 26ha park on the Glenbow Reservoir. Step back in time as you stroll through a real 1910 town of historic houses decorated with period furniture, wooden sidewalks, a working blacksmith, a teepee, an old schoolhouse, a post office, a divine candy store and the Gilbert and Jay Bakery, known for its sourdough bread. Staff in period dress play piano in the houses and take on the role of suffragettes speaking out for women's equality in the Wainwright Hotel. Other areas in the park recreate an 1880s settlement, a fur trading post, a ranch, a farm and the coming of the railroad. Not only is this a magical place for children, with rides in a steam engine and a paddlewheeler on the reservoir, but it is also a relaxing place to escape the city and enjoy a picnic.

Continue south on 14th Street SW and turn right on Anderson Road to reach the Tsuu T'Ina Museum, or take the Anderson C-Train south to the end of the line and then bus #504.

The **Tsuu T'Ina Museum ★** (*donation; Mon to Fri 8am to 4pm; 3700 Anderson Rd. SW, ☎238-2677*) commemorates the history of the Tsuu T'Ina First nation, who are Sarcee. Tsuu T'Ina means "great number of people" in their language. Nearly wiped out several times in the 1800s by diseases brought by Europeans, the Tsuu T'Ina were shuffled around reserves for many years but persevered and were eventually awarded their reserve on the outskirts of Calgary in 1881. They held on to the land, spurning pressure to sell it. Some of the pieces on display were donated by Calgary families who used to trade with the Tsuu T'Ina, whose reserve lies immediately to the west of the museum. Other items, including a teepee and two headdresses from the 1930s, were retrieved from the Provincial Museum in Edmonton.

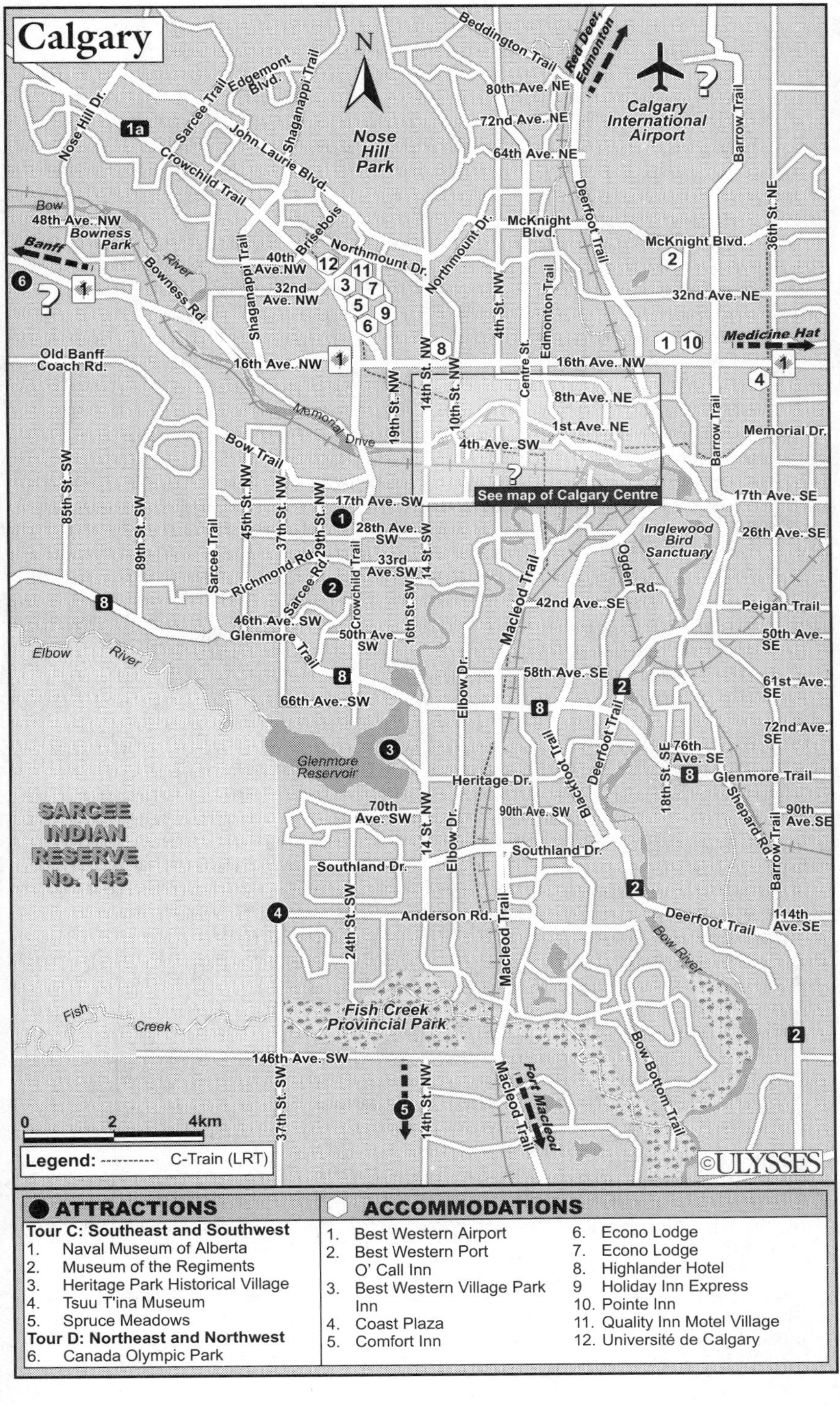
Calgary
N
Beddington Trail
Red Deer, Edmonton
80th Ave. NE
72nd Ave. NE
64th Ave. NE
Calgary International Airport
Barrow Trail
Nose Hill Park
Edgemont Blvd.
Shaganappi Trail
Sarcee Trail
Nose Hill Dr.
1a
John Laurie Blvd.
Crowchild Trail
Bow
48th Ave. NW
Bowness Park
Banff
River
Bowness Rd.
Brisebois
40th Ave.NW
32nd Ave. NW
Northmount Dr.
McKnight Blvd.
Deerfoot Trail
36th St. NE
32nd Ave. NE
4th St. NW
Edmonton Trail
Centre St.
Medicine Hat
Old Banff Coach Rd.
16th Ave. NW
14th St. NW
10th St. NW
19th St. NW
8th Ave. NE
1st Ave. NE
4th Ave. SW
Memorial Drive
Memorial Dr.
Bow Trail
See map of Calgary Centre
17th Ave. SW
17th Ave. SE
85th St. SW
69th St. SW
45th St. NW
37th St. NW
29th St. NW
Sarcee Trail
28th Ave. SW
33rd Ave.SW
Richmond Rd.
Sarcee Rd.
Crowchild Trail
14 St. SW
Inglewood Bird Sanctuary
26th Ave. SE
Ogden Rd.
42nd Ave. SE
Peigan Trail
Macleod Trail
46th Ave. SW
Glenmore Trail
50th Ave. SW
16th St. SW
Elbow Dr.
50th Ave. SE
Elbow River
58th Ave. SE
61st Ave. SE
66th Ave. SW
72nd Ave. SE
Glenmore Reservoir
Heritage Dr.
Blackfoot Trail
Deerfoot Trail
18th St. SE
76th Ave. SE
Glenmore Trail
Shepard Rd.
SARCEE INDIAN RESERVE No. 145
70th Ave. SW
90th Ave. SW
90th Ave.SE
Barrow Trail
Southland Dr.
Elbow Dr.
14 St. NW
24th St. SW
Anderson Rd.
Deerfoot Trail
114th Ave.SE
Bow River
Fish Creek
Fish Creek Provincial Park
146th Ave. SW
37th St. SW
Fort Macleod
Macleod Trail
Bow Bottom Trail
0 2 4km
Legend: C-Train (LRT)
©ULYSSES
ATTRACTIONS
Tour C: Southeast and Southwest
1. Naval Museum of Alberta
2. Museum of the Regiments
3. Heritage Park Historical Village
4. Tsuu T'ina Museum
5. Spruce Meadows
Tour D: Northeast and Northwest
6. Canada Olympic Park
ACCOMMODATIONS
1. Best Western Airport
2. Best Western Port O' Call Inn
3. Best Western Village Park Inn
4. Coast Plaza
5. Comfort Inn
6. Econo Lodge
7. Econo Lodge
8. Highlander Hotel
9 Holiday Inn Express
10. Pointe Inn
11. Quality Inn Motel Village
12. Université de Calgary

If show jumping is your thing you may want to take a little trip even farther south **Spruce Meadows** (*Marquis de Lorne Tr., ☎974-4200*). Four equestrian events take place here during the months of June, July and September. The rest of the year, visitors are welcome to look around.

Tour D: Northeast and Northwest

North of the Bow River, the biggest draws in the Northwest are Canada Olympic Park, Nose Hill Park (see p 373) and Bowness Park (see p 373); in the Northeast there isn't much besides the airport.

To reach Canada Olympic Park take Bow Trail, Sarcee Trail and 16th Ave. NW northwest.

Canada Olympic Park ★★★ (*museum $7, tours $10; summer every day 9am to 10pm, winter every day 9am to 6pm; on 16th Ave. NW, ☎247-5452*), or COP, built for the 1988 Winter Olympic Games, lies on the western outskirts of Calgary. This was the site of the ski-jumping, bobsleigh, luge, freestyle skiing and disabled events during the games, and it is now a world-class facility for training and competition. Artificial snow keeps the downhill ski slopes busy in the winter, and the park also offers tours year-round and the chance to try the luge in the summertime (*$13 for one ride, $22 for two*) or the bobsleigh in the winter, or view summer ski-jumping.

Visitors to COP have the choice of seven different guided tour packages ranging from a self-guided walking booklet to the Grand Olympic Tour for $10, which includes a guided bus tour, chairlift ride, the Olympic Hall of Fame and the tower. It is worth taking the bus up to the observation deck of the 90m ski jump tower visible from all over the city. You'll learn about the refrigeration system, which can make 1,250 tonnes of snow and ice in 24hrs, the infamous Jamaican bobsleigh team, the 90- and 70m towers and the plastic-surface landing material used in the summer. If you do decide to take the bus, sit on the left for a better view of the towers and tracks. The **Naturbahn Teahouse** (*☎247-5465*) is located in the former starthouse for the luge. Delicious treats and a scrumptious Sunday brunch are served, but be sure to make reservations. The **Olympic Hall of Fame and Museum** (*$3.75; mid-May to Sep every day 8am to 9pm, call ahead for winter hours; ☎247-5452*) is North America's largest museum devoted to the Olympics. The whole history of the games is presented with exhibits, videos, costumes, memorabilia and a bobsleigh and ski-jump simulator. You'll find a tourist information office and a gift shop near the entrance.

Parks

Prince's Island Park lies across the bridge at the end of Third Street SW. It is a small haven of tranquillity that is perfect for a picnic or a morning jog, and just 2min from downtown.

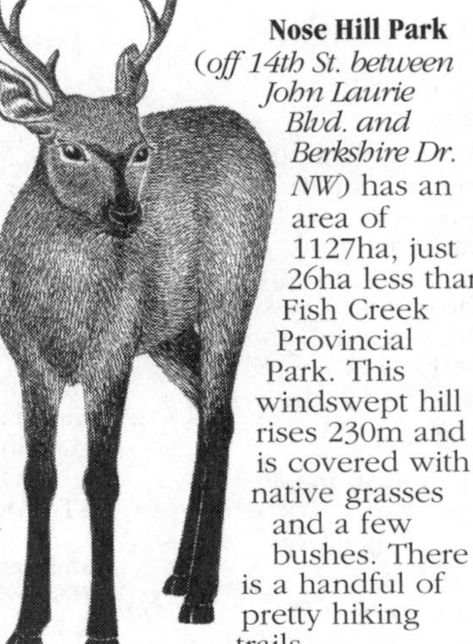

Fish Creek Provincial Park (*from 37th St. W to the Bow River*) lies south of the city. Take Macleod Trail south and turn left on Canyon Meadows Drive then right on Bow Bottom Trail, the information centre is located here (☎*297-5293*). It is the largest urban park in Canada and boasts paved and shale trails that lead walkers, joggers and cyclists through stands of aspen and spruce, prairie grasslands and floodplains dotted with poplar and willow trees. An abundance of wildflowers can be found in the park as can mule deer, white-tailed deer and coyotes. An interpretive trail, artificial lake and beach, playground and picnic areas are some of the facilities. Fishing is exceptional; you are virtually guaranteed to catch something. Horses may also be rented.

Bowness Park (*off 85th St. at 48th Ave. NW*) has always been a favourite escape for Calgarians. You can paddle around its pretty lagoons in the summer, while in the winter they freeze up to form the city's largest skating rink.

Nose Hill Park (*off 14th St. between John Laurie Blvd. and Berkshire Dr. NW*) has an area of 1127ha, just 26ha less than Fish Creek Provincial Park. This windswept hill rises 230m and is covered with native grasses and a few bushes. There is a handful of pretty hiking trails.

Outdoor Activities

Golf

The **Mapleridge Golf Course** (*1240 Mapleglade Dr. SE,* ☎*974-1825*) and the **Shaganappi Golf Course** (*1200 26th St. SW,* ☎*974-1810*) are two of the nicer municipal golf courses in Calgary. Tee times for all City of Calgary courses can be booked one day in advance by calling ☎*221-3510.*

Skating

For the chance to skate on Olympic ice, head to Calgary's **Olympic Oval**. This world-class facility, built for the '88 Winter Olympics, is now used as a training centre. The public skating hours vary, but generally the rink is open to the public in the afternoon from noon to 1pm and in the evenings. It is a good idea to call ahead (☎*220-7890*).

For outdoor skating, nothing beats the frozen lagoons of Bowness Park.

Hiking

Calgary's trail system is extensive. There are marked paths all along the Bow River, the Elbow River, Nose Creek, around the Glenmore Reservoir and in Nose Hill Park.

Bird-Watching

Inglewood Bird Sanctuary (*donation; Mon to Thu 10am to 5pm, Fri to Sun 10am to 5pm; 2429 Ninth Ave. SE,* ☎*269-6688*) is 32ha of riverside land where more than 250 species of birds have been spotted over the years. There is an interpretive centre for information on these species and on Calgary's other wildlife.

Accommodations

There are often two rates for Calgary hotels and motels: a Stampede rate and a rest-of-the-year rate. The difference between the two can be substantial in some cases.

Tour A: Downtown

Calgary International Hostel
$16 members
$20 non-members
520 Seventh Ave. SE, T2G 0J6
☎***269-8239***
⇄***283-6503***
The Calgary International Hostel can accommodate up to 114 people in dormitory-style rooms. Two family rooms are also available in winter. Guests have access to laundry and kitchen facilities, as well as to a game room and a snack bar. The hostel is advantageously located two blocks east of City Hall and Olympic Plaza. Reservations are recommended.

The youth hostel is located a stone's throw from downtown, but it is also in a rather seedy – although safe – part of town. If the hostel is full, there are others in the area to chose from. However, be aware that these places are not very pleasant. Their only redeeming feature is their price.

St-Louis Hotel
$35
430 Eighth Ave. SE
☎***266-6341***
Among these hotels is the St-Louis Hotel, which is guarded by a gate that controls the comings and goings in the hotel. Considering the price and the area, nothing is comparable (except for the youth hostel).

Plaza Regis Hotel
$69
124 Seventh Ave. SE
☎***262-4641***
⇄***262-1125***
The Plaza Regis Hotel moves into the superior category. The 100 rooms are spacious, the beds are comfortable and the decor is attractive.

Inglewood Bed & Breakfast
$70-$95
1006 Eighth Ave. SE, T2G 0M4
☎/⇄***262-6570***
One of the most charming places recommended by the Bed & Breakfast Association of Calgary is the Inglewood Bed & Breakfast. Not far from downtown, this lovely Victorian house is also close to the Bow River's pathway system. Breakfast is prepared by Chef Valinda.

Tour B: Along the Bow

Lord Nelson Inn
$79-$95
ℜ, ≡, ⊛, *tv*, ℝ
1020 Eighth Ave. SW, T2P 1J2
☎***269-8262***
☎***800-661-6017***
⇄***269-4868***
The Lord Nelson offers reasonably priced hotel accommodation close to downtown and the C-Train.

Sandman Hotel
$109
ℜ, ≡, ≈, ⊛, *tv*, ⊙, ⌂
888 Seventh Ave. SW, T2P 3J3, Calgary
☎***237-8626***
☎***800-726-3626***
⇄***290-1238***
Travellers in search of a hotel with facilities and quality rooms should check out the Sandman Hotel. The heated parking and 24hr food services can come in handy.

Best Western Suites Calgary Centre
$89-$149
ℜ, ≡, *tv*, *K*, ⊙, ⌂, 🐕
1330 Eighth St. SW, T2R 1B6
☎***228-6900***
☎***800-981-2555***
⇄***228-5535***
This is perhaps one of the best values near the downtown area. All the rooms are suites with one or two bedrooms and kitchenettes.

Prince Royal Inn
$120-$155
ℜ, ⌂, ⏲, *tv, K*
618 Fifth Ave. SW, T2P 0M7
☎***263-0520***
☎***800-661-1592***
⇄***298-4888***
The weekly, corporate and group rates of the all-suite Prince Royal Inn make this perhaps the least expensive hotel accommodation right downtown. The fully equipped kitchens also help keep costs down.

Calgary Mariott Hotel
$149-$179
ℜ, ≈, ≡, ⊛, ⌂, ⏲, *tv*, 🐕, ♿
110 Ninth Ave. SE, T2G 5A6
☎***266-7331***
☎***800-228-9290***
⇄***262-8442***
The business-class Calgary Mariott Hotel is one of the biggest of the downtown hotels. Its spacious rooms are decorated with warm colours and comfortable furnishings.

The Palliser
$289-$368
ℜ, ≡, ⊛, ⌂, ⏲, *tv*, 🐕, ♿
133 Ninth Ave. SW, T2P 2M3
☎***262-1234***
☎***800-441-1414***
⇄***260-1260***
The Palliser offers distinguished, classic accommodations in true Canadian Pacific style. The hotel was built in 1914, and the lofty lobby, restored in 1997, retains its original marble staircase, solid-brass doors and superb chandelier. The rooms are a bit small but have high ceilings and are magnificently decorated in classic styles.

Tour D: Northeast and Northwest

Northeast (Near the airport)

Pointe Inn
$80
ℜ, ≡, *tv*, 🐕
1808 19th St. NE, T2E 4Y3
☎***291-4681***
☎***800-661-8164***
⇄***291-4576***
Travellers just passing through or who have early or late flight connections to make should consider the convenience and reasonable prices of the Pointe Inn. From their fresh appearance, you can tell that the rooms were recently renovated (1998). Laundry facilities.

Best Western Airport
$79-$109
ℜ, ≡, ≈, *tv*, 🐕
1947 18th Ave. NE, T2E 2T8
☎***250-5015***
☎***800-528-1234***
⇄***250-5019***
The Best Western offers similar accommodations, plus an outdoor pool.

Best Western Port O' Call Inn
$124-$129
ℜ, ≡, ≈, ⊛, *tv*, ♿
1935 McKnight Blvd. NE, Calgary, T2E 6V4
☎***291-4600***
☎***800-661-1161***
⇄***250-6827***
This Best Western is a full-service hotel with 24hr shuttle service to the airport, located close by. Facilities include an indoor pool and a racquetball court.

Coast Plaza Hotel
$165
ℜ, ≡, ≈, ⊛
1316 33rd Street NE
☎***248-8888***
☎***800-663-1144***
⇄***248-0749***
The Coast Plaza Hotel offers luxurious accommodations near the airport and is located a short distance from the C-train. The 248 rooms are spacious and comfortable, and the service is impeccable.

Northwest

Another inexpensive accommodation option, only available in summer, is to stay at the residences of the **University of Calgary** (*$20/person in the dormitories, $32/room and $50/suite; 3330 24th Ave. NW, Calgary,* ☎*220-3203*).

Calgary's Motel Village is quite something: car-rental offices, countless chain motels and hotels, fast-food and family-style restaurants and the Banff Trail C-Train stop. The majority of the hotels and motels look the same, but the more expensive ones are usually newer and offer more facilities. Most places charge considerably higher rates during Stampede Week.

The Red Carpet Motor Hotel
$49-$89
≡, ℝ, *tv*
4635 16th Ave. NW, T3B 0M7
☎286-5111
⇄247-9239
The Red Carpet Motor Hotel is one of the best values in Motel Village. Some suites have small refrigerators.

EconoLodge
$75
≡, ⌂, ⏲, *tv*
2440 16th Ave. NW, T2M 0M5
☎289-2561
⇄282-9713
The Econolodge offers clean, typical motel rooms with queen-size beds. There is no charge for local calls.

Comfort Inn
$78-$88
≡, ≈, ⌂, *tv*
2363 Banff Tr. NW, T2M 4L2
☎289-2581
☎800-228-5150
⇄284-3897
Rates at the Comfort Inn include a continental breakfast. Regular rooms are spacious and comfortable; suites are also available.

Highlander Hotel
$59-$149
ℜ, ≡, ≈, *tv*
1818 16th Ave., T2M 0L8
☎289-1961
☎800-661-9564
⇄289-3901
The Scottish decor of the Highlander Hotel is a nice change from the typically drab motel experience. Close to services and a shopping mall. Airport shuttle service available.

Econo Lodge
$89
ℜ, ≡, ≈, *K*, *tv*
2231 Banff Tr. NW, T2M 4L2
☎289-1921
⇄282-2149
Not to be confused with the other hotel of (almost) the same name above, the Econo Lodge is a good place for families. Children will enjoy the outdoor pool and playground, while the laundry facilities and large units with kitchenettes are very practical. The Louisiana family restaurant serves inexpensive ($) Cajun and Creole food.

Holiday Inn Express
$95
≡, ≈, ⊛, ⌂, ⏲, *tv*
2227 Banff Tr. NW, T2M 4L2
☎289-6600
☎800-HOLIDAY
⇄289-6767
The Holiday Inn express offers quality accommodations at affordable prices. Rooms are furnished with king- and queen-size beds, and a complimentary continental breakfast is served.

Quality Inn Motel Village
$109-$159
ℜ, ≈, ≡, ⊛, ⌂, ⏲, *tv*
2359 Banff Tr. NW, T2M 4L2
☎289-1973
☎800-221-2222
☎800-661-4667
⇄282-1241
The Quality Inn has a nice lobby and an atrium restaurant and lounge. Both rooms and suites are available. Good value for the price.

The Best Western Village Park Inn
$129-$149
ℜ, ≡, ≈, ⊛, *tv*, ♿
1804 Crowchild Tr. NW, Calgary, T2M 3Y7
☎289-0241
☎800-774-7716
☎800-528-1234
⇄289-4645
Another member of this well-known chain. Guests enjoy many services, including Budget car-rental offices. Rooms are nicely furnished with up-to-date colour schemes.

Restaurants

Tour A: Downtown

Schwartzie's Bagel Noshery
$
Eighth Ave. SW
☎296-1353
If you don't think you'll last until dinner, grab a bagel to go from Schwartzie's Bagel Noshery. Imagine the most typical and the most original bagels you can and they probably have one. You can also eat in; the interior is inviting and comfortable.

Drinkwaters Grill
$$
237 Eighth Ave. SE
☎264-9494
The new kid on the block when it comes to steakhouses in Calgary, its self-billing as "contemporary" is appropriate. The huge sky-blue-

coloured columns, modern tableaux, classic dark wooden chairs and upholstered banquettes are appealing. On the menu, there is everything from thin-crust pizza to spinach and strawberry salad, Chilean sea bass and, of course, a range of very acceptable sirloins, strips and other fine cuts, each with original accompaniments. They have theatre specials and a Happy Hour from 3:30pm to 7pm, Monday to Friday.

Grand Isle
$$
128 Second St. SE
☎***269-7783***
Grand Isle prepares many of the favourites of Cantonese cooking but prides itself on its fresh and light dishes and its Szechuan-inspired flavouring. The decor is understated and the staff particularly friendly.

The Silver Dragon
$$
106 Third Ave. SE
☎***264-5326***
This is one of the best of the many Chinese restaurants in Chinatown. The staff is particularly friendly and the dumplings particularly tasty.

Teatro
$$$
200 Eighth Ave. SE
☎***290-1012***
Right next to Olympic Plaza in the old Dominion Bank Building, boasts a great setting and stylish atmosphere. Traditional "Italian Market Cuisine", prepared in a wood-burning oven, becomes innovative and exciting at the hands of Teatro's chef Dany Lamote.

Caesar's Steakhouse
$$$$
512 Fourth Ave. SW
☎***264-1222***
and 10816 Macleod Tr. S
☎***278-3930***
One of Calgary's most popular spots to dig in to a big juicy steak, though they also serve good seafood. The elegant decor features Roman columns and soft lighting.

Hy's
$$$$
316 Fourth Ave. SW
☎***263-2222***
Hy's, around since 1955, is the other favourite for steaks. The main dishes are just slightly less expensive than Caesar's and the atmosphere is a bit more relaxed, thanks to wood panelling. Reservations are recommended.

Owl's Nest
$$$$
In the Westin Hotel, Fourth Ave. and Third St. SW
☎***266-1611***
Fine French and European dishes are artfully prepared at the Owl's Nest. Some are even prepared at your table and flambéed right in front of you. All of the ladies get a rose at this fancy dining establishment.

The Rimrock Room
$$$$
In the Palliser Hotel, 133 Ninth Ave. SW
☎***262-1234***
The Palliser Hotel's Rimrock Room serves a fantastic Sunday brunch and of course healthy portions of prime Alberta beef. The Palliser's classic surroundings and fine food coalesce into one of Calgary's most elegant dining experiences.

Tour B: Along the Bow

Good Earth Café
$
at Eau Claire Market, 200 Barclay Parade SW
☎***237-8684***
Good Earth Café is a wonderful coffee shop with tasty wholesome goodies all made from scratch. Besides being a choice spot for lunch, this is also a good source of picnic fixings.

Heartland Café
$$
corner of 940 Second Ave. NW and Ninth St. NW
☎ ***270-4541***
The café au lait whipped up by the Heartland Café is one of the best in town. They also have cinnamon buns and delicious soups, served in a warm decor accented by old varnished wood.

CJ'S Pizza Place
$$
1117B Kensington Rd., near 10th St. NW
☎ ***270-9787***
CJ'S Pizza Place is one of those rare places where pizza is the work of skilled hands. It's hard to chose between the vegetarian pine-nut pizza and the Louisiana Cajun chicken pizza…mmmmm!

 **The 1886 Café**
$-$$
every day 7am to 3pm; breakfast only
187 Barclay Parade SW
☎***269-9255***
The 1886 is right next door to the market and located in the old Eau Claire & Bow River Lumber Company building. Buffalo heads and a large collection of old clocks decorate the interior. Huge breakfast portions are served all day long.

Sam's Original Deli and Restaurant
$-$$
1160 Memorial Dr. NW
☎***270-3880***
This is a good spot for lunch while strolling through Kensington. Yummy chicken sandwiches, gourmet burgers, and Montreal-style smoked meat are among the main-course offerings, while for dessert there is cheesecake, double-fudge cake and to-die-for apple crisp. The good, solid food far outweighs the mediocre decor as a reason to choose Sam's. Also located at 933 17th Ave. SW and 2208 Fourth Street SW.

The Barley Mill
$$
201 Barclay Parade SW, next to the Eau Claire Market
☎***290-1500***
The Barley Mill is located in what appears to be a historic building, but is actually a new construction. An old-fashioned interior is successfully achieved with worn-down hardwood floors, a grand fireplace, an old cash register and a bar that comes all the way from Scotland. The menu includes pasta, meat and chicken dishes, as well as several imported beers on tap.

Cajun Charlie's
$$
Eau Claire Market
☎***233-8101***
In the market, Cajun Charlie's with its Mardi Gras masks, trombone and giant alligator crawling out of the wall, is a real hoot. Gumbo and jambalaya are, of course, among the offerings, but so are "voodoo wings" and Po'Boy sandwiches. Blues music adds to the ambience.

Deane House Restaurant
$$
year-round, Wed to Sun 11am to 2pm
806 Ninth Ave. SE, just across the bridge from Fort Calgary
☎***269-7747***
The Historic Deane House Restaurant is a pleasant tearoom located in the house of former RCMP commanding officer Richard Burton Deane. Soups and salads figure prominently on the menu.

Joey Tomato's
$$
208 Barclay Place SW, next to the Eau Claire Market
☎***263-6336***
The open concept design makes for a lively atmosphere. The patio can hold a large crowd. The food is Italian and includes a great selection of pastas, topped, by, among other things, original tomato sauces.

Stromboli Inn
$$
1147 Kensington Cresc. NW
☎***283-1166***
The Stromboli offers unpretentious service and ambiance and classic Italian cuisine. Locals recommend it for its pizza, though the menu also includes handmade gnocchi, plump ravioli and a delicious veal gorgonzola.

The River Café
$$-$$$
closed Jan and Feb
Prince's Island Park
☎***261-7670***
The River Café is only open during warm summer months, when brunch or lunch can be enjoyed outdoors in beautiful Prince's Island Park. Located in an old boathouse, this gem of a restaurant is the perfect escape from urban downtown Calgary, just across the Bow River. Reservations are highly recommended.

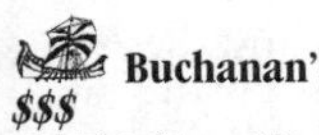 **Buchanan's**
$$$
738 Third Ave. SW
☎261-4646
Buchanan's gets the nod not only for its innovative steaks and chops in blue cheese sauce, but also for its excellent wine list (fine choices by the glass) and impressive selection of single malt scotches. This is a power-lunch favourite of Calgary's business crowd.

Tour C: Southeast and Southwest

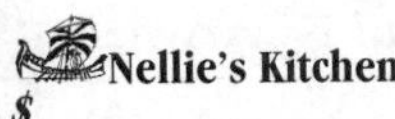 **Nellie's Kitchen**
$
17th Ave. SW between Seventh and Sixth St. SW
Everything is made from scratch at the informal Nellie's Kitchen, a neat little rendez vous for lunch and people-watching.

Wicked Wedge Pizza
$
618 17th Ave. SW
☎ 288-1024
The best slice of pizza south of the Bow River is served at Wicked Wedge Pizza. They concoct three different kinds of pizza every day using a variety of ingredients – from Mexican hot peppers, to tahini sauce, to marinated artichoke hearts.

Galaxie Diner
$
every day 8:00am to 4:00pm
11th St. SW, near 15th Ave. SW
For inexpensive breakfasts served at any time of day, go to Galaxie Diner. The decor doesn't look like it's changed here in 50 years. They serve hearty breakfasts as well as mouthwatering, home-made burgers.

4th Street Rose
$$
2116 Fourth St. SW
☎228-5377
The 4th Street Rose is a favourite. The fusion cuisine is very California and features lots of tasty vegetarian selections like Thai stir-fries and wraps, pasta dishes with wonderfully fresh ingredients and sinfully sweet desserts to finish it off. On warm summer days, the terrace is the place to be.

The King & I Thai Restaurant
$$
820 11th Ave. SW
☎264-7241
The King & I Thai Restaurant features an extensive menu of exotic dishes including delicious Chu Chu Kai. The ambience is modern and elegant.

Kremlin
$$
2004 Fourth St. SW
☎228-6068
This tiny restaurant serves Russian "love food" that you will fall in love with. The hearty borscht with herb bread is a real deal, or maybe you'll go for the perogies with their filling of the day or the oh-so-tender tenderloin with rosemary, red wine and honey. For dessert, who could say no to perogies filled with Saskatoon berries and topped with orange brandy cream sauce? The decor is eclectic, cosy and perfect for "love food."

Pongo
$$
524 17th Ave. SW
☎ 209-1073
Opening onto the street, the Pongo restaurant does not go unnoticed. Its modern Art-Deco design is extraordinary. The round white decorations everywhere create a science-fiction-like atmosphere, and the guests are lulled to the sound of jazz. The oriental cuisine is decent. Try the scrumptious chicken coconut curry.

Moti Mahal Restaurant
$$
1805 14th St. SW
☎ 228-9990
The Moti Mahal Restaurant offers good value for your dollar. It is, in fact, an all-you-can-eat Indian buffet. Unlike most restaurants of its kind, the food here is good quality (try the rice pudding at least twice) and the Indian-style decor is elegant. Reservations are recommended if you plan to go there for dinner.

Passage To India
$$
1325 Ninth Ave. SE
☎ ***263-4440***
The owner of Passage To India left India 30 years ago to come to Canada and brought his secret recipes along in his luggage. He recently left his job as a civil servant to devote himself full time to his culinary passion. The great variety of impressive dishes on the menu will definitely satisfy lovers of Indian cuisine (beef, chicken, vegetables, etc.). Even the wine and beer come from India.

The Mongolie Grill
$$
1108 Fourth St. SW
☎***262-7773***
The Mongolie Grill is truly a culinary experience. Diners choose meats and vegetables from a fresh food bar, the combination is then weighed (to determine the cost) and grilled right before your eyes. Roll it all up in a Mongolian wrap with some rice and hoisin sauce and there you go!

Entre Nous
$$-$$$
2206 Fourth St. SW
☎***228-5525***
Entre Nous, which means between us, boasts a friendly and intimate bistro atmosphere, perfect for savouring some good French food. Special attention to detail, from the hand-selected ingredients to the *table d'hôte* menu, make for a memorable dining experience. Reservations recommended.

Cannery Row
$$$
317 10th Ave. SW
☎***269-8889***
Cannery Row serves this landlocked city's best seafood. An oyster bar and casual atmosphere is intended to make you feel like you're by the sea, and it works. Fresh halibut, salmon and swordfish are prepared in a variety of ways. **McQueen's Upstairs** (***$$$***; *upstairs*, ☎*269-4722*) has a similar seafood-oriented menu but is slightly more upscale.

Mescalero
$$$
1315 First St. SW
☎***266-3339***
Mescalero serves up an eclectic blend of Southwestern, Mexican and Spanish cuisine, including simply divine veal cheeks, all cooked on an apple-wood-fired grill. They have a great courtyard, but unfortunately the service can be iffy at times.

The Casablancan Chef at the Sultan's Tent
$$$
909 17th Ave. SW
☎***244-2333***
This is the place for fine authentic Moroccan cuisine. In keeping with tradition, guests are greeted upon arrival with a basin of scented water with which to wash their hands. The room is decorated with myriad plush cushions and tapestries and the mood is set with lanterns and soft Arabic music. (Remember it is traditional to eat with your right hand as your left one is considered unclean.)

The Inn on Lake Bonavista
$$$$
747 Lake Bonavista Dr. SE
☎***271-6711***
This is one of Calgary's finest dining rooms with fine menu selections like filet mignon and Châteaubriand, complemented by fine views over the lake.

Tour D: Northeast and Northwest

The Blue House Cafe
$$
3843 19th St. NW
☎***284-9111***
The Blue House doesn't look like much, but the chef's Argentinian creations, especially the fish and seafood dishes, more than make up for it. Another plus is the flamenco and three-finger guitar performances on some evenings. The mood it fairly casual, but a bit dressier in the evenings.

The Naturbahn Teahouse
$$
Sunday brunch and tea
Canada Olympic Park
☎***247-5465***
Located at the top of the luge and bobsleigh tracks at Canada Olympic Park, this is actually in the former starthouse. The Naturbahn, which means natural

track, no longer serves up luges; nowadays the menu features an interesting Sunday brunch. Reservations essential.

Mamma's Ristorante
$$$
320 16th St., NW
☎276-9744
Mamma's has been serving Italian cuisine to Calgarians for more than 20 years. The ambiance and menu offerings are both equally refined, the latter including home-made pasta, veal and seafood dishes.

Entertainment

Avenue is a monthly publications that lists what's on throughout Calgary, including live acts around town and theatre offerings. It is available free of charge throughout the city. **The Calgary Mirror** and **ffwd** are free news and entertainment weeklies.

Bars and Nightclubs

Things have changed since the heyday of **Electric Avenue** (*11th Avenue SW*); the downtown core is picking up, as are 12th Avenue and 17th Avenue. **Senor Frog's** and **Crazy Horse** are popular with young professionals, with dance tunes at the former and classic rock and roll at the latter. **The Republic** (*219 17th Ave. SW, ☎244-1884*) and **The Warehouse** (*733 10th Ave. SW, ☎264-0535*) offers more "alternative" alternative.

Day and night, the terrace of the popular **Ship & Anchor Pub** (534 17th Ave. SW, ☎245-3333) is always overflowing with people. It seems that any excuse is good enough for the 20-something crowd to come here and guzzle down one of the many beers on tap. Light fare available.

The cocktail craze has hit Calgary, and the best places to lounge and sip martinis are the **Auburn Saloon** (*200 Eighth Ave. SW, ☎290-1012*), the **Embassy** (*516C Ninth Ave., ☎213-3970*), **Quincy's** (*609 Seventh Ave. SW, ☎264-1000*), which also has cigars, and finally **Diva** (*1154 Kensington Cresc., ☎270-3739*), in Kensington.

Boystown (*213 10th Ave. SW, ☎265-2028*) attracts a gay crowd, while **The 318** and **Victoria's Restaurant** (*17th Ave. at Second St. SW*), both located in the same building, cater to mixed crowds. **Rook's** is a relaxed bar with great 25¢ chicken wings and a mostly lesbian clientele.

Kaos Jazz Bar (*718 17th Ave. SW, ☎228-9997*) is a popular jazz club with live shows Thursday to Saturday; it is also a fun café with an interesting menu.

If you're itchin' to two-step then you're in luck. Calgary has two great country bars. At **The Ranchman's** (*9615 Macleod Tr. SW, ☎253-1100*), the horseshoe-shaped dance floor is the scene of two-step lessons on Tuesdays and line-dancing lessons on Wednesdays; the rest of the week it is packed. The **Rockin' Horse Saloon** (*7400 Macleod Tr. SE, ☎255-4646*) is where the real cowboys and cowgirls hang out. For some two-stepping downtown head to **Cowboy's** (*826 Fifth St. SW, ☎265-0699*).

Cultural Activities

Alberta Theatre Projects (*☎294-7475*) is an excellent troupe that performs great contemporary plays.

Those in need of some culture may want to inquire about performances of the **Calgary Opera** (*☎262-7286*), the **Calgary Philharmonic Orchestra** (*☎571-0270*) and the **Alberta Ballet** (*☎245-2274*).

Calgary has an **IMAX** theatre in the Eau-Claire Market (*☎974-IMAX or 974-4700*).

Uptown Screen (*612 Eighth Ave.,* ☎*265-0120*) shows foreign films in an old revamped theatre downtown. First-run movies can be seen at movie theatres throughout the city. Pick up a newspaper for schedules and locations, or call the **Talking Yellow Pages**(☎*521-5222*) (see p 362).

Festivals and Events

The **Calgary Exhibition and Stampede** is deservedly called the "Greatest Show on Earth." It began in 1912, at a time when many people expected that the wheat industry would eventually supercede the cattle industry and was intended to be a one-time showcase for traditional cowboy skills. Of course the cattle industry thrived, and the show has been a huge success ever since.

Every July, around 100,000 people descend on Stampede Park for the extravaganza. It begins with a parade, which starts at Sixth Avenue SE and Second Street SE at 9am, but get there early (by 7am) if you want to see anything. The main attraction is of course the rodeo where cowboys and cowgirls show off their skills.

The trials take place every afternoon at 1:30pm and the big final is held on the last weekend. Reserved seats for this event sell out quickly and you are better off ordering tickets in advance if you have your heart set on seeing the big event. There are also chuckwagon races; heats for the Rangeland Derby are held every evening at 8pm, and the final on the last weekend. **Olympic Plaza** is transformed into **Rope Square**, where free breakfast is served every morning from the backs of chuck wagons. Festivities continue throughout the day in the Plaza.

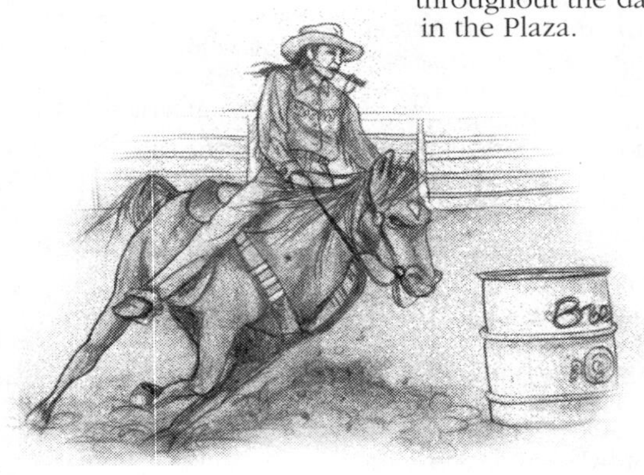

Back at Stampede Park, an "Indian Village" and agricultural fair are among the exhibits to explore.

Evening performances often showcase some of the biggest stars in country music. A gate admission fee of $8 is charged and allows access to all live entertainment, except shows at the Saddledome, for which tickets must be purchased in advance. For information on the good rodeo seats write to:

Calgary Exhibition and Stampede
Box 1060, Station M, Calgary, Alberta, T2P 2L8
or call
☎*261-0101*
☎*800-661-1260*

The **Calgary International Jazz Festival** (☎*233-2628*) takes place the last week of June. The **International Native Arts Festival** (☎*233-0022*) and **Afrikadey** (☎*283-7119*) both take place the third week of August, and both highlight entertainment and art from a variety of cultures from all over the world. The **Calgary Winter Festival** (☎*543-5480*) takes place in late January or February.

Spruce Meadows, located southwest of the city, is Canada's premier equestrian facility. There are actually three annual events here, the National in early June, the North American in

July (same time as Stampede) and the **Spruce Meadows Masters** during the second week in September. The winner of the **Du Maurier International** during this last event takes home the biggest purse of any equestrian event anywhere. For information call ☎*947-4200*.

Tsuu T'Ina Nation holds its annual powwow the last weekend of July. This is a more low-key event than the famous Stampede, but also much more intimate. For only $7 you'll see a real rodeo, plus you'll experience Aboriginal culture. For information ☎*974-1400*.

Spectator Sports

The Canadian Football League's **Calgary Stampeders** play their home games in **McMahon Stadium** (*1817 Crowchild Tr. NW,* ☎*289-0205* ☎*800-667-FANS*) from July to November. The National Hockey League's **Calgary Flames** play at the **Olympic Saddledome** (*17th Ave. and Second St. SE,* ☎*777-4646 or 777-2177*) from October to April.

Shopping

The **Eaton Centre, TD Square, Scotia Centre** and **The Bay** department stores line Eighth Avenue SW, as does a collection of swanky upscale shops including **Holt Renfrew** and the boutiques in **Penny Lane Hall**.

The **Eau-Claire Market** is a wonderful spot to pick up just about anything. Imported goods, including Peruvian sweaters and southwestern-style decorating items, are all sold right next to fresh fish and produce. **Sandpiper Books** (also located on 10th Avenue) on the upper level is a marvellous bookshop with a good collection of books on Alberta.

Not only are **Kensington Avenue** and the surrounding streets a pleasant place to stroll, but the area is also full of interesting specialty shops that are worth a look. One of these is **Heartland Country Store** (*940 Second Ave. NW*) which sells beautiful pottery. There is a collection of shops, cafés and galleries along 17th Avenue SW, with a distinctly upbeat atmosphere. Along Ninth Avenue SE, east of the Elbow River, in Inglewood, gentrified houses now contain antique shops and cafés.

The **Alberta Boot Co.** (*614 10th Ave. SW*) is the place to outfit yourself for the Stampede, with boots in all sizes and styles, just to make sure you fit in!

The kingdom of records, cassettes and movies in Calgary is called **Recordland** (*1204 Ninth Ave. SE, near 11th St. SE*). They have every style of music here--and at unbeatable prices: three CDs for just $25!

Mountain Equipment Co-op (*830 10th Ave. SW,* ☎*269-2420*) is a cooperative that is essentially open only to its members, but it only costs $5 to join, and it is well worth it. High-quality camping and outdoor equipment, clothing and accessories are sold at very reasonable prices.

Arnold Churgin Shoes (*221 Eighth Ave. SW,* ☎*262-3366 and at the Chinook Centre, Macleod Tr. at Glenmore Tr.,* ☎*258-1818*) sells high-quality women's shoes at reasonable prices and offers excellent service, a must for those with a weakness for footwear!

Callebaut Chocolates (*1313 First St. SE,* ☎*265-5777*) makes delicious Belgian chocolates right here in Calgary. They are available throughout the city, but at the head office in the Southeast you can see them being made.

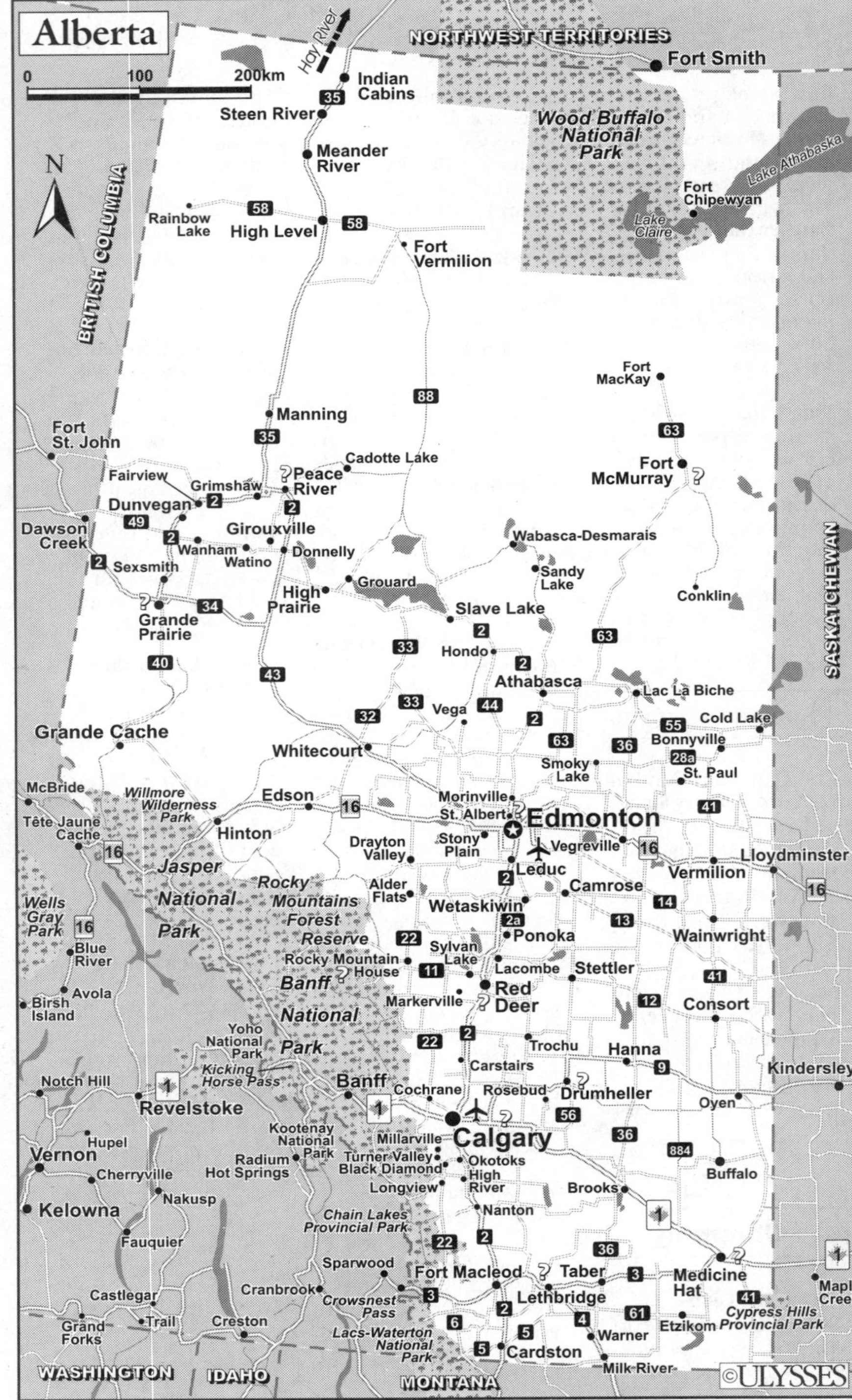

Alberta
0
100
200km
N
NORTHWEST TERRITORIES
BRITISH COLUMBIA
SASKATCHEWAN
WASHINGTON
IDAHO
MONTANA
Hay River
Fort Smith
Indian Cabins
Steen River
Meander River
Wood Buffalo National Park
Lake Athabaska
Fort Chipewyan
Lake Claire
Rainbow Lake
High Level
Fort Vermilion
Fort MacKay
Manning
Fort St. John
Cadotte Lake
Fort McMurray
Fairview
Grimshaw
Peace River
Dunvegan
Dawson Creek
Girouxville
Wanham
Watino
Donnelly
Wabasca-Desmarais
Sandy Lake
Sexsmith
Grouard
High Prairie
Conklin
Grande Prairie
Slave Lake
Hondo
Athabasca
Lac La Biche
Vega
Cold Lake
Bonnyville
Grande Cache
Whitecourt
Smoky Lake
St. Paul
McBride
Willmore Wilderness Park
Edson
Morinville
St. Albert
Edmonton
Tête Jaune Cache
Hinton
Drayton Valley
Stony Plain
Vegreville
Lloydminster
Jasper National Park
Leduc
Vermilion
Rocky Mountains Forest Reserve
Alder Flats
Camrose
Wells Gray Park
Wetaskiwin
Ponoka
Wainwright
Blue River
Sylvan Lake
Rocky Mountain House
Lacombe
Stettler
Banff National Park
Red Deer
Avola
Markerville
Consort
Birsh Island
Yoho National Park
Trochu
Hanna
Kicking Horse Pass
Carstairs
Kindersley
Notch Hill
Banff
Cochrane
Rosebud
Drumheller
Revelstoke
Oyen
Calgary
Kootenay National Park
Millarville
Hupel
Vernon
Radium Hot Springs
Turner Valley
Black Diamond
Okotoks
High River
Buffalo
Cherryville
Longview
Brooks
Nakusp
Kelowna
Nanton
Chain Lakes Provincial Park
Fauquier
Sparwood
Fort Macleod
Taber
Medicine Hat
Maple Creek
Castlegar
Cranbrook
Crowsnest Pass
Lethbridge
Cypress Hills Provincial Park
Grand Forks
Trail
Creston
Etzikom
Lacs-Waterton National Park
Warner
Cardston
Milk River
©ULYSSES

Freshly cut bundles of hay dot Prairie fields, with the Rockies rising up in the distance.
- Troy & Mary Parlee

Like other western capitals, Edmonton boasts a magnificent parliament.
- Troy & Mary Parlee

Diverse landscapes, such as these sandy plains in Saskatchewan, stretch across Western Canada.
- M. Michaelnuk

Southern Alberta

When departing Calgary it is difficult to resist the pull of the Rocky Mountains and head south.

However, southern Alberta boasts some of the best sights and scenery of the whole province, from Waterton Lakes National Park and the mining towns of Crowsnest Pass to the historic native gathering place at Head-Smashed-In Buffalo Jump, and the edge of the endless prairies.

The vast expanses and sometimes desert-like conditions you'll traverse while making your way from west to east in Southern Alberta are in stark contrast to the looming, snow-capped Rocky Mountains to the west. Neat rows of wheat and other grains, perfectly round bales of hay, and the occasional grain elevator are about the extent of the relief across the slow-rolling terrain of this part of the province.

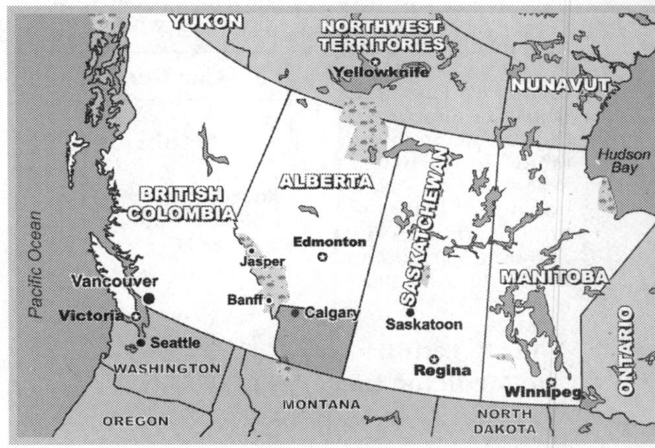

This chapter is divided into two driving tours:

Tour A: Southern Foothills ★★

Tour B: Lethbridge to Medicine Hat ★★

Finding Your Way Around

By Car

Tour A: The Southern Foothills

Although Hwy. 2 is the quickest route from Calgary to Fort Macleod, the superb scenery along Hwy. 22, referred to by some as God's country, is well worth the extra time.

This quiet two-lane highway first heads southwest from Calgary through an area synonymous with Alberta's oil-and-gas boom, and then runs through stunning historic ranchlands, with the Rocky Mountains as a backdrop. The community of Crowsnest Pass lies to the west of the junction with Hwy. 3, and beyond it are Crowsnest Pass and British Columbia. To the east, the tour continues down Hwy. 6 to Waterton Lakes National Park before returning north on Hwy. 2 to Fort Macleod and Lethbridge, the starting point of Tour B.

Tour B: Lethbridge to Medicine Hat

There is a quick, fairly scenic way to get from Lethbridge to Medicine Hat, but a detour south to Writing on Stone Provincial Park and then a peaceful drive along Hwys. 501, 879 and 61 is well worth the extra time and promises even better scenery.

Cypress Hill Interprovincial Park lies about 20km south of Medicine Hat on Hwy. 41. The park is also accessible via a gravel road running east from Orion; this road is in fairly good condition, but there are no service stations along it and it is slow going.

Lethbridge and Medicine Hat both have numbered street systems. Most of Lethbridge's hotels and motels are located along Mayor Magrath Drive, on your way into town on Hwy. 5. Medicine Hat's motel and hotel strip is located on the Trans-Canada, east of downtown.

Car Rentals

Lethbridge

Budget:
1718 Third Ave. S
☎***328-6555***

Avis:
at the airport
☎***382-4880***

Tilden:
2351 Second Ave. N
☎***380-3070***

Medicine Hat

Budget (Airport):
49 Viscount Ave. SW
☎***527-7368***

Budget (Downtown):
1566 Gershaw Drive SW
☎***527 7368***

Tilden (Airport):
☎***527-5665***

By Bus

Lethbridge Greyhound Bus Depot
411 Fifth St. S
☎***327-1551***
services: restaurant, lockers.

Medicine Hat Greyhound Bus Depot
557 Second St. SE
☎***527-4418***

Practical Information

Tourist Information

Travel Alberta South:
☎***(800) 661-1222***

Lethbridge Tourist Information Centre:
2805 Scenic Dr.
☎***320-1222***

Medicine Hat Tourist Information:
8 Gehring Rd. SE
☎***527-6422***

Drumheller Tourist Information:
60 First Ave. W
☎***823-1331***

Big Country Tourist Association:
170 Centre St., #28 Drumheller
☎***823-5885***
⇄***823-7942***

High Country B&B Association:
Box 772, Turner Valley, T0L 2A0
☎***933-4174*** or
888-933-4183
⇄***933-2870***
(*covers the area southwest of Calgary, from Priddis to Waterton Lakes National Park*)

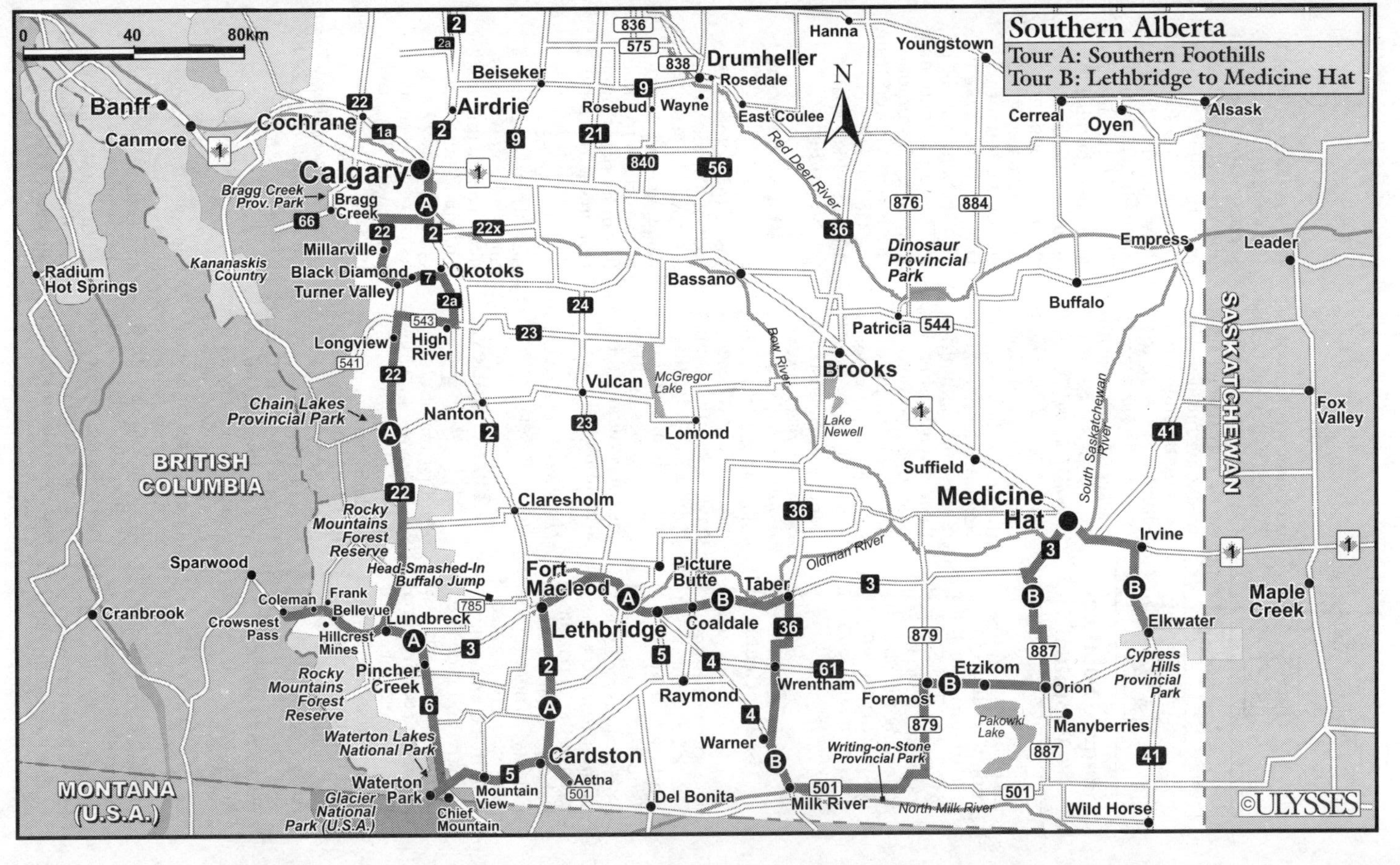

Southern Alberta
Tour A: Southern Foothills
Tour B: Lethbridge to Medicine Hat
0
40
80km
Banff
Canmore
Cochrane
Calgary
Airdrie
Beiseker
Drumheller
Rosedale
Rosebud
Wayne
East Coulee
Hanna
Youngstown
Cerreal
Oyen
Alsask
Bragg Creek Prov. Park
Bragg Creek
Millarville
Black Diamond
Turner Valley
Okotoks
Radium Hot Springs
Kananaskis Country
Longview
High River
Chain Lakes Provincial Park
Nanton
Vulcan
McGregor Lake
Lomond
Bassano
Red Deer River
Bow River
Dinosaur Provincial Park
Empress
Leader
Buffalo
Patricia
Brooks
Lake Newell
Suffield
Medicine Hat
South Saskatchewan River
Fox Valley
Maple Creek
Irvine
Elkwater
Cypress Hills Provincial Park
SASKATCHEWAN
BRITISH COLUMBIA
Claresholm
Rocky Mountains Forest Reserve
Head-Smashed-In Buffalo Jump
Fort Macleod
Lethbridge
Picture Butte
Coaldale
Taber
Oldman River
Sparwood
Coleman
Frank
Bellevue
Crowsnest Pass
Hillcrest Mines
Lundbreck
Cranbrook
Pincher Creek
Waterton Lakes National Park
Waterton Park
Glacier National Park (U.S.A.)
Chief Mountain
Mountain View
Cardston
Aetna
Raymond
Wrentham
Warner
Del Bonita
Milk River
Writing-on-Stone Provincial Park
North Milk River
Foremost
Etzikom
Orion
Pakowki Lake
Manyberries
Wild Horse
MONTANA (U.S.A.)
©ULYSSES

Exploring

Tour A: Southern Foothills

Like the tour of the central foothills (see p 416), this tour follows Hwy. 22. These two tours can be joined by following the stretch of Hwy. 22 between Cochrane and Bragg Creek Provincial Park.

★
Bragg Creek

The town of Bragg Creek lies right next to land owned by the Tsuu T'ina First Nation. The eastern extremity of their reserve butts up against the expanding suburbs of Southwest Calgary. There are two very good reasons to visit this community: scenery and pie. The former can be enjoyed at **Bragg Creek Provincial Park**, a pretty place for short walks or picnics and the latter can be had at **Pies Plus** (*☎949-3450*).

Head south on Hwy. 752 to Millarville.

Millarville

Home of the historic **Millarville Racetrack**, this town is the only one left of five that were built to accommodate transient workers of the Turner Valley oil fields. There is not much to see in this hamlet on a weekday, but if you're passing through on a Saturday, be sure to stop at the **Farmer's Market** (*$1 parking; Jun to Sep, Sat 8:30am to noon; Millarville Racetrack, ☎931-2404*). Vendors from throughout the area sell crafts, fresh produce, baked goods and clothing. A three-day Christmas market is also held the first weekend in November, as is an agricultural fair the third Sunday in August. The **races** (*$4; first weekend in Jul, Sat and Sun 1pm*) take place at the beginning of July. These have been running for 90 years, but betting was only allowed in 1995. Games and festivities accompany the annual races.

Head south on Hwy. 22 to Turner Valley.

Turner Valley

The first major crude oil discovery in Alberta (and Canada), was made in Turner Valley in 1914, but it is natural gas, discovered 11 years earlier that is the claim to fame of Turner Valley. **Dingman No. 1** was Turner Valley's first producing well. It was named after a Calgary businessman who was brought, along with R. B. Bennett, who was later elected prime minister of Canada, to the site by William Herron in 1903. Herron lit a flame using the gas seepage from the earth and cooked the three men breakfast. Dingman and Bennett thus agreed to finance the well, which lasted until 1952. An area known as **burning ground**, where gas flares still burn round the clock, is actually the site of the former Dingman No. 2 well. The seepage was lit in 1977 as a precautionary measure. This unique site is best viewed from the Hell's Half Acre Bridge, which spans the Sheep River.

Black Diamond

Just a few kilometres east of Turner Valley is the town of **Black Diamond**, another town whose claim to fame lies in its rich natural resources. The false fronts of this town's main street bear witness to prosperous times when coal was like black diamonds. The mine here was opened in 1899, and at its peak 650 tonnes of coal a year were extracted.

Head east along Hwy. 7, then north on Hwy. 2A to Okotoks.

Okotoks

Okotoks is the largest city between Calgary and Lethbridge. It is also home to several antique and craft shops. The **Ginger Tea Room and Gift Shop** (*43 Riverside*

Dr., ☎*938-2907*) is a Victorian mansion, where afternoon tea is served on weekdays and two floors of collectibles and crafts can be admired or purchased (see "Restaurants" section, p. 410). A walking tour map is available at the tourist office (*53 N. Railway St.,* ☎*938-3204*) and includes several historic buildings which date from when the town was a rest stop along the Macleod Trail between Fort Calgary and Fort Macleod.

The town's name comes from the Blackfoot word *okatok*, which means rock, and refers to the **Big Rock**, one of the largest glacial erratics found in North America and the town's biggest attraction. This 18,000-ton rock was deposited 7km west of Okotoks during the Ice Age after it landed on an advancing glacier during a landslide in what is now Jasper National Park.

Okotoks is also home to the **Okotoks Bird Sanctuary**, where geese, ducks and other waterfowl can be observed from an elevated observation deck. The sanctuary is an ongoing project of the Fish and Game Association.

Ducks

High River

Another rest stop along the Macleod Trail, **High River**, 24km south of Okotoks along Hwy. 2A, was the only place people, horses, cattle and wagons could cross the Highwood River. High River is now a small ranching community with an interesting local museum, the **Museum of the Highwood** (*$3; May to Sep, every day 10am to 5pm, Oct to May, Tue to Sat noon to 4pm, Sun 1pm to 5pm; 406 First St. W.*). The North American Chuckwagon Racing Championships are held here in late June. It is also the birthplace of Canada's 16th prime minister, Joe Clark.

Backtrack from High River along Hwy. 543 then take Hwy. 22 south to Longview and the Bar U Ranch.

Longview

The **Bar U Ranch National Historic Site ★★** (*$6; mid May to mid-Oct, every day 10am to 6pm; winter, call for group reservations; Longview, Alberta,* ☎*395-2212 or 800-568-4996*) opened in the summer of 1995 and commemorates the contribution of ranching to the development of Canada. It is one of four ranches that once covered almost all of Alberta, and until recently it was still a working ranch. Now, people are able to wander freely around the ranch and observe ranching operations on a scaled-down, demonstration level. "Bar U" refers to the symbol branded on cattle from this ranch. A beautiful new visitors centre features an interpretive display on breeds of cattle, the roundup, branding and what exactly a quirt is. A 15min video on the Mighty Bar U conveys the romance of the cowboy way of life and also explains how the native grasslands and Chinook winds unique to Alberta have been a perpetual cornerstone of ranching. The centre also houses a gift shop and a restaurant where you can savour an authentic buffalo burger.

Continue south along Hwy. 22 for another 100km or so to Hwy. 3.

Chain Lakes Provincial Park ★ (see Parks section, p. 402) is the only real attraction along this stretch of Hwy.. It sits between the Rocky Mountains and the Porcupine Hills in a transition zone of spring-fed lakes. There is a campground (see p. 406). Farther south, the splendid pale yellow grasslands, dotted occasionally by deep blue lakes, roll up into the distant Rocky Mountains. There is an otherworldly look about the mountains looming on the horizon.

Head west once you reach Hwy. 3, another stretch of scenic highway. It leads deeper into the foothills and through a series of mining towns to Crowsnest Pass and British Columbia.

★

Crowsnest Pass

The area along Hwy. 3 between Pincher Creek and the continental divide is known as the Municipality of Crowsnest Pass. A number of once thriving coal-mining communities along the highway are now home to a handful of sites offering an interesting historical perspective on the local mining industry. Coal was first discovered here in 1845, but it wasn't until 1898, when the CPR built a line through the pass, that towns were really settled. Coal was the only industry in the area, and when the mineral turned out to be of inferior quality and hard to get at, troubled times set in. Local coal fetched lower prices than that of British Columbia, and by 1915 the first mine had closed; the others soon followed. The municipality is Alberta's only ecomuseum and was declared a Historic District in 1988.

The first site you will come across as you head west along Hwy. 3 is the **Lietch Collieries** (*$2; guided tours mid-May to Sep, 10am to 4pm, self-guided Sep to May; ☎562-7388*). This was the only Canadian-owned mine in the Pass and the first to close in 1915. Various information panels explain the extraction process while a path leads through the mine ruins.

Farther down Hwy. 3, follow the signs toward Hillcrest.

On June 19, 1914, **Hillcrest** was the site of the worst mining disaster in Canadian history when an explosion ripped through the tunnels of the mine trapping 235 men underground. Many that had survived the blast eventually died of asphyxiation from the afterdamp (the carbon dioxide and carbon monoxide left over after the explosion has used all available oxygen), which, along with smoke, also forced back rescuers. The mine has been sealed since it shut down in 1939, and there isn't much to see except the closed-off entrance. The 189 victims of the disaster were buried in a mass grave in a cemetery located 1km along the road from Hwy. 3.

Continue west through Hillcrest, and cross Hwy. 3 to the Bellevue Mine.

The **Bellevue Mine** opened in 1903 and had been operating for seven years without incident, when it was rocked by an underground explosion on December 9, 1910. Afterdamp poisoning lead to the deaths of 30 miners. The mine reopened and remained operational until 1962. Today visitors are given hard hats and miner's lamps and follow a **guided tour** ★★ (*$4; mid-May to early Sep, tours every half hour 10am to 5:30pm*) through about 100m of dark, cool and damp underground mine tunnels. This is the only mine in the Pass open to visitors and is a real treat for both young and old. Bring a sweater, as it can get quite cold in the mine.

Continuing along Hwy. 3, you'll notice a very drastic change in the landscape. Extending on both sides of the

The Chinook Wind

A Chinook occurs when moisture-laden winds from the Pacific Ocean strike the Rocky Mountains and are forced to precipitate their moisture as rain or snow. This leaves the winds cold and dry.

However, as the air descends the eastern slopes it remains dry but is condensed by the increase in atmospheric pressure and warms up. This warm, dry wind brings mild conditions that can melt 30cm of snow in a few hours.

It is essentially because of the Chinook that Alberta's native grasses survive the winter and that cattle can graze on the prairies year-round.

The warm, dry breath of the Chinook is a fabled part of Alberta history. It is the stuff of legend, with stories of farmers rushing home at the sight of the telltale Chinook arch (an arch-shaped cloud formed when the air pushes the cloud cover to the west), with their horses' front legs in the snow and hind legs in mud!

highway, covering 3km², debris of the Frank Slide creates a spectacular, almost lunar landscape. Consisting mostly of limestone, these boulders are on average 14m deep, but exceed 30m in some places. The **Frank Slide Interpretive Centre** ★★ (*$4; Jun to early Sep, every day 9am to 8pm; Sep to May 10am to 4pm; turn right off highway, ☎562-7388, ⇄562-8635*), located north of the highway on a slight rise, presents an audiovisual account of the growth of the town and of the slide itself. It explains the various theories about what caused the slide on April 29, 1903 that sent 82 million tonnes of limestone crashing from the summit of Turtle Mountain onto the town of Frank, which at the time lay south of the highway at the foot of the mountain. All that remains of the town is an old fire hydrant. The mountain's unstable structure, mining, water and severe weather are believed to have contributed to the disaster.

A self-guided trail through the slide area provides an interesting perspective of the scope of the slide. Sixty-eight of the town's residents were buried, but the disaster might have been worse if it hadn't been for a CPR brakeman who amazingly raced across the rocks to stop an approaching passenger train. Those who dare can climb Turtle Mountain to examine fissures and cracks near the summit that still pose a threat. The trail is not too difficult and takes between 2 to 3hrs each way.

The town of Coleman lies farther north. The Coleman Colliery closed in 1983, and the town's main street is a testament to the hard times that set in afterward. The **Crowsnest Museum** ★ (*$3; May to Sep, every day 10am to noon and 1pm to 5pm; Sep to May, Mon to Fri 10am to 4pm; 7701 18th Ave., Coleman, ☎563-5434*) recounts the history of the Pass from 1899 to 1950. There are models of coal mining rescues, coal cars from the Greenhill Mine plus a diorama of the fish and wildlife of Crowsnest Pass.

From Coleman, backtrack east along Hwy. 3 to Pincher Creek. Take Hwy. 6 south toward Waterton Lakes National Park.

Pincher Creek is reputed to be the windiest spot in Alberta, which explains all the windmills in the vicinity. This town is a gateway to Waterton Lakes National Park.

★★★ Waterton Lakes National Park

Waterton Lakes National Park, along with Glacier National Park in Montana, is part of the world's first International Peace Park. With stunning scenery, an exceptional choice of outdoor activities and varied wildlife, Waterton is not to be missed. Its main attraction, however, is its ambience. Many say it is like Banff and Jasper of 20 years ago – before the crowds and the mass commercialism. Waterton Townsite is home to restaurants, bars, shops, grocery stores, laundry facilities, a post office and hotels. There is also a marina, from which lake cruises depart. Things slow down considerably in the winter, though the cross-country skiing is outstanding. For more information see the Parks section, p 402.

From Waterton Lakes National Park take Hwy. 5 east to Cardston.

★ Cardston

Cardston is a prosperous-looking town nestled in the rolling foothills where the grasslands begin to give way to fields of wheat and the yellow glow of canola. The town was established by Mormon pioneers fleeing religious persecution in Utah. Their move here marked one of the last great covered-wagon migrations of the 19th century.

Cardston might not seem like much of a tourist town, but it is home to one of the most impressive monuments and one of the most unique museums in Alberta. The monument is the **Mormon Temple** (*free admission; every day 9am to 9pm; 348 Third St. W., ☎653-1696*), which seems a tad out of place rising from the prairie. This truly majestic edifice took 10 years to construct and was the first temple built by the church outside the United States. The marble comes from Italy and the granite was quarried in Nelson, B.C. When it came time to do renovations recently, a problem arose because there was no granite left in Nelson; luckily, several blocks were found in a farmer's field nearby, having been left there in storage when the temple was built. Only Mormons in good standing may enter the temple itself, but the photographs and video presented at the visitors centre should satisfy your curiosity. A walk on the beautiful grounds adjacent to the temple is also highly recommended.

The **Southern Alberta Art Gallery** (*free; Tue to Sat; 10am to 5pm, Sun 1pm to 5pm; 601 Third Ave. South, ☎327-8770,* ⇌328-3913) enjoys an international reputation, thanks to the 15 exhibitions it puts on every year. Each of the three art spaces has different architecture. Other events take place here regularly: music, theatre, film and conferences. Call ahead and check this place out.

The unique museum is the **Remington-Alberta Carriage Centre ★★★** (*$6.50; mid-May to early Sep, every day 9am to 8pm; Sep to May, every day 9am to 5pm; 623 Main St., ☎653-5139*), opened in 1993. "A museum on carriages?", you may ask. The subject matter may seem narrow, but this museum is definitely worth a visit. Forty-nine of the approximately 260 carriages were donated by Mr. Don Remington of Cardston on the condition that the Alberta government build an interpretive centre in which to display them. The wonderfully restored carriages and enthusiastic, dedicated staff at this magnificent facility make this exhibit first-rate.

Take a guided tour through the 1,675m² display gallery, where town mock-ups and

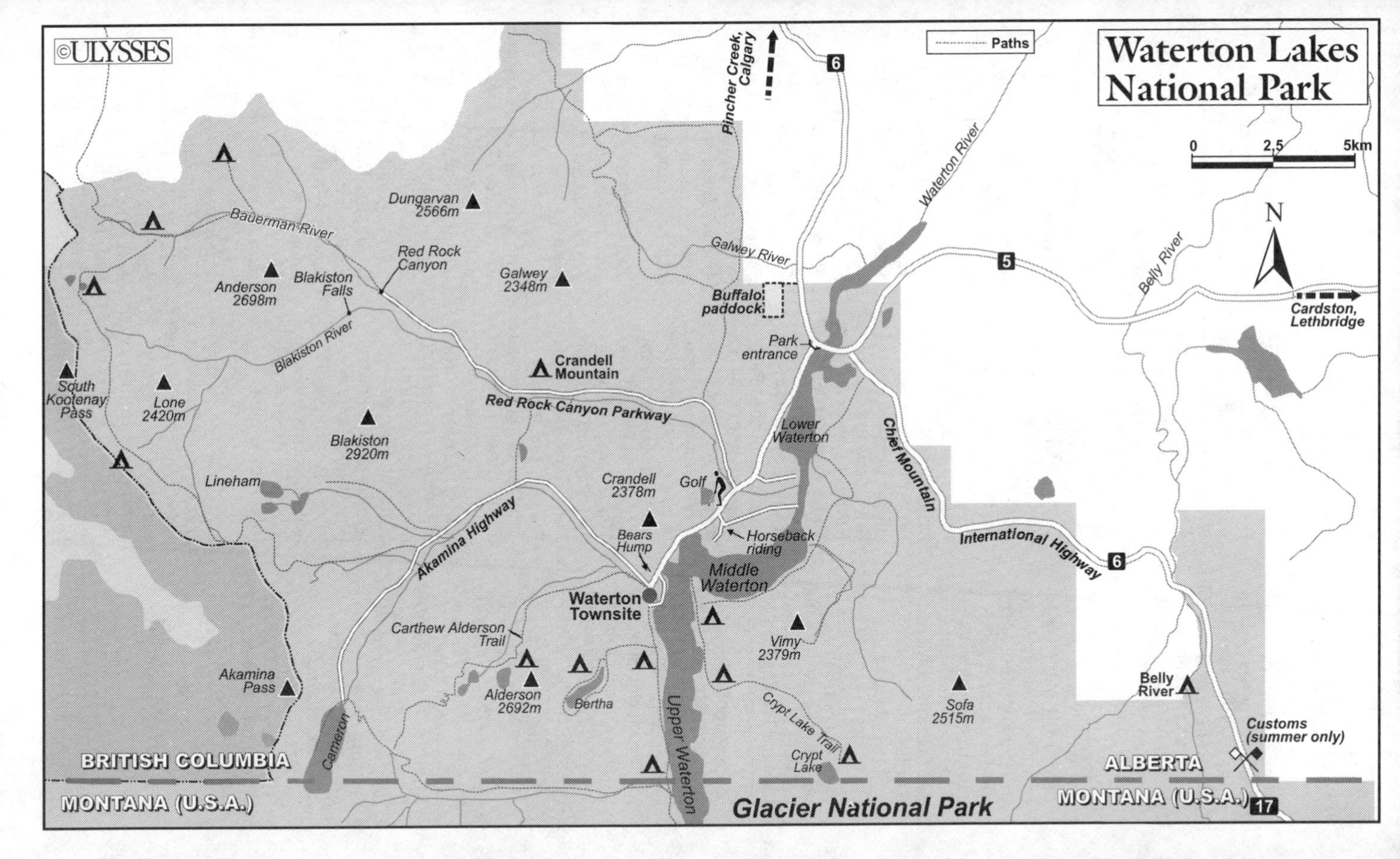

Waterton Lakes National Park
©ULYSSES
Paths
0
2,5
5km
N
Pincher Creek, Calgary
Cardston, Lethbridge
6
5
6
17
Waterton River
Belly River
Galwey River
Bauerman River
Blakiston River
Dungarvan 2566m
Red Rock Canyon
Galwey 2348m
Anderson 2698m
Blakiston Falls
Buffalo paddock
Park entrance
Crandell Mountain
South Kootenay Pass
Lone 2420m
Red Rock Canyon Parkway
Blakiston 2920m
Lower Waterton
Chief Mountain
Lineham
Crandell 2378m
Golf
Akamina Highway
Bears Hump
Horseback riding
International Highway
Middle Waterton
Waterton Townsite
Carthew Alderson Trail
Vimy 2379m
Akamina Pass
Alderson 2692m
Bertha
Upper Waterton
Crypt Lake Trail
Sofa 2515m
Belly River
Customs (summer only)
Cameron
Crypt Lake
BRITISH COLUMBIA
ALBERTA
MONTANA (U.S.A.)
Glacier National Park
MONTANA (U.S.A.)

animated street scenes provide the backdrop for the collection, one of the best in the world among elite carriage facilities. The interesting film *Wheels of Change* tells the story of this once huge industry, which was all but dead by 1922. Visitors can also learn how to drive a carriage, watch the restoration work in progress, take a carriage ride and have an old-fashioned picture taken.

Aetna

South of Cardston, just off Hwy. 2, is the once-thriving town of Aetna. **Jensen's Trading Post** (☎*653-2500*) has an interesting collection of antiques. Hwy. 2 continues to the American border and **Police Outpost Provincial Park**, named after a police outpost set up in 1891 to control smuggling. There is a campground in the park.

Head north of Cardston on Hwy. 2 to Fort Macleod and Head-Smashed-In Buffalo Jump. If it's getting late in the day, you may consider heading north on Hwy. 5, in order to spend the night in Lethbridge. Fort Macleod and Head-Smashed-In are both easily accessible from Lethbridge.

★ Fort Macleod

The town of Fort Macleod centres around the fort of the same name, first set up by the North West Mounted Police in an effort to stop the whisky trade. Troops were sent to raid Fort Whoop-Up (see p 396) in 1874, but got lost along the way, and by the time they got to Whoop-Up the traders had fled. They continued west to this spot by the Oldman River and established a permanent outpost. The original settlement was on an island 3km east of the present town, but persistent flooding forced its relocation in 1882. The fort as it stands now was reconstructed in 1956-1957 as a museum. The **Fort Museum** ★ (*$4.50; May and Jun, every day 9am to 5pm; Jul to Sep 9am to 8:30pm; Sep to mid-Oct, every day 9am to 5pm; mid-Oct to Dec 23 and Mar to May, weekdays 10am to 4pm; 219 25th St. at Third Ave.,* ☎*553-4703*) houses exhibits of pioneer life at the time of the settlement, dioramas of the fort, tombstones from the cemetery and an interesting section of artifacts and photographs of the Plains Blood and Peigan tribes. A Mounted Patrol performs a musical ride four times a day in July and August.

Fort Macleod's downtown area is very representative of a significant period in history. Most of the buildings were erected between 1897 and 1914, except the Kanouse cabin which lies inside the fort walls and dates from much earlier.

Walking-tour pamphlets are available at the tourist office. The tour includes such notable edifices as the **Empress Theatre**, which retains its original pressed-metal ceiling panels, stage and dressing rooms (complete with graffiti from 1913). Movies are still shown here, despite a ghost who occasionally gets upset with the way things are run. The **Silver Grill**, an old saloon across the street, has its original bar and bullet-pierced mirror, while the sandstone **Queen's Hotel** still rents rooms (reservations are not recommended!)

Drive northwest of Fort Macleod on Hwy. 785 to Head-Smashed-In Buffalo Jump.

The arrival of the horse in the mid-1700s signalled the end of a traditional way of hunting buffalo among Plains Indians. For 5,700 years before this, the Plains Indians had depended on **Head-Smashed-In Buffalo Jump** ★★★ (*$6.50; May to Sep, every day 9am to 7pm; Sep to May, every day 9am to 5pm; 15km northwest of Fort Macleod on Hwy. 785,* ☎*553-2731*). From it they got meat: fresh and dried for pemmican; hides for tipis, clothing and moccasins; and bones and horns for tools and decorations. Head-Smashed-In was an ideal spot for a jump, with a vast grazing area to the west. The Plains Indians would construct drive lines with stone cairns leading to the cliff. Some 500 people participated in the yearly hunt; men dressed in buffalo-calf robes and wolf skins lured the herd towards the precipice. Upon reaching the cliff, the leading buffalo were forced over the edge by the momentum of the stampeding herd behind them. The herd was not actually chased over the cliff, but rather fear in the herd led to a stampede. The area remains much as it was thousands of years ago, though the distance from the cliff to the ground drastically changed as the bones of butchered bison piled up, 10m deep in some places.

Today, the jump is the best preserved buffalo jump in North America and a UNESCO World Heritage Site. Many assume that the name comes from the crushed skulls of the buffalo, but it actually refers to a Peigan legend of a young brave who went under the jump to watch the buffalo topple in front of him. The kill was exceptionally good this particular day, and the brave was crushed by the animals. When his people were butchering the buffalos after the kill, they discovered the brave with his head smashed in — hence the name.

As you approach the jump, the cliff appears as a small ridge on a vast plain. Signs of civilization are few; in fact the interpretive centre blends in to the landscape so well that it is hardly noticeable. You almost expect to see a herd of buffalo just beyond the rise, and can envision what the natural plain must have been like before Europeans arrived. There is something truly mythical about the place.

The interpretive centre, built into the cliff, comprises five levels and is visited from the top down. Start off by following the trail along the top of the cliff for a spectacular view of the plain and the Calderwood Jump to the left. Marmots can be seen sunning themselves on the rocks below and generally contemplating the scene. Continuing through the centre you'll learn about Napi, the mythical creator of people according to the Blackfoot.

The centre leads through Napi's world, the people and their routines, the buffalo, the hunt, the contact of cultures and European settlement. An excellent film entitled *In Search of the Buffalo* is presented every 30min. The tour ends with an archaeological exhibit of the excavation work at the site. Back outside the centre you can follow a trail to the butchering site. The annual Buffalo Days celebrations take place here in July. The centre has a great gift shop and a small cafeteria that serves buffalo burgers.

The city of Lethbridge (see below) is about 20km from Fort Macleod along Hwy. 3.

Tour B: Lethbridge to Medicine Hat

★★ Lethbridge

Lethbridge, known affectionately by locals as "downtown L.A.," is Alberta's third largest city, and a pleasant urban oasis on the prairies. Steeped in history, the city boasts an extensive park system, pretty tree-lined streets, interesting sights and a diverse cultural community. You're as likely to meet ranchers as business people, Hutterites or Mormons on the streets of L.A.

Indian Battle Park ★★, in the Oldman River valley in the heart of town, is where Lethbridge's history comes alive; it is the site of Fort Whoop-Up and the was the setting of a terrible battle. On October 25, 1870, Cree, displaced by European settlers into Blackfoot territory, attacked a band of Blood Blackfoot camped on the banks of the Oldman River. In the ensuing battle, the Blood were aided by a group of Peigan Blackfoot nearby; by the end some 300 Cree and 50 Blackfoot were dead.

A year earlier, American whisky traders had moved into Southern Alberta from Fort Benton, Montana. t was illegal to sell alcohol to Aboriginal People in the United States, so the traders headed north into Canada, where there was no law enforcement. They set up Fort Hamilton nearby, at the confluence of the St. Mary's and Oldman rivers, and it became the headquarters of American activity in southern Alberta and Saskatchewan. This activity involved the trading of a particularly lethal brew which was passed off as whisky to the Aboriginal People; besides whisky, this firewater might also contain fortified grain alcohol, red pepper, chewing tobacco, Jamaican ginger and black molasses.

Fire destroyed the original fort, but a second, called **Fort Whoop-Up ★★**, was built and whisky and guns continued to be traded for buffalo hides and robes. Fort Whoop-Up was the first and most notorious of 44 whisky-trading posts. The American encroachment on Canadian territory, the illicit trading which had a demoralizing effect on the Aboriginal People, and news of the Cypress Hills massacre (see p. 405) prompted the Canadian government to form the North West Mounted Police. Led by scout Jerry Potts, the Mounties, under the command of Colonel Macleod, arrived at Fort Whoop-Up in October of 1874. Word of their arrival preceded them, however, and the place was empty by the time they arrived. A cairn marks the site of this fort. The present fort is a reconstruction and houses an interesting **interpretive centre** (*$2.50; summer, Mon to Sat 10am to 6pm, Sun noon to 5pm; winter, Tue to Fri 10am to 4pm, Sun 1pm to 4pm; Indian Battle Park, ☎329-0444*), where visitors can experience the exciting days of the whisky trade. You can also taste fresh bannock, a round, flat Scottish cake made from barley and oatmeal and cooked on a griddle. Guides in period costume offer tours.

After peace was restored (so to speak) by the Mounties, attention turned to an exposed coal seam along the east bank of the Oldman River. The first mine was called Coalbanks, and so was the town that eventually sprung up at the opening to the mine. The **Coalbanks Interpretive Site** now stands at the original mine entrance in Indian Battle Park.

With financing from his father, Sir Alexander Galt, Elliot Galt set up a major drift mine. It soon became clear that a railway was needed to haul the coal, and eventually the town of Lethbridge was settled on the benchlands above the river. The town was named after a man who had never even been to Alberta, but was a friend of Galt's and a major financial contributor to the whole operation.

With 62km of walking, biking and horseback riding trails, the recreation possibilities are endless in Indian Battle Park. There are also picnic shelters and playgrounds.

The **Lethbridge Nature Reserve** is also located in Indian Battle Park. This 82ha protected area preserves much of the Oldman River Valley and contains the **Helen Schuler Coulee Centre ★** (*summer, Sun to Thu 10am to 8pm, Fri and Sat 10am to 6pm;*

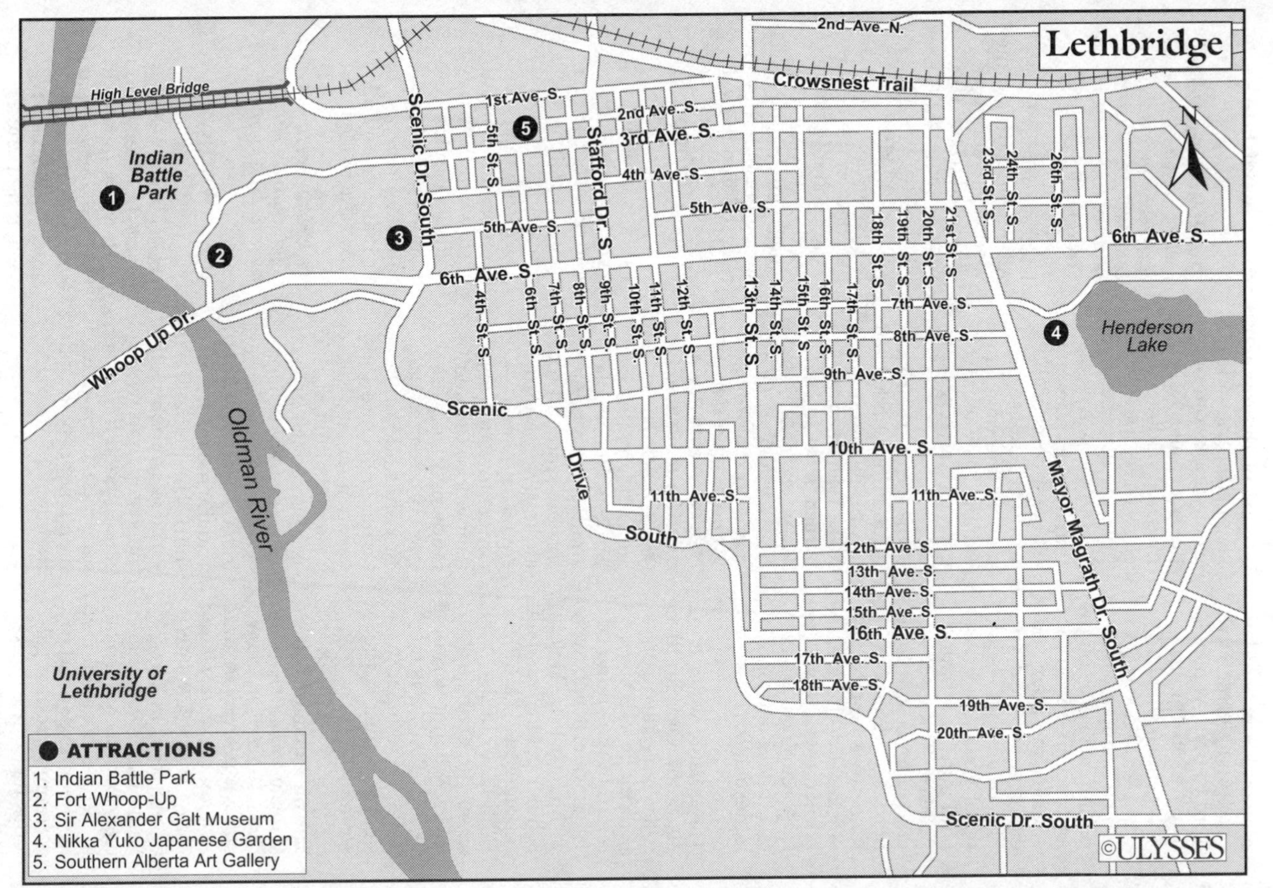
Lethbridge
N
2nd Ave. N.
Crowsnest Trail
High Level Bridge
1st Ave. S.
2nd Ave. S.
3rd Ave. S.
4th Ave. S.
5th Ave. S.
6th Ave. S.
7th Ave. S.
8th Ave. S.
9th Ave. S.
10th Ave. S.
11th Ave. S.
12th Ave. S.
13th Ave. S.
14th Ave. S.
15th Ave. S.
16th Ave. S.
17th Ave. S.
18th Ave. S.
19th Ave. S.
20th Ave. S.
4th St. S.
5th St. S.
6th St. S.
7th St. S.
8th St. S.
9th St. S.
10th St. S.
11th St. S.
12th St. S.
13th St. S.
14th St. S.
15th St. S.
16th St. S.
17th St. S.
18th St. S.
19th St. S.
20th St. S.
21st St. S.
23rd St. S.
24th St. S.
26th St. S.
Stafford Dr. S
Scenic Dr. South
Scenic Drive South
Mayor Magrath Dr. South
Whoop Up Dr.
Henderson Lake
Indian Battle Park
Oldman River
University of Lethbridge
ATTRACTIONS
1. Indian Battle Park
2. Fort Whoop-Up
3. Sir Alexander Galt Museum
4. Nikka Yuko Japanese Garden
5. Southern Alberta Art Gallery
©ULYSSES

May and Sep, Tue to Sat 1pm to 4pm, Sun 1pm to 6pm; winter, Tue to Sun 1pm to 4pm; Indian Battle Park, ☎320-3064), which features hands-on interactive displays and fact sheets on local animals and plant species that are great for kids of all ages — find out if you are a grassland guru or a prairie peewee. Three self-guided trails start from here. The reserve is home to Alberta's provincial bird, the great horned owl, as well as to porcupines, white-tailed deer and prairie rattlesnakes.

The volatile water levels of the Oldman River still wreak havoc on Lethbridge every so often. In the spring of 1995, water levels were so high that the Helen Schuler centre was half-submerged. The CPR High Level Bridge spans the Oldman River. When it was built in 1907-09, it was the longest and highest steel aqueduct in the world.

The **Sir Alexander Galt Museum** (*donation; every day 10am to 5pm, closed holidays between Sep and Apr; just off Scenic Dr. at Fifth Ave. S,* ☎*320-3898*), overlooking Indian Battle Park, was originally built as a hospital in 1910. Since then it has been expanded to accommodate five galleries that offer an excellent perspective on the human history of the city of Lethbridge. A particularly impressive glazed viewing gallery looks out onto the river valley. The museum outlines the city's development from the discovery of coal to the waves of immigration from many different parts of the world. There are permanent and travelling exhibits, as well as extensive archives.

Paths weave their way through five traditional Japanese gardens at the **Nikka Yuko Japanese Garden** ★★(*$4; mid-May to end of Jun, every day 9am to 5pm; Jul and Aug every day 9am to 9pm; Sep, every day 9am to 5pm; Seventh Ave. S and Mayor Magrath Dr.,* ☎*328-3511*). These aren't bright, flowery gardens, but simple arrangements of green shrubs, sand and rocks in the style of a true Japanese garden — perfect for quiet contemplation. Created by renowned Japanese garden designer Dr. Tadashi Kudo of the Osaka Prefecture University in Japan, Nikka Yuko was built in 1967 as a centennial project and a symbol of Japanese and Canadian friendship (*Nikka Yuko* actually means friendship). The bell at the gardens symbolizes this friendship, and when it is rung good things are supposed to happen simultaneously in both countries.

Head east on Hwy. 3 to Coaldale and then on to Taber.

Coaldale

The **Birds of Prey Centre** (*$4.75; May to Sep, every day 10am to 5pm; 2124 Burrowing Owl Lane, north of Hwy. 3 in Coaldale,* ☎*345-4262*) is a living museum populated with birds from Alberta and around the world. The centre is dedicated to the survival of birds of prey like hawks, falcons, eagles and great horned owls. Many of the birds in the centre were brought here injured or as young chicks. Once they are strong enough they are released into the wild.

Taber

Taber is famous for its sweet corn, which is sold all over the province. The city is also a centre for the food-processing industry. Corn season is in August, when the town holds its **Cornfest** celebrations featuring a pancake breakfast, hot-air balloons and all sorts of activities.

Backtrack on Hwy. 3 and head south on Hwy. 36 towards Milk River.

Warner

The town of Warner lies at the intersection of Hwy.s 4 and 36. In 1987, an amateur paleontologist discovered a clutch of **dinosaur eggs** containing perfectly formed embryonic hadrosaur bones. There are bus tours to this significant fossil site, and the eggs can also be viewed at the Royal Tyrell Museum in Drumheller (see p 420).

In Milk River take Hwy. 501, and watch for signs for Writing-on-Stone Provincial Park.

Milk River

The Milk River is the only river in western Canada on the east side of the continental divide that does not eventually empty into Hudson Bay; it flows south into the Missouri River and on into the Mississippi River and the Gulf of Mexico. As a result the area has been claimed by eight different governments and countries. When France claimed all lands that drained into the Mississippi, this part of Alberta was under French jurisdiction. The Spanish, British, Americans, and the Hudson's Bay Company have all staked their claim at some point in history.

★★

Writing-on-Stone Provincial Park

Writing-on-Stone protects fascinating examples of petroglyphs, some of which are believed to date back some 1,800 years. A wealth of animals and plant species call this arid parcel of land home. The province's hottest temperatures are recorded here in this almost desert-like setting. Great hiking is possible, but the best rock drawings lie within a restricted area that is only accessible through guided hikes. To avoid disappointment, call ahead to find out when the hikes are heading out (see p 403).

★★

Across the Prairie to Medicine Hat

Continue east on Hwy. 501, then go north on Hwy. 879. When you reach Hwy. 61, head east.

The prairies roll on and on as far as the eye can see along this stretch of highway surrounded by golden fields that are empty but for the occasional hamlet, grain elevator or abandoned farmhouse. Towns were set up every 16km because that was how far a farmer could haul his grain.

As you drive this road, you will come upon what was once the town of Nemiskam, about 16km out of Foremost. Another 16km down the road is Etzikom. With fewer than 100 inhabitants these days, Etzikom's days may be numbered. For a look at the way things used to be, and a chance to stretch your legs, stop in at the **Etzikom Museum ★** (*donation; May to Sep, Mon to Sat 10am to 5pm, Sun noon to 6pm; Etzikom, ☎666-3737, 666-3792 or 666-3915*). Local museums like this can be found throughout Alberta, but this is one of the best of its kind and makes for a pleasant stop off the highway.

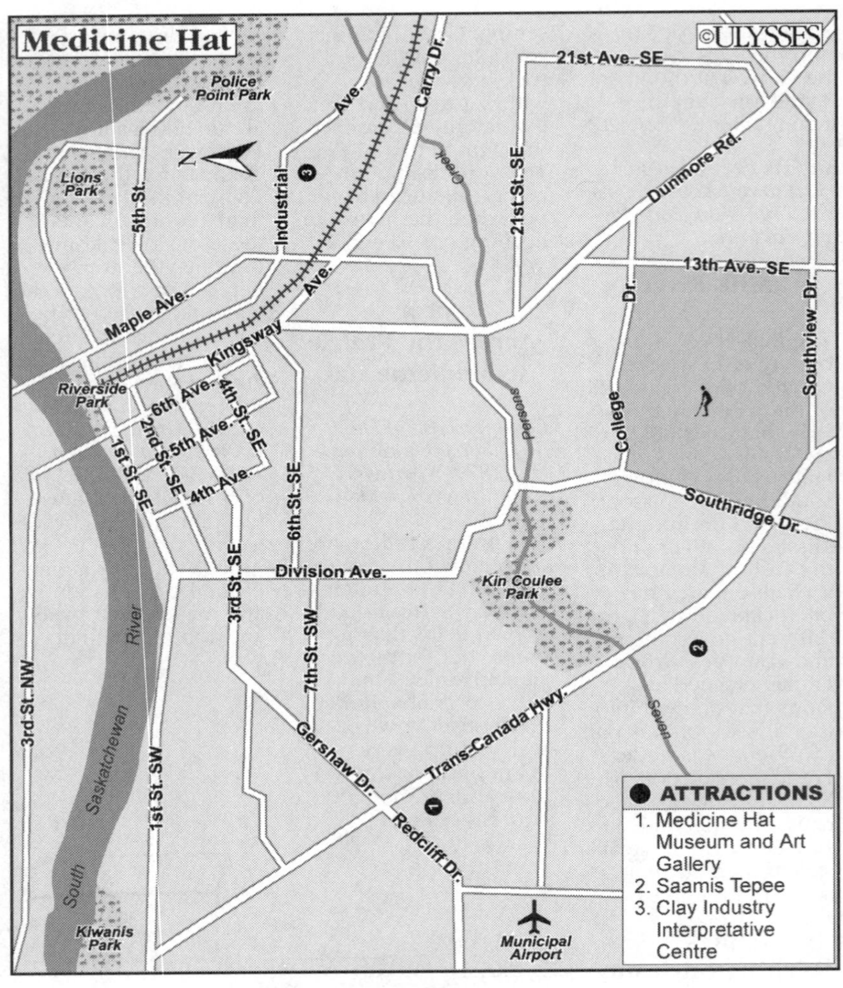

The museum is located in the Etzikom School, and houses a wonderful recreation of the Main Street of a typical town, complete with barber shop, general store and hotel. Outside is the Wind-power Interpretive Centre, a collection of windmills including one from Martha's Vineyard, Massachusetts, U.S.A.

Continue east along Hwy. 61, then head north on Hwy. 887, and east on Hwy. 3 into Medicine Hat. Cypress Hills Interprovincial Park is accessible along the dirt road running east of Orion, or by taking Hwy. 41 south of Medicine Hat.

★
Medicine Hat

Rudyard Kipling once called Medicine Hat "a city with all hell for a basement," in reference to Medicine Hat's location above some of western Canada's largest natural gas fields. The town prospered because of this natural resource, which now supplies a thriving petro-chemical industry. Clay deposits nearby also left their mark on the city, contributing to the city's once thriving pottery industry. Medicine Hat, like many towns in Alberta, boasts several parks. As for its name, legend has it that a great battle between the Cree and the Blackfoot took place here. During the battle the Cree medicine man deserted his people, and while fleeing across the river he lost his headdress in midstream. Believing this to be a bad omen the Cree abandoned the fight, and were massacred by the Blackfoot. The battle site was called Saamis, which means medicine man's hat. When the Mounties arrived years later, the name was translated and shortened to Medicine Hat.

The **Medicine Hat Museum and Art Gallery** (*donation; summer, Mon to Fri 9am to 5pm, Sat and Sun 1pm to 5pm; winter, Mon to Fri 10:30am to 5pm, Sat and Sun 1pm to 5pm; 1302 Bomford Crescent SW, ☎527-6266*) is a National Exhibition Centre with first-rate local, national and international exhibits. The museum has a permanent collection depicting the history of Medicine Hat, the Plains Indians, the NWMP, ranching, farming and the railway.

Continue along Hwy. 1 to the Saamis Tipi and Information Office.

The **Saamis Tipi** is the world's tallest tipi. It was constructed for the 1988 Calgary Winter Olympics, and then purchased by a Medicine Hat businessman following the Games. The tipi symbolizes the First Nations way of life, based on spirituality, the circle of life, family and the sacred home. It certainly is an architectural wonder, though its steel structure and sheer size do seem a bit inconsistent with native traditions. Below the Saamis Tipi is the **Saamis Archaeological Site**. Over 80 million artifacts are believed to be buried at the site. A self-guided walking tour leads through the site of a late winter and early spring buffalo camp and a meat-processing site.

Follow the signs to the Clay Industry Interpretive Centre.

You'll probably have seen the pamphlets for the **Great Wall of China**; this is not a replica of the real thing, but quite literally a wall of china produced by the potteries of Medicine Hat from 1912 to 1988. Though many of the pieces on display are priceless collector's items, the best part of the **Clay Interpretive Centre ★★** (*$3; summer 9am to 5:30pm, winter 8am to 4:30pm; ☎529-1070*) is the tour of the old Medalta plant and kilns. Medalta once supplied the fine china for all Canadian Pacific hotels. Today, workers' clothes and personal effects remain in the plant, which closed down unexpectedly in 1989. Medalta Potteries, Medicine Hat Potteries, Alberta Potteries and Hycroft China established Medicine Hat's reputation as an important pottery centre. Tour guides lead visitors through the plant and explain the intricate and labour-intensive work that went into each piece. The tour ends with a fascinating visit inside one of the six beehive kilns outside. Historic Walking Tour pamphlets are available at the information office for those interested in exploring the turn-of-the-century architecture of Medicine Hat's downtown core.

★★ Cypress Hills Provincial Park

Cypress Hills Provincial Park lies 65km southeast of Medicine Hat, near the Saskatchewan border. These hills were not covered by glaciers during the last ice age, and with a maximum elevation of 1,466m above sea level, they are the highest point in Canada between Banff and Labrador. This was the site of the Cypress Hills massacre in the winter of 1872-3, the result of which contributed to the formation of the North West Mounted Police. Animal and plant species found nowhere else in southern Alberta are the treasures of this park (see p 405).

From Medicine Hat, head northwest on Hwy. 1, the Trans-Canada, to Brooks.

Parks and Beaches

Tour A: Southern Foothills

Chain Lakes Provincial Park (☎*646-5887*) is open year-round and offers all sorts of possibilities for enjoying the outdoors: boating, summer (rainbow trout and Rocky Mountain whitefish) and ice-fishing, summer and winter camping and cross-country skiing. There is a boat ramp.

Waterton Lakes National Park ★★★ (*per car for one day: groups $8, $4; camping from $10 to $23; for information call ☎859-5133 or write Waterton Lakes National Park, c/o Superintendent, Waterton Park, Alberta, T0K 2M0. Note that reservations are not accepted for campgrounds.*) is located right on the US-Canadian border and forms one half of the world's first International Peace Park (the other half is Glacier National Park, Montana). Waterton boasts some of the best scenery in the province and is well worth the detour required to visit it. Characterized by a chain of deep glacial lakes and upside-down mountains with irregularly shaped summits, this area where the peaks meet the prairies offers wonderful hiking, cross-country skiing, camping and wildlife-viewing opportunities.

The unique geology of the area is formed by 1.5-billion-year-old sedimentary rock from the Rockies that was dumped on the 60-million-year-old shale of the prairie during the last ice age. Hardly any transition zone exists between these two regions that are home to abundant and varied wildlife, where species from a prairie habitat mix with those of subalpine and alpine regions (some 800 varieties of plants and 250 species of birds).

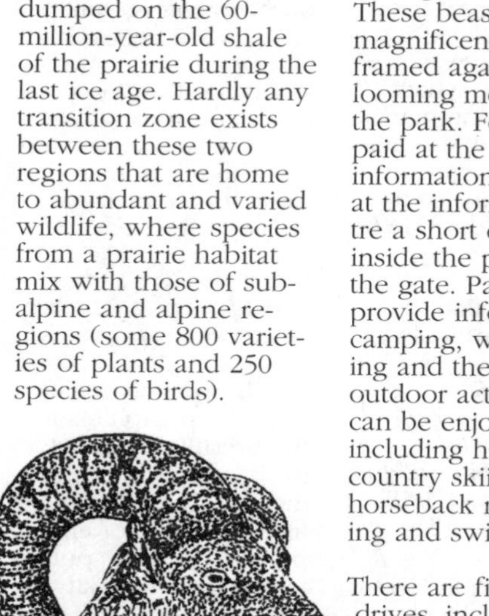

One thing to remember, and you will be reminded of it as you enter the park, is that wild animals here are just that — wild. While they may appear tame, they are unpredictable and potentially dangerous, and visitors are responsible for their own safety.

There is one park entrance accessible from Hwy. 6 or 5. On your way in from Hwy. 6, you will come upon a **buffalo paddock** shortly before the park gate. A small herd lives here and can be viewed by visitors from their cars along a loop road through the paddock. These beasts are truly magnificent, especially framed against the looming mountains of the park. Fees must be paid at the gate, and information is available at the information centre a short distance inside the park beyond the gate. Park staff can provide information on camping, wildlife-viewing and the various outdoor activities that can be enjoyed here, including hiking, cross-country skiing, golf, horseback riding, boating and swimming.

There are five scenic drives, including the **Akamina Highway**, which starts near the townsite and runs for 16km to Cameron Lake. About 1km beyond the junction of the park road is a viewpoint over the Bear's Hump, where you have a good chance of spotting some bighorn sheep. You'll find picnic areas as well as the site of Canada's first producing oil well and the city that never was. Mount Custer and the Herbst Glacier in the United States are visible from Cameron Lake, where canoes and pedal boats can be rented. This is the starting point of several trails.

The **Red Rock Canyon Parkway** is another scenic drive. It epitomizes the "prairies to peaks" region as it leads through the rolling prairie of Blakiston Valley to the rusty rocks of the water-carved gorge of Red Rock Canyon. Black bears and grizzlies can often be spotted on the slopes feeding on berries. You can also view the park's highest summit, Mount Blakiston. An interpretive trail leads into the canyon at the end of the parkway.

Another drive, the **Chief Mountain International Highway** leads through the park and into Glacier National Park in Montana. Travellers crossing the border into the United States must report to the Goat Haunt Ranger Station.

Waterton Lakes National Park was initially set aside as a forest reserve in 1895, with John George "Kootenay" Brown as its first warden. Brown got his nickname through his association with the Kootenay First Nation. He led an adventurous life, nearly losing it to the Blackfoot and his scalp to Chief Sitting Bull before turning to more conservationist pursuits.

In 1911, Waterton became a national park, and in 1932 it joined with Glacier National Park to form the first International Peace Park. The park was declared an International Biosphere Reserve in 1979. Waterton's history is also marked by a short-lived oil boom in 1901.

Unlike Banff and Jasper National Parks farther north, Waterton never had a rail link. This is still the case, with the result that Waterton remains small, pristine and unspoiled. It retains a genuine Rocky Mountain atmosphere, and so far is free of the heavy-handed, touristy commercialism that can mar any adventure into the Canadian Rockies.

The park's trademark **Prince of Wales Hotel** (see p. 408) was built in 1926-1927 by Louis Hill, head of the Great Northern Railway, to accommodate American tourists that the railway transported by bus from Montana to Jasper (today, the majority of visitors to the park are still American). Though the hotel has been sold twice, its ownership and operations are still based in the United States; furthermore, the view from the lobby over Upper Waterton Lake remains the same; the hotel still has 90 rooms and it is still open during the summer months only. Expansion and renovation plans for the hotel include the possibility of year-round operation. This would certainly change things, not only at the Prince of Wales, but in Waterton National Park as well, and the prospect of a more southerly version of Banff gets very mixed reviews. The Swiss chalet-style hotel was proclaimed a National Historic Site in 1994 by the Canadian government and is worth a visit even if you can't afford to stay here.

Tour B: Lethbridge to Medicine Hat

As you approach **Writing-on-Stone Provincial Park ★★** (*free admission; park office ☎647-2364*), located only about 10km from the U.S. border, you'll notice the carved out valley of the Milk River and in the distance the Sweetgrass Hills rising up in the state of Montana. The Milk River lies in a wide, green valley with strange rock formations and steep sandstone cliffs. The hoodoos, formed by iron-rich layers of sandstone that protect the softer underlying layers, appear like strange mushroom-shaped formations. These formations, along with the cliffs, were believed to house the powerful spirits of all things in the world, attracting Aboriginal people to this sacred place as many as 3,000 years ago.

Writing-on-Stone Provincial Park protects more rock art — petroglyphs (rock carvings) and picto-graphs (rock paintings) — than any other place on the North American plains. Dating of the rock art is difficult and based solely on styles of drawing and tell-tale objects; for example, horses and guns imply that the drawings continued into the 18th and 19th centuries. Some archaeological sites date from the Late Prehistoric Period, around 1,800 years ago.

Moose

Once, buffalo, wolves and grizzly bears could be seen in the park. Though they are gone, a great variety of wildlife and plants still thrive here. Watch for pronghorn antelope, white-tailed and mule deer, yellow-bellied marmots and beavers.

Catbirds, mourning doves, towhees and rock wrens also make their homes here. Finally, keep an ear out for rattlesnakes. These venomous critters are not dangerous unless provoked.

The North West Mounted Police also played a role in the history of the park, establishing a post here in 1889 to stop the whisky trade and fighting between Aboriginal peoples. During their time here, many officers carved their names into the sandstone cliffs. The 19th century post was washed away, but a reconstruction stands on the original site.

You must participate in a guided tour to view the post. The Battle Scene, one of the most elaborate petroglyphs in the park, can be viewed along the two self-guided interpretive trails.

The scene may depict a battle fought in 1866, but no one is sure. One of the trails, the Hoodoo Interpretive Trail, also leads through the unique natural environment of the park; a self-guiding trail brochure is available from the park office.

The majority of the rock art sites are located in the larger part of the provincial park, which is an archaeological preserve. Access is provided only through scheduled interpretive tours, and for this reason it is extremely important to call the park's **naturalist office** (☎*647-2364*) ahead of time to find out when the tours are heading out. They are given daily from mid-May to early September, and free tickets, limited in number, are required. These may be obtained from the naturalist office one hour before the tour begins. Wildlife checklists and fact sheets are also available at the naturalist office.

The park boasts an excellent campground (inquire at park office regarding fees). Visitors also have the opportunity to practise a whole slew of outdoor activities, including hiking and canoeing — this is a convenient place to start or end a canoe trip along the Milk River.

Cypress Hills Provincial Park ★★ is a wooded oasis of lodgepole pine rising out of the prairie grassland and harbouring a varied wildlife, including deer, elk and moose and some 215 species of bird (including wild turkeys). At least 18 species of orchid also thrive in the park. There are, however, no cypress trees in the park; the French word for lodgepole pine is *cypres*, and the name *montagnes de cyprès* was mistranslated to Cypress Hills.

This was also the site of the Cypress Hill Massacre. Two American whisky-trading posts were established in the hills in the early 1870s. During the winter of 1872-3, some Assiniboines were camped in the hills, close to these two posts, when a party of drunken American hunters, whose horses had been stolen, came upon the band of Assiniboine. Believing that they had taken the horses, the American hunters killed 20 innocent Assiniboine.

The incident contributed to the establishment of the North West Mounted Police to restore order. Three-hundred Mounties arrived at Fort Walsh, Saskatchewan, and the men responsible for the massacre were arrested. Though they were not convicted because of lack of evidence, the fact that white men had been arrested gave credence in the eyes of the Aboriginal people to this new police force.

This is Alberta's second largest provincial park and the only interprovincial park in the province. The park is rarely very busy, giving visitors the opportunity to enjoy great hiking and fishing in peace and quiet. It is open year-round. Visitors can rent boats, bicycles, play golf, go downhill skiing and go tobogganning. The park is also home to an abundance of stunning fragile orchids. Some bloom throughout the summer but the best time to see them is in mid-June. There are 13 campgrounds here. The visitors centre (*mid-May to early Sep, every day 10am to 5pm, information ☎893-3833*), is close to Elkwater Lake, at the townsite. In the off-season, visit the park administration office, at the eastern entrance to town, or write to *Box 12, Elkwater, Alberta, T0J 1C0, ☎893-3777.*

Outdoor Activities

Golf

Paradise Canyon (*185 Canyon Blvd; ☎381-7500, ⇄381-4300*) has a 71 par 18-hole course located in southwestern Lethbridge, between the rolling plains and Oldman River.

Waterton Lakes Golf Club (*☎859-2042*) was designed by Stanley Thompson and offers 18 holes of challenging and scenic golf. It is located 4km north of town. There is a pro shop where you can rent clubs.

Canoeing and Rafting

With hot summer temperatures and the possibility of spotting antelope, mule deer, white-tailed deer, coyotes, badger, beaver and cottontail rabbits, as well as several bird species, the Milk River is a great spot to explore by canoe. Set in arid southern Alberta, this river is the only one in Alberta that drains into the Gulf of Mexico. Canoes can be rented in Lethbridge.

Milk River Raft Tours (*Box 396 Milk River, Alberta, T0K 1M0, ☎647-3586*) organizes rafting trips along the river in the vicinity of Writing-on-Stone Provincial Park. Trips last from 2 to 6hrs, cost between $20 and $40 and can include lunch and hikes through the coulees.

Hiking

Waterton Lakes National Park has some of the most exceptional hiking in southern Alberta. Eight trails offer hikers and cross-country skiers the opportunity to explore the far reaches of this park, which lies at the meeting point between the mountains and the prairies. Complete descriptions of the trails are available at the park information centre, but take note that some of the best scenery is along the Crypt Lake Trail (8.7km one way) and the Carthew Alderson Trail (20km one way). There is also the shorter and very popular trail, the Bear's Hump (1.2km one way), which offers great views. Remember, not all of these trails are maintained for cross-country skiing, and you must register at the park office for all back-country exploring in the park, winter or summer (see p 402).

Horseback Riding

The **Willow Lane Ranch** (*$70 for B&B, $90 fb per person, weekend package $325 per person; Box 114, Granum, T0L 1A0, ☎687-2284, or (800) 665-0284, ⇌687-2409*) is a working ranch in the foothills of the Rockies about 20km north of Fort Macleod. City-slickers can join a real cattle drive (*four times a year; $225 for one week; reserve several months in advance*) or round-up, mend some fences, try their luck at calving and branding or take a day or overnight excursion into the Porcupine Hills. Accommodations are in the main ranch house (private floor) or in a cosy log cabin. Friendly service. Children must be 16 years of age or older. Enquire about various packages and their rates.

Blue Ridge Outfitters (*Box 1718, Cardston T0K 0K0, ☎653-2449*) also organizes pack trips. These can be anywhere from two to six days and usually go through the Rocky Mountains close to Waterton National Park. Accommodation is in tipis or tents, your choice. There are many different packages from weekends to excursions on horseback, call for details.

Accommodations

Tour A: Southern Foothills

Chain Lakes Provincial Park
$11 less during the week
pit toilets, water, no shower
Hwy. 22 and Hwy. 533
☎646-5887
Chain Lakes Provincial Park has over 150 campsites 12 of which are cleared in the winter ($5).

Crowsnest Pass

The Grand Union International Hostel
$15 members
$20 non-members
7719 17th Ave.
Box 1000, Coleman, T0K 0M0
☎563-3433
⇄563-3433
The Grand Union International Hostel is located in Coleman's original Grand Union Hotel, built in 1926. The interior was renovated by the Southern Alberta Hostelling Association and now houses standard hostel rooms and all the usual hostel facilities, including laundry machines and a common kitchen.

The Inn on the Lake
$45 bkfst. incl.
sb
$60 cabins
tv, K
2413 23rd Ave.
☎563-5111
The Inn on the Lake, a lovely country house on Crowsnest Lake, is a cosy place to enjoy a delicious hot breakfast.

Kosy Knest Kabins
$48
K, tv
Box 670,
Coleman, T0K 0M0
☎/⇄563-5155
You can stay at the Kosy Knest Kabins looking out over Crowsnest Lake, from May 1 to November 1. The 10 cabins are located 12km west of Coleman on Hwy. 3.

Waterton Townsite

Things slow down considerably during the winter months, when many hotels and motels close and others offer winter rates and packages.

Within the park proper there are many campsites:

Townsite Campground
$15-$20
☎859-2224
The Townsite Campground is by the lake and close to all the services in town. It is a full-service campground with hookups, showers and kitchen shelters.

Crandell Mountain Campground
$13
This campground is 10km up the Akamina Highway; it has 129 sites, no power, flush toilets and kitchen shelters.

Belly River Campground
$10
Belly River is more primitive, with pit toilets and shelters. There are also 13 back-country sites (*permit required*).

Two private campgrounds outside the park, **Waterton Homestead Campground** (*$10-$17; ≈; Hwy 5, east of park gate; ☎859-2247*) and **Waterton Riverside Campground** (*$10-$13*), offer services like showers, laundry and barbecue parties.

The Northland Lodge
$50
sb/pb, ℝ
on Evergreen Ave. Waterton Lakes National Park, T0K 2M0
☎859-2353
Open from mid-May to mid-October, The Northland Lodge is a converted house with nine cosy rooms. Some rooms have balconies and barbecues.

The Kilmorey Lodge
$86
♿, ℜ, *K*
117 Evergreen Ave. Box 100, Waterton Lakes National Park T0K 2M0
☎859-2334
⇄859-2342
The Kilmorey Lodge is open year-round. It is ideally located overlooking Emerald Bay, and many rooms have great views. Antiques and duvets contribute to the old-fashioned, homey feel. Two wheelchair-accessible suites have recently been added. The Kilmorey also boasts one of Waterton's finest restaurants, the Lamp Post Dining Room (see p 411).

Crandell Mountain Lodge
$116
K, tv, ♿; 102 Mountview Rd
Box 114
Waterton Lakes National Park, T0K 2M0
☎/⇄859-2288
The small Crandell Mountain Lodge is open from early April until the end of October. Its rustic, cosy country-inn atmosphere fits right in with the setting and is a nice

change from the motel scene. Four three-room suites with full kitchens are available, and four rooms have kitchenettes.

The Lodge at Waterton Lakes
$165
ℜ, ≈, ⌂, ⊙, K, tv
corner of Windflower and Cameron Falls Dr.
Box 4, T0K 2M0
☎***59-2151***
☎***(800) 985-6343***
⇄***859-2229***

The Lodge at Waterton Lakes is a new resort hotel in the townsite of Waterton Park. Completed in 1998, the complex has 80 rooms in nine two-storey buildings as well as 20 additional rooms affiliated with the YHA youth-hostel network. Each of the nine buildings has a theme (forests, lakes, birds, etc.) and the individual rooms are named and decorated accordingly. There are nature-education programs and a health spa, and some rooms have kitchenettes, whirlpool baths and fireplaces.

Prince of Wales Hotel
$175-$190 economy room
$347 suite
ℜ
Waterton Lakes National Park, T0K 2M0
☎***859-2231***
☎***(602) 207-6000***
⇄***859-2630***
reservations:
☎***236-3400***

The venerable Prince of Wales Hotel, open from mid-May until the end of September, is definitely the grandest place to stay in Waterton, with bellhops in kilts and high tea in Valerie's Tea Room, not to mention the unbeatable view. The lobby and rooms are all adorned with original wood panelling. The rooms are actually quite small and unspectacular, however, with tiny bathrooms and a rustic feel. Those on the third floor and higher have balconies. Try to request a room facing the lake, which is, after all, the reason people stay here. Things will certainly change here if the rumours about expanding the Prince of Wales are true (see p 403).

Fort Macleod

The Red Coat Inn
$40-$50
K, ≈, ⊛, tv
359 Col. Macleod Blvd. or Main St., Fort Macleod, T0L 0Z0
☎***553-4434***

The Red Coat Inn is one of the most reliable motel choices in Fort Macleod. Clean, pleasant rooms, kitchenettes and a pool make this a good deal.

The Mackenzie House Bed and Breakfast
$55
1623 Third Ave., Fort Macleod, T0L 0Z0
☎/⇄***553-3302***

The Mackenzie House is located in a historic house built in 1904 for an Alberta member of the legislature at the time the province was founded, in 1905. Tea and coffee are served in the afternoon, and guests are greeted in the morning with a delicious home-made breakfast.

Tour B: Lethbridge to Medicine Hat

Lethbridge

Art Deco Heritage House B&B
$50 bkfst incl.
sb
1115 Eighth Ave. S, T1J 1P7
☎***328-3824***
⇄***328-9011***

Built in 1937, the Art Deco Heritage House B&B is located on one of Lethbridge's pretty tree-lined residential streets, only a few minutes' walk from downtown. The guest rooms are uniquely decorated in accordance with the design of the house and include many of the house's original features. This house is an Alberta Provincial Historic Resource.

London Road B&B
$65
pb/sb
637 Ninth St. S, T1J 2L5
☎***381-2580***
fitzpatrick@uleth.ca

London Road B&B is a friendly place just a few blocks from downtown. The rooms are very prettily decorated with iron beds, lace and floral motifs, and duvet bedspreads. Guests are made to feel very welcome with full access to the kitchen, a lounge with a fireplace and a pretty backyard and terrace. Breakfasts are copious to say the least and might feature fruit salad, muffins, crab quiche or crispy bacon. No smoking.

Bartlett House B&B
$75
sb
318 12th St. S, T1J 2R1
☎328-4832
Bartlett House B&B is set in a large 1910 house with red shutters. Louise, your hostess, is originally from Québec and a few of the pieces of pine furniture, along with some of the art, come from her native province. At the top of the charmingly creaky stairs, one guest room has a gorgeous antique bed, and the bathroom has a lovely antique tub . Breakfast might be an Italian omelette with sausage, a baked apple pancake or a fruity biscuit, each accompanied by freshly made cappuccino. There is wine and cheese upon arrival and evening meals are available if requested ahead of time.

Days Inn
$64-$67 bkfst. incl.
≡, ⊛, *K*, ≈, ⊘, *tv*, 🐕, ♿
100 Third Ave. S, T1J 4L2
☎327-6000
☎(800) 661-8085
⇄320-2070
Days Inn is the best motel choice downtown. The typical motel-style rooms are non-descript, but modern and clean. A free continental breakfast is served. Coin laundry available. You can also take advantage of the brand new pool.

The Best Western Heidelberg Inn
$77-$80
≡, ⌂, ℜ, *bar, tv*
1303 Mayor Magrath Dr. S, T1K 2R1
☎329-0555
☎(800) 791-8488
☎(800) 528-1234
⇄328-8846
The Best Western Heidelberg Inn is an inexpensive, reliable option along the motel strip south of the city. Though the decor is a bit dated, the rooms are spotless, the staff is friendly and you get a complimentary newspaper in the morning.

Sandman Inn
$80
≡, ≈, ℜ, ⌂, *tv*
421 Mayor Magrath Dr. S, T1J 3L8
☎328-1111
☎(800) 726-3626
⇄329-9488
The Sandman Inn is another safe bet, with a nice indoor pool and clean, modern rooms.

Lethbridge Lodge Hotel
$119-$139
≡, ≈, ℜ, ⊛, *tv*, 🐕
320 Scenic Dr., T1J 4B4
☎328-1123
☎(800) 661-1232
⇄328-0002
The best hotel accommodation in Lethbridge is found at the Lethbridge Lodge Hotel overlooking the river valley. The comfortable rooms, decorated in warm and pleasant colours, seem almost luxurious when you consider the reasonable price. The rooms surround an interior tropical courtyard where small footbridges lead from the pool to the lounge and Anton's Restaurant (see p 412).

Medicine Hat

Groves B&B
$45 bkfst incl.
Box 998, T1A 7H1
☎529-6065
Groves B&B is located about 10km from downtown Medicine Hat in a peaceful spot near the South Saskatchewan River. Breakfast which includes home-made bread, can be taken on the deck outside. There are also walking trails nearby. From downtown take Holsom Road west, turn left on Range Road 70, drive 3.3km and turn right on #130.

The Sunny Holme B&B
$65 bkfst incl.
271 1st St. SE, T1A 0A3
☎526-5846
Besides the one central hotel, there is actually another, very pleasant place to stay that is close to downtown, along pretty First Street SE. The Sunny Holme B&B is in a grand western Georgian house with a Victorian interior, and the three rooms are decorated in the arts and crafts style, and each room has its own bathroom. A large leafy lot surrounds the house. Sourdough pan-

cakes are just one of the breakfast possibilities. Be sure to call ahead.

The Inn on Fourth
56-$65
≡, ℜ, *tv*
530 Fourth St. SE, T1A 0K8
☎526-1313
☎(800) 730-3887
⇄526-4189
The only hotel right downtown is the little The Inn on Fourth which only has 34 rooms. The rooms are clean and the hotel was completely renovated in 1997.

Best Western Inn
$99
ℜ, ⊙, ≡, ≈, ⌂, ⊛, *K*, *tv*, ;
1051 Ross Glen Dr.
☎529-2222
⇄529-1538
For about the same price, you can stay along the motel strip at the Best Western Inn where the surroundings may not be as pleasant, but the facilities and rooms are more modern. Guests have access to an indoor pool and laundry facilities, and can benefit (hopefully) from the only casino in town.

Medicine Hat Lodge
$79 bkfst incl.
tv, ≈, ≡, ℜ, ⊛, *pb*
1051 Ross Glen Dr. SE
T1B 3T8
☎529-2222
☎(800) 661-8095
⇄529-1538
Medicine Hat Lodge offers good value for the money. The rooms are standard but surprisingly pleasant with classic dark-wood furniture and pretty bedspreads. Some have sofas, and all have coffee machines and hairdryers. The hotel also has a waterslide to keep the kids happy. Its restaurant is recommended.

Elkwater

Cypress Hills Provincial Park
$11-$22
reservations
☎893-3782
Cypress Hills Provincial Park has 13 campsites for both tents and R.V.s, with or without services. Reservations are only required for two sites; for the 11 others, it's first come, first served.

Restaurants

Tour A: Southern Foothills

Okotoks

Ginger Tea Room and Gift Shop
$-$$
43 Riverside Dr.
☎938-2907
Ginger Tea Room and Gift Shop is a fanciful mix of sensible lunch fare and two floors of unique antiques and gifts. The menu includes sandwiches, soups, salads and an afternoon country tea with hot biscuits and jam. You can eat in or take out. "Romantic Dinners for Two" are also available.

La P'tite Table
$$
52 N. Railway St.
☎938-2224
www.la-ptite-table.com
La P'tite Table is so *petite* that reservations are a must. The chef once cooked at the Palliser and at La Chaumiere in Calgary. Classic bistro-style French cuisine and Alberta ingredients, including duck and ostrich, are served; perfect pastries and coffee finish the soiree.

Longview

Memories Inn
$-$$
Main St., Longview
☎558-3665
Memories Inn has been decorated with the props left behind from the filming of the Clint Eastwood film *Unforgiven*. The atmosphere can get rowdy, especially during the weekend buffets, which feature, among other things, succulent ribs, burgers and homemade pies.

Waterton

Borderline
$
305 Windflower Ave.
☎859-2284
Borderline is a friendly place for a hearty breakfast. The homemade soups and breads are delicious. Take-out lunches are available. The place stays busy

throughout the day, both inside and outside on the terrace. A section of the bookstore was converted into the coffee shop a while back, creating a particularly pleasant atmosphere.

The Waterton Park Café
$
Waterton Ave.
The Waterton Park Café is popular with the seasonal workers in the park as a place to eat and drink. Good sandwiches and lunch fare.

The Lamp Post Dining Room
$$$
in Kilmorey Lodge
☎*859-2334*
The Lamp Post offers what some argue is the best dining in Waterton. The traditional charm, coupled with award-winning food and relatively reasonable prices definitely make it one of the best.

Garden Court Dining Room
$$$$
☎*859-2231*
The atmosphere at the Garden Court Dining Room in the Prince of Wales Hotel is unbeatable. This formal dining room serves a complete menu and daily specials that often include delicious seafood or pasta. Reservations are not accepted. Also in the Prince of Wales, and enjoying an equally elegant ambience and a stunning view are the **Windsor Lounge** and **Valerie's Tea Room**, where afternoon tea and continental breakfast are both served.

Fort Macleod

The Silver Grill
$
24th St. between Second and Third Ave.
☎*553-3888*
The Silver Grill is an interesting alternative to the fast food joints near the motels. This historic saloon serves a mediocre Chinese buffet, called a "Smorg," and typical North American dishes, but it is the interior that makes it worth a stop. The original bar and a bullet-pierced mirror will make you feel like you should be watching your back!

Tour B: Lethbridge to Medicine Hat

Lethbridge

O'Sho Japanese Restaurant
$
1219 Third Ave. S
☎*327-8382*
For a change from Alberta beef try the O'Sho Japanese Restaurant where classic Japanese fare is enjoyed in traditional style from low tables set in partitioned rooms.

The Penny Coffee House
$
Ninth St. S, between Fifth and Sixth Ave. S
Located next to B. Maccabee's bookseller, The Penny Coffee House is the perfect place to enjoy a good book; don't worry if you haven't got one, there is plenty of interesting reading material on the walls. This café serves delicious hearty soups and chilis, filling sandwiches, a wonderful cheese and tomato scone, sodas and of course a great cup of Java.

Cupper's
$
309A Fifth St. S
☎/⇌*380-4555*
The Penny Coffee House just opened another café in the municipal library. The expansion didn't stop there; if you want to buy coffee or tea, the owner recently opened Cupper's, a little café where they roast and grind their own coffee beans. Coffees from all over the world are available.

Coco Pazzo
$$
1249 Third Ave. S
☎*329-8979*
The hip Mediterranean decor at Coco Pazzo certainly has something to do with this new Italian café's success, but so does the food. The Strascinati sauce, a tomato cream sauce of their own invention is good, though not too original. It compliments the veal with capicollo nicely in the Modo Mio dish. The vegetarian pizza is truly a veggie-lover's dream. Another house specialty is fettuccine del

Pescatore, prepared with scallops, clams and tiger prawns.

Showdowns Eatin' Adventures
$$
329 Fifth St. S
☎***329-8830***
Showdowns Eatin' Adventures is indeed an adventure with a gun-toting, can-can-girl act. Steaks and ribs figure prominently on the menu, which is rather ordinary.

Shanghaï
$$
610 Third Ave. S
☎***327-3552***
Despite an interior that could use a little freshening up, the Shanghaï restaurant offers a complete Chinese menu. They also serve north-American fare (club sandwiches, hamburgers, and the like). The chicken dishes are the chef's speciality.

Sven Ericksen's
$$-$$$
1714 Mayor Magrath Dr. S
☎***328-7756***
Sven Ericksen's is a family-style restaurant that stands out among the endless fast-food joints on Mayor Magrath Drive. This restaurant has been in business since 1948 and serves carefully prepared home-made dishes. The vast menu will please everyone.

Anton's
$$$$
Lethbridge Lodge
☎***328-1123***
The Lethbridge Lodge is home to Anton's, the city's finest restaurant. The pasta dishes are particularly well received, as is the setting, in the hotel's tropical indoor courtyard. Reservations are recommended.

Garden Café
$$
The Garden Café is a less expensive alternative in the Lethbridge Lodge with the same lovely surroundings. It is open from 6:30am to 11:30pm and serves a hearty breakfast, as well as truly divine desserts.

Medicine Hat

The City Bakery
$
Fifth Ave. SW, between Third and Fourth St. SW
☎***527-2800***
The City Bakery bakes up wonderful fresh breads and New York bagels.

At Damon Lane's Tearoom
$
10am to 4pm, closed Mon
730 Third St. SE
☎***529-2224***
At Damon Lane's Tearoom you can lunch on simple soups, salads and sandwiches, all home-made on the premises, or just stop in for a spot of tea and a bit of shopping. There are crafts, pottery, and decorative items for the home plus a small collection of antiques for sale.

Rustler's
$
901 Eighth St. SW
☎***526-8004***
Rustler's is another spot that transports you back to the lawless wild west — the restaurant boasts a blood-stained card table preserved under glass for all to gawk at! The menu features steaks, chicken, ribs, pasta and several Mexican dishes. Breakfasts are particularly busy and copious.

Caroline's Pub & Eatery
$-$$
101 Fourth Ave. SE
☎***529-5300***
For lunch, try Caroline's Pub & Eatery, a big, airy place that lacks ambience but serves good, inexpensive food.

Mamma's Restaurant
$$-$$$
at the Medicine Hat Lodge, 1051 Ross Glen Dr., SE
☎***529-2222***
Mamma's Restaurant offers a varied menu that features fine Alberta steaks and several pasta dishes. The food is recommended, but unfortunately the noise and chlorine smell from the hotel's waterslides is a little distracting.

Entertainment

Tour A: Southern Foothills

Fort Macleod

Main Street's **Empress Theatre** (*235 24th St., ☎553-4404 or 800-540-9229*) is an original theatre from 1912. In fact, it's one of the oldest theatres in the province. It presents popular films throughout the year. Depending on the time of year, musical concerts, plays and conferences alternate with the program of films.

Every year in mid-July the **Annual Pow-Wow** is held at Head-Smashed-In Buffalo Jump. A large tipi is set up on the grounds where visitors can see traditional native dancing and sample some native food. For information call ☎553-2731.

Tour B: Lethbridge to Medicine Hat

Lethbridge

The third week in July is time for **Whoop-Up Days** in Lethbridge. Parades, festivities in the streets, a casino, performances every night and, of course, a rodeo are just some of the highlights. For information call ☎328-4491.

Medicine Hat

The **Medicine Hat Exhibition and Stampede**, held the last weekend in July, is second only to Calgary's Stampede in grandeur and extravagance. For information call ☎527-1234.

Shopping

Lethbridge

B. Macabee's Bookseller (*Fourth Ave. S at Fifth St. S, ☎329-0771*) is a cosy little bookstore adjoining the Penny Coffee House (see p 411). Choose from an extensive selection of books about local issues by local writers. Not only is this a great place to pick up a good book, but it's also a great place to peruse your purchase.

Medicine Hat

The **Clay Interpretive Centre** (see p 401) sells replicas and originals of Hycroft China and Medalta potteries. Copies of the Medalta cauldrons, prized by antique collectors, are available.

Hockey

Canada's national sport, without a doubt, is ice hockey. The National Hockey League (NHL) originally had only six teams, two of which were in Canada: the Montréal Canadiens and the Toronto Maple Leafs.

During the 1960s and 1970s, expansions doubled the number of franchises, eventually bringing the number of teams up to 21. Today the league includes 28 teams divided between two associations. The Edmonton Oilers were a part of the second wave of expansion when the World Hockey Association (WHA) joined up with the NHL.

The Oilers and three other WHL teams joined the NHL in time for the 1979-80 hockey season. The Oilers were a well-managed, young team that knew how to scout recruits from the minor leagues. The team's owner even declared that his team would win the Stanley Cup (the trophy awarded to the winner of the finals) within five years or less. This was a bold prediction in a league where the championship title passed back and forth between the dynasties of the Montréal Canadiens and the New York Islanders.

But while those teams were ageing, the Oilers were building their future. Their captain, Wayne Gretzky, soon earned the nickname "The Great One" due to his incredible natural talent. He accumulated record after record, and even scored five goals in one game on December 30, 1981. That day, he became the first player in hockey history to score 50 goals in such a short period of time: 39 games. He ended the season with 92 goals and 120 assists, an unprecedented record.

However, Oilers fans had to wait until their players matured, and it was not until 1984 that the Oilers finally broke the domination of the New York Islanders, who had just won four consecutive championships. The rest is history: the Oilers won five Stanley Cups in seven years, broke numerous records and had the satisfaction of winning the coveted trophy again in 1990, while Gretzky had been playing for the Los Angeles Kings for two years.

Since these glory years, Canadian teams have remained competitive, but have not frequently won top honours in competition. Money prevailed over passion, and the teams with the largest budgets now attract the best players – nearly all of them millionaires – who all hope to run off with the Stanley Cup.

Canadian hockey in particular suffers from this new business environment since its markets are much smaller than those of the U.S. megalopolises, not to mention the weakness of the Canadian dollar against the U.S. currency. For these reasons, the Québec Nordiques and Winnipeg Jets had to move to the United States at the beginning of the 1990s.

Having broken every imaginable record, Wayne Gretzky retired from competition in 1999. After toying with the idea of renaming their town "Gretzkyville," Edmonton city officials instead decided to name a highway after him. And why not?! The highways are can turn to ice on cold winter days in northern Alberta!

Central Alberta

Central Alberta encompasses a vast swath of the province that includes the Red Deer River Valley, the foothills, the Rocky Mountains Forest Reserve and the heartland.

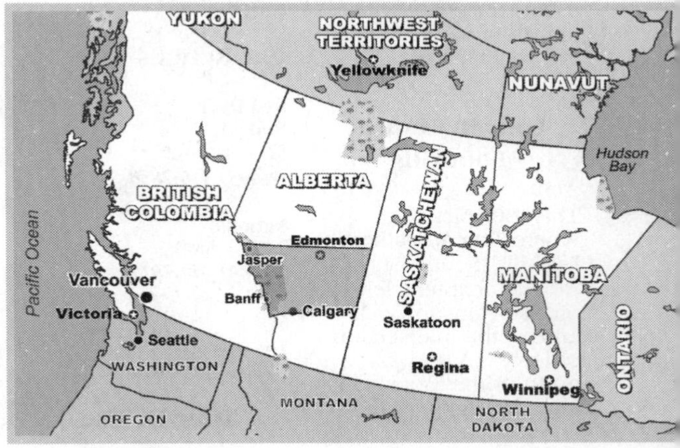

A region that holds an inestimable amount of natural resources, forestry, farming and oil drive the economy of this region, as does tourism which has been boosted by the occasional discovery of a dinosaur bone or two.

This chapter is divided into four driving tours:

Tour A:
Digging for Dinosaur Bones and Other Treasures ★★★

Tour B:
The Central Foothills ★

Tour C:
The Heartland ★

Tour D:
The Yellowhead ★★

Tour A and Tour C of this chapter can be combined loosely to form a meandering route between Alberta's two main cities, Calgary and Edmonton, while take this route there and a more direct route back.

This route also covers parts of the first three tours of this chapter and links up to the last one.

Tour B picks up where Tour A of the Southern Alberta chapter left off.

Finding Your Way Around

Visitors who want to go from Calgary to Edmonton have several options:

One of these, though indirect, consists of passing through the spectacular Rocky mountains following Rte. 93. Travellers can

By Car

Tour A: Digging for Dinosaur Bones and Other Treasures

This tour follows the Red Deer River Valley from Dinosaur Provincial Park to the vicinity of Drumheller. Dinosaur Provincial Park is north of the Trans-Canada (Hwy. 1), off Hwy. 876. From there, head west on Hwy. 550 then Hwy. 1. Head north on Hwy. 56 to Drumheller. To reach Rosebud head west on Hwy. 9 then south on Hwy. 840. The tour continues north of Drumheller on Hwy. 9 to Morrin and Rowley and then west on Hwy. 585 to Trochu.

Tour B: Central Foothills

This tour picks up where **Tour A: Southern Foothills** (Southern Alberta chapter), left off. It begins in Cochrane at the intersection of Hwy. 1A and 22, north of the Trans-Canada Highway 1. From Cochrane head north on Hwy. 22 then east on Hwy. 580 to Carstairs. Next head north on Hwy. 2A to Innisfail, then west on Hwy. 592 to Markerville, then north on Hwy. 781 to Sylvan Lake, and finally west on Hwy. 11 to Rocky Mountain House. Hwy. 11 is the David Thompson Highway and reaches Hwy. 93, the Icefields Parkway through the Rockies, at Saskatchewan River Crossing.

Tour C: Heartland

This tour starts in Olds, heads north toward Red Deer, and continues to Ponoka. From there, it returns towards Lacombe in the south before heading east on Hwy. 12 to Stettler, north on Hwy. 56 to Camrose, west on Hwy. 13 to Wetaskiwin, north on Hwy. 2A to Leduc, and finally west on Hwy. 39 and north on Hwy. 6 to Devon. Edmonton (see p 441) is another 15km north on Hwy. 60.

Car Rentals

Red Deer
Budget
5214 Gaetz Ave.
☎***(403) 346-7858***

National
2319 Taylor Dr.
☎***(403) 347-5811***

Avis
4702 51st Ave.
☎***(403) 343-7010***

Tour D: The Yellowhead

The Yellowhead Highway 16 crosses the province from east to west, leading from the city of Lloydminster to Jasper and the border of British Columbia at Yellowhead Pass.

By Bus

Drumheller Greyhound Bus Depot
308 Center St.
☎***823-7566***
Services: restaurant, tourist information.

Red Deer Greyhound Bus Depot
4303 Gaetz Ave. at 50th Ave. (across from the Red Deer Inn)
☎***343-8866***

Wetaskiwin Greyhound Bus Depot
4122 49th St.
☎***352-4713***

Lloydminster Greyhound Bus Depot
5217 51st St.
☎***875-9141***

Hinton Greyhound Bus Depot
128 North St., behind the Kentucky Fried Chicken
☎***865-3367***

By Train

Via trains follow the Yellowhead Route into Edmonton and then on to Jasper. For information on schedules and stops see p ?.

Alberta Prairie Railway Excursions: (☎*742-2811 for schedule and reservations*) operates a scenic train out of Stettler (see p 429)

Practical Information

Area Code: 403

Tourist Information

Heartland Office of Alberta Travel
☎***888-414-4139***

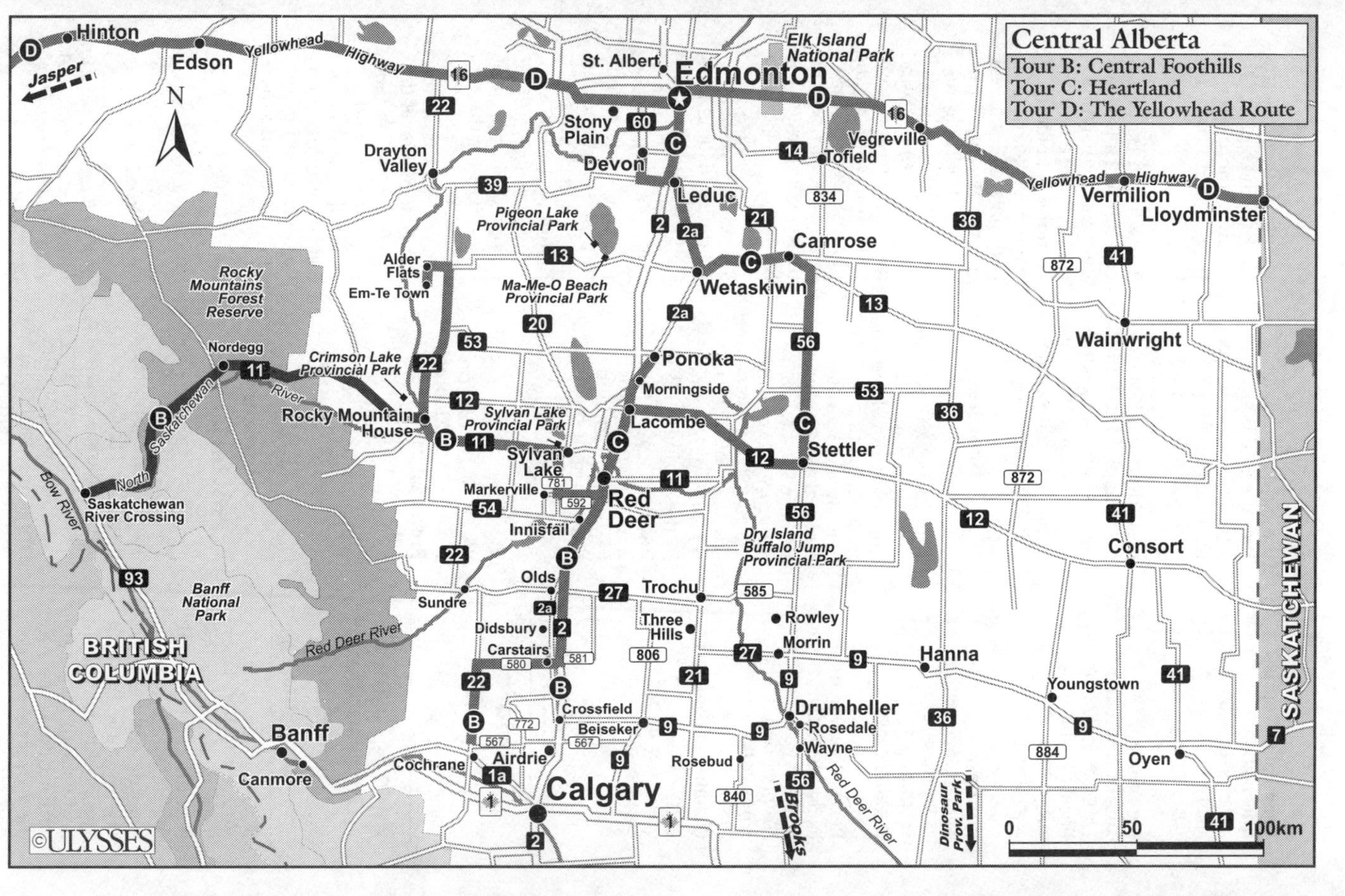

Central Alberta
Tour B: Central Foothills
Tour C: Heartland
Tour D: The Yellowhead Route
Hinton
Edson
Jasper
Yellowhead Highway
St. Albert
Edmonton
Elk Island National Park
Stony Plain
Devon
Drayton Valley
Leduc
Vegreville
Tofield
Vermilion
Lloydminster
Camrose
Wetaskiwin
Pigeon Lake Provincial Park
Ma-Me-O Beach Provincial Park
Alder Flats
Em-Te Town
Rocky Mountains Forest Reserve
Wainwright
Nordegg
Crimson Lake Provincial Park
Ponoka
Morningside
Lacombe
Rocky Mountain House
Sylvan Lake Provincial Park
Sylvan Lake
Stettler
North Saskatchewan River
Saskatchewan River Crossing
Bow River
Markerville
Red Deer
Innisfail
Dry Island Buffalo Jump Provincial Park
Consort
Banff National Park
Olds
Sundre
Trochu
Rowley
Didsbury
Three Hills
Morrin
Carstairs
Hanna
Red Deer River
British Columbia
Youngstown
Crossfield
Drumheller
Beiseker
Rosedale
Banff
Wayne
Airdrie
Rosebud
Oyen
Cochrane
Canmore
Calgary
Brooks
Dinosaur Prov. Park
Saskatchewan
0
50
100km
©ULYSSES

Drumheller Tourist Information
at the corner of Riverside Dr. and 1st St. W
☎***823-1331***

Big Country Tourist Association
170 Centre St., #28, Box 2308, Drumheller, T0J 0Y0
☎***823-5885***
⇌ ***823-7942***

Red Deer Tourist Information
25 Riverview Park
☎***346-0180***
☎***800-215-8946***

Rocky Mountain House
tourist information in a trailer north of town on Hwy. 11
summer only
☎***845-2414***

Chamber of Commerce
In Town Hall
open year round
☎***845-5450***

Exploring

Tour A: Digging for Dinosaur Bones and Other Treasures

Where the Red Deer River Valley now lies was once the coastal region of a vast inland sea; the climate probably resembled that of the Florida Everglades and was an ideal habitat for dinosaurs. After the extinction of the dinosaurs, ice covered the land. As the ice retreated 10,000 years ago, it carved out deep trenches in the prairie; this and subsequent erosion have uncovered dinosaur bones and shaped the fabulously interesting landscape of hoodoos and coulees you'll see on this Dinosaur odyssey.

Brooks

Brooks began as a railway stop in the 1880s, and soon developed a major irrigation system. The **Brooks Aqueduct National and Provincial Historic Site** (*$2; mid-May to Sep, every day 10am to 6pm; 3km southeast of Brooks,* ☎*362-4451*) began operating in the spring of 1915; at the time it was the longest concrete structure (3.2km) of its kind in the world. It was a vital part of the irrigation of southeastern Alberta for 65 years.

South of Brooks on Hwy. 873 is **Kinbrook Provincial Park** ★ and Lake Newell. The wildlife observation possibilities here are excellent. See Parks, p 431.

★★★ Dinosaur Provincial Park

The town of Brooks is also a great jumping-off point for Dinosaur Provincial Park, declared a UNESCO World Heritage Site in 1979. The landscape of this park consists of Badlands, called *mauvaises terres* by French explorers because there was neither food nor beavers there.

These eerie Badlands contain fossil beds of international significance, where over 300 complete skeletons have been found. Glacial meltwater carved out the Badlands from the soft bedrock, revealing hills laden with dinosaur bones. Wind and rain erosion continue today, providing a glimpse of how this landscape of hoodoos, mesas and gorges was formed.

There are two self-guided trails and a loop road, but the best way to see the park is to follow a guided-tour into the restricted nature preserve, though this requires a bit of planning. Unless you plan to arrive early, it is extremely important to call ahead for the times of the tours (see Parks, p 432). Visitors can tour the **Field Station of the Tyrell Museum** ★ (see p 432 for fee and schedule information) for an introduction to the excavation of dinosaur bones, and then head off on their own adventure.

The dinosaur odyssey continues in Drumheller. From Dinosaur Provincial Park take Hwy. 550 west to Bassano and then travel west on Hwy. 1. At Hwy. 56 head north to Drumheller.

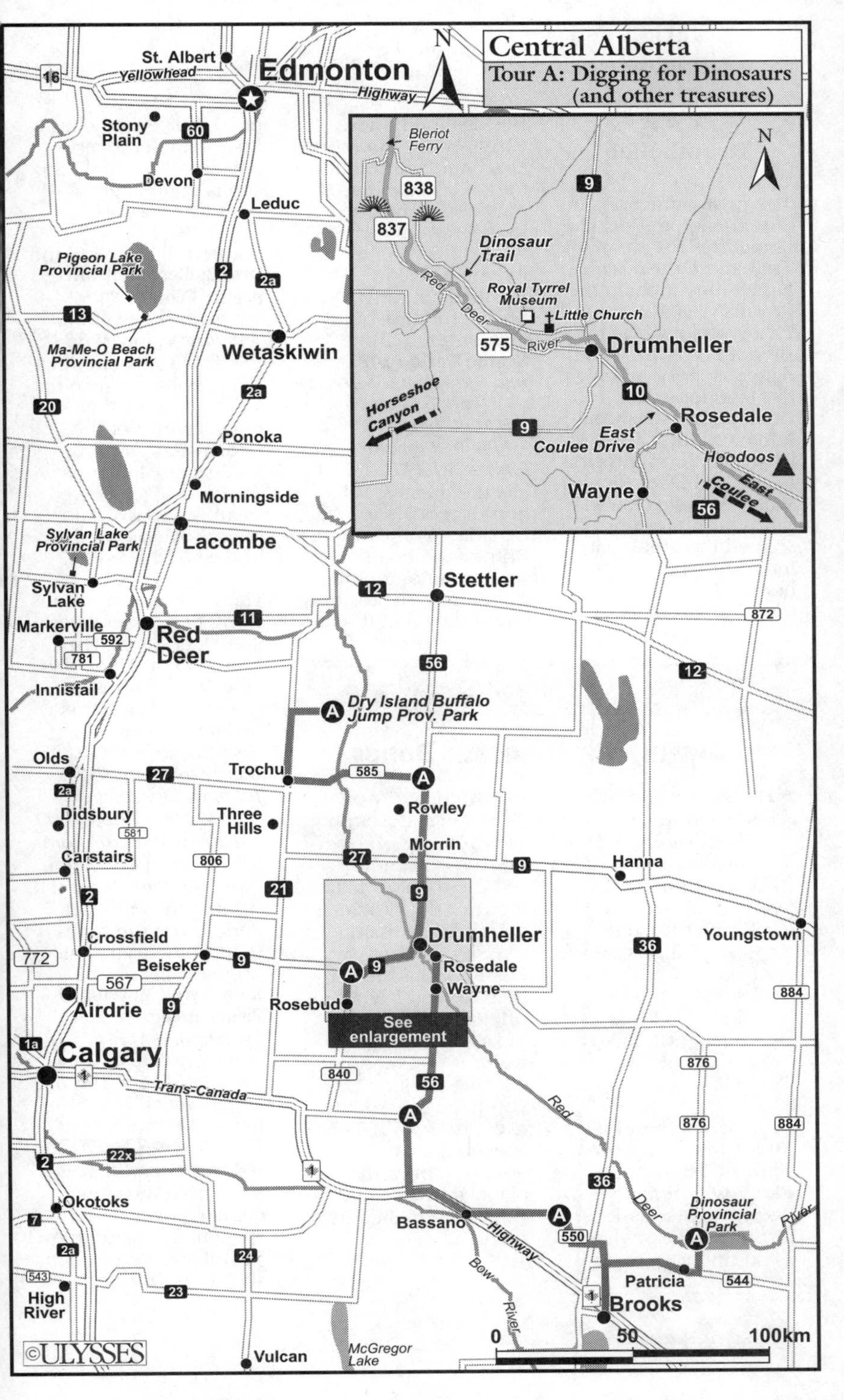

Central Alberta
Tour A: Digging for Dinosaurs (and other treasures)
Edmonton
St. Albert
Yellowhead Highway
Stony Plain
Devon
Leduc
Pigeon Lake Provincial Park
Ma-Me-O Beach Provincial Park
Wetaskiwin
Ponoka
Morningside
Lacombe
Sylvan Lake Provincial Park
Sylvan Lake
Markerville
Red Deer
Innisfail
Stettler
Dry Island Buffalo Jump Prov. Park
Olds
Trochu
Didsbury
Three Hills
Rowley
Morrin
Carstairs
Hanna
Drumheller
Crossfield
Beiseker
Rosedale
Wayne
Rosebud
Youngstown
Airdrie
See enlargement
Calgary
Trans-Canada
Red Deer River
Okotoks
Bassano
Highway
Dinosaur Provincial Park
Patricia
Bow River
Brooks
High River
Vulcan
McGregor Lake
0 50 100km
©ULYSSES
Bleriot Ferry
Dinosaur Trail
Royal Tyrrel Museum
Little Church
Red Deer River
Drumheller
Horseshoe Canyon
East Coulee Drive
Rosedale
Hoodoos
Wayne
East Coulee

★★★ Drumheller

The main attractions in Drumheller are located along the Dinosaur Trail and East Coulee Drive; they include the Royal Tyrell Museum of Palaeontology, the Bleriot Ferry, the Rosedale Suspension Bridge, the Hoodoos, East Coulee, the Atlas Coal Mine and the Last Chance Saloon. Erosion in the Red Deer River Valley has uncovered dinosaur bones and shaped the fabulously interesting landscape of hoodoos and coulees found in Drumheller.

Besides the bones, early settlers discovered coal. Agriculture and the oil and gas industries now drive the local economy.

As you arrive in Drumheller via Hwy. 9, one of the first buildings on the right is **Reptile World** (*$4.50; mid-May to mid-Sep every day 9am to 10pm, mid-Sep to mid-May Thu-Tue 10am to 6pm; Sun City Market, ☎823-8623*). It has the greatest selection of reptiles in Canada. You can meet Britney the boa constrictor, among others. Apparently snakes only bite if they feel threatened, but Britney has been handled every day since her birth, so she is completely at ease with visitors.

Located downtown, the **Drumheller Valley Interpretive Center** (*$3.50; every day 9am to 5pm; 335 First St. East, ☎823-2593*) is a museum that offers you a chance to learn about First Nations' culture of the Badlands. Dinosaur fossils and skeletons are on display as well as an instructive geological exhibit on the history of the valley.

The Dinosaur Trail runs along both sides of the Red Deer River. The first stop on Hwy. 838 (the North Dinosaur Trail), the **Homestead Antique Museum** (*$3; mid-May to mid-Oct, every day 9am to 5pm; Jul and Aug, every day 9am to 8pm; ☎823-2600, www.tyrellmuseum.com*), which has a collection of 4,000 items from the days of the early settlers, is not the highlight of the tour. That honour falls on the **Royal Tyrell Museum of Palaeontology ★★★** (*$6.50; mid-May to Sep every day 9am to 9pm; Oct to mid-May, Tue to Sun 10am to 5pm; 6km west of Drumheller on Hwy. 838, ☎823-7707 or ☎888-440-4240*). This mammoth museum contains over 80,000 specimens, including 50 full-size dinosaur skeletons.

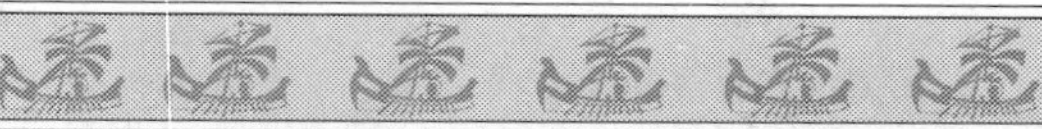

Digging for Dinosaur Bones

The very nature of the Red Deer River Valley means that every time it rains, more dinosaur bones are uncovered. As mentioned, the Royal Tyrell Museum organizes various digs for budding palaeontologists, but while exploring on this tour you may just make a discovery of your own.

Any items found on the surface and on private land can be kept with the landowner's permission. You can keep what you find as a custodian (ultimately ownership resides with the Province of Alberta), but you cannot sell the fossil or take it out of the province without permission.

Fossils should never be removed from their original stratigraphic position, however, without first mapping out that position, and you need a permit to excavate fossils. These treasures are an important part of the planet's history and should be treated as such.

There are hands-on exhibits and computers, fibre-optics and audio-visual presentations. The Royal Tyrell is also a major research centre, and visitors can watch scientists cleaning bones and preparing specimens for display. There is certainly a lot to thrill younger travellers here; however, the wealth of information to absorb can be a bit overwhelming. Special new displays are always being set up. You can participate in the **Day Dig** (*$85, children 10 to 15 $55, includes lunch, snacks, transportation and admission to the museum, reservations required; mid-May to late Jun, Sat and Sun, late Jun to end of Aug every day*), which offers an opportunity to visit a dinosaur quarry and excavate fossils yourself, or the **Dig Watch** (*$12, children 7 to 17 $8, under 7 free, families $30; daily departures from the museum at 10am, noon, 2pm*), a 90min guided tour to an actual working excavation site, where you'll see a dig in progress. Call ahead for tour times.

The next stop is the world's largest **Little Church**, which can accommodate "10,000 people, but only 6 at a time." The seven-by-eleven-foot house of worship, opened in 1958, seems to have been more popular with vandals than the devout and was rebuilt in 1990.

Continue along the Dinosaur Trail for breathtaking views over the Red Deer River at the **Horsethief Canyon Lookout**. There are paths to petrified oyster beds. The canyon got its name after it became an ideal hideout for horse thieves' booties in the early 1900s. Turn right onto Hwy. 838 to the **Bleriot Ferry**, one of the last cable-operated ferries in Alberta. The ferry was named after the famous French pilot and balloonist Louis Bleriot. The trail continues along the southern shore of the river with another great lookout, the **Orkney Hill Lookout**.

★★★ Hoodoo Trail/East Coulee Drive

Once back in Drumheller, get on East Coulee Drive, also called the Hoodoo Trail, which heads southeast along the Red Deer River. The town of **Rosedale** originally stood on the other side of the river next to the Star Mine. The suspension bridge across the Red Deer looks flimsy, but is said to be safe for those who want to venture across. Take a detour to cross the 11 bridges to get to **Wayne**. The bridges are perhaps the best part, as the main attraction in town, the Rosedeer Hotel, with its **Last Chance Saloon**, leaves something to be desired. Rooms are available for rent at $15/night, but settle for a beer and some nostalgia instead. You can also have a good steak cooked up on the grill. The fourth floor is closed because legend has it that the spirit of a murderer from the early 1900s still wanders there.

About halfway between Rosedale and East Coulee you'll see some of the most spectacular **hoodoos ★★★** in southern Alberta. These strange mushroom-shaped formations result when the softer underlying sandstone erodes. **East Coulee**, a town that almost disappeared, was once home to 3,000 people but only 200 residents remain. The **East Coulee School Museum** (*$2.15; summer, every day 9am to 6pm; winter, closed Sat and Sun; ☎822-3970*) occupies a 1930s school house. Inside are a small tea room and gallery. Although the Atlas Coal Mine ceased operations in 1955, the **Atlas Coal Mine Museum** (*$3; May to Oct, every day 9am to 6pm; ☎822-2220*) keeps the place alive to this day across the river from town. The last standing tipple (a device for emptying coal from mine cars) in Canada stands among the mine buildings, which you can explore on your own or as part of a guided tour. The colourful owner of the Wildhorse Saloon, in front of the mine, was instrumental in saving the School Museum and the Atlas Coal Mine. Don't drink anything that's not bottled in this place.

Horseshoe Canyon (*19km from Drumheller on Hwy. 9*) looks out over Alberta's version of the Grand Canyon. The terrific formations of volcanic and sedimentary rock can be observed up close on easy footpaths leading into the canyon from the lookout. **Horseshoe Canyon Tours** (*mid-May to end of mid-Oct, every day; ☎288-8788*) organizes 1hr "Terra-Bus" tours into the canyon.

Continue on Hwy. 9 and turn left on Hwy. 840 to reach Rosebud.

★ Rosebud

This town, which almost disappeared, is becoming a tourist attraction in its own right with the opening of the new Rosebud Country Inn (see p 435) and the increasing popularity of the its biggest claim to fame, the **Rosebud Theatre ★★★** (see p 439). The streets of this tiny town overlooking the Rosebud River are lined with **historic buildings ★** that will take you back in time. Most of these have markers.

North of Drumheller

North of Drumheller on Hwy. 56 are two curious towns. The first is **Morrin**, with its **Sod House and Historical Park** (*free admission; Jul and Aug, Wed to Sun 9:30am to 5:30pm*). The earth floor of this replica of the pioneers' original houses underlines the crude conditions they lived in.

Continuing north on Hwy. 56 and turning left on Range Road to **Rowley** is a must for movie buffs. Rowley's main drag looks like a ghost town, all the better for making movies: the street has been featured in several films. Of particular interest are an old country school, a refurbished train station, the Trading Post soda shop and Sam's Saloon, which doubles as the terminus of the Alberta Prairie Steam Train tour out of Stettler (see p 429).

Take Hwy. 585 West, then Hwy. 21 North to Trochu.

Trochu

The **St. Ann Ranch and Trading Company ★** (*$2; every day 9am to 9pm; on the southeast edge of Trochu, ☎442-3924*) was originally established in 1903 as part of a French-speaking settlement. The community thrived and grew to include a school, church and post office, but the onset of WWI prompted many settlers to return to their homeland of France. The ranch has been restored and is run by a descendent of one of the original settlers. A small museum displays historic pieces, while an adjoining tea room (*open every second weekend in Jul and Aug from 2pm to 4pm*) and *gîte* (*bed and breakfast, see p 435*) provide an opportunity for an experience *à la française*.

Thirty kilometres north of Trochu off Hwy. 21 you'll find **Dry Island Buffalo Jump Provincial Park**, a day-use park that highlights the dramatic contrast between the Red Deer River Valley floor and the surrounding farmland. The jump, once used by the Cree, is higher than most in Alberta; the buffalo herded over its cliffs fell about 50m and were then butchered by the Cree for their meat and hides.

Red Deer can be reached by heading east on Hwy. 590 and north on Hwy. 2, Calgary is south on Hwy. 2.

Tour B: Central Foothills

★ Cochrane

This friendly town lies on the northern edge of Alberta's ranchlands and was the site of the first big leasehold ranch in the province. Ranching is still a part of the local economy, but more and more residents are commuting into nearby Calgary, just 20min away.

The **Cochrane Ranche Historic Site** ★★ (*donation; visitors centre: mid-May to early Sep, every day 10am to 6pm; ranche site: open year-round; 0.5km west of Cochrane on Hwy. 1A, ☎932-3242 in summer, or ☎932-2902 in winter*) commemorates the establishment in 1881 of the Cochrane Ranche Company by Québec businessman Senator Matthew Cochrane, and the initiation of Alberta's cattle industry.

The company controlled 189,000ha of sweeping grasslands which, along with three other ranches including the Bar U (see p 389), covered most of Alberta. Though the ranch failed after two years, its legacy lives on. Travellers can relive those romantic days through interpretive programs at the visitors centre.

The **Western Heritage Centre** (*$7.50; mid-May to early Sep, every day 9am to 8pm; winter, every day 9am to 5pm; ☎932-3514, ⇄ 932-3515*) opened on the site in July 1996 in an attractive log building. It provides an overview of the cowboy way of life in the Canadian West, from the days of the frontier and the chuck wagon to rodeos, lariats and livestock auctions. The centre includes a restaurant, a gift shop, a lounge and a movie theatre, as well as hands-on exhibitions for young and old.

The **Studio West Art Foundry** (*every day 9am to 5pm; 205 Second Ave. SE, ☎932-2611*), in Cochrane's industrial park, is Western Canada's largest sculpture foundry. Artisans practise the age-old "lost wax", a bronze-casting technique that hasn't changed in 3,000 years. You can see the complete process of sculpting here, from the original concept to the final product. Wildlife and western bronze sculptures as well as woodcarvings and paintings are for sale.

While in Cochrane, don't miss the opportunity to savour some ice cream from **McKay's Ice Cream** ★, rated one of the best in Canada. You may even want to take a trip from Calgary just for a cone or stop in on your way to Banff.

Drive north on Hwy. 22 and then east on Hwy. 580 to Carstairs for a bit of shopping.

Carstairs

Two of Carstairs's most interesting attractions, which are essentially great shopping opportunities, lie on the outskirts of this town, whose streets are lined with grand old houses. The **Pa-Su Farm** lies 9km west of town on Hwy. 580, while the **Custom Woolen Mills** are about 20km ast on Hwy. 581 and then 4.5km orth on Hwy. 791. See the Shopping section, p 439.

Instead of boring old Hwy. 2, take the 2A, which runs parallel to the 2, then go west on Hwy. 592 to Markerville.

★ Markerville

The town of Markerville began in 1888 as an Icelandic settlement called Tindastoll, whose settlers arrived from Dakota. A year later another group of Icelanders arrived, including poet Stephan G. Stephansson (see below), and settled in a district they called

Hola. The area was chosen partly because of its isolation, for the settlers wished to preserve their language and customs.

In 1899, the federal government built the Markerville Creamery, and the village that grew up around it became something of an economic hub, attracting various groups of settlers including Danes, Swedes and Americans. The Icelandic culture nevertheless thrived into the 1920s. Eventually, however, intermarriage and migration changed things. Today less than 10% of the region's population is of Icelandic descent.

Once a leader in Alberta's dairy industry, the **Markerville Creamery** ★★ (*$2; late May to early Sep, Mon to Sat 10am to 5:30pm, Sun noon to 5:30pm; Creamery Way, Markerville,* ☎*728-3006*) is the only restored creamery in the province. It was opened in 1899 by the federal Department of Agriculture. An association of local Icelandic farmers maintained the building, and the government kept the books and hired a buttermaker. The buttermaker paid farmers depending on the butterfat of their cream. The creamery was the mainstay of the local economy until it closed in 1972, producing 90,000kg of butter at its peak. It is now a Provincial Historic Resource and has been restored to its circa-1934. Visitors can take a guided tour to learn about the operation of the creamery and its equipment, which includes old pasteurizers. Adjoining the building are two neat gift shops, as well as the "Kaffistofa", where you can sample *vinarterta*, Icelandic layer cake.

To reach Stephansson House, continue west on the 364A across the Medicine River; shortly after the river turn right on an unnamed road. Follow this road to the 371, turn right, cross the river again, and you'll soon see the entrance to the house on your left.

Stephansson House ★ (*$2; mid-May to early Sep, every day 10am to 6pm;* ☎*728-3929*). Stephan G. Stephansson was among the second group of Icelandic settlers who came to the area now known as Markerville from Dakota in 1889. Few people have heard of Stephansson, perhaps one of Canada's most prolific poets, because he wrote in his native Icelandic.

His original log house quickly proved too small, so a study, front room, upstairs, kitchen and front bedroom were gradually added. The house, with its newspaper insulation and attempts to copy the picturesque style, is representative of a typical struggling Canadian farm family.

Stephansson, like the other Icelandic settlers, was particularly concerned with preserving his native culture and he perpetuated it with his strong views and mastery of the language. The most famous of his works to have been translated is *Androkur*, or *Wakeful Nights* (Stephansson was an insomniac). Guides give tours of the house and light the stove every day to bake delicious Icelandic cookies called *astarbollur*, "love buns."

Head north on Hwy. 781 to Sylvan Lake.

★ Sylvan Lake

This lakeside town, with its marina, beach, souvenir shops, hotels, waterslide and shingled buildings, looks almost like an Atlantic coast beach resort. **Sylvan Lake Provincial Park** ★ (☎*887-5575*) is a day-use area for sunbathing, swimming and picnicking (see p x).

Jarvis Bay Provincial Park (*camping reservations* ☎*887-5522*) is also located on Sylvan Lake and, like the former, is popular on weekends. Hiking trails lead through the aspen parkland, and provide some good bird-watching.

You may want to overnight in Red Deer, which has a lot of hotels, before continuing west, if so head east on Hwy. 11, otherwise head west to Rocky Mountain House.

Rocky Mountain House

Despite its evocative name, Rocky Mountain House is not a picturesque log cabin in the woods but rather a gateway town into the majestic Rocky Mountains. The town, known locally as Rocky, is home to just under 6,000 people and represents a transition zone between the aspen parkland and the mountains. The exceptional setting is certainly one of the town's major attractions, which otherwise offers the gamut of services — hotels, gas stations and restaurants. Just outside Rocky lies the town's namesake, Rocky Mountain House National Historic Site, along with a wealth of outdoor possibilities, including river trips in voyageur canoes and fishing, hiking and cross-country skiing at Crimson Lake Provincial Park (see p 432).

The **Rocky Mountain House National Historic Park ★★** (*$2.25; May to Sep, every day 10am to 6pm, call for winter hours; 4.8km southwest of Rocky on Hwy. 11A, ☎845-2412*) is Alberta's only National Historic Park and the site of four known historic sites. Rocky Mountain House is interesting because it exemplifies, perhaps better than any other trading post, the inextricable link between the fur trade and the discovery and exploration of Canada.

Two rival forts were set up here in 1799, Rocky Mountain House by the North West Company and Acton House by the Hudson's Bay Company. Both companies were lured by the possibility of establishing lucrative trade with the Kootenay First Nation, west of the Rockies. It was after the merging of the Hudson's Bay Company and the North West Company in 1821, that the area was called Rocky Mountain House.

Trade with the Kootenay never did materialize; except for a brief period of trade with the Blackfoot in the 1820s, the fort never prospered, and actually closed down and was then rebuilt several occasions. It closed for good in 1875, after the North West Mounted Police made the area to the south safe for trading. The Hudson's Bay Company thus set up a post in the vicinity of Calgary. An interesting aside: the Hudson's Bay Company, today the department store The Bay, makes more money on its real estate holdings than on its retail operations.

The visitors centre presents a most informative exhibit on the fur-trading days at Rocky Mountain House, including a look at the clothing of the Plains Indians and how it changed with the arrival of fur traders as well as artifacts and testimonies of early explorers. Visitors can also choose to view one of several excellent National Film Board documentaries. Two interpretive trails lead through the site to listening posts (in English and French) along the swift-flowing North Saskatchewan River. Stops include a buffalo paddock and demonstration sites where tea is brewed and a York Boat, once used by Hudson's Bay Company traders, is displayed (the North West Company traders preferred the birchbark canoe, even though it was much slower). All that remains of the last fort are two chimneys.

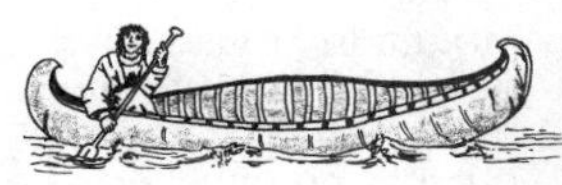

Rocky Mountain House was also a base for exploration. David Thompson, an explorer, surveyor and geographer for the North West Company who played an integral role in the North West Company's search for a route through the Rockies to the Pacific, was based at Rocky

David Thompson

David Thompson began at the Hudson's Bay Company in 1784 as a clerk stationed at several posts on Hudson Bay and the Saskatchewan River.

While laid up with a broken leg, he took an interest in surveying and practical astronomy. After years of exploring and surveying much of present-day northern Manitoba and Saskatchewan, he decided to switch camps and go to work for the North West Company in 1797.

The company enlisted his services in the "Columbia Enterprise," the search for a route through the Rockies. In 1806-07, Thompson made preparations to cross the Rockies at Rocky Mountain House. However, the Peigan First Nation, who frequented the post, opposed the project; if trade extended west of the Rockies, their enemies, the Kootenay and Flathead, would acquire guns. Thompson thus moved upriver from Rocky Mountain House to the Howse Pass in 1807.

In 1810, the race to the mouth of the Columbia came to a head when news of an American expedition reached Thompson. He immediately headed west but was blocked by the Peigan. He headed north again, skirting Peigan territory.

In 1811, he crossed the Athabasca Pass and reached the Pacific and the mouth of the Columbia River four months after the Americans had set up their post there.

Thompson later settled in Terrebonne, near Montreal, and worked on the establishment of the boundary between Upper and Lower Canada. He was unsuccessful in business and died in 1857, in poverty and virtual obscurity.

Mountain House for a time. Ultimately beaten by the Americans in his pursuit, he travelled 88,000km during his years in the fur trade, filling in the map of Western Canada along the way.

A detour north on Hwy. 22 leads to the tiny town of Alder Flats.

Alder Flats

Alder Flats itself is of little interest to visitors. A few kilometres south, however, is another town that is full of attractions, a place ironically called **Em-Te Town**. Here you'll find a saloon, jailhouse, harness shop, schoolhouse, church and emporium, located in a pretty setting at the end of a gravel road. Built from scratch in 1978, this is a neat place to experience life the way it was in the old west, with trail rides and home-cooked meals at the Lost Woman Hotel. Some may find the whole experience a bit contrived. In addition to the attractions, there are campsites and cabins for rent, as well as a restaurant.

★★★

David Thompson Highway

The drive west from Rocky Mountain House runs along the edge of

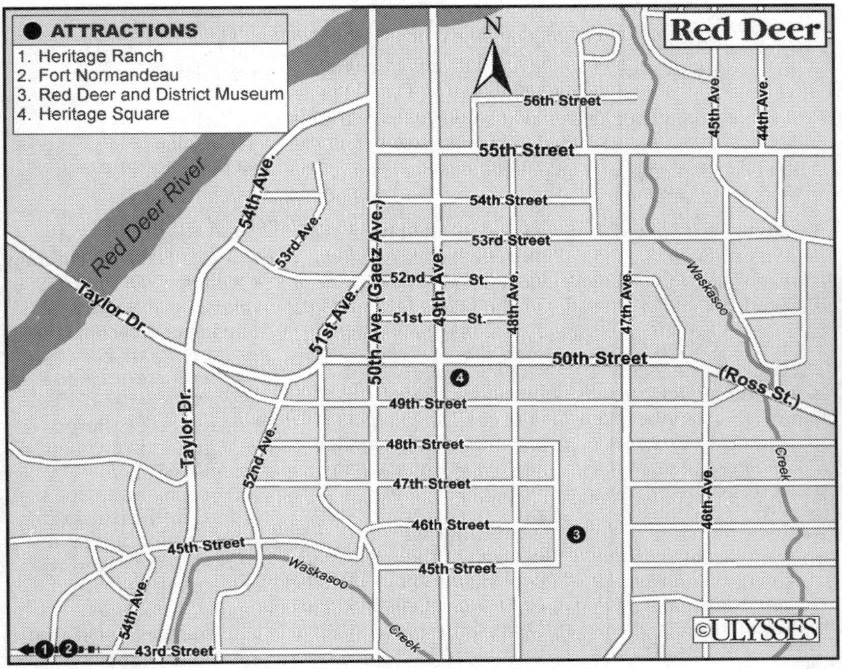

Red Deer

ATTRACTIONS

1. Heritage Ranch
2. Fort Normandeau
3. Red Deer and District Museum
4. Heritage Square

©ULYSSES

the Rocky Mountain Forest Reserve. Stunning views of the Rocky Mountains line the horizon. Hwy. 11, the David Thompson Highway, continues west from Rocky Mountain House up into the Aspen Parkland and on into Banff National Park (see p 296). The town of **Nordegg** lies at the halfway point of the highway. In addition to an interesting museum, the Nordegg Museum, the town offers access to great fishing, the Forestry Trunk Road and camping and is also home to the Shunda Creek Hostel (see p 436). The only services available west of Nordegg before the Hwy. 93 are at the David Thompson Resort (see p 436).

Tour C: The Heartland

Olds

Located about 30km south of Red Deer, Olds is a small agricultural town and the site of the **Agricultural College** (*4500 50th St., ☎556-8281 or 888-661-6537, www. oldscollege.ab.ca*), where you can learn more about agriculture by visiting the greenhouses and various research areas scattered around the enormous premises.

★

Red Deer

Red Deer, a city of 60,000 people, began as a stopover for early commercial travellers along the Calgary Edmonton Trail. Red Deer is an erroneous translation of *Waskasoo*, which means elk in Cree. The shores of the river were frequented by elk, and Scottish settlers thought the animals resembled red deer found in Scotland. During the Riel Rebellion of 1885, the Canadian militia built Fort Normandeau at this site. The post was later occupied by the North West Mounted Police. The railway, agriculture, oil and gas all contributed to the growth of Red Deer, at one point the fastest growing city in Canada.

Red Deer is another Alberta city whose extensive park system is one of its greatest attractions. The **Waskasoo Park System** weaves its way throughout the city and through the Red Deer River valley with walking and cycling trails. The information centre is located at **Heritage Ranch** (*25 Riverview Park, at the end of Cronquist Dr., ☎346-0180*) on the western edge of town; take the 32nd Street Exit from Hwy. 2, left on 60th Street and left on Cronquist Drive. Heritage Ranch also features, among other things, an equestrian centre, picnic shelters and access to trails in the park system.

Fort Normandeau ★ (*free; late May to end of Jun, every day 10am to 6pm; Jul to early Sep, every day noon to 8pm; ☎347-2010 or 347-7550*) is located west of Hwy. 2, along 32nd Street. The fort as it stands today is a replica of the original. A stopping house next to the river was fortified and enclosed in palisade walls by the **Carabiniers de Mont Royal** under Lieutenant J.E. Bédard Normandeau in anticipation of an attack by the Cree during the Louis Riel Rebellion of 1885. The fort was never attacked. An interpretive centre next to the fort describes Aboriginal, Metis and European settlement of the area. Visitors can see wool being spun, and rope, soap, candles and ice cream being made.

In downtown Red Deer, the **Red Deer and District Museum** (*donation; Jul to early Sep, every day 10am to 9pm; Sep to Jun, Mon to Thu noon to 5pm and 7pm to 9pm, Fri noon to 5pm, Sat and Sun 1pm to 5pm; 4525 47A Ave., ☎342-6844*) boasts different galleries featuring international and Canadian art, plus permanent exhibits dealing with the history of the area from prehistoric times. Walking tours of historic Red Deer depart from the museum.

Heritage Square, next to the museum, encloses a collection of historic buildings, including the unique Aspelund Laft Hus, a replica of a 17th- century sod-roofed Norwegian home. Northwest of Heritage Square is **City Hall Park ★**, a lovely garden filled with 45,000 blossoming annuals.

Head north of Red Deer on Hwy. 2A, turn right on Hwy. 12 East to reach Stettler, make a brief stop in the town of Lacombe.

Lacombe

Lacombe is a small agricultural town typical of central Alberta. At the turn of the century it was larger than Red Deer. Today, its population is only 8,000.

There are over 25 restored buildings in Lacombe's historic downtown. The town even has its own distinctive **Flat Iron Building** (*50th Ave.*). A block over is the **Roland Mitchener Museum** (*donations appreciated; summer, every day 10am to 4pm; ☎782-3933*), the birthplace of the governor general of Canada from 1967-1974. The house has been restored and furnished with family heirlooms, period pieces and old photographs.

The museum also manages the **Blacksmith Museum** (*donations welcome; Jun to Sep, Mon to Fri, 10am to 4pm or by appointment; 5020 49th St., ☎782-3933*), located two streets away. It's one of the rare original blacksmith workshops remaining in Alberta. You can watch as the blacksmith carefully moulds the hot iron the same way it was done in the early 1900s. At that time, the blacksmith workshop was essential since it repaired heavy machinery and made the hooves for horses.

Two other attractions are found on the way from Stettler. The **Ellis Bird Farm** (*$5; drive 8km towards Stettler on Hwy. 12, then 8km south on Prentiss Road*) has looked after endangered species of birds for nearly 50 years. The protected wildlife reserves on this interesting property ensure the survival of the flora and fauna, and the many hiking trails offer an opportunity to appreciate its beauty.

Continue down Hwy. 12 east for a few minutes (instead of turning on Prentiss Road) and you arrive at **Doug's Exotic Zoo** (*$5; every day; 10am to 7pm; ☎784-3400, ⇌784-3401*). There are 54 different kinds of animals here, from the hedgehog, to the zebra, to the Siberian tiger. Unfortunately, some of the cages are cramped.

Ponoka

If you are travelling through this region in late June or early July make a detour to Ponoka (north of Lacombe on Hwy. 2A), home of the province's second largest rodeo after the Calgary Stampede. **The Ponoka Stampede** ★ takes place the last weekend in June and first weekend in July, just as it has for more than 60 years.

Return toward Lacombe and take Hwy. 12 East to Stettler.

Stettler

For a trip across the wonderful prairie landscape **Alberta Prairie Railway Excursions** ★ (*47th Ave. and 47th St.; ☎742-2811 for schedule and reservations*) organizes trips aboard a vintage 1920s steam locomotive, which departs from Stettler for small towns like Halkirk, Castor and Coronation to the east or even Big Valley to the south. Full and half-day excursions include one or two meals, and special trips include murder-mystery trains and casino trains. The trains run from May to October and on selected weekends from November to April.

Take Hwy. 56 north to Camrose.

Camrose

Alberta's Littlest Airport (*donation; Jun to Aug, Wed to Sun, noon to 8pm; from Camrose, 22km east on Hwy. 13 then 4km south on Kelsey Rd., ☎373-3953*) has mini-runways where radio-controlled planes land and take-off. Camrose is also the setting for the Big Valley Jamboree in early August, a terrific country music festival with big names from the United States and Canada.

Take Hwy. 26 west to Wetaskiwin.

★ Wetaskiwin

The city of Wetaskiwin is home to one of the finest museums in the province. Like the Remington-Alberta Carriage Centre in Cardston, the Reynolds-Alberta Museum proves again that there is more to Alberta than Calgary, Edmonton and the Rockies. Though there isn't much to see in Wetaskiwin besides the Reynolds-Alberta and the Aviation Hall of Fame, this pleasant city has an interesting main street, and respectable restaurants and hotels.

The **Reynolds-Alberta Museum** ★★★ (*$6.50; Late Jun to early Sep, 9am to 7pm; Sep to Jun, Tue to Sun 9am to 5pm; west of Wetaskiwin on Hwy. 13, ☎361-1351 or 800-661-4726*) celebrates the "spirit of the machine" and is a wonderful place to explore. Interactive programs for children bring everything alive. A top-notch collection of restored automobiles, trucks, bicycles, tractors and related machinery is on display.

Among the vintage cars is one of about 470 Model J Duesenberg Phaeton Royales. This one-of-a-kind automobile cost $20,000 when it was purchased in 1929. Visitors to the museum will also learn how a grain elevator works, and can observe the goings-on in the restoration workshop through a large picture window. Tours of the warehouse, where over 800 pieces are waiting to be restored, are offered twice daily (*$1, call ahead for times, sign up at front desk*); pre-booked 1hr guided tours are also available.

Canada's Aviation Hall of Fame, located on the site of the Reynolds-Alberta, pays tribute to the pioneers of Canadian aviation. Photographs, artifacts, personal memorabilia and the favourite aircraft of the over 140 members of the Hall of Fame are displayed. These people include military and civilian pilots, doctors, scientists, inventors, aeronautical engineers and administrators.

Continue north on Hwy. 2A to Leduc, site of the biggest oil discovery in the world.

Leduc

Alberta came into its own when crude oil was discovered south of Edmonton. **Leduc Oil Well #1** (*donation; open year-round; 2km south of Devon on Hwy 60, ☎780-987-3435*) blew in on February 13, 1947, signalling the start of the oil boom. The oil was actually discovered on a farm northwest of Leduc in what was to become the town of Devon. A replica of the original 174-foot conventional derrick now stands on the site. Visitors get a first-hand look at equipment by climbing down to the drilling floor.

Head west on Hwy. 39 and then north on Hwy. 60 to Devon.

Devon

Devon and its **University of Alberta Devonian Botanic Garden** (*$5, seniors $4, children $3; May to Sep, every day 10am to 7pm; Sep and Oct, every day 10am to 4pm; Hwy. 60, ☎987-3054 or 987-3055*) are named for the Devonian rock formation in which oil was struck in the 1940s. Native species, a Japanese garden and the Butterfly House, full of fluttering tropical beauties, occupy 110 acres. *Edmonton is 30min north on Hwy. 60.*

Tour D: The Yellowhead

The scenic **Yellowhead Route** follows Hwy. 16 west from Winnipeg, Manitoba and across the prairies through Saskatoon, Saskatchewan, before reaching the Alberta border at Lloydminster. It crosses Alberta, passing the provincial capital, Edmonton, and Jasper along the way. Once in British Columbia it splits, heading south on Hwy. 5 to Merritt and continuing on the 16 west all the way to Prince Rupert.

Lloydminster

Lloydminster was settled in 1903 when the region was part of the vast Northwest Territories. In 1930, 25 years after the creation of the provinces of Saskatchewan and Alberta, the two communities merged to form the only city with a single corporate body in two provinces. The different costs of living in each province make life interesting in Lloydminster: there is no sales tax in Alberta; the minimum wage is higher in Saskatchewan, but so are the income taxes; the drinking age in Saskatchewan is 19, in Alberta it is 18, and so on.

The **Barr Colony Heritage Centre** (*$3; mid-May to end of Aug every day 10am to 8pm, Sep to mid-May Wed to Fri noon to 5pm, Sat and Sun 1pm to 5pm; Hwy. 16 at 45th Ave.*) recalls the original settlement of Lloydminster in 1903 when 2,000 British colonists arrived with Reverend Isaac Barr. It houses five art galleries.

Bud Miller Park (*every day 7am to 11pm; 59th Ave., south of Hwy. 16, ☎780-875-4499 or 875-4497*) is 81ha of nature trails and aspen stands. There are also lawn bowling greens, a tree maze, a formal garden and Canada's largest sundial.

Head west on Hwy. 16 through Vermillion, named for the reddish deposits of the river, and on to Vegreville.

Vegreville

Vegreville was first settled by French farmers migrating from Kansas. These days it is better known for its Ukrainian community and its rather curious landmark, the world's largest pysanka. The traditional Ukrainian Easter egg is 7m long and it actually turns in the wind, like a giant weathervane.

Continuing west on Hwy. 16, you will soon come upon the **Ukrainian Cultural Heritage Village** ★★ (*$6.50, reduced rates in the off-season and by reservation only; mid-May to early Sep every day 10am to 6pm; Sep to mid-Oct every day 10am to 4pm; on Hwy. 16 about 30km east of Edmonton,* ☎*780-662-3640*), where the fascinating story of the region's Ukrainian settlers is brought to life. Life at the Bloc settlement in East Central Alberta from 1892 to 1930 is recreated with staff in period costume and a whole historic townsite. Driven from their homeland, these settlers fled to the Canadian prairies, where land was practically being given away. They dressed and worked as they had in the old country, thereby enriching the Canadian cultural landscape. Late August is the time for the **Harvest of the Past**, featuring *tsymbaly* entertainment and pirogi (potato dumpling) eating contests.

★★

Elk Island National Park

Heading west on Hwy. 16 (the Yellowhead Highway) the next stop is Elk Island National Park. This island wilderness in a sea of grass preserves two herds of buffalo, plains bison and the rare wood bison. It is also home to a multitude of animals species. There are campgrounds, while trails and a lake offer the possibility of all sorts of outdoor activities (see p 432).

Edmonton lies 27km west. Continuing on the Yellowhead, Stony Plain is 40km west of the provincial capital.

Stony Plain

The **Andrew Wolf Wine Cellar** (*Mon to Sat 10am to 6pm; Stony Plain,* ☎*780-963-7717*) is Alberta's only winery, and the wine actually comes from California. The final aging is done here in oak vats. Wine-tastings are possible, and you can also purchase fine bottles for very reasonable prices at the gift boutique.

The Yellowhead West to Jasper

Another 160km west of Stony Plain is the town of **Edson** – not much to look at but nonetheless home to two small museums on the history of the region, the **Galloway Station Museum** (*$1; mid-May to Aug, Fri to Tue 10am to 5pm; 5425 3rd Ave.,* ☎*723-5696*) and the **Red Brick Arts Centre and Museum** (*$1; Mon to Fri 9am to 4:30pm; 4818 Seventh Ave.,* ☎*780-723-3582*), in a 1913 schoolhouse.

Hinton lies on the Jasper National Park's doorstep and offers an inexpensive alternative for accommodations and services (see p 437). The **Alberta Forest Service Museum** (*free admission; Mon to Fri 8:15am to 4:30pm; 1176 Switzer Dr.,* ☎*780-865-8200*) covers the forestry industry in Alberta. Spectacular wilderness surrounds Hinton including the **Cadomin Caves** (excursions can be arranged in town), the best known and most accessible in the province.

Parks

Tour A: Digging for Dinosaur Bones and Other Treasures

★

Kinbrook Island Provincial Park

The shores of Lake Newell, the largest artificial lake in the province, are home to over 250 species of birds and fowl. Colonies of double-crested cormorants and American white pelicans occupy several of the protected islands on the lake. The best wildlife viewing is from the eastern shore. There are also walking trails through nearby Kinbrook Marsh. For information and reservations: ☎*362-2962*.

★★★

Dinosaur Provincial Park

Dinosaur Provincial Park offers amateur palaeontologists the opportunity to walk through the land of the dinosaurs. Declared a UNESCO World Heritage Site in 1979, this nature preserve harbours a wealth of information on these formidable former inhabitants of the planet. Today, the park is also home to more than 35 species of animals.

The small museum at the **Field Station of the Tyrell Museum** (*$4.50; mid-May to early Sep, every day 9am to 9pm; Sep to May, Mon to Fri, 8:15am to 4:30pm;* ☎*378-4342 or 378-4344 for bus tour reservations*), the loop road and the two self-guided trails (the **Cottonwood Flats Trail** and the **Badlands Trail**) will give you a summary introduction to the park. Two exposed skeletons left where they were discovered can be viewed. The best way to see the park, however, is on one of the guided tours into the restricted nature preserve that makes up most of the park. The 90min **Badlands Bus Tour** leads into the heart of the preserve for unforgettable scenery, skeletons and wildlife; the **Centrosaurus Bone Bed Hike** and **Fossil Safari Hike** offer close-up looks at excavation sites. Tickets for all of these tours go on sale at 8:30am the day of the event at the field station and space is limited; arrive early in July and August. To avoid missing out, visitors are strongly advised to call ahead to find out when the tours leave.

The park also features campgrounds and a Dinosaur Service Centre with laundry, showers, picnic and food.

The cabin of John Ware, an ex-slave from Texas who became a well-respected Albertan cattle rancher, lies near the campground.

Tour B: Central Foothills

Crimson Lake Provincial Park

Crimson Lake Provincial Park (*information and camping reservations* ☎*845-2330, for emergencies, call the warden's office at* ☎*845-2340*) is located just west of Rocky Mountain House and features peaceful campsites and good fishing for rainbow trout. Extensive hiking trails become cross-country trails in the winter.

Ma-Me-O Beach Provincial Park

Ma-Me-O Beach Provincial Park (*day use only; park office* ☎*780-586-2645*) and **Pigeon Lake Provincial Park** (*park office* ☎*780-586-2645, camping reservations* ☎*586-2644*) are for those who have had enough of the mountains and are up for a day at the beach. Both offer excellent access to the great swimming (said to be the best in Alberta) and fishing on Pigeon Lake. Boats can be rented at the Zeiner campground in the Pigeon Lake Provincial Park.

Tour D: The Yellowhead

★★

Elk Island National Park

The magnificent **Elk Island National Park** (*$4; open year-round; park administration and warden Mon to Fri 8am to 4pm,* ☎*780-992-2950; camping* ☎*998-3161*) preserves part of the Beaver Hills area as it was before the arrival of settlers when Sarcee and Plains Cree hunted and trapped in these lands. The arrival of settlers endangered beaver, elk and bison populations, prompting local residents and conservationists to petition the government to set aside an elk reserve in 1906. The plains bison that live in the park actually ended up there by accident, having escaped from a herd placed there temporarily while a fence at Buffalo National Park in Wainwright, Alberta was being completed. The plains bison herd that inhabits the park began with those 50 escaped bison.

Elk Island is also home to a small herd of rare wood bison, North America's largest mammal. In 1940, pure wood buffalo were thought to be extinct, but by sheer luck a herd of about 200 wood buffalo were discovered in a remote part of the park in 1957. Part of that herd was sent to a fenced sanctuary in the Northwest Territories.

Today the smaller plains bison are found north of Hwy. 16, while the wood bison live south of the highway. While touring the park, remember that you are in bison country and that these animals are wild. Though they may look docile, they are dangerous, unpredictable and may charge without warning, so stay in your vehicle and keep a safe distance (50 to 75m).

Elk Island became a national park in 1930 and is now a 195km² sanctuary for 44 kinds of mammals, including moose, elk, deer, lynx, beaver and coyote. The park offers some of the best wildlife viewing in the province. It is crossed by major migratory fly ways; be on the look-out for trumpeter swans in the fall.

The park office at the South Gate, just north of Hwy. 16, can provide information on the two campgrounds, wildlife viewing and the 12 trails that run through the park, making for great hiking and cross-country skiing. Fishing and boating can be enjoyed on Astotin Lake, and the park even boasts a nine-hole golf course.

Beaches

Believe it or not, landlocked Alberta has a handful of beaches that are great for swimming and suntanning. In central Alberta and northern Alberta, countless lakes left behind by retreating glaciers now provide water fun for summer vacationers. **Pigeon Lake Provincial Park** has a long sandy beach with showers and picnic tables, while **Ma-Me-O Provincial Park** at the other end of Pigeon Lake, is a day-use area that's great for picnics and for catching some rays. **Sylvan Lake ★** is a veritable beach resort town. A beautiful beach lines one of Alberta's most spectacular lakes. Windsurfers and pedalboats can be rented.

Outdoor Activities

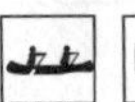 

Canoeing and Rafting

Alpenglow Mountain Adventures (*R.R. 1, Rocky Mountain House, T0M 1T0, ☎/⇄ 780-844-4715*) organizes rafting, kayaking and canoeing trips along the North Saskatchewan River between Nordegg and Rocky Mountain House. Full-day trips range from $39 to $64, while overnight trips from two to three days range from $149 to $249. This outfit also organizes trips along the Athabasca River. This outfit also offers ice-climbing excursions in winter.

Central Alberta

Also based in Rocky Mountain House, **Voyageur Adventure Tours** (*Box 278, Rocky Mountain House, T0M 1T0, ☎780-845-7878 or 780-932-7750*) organizes trips of one to several days in eight passenger voyageur canoes. Trips cost between $55 and $200.

Hiking and Cross-Country Skiing

Elk Island National Park offers the opportunity to view an exceptional variety of wildlife. The **Shoreline Trail** (3km one way) and **Lakeview Trail** (3.3km round trip) explore the area around Astotin Lake, where beavers are occasionally seen. The Wood Bison Trail (18.5km round trip) does a loop around Flying Shot Lake in the area of the park south of Hwy. 16, where wood buffalo roam. These three trails are maintained as cross-country trails in the winter.

Paragliding

Located 30min west of Calgary, just before the town of Cochrane, **Muller** (*Bigg Hill Road, P.O. Box 13, RR2, ☎/⇄ 932-6760, www. muller-hang-paraglide.com*) offers hang-gliding and paragliding classes. The beginners' course costs $100 and includes a few flights. Apparently the sensation of flying is incredible! The young instructor grew up on the slopes and today he participates in international competitions.

Accommodations

Tour A: Digging for Dinosaur Bones and Other Treasures

There are campsites at **Kinbrook Island Provincial Park** (*☎362-2962*) as well as at **Dinosaur Provincial Park** (*☎378-3700*). The latter has more facilities, including a snack bar, showers and a laundry.

Brooks

Tel-Star Motor Inn
$56
ℜ, ≡, ℝ, *K, tv*
813 Second St. W., on the way into town, Box 547, T1R 1B5
☎362-3466
☎800-260-6211
⇄362-8818
About 30min down the highway from Dinosaur Provincial Park is the town of Brooks and the Tel-Star Motor Inn. The rooms don't have much to recommend them aside from the fact that they are clean and each has a microwave and a refrigerator. The hotel also doesn't charge for local calls and has freezer facilities for your catch.

Douglas Country Inn
$77 bkfst incl.
ℜ, ≡
Box 463, T1R 1B5
☎362-2873
⇄ 362-2100
The Douglas Country Inn is 6.5km north of town on Hwy. 873. A casual country atmosphere is achieved in each of the seven beautifully appointed rooms and throughout the rest of the inn. The only television is in the small TV room, which is rarely used. Enjoy your complimentary sherry by the fire in the sitting room. The special occasion room *($99)* boasts a divine Japanese soaker tub with a view.

Drumheller

Alexandra International Hostel
members $15
non-members $20
30 Railway Ave. N, T0J 0Y0
☎823-6337
⇄ 823-5327
A converted downtown hotel now houses the Alexandra International Hostel. It opened in 1991 after renovations and is independently operated in cooperation with Hostelling International. Most dorm rooms have eight beds, though there are some with fewer, and several even have private bathrooms. There are kitchen and laundry

facilities on the premises, as well as all sorts of information brochures and a mountain-bike rental service.

Badlands Motel
$60
≡, ℜ, ℝ, *K, tv*
on the Dinosaur Trail
Box 2217, T0J 0Y0
☎***823-5155***
⇄ ***823-7653***
The Badlands Motel lies outside of town, along the scenic Dinosaur Trail. Rooms are typical, but the pancake restaurant next door is particularly noteworthy.

Waldorf Hotel
$25-$30
70 Railview Ave.
☎823-6687 or 823-2623
The Waldorf Hotel is in one of the oldest buildings in Drumheller. And it shows! The rooms are adequate, although they are in deplorable condition and smell musty. As for the decor, it isn't memorable – but the price is.

Newcastle Country Inn
$80, bkfst
≡
1130 Newcastle Trail
☎***823-8356***
The Newcastle Country Inn offers decently decorated, comfortable rooms. The breakfasts are filling and the staff is friendly. The plumbing, however, is sometimes noisy.

Taste the Past B&B
$79
sb, ⊗
281 Second St. W.
Box 865, T0J 0Y0
☎***823-5889***
The fittingly named Taste the Past B&B is a 1910 Victorian house decorated with antiques. Guests enjoy a large yard and veranda and a choice of breakfasts. They also have the use of a cosy bathrobe and slippers. In 1998, this establishment went from four to three rooms, giving its guests more privacy. Each room now has its own private bathroom.

Heartwood Manor
$79-$150
⊛, ≡, *tv*, 🐕, ♿
320 Railway Ave. E, T0J 0Y4
☎***823-6495***
☎***888-823-6495***
⇄ ***823-4935***
By far the prettiest place to stay in town is the Heartwood Manor, a bed and breakfast in a restored heritage building, where a striking use of colour creates a cosy and luxurious atmosphere. Nine of the ten rooms have whirlpool baths, and five even boast fireplaces. A spacious cottage and a two-bedroom suite is also available. Yummy homemade fruit syrups are served with the pancake breakfast. French and English spoken.

Best Western Jurassic Inn
$89-$129
≡, ≈, ⊛, ℜ
1103 Hwy. 9 S, T0J 0Y0
☎***823-7700***
☎***800-528-1234***
⇄ ***823-5002***
The Best Western has 49 guest rooms. They are standard, but very clean and very well equipped: they all have a fridge, microwave and hair dryer. Continental breakfast is included.

Trochu

St. Ann Ranch
$55-$75
Box 670, T0M 2C0
☎***442-3924***
Once the ranch of French cavalry men, the St. Ann Ranch country bed and breakfast offers travellers the chance to experience a true French *gîte*. Guests of the B&B have the choice of seven private, antique-furnished rooms (five with private baths) in the rambling 30-room ranch house or in the Pioneer Cottage and the use of a parlour with a fireplace, a library and patios. While you're here visit the tea house and museum (see p 422).

Rosebud

Rosebud Country Inn
$95
♿, *no smoking*
Box 631, T0J 2T0
☎***677-2211***
⇄ ***677-2106***
Rooms at the Rosebud Country Inn feature queen-size sleigh beds, designer linens, pedes-

tal sinks and balconies. Roses brighten up the interior space throughout. This inn boasts first-rate facilities and spotless accommodations. The tea room serves breakfast, Sunday brunch, lunch, supper and, of course, afternoon tea. The inn organizes murder-mystery packages in the winter. There are no televisions (by choice) and children are not permitted.

Tour B: Central Foothills

Cochrane

Dickens Inn
$75-$85 bkfst incl.
R.R. 1, T0L 0W0
2km west of Cochrane on the 1A, turn right on Horse Creek Rd. and continue for 7km, driveway to the right
☎932-3945
Take in the panoramic views of the mountains from the Dickens Inn, a Victorian house built as a B&B. Enjoy peaceful slumber in one of three guest rooms with queen-size four-poster beds and private bathrooms and then awaken to a copious breakfast featuring home-made preserves and fresh bread.

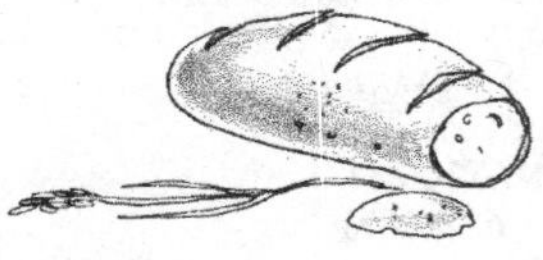

Sylvan Lake

Sylvan Lake Bed & Breakfast
$50 bkfst incl.
tv, sb
3723 50th Ave., T4S 1B5
☎887-3546
The Sylvan Lake B&B is run by a globetrotting couple who speak English, Swedish, Spanish and Portuguese. The rooms are simple but cosy, while outside the lovely yard is very peaceful. Only one block from the beach. For $60 you can have a suite with an extra room, as well as a sofa and television.

Rocky Mountain House

Voyageur Motel
$58
≡, K, ℝ, tv
on Hwy. 11 S, Box 1376, T0M 1T0
☎845-3381
☎888-845-3569
⇄ 845-6166
The Voyageur is a practical choice with spacious, clean rooms, each equipped with a refrigerator. Kitchenettes are also available for a surcharge. Each room has a VCR.

Walking Eagle Motor Inn
$75, cabins $35
≡, ℜ, tv, bar, fridge
on Hwy. 11, Box 1317, T0M 1T0
☎845-2804
⇄ 845-3685
The log exterior of the Walking Eagle Motor Inn encloses 63 clean and large rooms decorated in keeping with the hotel's name. The hotel owes its attractive appearance to a complete renovation and paint-job. In addition, a brand new 35-room motel ($80) was built right next door. There's a microwave and refrigerator in each one of the clean – but rather drab – rooms.

Nordegg

Shunda Creek Hostel
members $14
non-members $19
west of Nordegg, 3km north of Hwy. 11, on Shunda Creek Recreation Area Rd.
☎/⇄ 721-2140
Set against the stunning backdrop of the Rocky Mountains in David Thompson Country, surrounded by countless opportunities for outdoor activities is the Shunda Creek Hostel. The two-storey lodge encloses kitchen and laundry facilities, a common area with a fireplace and 10 rooms able to accommodate a total of 48 people; it also adjoins an outdoor hot tub. Hiking, mountain biking, fishing, canoeing, cross-country skiing and ice-climbing are possible nearby.

David Thompson Resort
$70
≡, ≈
☎721-2103
This is more of a motel and RV park than a resort, but regardless it is the only accommodation between Nordegg and Hwy. 93, the Icefields Parkway (see p 292), and you can't beat the scenery. The resort rents bicycles

and can organize helicopter tours of the area.

Tour C: Heartland

Red Deer

Many conventions are held in Red Deer, and as a result weekend rates in the many hotels are often less expensive.

The Super 8
$60
tv, ≡, ℜ,
7474 Gaetz Ave.
☎343-1102
⇄ 341-6532
The Super 8 is one of the many hotels between Gaetz Avenue and downtown. To justify sleeping in one of these pleasant rooms overlooking the parking lot, bring your car.

McIntosh Tea House Bed and Breakfast
$65
4631 50th St., T4N 1X1
☎346-1622
This is the former home of the great grandson of the creator of the McIntosh apple. Each of the three upstairs rooms of the red-brick historic Victorian is decorated with antiques. Guests can enjoy a game of apple checkers in the private parlour. Tea and coffee are served in the evening and a full breakfast in the morning.

Red Deer Lodge
$89-$149
≡, ≈, ℜ, *bar*, ⊛, *tv*,
4311 49th Ave., T4N 5Y7
☎346-8841
☎800-661-1657
⇄ 341-3220
The Red Deer Lodge is a favourite with convention-goers because of its modern and extensive amenities. As one would expect, the rooms are comfortable and spotless. The rooms surround a cheerful courtyard.

Wetaskiwin

The Rose Country Inn
$55
≡, ℜ, ℝ, *K*, *bar*, *tv*
4820 56th St., T9A 2G5
☎780-352-3600
⇄780-352-2127
Close to the Reynolds-Alberta Museum, on 56th Street, the Rose Country Inn is one of the best deals in town. Each of the recently renovated rooms has a refrigerator and microwave oven.

Tour D: The Yellowhead

Elk Island National Park

Elk Island National Park has two campgrounds (*camping reservations ☎780-992-2984*). The park office at the South Gate, just north of Hwy. 16, can provide information on registration and the sites.

Hinton

Black Cat Guest Ranch
$82 per person, fb
⊛
Box 6267, T7V 1X6
☎780-865-3084
☎800-859-6840
⇄780-865-1924
www.telusplanet.net/public/bcranch/
The Black Cat provides a peaceful retreat and lots of family fun, ideal for family get-togethers. There are guided trail rides, hiking trails and cross-country skiing in the winter. The accommodations are rustic and homey and each room has a mountain view. The scenery can also be enjoyed from the outdoor hot-tub. The ranch also offers theme weekends and organizes excursions. Special rates for children.

Restaurants

Tour A: Digging for Dinosaur Bones and Other Treasures

Brooks

Peggy Sue's Diner
$
603 Second St. W
Peggy Sue's is neat little family-run eatery. Smoked meat, burgers, great fries and delicious mud pie can be eaten in or taken out.

Drumheller

The Corner Stop Restaurant
$$
15 Third Ave. W
☎823-5440
The Corner Stop Restaurant is located in the middle of the city. The Greek-style décor is meticulous, and the menu includes salads, pizza, pasta, seafood and steaks.

Yavis Family Restaurant
$$
249 Third Ave.
☎823-8317
This restaurant has been around for years. The interior is fairly non-descript, and so is the menu. The selections are nonetheless pretty good, especially the great big breakfasts.

The Bridge
$$
71 Bridge St. N
☎823-2225
The Bridge is a Greek restaurant that serves a bit of everything, including steaks and pasta dishes. The Greek selections are the best – they are a bit on the greasy side but come in huge portions with tsatziki on the side (i.e. don't order more!). The interior was recently redone and, along with the Greek background music, is faintly reminiscent of the Mediterranean.

Sizzling House
$$
160 Centre St.
☎823-8098
The Sizzling House serves up tasty Thai cooking, and is recommended by locals. A good place for lunch, the service is quick and friendly.

Rosebud

The Rosebud Dinner Theatre is an entertaining way to spend an evening. The food is simple, but the plays are always well presented. Reservations are mandatory; for schedules and information call ☎*677-2001* or *800-267-7553* (see p 439).

Tour B: Central Foothills

Cochrane

Mackay's Ice Cream (*$*) scoops up what many claim is the best ice cream in the country. Be sure to stop in to see for yourself!

Home Quarter Restaurant & Pie Shoppe
$$
216 First St. W
☎932-2111
Cochrane's friendly Home Quarter Restaurant is the home of the ever-popular Rancher's Special breakfast with eggs, bacon and sausage. Home-made pies are available all day long to eat in or take out. The lunch and dinner menu includes filet mignon and chicken parmesan.

Tour C: Heartland

Red Deer

City Roast Coffee
$
4940 50th St.
☎347-0893
The City Roast serves hearty soup, sandwich lunches and good coffee. The walls are decorated with posters announcing local art shows and events.

Good Food Company
$-$$
at the corner of 50th St. and Gaetz Ave.
☎343-8185
This restaurant is located in the old Greene Block, a historic building in downtown Red Deer. Healthy meals including borscht and a peasant's platter are all served with home-made bread.

Cheesecake Café
$$
4320 Gaetz Ave.
☎341-7818
⇄ 341-7849
The Cheesecake Cafe has a vast selection of famous desserts. But there's more: a laid-back atmosphere, fast and friendly service, as well as an eclectic menu. You won't regret your visit.

Wetaskiwin

The MacEachern Tea House & Restaurant
$-$$
Mon to Sat until 4:30pm, Jul and Aug also open Sun 10am to 4pm
4719 50th Ave.
☎352-8308
Home to specialty coffees and over 20 teas. The menu boasts hearty home-made soups and chowders, as well as sandwiches and salads.

Tour D: The Yellowhead

Lloydminster

Lunch at Lorna's
$-$$
5008 50th St.
☎875-1152
Lorna's is a friendly spot near the downtown area. They serve simple fare like soups and sandwiches.

Greek Classic
$$-$$$
4402 52nd Ave.
☎875-3553
Probably the fanciest restaurant in Lloyd, though fancy might be pushing it. The menu might be small, but the food is very well prepared and nice and spicy!

Entertainment

Drumheller

The Canadian Badlands Passion Play
adults $18
children $9
late Jun to early Jul, for tickets write to Box 457, Drumheller, T0J 0Y0
☎823-7750
The badlands make an eerily fitting background for this moving open-air portrayal of the life, death and resurrection of Jesus Christ.

Rosebud

The **Rosebud Dinner Theatre**, is a splendid way to spend a fun evening with friends. Amusing plays are presented every day except Sunday, alternating from one day to the next between matinee and evening performances. Reservations are mandatory; for schedules and information call *☎677-2001* or *1-800-267-7553*. Rosebud is located about an hour from Calgary on Hwy. 840 about halfway to Drumheller.

Shopping

Tour B: Central Foothills

Markerville

Three gift shops can be found in the vicinity of the Markerville Creamery (see p 424), the **Gallery and Gift Shop** adjoins the creamery and sells pretty bric-a-brac and gifts. Next door the **Butterchurn** features a remarkable collection of wood-worked items, from small shelves to benches and tables.

Carstairs

Pa-Su Farm (*9km west of Carstairs on Hwy. 580, follow the signs, ☎337-2800*) is a working sheep farm with a collection of rare and endangered breeds of sheep. A 280m^2 gallery displays weavings from Africa and local sheepskin and woolen products. The working part of the farm is only open to scheduled tours. The Devonshire Tea Room serves delicious warm scones with tea.

On the other side of Carstairs, the **Custom Woolen Mills** (*21km east of Carstairs on Hwy. 581, then 4.5km north on Hwy. 791, ☎337-2221*) is a curious little spot. Raw wool is processed on machines that in some cases are more than 100 years old. Yarn and ready-made knitted articles can be purchased.

Tour C: The Heartland

Lacomb

The Gallery on the Main (*4910 50th Ave., 3rd floor, ☎782-3405*) exhibits an impressive variety of creations by local artists. The gallery represents 45 artists who use diverse mediums such as acrylic, oil, woodcarving and pottery. Come check out these fine works of art.

Edmonton

Edmonton ★★ seems to suffer from an image problem, and undeservedly so.

People have trouble getting past the boomtown atmosphere and the huge mall! Admittedly it is a boomtown: a city that grew out of the wealth of the natural resources that surround it. But this city of new money has more than made good with an attractive downtown core, a park system and cultural facilities, including theatres and many festivals (see p 457). With all this going for it, though, the city's biggest attraction still seems to be its gargantuan shopping mall. You be the judge!

Edmonton has actually experienced three booms: the first in fur, the second in gold and the third in oil. The area had long been frequented by Aboriginal peoples who searched for quartzite to make tools and who trapped abundant beaver and muskrat. It was the supply of fur that attracted traders to the area in the late 18th century. The Hudson's Bay Company established Fort Edmonton in 1795 next to the North West Company's Fort Augustus overlooking the North Saskatchewan River where the Legislative Building now stands. Trading at the fort involved Cree and Assiniboine from the north as well as Blackfoot from the south. These normally warring peoples could trade in safety essentially because the fierce Blackfoot were more peaceable when they were outside their own territory to the south.

Edmonton's fortunes rose and fell until the next boom. Merchants tried to attract prospectors of the Klondike Gold Rush to pass through Edmonton on their way to Dawson City. Prospectors were encouraged to outfit themselves in Edmonton and use this

"All-Canadian Route," which was an alternative to the Chilkoot Trail, thereby avoiding Alaska. The route turned out to be something of a scam, however, proving arduous and impractical. None of the some 1,600 prospectors lured to Edmonton actually reached the goldfields in time for the big rush of 1899. Some perished trying and some never left. Six years later, on September 1, 1905, the province of Alberta was founded and Edmonton was named the capital. Citizens of cities like Calgary, Cochrane, Wetaskiwin, Athabasca and Banff, among others, all claimed that this distinction should have been bestowed on their cities, but Edmonton prevailed. In 1912, the cities of Strathcona and Edmonton merged, pushing the total population over 50,000.

Agriculture remained the bread and butter of Alberta's capital until the well at Leduc (see p 430) blew in and the third boom, the oil boom, was on. Since then Edmonton has been one of Canada's fastest growing cities. Pipelines, refineries, derricks and oil tanks sprang up all around the city in farmers' fields. Some 10,000 wells were drilled and by 1965 Edmonton had become the oil capital of Canada. As the population grew so did the downtown core in order to accommodate the business community, which is still very much centred around oil though the boom is over. Fortunately the city took care not to overdevelop, and today this boomtown has an unusually sophisticated atmosphere (despite the shopping mall), with fine restaurants and a thriving arts community. Edmonton has become the technological, service and supply centre of Alberta.

Finding Your Way Around

By Car

Edmonton's streets are numbered; the avenues run east-west and the streets run north-south. The major arteries include **Calgary Trail**, which runs north into the city (northbound it is also known as 103rd Street and southbound as 104th Street); **Whitemud Drive** runs east-west: it lies south of the city centre providing access to West Edmonton Mall, Fort Edmonton Park and the Valley Zoo; **Jasper Avenue** runs east-west through downtown where 101st Avenue would naturally fall; Hwy. 16, the Yellowhead Highway, crosses the city north of downtown, providing access to points in the tour of northern Alberta (see also Tour D in Central Alberta, p 416).

A collection of hotels line Calgary Trail south of downtown and Stony Plain Road west of the city centre.

Car Rentals

Budget
Airport:
☎***(780) 448-2000***
Downtown:
10016 106th Street
☎***(780) 448-2001***

Hertz
Airport:
☎***(780) 890-4565***
Downtown:
☎***(780) 423-3431***

Tilden
Airport:
☎***(780) 890-7232***
Downtown:
☎***(780) 422-6097***

Avis
Airport:
☎***(780)890-7596***
Downtown:
Sheraton Hotel
10235 101st Street
☎***(780) 448-0066***

Discount
Downtown:
Hotel Macdonald
9925 Jasper Avenue
☎*(780) 448-3892*

Thrifty
Airport:
☎*(780) 890-4555*
Downtown:
10036 102nd Street
☎*(780) 428-8555*

By Plane

Edmonton International Airport is located south of the city centre and offers many services and facilities, including restaurants, an information centre, hotel courtesy phones, major car-rental counters, currency exchange and a bus tour operator.

Air Canada, Canadian Airlines International, American Airlines, Delta Airlines, Northwest Airlines, United Airlines and Lufthansa all have regular flights to the airport. Regional companies (Air B.C. and Canadian Regional) fly in and out of the municipal airport, located north of the city.

The **Sky Shuttle** (☎*465-8515*) travels to downtown hotels and to Edmonton's municipal airport. It passes every 20min on weekends and every 30min during the week. The trip is $11 one-way and $18 return.

A taxi from the airport to downtown costs about $30.

By Train

Via Rail's transcontinental railway passenger service makes a stop in Edmonton three times a week, continuing west to Jasper and Vancouver or east to Saskatoon and beyond. See also p 42. The new VIA train station is at 12360 121st Street, about 15min from downtown.

By Bus

Edmonton Greyhound Bus Depot
10324 103rd St.
☎*413-8747*
☎*420-2440*
☎*800-661-8747*
Services: restaurant, lockers. See also p 45.

Edmonton South Greyhound Bus Depot
5723 104th St., 2 blocks north of Whitemud Freeway on Calgary Trail
☎*433-1919*

Public Transit

Edmonton's public transit also combines buses and a light-rail transit system. The LRT runs east-west along Jasper Avenue, south to the university and then north to 139th Street. There are only 10 stops, and in the city centre the train runs underground. The LRT is free between Churchill and Grandin stops on weekdays from 9am to 3pm and Saturdays from 9am to 6pm. Fares are $1.60 for adults and a day pass is $4.75. Route and schedule information is available by calling ☎*496-1611*.

By Foot

Edmonton's downtown core has its own system of walkways known as the pedway system. It lies below and above ground and at street level and seems complicated at first, though is very well indicated and easy to negotiate once you have picked up a map at the tourist information centre.

Practical Information

Area code: 780

Information on everything from road conditions to movie listings to provincial parks is available from the Talking Yellow Pages. In Edmonton, call ☎*493-9000*. A series of recorded messages is accessible by dialling specific codes. The codes are listed in the front of the yellow pages phone books; usually found in phone booths.

● ATTRACTIONS

Tour A: Downtown and North of the North Saskatchewan River

1. Civic Centre
2. Francis Winsper Centre for Music
3. Edmonton Art Gallery
4. Edmonton Police Museum
5. St. Josephat's Ukrainian Catholic Cathedral
6. Ukrainian Canadian Archives and Museum of Alberta
7. Ukrainian Museum of Canada
8. Chinatown Gate
9. Canadian Country Music Hall of Fame
10. Hotel Macdonald
11. Alberta Legislature Building

Tour B : Old Strathcona and South of the North Saskatchewan

12. Rutherford House
13. John Walter Museum
14. Old Strathcona Model and Toy Museum
15. C&E Railway Museum
16. Telephone Historical Information Centre
17. Strathcona Farmer's Market

Tour C : Other Sights

18. Muttart Conservatory

⬡ ACCOMMODATIONS

1. Alberta Suite Hotel
2. Best Western City Centre
3. Days Inn Downtown
4. Delta Edmonton Centre Suite Hotel
5. Econo Lodge
6. Edmonton House Suite Hotel
7. Edmonton International Hostel
8. Grand Hotel
9. Hotel Macdonald
10. Inn on Seventh
11. Union Bank Inn Hotel
12. Varscona
13. Westin Edmonton

⬢ RESTAURANTS

1. Baraka Cafe
2. Bistro Praha
3. Café Select
4. Claude's on the River
5. Funky Pickle Pizza Co.
6. Hy's Steakloft
7. Madison Grill
8. Manifesto
9. Pacific Fish
10. Plantier's
11. Symposium
12. Vi's by the River

Tourist Information

Edmonton Tourism Civic Centre
1 Sir Winston Churchill Square; also in Gateway Park, south of downtown on Calgary Trail (Hwy. 2)
☎496-8423
☎800-463-4667

Bed and Breakfasts

Alberta Bed & Breakfast Association
15615 81st St., T5Z 2T6
☎/⇄456-5928
Represents various regional B&B associations across the province.

Alberta's Gem B&B and Reservation Agency
11216 48th Ave., T6H 0C7
☎/⇄434-6098
B&B bookings throughout the province.

Edmonton Bed & Breakfast
13824 110A Ave., T5M 2M9
☎455-2297

Exploring

Tour A: Downtown and North of the North Saskatchewan River

Begin your tour of Edmonton with a visit to the **Tourist Information Centre** (*Mon to Fri 8am to 5pm*) located in the **Civic Centre** (*1 Sir Winston Churchill Square*); the hours may not be very practical,

Edmonton Centre
Legend: LRT
Stadium
Churchill
Bay
Corona
Grandin
University
Clark Park
North Saskatchewan River
Heritage Trail
OLD STRATHCONA
Low Level Bridge
J.A. Macdonald Bridge
High Level Bridge
105th Street Bridge
Hill Creek Ravine
Kingsway Ave.
Princess Elisabeth Ave.
Norwood Blvd.
Jasper Ave.
River Valley Rd.
Fortway Dr.
Bellamy Hill Rd.
Grierson Hill
Rowland Rd.
Connors Rd.
Scona Rd.
Walterdale Rd.
Fort Hill
Saskatchewan Dr.
Whyte Ave. (82nd Ave.)
©ULYSSES

but the staff is very friendly and helpful. While there, pick up a *Ride Guide* to figure out the public transportation system. The impressive City Hall is the centrepiece of the **Edmonton Civic Centre**, a complex that occupies six city blocks and includes the Centennial Library, the Edmonton Art Gallery, Sir Winston Churchill Square, the Law Courts Building, the Convention Centre and the Citadel Theatre. City Hall, with its impressive eight-storey glass pyramid, opened in 1992 on the site of the old city hall.

While City Hall may be the centrepiece of the Civic Centre, its biggest star these days is certainly the brand new **Francis Winspear Centre for Music ★★** (*4 Sir Winston Churchill Square*), which will hopefully bring some life back to Edmonton's fading urban core. Built with a $6 million gift from Edmonton businessman Francis Winspear, the 1,900-seat hall is faced with Manitoba tyndall limestone to match City Hall and brick to match the neighbouring Stan Milner Library. The Edmonton Symphony Orchestra now makes its home here.

On the eastern side of Sir Winston Churchill Square lies the **Edmonton Art Gallery ★★** (*$3, free Thu pm; Mon to Wed 10:30am to 5pm, Thu and Fri 10:30am to 8pm, Sat and Sun 11am to 5pm; ☎422-6223*). Admission is free when the museum can find sponsorship. Fine art by local, Canadian and international artists is unfortunately a bit lost in this drab building, but a new curator and plans for exciting new shows promise to breathe new life into the gallery. Still, worth checking out.

Head east on 102A Avenue, turn left on 97th Street and right on 103A Avenue.

The **Edmonton Police Museum ★** (*free admission; Mon to Sat 9am to 3pm; 9620 103A Ave., ☎421-2274*) is a bit of a change from your typical museum excursion as it traces law enforcement in Alberta's history. Located on the second floor of the Police Service Headquarters it houses displays of uniforms, handcuffs, jail cells and the force's former furry mascot!

The stretch of 97th Street from 105th to 108th Avenue is Edmonton's original Chinatown with plenty of shops and restaurants. Along 107th Avenue, from 95th Street to 116th Street is an area known as the Avenue of Nations with shops and restaurants representing a variety of cultures from Asia, Europe and the Americas. Rickshaws provide transportation during the summer months.

At the corner of 97th Street and 108th Avenue is **St. Josephat's Ukrainian Catholic Cathedral ★**. Among Edmonton's several Ukrainian churches, this is the most elaborate and is worth a stop for its lovely decor and artwork. One block to the east, 96th Street is recognized in *Ripley's Believe It or Not* as the street with the highest concentration of churches. It is appropriately known as Church Street.

Head east to 96th Street then north to 110th Avenue to the **Ukrainian Canadian Archives and Museum of Alberta ★** (*donation; Tue to Fri 10am to 5pm, Sat noon to 5pm; 9543 110th Ave., ☎424-7580*) which houses one of the largest displays of Ukrainian archives in Canada. The lives of Ukrainian pioneers around the turn of the century are chronicled through artifacts and photographs. About 10 blocks to the west, the smaller **Ukrainian Museum of Canada ★** (*free admission; Jun to Aug, Mon to Fri 9am to 4pm, winter by appt; 10611 110th Ave., ☎483-5932*) displays a collection of Ukrainian costumes, Easter eggs, and household items.

Head south on 95th Street to 102 Avenue to Edmonton's new **Chinatown**, the focal point of which is the Chinatown Gate at 97th Street. The gate is also a symbol of the friendship between Edmonton and its sister city Harbin in China. Roll the ball in the lion's mouth for good luck.

Head south to the Edmonton Convention Centre for a great view of the North Saskatchewan River Valley and a visit to the **Canadian Country Music Hall of Fame** (*free admission; every day 9am to 9pm; pedway level, 9797 Jasper Ave., ☎421-9797*) which is actually a wall with plaques and photographs commemorating such greats as Hank Snow and Wilf Carter. After a trip through Alberta you may well have developed an appreciation for country music and want to know more.

In true Canadian Pacific tradition, the Chateau-style **Hotel Macdonald** ★★ is Edmonton's ritziest place to stay (see p 453) and was for many years the place to see and be seen in Edmonton. Completed in 1915 by the Grand Trunk Railway, it was designed by Montréal architects Ross and MacFarlane. The wrecker's ball came close to falling in 1983 when the hotel closed, but a $28-million restoration brought the Macdonald back in all its splendour. If you aren't staying here, at least pop in to use the facilities, or better yet, enjoy a drink overlooking the river from the hotel's suave bar, The Library.

The next stop on the tour is the Alberta Legislature Building. It is a fair walk to get there from the Hotel Macdonald, but nevertheless a pleasant one, along the tree-lined **Heritage Trail** ★★★. This historic fur-traders' route from Old Town to the site of Old Fort Edmonton is a 30min walk that follows the river bank for most of its length. A red brick sidewalk, antique light standards and street signs will keep you on the right track. The river views along Macdonald Drive are remarkable, especially at sunset.

The 16-storey vaulted dome of the Edwardian **Alberta Legislature Building** ★★ (*mid-May to early Sep weekdays 9am to 5pm, weekends 9am to 5 pm; Sep to May weekdays 9am to 4:30pm, weekends noon to 5pm; Nov to Feb closed Sat, Guided tours every hour on the hour in the morning and every 30min in the evening; 107th St. at 97th Ave., ☎427-7362*) is a landmark in Edmonton's skyline. Sandstone from Calgary, marble from Québec, Pennsylvania and Italy, and mahogany from Belize were used to build this, the seat of Alberta government, in 1912. At the time, the Legislature stood next to the original Fort Edmonton. Today it is surrounded by gardens and fountains; be sure to visit the government greenhouses on the south grounds. Tours begin at the Interpretive Centre where Alberta's and Canada's parliamentary tradition is explained.

Alberta Legislature Building

Tour B: Old Strathcona and South of the North Saskatchewan River

Cross the High Level Bridge, continue along 109th Street, turn right on 88th Avenue, turn right again on 110th Street, and then left on Saskatchewan Drive to Rutherford House.

Rutherford House ★ (*$2; mid-May to early Sep every day 10am to 6pm; Sep to May Tue to Sun noon to 5pm; 11153 Saskatchewan Dr., ☎427-3995*) is the classic Edwardian former home of Alberta's first premier, Dr. A.C. Rutherford. Guides in period costume bake scones in a wood stove, offer craft demonstrations, lead visitors through the elegantly restored mansion and operate a tea room in the summer (*☎422-2697*).

If it is Sunday, return to 88th Avenue and head east. It becomes Walterdale Road; follow it to Queen Elizabeth Park Road and turn left into the parking lot of the John Walter Museum.

The **John Walter Museum** (*free admission; Sun 1pm to 4pm, until 5pm in summer; 10627 93rd Ave., Kinsmen Park, ☎496-4852*) is in fact made up of three houses, each built by John Walter between 1874 and 1900. Walter manned a ferry across the North Saskatchewan River, and his first house was used as a rest spot for travellers. Exhibits outline the growth of Edmonton over this period.

Continue your tour by heading to **Old Strathcona ★★★**. Once a city independent of Edmonton, Strathcona was founded when the Calgary and Edmonton Railway Company's rail line ended here in 1891. Brick buildings from that era still remain in this historic district, which is the best-preserved in Edmonton. While the area north of the North Saskatchewan River is clean, crisp and new with the unfinished feel of a boom town, south of the river, in Old Strathcona, a sense of character is much more tangible. Here an artistic, cosmopolitan and historic atmosphere prevails. Walking tour brochures are available from the **Old Strathcona Foundation** (*Mon to Fri 8:30am to 4:30pm; 10324 Whyte Ave., suite 401, ☎433-5866*).

The **Old Strathcona Model and Toy Museum ★★** (*8603 104 St., ☎433-4512*) is housed in the Mackenzie Residence, one of the best-preserved buildings in Old Strathcona. Unfortunately, these childhood treasures from a bygone era have temporarily been stored away in some old forgotten chest. During our visit in June 1999, they were still waiting for a buyer to restore this ancient building.

Three other interesting stops along the way are the **C&E Railway Museum** (*donation; summer, Tue to Sat 10am to 4pm; 10447 86th Ave., ☎433-9739*), housed in a replica of the original railway station; the **Telephone Historical Information Centre ★** (*$3; Tue to Fri 10am to 4pm, Sat noon to 4pm; 10437 83rd Ave., ☎441-2077*), housed in the original telephone exchange, where you'll get the real story behind switchboards and manholes; and finally the **Strathcona Farmer's Market ★**(*year-round, Sat 8am to 3pm; in the summer Tue and Wed noon to 4pm in summer, also; 10310 83rd Ave., ☎439-1844*) on 83rd Avenue between 104th Street and 103rd Street, where fresh produce, crafts and plenty of little treasures can be bought. On the corner of Whyte Avenue and 103rd Street is the **Caboose Tourist Information Centre** where you can pick up brochures for walking tours of historic Old Strathcona.

Next take a stroll along **Whyte Avenue** *(82nd Avenue) to explore the shops and cafés and soak up the atmosphere.*

Tour C: Other Sights

The city has a handful of other sights that merit a visit and are best reached by public transit or by car.

The four glass-pyramid greenhouses of the **Muttart Conservatory ★★★** (*$4.50; Mon to Fri 9am to 6pm, Sat and Sun 11am to 6pm; 9626 96A St., off 98 Ave., ☎496-8755*) are another of the landmarks of Edmonton's skyline. Flourishing beneath three of these pyramids are floral displays of arid, temperate and tropical climates, respectively. Every month a new, vivid floral display is put together under the fourth pyramid. The conservatory is accessible from bus #51 south on 100th Street.

About 6km west as the crow flies, north of the river, is the **Provincial Museum and Archives of Alberta ★★** (*$6.50; every day 9am to 5pm; 12845 102 Ave., ☎453-9100, www.pma.edmonton.ab.ca*). The natural and human history of Alberta is traced from the Cretaceous period, through the Ice Age to the pictographs of the province's earliest Aboriginal peoples. The merging of their cultures and those of the early explorers and pioneers is explained in the native display. The habitat gallery reproduces Alberta's four natural regions, while the Bug Room is abuzz with exotic live insects. Travelling exhibits complement the permanent collection. The displays are a bit dated, but nonetheless provide an interesting overview of the world of contrasts that is Alberta.

Government House ★ (*Sun 1pm to 5pm; free guided tours every half-hour ☎427-2281*), the former residence of Alberta's lieutenant-governor, is located beside the Provincial Museum. The three-storey sandstone mansion features the original library, oak-panelling along with newly renovated conference rooms. Take bus #1 along Jasper Avenue, or bus #116 along 102 Avenue.

Also north of the river is the **Edmonton Space and Science Centre ★** (*$7; mid-Jun to Sep every day 10am to 6pm; Sep to mid-Jun, Tue to Sun 10am 6pm; 11211 142nd St., ☎451-3344*). All sorts of out-of-this-world stuff is sure to keep the young and old busy. You can embark on a simulated space mission at the Challenger Centre or create music on a giant piano. The Margeret Ziedler Star Theatre presents multimedia shows. An IMAX theatre is also on site (see p 459).

In the North Saskatchewan River Valley, off Whitemud and Fox Drives, lies **Fort Edmonton Park ★★★** (*$7; May and Jun, Mon to Fri 10am to 4pm, Sat and Sun 10am to 6pm; Jul to Aug, every day 10am to 6pm; over Christmas for sleigh rides; ☎496-8787*), Canada's largest historic park and home to an authentic reconstruction of Fort Edmonton as it stood in 1846. Four historic villages recreate different periods at the fort: the fur-trading era at the fort itself; the settlement era on 1885 Street; the municipal era on 1905 Street and the metropolitan era on 1920 Street. Period buildings, period dress, period automobiles and period shops, including a bazaar, a general store, a saloon and a bakery, bring you back in time.

Reed's Bazaar and Tea Room serves a "proper" English tea with scones from 12:30pm to 5pm. Theme programs for children are put on Saturday afternoons. Admission is free after 4:30pm, but don't arrive any later in order to catch the last train to the fort, and take note that you'll be tight for time if you choose this frugal option, so it depends how much you want to see.

For a lovely walk through the North Saskatchewan River Valley, follow the 4km-long self-guided interpretive trail that starts at the

John Janzen Nature Centre (*free admission; mid-May to Jun Mon to Fri 9am to 4pm, Sat and Sun 11am to 6pm; Jul and Aug Mon to Fri 9am to 4pm, Sat and Sun 11am to 6pm; rest of year Mon to Fri 9am to 4pm, Sat and Sun 1pm to 4pm; next to Fort Edmonton Park, ☎496-2939*). The Centre has hands-on displays and live animals, including a working beehive.

The Fort Edmonton Valley Zoo Shuttle operates from the University Transit Centre and between these two sights on Sundays and holidays between Victoria Day (3rd Sunday in May) and Labour Day (early September). Fares (one-way) are $1.60. Alternatively, bus #12 drops you at Buena Vista and 102nd Ave., from where you must walk 1.5km to the zoo.

Across the river is the **Valley Zoo** ★ (*$5.25, lower rate in winter; May to Jun every day 9:30am to 6pm; Jul and Aug until 8pm; Sep to mid-Oct weekdays 9:30am to 4pm, weekends 9:30am to 6pm; winter every day 9:30am to 4pm; at the end of Buena Vista Rd., corner 134th St., ☎496-6911*), a great place for kids. It apparently began with a story-book theme but has since grown to include an African veldt and winter quarters which permit it to stay open in the winter. The residents include Siberian tigers and white-handed gibbons along with more indigenous species. Kids enjoy run-of-the-mill pony rides and more exotic camel rides.

Last, but certainly not least, is Edmonton's pride and joy the **West Edmonton Mall** ★★★ (*87th Ave. between 170th St. and 178th St.*). You may scoff to hear that some visitors come to Edmonton and never leave the West Edmonton Mall, and then you may swear that you won't give in to the hype and visit it, but these reasons alone are enough to go, if only to say you've been.

There are real submarines at the Deep-Sea Adventure; dolphin shows; underwater caverns and barrier reefs; the largest indoor amusement park; a National Hockey League-size rink where you can watch the Edmonton Oilers practise; an 18-hole golf course; a waterpark complete with wave pool, waterslides, rapids, bungee jumping and whirlpools; a casino, bingo room and North America's largest billiard hall; fine dining on Bourbon Street; a life-size, hand-carved and painted replica of Columbus' flagship, the *Santa Maria*; replicas of England's crown jewels; a solid ivory pagoda; bronze sculptures; fabulous fountains, including one fashioned after a fountain at the Palace of Versailles, and finally, the Fantasyland Hotel (see p 454): lodging that truly lives up to its name... and, oh yeah, we almost forgot, there are also some 800 shops and services – this is a mall after all. It seems it is possible to come and never leave! Even though it is a shopping mall, the West Edmonton Mall simply has to be seen and therefore merits its three stars!

If you can't afford the extra money to stay in an igloo or a horse-drawn coach, at least take a tour of the theme rooms at the **Fantasyland Hotel** (*free tour; every day 2pm; reserve ahead ☎444-3000, see p 454*).

Parks and Beaches

The **River Valley Parks System** (*Edmonton Community Services, ☎496-4999*) lies along the North Saskatchewan River and consists of several small parks where you can bicycle, jog, go swimming, play golf or just generally enjoy the natural surroundings. The amount of land set aside for parks per capita is higher in Edmonton than anywhere else in the country. Bicyclists are encouraged to pick up a copy of the map *Cycle Edmonton* at one of the tourist information offices.

ATTRACTIONS

Tour C: Other Sights

1. Provincial Museum of Alberta
2. Edmonton Space and Science Centre
3. Fort Edmonton Park
4. John Janzen Nature Centre
5. Valley Zoo
6. West Edmonton Mall

RESTAURANTS

1. Syrtaki Greek Restaurant

ACCOMMODATIONS

1. Best Western Cedar Park Inn
2. Best Western Westwood Inn
3. Edmonton West Travelodge
4. Holgate House B&B
5. La Bohème B&B (R)
6. Southbend Motel
7. West Harvest Inn
8. University of Alberta

(R) property with restaurant (see description)

Outdoor Activities

Golf

The **Riverside Golf Course** (*8630 Rowland Rd., ☎496-4914*), overlooking the North Saskatchewan River in Edmonton, is one of the city's more than 30 courses.

Cycling

With its relatively flat terrain (besides, of course, the Rocky Mountains), Alberta is an ideal place to explore by bike. The **Alberta Bicycle Association** (*11759 Groat Rd., Edmonton, T5M 3K6, ☎453-8518*) can provide more information about bicycle touring in the province. There is also a map for bicycling in Edmonton called **Cycle Edmonton**, which is available at the tourist office.

Accommodations

Tour A: Downtown and North of the North Saskatchewan River

Downtown

Edmonton International Hostel
members $15
non-members $20
≡
10422 91st St., T5H 1S6
☎988-6836
⇄988-8698
This hostel is located close to the bus terminal, in a questionable area, so take care. The usual hostel facilities, including laundry machines, common kitchen and a common room with a fireplace are rounded out by a small food store and bike rentals.

The Days Inn Downtown
$50-$60
ℝ, ≡, ℜ, ⊛, ⌂, *tv, bar,* 🐕
10041 106th St., T5J 1G3
☎423-1925
☎800-267-2191
☎800-DAYS-INN
⇄424-5302
The Days Inn Dowtown boasts comfortable, modern rooms. This is another downtown spot with a good quality to price ratio.

Grand Hotel
$51, bkfst
10266 103rd St.,
corner of 103rd Ave.
☎422-6365
At the Grand Hotel you will be fascinated by Edmonton's cowboy past. With its tavern, diner, dance hall and 79 anonymous dark rooms, the Grand Hotel seems like it came right out of one of Lucky Lake's comic strips. Despite its minimal comfort and lacklustre appearance, people come here for the price and location (the Greyhound bus terminal is right across the street).

The Econo Lodge
$54-$59
, ≡, ℜ, ⊛, *tv, bar,* 🐕
10209 100th Ave., T5J 0A1
☎428-6442
☎800-613-7043
This Econo Lodge has 73 rooms including some suites featuring whirlpool baths. Parking and an airport shuttle service make this a good deal for those looking for lodging downtown. Rooms are nothing special, however.

Inn on Seventh
$70
≡, ℜ, ⊛, *tv, bar,* ⊘, 🐕
10001 107th St., T5J 1J1
☎429-2861
☎800-661-7327
⇄426-7225
Fifteen of the nearly 200 clean and modern rooms at the Inn on Seventh are "environmentally safe," though this just means they are non-smoking rooms on non-smoking floors.

Weekend rates are available. Facilities include coin-laundry machines.

Best Western City Centre
$89-$99
≡, ≈, ℜ, ⊛, *tv, bar,* ⌂
11310 109th St., T5G 2T7
☎***479-2042***
☎***800-666-5026***
☎***800-528-1234***
⇄***474-2204***
This Best Western is not quite in the city centre and has a rather dated exterior. The rooms are nevertheless very comfortable and pleasantly decorated with wooden furniture.

Alberta Suite Hotel
$90-$110
tv, ⊛ *, K,* ≡, ⊘, ⌂, ⊛
10049 102nd Street, near Jasper Avenue
☎***423-1565***
☎***800 661-3982***
⇄***426-6260***
www.albertaplace.com
As the name indicates, the Alberta Suite Hotel offers mini-apartments with kitchenettes and work areas. With its friendly staff and unpretentious, tastefully decorated rooms, this establishment is a perfect compromise between impersonal, luxury hotels and budget accommodation.

Edmonton Westin Hotel
$115-$155
≈, ≡, ℜ
10135 100th St.
☎***426-3636***
⇄***428-1454***
www.westin.ab.ca
The Edmonton Westin Hotel was built on the site of the first post office in Edmonton. This modern facility with 413 rooms is located in what is now the heart of the business district. The guests, mostly from the business district, enjoy the restaurant, pool and enormous terrace – all of which exude luxury.

Union Bank Inn Hotel
$125-$165, bkfst
≡, ⊛, ℜ;
10053 Jasper Avenue, between 100th and 101st Sts.
☎***423-3600***
☎***888-423-3601***
⇄***423-4623***
www.unionbank.com
The Union Bank, constructed in 1910, was the first bank built on Jasper Street. Relegated to pigeons and the homeless, it was transformed into the Union Bank Inn Hotel after a major facelift in 1997. Each of the 14 magnificent and inviting rooms is the work of a different decorator. Every room has a fireplace and a whirlpool. The delicious Madison's Grill is on the main floor.

The Edmonton House Suite Hotel
$140-$195
ℜ, *K,* ≈, ⌂, *tv,* ⊘, 🐕
10205 100th Ave., T5J 4B5
☎***420-4000***
☎***800-661-6562***
⇄***420-4008***
The Edmonton House is actually an apartment-hotel with suites that boast kitchens and balconies. This is one of the better apartment-hotel options in town. Reservations are recommended.

Delta Edmonton Centre Suite Hotel
$154-$220
ℜ, ⊛, ⌂, *tv, bar,* ≡, ⊘, 🐕
10222 102nd St., T5J 4C5
☎***429-3900***
☎***800-661-6655***
⇄***426-0562***
This Delta is part of the downtown Eaton Centre shopping mall. This means that apart from the hotel's extensive facilities, guests have access to shops and cinemas. Rooms are comfortable and the suites are lavishly decorated.

Hotel MacDonald
$249-$295
≡, ℜ, ≈, ⊛, ⌂, ⊘, *tv, bar,* 🐕, ♿
10065 100th St., T5J 0N6
☎***424-5181***
☎***800-441-1414***
⇄***424-8017***
www.cphotels.com
Edmonton's grand chateau-style Hotel MacDonald is stunning. Classic styling from the guest rooms to the dining rooms make this an exquisite place to stay. A variety of weekend packages are available, including golf packages and romantic getaways. Call for details.

West of Downtown

West Harvest Inn
$72-$79
≡, ℜ, ⊛, *tv*
17803 Stony Plain Rd., T5S 1B4
☎***484-8000***
☎***800-661-6993***
⇄***486-6060***
The West Harvest Inn is the other inexpensive choice within striking distance of the mall. This hotel is relatively

quiet and receives quite a few business travellers.

Best Western Westwood Inn
$79
≡, ⌂, ⊙, ≈, ℜ, *tv*
18035 Stony Plain Rd., T5S 1B2
☎***483-7770***
☎***800-557-4767***
☎***800-528-1234***
⇄***486-1769***
The Best Western Westwood Inn is also close to the mall. The rooms are more expensive here but they are also much larger and noticeably more comfortable and more pleasantly decorated.

Edmonton West Travelodge
$79-$89
≈, ≡, ⊛, *tv*,
18320 Stony Plain Rd., T5S 1A7
☎***483-6031***
☎***800-578-7878***
⇄***484-2358***
For those who want to be close to the shopping, but aren't necessarily big spenders, the Edmonton West Travelodge is one of two relatively inexpensive hotels located close to the West Edmonton Mall. The rooms were recently redone and there is a big indoor pool.

Fantasyland Hotel & Resort
$165
⊙, , ≡, ℜ, ⊛, ⌂, *tv, bar*
17700 87th Ave., T5T 4V4
☎***444-3000***
☎***800-661-6454***
⇄***444-3294***
www.fantasylandhotel.com
Travellers on a shopping vacation will certainly want to be as close to the West Edmonton Mall as possible, making the Fantasyland Hotel & Resort the obvious choice. Of course, you might also choose to stay here just for the sheer delight of spending the night under African or Arabian skies or in the back of a pick-up truck!

East of Downtown

Holgate House B&B
$85
≡
6210 Ada Blvd, T5W 4P1
☎/⇄***471-1185***
The Holgate House B&B is located nearby in the historic Highlands district. It offers two exquisite rooms decorated in the "arts and crafts" style, one with private bath and the other boasting an ensuite bathroom complete with a six-foot soaker tub. After exploring the scenic streets that surround the house and overlook the Saskatchewan River Valley, guests can relax on the lovely front verandah, in the sitting room by a roaring fire or in the morning room with a good book.

La Boheme B&B
$140
K
6427 112th Ave., T5W 0N9
☎***474-5693***
⇄***479-1871***
geceventures.com/laboheme
Set on the second floor of the historic Gibbard Building and upstairs from the restaurant of the same name, La Boheme B&B occupies the rooms of a former luxury apartment building. All the rooms are charmingly decorated and equipped with kitchenettes, but you will find it hard to resist the gastronomical delights at the restaurant downstairs.

Tour B: Old Strathcona and South of the North Saskatchewan River

The cheaper hotels are situated in Strathcona. We found two that we liked. With its 40 rooms located in one of the oldest wooden buildings in Edmonton, the **Strathcona Hotel** (*$28; sb/pb, 10302 82nd Ave, near 103rd Street;* ☎*439-1992*) is less expensive and more attractive than its neighbour across the street, the **Commercial Hotel** (*$31; sb/pb; 10329 82nd Ave.;* ☎*439-3981*), which is clean and comfortable, but sometimes noisy. In both of these establishments, expect to pay extra for a private bathroom.

University of Alberta
$30-40
116th St. at 87th Ave., T6G 2H6
☎***492-4281***
⇄***492-7032***
Student residences at the University of Alberta are available May to August only. They have pleasant youth–hostel–style dormitories. Reservations recommended.

Southbend Motel
$44
K, tv, 🐕
5130 Calgary Tr. Northbound, T6H 2H4
☎434-1418
⇄435-1525
For a very reasonable rate, guests can stay at the Southbend Motel, where rooms are admittedly a bit dated, and for no extra charge use all the facilities at the Best Western Cedar Park Inn next door (see below). These include a pool, a sauna and an exercise room.

The Best Western Cedar Park Inn
$104-$149
≡, ℜ, ≈, ⌂, ⏲, *tv,* 🐕
5116 Calgary Tr. Northbound
☎434-7411
☎800-661-9461
☎800-528-1234
⇄437-4836
The Cedar Park Inn is a large hotel with 190 equally spacious rooms. Some of these are called theme rooms ($150), which essentially means there is a hot-tub for two, a king-size bed, a living room and a fancier decor. Weekend and family rates are available, and there is a courtesy limo service to the airports or the West Edmonton Mall.

Varscona
$89
≡, ℜ, ⌂, *tv, bar*
10620 Whyte Ave., T6E 2A7
☎434-6111
☎888-515-3355
⇄439-1195
The newly renovated Varscona offers guests king-size beds, wine and cheese upon arrival and a cosy fireplace for those cold Edmonton winters. In the heart of Old Strathcona, it is easily one of the city's best-located hotels.

Restaurants

Tour A: Downtown and North of the North Saskatchewan River

Baraka Café
$
corner of Jasper Avenue and 101st St.
☎423-1819
Ideally located, the Baraka Café offers a laid-back atmosphere where clients of all ages and backgrounds mingle. People come here to drink fresh juice, good coffee or bite into one of their many delicious sandwiches.

Manifesto
$
10043 102nd St., near Jasper Avenue
☎423-7901
An arts space, café, as well as a second-hand bookstore, Manifesto is purely underground. They serve light fare, such as soup and bagels. A few large, inviting couches complete the picture. All sorts of gatherings take place here on weekends: from the launching of a new CD, to art expositions, to a performance of video scratch.

Cheesecake Café Bakery Restaurant
$
17011 100th Ave.
☎486-0440
10390 51st Ave.
☎437-5011
A huge variety of cheesecakes — need we say more?

Levis by the River
$$
9712 111th St.
☎482-6402
Levis is located in a converted house overlooking the North Saskatchewan River Valley. Innovative and delicious dishes are served in its several small dining rooms and, in the summer, on the terrace, from which you can enjoy great views and spectacular sunsets. Service can be slow if they are really busy, but the chocolate pecan pie on the dessert menu is worth the wait!

The **West Edmonton Mall's** Bourbon Street harbours a collection of moderately priced restaurants. **Café Orleans** (**$$**; ☎*444-2202*) serves Cajun and Creole specialties; **Sherlock Holmes** (**$$**; ☎*444-1752*) serves typical English pub grub; **Albert's Family Restaurant** (**$**; ☎*444-1179*) serves Montréal-style smoked meat; the **Modern Art Café** (**$-$$**; ☎*444-2233*) is a new-world bistro with pizzas, pasta and

Edmonton

steaks where everything (the art, the furniture) is for sale.

Pacific Fish
$$-$$$
10020 101A Ave.
☎422-0282
Also known as Frank's Place, this is perhaps Edmonton's best seafood restaurant, with fresh fish arriving daily. Reservations are recommended.

Syrtaki Greek Restaurant
$$-$$$
16313 111th Ave.
☎484-2473
The whitewashed and blue decor of the Syrtaki Greek Restaurant is enough to make you forget you are in Edmonton. Belly dancers animate the evening on Fridays and Saturdays. Fresh game, seafood, meat, chicken and vegetables are all prepared according to authentic Greek recipes.

Bistro Praha
$$$
10168 100A St.
☎424-4218
Edmonton's first European bistro, Bistro Praha is very popular and charges in accordance. Favourites like cabbage soup, Wiener schnitzel, filet mignon, tortes and strudels are served in a refined but comfortable setting.

Madison Grill
$$$
10053 Jasper Ave.
☎423-3600
The Madison Grill is the Union Bank Inn Hotel's magnificent restaurant. The dining room is as impeccably decorated as the rooms. Its high quality food, from the four corners of the globe, has earned it a place among the top 100 restaurants in the country.

La Bohème
$$$
6427 112th Ave.
☎474-5693
La Bohème is set in the splendidly restored Gibbard Building. A delicious variety of classic yet original French appetizers and entrées are enjoyed in a romantic setting complete with a cosy fire. Bed and breakfast accommodation is also offered upstairs (see p 454).

Café Select
$$$
10018 106th St.
☎423-0419
The posh ambience at the Café Select is deceiving. The atmosphere is actually elegantly unpretentious, all the better to enjoy the delicious entrées featured on the evening menu of the week. With a 2am closing time on Fridays and Saturdays, this is the place for a fashionably late meal.

Plantier's
$$$
10807 106th Ave.
☎990-1992
Plantier's serves up flavourful French creations like spiced, roasted salmon and sublime escargots. For dessert, try delicate French pastries or their specialty, créme brûlée. Friendly service.

Claude's on the River
$$$$
9797 Jasper Ave.
☎429-2900
This is one of Edmonton's finest restaurants. An exceptional river-valley view, menu offerings like Australian rack of lamb in a provençale crust and other distinguished French dishes, as well as an extensive wine list explain why.

Hy's Steakloft
$$$$
10013 101A Ave.
☎424-4444
Like its Calgary counterpart, Hy's Steakloft serves up juicy Alberta steaks done to perfection. Chicken and pasta dishes round out the menu. A beautiful skylight is the centrepiece of the restaurant's classy decor.

Tour B: Old Strathcona and South of the North Saskatchewan River

Bagel Tree
$
10354 Whyte Ave
☎439-9604
As one would expect, the Bagel Tree makes its own bagels, but it also sells bagels imported from Fairmount Bagels in Montréal, arguably the best bagels around.

Barb and Ernie's
$
9906 72nd Ave.
☎*433-3242*
This is an exceptionally popular diner-style restaurant with good food, good prices and a friendly, unpretentious ambience. Breakfast is a particularly busy time, expect to have to wait a bit for a table in the morning, though you can always come later since breakfast is served until 4pm.

Bee-Bell Health Bakery
$
10416 80th Ave.
☎*439-3247*
Wonderful breads and pastries.

Block 1912
$
10361 Whyte Ave.
☎*433-6575*
Block 1912 is a European café that won an award for its effort to beautify the Strathcona area. The interior is like a living room, with an eclectic mix of tables, chairs and sofas. Lasagna is one of the simple menu's best offerings. Soothing music and a relaxed mood are conducive to a chat with friends or the enjoyment of a good book.

Café La Gare
$
10308A 81st Ave.
☎*439-2969*
Among the many cafés in Old Strathcona, the Café La Gare seems to be the place to be. Outdoor chairs and tables are reminiscent of a Parisian café. The only food available are bagels and scones. An intriguing intellectual atmosphere prevails.

Funky Pickle Pizza Co.
$
10041 Whyte Ave.
☎*433-3863*
At Funky Pickle Pizza Co., the art of pizza making is brought to unparalleled heights. Of course, at $3.50 a slice, it's not cheap. But the price is quickly forgotten as soon as your teeth sink into the whole-wheat crust, home-made sauce, blend of cheeses, fresh vegetables and spices — a sheer delight. Since the place is not much bigger than a counter, it's best to take out.

Symposium
$$
10039 Whyte Ave.
☎*433-7912*
Right above Funky Pickle Pizza is Symposium, a Greek restaurant whose pleasant terrace opens onto Whyte Avenue. The friendly staff serves dishes that go far beyond simply souvlaki and Greek salad. Try the shrimp salad on pita!

Café Soleil
$$
10360 Whyte Ave.
☎*438-4848*
Casual French dining is the theme at Café Soleil, where the menu includes a good selection of stuffed dinner crepes and desserts.

Chianti Café
$$
10501 82nd Ave.
☎*439-9829*
More than 20 varieties of pasta are served at Chianti Café located in Old Strathcona's former post office. Reservations are recommended on weekends.

Julio's Barrio
$$
10450 82nd Ave.
☎*431-0774*
Julio's boasts an original Mexican-Southwest decor with *piñatas* hanging from the ceiling, cactus coat racks and soft leather chairs. The menu features a good selection of nachos and soups, plus all the regular Mexican fare. Servings are huge and the service is quick.

Packrat Louie Kitchen & Bar
$$
10335 83rd Ave.
☎*433-0123*
A good selection of wines and a nice atmosphere are mixed with interesting music. The menu offerings are varied and generally well prepared.

Turtle Creek
$$
8404 109th St.
☎*433-4202*
Turtle Creek is an Edmonton favourite for several reasons, not the least of which are its California wines and its relaxed ambiance. The dishes follow the latest trends in Californian and fusion cuisine very

well, though a little predictably. The weekend brunch is a good deal. Free indoor parking.

The Unheard of Restaurant
$$$$
9602 82nd Ave.
☎432-0480
The name fits and it doesn't. This restaurant is no longer unheard of, yet it is an exception to Edmonton's dining norm. Recently expanded, it offers both à la carte and table d'hôte menus. The menu changes every two weeks, but usually features fresh game in the fall and chicken or beef the rest of the year. Inventive vegetarian dishes are also available. The food is exquisite and refined. Reservations are required.

Entertainment

Vue Weekly is a free news and entertainment weekly that outlines what's on throughout the city.

Bars and Nightlife

Barry T's on 104th Street is a sports pub that attracts a young crowd with a mix of country and popular music. **Club Malibu** at 10310 85th Avenue attracts crowds of young professionals. **The Thunderdome** is another hot spot with top name rock'n'roll acts. There is always something happening at the **Sidetrack Cafe** (*10333 112th St., ☎421-1326*) resto-bar with its mix of comedy, rock and jazz acts.

The **Sherlock Holmes** (*10012 101A Ave., ☎426-7784*) has an impressive choice of British and Irish ales on tap. The relaxed atmosphere seems to attract a mixed crowd. The **Yardbird Suite** (*10203 86th Ave., ☎432-0428*) is the home base of the local Jazz Society, with live performances every night of the week. A small admission fee is charged. **Blues on Whyte** (*10329 82nd Ave., ☎439-5058*) showcases live acts.

The Rebar (*10551 Whyte Ave., ☎433-3600*) is an exquisitely decorated bar that often welcomes techno musicians. Many DJs as well as alternative music groups file through here every week.

The Roost (*10345 104th St., ☎426-3150*) is one of the few gay bars in Edmonton.

Well known as Edmonton's premiere country bar, the **Cook County Saloon** (*8010 103rd St., ☎432-2665*) offers lessons for amateur line-dancers and a mechanical bull for those closet cowboys looking for a wild eight seconds.

Cultural Activities

The **Citadel Theatre** is a huge facility with five theatres inside. A variety of shows are put on from children's theatre to experimental and major productions. For information contact the box office at *☎426-4811 or 425-1820.*

The **Northern Light Theatre** (*☎471-1586*) stages innovative and interesting works.

For some more classical culture, check out the offerings of the **Edmonton Opera** (*☎429-1000*), the **Edmonton Symphony Orchestra** (*in the Francis Winspear Centre for Music, box office ☎428-1414*) and the **Alberta Ballet** (*☎428-6839*).

First-run movies are shown throughout the city; for locations and schedules pick up a newspaper or call the **Talking Yellow Pages** *☎493-9000* (see p 443).

The new cinema megacomplex **Silver City** (*West Edmonton Mall; ☎444-1242*) opened its doors in May 1999. The 12 comfortable, modern theatres offer all the latest predictable Hollywood productions. There is also an IMAX.

More spectacular cinematic events occur at the giant **IMAX** (*$8; 11211 142nd St., ☎451-3344*) theatre at the **Edmonton Space and Science Centre** (see p 449).

Calendar of Events

Edmonton is touted as a city of festivals, and **Edmonton's Klondike Days** is possibly the city's biggest event. During the Yukon gold-rush, gold diggers were attracted to the "All-Canadian Route," which departed from here. The route proved almost impassable and none of the prospectors made it to the Yukon before the rush was over. This tenuous link to the gold rush is, nevertheless, reason enough for Edmontonians to celebrate for 10 days in July. Starting the third Thursday in July, festivities, parades, bathtub road races, sourdough raft races and a casino bring the city to life. Every morning, free pancake breakfasts are served throughout the city. For information call *☎423-2822.*

Other festival highlights include the **Jazz City International Festival** (*☎432-7166*), which takes place during the last week in June. In late June and early July, **The Works: A Visual Arts Celebration** (*☎426-2122*) sees art exhibits take to the streets.

The **Edmonton Heritage Festival** (*☎488-3378*) features international singing and dancing during the first week in August. The **Edmonton Folk Music Festival** (*☎429-1899*) takes place the second week in August and tickets are recommended. The **Fringe Theatre Festival** (*☎448-9000*) is one of North America's largest alternative-theatre events; it takes place throughout Old Strathcona starting the second Friday in August for ten days. **The Dreamspeakers Festival** (*☎451-5033*) at the end of May celebrates native arts and culture.

Sports

The National Hockey League's **Edmonton Oilers** play at the **Northland Coliseum** (*118th Ave. and 74th St., ☎471-2191 or 414-4400*); the season lasts from October to April.

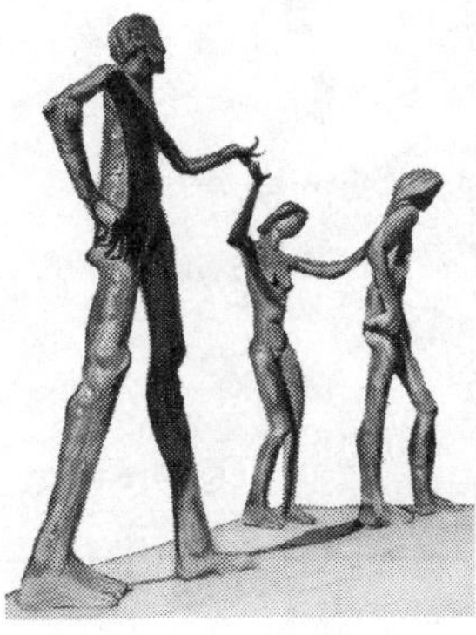

Shopping

Besides the obvious, the **West Edmonton Mall** (see Exploring, p 450) and its 800 shops and services located at 87th Avenue and 170th Street, there are regular malls scattered north, south and west of the city centre.

Downtown, the **Eaton Centre** and **The Bay** boast the usual department store offerings.

Old Strathcona makes for a much more pleasant shopping experience, with some funky specialty shops, bookstores and women's clothing stores along **Whyte Avenue** (*82nd Avenue*), including **Avenue Clothing Co.** and **Etzio**, and along 104th Street. **Strathcona Square** (*8150 105th St.*) is located in an old converted post office and boasts a bright assortment of cafés and boutiques all set in a cheery market atmosphere. The **Treasure Barrel** (*8216 104th St.*) is like a permanent craft fair showcasing arts and crafts of all kinds and for all tastes.

High Street at 124th Street (*124th St. and 125th St. between 102nd Ave. and 109th Ave.*) is an outdoor shopping arcade with galleries, cafés and shops located in a pretty residential area.

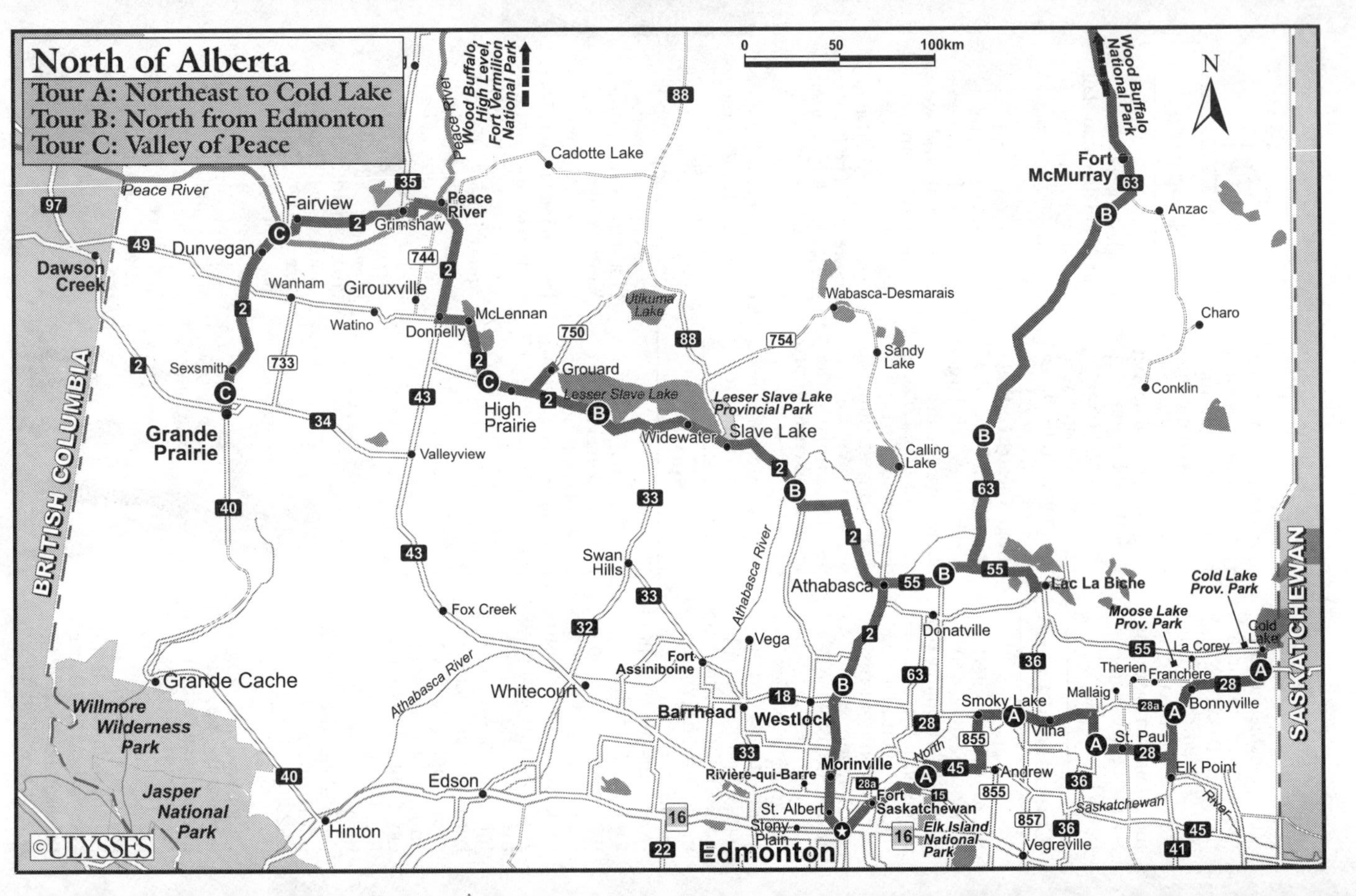
North of Alberta
Tour A: Northeast to Cold Lake
Tour B: North from Edmonton
Tour C: Valley of Peace
0
50
100km
N
Wood Buffalo, High Level, Fort Vermilion National Park
Wood Buffalo National Park
Fort McMurray
Anzac
Charo
Conklin
Cadotte Lake
Peace River
Fairview
Grimshaw
Dunvegan
Dawson Creek
Wanham
Girouxville
Watino
Donnelly
McLennan
Grouard
Utikuma Lake
Lesser Slave Lake
Leeser Slave Lake Provincial Park
Slave Lake
Widewater
High Prairie
Wabasca-Desmarais
Sandy Lake
Calling Lake
Sexsmith
Grande Prairie
Valleyview
Swan Hills
Fox Creek
Athabasca River
Athabasca
Lac La Biche
Cold Lake Prov. Park
Moose Lake Prov. Park
Cold Lake
La Corey
Therien
Franchere
Mallaig
Bonnyville
St. Paul
Elk Point
Smoky Lake
Vilna
Donatville
Vega
Fort Assiniboine
Barrhead
Westlock
Whitecourt
Grande Cache
Willmore Wilderness Park
Jasper National Park
Hinton
Edson
Morinville
Rivière-qui-Barre
St. Albert
Stony Plain
Edmonton
Fort Saskatchewan
Elk Island National Park
Andrew
Vegreville
North Saskatchewan River
BRITISH COLUMBIA
SASKATCHEWAN
©ULYSSES

Northern Alberta

Northern Alberta, as described in this chapter, covers more than half the province.

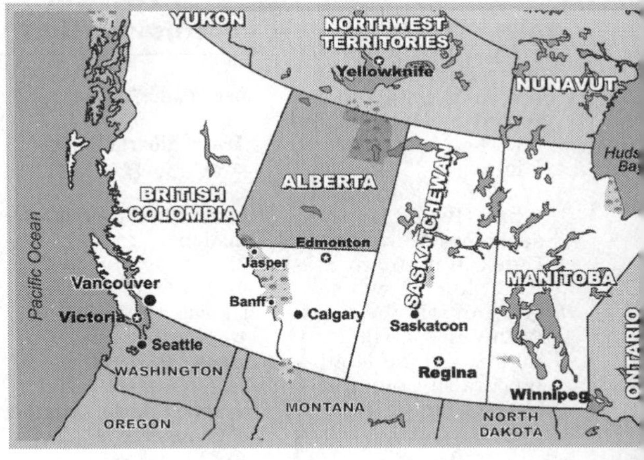

This vast hinterland offers excellent opportunities for outdoor pursuits as well as the chance to discover some of Alberta's cultural communities. Distances are so great, however, that it is inconceivable to imagine touring the whole region unless you have all sorts of time and a car.

The following three tours:

Tour A: Northeast to Cold Lake

Tour B: North of Edmonton ★

Tour C: The Valley of the Peace ★

Explore the northern frontiers of Alberta, passing major attractions along the way. They run northeast to Cold Lake at the Saskatchewan border; north to Fort McMurray with its Oil Sands Interpretive Centre and then on to Wood Buffalo National Park; and northwest, to the valley of the Peace River and then up the Mackenzie Highway or into northern British Columbia (see p 237).

Finding Your Way Around

By Car

Tour A: Northeast to Cold Lake

From Edmonton head north on Hwy. 15, then Hwy. 45. Continue on the 45 and then north on Hwy. 855 to the Victoria Settlement Historic Site and Smoky Lake at Hwy. 28. Remain on Hwy. 28 all the way to St. Paul. At Hwy. 41 head south to Elk Point. Head back up Hwy. 41 to the 28 and on to Bonnyville and Cold Lake.

Tour B: North of Edmonton

This is an ambitious tour that cannot be done entirely by car. Fort McMurray is accessible by car, but Wood Buffalo National Park is best reached from the communities of Fort Chipewyan, Alberta or Fort Smith, Northwest Territories. The tour starts on Hwy. 2, north of Edmonton. At Hwy. 55 it splits, with one leg heading east and north to Lac La Biche and Fort McMurray and the other heading west for a scenic drive to High Prairie.

Tour C: Valley of the Peace

This loop tour follows Hwy. 2 from High Prairie to Grande Prairie, the circle being completed by Hwy. 32 and 43. The Mackenzie Highway (35) heads north from Grimshaw, while Hwy. 2 is the scenic route to Dawson Creek in northern British Columbia, where you can join the tours of the Alaska Highway outlined in the Northern British Columbia chapter (see p 239).

By Bus

Lac La Biche Greyhound Bus Depot
Almac Motor Inn
☎*623-4123*

Cold Lake Greyhound Bus Depot
5504 55th St.
☎*594-2777*

Slave Lake Greyhound Bus Depot
Sawridge Truck Stop, Hwy. 88
☎*849-4003*

High Prairie Greyhound Bus Depot
4853 52nd Ave.
☎*523-3733*

Peace River Greyhound Bus Depot
9801 97th Ave.
☎*624-2558*

Grande Prairie Greyhound Bus Depot
9918 121st Ave., north of the Prairie Mall
☎*539-1111*

Practical Information

Area Code: 780

Travel Alberta North
☎*800-756-4351*

Peace River Tourist Information
open in summer only
9309 100th St., or in the log building at town entrance
☎*624-4042*
☎*800-215-4535.*

Grande Prairie: Chamber of Commerce
10632 102nd Ave.
☎*532-5340*

Fort McMurray Visitors Centre
just north of Oil Sands Centre
☎*791-4336*
☎*800-565-3947*

North Eastern B&B Association
between 5pm and 7pm
☎*826-1786*

Exploring

Tour A: Northeast to Cold Lake

Fort Saskatchewan

Established by the North West Mounted Police in 1875, Fort Saskatchewan, overlooking the North Saskatchewan River, was demolished in 1913, when it was taken over by the city of Edmonton. Fort Saskatchewan became an independent city in 1985.

The **Fort Saskatchewan Museum** (*$2; Jan to Mar Mon to Fri 11am to 3pm; Apr to Jun and Sep to Dec every day 11am to 3pm; Jul and Aug, every day 10am to 6pm; 10104 101st St.,* ☎*998-1750*) takes you back to the old town. It features nine buildings dating from 1900 to 1920, including the original courthouse, a schoolhouse, a country church, a blacksmith's shop and a great old log farm. There are tours in the summer.

Drive north on Hwy. 855 to the Victoria Settlement Provincial Historic Site and Smoky Lake.

Smoky Lake

Before reaching Smoky Lake itself, watch for signs for the Victoria Settlement Provincial Historic Site, about 16km south of Smoky Lake.

Victoria Settlement Provincial Historic Site ★ (*$5.50; mid-May to early Sep every day 10am to 6pm, ☎645-6256, ⇌645-4760*). A Methodist mission was established here in 1862, and two years later the Hudson's Bay Company set up Fort Victoria to compete with free traders at the settlement. This wonderfully peaceful spot along the Saskatchewan River, once a bustling village, was also the centre of a Metis community.

The town was called Pakan, after a Cree chief who was loyal to the Riel Rebellion. When the railway moved to Smoky Lake, all the buildings were relocated; only the clerk's quarters were left behind. Exhibits and trails point out the highlights of this once thriving village that has all but disappeared. The tranquil atmosphere makes this a nice place for a picnic.

The little **Smoky Lake Museum** (*donation; mid-May to Sep, Mon to Sat 10am to 4pm, Sun 10am to 5pm*) holds a quaint and curious collection of pioneer artifacts that puts faces on all those courageous settlers. Photos, old dresses and linens, early farm equipment and stuffed, mounted wildlife are proudly displayed in an old rural school.

A drive east on Hwy. 28 toward the Saskatchewan border leads through a region of francophone communities. These include **St. Paul**, **Mallaig**, **Therien**, **Franchère**, **La Corey** and **Bonnyville**.

★

St. Paul

The town of St. Paul began in 1896 when Father Albert Lacombe established a Metis settlement here hoping to attract Metis from all over Western Canada. Only 330 Metis, who had been continuously ignored by the government, responded to his invitation. Eventually settlers from a variety of cultural backgrounds arrived. The **St. Paul Culture Centre** (*Mon to Fri 8:30am to 4:30pm; 4537 50th Ave., ☎645-4800*) examines the area's diverse cultural background. The **old Rectory** still stands a few blocks away (*5015 47th St.*).

These days, residents of St. Paul are attempting to attract a whole other kind of visitor to their part of the world, something that may someday diversify the cultural make-up of St. Paul even more, that is if the **UFO Landing Pad ★** (*every day 9am to 5pm; near the tourist information centre at 50th Ave. and 53rd St.*) in town is ever put to use!

Continue east on Hwy. 28 then south on Hwy. 41 to the junction of Hwy. 646 and Elk Point.

Elk Point

For an idea of this town's history and culture one only needs to check out the colourful **100 Foot Historical Mural** (*west of Hwy. 41 on 50th Ave.*). From the mural drive east on Hwy. 646 to Fort George - **Buckingham House Provincial Historic Site ★** (*$3; mid-May to Sep every day 10am to 6pm; ☎724-2611*), which marks the location of two rival fur-trading posts. Both built in 1792, the North West Company held the former and the Hudson's Bay the latter. They were abandoned shortly after the turn of the century and there isn't much to see today, save a few depressions in the ground and piles of stones. An interpretive centre does a good job, nonetheless, explaining the excavations and the posts' histories. The North Saskatchewan River is close by and short trails lead around the site.

Drive north on Hwy. 41 to the 28, turn right toward Bonnyville.

Perogi (Ukrainian potato and onion dumpling) fans might want to take a jog left to Glendon where that increasingly popular fashion for huge sculptures of inane objects has struck again: Glendon is home to the world's largest perogi!

Bonnyville

Bonnyville used to be known as St. Louis de Moose Lake and today provides access to lovely natural areas. **Jessie Lake** is a wetland area that is great for birdwatching (see p 470) and **Moose Lake Provincial Park** has swimming, boating, walking and fishing.

Cold Lake

Home to Canadian Forces Base Cold Lake, this town actually relies on the nearby oil sands for its economic well-being. The nearby town of Medley is really just the post office, while Grand Centre is where all the shops are.

The lake is the seventh largest in the province with an area of 370 km^2. Its name is fitting when you consider that the surface remains frozen for five months of the year. The 100m depths are home to some prize fish (see Outdoor Activities p 470).

The **Kinosoo Totem Poles** are two 6.7m totems carved out of cedar trees by Chief Ovide Jacko. They overlook Kinosoo Beach, a popular picnicking spot on the shores of Cold Lake.

Cold Lake Provincial Park (see p 469) has fishing, wildlife viewing, beaches and camping.

Tour B: North of Edmonton

★★ St. Albert

Just north of Edmonton lies the community of St. Albert, the oldest farming settlement in Alberta. It began as a small log chapel in 1861, built by the Mary Immaculate Mission and Father Albert Lacombe. Born in Québec in 1827, Albert Lacombe began his missionary work in St. Boniface near present-day Winnipeg. He convinced Bishop Alexandre Taché of the need for a mission dedicated to the Metis population, and St. Albert thus came into existence.

Father Lacombe only stayed at the new mission for four years, and then continued his work throughout the prairies. Bishop Vital Grandin moved his headquarters to St. Albert in 1868 and brought a group of skilled Oblate Brothers with him, making St. Albert the centre of missionary work in Alberta. Grandin played an important role in lobbying Ottawa for fair treatment of Aboriginal people, Metis and French Canadian settlers.

The **Father Lacombe Chapel** ★★ (*$2; mid-May to early Sep every day 10am to 6pm; St. Vital Avenue, St. Albert, ☎457-7663*) is the oldest known standing structure in Alberta. This humble log chapel, built in 1861, was the centre of the busy Metis settlement. It was restored in 1929 by being enclosed in a brick structure. In 1980 it was once again restored and moved to its present site on Mission Hill, where it enjoys a sweeping view out over the fields and the Sturgeon River Valley. Mission Hill is also the site of the residence of Bishop Grandin, now known as the Vital Grandin Centre.

The **Musée Heritage Museum** ★ (*free admission; Jun to Aug, Mon to Thu 9:30am to 5pm, Fri 9:30am to 8pm, Sat and Sun 10am to 5pm; Sep to May, Mon to Fri 10am to 5pm, Sat noon to 5pm; 5 St. Ann St., St. Albert, ☎459-1528*) is located in an interesting, contoured brick building called St. Ann Place. The museum houses an exceptional exhibit of artifacts and objects related to the history of the first citizens of St. Albert, including the Metis, Aboriginal people, missionaries and pioneers. Tours are available in both French and English.

Continuing north on Hwy. 2, you'll soon reach another area of francophone communities, some with poetic names like Rivière Qui Barre, before arriving in **Morinville**. The **St. Jean Baptiste Church** (*☎939-4412 for tours*) in town was erected in 1907, while the original chapel was built in 1891 under direction of Father Jean Baptiste Morin. There are a Casavant organ and large murals adorning its interior.

★

Athabasca

A little over 100km farther north is the town of Athabasca, located close to the geographic centre of Alberta. The Athabasca River, which flows through the town, was the main corridor to the north, and the town of Athabasca was once a candidate for provincial capital.

The town began as Athabasca Landing, a Hudson's Bay Company trading post, and a point along one of the river trails that led north. Traders and explorers headed west on the North Saskatchewan River to present-day Edmonton, then overland on a hazardous 130km portage, cut in 1823, to the Athabasca River at Fort Assiniboine, southwest of the present-day town of Athabasca.

It was this pitiful trail that spelt disaster for Klondikers in 1897-98 on the "All-Canadian Route" from Edmonton (see p 442). A new trail, the Athabasca Landing Trail, was created in 1877. It soon became the major highway to the north and a transshipment point for northern posts and Peace River.

Hudson's Bay Company scows built in Athabasca were manned by a group known as the Athabasca Brigade, composed mainly of Cree and Metis. This brigade handily guided the scows down the Athabasca River through rapids and shallow waters to points north. Most scows were broken up at their destination and used in building, but those that returned had to be pulled by the brigades. Paddle-wheelers eventually replaced these scows.

The town was known as a jumping-off point for traders and adventurers heading north, and to this day, it is still a good jumping-off point for outdoor adventurers as it lies right on the fringe of the northern hinterland, yet is only 1.5hrs north of Edmonton. Cross-country skiing in winter, river adventures, fishing and even golf on a beautiful new 18-hole course in summer are some of the possibilities. A pamphlet featuring a historic walking tour is available at the tourist office, located in an old train car on 50th Avenue *(mid-May to mid-Sep every day 10am to 6pm)*. Athabasca is also home to Athabasca University, Canada's most northerly university, reputed for its distance-education programs.

Lac La Biche

East on Hwy. 55 lies Lac La Biche, located on a divide separating the Athabasca River system, which drains into the Pacific, and the Churchill River system, which drains into Hudson Bay. This portage was a vital link on the transcontinental fur-trading route and was used by voyageurs to cross the 5kms between Beaver Lake and Lac La Biche. The North West Company and the Hudson's Bay Company each built trading posts here around 1800, but these were both abandoned when a shorter route was found along the North Saskatchewan River through Edmonton.

In 1853, Father René Remas organized the building of the **Lac La Biche Mission** (*May to Sep every day 9am to 6pm, ☎623-3274*). The present restored mission lies 11km from the original site, having been moved in 1855. The original buildings, including the oldest lumber building in Alberta, are still standing. The mission served as a supply centre for voyageurs and other missions in the area and expanded to include a sawmill, gristmill, printing-press and boat-yard. An hour-long guided tour is available.

★★ Fort McMurray

About 250km north on Hwy. 63 lies the town of Fort McMurray, which grew up around the Athabasca oil sands, the largest single oil deposit in the world. The oil is actually bitumen, a heavy oil whose extraction requires an expensive, lengthy process; the deposits consist of compacted sand mixed with the bitumen. The sand is brought to the surface, where the bitumen is separated and treated to produce a lighter, more useful oil. The one trillion barrels of bitumen in the sands promise a vital supply of future energy needs.

The **Fort McMurray Oil Sands Interpretive Centre** ★★ (*$3; mid-May to early Sep, every day 10am to 6pm; Sep to May, every day 10am to 4pm; 515 Mackenzie Blvd., ☎743-7167*) explains the extraction process, and much more, through colourful hands-on exhibits. The sheer size and potential of the operations are evident from the mining equipment and seven-storey bucket-wheel extractor on display. Tours of the **Suncor/Syncrude Sand Plant** are also possible (*$15; every day 8:30am to 4:30pm; Jun to Aug every day 8:30am to 8:30pm, contact Visitors Centre, 440 Saskitawaw Trail, ☎791-4336 or 1-800-565-3947*).

★★ Wood Buffalo National Park

The boundary of Wood Buffalo National Park is approximately 130km due north as the crow flies. Though this does not seem that far, the park is difficult to access. Furthermore, only people with back-country experience should consider such a trip. Resourceful travellers who choose to venture to Wood Buffalo should do so from the communities of Fort Chipewyan, Alberta, or Fort Smith, Northwest Territories. For more information see "Parks", p 469.

Back in Athabasca, take Hwy. 2 west to Slave Lake.

★ Slave Lake

Lesser Slave Lake is Alberta's third largest lake, with an area of 1,150ha; on its south-eastern shore lies the town of Slave Lake, once a busy centre on the route towards the Yukon goldfields. There isn't much to see in town, except of course the spectacular scenery across the lake, which seems like a veritable inland sea in this landlocked province. Its shallow waters are teeming with huge northern pike, walleye and whitefish.

Continue west on Hwy. 2 to Hwy. 750 and Grouard.

Grouard

Founded in 1884 as the St. Bernard Mission by Father Émile Grouard, the village of Grouard, with a population fo under 400, lies at the northeastern end of Lesser Slave Lake. Father Grouard worked in northern Alberta as a linguist, pioneer missionary and translator for 69 years. He is buried in the cemetery adjoining the mission (*for a tour call the Grouard Native Art Museum, see below*). A display of artifacts lies at the back of the church, which has been declared a Historic Site.

The **Grouard Native Art Museum** (*donation; Mon to Fri 9am to 4pm; in Moosehorn Lodge Building, Alberta Vocational College, ☎751-3306*) is an interesting little museum whose aim is to promote an understanding of North America's Aboriginal cultures through arts and crafts exhibits. Artifacts on display include birch-bark work, decorative arts and contemporary clothing.

Tour C: Peace Valley

From Grouard, the final stop on Tour B, continue on Hwy. 2 through **High Prairie**, home to great walleye fishing (see p 470), and **McLennan**, the "bird capital of Canada" (see p 470), to Donnelly.

Donnelly

Donnelly is home to the **Société Historique et Généalogique** (*$5; Mon to Fri 10am to 4pm, ☎925-3801*) which has traced the history of French settlement in Alberta. There isn't much to see, except perhaps an interesting map of the province that indicates the principle French settlements. Extensive archives are available for anyone who wants to trace their family tree.

Continue north on Hwy. 2 to Peace River.

★★ Peace River

The mighty Peace River makes its way from British Columbia's interior to Lake Athabasca in northeastern Alberta. Fur trappers and traders used the river to get upstream from Fort Forks to posts at Dunvegan and Fort Vermillion. Fort Forks was established by Alexander Mackenzie in 1792 where the town of Peace River now stands. Mackenzie was the first person to cross what is now Canada and reach the Pacific Ocean. Exceptional scenery greets any who visits this area, and legend has it that anyone who drinks from the Peace will return.

In town, the **Peace River Centennial Museum** (*$3; mid-May to early Sep, Mon to Wed 9am to 5pm, Thu and Fri 9am to 8pm, Sat noon to 8pm, Sun 1pm to 5pm; Sep to May, Mon to Fri 9am to 5pm, 3rd Sun of the month free 1pm to 5pm; 10302 99th St., near the corner of 100th St. and 103rd Ave., ☎624-4261*) features an interpretive display on the Abroiginal Peoples of the area, the fur trade, early explorers and the growth of the town. All sorts of old photographs do a good job of evoking life in the frontier town.

Aboriginals, explorers, shipbuilders, traders, missionaries and Klondikers all passed through what is now the town of Peace River when they took the **Shaftesbury Trail** which follows Hwy. 684 on the west side of the river. Take the **Shaftesbury Ferry** (*in summer, every day 7am to midnight*) from Blakely's Landing to the historic Shaftesbury settlement.

Twelve Foot Davis ★ was not a 12-foot-tall man, but rather a gold-digger and free-trader named Henry Fuller who made a $15,000 strike on a 12-foot claim in the Cariboo Goldfields of British Columbia. He is buried on Grouard Hill, above the town. A breathtaking view of the confluence of the Peace, Smoky and Heart Rivers can be had from the **Twelve Foot Davis Historical Site** accessible by continuing to the end of 100th Avenue. Another lookout, called the **Sagitawa Lookout** (*Judah Hill Road*) also affords an exceptional view of the surroundings.

The Mackenzie Highway starts in the town of **Grimshaw** and continues through the larger centres of **Manning** and **High Level** where a variety of services including gas and lodging are available.

Fort Vermilion is the second oldest settlement in Alberta. It was established by the North West Company in 1788, the same year Fort Chipewyan was established on Lake Athabasca. Nothing remains of the original fort.

Beyond this, the towns of **Meander River**, **Steen River** and **Indian Cabins** do not have much in the way of services besides campgrounds; the next big centre is **Hay River**, near the shores of Great Slave Lake in the Northwest Territories.

Heading west of Peace River, Hwy. 2 leads eventually to historic Dunvegan.

★

Dunvegan

With Alberta's longest suspension bridge as a backdrop, **Historic Dunvegan ★** (*$3; mid-May to early Sep every day 10am to 6pm; off Hwy. 2 just north of the Peace River, ☎835-7150 or 835-5244*) peacefully overlooks the Peace River. Once part of the territory of the Dunne-za (Beaver) First Nation, this site was chosen in 1805 for a North West Company fort, later a Hudson's Bay Company fort. Dunvegan became a major trade and provisioning centre for the Upper Peace River and later the Hudson's Bay headquarters for the Athabasca district.

By the 1840s Catholic missionaries were visiting Dunvegan, including a visit by the eminent Father Albert Lacombe (see p 464) in 1855. In 1867, the Catholic St. Charles Mission was established, and in 1879 the Anglican St. Savior's Mission, making Dunvegan a centre for missionary activity. The missions were ultimately abandoned following the discovery of gold and the signing of Treaty No. 8, at which point the Dunne-za began leaving the area.

The fort operated right up until 1918, when homesteading became more important than trading, hunting and trapping. The mission church (1884), the rectory (1889) and the Hudson's Bay Company factor's house (1877) still stand on the site, as does an informative interpretive centre that is unfortunately housed in a rather ugly modern building. Dunvegan also has some camping sites.

Continue south to the town of Grande Prairie.

★★

Grande Prairie

As Alberta's fastest growing city, Canada's forest capital and the Swan City, Grande Prairie is a major business and service centre in northern Alberta, thanks to natural gas reserves in the area. The town is so named because of *la grande prairie*, highly fertile agricultural lands that are exceptional this far north. Unlike most towns in Alberta's north, Grande Prairie is not what was left behind when the trading post closed. From the start, homesteaders were attracted to the area's fertile farmland.

The **Pioneer Village at Grande Prairie Museum** (*$2; May to Sep every day 10am to 6pm; winter, museum only, Sun to Fri 1pm to 4pm; corner of 102nd Ave. and 102nd St., ☎532-5482*) offers a glimpse of life in Peace Country at the turn of the century with historic buildings, guides in period dress, artifacts and an extensive wildlife collection.

The museum is located near **Muskoseepi Park** a 446ha urban park with an interpretive trail and some 40km of walking and cycling trails.

The landmark design of **Grande Prairie Regional College** (*10726 106th Ave.*), with its curved red brick exterior, is the work of aboriginal architect Douglas Cardinal.

The **Prairie Gallery ★** (*Wed to Fri 10am to 5pm, Sat and Sun 1pm to 5pm; 10209 99th St., ☎532-8111*) exhibits a very respectable collection of Canadian and international art.

The town of **Dawson Creek** (see p 251) is kilometre/mile zero (0) of the Alaska Highway. It is reached by continuing west on Hwy. 2.

Parks

Tour A: Northeast to Cold Lake

Moose Lake Provincial Park

There was a Northwest Company post on the shores of this shallow lake in 1789. Trails skirt the shoreline and small beach, and a small marshy area is home to lots of birds. You can also fish for walleye and pike in the lake. Camping is possible (☎*826-5853, in the off season contact Cold Lake Provincial Park, see below*).

Cold Lake Provincial Park

This is a small park on a spit of land south of town. Mostly forested with balsam fir and white spruce, it is the domain of moose, muskrats and minks. Hall's Lagoon in the park is good for birding. Camping is possible (☎*639-3341*).

Tour B: North of Edmonton

★★ Wood Buffalo National Park

Wood Buffalo National Park is accessible from the communities of Fort Chipewyan, Alberta, and Fort Smith, Northwest Territories. Fort Chipewyan can be reached by plane from Fort McMurray twice a day, Sunday through Friday; in summer, motorboats travel the Athabasca and Embarras Rivers; there is a winter road open from December to March between Fort McMurray and Fort Chipewyan but it is not recommended; and finally, for the really adventurous, it is possible to enter the park by canoe on the Peace and Athabasca Rivers.

The park is home to the largest, free-roaming, self-regulating herd of bison in the world; it is also the only remaining nesting ground of the whooping crane. These two facts contributed to Wood Buffalo being designated a World Heritage Site.

The park was initially established to protect the last remaining herd of wood bison in northern Canada. But when plains bison were shipped to the park between 1925 and 1928, due to overgrazing, Buffalo National Park in Wainwright, Alberta, the plains bison interbred with the wood bison, causing the extinction of pure wood bison. Or so it was thought. A herd was discovered in Elk Island National Park (see p 432), some of which were shipped to Mackenzie Bison Sanctuary in the Northwest Territories. As a result, there are actually no pure wood buffalo in Wood Buffalo National Park.

Those who make the effort will enjoy hiking (most trails are in the vicinity of Fort Smith), excellent canoeing and camping and the chance to experience Canada's northern wilderness in the country's largest national park. Advance planning is essential to a successful trip to this huge wilderness area and a Park Use Permit is required for all overnight stays in the park. Also remember to bring lots of insect repellent. For more information contact the park (*Box 750, Fort Smith, NWT, X0E 0P0,* ☎*867-872-7900, or Fort Chipewyan 697-3662,* ☎*6*

Beaches

Tour B: North of Edmonton

Lesser Slave Lake Provincial Park ★, next to Alberta's third largest lake, offers all sorts of opportunities for aquatic pursuits, including Devonshire Beach, a 7km stretch of beautiful sand.

Outdoor Activities

Golf

The **Athabasca Golf & Country Club** (*just outside Athabaska, on the north side of the Athabasca River, ☎675-4599*) is a new course with beautiful scenery and 18 challenging holes.

Birdwatching

McLennan is the bird capital of Canada. Three major migratory fly ways converge here, giving birdwatchers the chance to see over 200 different species.

The town has an interesting interpretive centre and boardwalk that leads to a bird blind.

The town of Bonnyville lies on the north shoes of **Jessie Lake**. These wetlands harbour more than 230 species of birds. The Wetlands Viewing Trail leads through them to a series of viewing platforms. In the spring and fall, the best time to birdwatch here, you may spot osprey, bald eagles and golden eagles.

Fishing

Real fans may want to try their luck in the Golden Walleye Classic, which takes place in **High Prairie** the third week in August. With a thousands of dollars in prize money it just may be worth your while. Anyone can join. For information call ☎523-3505.

Northern pike, walleye and trout are the catches of the day in **Cold Lake**. Boats and tackle can be hired at the Cold Lake Marina at the end of Main Street.

To fish **Lesser Slave Lake**, your best bet is to head out onto the lake. Boats can be hired at the Sawridge Recreation Area on Caribou Trail.

Accommodations

Tour A: Northeast to Cold Lake

St. Paul

King's Motel and Restaurant
$48 bkfst incl.
≡, ℜ, ℝ, *tv*, ♿
5638 50th Ave., Box 1685, T0A 3A0
☎645-5656
☎800-265-7407
⇄645-5107
King's Motel offers decent, clean rooms, most of which have refrigerators. Breakfast at the restaurant is included in the price.

Smoky Lake

Countrylane Bed & Breakfast
$65
sb
Box 38, T0A 3C0, off Hwy 28, watch for signs at R.R. 36
☎656-2277
Each of the six rooms at the Countrylane Bed & Breakfast are named after the six girls that were born in the house. The sound of birds chirping and a sunny balcony are among the extras found throughout the rest of

the house. An evening meal can be arranged with advance notice and group rates are available. An old schoolhouse dating from 1913 has now been renovated and added to Countrylane's facilities. It's an ideal spot to host business meetings or family celebrations.

Inn at the Ranch
$70
tv, ⊗
Box 562, T0A 3C0, Hwy. 855, 22km north of Hwy. 28, follow the signs
☎***656-2474***
☎***800-974-2474***
⇄***656-3094***
Smoky Lake is home to another charming bed and breakfast, the Inn at the Ranch. This working bison-elk ranch has two lovely rooms. The newly built mansion is surrounded by a veritable birdwatcher's paradise.

Cold Lake

Harbour House B&B
$80
615 Lakeshore Dr.
☎***639-2337***
The Harbour House is a lovely spot on the shores of Cold Lake. Each room has a theme, ask for the one with the fireplace and canopy bed. A real gem! There is also an adjoining tea room (see p 473). Each room now has its own bathroom, and a family restaurant offers breakfast, lunch and dinner.

Tour B: North of Edmonton

Athabasca

The Athabasca Inn
$99
≡, ℜ, ⊙, *tv*, 🐕
5211 41 Ave., T9S 1A5
☎***675-2294***
☎***800-567-5718***
⇄***675-3890***
The Athabasca Inn features non-smoking rooms with filtered air. Business people make up the bulk of its guests. Rooms are clean and spacious.

Donatville

Donatberry Inn B&B
$75
⊛, ⌂
R.R. 1, Boyle, T0A 0M0
☎***689-3639***
⇄***689-3380***
Located about halfway between Lac La Biche and Athabasca on Hwy. 63 is the small town of Donatville, home of the Donatberry Inn B&B. This newly built house is set on a large property with a northern berry orchard nearby (home-made preserves of these berries are served at breakfast). The large, bright rooms all have private bathrooms, and guests also have access to a whirlpool and a steam room.

Lac La Biche

Parkland Motel
$60
≡, *K*, *tv*, ⊛, ♿
9112 101 Ave., Box 659, T0A 2C0
☎***623-4424***
☎***888-884-8886***
⇄***623-4599***
the Parkland Hotel features regular rooms and kitchenette suites, some of which have fireplaces and lofts. Good value.

Fort McMurray

Mackenzie Park Inn
$84
≡, ≈, ℜ, ⊛, *tv*, *bar*
424 Gregoire Dr., T9H 3R2
☎***791-7200***
☎***800-582-3273***
⇄***790-1658***
With a good restaurant and lounge as well as a pool and a casino, the Mackenzie Park Inn is the most reliable hotel or motel choice in town. It is located about 4km south of the centre of town.

Slave Lake

Sawridge Hotel
$75
≡, ℜ, ⌂, ⊛, ℝ, *tv*, ⊙, ♿
Box 879, T0G 2A0, just off Hwy 2 on Main St.
☎***849-4101***
☎***800-661-6657***
⇄***849-3426***
The rather interesting exterior of the Sawridge Hotel houses some rather ordinary rooms that are just a tad outdated. Several of the rooms have refrigerators.

Northwest Inn
$84
ℝ, ≡, ℜ, *K*, ⊛, △, ⊘, *tv*
Box 2459, T0G 2A0
☎849-3300
⇄849-2667
Farther along Main Street towards town is the newest hotel in town, the Northwest Inn. The rooms, though clean and modern, are unfortunately very bare. Some are equipped with refrigerators.

Tour C: Valley of the Peace

Peace River

Crescent Motor Inn Best Canadian
$49
≡, *K*, *tv*
9810 98th St., T8S 1J3
☎624-2586
⇄624-1888
The Crescent Motor Inn is located close to the centre of town and offers clean, rather ordinary rooms. Family suites with kitchenettes are certainly an economical choice. A pool and restaurant are scheduled to open in the summer of 2000.

Kozy Quarters B&B
$60
sb
11015 99th St., Box 7493, T8S 1T1
☎624-2807
This historic two-storey structure is located on the waterfront. It was built by the RCMP, but today houses cosy and spacious guest rooms. A choice of breakfasts is offered each morning.

Traveller's Motor Hotel
$61
≡, ℜ, *K*, △, *tv, bar*
Box 7290, T8S 1S9
☎624-3621
☎800-661-3227
⇄624-4855
The Traveller's Motor Hotel offers ordinary hotel-motel rooms as well as suite rooms. With a nightclub in the hotel, this isn't the quietest place in town. All rooms are newly renovated. Note that the price includes a special pass allowing free access to the golf course, municipal pool and the Peace River Sports Club.

Grande Prairie

Canadian Motor Inn
$62
≡, ℝ, *K*, *tv*, ⊛, 🐕
10901 100th Ave., T8V 3J9
☎532-1680
☎800-291-7893
⇄532-1245
Grande Prairie's best hotel and motel bet is the Canadian Motor Inn, where each room has two queen-size beds, a refrigerator and a large-screen television. Rooms with fully equipped kitchenettes are available ($68) and there is also an executive suite with a whirlpool bath ($150-$200). The hotel was recently completely renovated and the result is spotless, modern, yet very comfortable accommodations.

Fieldstone Inn B&B
$80 bkfst incl.
Box 295, T8V 3A4
☎532-7529
Set on a secluded lakeside property, the Fieldstone Inn is a great find, as long as you have no problem with their new "celebrating marriage" policy (unmarried couples must stay in separate rooms). This newly built fieldstone house has a homey feel, thanks to the old-fashioned decor and classic styling. Some rooms have whirlpool baths or fireplaces.

Golden Inn
$84
≡, ℜ, *K*, *tv, bar*
11201 100th Ave., T8V 5M6
☎539-6000
☎800-661-7954
⇄532-1961
The Golden Inn lies north of the city centre with services and shops nearby. The decor of the rooms and lobby is slightly outdated.

Restaurants

Tour A: Northeast to Cold Lake

St. Paul

The King's Motel
$
5638 50th Ave.
The motel's restaurant serves hot pancakes and French toast breakfasts, as well as lunch and dinner. The atmo-

sphere is nothing special, but the food is good and inexpensive (breakfast is free if you're staying at the motel).

Corfou Villa Restaurant
$$
5010 50th Ave.
☎645-2948
The Corfou serves Greek food, as its name suggests, but also dishes up Italian and Spanish specialities.

Cold Lake

Harbour House Tea Room
$
615 Lakeshore Dr.
☎639-2337
the Harbour House serves light fare like sandwiches and cakes each afternoon.

Roundel Hotel
$-$$
902 Eighth Ave.
☎639-3261
While not recommended as a place to stay, the Roundel Hotel serves standard fare all day long.

Tour B: North of Edmonton

Athabasca

Green Spot
$
4820 51st St.
☎675-3040
The Green Spot is open from breakfast to dinner and serves a bit of everything, from healthy soups and sandwiches (as its name suggests) to big juicy burgers.

Fort McMurray

Garden Café
$
9924 Biggs Ave.
☎791-6665
This is a fresh and cheery place to enjoy soups, sandwiches and good desserts. It is open all day and all night.

Mapletree Pancake House
$$
424 Gregoire Dr.
☎791-7200
This restaurant at the Mackenzie Park Inn is known for its huge Sunday brunch and of course, its pancakes.

Slave Lake

Joey's Incredible Edibles
$-$$
at the corner of Third Ave. and Main St.
☎849-5577
Joey's is a pleasant family-style restaurant with a complete menu including a wide choice of juicy hamburgers.

Tour C: Valley of the Peace

Peace River

Peace Garden
$$
10016 100th St.
☎624-1048
The best of the handful of Chinese restaurants in town, the Peace Garden serves good seafood dishes, as well as North American standards like steak and pizza.

Grande Prairie

Java Junction
$
9931 100th Ave.
☎539-5070
Java Junction is a funky spot in the small downtown area with hearty and inexpensive muffins, soups and sandwiches.

Earl's
$$
9825 100th St.
☎538-3275
Grande Prairie is home to one of Alberta's several Earl's restaurant outlets. With its outdoor terrace and reliable and varied menu, it is a favourite in town.

Entertainment

Grande Prairie

The **Grande Prairie Little Theatre** is a small, but popular, theatre company. For information call ☎538-1616.

Saskatchewan

In the popular imagination, Saskatchewan is but one continuous wheat field, a place with little topography or cultural diversity.

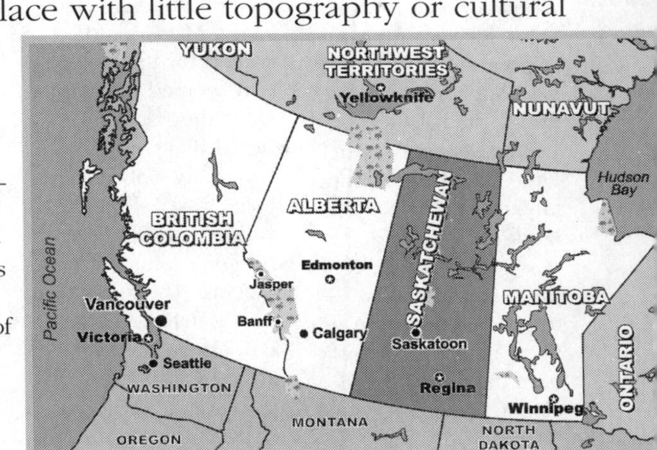

And the traveller passing through parts of southern Saskatchewan in late summer can hardly be forgiven for thinking otherwise: this is Canada's breadbasket, after all, producing a full 60% of the nation's wheat in acres of golden fields that literally stretch to the horizon.

It is for this reason that the place is usually portrayed as nothing more than a cold monotonous patch of grassland between the lakes of Manitoba and the mountains of Alberta. And it's true: the entire province is subject to such bitterly cold winters that "plug-ins" – electric connections that keep a car battery warm overnight – are standard at a good hotel.

However, a little probing reveals a much richer identity than the stereotype indicates. The spectacular Qu'Appelle Valley cuts across two thirds of the province, slicing into the level plain with deep glacial creases running down to the river. Venture to Saskatchewan's two major cities and surprising architectural touches are revealed. In other areas, a preponderance of Eastern European churches crop up – painted church domes rising from the prairie like delicately painted Easter eggs, testifying to the province's solid Ukrainian influence.

Farther north, the prairies abruptly give way to foothills and then genuine mountains, woods and lakes – making it a bit less surprising to learn that there is more forest here – half a province worth, in fact – than farmland. All of the major rivers in the province flow east into Manitoba, eventually emptying into Hudson Bay.

Saskatchewan's First Nations include the Assiniboine and the Blackfoot. Later, the Cree took on the most active role, pushing aggressively westward to satisfy traders' voracious appetite for furs. Later, Sitting Bull came to southern Saskatchewan after routing General Custer of the United States Army at Little Big Horn. Eventually, most First Nations land in the province was sold or ceded to the government by treaty, but there are still more native reserves here than anywhere else in Canada.

Louis Riel and the Metis, descendants of French voyageurs and Aboriginal people, made a significant mark on prairie history here in the hills and valleys of Saskatchewan. In 1884, after fighting for the rights of the Metis and being exiled to the United States, Riel was called up by the settlers of present-day Saskatchewan, which at the time was part of the vast Northwest Territories. Riel's small band, fighting for provincial status for Saskatchewan and better treatment of Aboriginals and Metis, defeated Dominion troops in several early skirmishes. But Riel never wanted a military conflict; rather, he hoped for negotiation.

The Canadians, led by MacDonald, waited for the victory that seemed inevitable, since they outnumbered Riel's force – especially since a new coast-to-coast railroad was now capable of bringing reinforcements quickly. The Metis were finally defeated at Batoche in the last armed conflict on Canadian soil, and Riel was hanged as a traitor; he is still a hero in some quarters of the province because of his unswerving determination to retain his people's sovereignty. Saskatchewan joined Confederation in 1905.

Since Riel's time, few other individuals have made such a personal mark on the province, save John Diefenbaker. Diefenbaker, who grew up in a tiny homestead near the Saskatchewan River, rose from the post of a country lawyer to become Prime Minister of Canada in the early 1960s. His law office, boyhood home, adult home and university office are all well-visited attractions. A lake also bears his name. Popular folk singer Joni Mitchell (born Joan Anderson) is probably the most famous contemporary daughter of the province.

Generally speaking, however, time still moves slowly in Saskatchewan. Today, farmers are diversifying and growing such crops as flax, and the mining of potash and the damming of rivers provide steady jobs, though wheat and oil continue to power the economy. The province's two major cities both contain just over 200,000 residents and strive to fill the short summer with festivities. Regina is the elegant capital, so English it appears never to have left the Crown, while Saskatoon has a large university and a thriving cultural scene, as well as proximity to many of the province's natural attractions.

Finding Your Way Around

By Plane

The province's two largest airports are located in Regina and Saskatoon; several major carriers serve the province, shuttling to and from Calgary, Toronto, Vancouver and other Canadian cities.

Air Canada's offices in Regina (☎*525-4711*) and Saskatoon (☎*652-4181*) are both located at the city airport.

Canadian Regional Airlines also has offices in Regina (☎*569-2307*) and in Saskatoon (☎*800-665-1177*), both located at the airport.

To get to **Saskatoon's John G. Diefenbaker Airport**, head directly north of the city approximately 7km. A chain of motels marks the approach. It is about a $12 taxi ride from downtown.

Regina Airport lies just southwest of the city, about 5km away; a cab costs about $10.

By Bus

Greyhound Canada (☎*800-661-8747*) serves the province's major destinations. In Regina, the bus depot (☎*787-3340*) is located at 2041 Hamilton St. In Saskatoon, the depot (☎*933-8000*) is at 50 23rd St. E, corner of Pacific Avenue.

The **Saskatchewan Transportation Company** also serves lesser-visited parts of the province. In Regina, STC buses (☎*787-3340*) depart from the same depot at 2041 Hamilton St.; in Saskatoon, call ☎*933-8000* to reach the company.

By Train

VIA Rail's (☎*800-561-8630 from western Canada*) cross-country Canadian service passes through the province during the night, making a stop here difficult, although not impossible; coming from the east, for example, the thrice-weekly train stops in Saskatoon at 2:40am. Eastbound trains pass through at 2:45am.

The Saskatoon Station (☎*800-561-8630*), located in the extreme southwest of the city at Cassino Avenue and Chappell Drive, is the largest station and the usual point of embarking or disembarking in Saskatchewan; the cross-country train no longer runs through Regina. Smaller stations exist at Watrous and Biggar, stopping only on passenger request.

There is no train service to Regina.

Public Transportation

Regina Transit (*333 Winnipeg St.,* ☎*777-7433*) serves the capital city and offers discounts if you buy a booklet of tickets.

Saskatoon Transit (☎*975-3100*) operates buses around that city.

Taxis

Capital Cab (☎*791-2225*) operates throughout Regina. In Saskatoon, try **Radio Cabs** (☎*242-1221*).

Practical Information

Area Code: ***306***.

Tourist Information Offices

Tourism Saskatchewan (☎*800-667-7191, www.sasktourism.com*) can be reached year-round. Provincial tourism information centres, scattered around the province on major highways, are only open during the summers; the lone exception is the centre in downtown Regina (*1900 Albert St., ☎787-2300*), which remains open all year.

Local tourism office hours vary a great deal, but the larger ones are open year-round.

Tourism Regina (*Trans-Canada Hwy. 1, ☎789-5099 or 800-661-5099*) is way out on the eastern fringe of the city, impossible to reach except by driving; it is well-stocked and friendly. It is open all day on weekdays year-round, and all day on weekends from May through August.

Tourism Saskatoon (*#6-305 Idylwyld Dr. N., ☎242-1206 or 800-567-2444*) is located downtown and remains open weekdays all year. In summer months, it is open on weekends as well.

Post Offices

The main **post offices** are located at 2200 Saskatchewan Dr. in Regina and at the corner of Fourth Avenue N and 23rd St. E in Saskatoon.

Safety

The province is quite safe, even in its few urban areas. In case of mishaps, the **Regina Police Station** (*1717 Osler St., ☎777-6500*) and **Saskatoon Police Station** (*130 Fourth Ave. N, ☎975-8300*) are the places to call. There is also a **Royal Canadian Mounted Police** (*1721 Eighth St. E, ☎975-5173*) detachment in Saskatoon and Regina (*1601 Dewdney Ave. W, same telephone no.*)

The **Canadian Automobile Association** maintains offices in the province's most populous areas, offering roadside assistance and information to members.

In Regina, offices are located at:

200 Albert St. N
☎791-4321

208 University Park Dr.
☎791-4323

3806 Albert St.
☎791-4322

In Saskatoon, they are located at:

204-3929 Eighth St. E
☎668-3770

321 Fourth Ave. N
☎668-3737

Other offices are located in:

Moose Jaw
80 Caribou St. W
☎693-5195

North Battleford
2002-100th St.
☎445-9451

Prince Albert
68-13th St. W
☎764-6818

Swift Current
15 Dufferin St. W
☎773-3193

Weyburn
110 Souris Ave.
☎842-6651

Yorkton
159 Broadway St. E
☎783-6536

Climate

Summers are generally warm and dry, with a great deal of sunshine. Winter, however, can bring dangerously low temperatures and blinding snowstorms; Temperatures can plunge to below -30°C, with the windchill making it feel even colder. Travellers should take the appropriate precautions.

For updated weather forecast information in Regina, call *☎780-5744*; in Saskatoon, call *☎975-4266*.

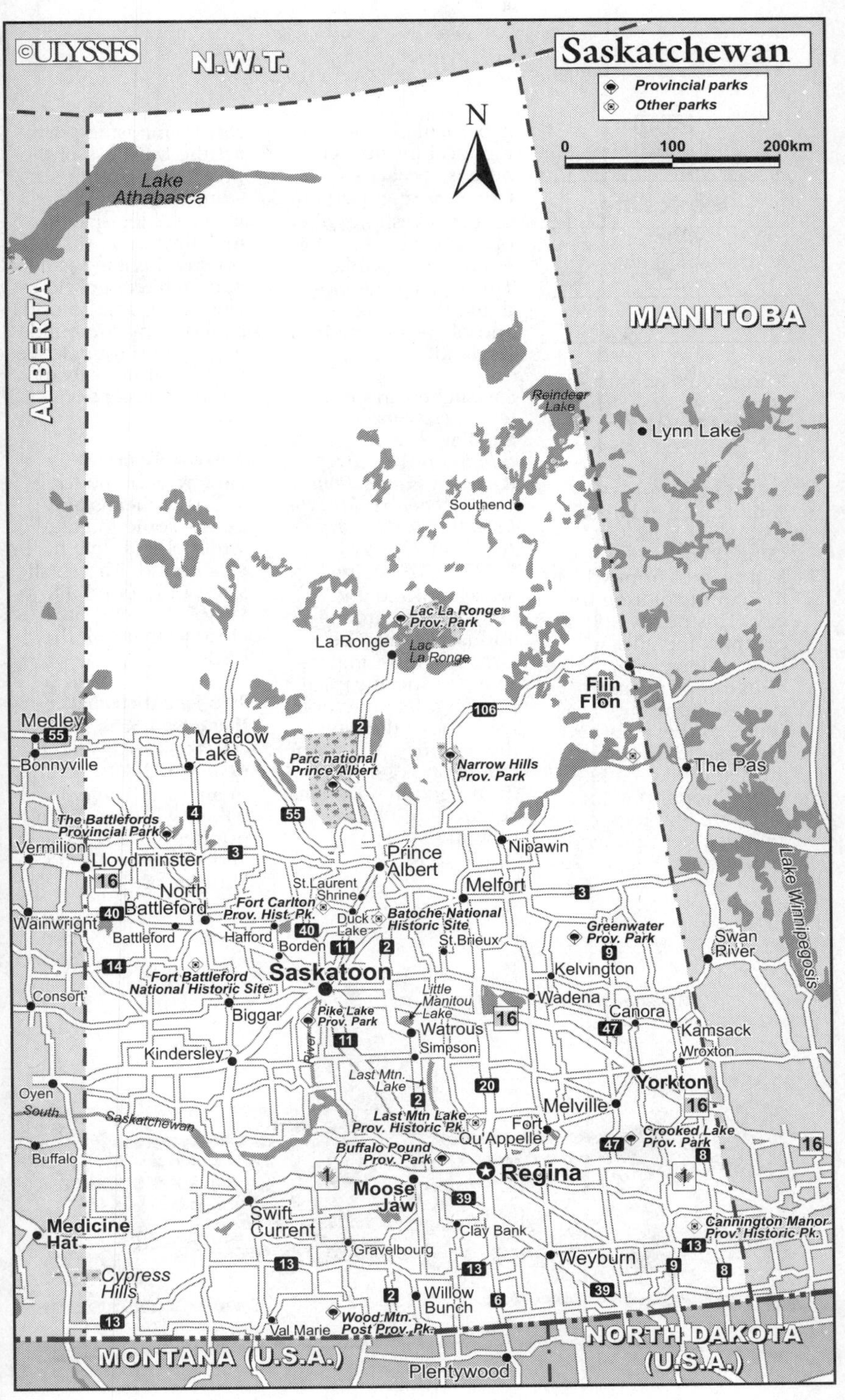

©ULYSSES
Saskatchewan
Provincial parks
Other parks
0
100
200km
N
N.W.T.
ALBERTA
MANITOBA
Lake Athabasca
Reindeer Lake
Lynn Lake
Southend
Lac La Ronge Prov. Park
La Ronge
Lac La Ronge
Flin Flon
106
2
Medley
55
Bonnyville
Meadow Lake
Parc national Prince Albert
Narrow Hills Prov. Park
The Pas
4
55
The Battlefords Provincial Park
Vermilion
Lloydminster
3
Prince Albert
Nipawin
16
North Battleford
St.Laurent Shrine
Melfort
3
Lake Winnipegosis
40
Wainwright
Fort Carlton Prov. Hist. Pk.
Duck Lake
Batoche National Historic Site
Greenwater Prov. Park
Battleford
Hafford
40
Borden
11
2
St.Brieux
9
Swan River
14
Saskatoon
Kelvington
Fort Battleford National Historic Site
Consort
Little Manitou Lake
Wadena
Biggar
Pike Lake Prov. Park
16
Canora
Watrous
47
Kamsack
11
Kindersley
River
Simpson
Wroxton
Yorkton
Last Mtn. Lake
20
Oyen
2
Melville
16
South
Saskatchewan
Last Mtn Lake Prov. Historic Pk.
Fort Qu'Appelle
47
Crooked Lake Prov. Park
Buffalo
Buffalo Pound Prov. Park
8
16
1
Regina
1
Moose Jaw
39
Swift Current
Medicine Hat
Clay Bank
Cannington Manor Prov. Historic Pk.
Gravelbourg
13
13
Weyburn
9
8
13
Cypress Hills
2
Willow Bunch
6
39
13
Val Marie
Wood Mtn. Post Prov. Pk.
NORTH DAKOTA (U.S.A.)
MONTANA (U.S.A.)
Plentywood

Exploring

Regina

Though it's hard to see from downtown, the **Wascana Centre ★★★** is a huge green space – reputedly the largest urban park in North America; even larger than New York City's Central Park – and the logical spot from which to begin exploring the city. This nearly 400ha complex includes a lake, a university, bridges, lawns, gardens, a convention centre and even a bird sanctuary. Walking trails and bike paths wind throughout, and there are ample parking and well-kept public washrooms.

A particularly interesting local institution here is **Speaker's Corner ★★**, a podium on the lakeshore where opinions may be proffered to the public. This is a serious podium: the gas lamps and birches come from England.

Saskatchewan's cruciform **Legislative Building ★★★** (*free admission; May to Sep every day 8am to 9pm; Oct to Apr every day 8am to 5pm; Albert St. and Legislative Dr.,* ☎*787-5358*), facing Wascana Lake and landscaped gardens and lawns, may be Canada's most impressive provincial capital building. Its huge dome rises above the city; at the entrance, the fountain is one of a pair from London's Trafalgar Square (the other is now in Ottawa). Inside, ministers transact the business of the province – and in session, it's possible to sit in on the legislative machinations. An Aboriginal heritage gallery and architectural flourishes such as a rotunda also occupy the building; guided tours leave every half hour from the front reception desk.

Wascana Waterfowl Park ★ is home to swans, pelicans and geese; some migrate while others live here year-round. The small size of the pond allows visitors to get quite close to many of the birds.

The **John Diefenbaker Homestead ★★** (*May to Sep every day 9am to 6pm;* ☎*522-3661*) commemorates Diefenbaker, who was born in northern Saskatchewan and served as Prime Minister of Canada.

Legislature Building

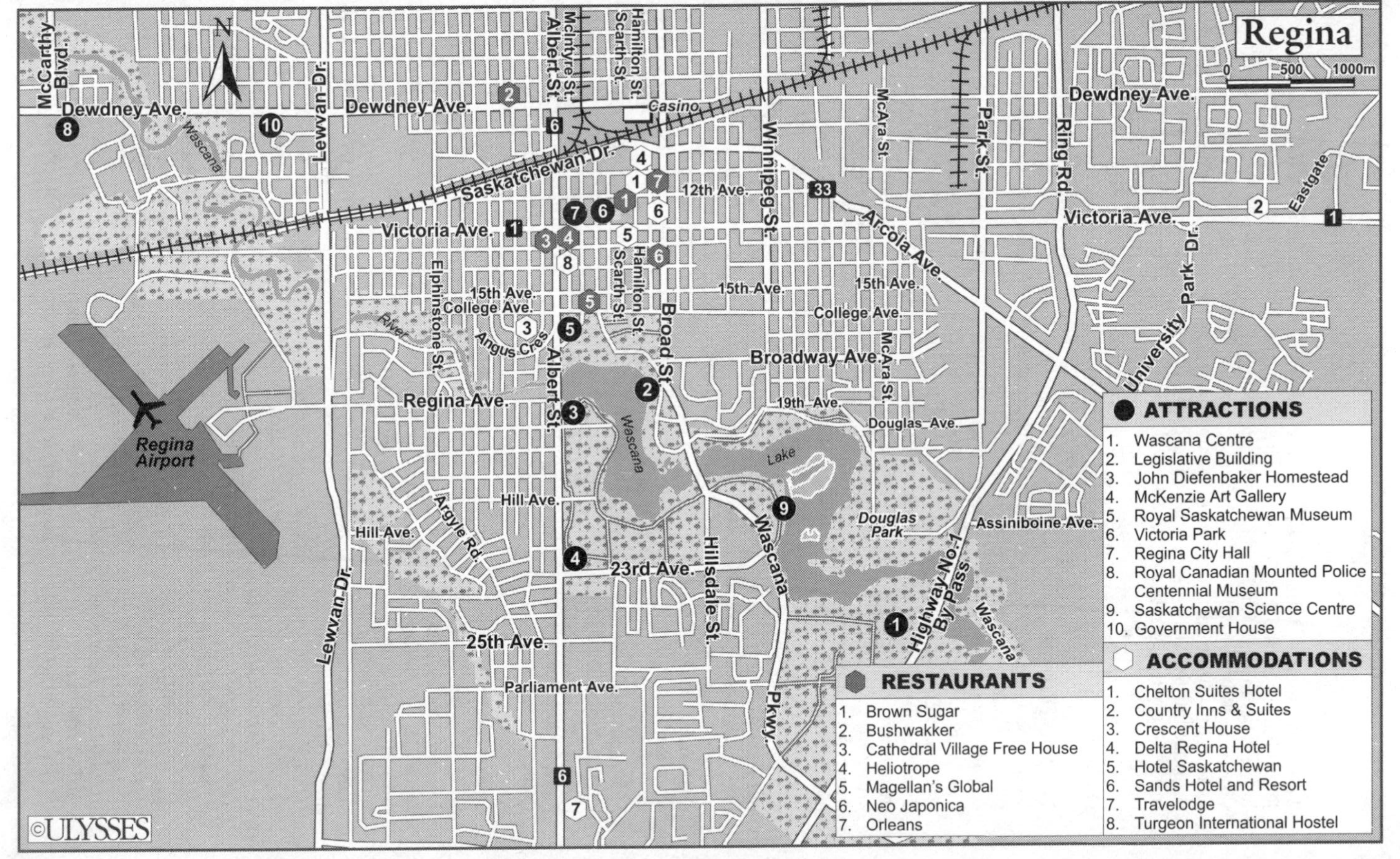

Regina
0 500 1000m
ATTRACTIONS
1. Wascana Centre
2. Legislative Building
3. John Diefenbaker Homestead
4. McKenzie Art Gallery
5. Royal Saskatchewan Museum
6. Victoria Park
7. Regina City Hall
8. Royal Canadian Mounted Police Centennial Museum
9. Saskatchewan Science Centre
10. Government House
ACCOMMODATIONS
1. Chelton Suites Hotel
2. Country Inns & Suites
3. Crescent House
4. Delta Regina Hotel
5. Hotel Saskatchewan
6. Sands Hotel and Resort
7. Travelodge
8. Turgeon International Hostel
RESTAURANTS
1. Brown Sugar
2. Bushwakker
3. Cathedral Village Free House
4. Heliotrope
5. Magellan's Global
6. Neo Japonica
7. Orleans
McCarthy Blvd.
Dewdney Ave.
Lewvan Dr.
Albert St.
McIntyre St.
Scarth St.
Hamilton St.
Casino
Broad St.
Winnipeg St.
McAra St.
Park St.
Ring Rd.
Eastgate
Saskatchewan Dr.
12th Ave.
Victoria Ave.
Arcola Ave.
University Park Dr.
15th Ave.
College Ave.
Elphinstone St.
Angus Cres.
River
Broadway Ave.
19th Ave.
Douglas Ave.
Regina Ave.
Wascana
Lake
Douglas Park
Assiniboine Ave.
Hill Ave.
Argyle Rd.
23rd Ave.
Hillsdale St.
Wascana Pkwy.
Highway No.1 By Pass
25th Ave.
Parliament Ave.
Regina Airport
©ULYSSES

The homestead – which Diefenbaker actually helped his father build when he was just 10 years old – includes original family furnishings. A second, smaller building on the property belonged to Diefenbaker's uncle.

The **MacKenzie Art Gallery** ★ (*free admission; every day 11am to 6pm; Wed and Thu until 10pm; 3475 Albert St., ☎522-4242*), located in the Wascana Centre at the corner of Albert St. and 23rd Avenue, showcases travelling exhibitions and a permanent collection. The gallery, funded by the bequest of a local attorney, includes a painted bronze statue of John Diefenbaker standing on a chair.

Moving across the Prince Albert Bridge toward downtown, the **Royal Saskatchewan Museum** ★ (*free admission; every day 9am to 4:30pm; College Ave. and Albert St., ☎787-2815*) occupies a nice corner of parkland. This is Regina's natural history museum; the exhibits are heavy on sandbox-style dioramas of dinosaurs accompanied by stentorian voice-overs, and there's more Saskatchewan geology here than a visitor could ever want or need to know. Still, this is the best place in town to see aboriginal Canadian artifacts and hear recorded Aboriginal voices. An impressive selection of black-and-white photographs of native leaders, along with videotape of some dances and ceremonies, makes a fitting closing to the walk.

A few blocks north of the museum, toward downtown, you will come across lovely **Victoria Park** ★★★ – an outstanding urban green space, the best on the prairies, right in the centre of Regina with a fantastic view of downtown's modern skyscrapers. A series of pathways radiate like spokes of a wheel outward from the war memorial at the centre; spruce trees add a lovely contrast to the grass and gardens.

Nearby, Regina's **city hall** ★★ (*free admission; Mon to Fri 8am to 4:30pm; 2476 Victoria Ave., ☎777-7305*) is also worth a look while downtown. The lights on the roof are designed to resemble a queen's crown at night; tours, which must be booked in advance, offer a glimpse of the council chambers, foyer and forum.

There is also a souvenir shop on the premises.

Scarth Street is downtown's pedestrian mall, which ends at a large forgettable shopping centre called the Cornwall Centre. Just a few doors before the centre, the **Regina Plains Museum** ★★ (*$2; Apr to Sep every day 10am to 4pm; Oct to Mar every day Mon to Fri 10am to 4pm; 1801 Scarth St., ☎780-9435*) is a bit hard to find but worth the trip. Located four floors up in the same downtown building that houses the Globe Theatre, this stop makes a good introduction to life on the plains.

The museum contains the obligatory recreations of a plains chapel, schoolhouse, bedroom and post office. More interesting are a small display describing the migrations of Aboriginal people through the province; an elegant glass sculpture of a wheatfield; a display on Louis Riel's trial; period surveyor's tools that were used to carve up the prairie (on paper, at least); and an old police mug book containing criminals' photographs. The cons' offenses, described in cursive handwriting as "cheating at cards," "resident of a bawdy house," and the like, make for entertaining reading.

The only two major sites requiring a drive are just a few minutes west of downtown and nearly adjacent to each other. The **Royal Canadian Mounted Police Centennial Museum** ★★★ (*free admission; Jun to Sep 15 every day 8am to 6:45pm; Sep 15 to May every day 10am to 4:45pm; Dewdney Ave. W, ☎780-5838*) is a popular, well-laid-out attraction located on the grounds of the RCMP's training academy. Exhibits at this walk-through museum include many rifles, red-serge uniforms and other police artifacts dating from the formation of the R.C.M.P. force in 1873 to keep order and quell bootleggers in the Canadian Northwest. The story of the force's creation, march west across the prairies – their inaugural 3,200km walk from Montreal – and eventual relocation to the Regina post are all traced in detail here.

The museum is obviously strong on military items from all historical periods, but as a bonus it also contains some truly interesting material relating to the darker side of the pioneers' resettling of the west: First Nations land treaties, a buffalo skin incised with victories, Sitting Bull's rifle case, a buffalo skull paired with an ironic quote about the native buffalo hunt, the personal effects of Louis Riel, and so forth.

Government House ★ (*free admission; Tue to Sun, 1pm to 4pm; 4607 Dewdney Ave. W., ☎787-5773*), near the RCMP training grounds, has been home to some of the province's highest officials since the late 19th century. It is still the private home of Saskatchewan's lieutenant governor, but tours are offered. On some summer weekend afternoons, the staff also serves tea.

The **Saskatchewan Science Centre ★** (*at Winnipeg St. and Wascana Dr., Wascana Centre, ☎800-667-6300 or 352-5811*) is best known for its 17m IMAX cinema with sound on all sides. Another section of the museum, the **Powerhouse of Discovery** (*$6.50*), presents exhibits and live talks.

Southern Saskatchewan

The Trans-Canada Highway runs east to west through southern Saskatchewan, crossing wheatfields and the occasional town. East of Regina, it gives no hint of the spectacular vista that lies just a few kilometres to the north, in the Qu'Appelle Valley, which runs parallel to it at this point. West of Regina the land is perfectly flat; this is the scenery for which Saskatchewan is best known, making humans feel, as the popular saying goes, like a fly on a plate.

★★★ Qu'Appelle River Valley

The Fort Qu'Appelle River Valley makes for a surprising detour: the river has cut a little valley in the otherwise flat countryside. **Route 247** (*north of the Trans-Canada between Whitewood and Grenfell*), barely known by tourists, runs along the river as it dips through the brown and green hills. It passes **Round Lake ★★** and then **Crooked Lake Provincial Park ★★**, beautiful lakes for swimming, fishing and sightseeing. A string of tiny tree-shaded resort towns provides campgrounds and the odd country store.

Continuing along the very poorly maintained Rte. 22 takes you to a worthwhile, if isolated, destination: the **Motherwell Homestead National Historic Site ★★** (*$4; summer every day 10am to 6pm; Box 247, Abernethy, ☎333-2116, ⇄333-2210*). This impressive Victorian fieldstone house with gingerbread trim was built by W.R. Motherwell, famous for developing innovative dryland farming techniques at the turn of the century. The property, which more or less amounts to an estate, does not lack for anything: the grounds encompass a tennis court, croquet lawn, arbours, a herb garden and barnyard. The interior of the house is just as astonishing an example of high living in the midst of deserted prairie. Visitors can tour the house and grounds, and are even invited to help with the farm chores. There is a food concession stand on the premises.

At a bend in the valley, where the river feeds into a series of lakes, the small town of **Fort Qu'Appelle** charms visitors with its setting – tucked among hills – as well as a smattering of historic sites. The tourist information centre is situated inside a former train station; a former Hudson's Bay Company log cabin for which the town is named is now a small **museum** ★ (*$2; early June to late Aug 10am to 5pm; Bay Ave. and Third St., ☎332-6443 or 332-4319*). The fort was the site of a historic treaty ceding vast tracts of First Nation lands in Saskatchewan to the Canadian government.

Moose Jaw

Moose Jaw (pop. 30,000), a former bootlegging capital during US prohibition years, sprouts up in the flatlands west of Regina and offers visitors a glimpse into little-known aspects of the province's past. While it is now a sleepy little town where the parking meters still accept nickels, impressive bank buildings and the ornate city hall attest to its more glamorous past.

The **Western Development Museum's Transportation Museum** ★ (*$5;every day 9am to 6pm; Jan to Mar Mon closed; 50 Diefenbaker Dr., ☎693-5989*), in a somewhat forlorn location north of downtown, serves up the history of Canadian transportation – everything from canoes, Red River carts and pack horses to vintage rail cars, automobiles and airplanes. A narrow-gauge railway runs behind the museum on weekends and holidays from late May to Labour Day.

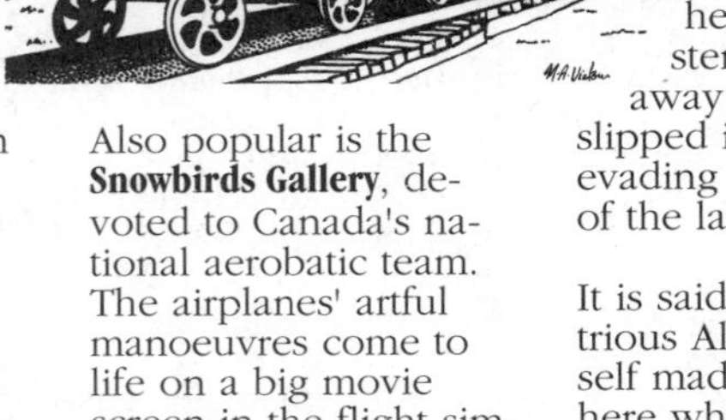

Also popular is the **Snowbirds Gallery**, devoted to Canada's national aerobatic team. The airplanes' artful manoeuvres come to life on a big movie screen in the flight simulator, in the museum's cinema (*$1.50*).

Crescent Park ★, just east of downtown, is on the banks of the Moose Jaw River and is a pleasant place for a short walk beneath trees and over a picturesque bridge. The secret underground passages of Moose Jaw were but a rumour until a car plunged through the pavement and wound up 4m below street level, in what are now referred to as the **Tunnels of Little Chicago** ★★★ (*$7; 108 Main St. N., ☎693-5261*). Today, a guided tour takes visitors through a small portion of the vast hidden network, and interpreters explain how they were built by the Chinese labourers who had come to work on the railway and decided to go "underground," in this case literally, when Canada went back on its promise to grant them citizenship once the task was completed. Later, the passages were used as hideouts of a different kind as bootlegging operations were set up here and gangsters from as far away as Chicago slipped into town, evading the long arm of the law.

It is said that the illustrious Al Capone himself made appearances here when the heat became too strong south of the border. The tour evokes both the abysmal living conditions endured by the Chinese in these dark, cramped quarters and the scintillating era of speakeasies and corruption. While the adjacent museum is of lesser interest, the tour of the tunnels is an excellent way to become immersed in the history of this once-electrifying town.

Claybank

Southeast of Moose Jaw, on Hwy. 339, is little Claybank and its historic **Claybank Brick Plant** ★ (*$3; Jul to Aug Sat and Sun 10am to 4pm; ☎306-868-4774*). The plant operated from 1914 until 1989, one of Canada's two major plants of this kind during that time; its bricks were used in such buildings as Quebec City's Chateau Frontenac. The complex of high chimneys and dome-like kilns can be toured by arrangement, and there is also a tea room on the premises.

Gravelbourg

Southwest of Moose Jaw, a 115km detour off the Trans-Canada down Rtes. 2 and then 43, Gravelbourg is the acknowledged centre of French culture in Saskatchewan. A French-Canadian cultural centre and dance troupe both make their homes here. Most prominent among downtown buildings is the **Cathédrale Notre-Dame de l'Assomption** ★★ (*free admission; every day 9am to 5pm, guided tours Jul and Aug, $2; ☎648-3322*). Built in 1918, the church is a historic property and features wonderful interior murals painted by Charles Maillard, its founding pastor, over a 10-year period.

Nearby, on Fifth Avenue East, the **Musée de Gravelbourg** ★ (*Jul and Aug 1pm to 5pm, 5th Ave. E., ☎648-3301*) preserves mementoes from the original French-speaking settlers of the region, including the missionary Father L.P. Gravel, for whom the town is named.

Other Sights

Nearby, **Wood Mountain Post Provincial Historic Park** ★★ (*donation; Jun to mid-Aug everyday 10am to 5pm; ☎694-3659*), a former Mountie post, is interesting particularly for its association with the Sioux chief Sitting Bull and his people. Sitting Bull came here in the spring of 1877 after defeating the United States Army at the battle of Little Big Horn; as many as 5,000 Sioux were already hiding in the surrounding hills.

The chief quickly forged a friendship with police Major James Walsh, but political pressure from both the Canadian and United States governments replaced Walsh with another officer who began a siege against the Sioux. The two buildings here, staffed with interpreters, recount the story in more detail.

Sitting Bull's former camp is located near the village of Willow Bunch in **Jean-Louis Legare Park** ★. Legare, a Metis trader, supplied food to the Sioux during their exile and also provisioned them for their long march back to the United States in 1881.

Approximately 40km north of Regina on Rte. 20 is **Last Mountain House Provincial Park** ★ (*free admission; Jul to Sep, ☎787-2080*), a small but interesting recreation of a short-lived Hudson's Bay Company fur post. Built of wood and local white clay, the post was established near a buffalo herd in the adjacent river valley in 1869. However, the buffalo moved west the following year, never to return.

Today the windswept park's displays include a fur press, trading store, icehouse for preserving meat, bunkhouse quarters for trappers and the more spacious quarters of the officers. During the summer, park interpreters are on hand to recreate the experience.

Saskatoon

Set on the banks of the South Saskatchewan River, Saskatoon is Saskatchewan's hip address. Home to a large university, and a world leader in agricultural biotechnology, the city also offers a host of outdoor activities and cultural events year-round, including a jazz festival, fringe and folk festivals, and the famous Shakespeare on the Saskatchewan theatre series. Once a major stop on the trans-Canadian rail network, the downtown still has some impressive buildings from that era.

Among the city's most striking buildings is the castle-like railway hotel, the **Bessborough**, which was built by relief workers during the depression era, as were the graceful arched bridges that span the river from downtown.

While the Bessborough is Saskatoon's best-known of hotel, the **Hotel Senator** (*243 21st St. E.*) is its oldest. Built in 1908 as the Flanagan Hotel, it boasted such extravagances as steam heating, hot and cold running water, and a telephone in each room. Although the Senator can no longer be considered a luxury hotel by any stretch of the imagination, some of its former glory is still in evidence; the marble pillar at the foot of the staircase, the wood-panelled dining room with its original chandelier, and the marble floor of the lobby recall a more prosperous era in the hotel's history.

Saskatoon's most interesting commercial street is **Broadway Avenue**, south of the river. Downtown, **Second Avenue** is lined with small shops selling everything from CDs and LPs to books, pottery and international crafts. It intersects with **21st St. E**, which boasts the major banks, a few slightly more upscale shops, and some attractive older storefronts including the Art Deco facade of the former Eaton's department store (now housing an Army Navy and Surplus store).

At the corner of 21st St. E and First Ave. is an interesting sculpture commemorating a chance meeting of two of the most prominent figures in Canadian history; it depicts Sir Wilfrid Laurier buying a newspaper from a young John Diefenbaker, circa 1910.

Historical sites are harder to find. The city is, in fact, rather short on cultural attractions. Nearly all of the good ones are concentrated downtown along the river. It's possible to see everything of note in a single busy day.

The **Ukrainian Museum of Canada** ★★ (*$2; Tue to Sat 10am to 5pm, Sun 1pm to 5pm; 910 Spadina Cr. E, ☎244-3800*) is a surprisingly good history lesson beneath a small roof. Through a series of walk-through rooms, the museum uses texts and simple articles to describe the Ukrainian people's Eastern European origins and persecution, their migration to North America, their settlement of the prairies, and their subsequent endurance as a people.

Highlights among the displays include a large section on the deep religious significance of the beautiful art of *pysanka* (Easter-egg decoration), a careful explanation of the distinctively domed Ukrainian churches and a delineation of where and why the Ukrainians settled where they did. Some intricate ornamental breads and examples of *rozpys* – the decorative painting of furnishings, walls and doors – are also nice touches. The **Mendel Art Gallery and Arts Centre** ★★★ (*free admission; summer every day 9am to 9pm, winter every day noon to 9pm; 950 Spadina Cr. E, ☎975-7610*) is the province's best art museum. Its exhibits rotate quite regularly, and whether drawn from the permanent collection or just

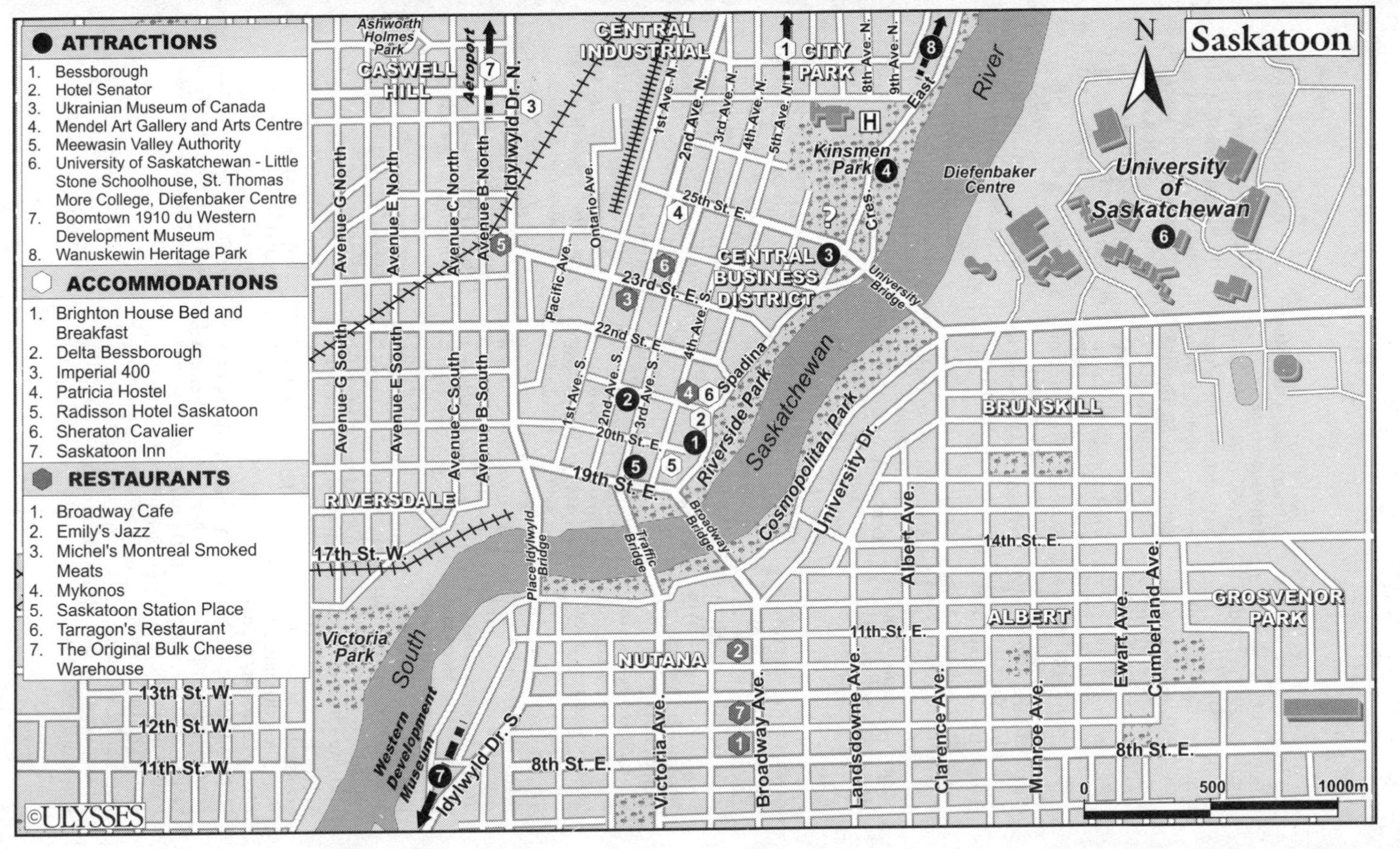

Saskatoon
ATTRACTIONS
1. Bessborough
2. Hotel Senator
3. Ukrainian Museum of Canada
4. Mendel Art Gallery and Arts Centre
5. Meewasin Valley Authority
6. University of Saskatchewan - Little Stone Schoolhouse, St. Thomas More College, Diefenbaker Centre
7. Boomtown 1910 du Western Development Museum
8. Wanuskewin Heritage Park
ACCOMMODATIONS
1. Brighton House Bed and Breakfast
2. Delta Bessborough
3. Imperial 400
4. Patricia Hostel
5. Radisson Hotel Saskatoon
6. Sheraton Cavalier
7. Saskatoon Inn
RESTAURANTS
1. Broadway Cafe
2. Emily's Jazz
3. Michel's Montreal Smoked Meats
4. Mykonos
5. Saskatoon Station Place
6. Tarragon's Restaurant
7. The Original Bulk Cheese Warehouse
Ashworth Holmes Park
CASWELL HILL
Aeroport
CENTRAL INDUSTRIAL
CITY PARK
CENTRAL BUSINESS DISTRICT
Kinsmen Park
Diefenbaker Centre
University of Saskatchewan
River
Saskatchewan
South
East
University Bridge
Broadway Bridge
Traffic Bridge
Place Idylwyld Bridge
Riverside Park
Cosmopolitan Park
University Dr.
Spadina
Cres.
BRUNSKILL
ALBERT
GROSVENOR PARK
NUTANA
RIVERSDALE
Victoria Park
Western Development Museum
Idylwyld Dr. N.
Idylwyld Dr. S.
Avenue G North
Avenue E North
Avenue C North
Avenue B North
Avenue G South
Avenue E South
Avenue C South
Avenue B South
Pacific Ave.
Ontario Ave.
1st Ave. N.
2nd Ave. N.
3rd Ave. N.
4th Ave. N.
5th Ave. N.
8th Ave. N.
9th Ave. N.
25th St. E.
23rd St. E.
22nd St. E.
20th St. E.
19th St. E.
1st Ave. S.
2nd Ave. S.
3rd Ave. S.
4th Ave. S.
17th St. W.
13th St. W.
12th St. W.
11th St. W.
14th St. E.
11th St. E.
8th St. E.
Victoria Ave.
Broadway Ave.
Landsdowne Ave.
Clarence Ave.
Albert Ave.
Munroe Ave.
Ewart Ave.
Cumberland Ave.
N
0
500
1000m
©ULYSSES

on loan, they're always interesting; concurrently showing might be American James Walsh's astonishingly thick acrylics in one gallery, several different multimedia installations occupying another and a collection of modern prints, paintings and other media works by First Nations artists sprinkled throughout. The museum also contains such amenities as a children's room, coffee shop, a good gift shop and a small but lovely conservatory.

A footpath from the back of the centre leads down to the river, hooking up with an extensive network of trails running north and south along both river banks. The **Meewasin Valley Trails** ★★ (*www.lights.com/meewasin*) extend more than 50km along the river, a joy for cyclists and walkers. The valley's other amenities include an outdoor skating rink and an urban grassland reserve. The **Meewasin Valley Authority Headquarters** ★ (*402 Third Ave. S, ☎665-6888*) provide an introduction to the river and the city.

Southeast, across the river, lies the large and pretty **University of Saskatchewan** ★★ campus. Several attractions of historic interest are found here, though some are only open during the summer when school is out of session. Especially quaint is the **Little Stone Schoolhouse** ★ (*☎966-8384*), Saskatoon's first schoolhouse – it dates from 1887. The **St. Thomas More College chapel** ★ (*☎966-8900*) is worth a look for its mural by Canadian artist William Kurelek, and the university **observatory** (*☎966-6429*) opens to the public Saturday evenings.

Also not to be missed, the **Diefenbaker Centre** ★ (*$2; Mon to Fri 9:30am to 4:30pm, Tue and Thr 9:30am to 8pm, Sun 12:30pm to 5pm; ☎966-8384*) preserves many of Diefenbaker's personal papers and effects, and his gravestone is located nearby on the university campus. Other displays include replicas of the former Prime Minister's office and Privy Council chamber. The centre – splendidly located with a view of the river and the downtown – is also famous for housing what is probably the most renowned piece of furniture in the province: a simple maple desk that once belonged to John A. Macdonald, the man considered the father of Canadian confederation.

On the outskirts of town sits the **Western Development Museum's Boomtown 1910** ★ (*$5; every day 9am to 5pm; 2610 Lorne Ave. S., ☎931-1910*), which reconstructs a typical western mining town's main street in movie-set fashion. More than 30 buildings make up the complex; like many of the province's museums, its exhibits lean toward agricultural equipment and farm implements. Also outside the city, about 4km away, is **Valley Road**, an agricultural drive leading to a number of fruit, vegetable and herb farms in the area.

Finally, a 10min drive to the north leads to the wonderful **Wanuskewin Heritage Park** ★★★ (*$6; May to Sep every day 9am to 9pm; Oct to Apr everyday 9am to 5pm; ☎931-6767*), perhaps the best native museum in the prairies. The area around Saskatoon was settled continuously for thousands of years before the first white settlers arrived; a river valley just north of the city was long used as a "buffalo jump" where local First Nations hunted and established winter camps. Now the property is open to the public as a series of archaeological sites – ancient tipi rings and a medicine wheel, for instance, can be walked to – plus an indoor museum and interpretive centre dealing with the history of First Nations people here.

"A people without history is like wind in the buffalo grass," says a panel in the museum, and the museum does indeed throw much light onto the Aboriginal peoples of the Plains. The differences among Cree, Dene, Lakota, Dakota and Assiniboine are carefully explained in one display, and their recorded voices can be heard by pressing a button. Other rooms in the centre host art exhibits and slide shows; talks and conferences; and an Aboriginal-foods café. Ongoing archaeological research is also conducted on the grounds.

Yellowhead Highway

Yorkton

Yorkton would be rather uninteresting but for the **Western Development Museum's "Story of People" museum ★★** (*$5; May to Sep every day 9am to 6pm; Hwy. 16, ☎783-8361*), which traces the history of the various immigrant populations that have made the province as colourful as it is.

Yorkton is also the site of western Canada's first brick Ukrainian church. **St. Mary's Ukrainian Catholic Church ★★** (*155 Catherine St., ☎783-4594*), built in 1914, is topped with a distinctive 21m-high cathedral dome. The dome was painted in 1939-41 by Steven Meush and is considered one of the most beautiful on the continent. Inside, there is beautiful icon work by Ihor Suhacev. If the church is not open, visitors can ask at the adjacent rectory for a look inside. The church also hosts an annual "Vid Pust" (Pilgrimage Day) celebration each June.

Veregin

Approximately 50km north off the Yellowhead, Veregin houses the **National Doukhobour Heritage Village ★★** (*$3; mid-May to mid-Sep every day 10am to 6pm; mid-Sep to mid-May Mon to Fri, 10am to 4pm; ☎542-4441*), an 11-building complex that throws light on one of the province's most intriguing immigrant groups. The Doukhobours came to Saskatchewan in 1899 and established a short-lived community here, eschewing meat, alcohol and tobacco in favour of an agrarian existence. They soon moved farther west, but this museum preserves the original prayer home and machinery shop. Also on display are a brick oven, bath house, agricultural equipment and blacksmith's shop.

Canora

Just 25km west of Veregin, Canora welcomes travellers with a 7.6m statue in Slavic dress. A tourist booth next to the statue operates from June until September to orient visitors to local attractions. This little village is also home to a fine restored **Ukrainian Orthodox Heritage Church ★** (*Jun to mid-Sep every day 8am to 6pm; 710 Main St., ☎563-5662*) Built in 1928, the church displays Kiev architecture and stained glass; visitors can obtain a key next door at 720 Main St. when the church isn't open.

Wroxton

Wroxton is some distance from the Yellowhead – 35km north – but interesting for its two Ukrainian churches on opposite ends of the village. Both domes are visible just north of the main highway, and can be reached by driving along one of the town's several dirt roads.

Around Wadena

In the Wadena area, **Big Quill Lake** and various other marshes on both sides of the Yellowhead offer good opportunities to view birds. The advocacy group Ducks Unlimited helps preserve many of these lands and interprets them for the general public. **Little Quill Lake Heritage Marsh** ★, best reached from Hwy. 35, was designated an international shorebird reserve in 1994 and is open year-round. This marsh hosts more than 800,000 migrating and resident shorebirds each year; visitors can hike, learn from interpretive signs and climb an observation tower.

St. Brieux

St. Brieux features a little **museum** ★ (*mid-May to Aug everyday 10am to 4pm; 300 Barbier Dr., ☎275-2229*) in a former Roman Catholic rectory. It contains artifacts of early settlers from Quebec, France and Hungary; tours here are conducted in both English and French.

Muenster

Continuing west, also near the Yellowhead, the small town of Muenster is notable for a beautiful twin-towered cathedral and adjoining monastery. **St. Peter's Cathedral** ★★ (*free; Mar to Dec 9am to 9pm; closed Jan and Feb, ☎682-5484*), built in 1910, features paintings by Berthold Imhoff, a German-born count who later moved to St. Walburg, Saskatchewan, and became an artist. Approximately 80 life-sized figures grace the cathedral, with saints and religious scenes making up the interior. **St. Peter's Abbey** ★★ (*March 1 to Dec 31, 8am to dusk; ☎682-1777*) gives a sense of what the monastic life is like: a self-guided tour reveals the abbey's farm, gardens, print shop and so on. It's also possible to sleep a night in the monastery for a small donation.

★ Little Manitou Lake

For centuries, travellers have been making a trip to Little Manitou Lake to "take the waters." This lake is so high in natural mineral salts that a person swimming can't sink. In fact, the water is even saltier here than in the Dead Sea, or in any ocean on Earth – and the salts are reputed to have restorative powers. That's why a strange little tourist town has sprung up around the lake, itself oddly placed among barren hills.

Borden

Borden, the boyhood home of John Diefenbaker – his house has been moved to downtown Regina – is interesting as a stop because you can tour a local **United Grain Growers (UGG) grain elevator** ★ (*every day 8am to 5pm; ☎997-2010*) year-round. Guests are requested to phone ahead, however, to arrange these tours.

The Battlefords

Battleford (pop. 4,000), former capital of the Northwest Territories, was once important but is today overshadowed by its twin city of North Battleford across the Saskatchewan River. As usual, railway politics decided the fate of the twin towns. **Fort Battleford National Historic Site** (*$4; mid-May to mid-Oct every day 9am to 5pm; ☎937-2621*) recalls the original impetus for the townsite – a Mountie post – complete with four restored period buildings. The barracks house contains additional displays of historical interest, explained by guides in period police costume.

North Battleford (pop. 14,000) is often visited for the **Western Development Museum's Heritage Farm and Village** ★ (*$5; May to mid-Sep every day 8:30am to 6:30pm; the rest of the year Tue to Sun 1pm to 5pm, ☎445-8033*), a mostly agricultural museum featuring plenty of period farm machinery.

The town is also famous as home to artist Allan Sapp. The **Allan Sapp Gallery** ★ (*free admission; May to Sep every day 1pm to 5pm; Oct to May Wed to Sun 1pm to 5pm; ☎445-1760*) showcases the work of the prairies' best-known and loved

Aboriginal artist. Sapp's paintings, recollections of Aboriginal life from a half-century ago, hang in the important museums of Canada and are displayed and sold here; the gallery, located on the ground floor of a restored Carnegie library, also contains hundreds of works by Sapp's mentor Allan Gonor.

West Central Saskatchewan

Poundmaker Trail

Rte. 40, also called Poundmaker Trail, is the former stronghold of the Poundmaker Cree Nation. **Cut Knife** sports what is said to be Canada's largest tomohawk, a suspended sculpture of wood and fiberglass whose fir handle is more than 16m long and supports a six-tonne blade. The surrounding park contains the obligatory small museum. The legendary **Chief Poundmaker's** (*www.wbm.ca/wilderness/poundmake*) grave is also in town, on the Cree Reserve. It is a testament to a man who favoured peace over war and surrendered his force of natives to the Mounties rather than continue to shed blood.

Hafford

Just northeast of Saskatoon, near the village of Hafford, the **Redberry Project Highway 40** ★ (*☎549-2400*) maintains one of the province's best waterfowl projects in a federal migratory bird sanctuary on Redberry Lake. Their motto is "we have friends in wet places," and the specialty here is pelicans. More than 1000 American white pelicans nest on the lake's New Tern Island; it's just one of 14 colonies of the birds in Saskatchewan. Boat tours are also available, and cost about $15 for approximately 1.5hrs.

Prince Albert

Prince Albert (pop. 39,000), the oldest city in the province, is a gateway in more ways than one. It is the largest town near **Prince Albert Provincial Park** ★★★ (*☎663-4512*), the site of a huge mill that converts the northern forests into pulp and paper, and the source of three Canadian Prime Ministers (see p 494). Though the town began as a fur post for Northwestern explorer Peter Pond in 1776, the town as it exists today was established nearly a full century later by the Reverend James Nisbet as a mission for local Cree.

The **Diefenbaker House Museum** (*free admission; mid-May to early Aug Mon to Sat 10am to 6pm, Sun 10am to 9pm; 246 19th St. W., ☎953-4863*) is probably the most famous stop in town. It contains many of the former Canadian Prime Minister's personal effects and furnishings, and describes his relationship to the city.

The **Prince Albert Historical Museum** (*$1; River St. and Central Ave.; mid-May to early Aug Mon to Sat 10am to 6pm, Sun10am to 9pm; ☎764-2992*) brings local history into focus, beginning with native and fur-trader culture from the mid-1800s. There is a second-floor tearoom with a balcony overlooking the North Saskatchewan River, as well.

Several other museums in Prince Albert are also worth a look. The **Evolution of Education Museum** (*free admission; mid-May to early Sep every day 10am to 8pm; ☎953-4385*) is located in a former one-room schoolhouse, and the **Rotary Museum of Police and Corrections** (*free admission; mid-May to Sep 10am to 8pm; ☎922-3313*) is inside a former North West Mounted Police guardhouse and includes a fascinating display of weapons fashioned by prisoners trying to break out of provincial jails.

Around Duck Lake

Southwest of Prince Albert, **Duck Lake** was the site of one of the most famous events in Saskatchewan history: the battle between Louis Riel and his band of Metis and the North West Police. The **Duck Lake Regional Interpretive Centre** ★★ (*$4; 5 Anderson Ave.; mid-May to early Sep every day 10am to 5:30pm; ☎467-2057*) describes the events as they unfolded, displaying artifacts from the Metis Resistance campaign, you can also climb a viewing tower of the battlefield grounds. A series of painted outdoor murals welcome the visitor.

About 25km west of Duck Lake, **Fort Carlton Provincial Historic Park** ★★ (*$2.50; mid-May to early Sep; every day 10am to 6pm; ☎467-4512*) dates from 1810, another in the string of Hudson's Bay Company posts in Saskatchewan. An important land treaty was also signed here. Today the site consists of a reconstructed stockade and buildings; interpretive staff lead tours and explain how the fort was a Mountie post until the Battle of Duck Lake. Just outside the fort, a Plains Cree encampment – three tipis furnished in typical late-19th-century fashion – give a sense of what and how the natives traded with the English. The objects in these tipis include robes, skins, pipes, weapons and other ceremonial objects.

St. Laurent

St. Laurent Shrine ★ (*May 1 to Aug 31; ☎467-2212*) makes for an enjoyable side trip in the area. Built in 1874 as an Order of the Oblate mission right on the South Saskatchewan River, and quite similar to the Our Lady of Lourdes shrine in France, it holds Sunday services at 4pm during July and August. Annual pilgrimages also take place during those months; the tradition dates back to 1893, when one Brother Guillet's leg miraculously healed after he prayed to the shrine.

Batoche National Historic Park ★★★ (*$4; May 18 to Oct 14 9am to 5pm; ☎423-6227*) is where Riel's story came to its end in March of 1885. The site, a peaceful agricultural valley where the Metis had settled after moving westwards, became capital of the Metis resistance when Riel challenged the English. Today, a walking path, museum and interpretive staff guide visitors through the remains of the village of Batoche, including the restored St. Antoine de Padoue church and rectory. There are also trenches and rifle pits used by the Mountie forces during their four-day siege of Batoche.

Parks

Southern Saskatchewan

Buffalo Pound Provincial Park ★ (*☎694-3659*), 23km northeast of Moose Jaw, presents a variety of recreational choices, including – most popularly – a chance to view grazing bison. A number of hiking trails wind through the dips and rises of the Qu'Appelle Valley: the trail tells the story of the Charles Nicolle Homestead, a stone dwelling built in 1930; another proceeds through a marsh; yet another traverses the junction of two rivers, an area rich with such wildlife as painted turtles, deer and great blue herons. The river is a popular beach and boating destination, as well.

Cannington Manor Provincial Historic Park ★ (*free admission; May to Sep 10am to 6pm; ☎577-2131*) recounts a short-lived experiment by the Englishman Captain Edward Pierce. Pierce tried to form a utopian colony based on agriculture here, and for a while it worked. A combination of days working the fields and diversions such as fox hunts, cricket, horse races and afternoon tea. The experiment did not survive, but the manor features period antiques and farm tools used on the site. Six other buildings – some original, some reconstructed – complete the park.

Last Mountain Lake National Wildlife Area ★★ (*free admission; May 1 to Oct 31; ☎836-2022*), occupying the northern end of the lake with the same name, is believed to be the oldest bird sanctuary on the North American continent. More than 250 species of bird touch down here during their annual migrations south, including the spectacular whooping crane. These migrations are most spectacular during spring (mid-May) and fall (September); visitors either choose to follow a scripted tour by car or climb the observation tower and take the two hiking trails on foot. The preserve is best reached by turning east off Hwy. 2 at the town of Simpson, then following signs to the lakeshore. There is talk that the site's administrators may soon begin charging a fee to visit the preserve.

Grasslands National Park ★★ (*year-round; between Val Marie and Killdeer, south of Hwy. 18; ☎298-2257*) was the first representative portion of original mixed-grass prairie set aside in North America. Among the variety of habitats represented here are grasslands, buttes, badlands and the Frenchman River Valley; spectacular views can be had from some of the butte tops, while the wildlife includes the rare swift fox, pronghorn antelopes and golden eagles. Most interesting, though, is the unique **prairie dog town ★★**, where colonies of black-tailed prairie dogs still live in their natural environment.

Guided hikes are given from the park office in Val Marie on summer Sundays, and wilderness camping is permitted in the park – but permission must be obtained from private landowners to access certain parts of it.

Pike Lake Park ★ (*☎933-6966*), a small recreational park about 30km southwest of Saskatoon, is a popular day trip for residents of Saskatchewan's largest city. The terrain here includes lawns shaded by aspen, ash and birch trees, a good beach and lots of wildlife. Watersports facilities include a pool, waterslide and canoes for hire; hiking trails, tennis courts, golf and mini-golf are also available here.

The Yellowhead Highway

Cumberland House Provincial Historic Park ★★★ (*☎888-2077*), on an island in the North Saskatchewan River near the Manitoba border, was quite important historically: it was the first Hudson's Bay Company fur post in western Canada. Later, it served as a port for steamboat traffic along the river. An 1890s-era powderhouse and part of a sternwheeler paddleboat are all that remain, but it's still a fascinating stop.

Duck Mountain Provincial Park ★★ (*☎542-5500*) sits 25km east of Kamsack, right on the Manitoba border. Open year-round, the park completely surrounds popular Madge Lake. The mountain itself rises 240m above the surrounding terrain, covered with aspens. Full recreational facilities are here, including a campground, golf course, mini-golf course, fishing gear and beach. A lodge within park grounds provides accommodations.

The Battlefords Provincial Park ★ (☎*386-2212*) is considered one of the recreational jewels of the province. Its location on the northeast shore of Jackfish Lake provides easy access to fishing and sailing. Equipment is available for these watersports; there are also a golf course and mini-golf course on premises, as well as a store and year-round resort-style accommodations.

Greenwater Lake Provincial Park ★ (☎*278-2972*) is on Hwy. 38, north of Kelvington in the province's eastern Porcupine Forest. There is a marina with boat rentals and fishing gear in the summer, as well as tennis, golf, and horseback-riding facilities; in winter, the park becomes a destination for cross-country skiers. Nice log cabins are available for rent, too.

West-Central Saskatchewan

Prince Albert National Park ★★★ (☎*663-4522*), encompassing 400,000ha, is one of Saskatchewan's finest parks. Entering from the south entrance on Rte. 263, you will pass through grassland and fields, then aspen parklands and finally forests.

Waskesiu Lake is the park area's largest and most popular body of water, and is where most of the services, beaches and activities are located. Farther off the beaten track, the park is noted for several good canoe routes and hiking trails that provide access to bird and plant life: bird enthusiasts, for instance, come to glimpse Canada's second-largest colony of American white pelicans, who nest on Lavallee Lake. Wolves, elk and buffalo also live here. Hikers often choose to explore Boundary Bog Trail, which penetrates the park's muskeg territory and includes carnivorous pitcher plants and dwarf stands of larch more than a century old, or the Treebeard Trail which winds through tall, aromatic groves of balsam fir and white spruce.

The park is most famous, however, for wise old Archibald Bellaney, an Englishman who came here in 1931, took the name of Grey Owl, and lived on a remote lake. **Grey Owl's Cabin ★**, a one-room log cabin on Ajawaan Lake, can only be reached by boat, canoe or – during summer – on foot via a 20km trail. Grey Owl lived here for seven years. Tours are available from park staff.

Lac La Ronge Provincial Park ★★★ (☎*800-772-4064 or 425-4244*) lies just north of Prince Albert Park on Rte. 2, providing similar scenery – and more of it, as this is the province's largest provincial park – than its more well-known neighbour. There are more than 100 lakes here, including enormous Lac La Ronge, dotted with what are said to be more than 1,000 islands. Cliffs, rock paintings and sand beaches can also be found in the park.

Additionally, Lac La Ronge Park contains one of the province's showcase historic sites, the **Holy Trinity Anglican Church Historic Site ★★★** – Saskatchewan's oldest standing building, an enormous structure in an oddly remote location. Built in the late 1850s from local wood, then completed with stained-glass windows shipped from England, the church was part of the historic Stanley Mission.

Narrow Hills Provincial Park ★★ (☎*426-2622*) lies just to the east of Prince Albert Park, although there is no direct connecting route; it can only be reached by a series of roads. It is famous for its eskers – the long, narrow glacially deposited hills that give the park its name – and more than 25 bodies of water, harbouring a number of species of game fish. One esker is topped by a fire tower, and its main building includes a small museum.

Scenic **Anglin Lake ★★**, southwest of Prince Albert Park, has at least on particularly distinguishing feature: it harbours the continent's largest nesting loon population.

Accommodations

Regina

Turgeon International Hostel
$18
K, tv, sb, ⊗
2310 McIntyre St., S4P 2S2
☎800-467-8357
☎791-8165
⇄721-2667
A great value for the guest who enjoys interacting with other travellers, this friendly hostel provides dorm rooms, a family room with space for five and a room for groups. The house once belonged to William Turgeon, an Acadian from New Brunswick who came to Regina and ran a successful law practice for many years; it was later purchased by Hostelling International and moved on a flatbed trailer.

Its location is superb – the Royal Saskatchewan Museum is visible at the end of the street – and the family room is a super bargain. There's also a huge self-catering kitchen, delightful travel library, airy television room and great manager. The neighbourhood is within walking distance of all the city's major attractions and restaurants, as well. The office is closed during the day, however, and the facility closes completely during January.

Crescent House
$50 bkfst incl.
sb
180 Angus Cr.
☎352-5995
cheryl.mogg@dlcwest.com
Crescent House is a Bed and Breakfast located on a crescent-shaped street just minutes from most of Regina's major attractions on foot. Special touches include a fireplace, three friendly terrier dogs, and a backyard shaded by 17m ash and elm trees.

Country Inns & Suites
room $76
suites $91 bkfst incl.
tv, ≡, *K,* 🐕, *P*
3321 Eastgate Bay, S4Z 1A4
☎800-456-4000
☎789-9117
⇄789-3010
This hotel chain strives to offer a more homey atmosphere than most chains; rooms are done up with brass beds and duvets resembling quilts. Most rooms have mini-bars on the honour system; all guests receive free newspapers and can make free local calls. Suites come

with a sitting room, sofa bed and microwave as well, and continental breakfast is included. Located just off Hwy. 1, at the eastern edge of town.

Chelton Suites Hotel
$79-$125
tv, ≡, ⊙, ℝ, *K*, 🐕, *P*
1907-11th Ave., S4P 0J2
☎800-667-9922
☎569-4600
⇄569-3531
The Chelton Suites Hotel rents out attractive and very spacious suites that come fully equipped with kitchenettes, desks and couches, everything you could need for a longer stay. The attractive red brick building and large windows give it a distinctive look.

Sands Resort and Hotel
$85
tv, ≡, ℜ, 🐕, ≈, ⌂, ⊙
1818 Victoria Ave., S4P 0R1
☎800-667-6500
☎569-1666
⇄352-6339
The Sands Resort and Hotel was in the process of becoming a Ramada resort at the time of our visit. Extensive renovations make this centrally located hotel one of the most attractive places to stay in Regina. Additional perks include suites with whirlpools and all the amenities expected of an upscale hotel.

Travelodge
$91
⊛, *tv*, ≡, ℜ, ≈, ⊙
4177 Albert St. S, S4S 3R6
☎800-578-7878
☎586-3443
⇄586-9311
Unlike many other hotels in this chain, Regina's Travelodge has a unique character; a California theme pervades the building, from the attractive pastel lobby with its glitzy chandelier to the fake rocks and greenery in the pool area. The rooms provide exceptional comfort, and the Hollywood-themed restaurant is sure to be a hit with the kids and star(let)s-in-the-making.

Delta Regina Hotel
$119
P, ♿, ℝ, 🐕, ⊛, ⌂
The Delta Regina Hotel offers guests luxurious accommodations, right near downtown. The rooms have a muted yet stylish decor, and most offer fine views of the city. The friendly and professional service, complete list of amenities, attractive pool area and overall elegance combine to pamper business travellers and vacationers alike.

Regina Inn Hotel and Convention Centre
$139
tv, ≡, ℜ, ⊛, ⊙, 🐕 ♿
1975 Broad St., S4P 1Y2
☎525-6767
☎800-667-8162
⇄525-3630
Another centrally located luxury hotel, its amenities include a dinner theatre, suites with whirlpools, a health club and winter plug-ins. Guests can choose from four on-site restaurants and lounges catering to fine or casual diners. All rooms have balconies.

Hotel Saskatchewan-Radisson Plaza
$134-$144
tv, ≡, ℜ, ⌂, ⊙, ⊛
2125 Victoria Ave., S4P 0S3
☎800-333-3333
☎522-7691
⇄522-8988
This hotel's fabulous location along one side of pretty Victoria Park, facing the city skyline, is only the beginning of the luxury that makes it Regina's crown jewel of accommodations. Built in 1927 by the Canadian Pacific Railroad, the hotel features such decorative notes as a chandelier from the Imperial Palace in St. Petersburg. More touches were added during a $28-million renovation in the early 1990s. There's also the original barbershop, a health club, massage therapists and an elegant dining room. How classy is it? Queen Elizabeth and Richard Chamberlain stay here whenever they're in town – not at the same time, of course – in the $995-per-night Royal Suite, where a special device heats towels as occupants bubble in the tub and the windows are fitted with bulletproof glass. It's 3,000 square feet of luxury and history.

Southern Saskatchewan

Swift Current

Heritage Inn Bed and Breakfast
$50
sb
Hwy. 4 bypass to Waker Rd., Box 1301
☎773-6305
⇄773-0135
Archaeologists and equine enthusiasts like this small Bed and Breakfast for its horses and Swift Current Petroglyph complex – both located on the property. There are two rooms containing queen-size beds, and a family-style room with a set of bunks and a single bed.

Fort Qu'Appelle

Company House Bed and Breakfast
$50-60 bkfst incl.
sb/pb
Box 159, 172 Company Ave., S0G 1S0
☎332-6333
cbbbt@sk.sympatico.ca
The Company House Bed and Breakfast is in a turn-of-the-century home with three attractive guest rooms and fully renovated bathrooms. Guests can relax by the beautiful fireplace in the living room, or in the wicker chairs on the porch. Friendly hosts Jill and Jerry Whiting are happy to share their knowledge and enthusiasm for the surrounding region with guests. Reservations recommended.

Country Squire Inn
$65
tv, ✈, *P*, ≡, ℜ
Hwy. 10, S0G 1S0
☎332-5603
⇄332-6708
Probably the best affordable hotel-motel in the Fort Qu'Appelle Valley. Big clean rooms, cheerful help and a good restaurant (see p 501) all add up to an enjoyable experience. Short hiking trails beginning behind the place climb to the top of surrounding hills. There is lounge, a bar and 'offsales' – on-premises sale of beer – here, as well.

Moose Jaw

Temple Gardens Mineral Spa Hotel and Resort
$89
tv, ≡, ℜ, ≈, ⌂, ⊙
24 Fairford St. E., Moose Jaw
☎800-718-7727
☎694-5055
⇄694-8310
This resort, tucked improbably down a sidestreet off Moose Jaw's slow-moving main drag, offers true luxuries to the dusty prairie traveller. The big open lobby gives a hint of what's to come. Regular hotel rooms here are roomy enough, with big sofas, but the 25 full suites are the real hit: king-sized beds, cotton robes, tables, enormous walk-in bathrooms and a two-person mineral water whirlpools create a romantic experience in each. Furthermore, all resort guests have free access to the resort's fourth-floor, 2000m^2 pool of mineral water. There is also a small health club featuring Nautilus machines and treadmills, a poolside café and a restaurant.

Saskatoon

Patricia Hotel Hostel
$12 members, $17 non-members
sb, ℝ
345 Second Ave. N., S7K 2B8
☎242-8861
⇄664-1119
For hostel prices, visitors get very basic accommodations in a hotel that has frankly seen better days. The advantage here is the low, low price and the location close to downtown. However, there are no kitchen facilities or special touches, save a local bar beneath the dorm rooms. Rooms are very basic, with two bunkbeds and shared washrooms. Some single rooms are available, however; these are in slightly better condition and all have a television and private bathroom (*$30 per person, $34 for two*).

Ramblin' Rose Bed and Breakfast
$45, bkst
sb/pb, tv, ⊛
Box 46, R.R. 3, S7K 3J6
☎668-4582
Located south of Saskatoon, near popular Pike Lake Provincial Park, this cedar home

offers two private suites with private baths and two with shared baths. Extras are plentiful – a whirlpool, tv/vcr, video and book library among them. Pets are welcome here, and guests are also welcome to hike any of several nature trails on the property. Rooms are comfortable, but try to book one on the main floor, rather than in the semi-basement.

Brighton House Bed and Breakfast
$45 bkfst incl.
sb/pb, tv, ⊛
1308 Fifth Ave. N, S7K 2S2
☎***664-3278***
⇄***664-6822***
brighton.house@eudoramail.com

The Brighton House Bed and Breakfast is in a lovely white clapboard house with blue and pink trim, located outside the downtown area and surrounded by a well-tended garden. All the rooms are delightfully furnished with floral prints and antiques, and the "honeymoon suite" comes with a private bathroom and sun porch. Hosts Barb and Lynne are sure to make you feel right at home. Extra touches include the family suite on the top floor, which provides ample space for children to play, and the outdoor hot tub and croquet set at guests' disposal.

Imperial 400
$59-$67
tv, K, ≡, ℜ, ≈, ⊛
610 Idylwyld Dr. N, S7L 0Z2
☎***800-781-2268***
☎***244-2901***
⇄***244-6063***

This 176-room motel features an indoor recreation complex with a whirlpool and (leaky) water-slide, and in-house movies, making it a good deal for families. Even more attractive are kitchenettes in some rooms. There is also a restaurant on premises.

Radisson Hotel Saskatoon
$84-$119
tv, ≡, ℜ, ≈, ⌂, ⊛, ♿, ⊘
405-20th St. E, S7K 6X6
☎***800-333-3333***
☎***665-3322***
⇄***665-5531***

This elegant and newly renovated high-rise luxury hotel caters to everyone: there are three executive floors and six meeting rooms, not to mention waterslides, a sauna, whirlpool and gym. Its location right on the South Saskatchewan River means good access to outdoor recreation. It includes 14 deluxe suites complete with a bar and an extra telephone connection and modem hook-up for your computer.

Delta Bessborough
$109
tv, ≡, ℜ, ≈, ⌂, ⊛, ⊘
601 Spadina Cr. E, S7K 3G8
☎***244-5521***
⇄***653-2458***

One of Saskatoon's most distinguishing landmarks, the Delta Bessborough is a former CN hotel in the *faux* French *château* style, with many turrets and gables. While the renovated lobby and restaurant do not do justice to the grand old edifice, the rooms are comfortable, if somewhat dark, and have retained such luxurious touches as the original bathroom fixtures and deep ceramic tubs. Modern conveniences such as in-room coffee makers, voicemail and hairdryers have, of course, been added. The elegant ballrooms and extensive river property are among Saskatoon's most prized sites for all kinds of functions and receptions.

Saskatoon Inn
$109-129
≡, *tv,* ≈, ⊛, ♿
2002 Airport Dr., S2L 6M4
☎***800-667-8789***
☎***242-1440***
⇄***224-2779***

Conveniently located right by the airport, the Saskatoon Inn offers spacious, attractive rooms with all the comforts and conveniences, as well as a unique recreation area with a swimming pool and ping pong table set amid a profusion of greenery traversed by winding walkways. The adjoining restaurant and lounge elaborate on the tropical theme, providing a sort of indoor oasis that is especially welcome in the dead of a northern Saskatchewan winter!

Sheraton Cavalier
$119-$129
tv, ≡, ℜ, ≈, ⌂, ⊛, ♿, ⊙, ⌂
621 Spadina Cr. E, S7K 3G9
☎800-325-3535
☎652-6770
⇄244-1739
Beautifully set on the river, the Sheraton Cavalier is a glamorous hotel with a sophisticated contemporary style. The rooms have all the comforts and conveniences, and the friendly and efficient service ensures a pleasant stay. The hotel's amenities include two indoor waterslides, a ballroom, a cigar lounge and mountain bike rentals.

The Yellowhead Highway

Manitou Beach

Manitou Springs Resort
$79
tv, ≡, ⊛, ⊙
MacLachlan Ave., S0K 4T0
☎800-667-7672
☎946-2233
⇄946-2554
An old and well-known resort in western Canada, this facility is famous for its three pools of heated mineral water drawn from Little Manitou Lake. Other services at the resort include massage therapy, reflexology, and a fitness centre.

West Central Saskatchewan

North Battleford

Battlefords Inn
$54
tv, ≡, ℜ, ≈, ⌂
11212 Railway Ave. E, S9A 2R7
☎800-691-6076
☎445-1515
⇄445-1541
Known for spacious rooms, this inn provides king- and queen-size beds, free local phone calls and free in-room coffee. Meals can be taken in the on-site restaurant, and alcohol can be purchased in the licensed beverage room.

Prince Albert

South Hill Inn
$65
tv, ≡, ℜ, ⊛
3245 Second Ave. W, S6V 5G1
☎800-363-4466
☎922-1333
⇄763-6408
Highlights of this conveniently located inn include big comfortable rooms, televisions with the option of in-house movies and free coffee. There is also a licensed restaurant on the premises.

Restaurants

Regina

Magellan's Global Coffee House
$
1800 College Ave.
☎789-0009
magellan@magellanscafe.com
A coffee place in a remodelled fieldstone house at the edge of Wascana Park, Magellan's Global Coffee House is where the upwardly mobile congregate for their java fix.

Bushwakker
$-$$
closed Sun
2206 Dewdney Ave.
☎359-7276
A fun brewpub on the edge of an industrial area. Locals don't think twice about motoring over here to try the latest batch of Harvest Ale or some other concoction, buffered by a fancy hamburger or other typical bar fare. The bar also offers offsales (small and very large bottles of the brewery's beer) in addition to the usual taps.

Heliotrope
$-$$
2204 McIntyre St.
☎569-3373
Heliotrope is the only vegetarian restaurant in Saskatchewan, and quite possibly one of

the best in all Canada. The chairs and tables in this brick house are cozy. In the winter a fireplace keeps things warm, and in summer there's a great outdoor patio. Entrees are expertly handled, everything from lunches of falafel, vegetables and burgers to dinners of Moroccan stew, Thai curries and *gado gado.* Dessert is a real stunner, with in-season fruit cheesecake and homemade gelato that consists only of fresh fruit and water.

Brown Sugar
$$
closed Sun
1941 Scarth St.
☎359-7355
A Caribbean eatery in the middle of the prairies? Absolutely. This blue-trimmed place, decorated in Caribbean prints, delivers authentic rotis (meat-filled pastry pockets), jerk chicken and dishes like fish cutter (fish on a bun) and ackee and salt fish that are otherwise impossible to find in western Canada. There's a great selection of imported Caribbean soft drinks and home-made libations such as ginger beer, mauby, sorrel and banana cow to consider, as well. The meal isn't over until the knockout tropical ice cream has been tasted.

Cathedral Village Free House
$$
2062 Albert St.
☎359-1661
Filling contemporary fare from all over the map – a concept that doesn't always work, but satisfies some of the time. Lunch might consist of straightforward buffalo burgers, salads, stir-fried vegetables, wood-fired oven pizza and the like; dinner leans toward pasta and other Italian dishes. The place gets extra points for having eight beers on tap. The crowd here is young and hip despite the stodgy name, possibly explaining the erratic service; at least the location is central, and the decor, with bold colours and tiled floor, is welcoming.

Neo Japonica
$$
2167 Hamilton St.
☎359-7669
The all-around most charming restaurant in Regina, Neo Japonica serves exquisite Japanese cuisine in a small, unassuming house with an inviting decor. The food's artistic presentation is matched only by its expert preparation. If you order the special plate you can sample the teriyaki chicken, vegetable and shrimp tempura, nigri sushi and Japanese tea for under $10. Homemade green tea and ginger ice cream are the perfect finale for any meal.

Danbry's
$$-$$$
1925 Victoria Ave.
☎525-8777
⇄525-3635
Danbry's successfully blends the luxurious historic character of one of Canada's oldest private clubs, which used to be located here, with contemporary style. From the wood-panelled main dining room to private dining rooms, a lounge and cigar lounge, care has been taken to maintain an atmosphere of comfort and sophistication. The menu features such delicacies as grilled salmon and asparagus salad with dijon dressing and roasted duck with sour cherry sauce. The service is exceptionally friendly.

Orleans
$$$
1907 11th Ave.
☎525-3636
A dash of Cajun cuisine on a busy downtown street, you'll find a sampling of the dishes that make the real New Orleans a mouth-watering destination; jambalaya, gumbo and *étoufée*, are all on the menu. Unfortunately, the original recipes have been somewhat altered to cater to North American tastes. However, the special dijon sauce (not listed on the menu – ask your server) and live jazz on Wednesdays make this place worthwhile.

Southern Saskatchewan

Fort Qu'Appelle

The Country Squire
$$
Hwy. 10
☎332-5603
⇌332-6708
Attached to the inn of the same name, this restaurant serves tasty, hearty portions in a convivial atmosphere; locals often drop by for a bite of grilled salmon, burgers (choose from elk, bison, hamburger or ostrich!), salad or fish and chips.

Caronport

The Pilgrim
$-$$
7am to 11pm
Trans-Canada Hwy. 1
☎756-3335
Yet another restaurant in a gas station, this one is located in the small town of Caronport, just west of Moose Jaw. This place serves family fare and a salad bar. Its reputation for hearty prairie cooking and a 60-item salad and soup bar is solid.

Saskatoon

The Original Bulk Cheese Warehouse
732 Broadway Ave.
☎652-8008
The Original Bulk Cheese Warehouse is the place to load up on picnic provisions like from samosas, quiche, salads, fresh shrimp cocktails, desserts, and, of course, an impressive selection of cheeses, including a local buffalo mozzarella.

Chocolatier Bernard Callebaut
$
125 Second Ave. N.
☎652-0909
Right in the centre of downtown Saskatoon, a small Canadian chain based in Calgary serves up artful cream chocolates and bars of baking chocolate made of all-natural ingredients. A special treat here are the hand-dipped chocolate ice cream bars – delicious beyond words, and only a few dollars apiece.

Broadway Café
$
814 Broadway Ave.
☎652-8244
This restaurant is located right in the heart of Saskatoon's hippest district. However, that's a bit misleading: this is merely a diner that serves up burgers, eggs and the like to swarms of locals. The snappy service is cheerful but a bit off-putting out here in laid-back Saskatchewan, and daring entrées should definitely be avoided. Diners will also want to note that the owner does not accept credit cards. Nevertheless, an authentic local experience.

Emily's Jazz
$
616 10th St. E
☎664-1953
Emily's Jazz, just off Broadway, is a small, inviting neighbourhood café with pretty blue walls and mismatched wooden furniture. Enjoy delicious home-made food such as borscht (Ukrainian beet soup), perogies and healthy sandwiches in a homey atmosphere. The melt-in-your-mouth flapper pie is sensational! The service is very friendly, and there is live jazz here on some nights.

Michel's Montreal Smoked Meats
$
closed Sun
101-129 Second Ave. N
☎384-6664
Fortuitously placed right next to Saskatoon's Belgian chocolate shop, this enterprising French-Canadian tries to match Montréal quality from 3,000km away – and nearly succeeds. The peppery smoked meat, stuffed between two slices of rye bread and embellished with generous squirts of mustard, doesn't have quite the bite of its Québec counterpart, but it's still very good. Other great touches include home-made sour pickles, a very basic (and therefore good and crunchy) coleslaw, and black-cherry cola and spruce beer imported from Quebec.

Wanuskewin Café
$
R.R 4
☎*931-6767*
Located in the native heritage park of the same name, just north of Saskatoon, this little café offers a good quick sampling of native-style cookery. Entrées aren't large here but they are tasty; the fare ranges from a warming, hearty cup of bison stew with a side of bannock (bread), to bison with wild rice. Dessert offerings include pastries featuring the tart local Saskatoon berry, while the line of First Nation soft drinks – bottled by an Aboriginal-owned company – are among the beverages offered.

Berry Barn
$-$$
830 Valley Rd.
☎*978-9797*
Located approximately 10km south of the city, the Berry Barn makes for a pleasant excursion to the country. Saskatoon berry bushes line the parking lot, hinting at the delights to come: berry pies, waffles, syrup and tea accompany hearty meals of perogies and farmer's sausage. The rustic pine-finished dining room has a great view of the river. After your meal you can browse in the gift shop for still more berry products or pick some berries yourself at the you-pick farm. Reservations recommended.

Genesis
$-$$
901D 22nd St. W., Saskatoon
☎*244-5516*
Widely acclaimed as Saskatoon's best healthy food, the menu leans toward Chinese food and macrobiotic cooking. Dim sum is available at lunchtime.

Mykonos
$$-$$$
416-21st St. E.
☎*244-2499*
Mykonos serves the usual kebabs, seafood, lamb and moussaka, but the overall flavour is not exactly authentic. The formal dining room has a maritime décor that is attractive, though, like the food, not exactly Greek. Overpriced, but still one of the better restaurants in town. The friendly service adds to the dining experience.

Saskatoon Station Place
$$-$$$
221 South Idylwyld Dr.
☎*244-7777*
Saskatoon Station Place draws guests with its railway motif; plush dining cars with mahogany trim surround a mock train station. While the Belle Epoque reigns supreme in the decor, the restaurant service and menu is more family-style, and dishes cover the basics of burgers, steak and pasta. Still, a good choice for an evening out. Be sure to stop in at the lounge for a pre-dinner drink.

Tarragon's Restaurant
$$$
closed Mon
119 Third Ave. S.
☎*664-3599*
Tarragon's is Saskatoon's most lauded restaurant. Owner and chef David Powell concocts such delights as Alaskan King Crab, Gazpacho and Gulf Shrimp Provençale for guests to enjoy in the spacious, multi-level dining room.

West Central Saskatchewan

North Battleford

DaVinci's Ristorante Italiano
$$
1001 Hwy. 16
☎*446-4700*
Leonardo himself might be surprised that the menu here is not exclusively Italian. Traditional Louisiana and continental European dishes are served.

Prince Albert

Amy's on Second
$$
2990 Second Ave.
☎*763-1515*
Fresh ingredients and a healthy approach to cooking make this restaurant a popular switch from the many local fast-food joints. Salads are made to order, and come with home-made soups. Also featured are steak, chicken and pasta dishes.

Entertainment

Regina

The **Buffalo Days** festival occupies one week each summer, usually beginning in late July and lasting into early August. Festivities kick off with a Sunday picnic in lovely Wascana Park; from there, it's on to a raft of shows and, eventually, fireworks.

Southern Saskatchewan

Saskatoon

Most of the pubs and clubs in Saskatoon are concentrated along Second Avenue South.

The **SaskTel Saskatchewan Jazz Festival** (☎*652-1421*) brings world-class jazz, gospel and world music to Saskatoon's riverbanks for 11 days each June. Musicians range from international stars to local artists. Some performances are held in the Delta Bessborough Gardens, adjacent to the landmark hotel. The **Great Northern River Roar** is either an abomination or a great time, depending on your opinion of powerboats tearing up and down the river. Either way, there's no avoiding these races when they arrive in Saskatoon each July. Some 60,000 spectators are said to watch as the powerboats charge around courses at speeds of up to 225km/h.

Shopping

Regina

Shopping is concentrated downtown, with the **Scarth Street Mall** the usual starting point. All the major stores are nearby.

Saskatoon

Shopping in Saskatoon is easy, with several downtown malls and streets dedicated to the activity. Perhaps the most popular area is the **Bayside Mall** (*225 Second Ave. N*), next to and including The Bay department store. The **Midtown Plaza**, on First Avenue South between 22nd St. E and 20th St. E, is another good option. **Second Avenue South** is the place to go for all the pubs, clubs and street life.

Manitoba

Mention the word Manitoba and two images swiftly come to mind: professional hockey's Winnipeg Jets, who don't even reside here anymore, and polar bears – which definitely do.

The popular impression of Manitoba seems to be that it is mostly a place for passing through. But in fact, visitors have been coming to Manitoba – and staying – for more than a century, swelling its capital city of Winnipeg into Canada's fourth-largest city and creating a surprising mix of immigrant culture more diverse than anywhere else between Vancouver and Toronto.

In the beginning, the province was occupied by several Aboriginal groups. It was they who gave the province its name: Manitou was a highly revered spirit among the First Nations who lived there, and the rapids of Lake Manitoba were believed to be his voice.

Once the English and French arrived, however, the story of Manitoba swiftly became the story of a running feud between two rival fur-trading companies: the English-owned Hudson's Bay Company on the one hand and the French-Indian North West Company – which emerged later and, for a time, successfully competed against the British – on the other.

The French-Canadian explorer Pierre de la Vérendrye made quite a mark on the region's fur trade. La Vérendrye was the first European to penetrate the grasslands of Manitoba; his trading posts established populations in what would eventually become the communities of Dauphin, The Pas, Selkirk and Portage la Prairie. This French influence is still evident today; in fact, the eastern Winnipeg suburb of St. Boniface, which was a separate city before it was amalgamated in 1972, is the largest French settlement in Canada outside of Québec.

The Metis made up a considerable part of this French-speaking population. The descendants of French trappers and Aboriginal people, the French-speaking, Catholic Metis lived on the Red and Assiniboine Rivers, in settlements which were annexed to Canada in 1869. Fearing for their language, education, land and religious rights, they were led by Louis Riel in their pursuit of responsible government for the territory. What little they had was slowly being taken away, leading settlers, both white and Metis, to set up their own provisional government.

The outrage over the trial and execution of Ontarian Orangeman Thomas Scott for defying the authority of the said government forced Riel into exile in the United States. He did return to Canada, to Saskatchewan this time, to continue his fight and lead the Northwest Rebellion. Riel, the man who might have been the first premier of Manitoba, was executed for treason in 1885 and has been seen as a martyr by many ever since.

There are also considerable Ukrainian and Mennonite influences in Manitoba, as well as a sizeable population of Icelandic immigrants. The beginning of the latter influx can be precisely dated: in 1875 a string of volcanic eruptions drove Icelanders to North America in search of another home. Many of them settled in the Interlake district, on the shores of Lakes Winnipeg and Manitoba, where they traded in their skills at saltwater fishing for the taking of whitefish.

Manitobans have gone to great lengths to preserve all these immigrants' stories, keeping their history alive through numerous museums and historic parks.

It is certainly true that the southern portion of the province is flat, levelled by great glaciers during the most recent Ice Age. Where thousands of square kilometres of uninterrupted tallgrass prairie once rolled under the press of the wind, colourful fields of hard wheat, flax, canola and sunflowers thrive today. In wet areas, pocket marshes teeming with resident and migrating waterfowl replace the fields.

But whatever Manitoba lacks in varied topography it makes up for with its fertile farmland and immense lakes that are home to countless birds. In fact, only about 40% of the province is flat. The rest is comprised of hills and waterways carved out of the Canadian Shield, a mass of hard ancient rock surrounding Hudson Bay that surfaces most obviously here and in northern Ontario. This land is shot through with deep pine forests, cliffs, and lakes; it is not unusual to see elk, caribou and bears in this rugged landscape.

In the sparsely populated far north, tundra becomes predominant and the wildlife grows more spectacular still, with the singular light of the luminous sub-Arctic summers, white whales and polar bears.

Finding Your Way Around

By Plane

Winnipeg International Airport is situated surprisingly close to the downtown area, only about 5km away.

Two major airlines handle traffic from both coasts: **Air Canada** (☎*943-9361*) and **Canadian Airlines** (☎*632-1250*) are both located in the airport.

By Bus

Greyhound Canada (☎*800-661-8747*) runs to the major towns and cities. In Winnipeg, the terminal is located at the corner of Portage Avenue and Colony Street.

By Train

VIA Rail's (☎*800-561-8630 from western Canada*) cross-country Canadian service passes through the province, usually stopping in Winnipeg around 5pm (westbound) or 12:50pm (eastbound); if the train is on time, it can be an excellent way to arrive in Winnipeg before dinner. Winnipeg's grand **Union Station** (*132 Main St.*), located right in the centre of downtown at the major intersection of Broadway and Main Street, is the largest station in Manitoba and the usual stopping point.

Smaller stations are located in Brandon, Portage la Prairie and other towns roughly parallel to the Trans-Canada Highway.

Public Transportation

Winnipeg Transit (☎*986-5054*), located in an underground facility at the corner of Portage and Main, runs a decent bus system around the city; rides cost $1.55, slightly less if purchased in bulk-ticket blocks. The city also maintains a transit information line (☎*986-5700*).

Taxis

Unicity (☎*947-6611*) is the main taxi company in Winnipeg.

Practical Information

Area Code: ***204***.

Tourist Information

Winnipeg Tourism
279 Portage Ave., Winnipeg
☎(800) 665-0204
☎943-1970
www.tourism.winnipeg.mb.ca
Winnipeg Tourism runs a year-round information centre that is open weekdays all year, and seven days a week during the summer months.

Manitoba Travel Ideas Centre
Travel Manitoba, 24 Forks Market Rd., Winnipeg, R3C 3H8
☎(800) 665-0040
☎945-3777
www.travelmanitoba.com
The Manitoba Ideas Centre, beside The Forks Market, is open year round and has longer hours. In other parts of the province, tourism office hours vary a great deal, but the larger ones are open year round.

Post Office

The main **post office** (*266 Graham Ave.,* ☎*987-5054*) is located right downtown.

Safety

Manitoba is generally safe, although much of downtown Winnipeg becomes deserted after dark, so some caution is advised. The city's police department maintains 17 stations in six districts around the city; dial ***911*** for emergencies. There is also a **Royal Canadian Mounted Police** detachment (*1091 Portage Ave.,* ☎*983-5420*) in the city.

The **Canadian Automobile Association** maintains offices in the province's most populous areas, offering roadside assistance and information to members. Its offices are located at:

Winnipeg
870 Empress St.
☎987-6161
501 St. Anne's Rd.
☎987-6201
1353 McPhillips St.
☎987-6226

Brandon
20-1300 18th St.
☎727-1394

Altona
61 Second Ave. NE
☎324-8474

Climate

Summers are warm and dry. Winter, however, can bring dangerously low temperatures and blinding snowstorms; temperatures can plunge to below -30°C, with the windchill making it feel even colder. Thus, you should take the necessary precautions, especially if you are planning to drive outside of town in the winter. For updated weather forecast information in Winnipeg, call ☎*983-2050*.

Exploring

Downtown Winnipeg

Manitoba boasts the largest city in the prairies: Winnipeg, a bona fide metropolis of more than 700,000, it rises improbably from the plains at the convergence of three rivers; it is the likely starting point for most visitors' journeys around the province.

The city was settled by a Scotsman named Thomas Douglas, fifth Earl of Selkirk, as a $187,000km^2$ settlement called the Red River Colony (a monument at the end of Alexander Avenue marks the exact spot). Douglas was an emissary of the Hudson's Bay Company.

All roads in Winnipeg seem to lead to **The Forks** ★★ (*behind Union Station, corner of Mark St. And Broadway Ave.*), which have always been a focal point

Getting to Northen Manitoba

Special arrangements are required to reach Manitoba's far north. VIA Rail runs regular trains from Winnipeg to Churchill three times a week, taking a full day and two nights each way.

Canadian Airlines and its partner **Calm Air** (☎*632-1250*) operate regularly scheduled flights from Winnipeg everyday except Saturday year-round; in autumn, during polar bear season, there are additional flights on weekends.

Once in Churchill, a variety of charter air and bus services can be hired for excursions out onto the tundra.

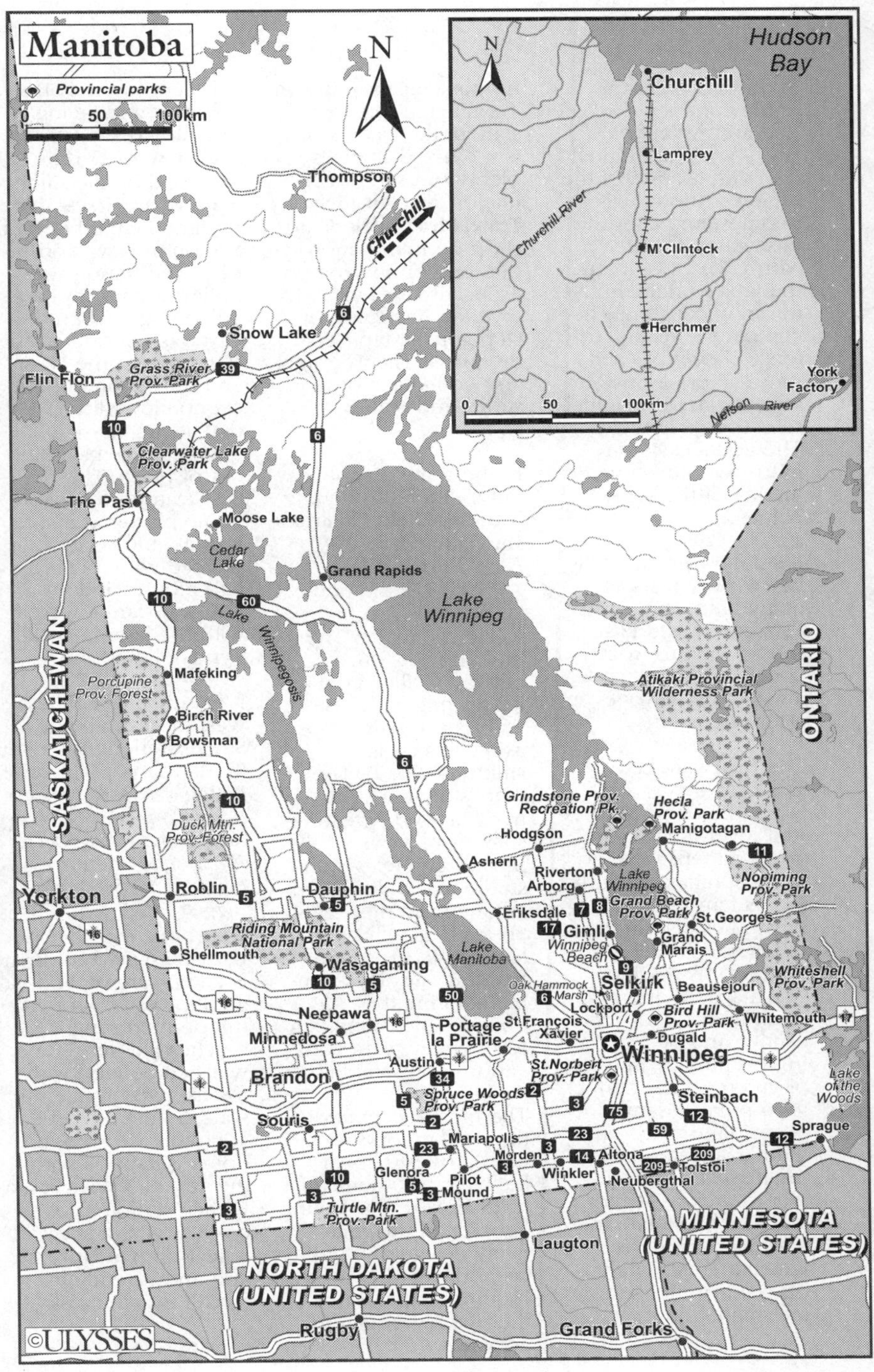

Manitoba
Provincial parks
0
50
100km
N
Hudson Bay
Churchill
Lamprey
Churchill River
M'Clintock
Herchmer
York Factory
Nelson River
Thompson
Churchill
Snow Lake
Flin Flon
Grass River Prov. Park
Clearwater Lake Prov. Park
The Pas
Moose Lake
Cedar Lake
Grand Rapids
Lake Winnipeg
Lake Winnipegosis
SASKATCHEWAN
ONTARIO
Mafeking
Porcupine Prov. Forest
Birch River
Bowsman
Atikaki Provincial Wilderness Park
Duck Mtn. Prov. Forest
Grindstone Prov. Recreation Pk.
Hecla Prov. Park
Manigotagan
Hodgson
Ashern
Riverton
Arborg
Lake Winnipeg
Grand Beach Prov. Park
Nopiming Prov. Park
Yorkton
Roblin
Dauphin
Eriksdale
Gimli
St.Georges
Riding Mountain National Park
Shellmouth
Lake Manitoba
Winnipeg Beach
Grand Marais
Wasagaming
Selkirk
Beausejour
Whiteshell Prov. Park
Oak Hammock Marsh
Lockport
Bird Hill Prov. Park
Whitemouth
Neepawa
Minnedosa
Portage la Prairie
St.François Xavier
Dugald
Winnipeg
Austin
Brandon
St.Norbert Prov. Park
Lake of the Woods
Spruce Woods Prov. Park
Steinbach
Souris
Sprague
Mariapolis
Morden
Altona
Winkler
Tolstoi
Glenora
Pilot Mound
Neubergthal
Turtle Mtn. Prov. Park
MINNESOTA (UNITED STATES)
Laugton
NORTH DAKOTA (UNITED STATES)
Rugby
Grand Forks
©ULYSSES

in the province: this fertile confluence of the Red and Assiniboine rivers was the original camping ground of the region's Aboriginal peoples, and later the base camp for the North West Company, the area's original fur-trapping concern. The company's headquarters (*77 Main St.*) still stand across a busy street from the original site. Today, however, The Forks is synonymous with the covered market of the same name.

Inside, dozens of stalls house purveyors of everything from fresh fish, candy and East-Indian food to frozen yogurt and handmade jewellery. There's even a fortune teller.

The riverwalk takes you on a lovely stroll along the banks of the Red River, and gives you a superb view of Saint Boniface, including its famous basilica, which lies just on the other side. There are many picnic-perfect green spaces and a small marina that rents canoes and pedal-boats in the summer, and lots of green spaces perfect for a picnic. Many events take place on the plaza just outside the market, in the summer as well as winter, and several restaurants have terraces here, which are extremely pleasant on hot summer nights.

In the adjacent Johnson Terminal, a former rail station, the city's tourism office dispenses plenty of useful information. The **Manitoba Travel Idea Centre** ★ is short on information but long on inspiration, especially for kids, who love the intriguing (if strangely juxtaposed) dioramas. The Terminal also contains more stores and coffee shops.

In the same complex but a different building is the **Manitoba Children's Museum** ★★★ (*$4; 45 Forks Market Rd., ☎956-5437*), the only children's museum in western Canada. The building was once a railway facility, containing an engine house and train repair shops as well as a blacksmith's shop. Today, there's a whimsical hand at work, creating such displays as a fully functioning television studio and a diesel engine from the 1950s. Sports fans will be interested in the "Goals for Kids" display, commemorating the now-defunct Winnipeg Jets hockey team with various memorabilia.

The most recent addition to the Forks are the CanWest Global ballpark and the Manitoba Theatre For Young People, an imaginatively designed building on Forks Market Road. Inquire within about their family-oriented activities.

Adjacent to the Forks complex and facing downtown sits **Union Station** ★ (*132 Main St.*), designed by the same team of architects that designed Grand Central Station in New York City. The station was built during Winnipeg's golden age, when the city was considered the "Gateway to the West," and thus an important economic centre. Today, its impressive grandeur seems a little out of place. The station features a huge dome plastered inside in pink and white, pierced with arching half-moon windows. The walls are covered with the famous local Tyndall limestone.

It is only a few blocks west up Assiniboine Street or along the river to Manitoba's **Legislative Building** ★★★ (*free admission, Jul to Sep every day, 9am to 6pm, Oct to Jun Mon to Fri by appointment; 450 Broadway, ☎945-5813*). This is where the province's parliamentary business is taken care of, and it's an impressive property, full of interesting touches like limestone walls embedded with fossils, two bronze bisons, a bust of Cartier and more. Up top, the dome is capped with the 4m-tall **Golden Boy**, a French sculpture of a boy carrying a sheaf of wheat underneath one arm and extending a torch toward the sky

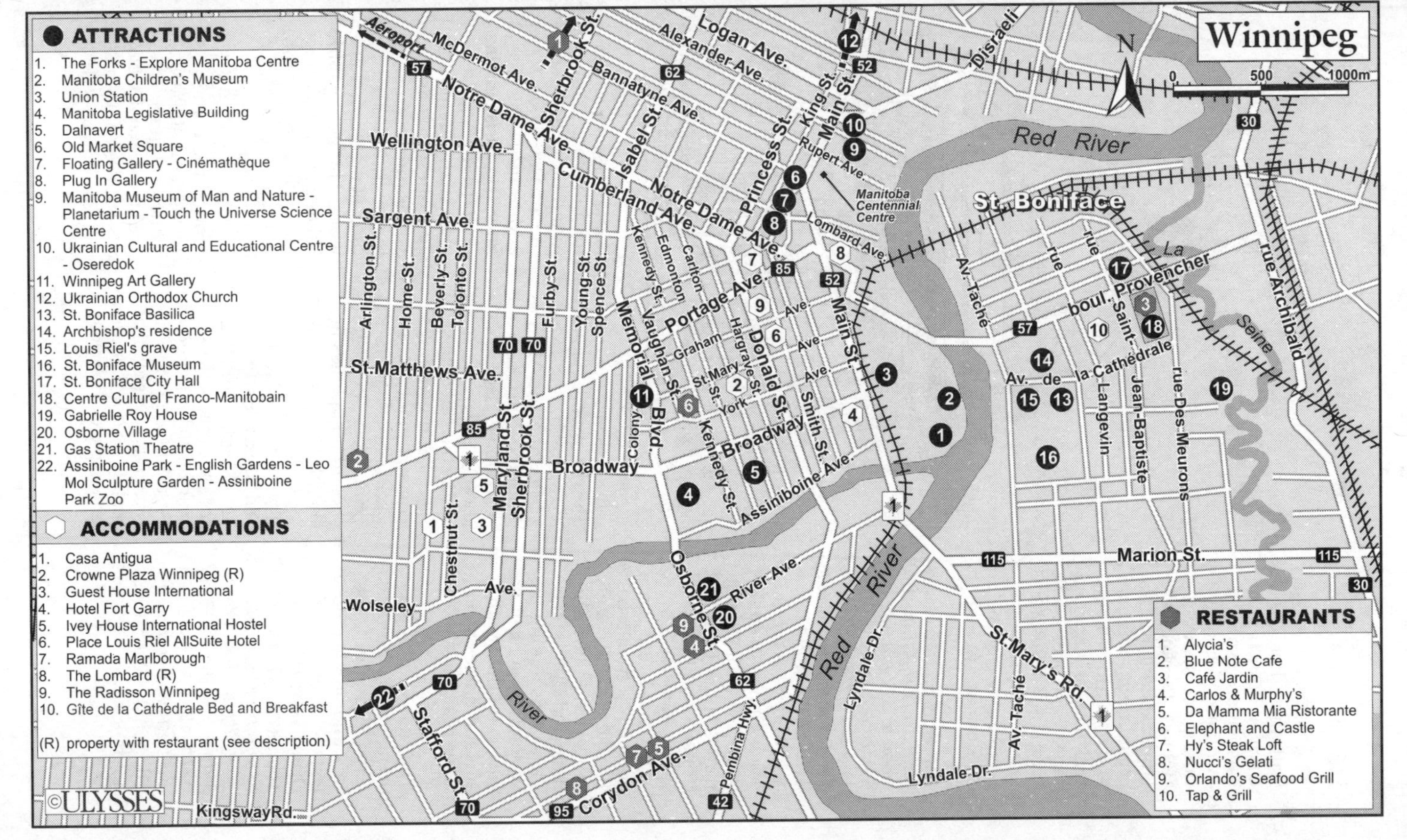

Winnipeg
N
0
500
1000m
ATTRACTIONS
1. The Forks - Explore Manitoba Centre
2. Manitoba Children's Museum
3. Union Station
4. Manitoba Legislative Building
5. Dalnavert
6. Old Market Square
7. Floating Gallery - Cinémathèque
8. Plug In Gallery
9. Manitoba Museum of Man and Nature - Planetarium - Touch the Universe Science Centre
10. Ukrainian Cultural and Educational Centre - Oseredok
11. Winnipeg Art Gallery
12. Ukrainian Orthodox Church
13. St. Boniface Basilica
14. Archbishop's residence
15. Louis Riel's grave
16. St. Boniface Museum
17. St. Boniface City Hall
18. Centre Culturel Franco-Manitobain
19. Gabrielle Roy House
20. Osborne Village
21. Gas Station Theatre
22. Assiniboine Park - English Gardens - Leo Mol Sculpture Garden - Assiniboine Park Zoo
ACCOMMODATIONS
1. Casa Antigua
2. Crowne Plaza Winnipeg (R)
3. Guest House International
4. Hotel Fort Garry
5. Ivey House International Hostel
6. Place Louis Riel AllSuite Hotel
7. Ramada Marlborough
8. The Lombard (R)
9. The Radisson Winnipeg
10. Gîte de la Cathédrale Bed and Breakfast
(R) property with restaurant (see description)
RESTAURANTS
1. Alycia's
2. Blue Note Cafe
3. Café Jardin
4. Carlos & Murphy's
5. Da Mamma Mia Ristorante
6. Elephant and Castle
7. Hy's Steak Loft
8. Nucci's Gelati
9. Orlando's Seafood Grill
10. Tap & Grill
Aéroport
McDermot Ave.
Sherbrook St.
Logan Ave.
Alexander Ave.
Bannatyne Ave.
Notre Dame Ave.
Wellington Ave.
Isabel St.
Cumberland Ave.
Princess St.
King St.
Main St.
Rupert Ave.
Manitoba Centennial Centre
Lombard Ave.
Disraeli
Red River
St. Boniface
Sargent Ave.
Arlington St.
Home St.
Beverly St.
Toronto St.
Furby St.
Young St.
Spence St.
Kennedy St.
Edmonton
Carlton
Portage Ave.
Graham
Hargrave St.
Donald St.
Ave.
St.Mary
York
Smith St.
St.Matthews Ave.
Memorial Blvd.
Vaughan St.
Colony
Broadway
Maryland St.
Assiniboine Ave.
Chestnut St.
Wolseley Ave.
Osborne St.
River Ave.
River
Stafford St.
Corydon Ave.
Pembina Hwy.
Kingsway Rd.
Av. Taché
rue
boul. Provencher
La Seine
rue Archibald
Saint-
Av. de la Cathédrale
Langevin
Jean-Baptiste
rue Des Meurons
Marion St.
St.Mary's Rd.
Lyndale Dr.
Red River
©ULYSSES

with the other. Guided tours in French and English are available throughout the day during the summer. Behind "the Leg" are landscaped gardens containing a fountain and a statue of Louis Riel. The original and more controversial sculpture of this Metis leader now stands across the river, behind St. Boniface College.

Manitoba's Legislative Building

Dalnavert ★ (*$4; closed Mon and Fri, Jun to Aug noon to 4:30pm, Sep to Dec and Mar to May noon to 4:30pm, Jan and Feb Sat and Sun noon to 4:30; 61 Carlton St., ☎943-2835*) is an old brick Queen-Anne-Revival-style home built for Sir Hugh John Macdonald, son of former Prime Minister John A. Macdonald, and former premier of Manitoba. Its interest lies mainly in its period furnishings, and in the fact that it was among the very first homes in the city to be built with such amenities as indoor plumbing.

The best way to get acquainted with downtown Winnipeg's history and architecture is to take one of the **Exchange District Walking Tours** (*Closed Mon, May to Sep every hour 10am to 3pm, depart from Old Market Square; $5; ☎942-6716, ⇌943-8741; exchbiz@mb.sympatico.ca*). The tours are 1.5 to 2 hours long.

The **Exchange District** ★★★, close to downtown, northwest of Portage and Main, is Winnipeg's former warehouse district – though today the smart industrial buildings have been given fresh coats of paint and new occupants, such as print shops, bookstores, theatre companies and the like have moved in.

The district surrounds **Old Market Square**, a small park with a stage for outdoor performances. The Fringe Festival (see p 533) is one of the events that makes use of this urban greenspace each year.

Some of the most striking buildings can be found by walking in the area of Albert Street and Notre Dame Avenue. The **Paris Building** (*269 Portage Ave.*) features many architectural flourishes such as scrolls, urns, Cupid figurines and other ornamental terra cotta work. The nearby **Birks Building**, across Portage (*at Smith St. and Portage Ave.*) displays an Egyptian mosaic.

Around the corner, away from the busy traffic of Portage Avenue, the **Alexander Block** (*78-86 Albert St.*) was the first Edwardian-style construction in the neighbourhood and the only residence built here in that style; it was once a businessman's home. Finally, a few paces up Albert, the spectacular **Notre Dame Chambers** (*213 Notre Dame Ave.*), also known as the Electric Railway Chambers Building, is a terra cotta building with arches along the top, lit up brightly with some 6,000 white lights at night.

The Exchange District is also home to a number of small, independent galleries that specialize in contemporary art. Among these, the **Floating Gallery** (*218-100 Arthur St.; ☎942-8183*) is notable for its photograph exhibits. The gallery is located right on Old Market Square, in the Artspace building which also houses the **Cinematheque**, a venue for independent films. You can always find truly avant-garde multimedia installations in the no-frills warehouse space at the **Plug In Gallery** (*286 McDermot Ave., ☎942-1043, www.plugin.mb.ca*), only a few blocks away.

The city's finest museums are also very close to the Exchange District. Located within a complex of science attractions in the same downtown building, the **Manitoba Museum of Man and Nature** ★★★ (*$5; mid-May to early Sep 10am to 6pm; rest of the year, Tue to Fri 10am to 4pm, Sat, Sun, Mon and holidays 10am to 5pm; 190 Rupert Ave., ☎956-2830*), is Winnipeg's showcase museum, a tour-de-force emphasizing Manitoba's natural and social history. Separate galleries teach the visitor about the province's geology, grasslands ecology, Arctic ecology – a polar bear diorama is the star here – and Aboriginal history. Other special exhibit rooms describe the voyage of the English ship the **Nonsuch** (which established the Hudson's Bay Company's presence in western Canada in 1670) with a replica of the ship, which visitors can board to explore the cabins and deck, and the construction of the railroad to the far northern Manitoba port town of Churchill.

The tour ends with a very popular and well-designed two-storey recreation of late-1800s downtown Winnipeg, including a cobbler, chapel, movie theatre and much more. Museum officials are excited about a new display slated to open in May 2000, show-casing an impressive number of Hudson's Bay Company items; but even before it arrives this museum is still a must-see. Other attractions on the lower floor of the same building include a **Planetarium** (*$4; Tue to Fri 3pm Sat to Sun 11am to 4pm; high season, every day, 11am to 6pm, ☎943-3139*) and the **Touch the Universe Science Centre** (*same hours as museum; $4*), where visitors can learn about science and technology through "hands-on" activities. It is especially popular with children.

Nearby, the **Ukrainian Cultural and Educational Centre** ★★ (*free; Tue to Sat 10am to 4pm, Sun 2pm to 5pm; 184 Alexander Ave. E., ☎942-0218*), also known as **Oseredok**, houses a number of Ukrainian-related services and exhibits under one roof, including a library, art gallery, gift shop and outreach program offices. The museum, located on the fifth floor, shows typical Ukrainian-decorated Easter eggs and other folk arts such as carving and embroidery.

Housed in a striking triangular building of pale limestone, the **Winnipeg Art Gallery** ★★ (*$4, every day 11am to 5pm; free admission Wed 11am to 9pm; Winter closed Mon; 300 Memorial Blvd., ☎786-6641*) is best known for its vast collection of Inuit art and sculptures. Founded in 1912, the museum boasts everything from 16th-century Flemish tapestry to modern art; it is particularly strong on Canadian artists, decorative porcelains and silver, and collections acquired from the Federal Department of Indian and Northern Affairs and the Hudson's Bay Company. Aboriginal works are displayed in changing exhibits on the mezzanine level. There is an interesting gift shop, as well as a pleasant rooftop restaurant with a terrace, open only at lunch.

In the city's north end, on north Main Street, the **Ukrainian Orthodox Church ★★** is one of the city's most distinctive landmarks, decked in handsome burgundy and gold paint and possessing the trademark Ukrainian dome

St. Boniface

Just across the Red River in St. Boniface, the distinctive ruins of the **St. Boniface Cathedral ★★★** (*190 Ave. de la Cathédrale*) are a must-see. The walls are all that remain of the church, which burned in 1968, but they are still very impressive. This was actually the fourth cathedral to stand on this spot. No wonder it remains a kind of shrine for Canada's largest French-speaking population outside of Quebec. The giant circular opening in the stone once contained a giant roseate stained-glass window. The beautiful **Archbishop's residence** (*141 Ave. de la Cathédrale*) right next door is one of the oldest remaining stone buildings in western Canada.

In the cemetery in front of the basilica, **Louis Riel's grave** is marked by a simple red stone that belies the renown of the man who lies beneath it. Other stones on the lawn mark the graves of French settlers and Metis, including Chief One Arrow. There's also a glorious view of the river and the city skyline from this vantage point.

Behind the cathedral stands the silver-domed **St. Boniface College** (*200 Ave. de la Cathédrale*), established in the 1800s. A scultpure of Louis Riel stands at its northern entrance.

Next door to the cathedral, the **St. Boniface Museum ★★** (*$2; Jul to Sep Mon to Fri 9am to 5pm, Sat 10am to 4pm, Sun 10am to 8pm, closed weekends Oct to Jun; 494 Tache Ave., St. Boniface; ☎237-4500*) was built as a convent in 1846 and tells a number of fascinating stories about the city's French roots; it is the oldest building in Winnipeg and its largest log structure. Of particular note is the tale of the four Grey Nuns (*Les Soeurs Grises*) who founded the convent – they travelled some 2,400km by canoe from Montréal, taking nearly two full months to complete the arduous journey.

Other highlights in the museum include holy-water vessels and church objects, and western Canada's oldest statue, a papier mâché Virgin Mary, decked in a blue shawl. It was crafted by the artistic Sister Lagrave, one of the original Grey Nuns.

Strolling north along the river brings you to the Provencher Bridge where you can stop for a snack at the crêperie located right in the middle of the bridge, in the former gatehouse. The bridge leads onto Provencher Boulevard, the main shopping and entertainment area in St. Boniface, lined with some interesting shops and locales. The old **St. Boniface City Hall** (*219 Provencher Blvd.*) and the modern **Centre Culturel Franco-manitobain** (*340 Provencher Blvd.*) are located on this street.

Fans of Gabrielle Roy can see the house in which she grew up and where several of her works, including one of her most famous novels, *Rue Deschambault*, are set. Distinguished by a commemorative plaque, the **Gabrielle Roy House** at 375 Rue Deschambault cannot be toured, as it is a private home.

East of St. Boniface, on the edge of the city, sits the ultra-modern **Royal Canadian Mint** ★ (*May to Aug Mon to Fri, 9am to 4pm; Sep to Apr Mon to Fri 10am to 2pm; 520 Lagimodière Blvd., ☎257-3359*), where all of Canada's circulation coinage is minted. Tours and observation areas give insight into the process.

Greater Winnipeg

South of the Assiniboine River but easily accessible from Memorial Boulevard by crossing the Osborne Bridge, **Osborne Village** is considered by some the city's hippest address, with its trendy shops and restaurants. People come here to browse or meet for coffee, or to take in one of the varied shows at the **Gas Station Theatre** (*454 River Ave., ☎284-9477*) which hosts everything from live theatre to music, contemporary dance and improv comedy.

Assiniboine Park ★★ (*☎986-6921*) is a popular walking and cycling destination. Its extensive tree-lined paths wind along the river of the same name, and are surrounded by wide open lawns where families come to picnic or play frisbee. During the winter, you can skate to piped music on the **Duck Pond**, or use the cross-country ski trails.

The park's **English Gardens** are a wonderful surprise when in bloom: colourful carpets of daisies, marigolds, begonias, and more, artfully arranged beneath dark, shaggy columns of spruce trees. This garden blends almost seamlessly into the **Leo Mol Sculpture Garden** ★★, an adjacent area containing the works of a single sculptor. Mol, a Ukrainian who immigrated to the city in 1949, has created whimsical bears, deer and nude bathers, among other forms. A glass-walled **gallery** (*free; early Jun to late Sep noon to 8pm, ☎986-6531*) displays hundreds more pieces of his work, while a reflecting pool catches the grace of several posed figures. Mol's studio, moved to a new home just behind the gallery, can be viewed.

The park's most popular feature is the **Assiniboine Park Zoo** ★★★ (*$3; everyday 10am to 4pm, in summer until sundown; ☎986-6921*). More than 1,300 animals live here, including Russian lynx, a polar bear, kangaroo, snowy and great horned owls – even imported residents like the *vicuña* (a kind of South American camel) and Siberian tigers. A statue of "Winnie-the-Bear" on the zoo grounds honours the famous Pooh's origins as a bear cub purchased by a Winnipeg soldier in Ontario and carried to England, where author A.A. Milne saw it and brought its story to a worldwide audience of children.

The **Prairie Dog Central** (*$13; Jul and Aug Sat and Sun 11am and 3pm, Sep Sun only; 0.5 km north of Inkster Blvd. on Prairie Dog Trail, ☎780-7328 to reserve or 453-8796 for info*) is a vintage steam train dating back to circa 1900 that welcomes visitors aboard for a unique 2.5hr excursion to Warren, northwest of Winnipeg.

Living Prairie Museum, in a suburb west of downtown, is said to contain the last significant pocket of tallgrass prairie in Canada. If so, these 12ha are a stark testament to the loss of the once vast prairie, for this is a rather small plot surrounded by an airfield, a school and housing developments, making it hard to imagine the wide open plains.

However, the adjacent **nature centre ★** (*free entry; Jul and Aug every day 10am to 5pm; 2795 Ness Ave., ☎832-0167*) does an adequate job of explaining and recapturing what once existed here. An annual festival, in August, draws further attention to the ecosystem.

Southwest of downtown, the **Fort Whyte Nature Centre ★★** (*$4; Jun to Oct Mon to Tue 9am to 5pm, Wed to Fri 9am to 9pm, Sat and Sun 10am to 9pm; Nov to May Mon to Fri 9am to 5pm, Sat and Sun 10am to 5pm; 1961 McCreary Rd., ☎989-8355*) is a pocket of wilderness that's a bit more vital: its animal life includes foxes and muskrats; a number of birds are also present. An interpretive centre on the premises features an aquarium, demonstration beehive and other exhibits designed with children in mind.

Tiny **Riel House ★★** (*suggested donation $2; mid-May to early Sep every day 10am to 6pm; 330 River Rd., just south of Bishop Grandin Blvd., St. Vital; ☎257-1783*) is set on a narrow river lot along the Red River. This building was home to famous Metis leader Louis Riel and his family for several years, and belonged to his descendants until 1969. Riel's body lay in state here after he was executed for treason in 1885. In addition to its connection with Riel, the museum paints a vivid picture of what life was like for the Metis in the Red River Settlement. Guided tours are available.

The **St. Norbert Farmers Market** (*late Jun to Thanksgiving Sat 8am to 3pm, Jul and Aug Wed 3pm to dusk; ☎275-8349*) is just south of the perimeter, on the east side of Pembina Highway. During the summer, people come from all over southern Manitoba to sell their products at the outdoor stalls. Locally grown fruits and vegetables, home-made bread and baking, plants, crafts and traditional Mennonite farmer's sausage are all sold here.

Eastern Manitoba

Dugald

Just east of Winnipeg, in the small town of Dugald, is the **Dugald Costume Museum ★** (*$4; Jun to Aug 10am to 5pm, May and Sep Wed to Fri 10am to 5pm, Sat and Sun noon to 5pm; $4; at the intersection of Hwy. 15 and Dugald Rd., ☎853-2166, ⇄853-2077*), the first of its kind in Canada. A 35,000-piece collection of costumes dating back to 1765 is displayed in tableaus, housed in an 1886 pioneer home. Special exhibits illustrate aspects of costume; one recent exhibit, for instance, explained the long history of the silk trade. The museum somehow has also acquired some of Queen Elizabeth I's linen napkins dating from the late 16th century.

Oak Hammock

Birds are the most satisfied visitors to **Oak Hammock Marsh and Conservation Centre ★★** (*$3.75; May to Sep every day 10am to 8pm, Oct to Apr every day 10am to 4:30pm, head north on Hwy. 8, then east on Hwy. 67, ☎467-3300*), a protected wetland (it was once farmland) a few kilometres north of downtown Winnipeg. Among the annual arrivals are Canada geese, ducks and more than 250 other species; mammals like the park, too, and all are visible while walking the centre's boardwalks (constructed so as not to disturb the marsh) and dikes. Special guided tours and canoe excursions are also available.

An excellent **interpretive centre ★** on site explains the value of the wetland and allows visitors to see it via remote-controlled cameras installed in the marsh. The Canadian headquarters of Ducks Unlimited are also located here.

Red River Heritage Road

From Rte. 9 heading north, the **Red River Heritage Road ★★** makes a nice meander off the beaten track. This territory once formed the heart of Thomas Douglas's "lower settlement" of Hudson's Bay Company charges; the dirt heritage road is beautifully laid out along the river banks and is well-marked with historic sites. It passes a number of old limestone buildings, including the William Scott farmhouse and the **Captain Kennedy Museum and Tea House ★★** (*free admission; Mon to Sat 11am to 4:30pm, Sun 11am to 6pm; ☎334-2498*), built by trader Captain William Kennedy in 1866 with three restored period rooms, English gardens and a superb view of the river. There is a pleasant restaurant where you can have a lovely English-style tea with scones.

Near the end of the road, the **St. Andrews-on-the-Red Anglican Church ★★★** is the oldest stone church in western Canada still being used for public worship. It is handsome, with typical English pointed windows – the stained glass was supposedly shipped in molasses from England to protect it from breaking – and massive stone walls. Inside, benches are still lined with the original buffalo hide.

Just south of the church, **St. Andrews Rectory ★★** (*☎334-6405 or 785-6050*), a striking little building that is now a national historic park. Signs on the grounds tell the story, and interpreters are available during summertime to discuss the rectory's function.

Selkirk

On Rte. 9A, Selkirk, a small river town marked by a giant green fish, is home to several important attractions. **Lower Fort Garry ★** (*$5.50; mid-May to early Sep, 10am to 6pm; PO 37, off Hwy. 9, just south of Selkirk, ☎785-6050*), just south of town, is a recreated trading post. It recalls the former importance of this post, built to replace the original Fort Garry in Winnipeg after it was carried away by flood waters. Exhibits include a recreated doctor's office, powder magazine, Aboriginal encampment and blacksmith's shop. The main attraction, however, is the big stone house at the centre of the property, constructed for the governor of the Hudson's Bay Company. It displays many interesting artefacts, including housewares and an old piano transported here from Montréal by canoe. Costumed characters interact with visitors while baking, trading and otherwise acting out their roles.

Several bridges across the Red River provide good views of the surrounding landscape. Downtown, hugging the river, lies **Selkirk Park** (see p 524). The world's largest Red River Ox Cart (6.5m high and 13.7m long) stands here, and the **Marine Museum of Manitoba ★★** (*$3.50; May to Sep every day 9am to 5pm; 490 Evelyn St., ☎482-7761*) occupies six ships – including Manitoba's oldest steamship – at the park entrance. An actual lighthouse that once stood on Lake Winnipeg is also located here.

St. Peter's Dynevor Church ★ sits just across the Red River, and has a lovely view of it. The stone church, built in 1854, is a reminder of the first agricultural colony in Western Canada; it employed a combination of missionaries and First Nations. **Chief Peguis** is buried in the churchyard, as are other settlers of the colony.

North of Selkirk on Rte. 9, the **Little Britain**

Church ★ is one of just five surviving Red River Settlement stone churches that remain standing in the province. It was constructed between 1872 and 1874.

Lockport

East of town, in Lockport at the foot of the large bridge, a park is home to the **Kenosewun Centre** (*free admission; mid-May to mid-Sep 11am to 6:30pm;* ☎*757-2902*). The name means "there are many fishes" in the Cree language; the centre displays Aboriginal horticultural artifacts and material on the history of the town, and offers tourist information. Pathways lead to the St. Andrews lock and dam.

Driving northeast from Selkirk, you will reach a series of beautiful white sandy beaches; some of the province's finest, including Winnipeg Beach (see p 523) and Camp Morton.

Gimli

Situated on the shores of Lake Winnipeg, Gimli is still the heart of Manitoba's Icelandic population; a Viking statue welcomes visitors to the centre of town. The town was once the capital of a sovereign republic known as New Iceland. A maritime ambiance still pervades the streets, though today it is mainly sailboats and windsurfers that set out from the marina and beach, while the history of the town's fishing industry and the lake's geological formation are recounted at the **Lake Winnipeg Visitor Centre** (*at the harbour,* ☎*642-7974.*)

The region's Icelandic heritage is commemorated with an annual festival and is also on display at the **New Icelandic Heritage Museum** (☎*642-7974*), scheduled to open at its new location at the Betel Waterfront Centre in the late summer of 2000. The museum will recount the history of the first Icelandic settlers to arrive on the shores of Lake Winnipeg and the collection will include interesting historical artifacts. In the meantime, a small temporary exhibit on the Vikings may be viewed at Gimli's school (*free admission; 2nd floor, 62 Second Ave*).

Around Lake Winnipeg

On the eastern side of Lake Winnipeg, Rte. 59 passes through resort towns located on some of the province's best beaches: **Grand Beach ★★★**, **Grand Marais** and **Victoria Beach ★** are the places to go during the summer for stunning white sand. Turning southeast again on Rte. 11, angling toward the Ontario border, the province's seemingly endless flatlands suddenly drop away and are replaced by rocks, rushing rivers and trees. As the road proceeds east, the towns become increasingly woodsy, while the fishing, canoeing and hiking become truly spectacular.

Pinawa is known for a paper mill and a festival celebrating paper, hydroelectric power and fish, while **Lac du Bonnet** is home to an underground nuclear research facility. A string of increasingly remote provincial parks compete for the attention of the traveller seeking off-the-beaten track Manitoba.

Southern Manitoba

Directly south of Winnipeg, between the city and the United States border, lies the Pembina Valley – the province's Mennonite country. The drive is absolutely flat, and the endless fields are interrupted only by the leafy oases of towns such as **Altona**. The town is famous for its fields of sunflowers and an annual festival that celebrates them (see p 534).

Steinbach

Southeast of Winnipeg, Steinbach is the largest town in the region and features the popular **Mennonite Heritage Village ★★** (*$5; Jul to Aug Mon to Sat 10am to 7pm, Sun noon to 5pm; May, Jun, Sep Mon to Sat 10am to 5pm, Sun noon to 5pm; Oct to May by appointment only, interpretive centre weekdays 10am to 4pm; Hwy. 12, ☎326-9661*). A 16ha village is laid out in the traditional pattern. The buildings focus on the lives of Mennonites, people of Dutch origin who emigrated to the province from Russia beginning in 1874.

Attractions include a restaurant offering authentic Mennonite food (plums and meat are featured); a general store selling such goods as stone-ground flour and old-fashioned candy; sod and log houses; an interpretative building; exhibition galleries, and a windmill with 20m-high sails.

Mariopolis

In Mariopolis, an unusually beautiful church reminds visitors of the strong French and Belgian culture in the province. **Our Lady of the Assumption Roman Catholic Church ★★★** combines careful brickwork with a striking steeple whose alternating bands of black and white draw the eye upward to a simple cross.

Morden

Morden, another Mennonite stronghold, is known for its attractive agricultural research facility and streets of graceful fieldstone mansions; various local tour operators will point out the homes for a small fee. The **Morden and District Museum ★** (*$2; Jun to Aug every day 1pm to 5pm; Sep to May Wed to Sun 1pm to 5pm; 111B Gilmour Ave., ☎822-3406*) displays a good collection of prehistoric marine fossils, reminders of the vast inland sea that once covered North America. Also in town, the **Agriculture Canada Research Station** (*Mon to Fri 8am to 5pm; ☎822-4471*) has impressive ornamental gardens.

Winkler

A bit farther east on Rte. 14, Winkler is home to the unusual **Pembina Thresherman's Museum ★** (*$3; closed in winter; Mon to Fri 9am to 5pm, Sat and Sun 1pm to 5pm; ☎325-7497*), filled with tools and machines from another era.

Neubergthal

Just southeast of Altona, Neubergthal is one of the province's best-preserved Mennonite towns, with its distinctive layout (just one long street lined with houses) and equally distinctive architecture, featuring thatched roofing and barns connected to houses.

Tolstoi

Just east of the small town of Tolstoi on Rte. 209, a 128ha **patch of tallgrass prairie ★★** (*☎945-7775*) is maintained by the Manitoba Naturalists Society; this is the largest remaining tract of this kind being protected in Canada.

Central Manitoba

Two main Rte.s pass across central Manitoba. The **Trans-Canada Highway** (*Hwy. 1*) is the faster of the two; though less visually rewarding, it does pass through the major population centres of Brandon and Portage La Prairie. The **Yellowhead Highway** (*Hwy. 16*) is a somewhat more scenic journey.

St. François-Xavier

Taking the Trans-Canada west from Winnipeg, it's not far to St. François-Xavier, a solidly French-Canadian village featuring two of Manitoba's most interesting restaurants as well as an intriguing Cree legend of a white horse. This is the oldest Metis settlement in the province, established in 1820 by **Cuthbert Grant**. Grant, legendary for his acumen at hunting buffalo, is buried inside the town's Roman Catholic church. The picturesque setting along a bow of the Assiniboine River makes this an excellent destination for a short excursion out of the city.

From here, **Rte. 26** makes a short scenic detour along the tree-lined Assiniboine River, once home to a string of trapping posts.

Portage La Prairie

A little farther west lies Portage La Prairie (pop. 20,000), founded in 1738 by French-Canadian explorer Pierre Gaultier de la Vérendrye as a resting stop on the riverine canoe journey to Lake Manitoba. The town's most interesting natural attraction is the crescent-shaped lake, a cutoff bow of the Assiniboine River that nearly encircles the entire downtown. **Island Park** ★ sits inside that crescent, providing beautiful tree-shaded picnic spots by the water and a host of attractions, including a golf course, playground, deer and waterfowl sanctuary (watch for the Canada geese), fairgrounds and a "you-pick" strawberry farm. Canoeing is excellent here. Good relief from the heat and glare of driving.

The limestone **city hall** ★★, a former post office right on the main street, was designed by the same architect who planned Canada's first Parliament Buildings. It is surprisingly ornate, and has been declared a federal historic site.

Fort la Reine Museum and Pioneer Village ★★★ (*$3; May to mid-Sep Mon to Fri 9am to 6pm, Sat to Sun 10am to 6pm; at Hwys. 26 and 1A, ☎857-3259*) is not, in fact, a fort, but rather an eclectic mix of old prairie buildings set on a small lot just east of town. This is not to say that it is not worth a visit; in fact, its small size makes the museum more manageable, and the varied collection is often surprising. Finery, such as mink stoles and gramophones tells of the aspirations of the people who once lived in this small prairie city and forms a stark contrast to the wash tubs, well-worn highchairs and rusted gas pumps found elsewhere in the museum, which give an excellent sense of the typical life of the average settler. It includes everything from a small trading post, trapper's cabin, school, church and barn to weathered houses like those prairie travellers see standing abandoned and on the verge of collapse in the flat, endless landscape.

Perhaps the museum's most remarkable piece is the luxurious and well-equipped railway car specially fitted for William Van Horne of the Canadian Pacific Railway, who traveled in it while overseeing the construction of the rail line. Next to it is one of the humble cabooses which are fast disappearing from the ends of trains across Canada. Children especially will enjoy climbing into the lookout dome of this relic from the past!

Austin

The highway west then passes through more fields and towns, reminders of the richness of the local farmland. A short distance south of the one-street town of Austin, the **Manitoba Agricultural Museum** ★ (*$5; mid-May to early Oct every day 9am to 5pm; Box 10, R0H 0C0, ☎637-2354, ⇌637-2395*) is particularly strong on farm equipment and old vehicles; John Deere tractors and implements and ancient snowmobiles are typical of the collection, which is the largest operating vintage farm machinery in Canada. An old prairie schoolhouse, train station, general store and amateur radio museum have also been moved here to add atmosphere.

Every summer, the **Thresherman's Reunion and Stampede** brings the place alive with farm contests and a race between a turtle and an old-fashioned tractor. (Sometimes the turtle wins!).

Glenboro

A detour 40km south of the Trans-Canada takes you to **Glenboro**, gateway to Spruce Woods Provincial Park (see p 524) And home to **Grund Church** ★, the oldest Icelandic Lutheran church in Canada. Manitoba's last remaining cable ferry still crosses the Assiniboine River here.

Brandon

Brandon (pop. 40,000) is Manitoba's second-largest city, a city so tied to the fortunes of the surrounding wheatfields that wheat is still grown experimentally right near centre of town. Many gracious Victorian homes stand in the residential area just south of downtown.

The handsome 1911 **Central Fire Station** ★(*637 Princess Ave*) and neoclassical **Courthouse** (*Princess Ave. and 11th St.*) Are both on Princess Avenue, one of the city's main streets.

Turn right on 18th St. to reach the **Daly House Museum** ★★ (*$2; Mon to Sat 10am to 5pm, Sun noon to 5pm; 122-18th St., ☎727-1722*) is the best place to get a feel for Brandon's history. Once home to Brandon's mayor, the house today includes a grocery store, recreated City Council chamber and research centre. A little farther is the attractive campus of **Brandon University**.

Heading north along 18th St. leads you to Grand Valley Road, which takes you to the **Experimental Research Farm** ★★ (*every day 8am to 4:30pm; Gran Valley Rd., ☎7267650*), whose scenic grounds and striking modern glass building are set in an idyllic location with a view of the valley. Guided tours are available Tuesdays and Thursdays at 1:30pm and 3:30pm.

Finally, there's an interesting aircraft museum housed in Hangar No. 1 of the city airport on the northern outskirts of Brandon. The **Commonwealth Air Training Plan Museum** ★ (*$3; May to Sep, Mon to Sun 10am to 4pm, Oct to Apr 1pm to 4pm; Box 3, R.R. 5, Brandon, ☎727-2444*) features vintage planes from WWII Royal Canadian Air Force training schools that were held here; some of the more interesting articles include a restored vintage flight simulator, memorials, official telegrams announcing casualties and losses and biographies of flyers.

Souris

Southwest of Brandon, Souris is known for its **swinging suspension bridge** ★, Canada's longest at 177m; the bridge was constructed at the turn of the century and restored after a 1976 flood swept it away. The adjacent **Hillcrest Museum** (*$2; Jun Sun 2pm to 5pm; Jul to early Sep every day 10am to 6pm; ☎483-2008 or 483-3138*) preserves items of local historical interest.

Neepawa

Another choice for touring central Manitoba is the Yellowhead Highway (Hwy. 16). Lying to the west of Winnipeg, Neepawa touts itself as "Manitoba's Loveliest Town." This is no idle boast, especially in lily season, when this pretty little town blooms. The oldest operating courthouse in Manitoba is here, as is the **Margaret Laurence Home** (*$2; May 1 to Aug Mon to Fri 10am to 5pm, weekends noon to 6pm, Sep to Oct every day* *noon to 5pm; 312 First Ave., ☎476-3612*), dedicated to the beloved author who was born here. Laurence's typewriter and furniture are the highlights.

Minnedosa

Minnedosa, a tiny town to the west, surprises with its Czechoslavakian population. A series of prairie potholes, glacier-made depressions in the earth that later filled with rainwater, lie south of town on Rte. 262 and provide optimum conditions for waterfowl such as drake, mallards and teal. Continuing north of Minnedosa on Rte. 262, the road enters a valley good for spotting white-tailed deer; a wildlife viewing tower provides even better opportunities to do so.

Dauphin

Just north of the Yellowhead, Dauphin is transformed into the famous **Selo Ukrainia** ("Ukrainian Village") during the **National Ukrainian Festival** (see p 534) each summer. The event draws thousands to the town in late July.

Also in Dauphin, the **Fort Dauphin Museum ★** (*$3; May to Sep Mon to Fri 9am to 5 pm, also on weekends Jul and Aug; 140 Jackson St., ☎638-6630*) recreates one of the area's French-run North West Company trading posts, showcasing fur trapping and other pioneer activities. The displays and buildings include a trapper's cabin, blacksmith's shop, one-room rural schoolhouse, Anglican church and the trading post. There's even a birch-bark canoe made entirely from natural materials, and a collection of fossils such as a bison horn, mammoth tusk and an ancient canine skull.

Northern Manitoba

The Pas

The so-called Woods and Water Rte. shows another side of Manitoba. The Pas home to a large Aboriginal population, hosts an important annual gathering of trappers and has an exceedingly clear lake. Most visitors head for the **Sam Waller Museum ★★** (*$2; mid-May to Aug Mon to Sat 10am to 7pm, Sun noon to 5pm; Sep to mid-May every day 1pm to 5pm; 306 Fischer Ave., ☎623-3802*). Built in 1916 and occupying the town's former courthouse, it covers local natural and cultural history, based on the eclectic collection of Sam Waller. Walking tours are offered.

A wall of **Christ Church ★★** (*Edwards Ave., ☎623-2119*) is inscribed with the Ten Commandments in the Cree language. The church was built in 1840 by Henry Budd, the first Aboriginal in Canada ordained to the Anglican ministry, and still retains some furnishings fashioned by ships' carpenters and brought here during an 1847 expedition.

Flin Flon

Flin Flon is Canada's most whimsically named municipality and greets visitors with a jumble of streets climbing the rocky hills. Located mostly in Manitoba, with a smaller part spilling over into Saskatchewan, Flin Flon is the most important mining centre in this part of the country, and has grown to become the province's sixth-largest city.

Flin Flon was named by a group of gold prospectors in 1915 who found a copy of the mass-market science fiction paperback of the same name during a northern Manitoba portage. Later, on a lakeshore near here, they staked a mining claim and named it for the book's main character, Josiah Flintabbatey Flonatin, or "Flinty" to locals. Thus, the green 7.5m-tall **Josiah Flintabbatey Flonatin statue** presides over the city's entrance. It was designed for the city by the renowned American cartoonist Al Capp.

A walk around town reveals old boomtown-era hotels, bright red headframes indicating mine shafts, and historic redwood cabins. Of all these historic sites, though, the **Flin Flon Station Museum** ★★ (*$2; mid-May to early Sept every day 11am to 7pm; ☎687-2946*) might be the best. It has a small collection of local mining artifacts, including a diving suit and helmet for underwater prospecting, a Linn tractor, a train sweeper and an ore car. The collection also includes a stuffed 9kg lake trout that was caught near here.

Churchill

Special arrangements are required to reach the far north of Manitoba. Isolated and cold, Churchill nevertheless beguiles travellers with its remoteness and stunning wildlife. The place is important historically as well, having helped the English first establish a foothold in Manitoba. They chose the site because of a superb natural harbour, so it's fitting that the town's dominant feature today is a huge **grain elevator** beside the docks.

The townsite is also located right in the middle of the migratory path of the area's **polar bear** population, which is a mixed blessing for the town's inhabitants. While these majestic animals attract visitors from around the world to this remote spot every autumn, they also wander right into town occasionally, posing a potential risk to anyone who crosses their path. In addition to the bears, people also come here. They come to see caribou, seals, birds and especially white **beluga whales** in summer. And there is always the possibility of an astonishing display of the aurora borealis, or northern lights.

The **Visitor Reception Centre**, in Bayport Plaza, orients visitors with an overview of the fur posts and forts. **Fort Prince of Wales** ★★ (*$5; Box 127, R0B 0E0, ☎675-8863, ⇄675-2026*), an enormous, diamond-shaped stone battlement located at the mouth of the Churchill River, is historically interesting: after four decades of steady construction by the English it was surrendered to Canadian forces without a fight. The fort can only be reached by boat or helicopter; in summer, park staff lead interpretive tours of the site.

Sloop's Cove National Historic Site ★★ (*☎675-8863*), 4km upstream from the fort, is a natural harbour that provided safe haven for huge wooden sailing ships at least as far back as 1689. When the Hudson's Bay Company set up shop here, its sloops were moored to these rocks with iron rings. Some of the rocks still bear inscriptions from the men posted there – men like explorer Samuel Hearne, who presided over the company in its heyday. Like Fort Prince of Wales, the site can only be reached by boat or helicopter.

Across the river, **Cape Merry National Historic Site** ★ (*☎675-8863*) preserves a gunpowder magazine, the only remnant of a battery built here back in 1746. It is reached via the Centennial Parkway.

The **Eskimo Museum** ★★★ (*free admission; summer Mon 1pm to 5pm, Tue to Sat 9am to noon and 1pm to 5pm; winter Mon and Sat 1pm to 4:30pm, Tue to Fri 10:30am to 4:30 pm, Sat 1am to 4:30pm; 242 La Vérendrye Ave., R0B 0E0, ☎675-2030*) maintains one of the world's pre-eminent collections of

Inuit artifacts. Founded in 1944 by the local Roman Catholic Diocese, it contains artifacts dating from as far back as 1700BC. A set of ornately carved walrus tusks is among its most impressive pieces.

The **Northern Studies Centre** (*Launch Rd., ☎675-2307*), 25km east of Churchill proper, is located in a former rocket test-range. Today, students come here to study the northern lights, Arctic ecology, botany, meteorology, geology and more. Guided tours are available for $5. It is best to call ahead.

York Factory National Historic Site ★★★ (*Box 127, R0B 0E0, ☎675-8863, ⇄675-2026*), 240km southeast of Churchill, is what remains of the Hudson Bay Company fur-trade post that first established the English in western Canada. A wooden depot built in 1832 still stands here, and there are ruins of a stone gunpowder magazine and a cemetery with markers dating back to the 1700s. Access can only be gained by charter plane or canoe, however; some guided tours are also offered in summer through Parks Canada.

Finally, there are the spectacular **polar bears** ★★★, easily Churchill's premier attraction. Autumn is the time to observe them, and the only way is as part of a guided tour. There are at least a dozen operators in Churchill The options include:

North Star Tours and Travel Agency (*Box 520, Churchill, ☎800-665-0690 or 675-2629; ⇄675-2852*). Mark Ingebrigtson leads natural history – and sometimes aboriginal culture – package tours along the shores of Hudson Bay.

Tundra Buggy Tours (*Box 662, Churchill, ☎800-544-5049 or 675-2121; ⇄675-2877*). Len and Beverly Smith lead polar bear safaris in both English and French; vehicles are specially outfitted to accommodate photographers.

Seal River Heritage Lodge (*Box 1034, Churchill, ☎800-665-0476 or 675-8875; ⇄675-2386*). Mike Reimer runs ecotours out of a remote wilderness lodge in the north country; sights include caribou, polar bears, beluga whales and seals.

Parks

Greater Winnipeg

Birds Hill Provincial Park, just north of Winnipeg, sits on a gentle rise deposited by retreating glaciers. It makes for easy and popular cross-country skiing. In summer, visitors bike and hike the park's trails (one of which is wheelchair-accessible) to view prairie wildflowers – including several species of rare orchid – or head for a small beach. The park is also the site of the city's annual folk-music extravaganza.

Grand Beach Provincial Park is the most popular beach in Manitoba, hands down. Situated on Lake Winnipeg's eastern shore, it consists of lovely white sand and grassy 8m-high dunes that seem to have been lifted directly from Cape Cod. As a bonus, the beach is wheelchair-accessible. Three self-guiding trails wind through the park – Spirit Rock Trail, Wild Wings Trail and the Ancient Beach Trail – enlightening beach goers before they slap on the sunblock.

This is a good spot for windsurfing, as well. There are full tourist facilities here, including a restaurant, campground and outdoor amphitheatre for concerts. A golf course lies just outside the park.

St. Norbert Provincial Park (*free, mid-May to Sep, Thu to Mon, 10:30am to 5:30 pm; 40 Turnbull Dr., ☎269-5377*) is a 6.8ha, south-Winnipeg complex of buildings, a former Metis and then French-Canadian settlement at the juncture of the Red and La Salle rivers. The restored gambrel-roofed Bohémier farmhouse and two other homes are on display and there is also a self-guided trail.

Eastern Manitoba

Winnipeg Beach Provincial Recreational Park ★★ (*☎389-2752*) has long been a favourite summer getaway for Winnipeg residents. Besides the well-known beach and a boardwalk, the park's grounds also include a marina, campground and bay that's a favourite with windsurfers.

Whiteshell Provincial Park ★★★ (*from Winnipeg, take Hwy. 1 east to Falcon Lake or West Hawk Lake; or, farther north, take Provincial Rd. 307 to Seven Sisters Falls, or Hwy. 44 to Rennie, www.whiteshell.mb.ca*) is one Manitoba's largest and best. Occupying some 2,500km^2, it is rich in lakes, rapids, waterfalls, fish and birds. There's something for everyone: **Alf Hole Goose Sanctuary ★** (*☎369-5470*) is among the best places in the province to see Canada geese, especially during migration; the rocks at **Bannock Point ★**, laid out by local First Nations to resemble the forms of snakes, fish, turtles and birds, are of archaeological interest; the cliffs of **Lily Pond ★** are 3.75 billion years old. This is also the location of the province's deepest lake, which is popular with scuba divers. **Hiking** is also good in Whiteshell. Hikes include the Forester's Footsteps Trail, an easy walk through jackpine forest and then up a granite ridge, the Pine Point Trail, which is suited for cross-country skiing in winter, and the White Pine trail.

A **Visitor Centre** and the **Whiteshell Natural History Museum** (*free, May to Sep every day 9am to 5pm, ☎348-2846, www.whiteshell.mb.ca*) help orient travellers and explain the park's ecology, geology and wildlife.

Nopiming Provincial Park (*from Winnipeg, take Hwy. 59 north to Hwy. 44; continue east along Hwy. 11, before turning onto Provincial Rd. 313 north and finally taking Provincial Rd. 315 east to Bird Lake, which lies just south of the park*) shows a whole different side of Manitoba; a place of huge granite outcrops and hundreds of lakes. The surprising presence of woodland caribou here is an added bonus, as are the fly-in and drive-in **fishing lodges** scattered through the park. "Nopiming" is an Anishinabe (Ojibwa and Cree) word meaning "entrance to the wilderness."

Atikaki Provincial Wilderness Park ★★★ (*from Winnipeg, take Hwy. 59 N, then turn onto Provincial Rd. 304*), in the east of the province along the Ontario border, consists of a 400,000ha hodgepodge of cliffs, rock formations, pristine lakes and cascading rivers. It is extremely difficult to get to, however, requiring a canoe, floatplane or a hike of several days to reach its interior; as a result, it contains the most unspoiled wilderness in the province's major parklands. Among the highlights are a series of rock murals painted by Aboriginals and a 20m waterfall well suited for whitewater canoeing. As Atikaki means "country of the caribou," moose and caribou sightings are quite possible.

Hecla Provincial Park ★★ (*from Winnipeg, take Hwy. 8 North along Lake Winnipeg to Gull Harbour,* ☎*279-2056*) is a beautiful and interesting park, combining lake ecology with dramatic island geology and the colours and creatures of the forest. Interpretive programs take place year-round, and there is a tower for viewing and photographing wildlife. The park's **Hecla Village** ★ adds a short trail with points of historical interest relating to Icelandic culture and architecture and a **heritage home museum** ★★ (*Thurs to Mon 11am to 5pm*), a restored 1920s home. Adjacent **Grindstone Provincial Park** ★★ is still being developed, and therein lies its beauty: it is not nearly as busy as Hecla.

East of Lake Winnipeg, the **Narcisse Wildlife Management Area** on Rte. 17 becomes wildly popular late each April when thousands of resident red-sided garter snakes emerge from their limestone dens to participate in a visceral mating ritual.

Selkirk Park, a riverside park in downtown Selkirk, has lots of recreational opportunities. There are campgrounds, boat-launching pads and an outdoor swimming pool. Snowshoeing and ice fishing are possible in winter; in spring and summer, the park is home to a bird sanctuary with an observation deck for viewing Canada geese and other birds.

Central Manitoba

Grand Valley Provincial Recreation Park ★ (*just west of Brandon on Hwy. 1*) is best known for the **Stott Site** ★★, a designated provincial heritage site. Bones and artifacts from at least 1,200 years ago have been discovered here. A bison enclosure and camp have been reconstructed.

North of Portage La Prairie, on the shore of Lake Manitoba, lies the 18,000ha **Delta Marsh**, one of the largest waterfowl staging marshes in North America, stretching 8km along the lake and a great place to bring binoculars. At Delta Beach, a waterfowl and wetlands research station studies ecological questions in a natural environment.

Approximately 23km south of Roblin, the **Frank Skinner Arboretum Trail** commemorates the work of Dr. Frank Leith Skinner, a famous Canadian horticulturist. This farm served as Skinner's laboratory for breeding new strains of plants; visitors can walk atop a former dike, visit Skinner's greenhouse, and walk the Wild Willow Trail.

Western Manitoba

The "Spirit Sands," a desert landscape of immense sand dunes in **Spruce Woods Provincial Park** ★★ (*take the Trans-Canada Hwy. 1 west to Carberry, then take Hwy. 5 south; from May to Sep* ☎*827-2543, from Sep to May* ☎*834-3223*) never fails to take visitors by surprise.

Self-guided trails take hikers through the dunes and the surrounding spruce forests and prairie, and to the "Devil's Punch Bowl," an unusual pond created by underground streams. Campgrounds and a sandy beach for swimming make this large park popular in the summer.

Turtle Mountain National Park ★★ (*from Brandon, travel 100km on Hwy. 10 South until you reach the park*), composed of compacted coal and glacial deposits, rises more than 250m above the surrounding prairie land. Explorer La Vérendrye called it the "blue jewel of the plains," and its gentle hills lend themselves to mountain biking, horseback riding and hiking. There is also, of course, a considerable population of the beautiful painted turtles that give the mountain its name. Camping is available at three lakes here.

Riding Mountain National Park ★★★ (*☎800-707-8480 or 848-7275*) rises majestically from the plains with aspen-covered slopes that are habitats for wild animals such as elk, moose, deer, wolves and lynx. The largest black bear ever seen in North America was killed here by a poacher in 1992, and bison are contained within a large **bison enclosure ★★** near Lake Audy. Rte. 10, running north-south, passes directly through the heart of the park and past the shores of its most beautiful lakes. The 12m-high wooden Agassiz lookout tower here gives a superb view of the surrounding territory. The remains of an old sawmill also fall within park boundaries, as does a series of geological formations called beach ridges – former edges of a giant lake.

The local Aboriginal people own and operate a traditional **Anishinabe Village★★** (*Southquill Camp; ☎204-925-2030, ⇄204-925-2027; www.wredco.com; On site May 15 to Sep 15; ☎/⇄204-848-2815*) in the park which offers visitors the opportiunity to learn about Anishinabe culture. The camp features tipi accommodations and campsites, walking tours, traditional teachings, performances and local crafts.

Rte. 19 begins in the centre of the park and travels a switchback path up (or down) the park's steepest ridge. The naturalist Grey Owl, an Englishman who passed himself off as an Aboriginal person, lived here for six months, giving talks with his two tamed beavers (he spent most of his time in Prince Albert National Park, however, see p 492); his remote **cabin ★** is located 17km up a hiking trail off Rte. 19. More than 400km of trails have been cleared at Riding Mountain National Park, including the North Escarpment Loop, best for views, Whitewater Lake, giving a history of the prisoner-of-war camp that was once here, and the Strathclair Trail, formerly a fur trappers' Rte. through the wooded hills. The park is also dotted with a number of pristine lakes superb for swimming. The sand beach at Wasagaming on **Clear Lake★★** is a hub of activity. There is also a superb **golf course**.

Duck Mountain Provincial Park ★★★ (*from Dauphin, take Hwy. 5 West, then Provincial Rd. 366 North*) rises in long hills near the Manitoba-Saskatchewan border; forests, meadows and lakes appear where the land has wrinkled upward in the Manitoba Escarpment formation. This is the home of **Baldy Mountain ★★**, the highest mountain in the province at 831m (there is also a tower at the top to get a still better view), as well as six hiking trails and a lake so clear the bottom, 10m below, can be seen from its surface.

Northern Manitoba

At **Clearwater Lake Provincial Park ★** (*from The Pas, take Hwy. 10 North to Provincial Hwy. 287, then head east to the park*), the lake water is so clear that the bottom is visible 11m below the surface, making it one of the clearest lakes in the world. It is well known for its lake trout and northern pike. Also interesting is a series of enormous limestone slabs on the south shore; known as "the caves," they splintered off from the nearby cliffs and can be reached by a trail.

The newly-created Wapusk National Park lies within the **Cape Churchill Wildlife Management Area ★★** which, together with the **Cape Tatnam Wildlife Management Area ★★**, takes in the coastline of Hudson Bay from Churchill to the Ontario border – a tremendous stretch of wild country, nearly 2.4 million hectares of land in all, harbouring polar bears, woodland caribou and many more birds and animals. They are accessible only by plane.

The region of **Grass River Provincial Park ★★** (*from Flin Flon, take Hwy. 10 South, turn left onto Hwy. 39 which takes you to the park*) was used by the Aboriginal peoples for thousands of years, then explored anew by the English. Countless islands and some 150 lakes interrupt the river. A Karst spring, which gushes from a rock cliff is one of the park's most fascinating sites.

Outdoor Activities

Bird-Watching

Eastern Manitoba

The **Netley Marsh Provincial Recreational Park ★** (*Rte. 320, 16km north of Selkirk*) is one of the most frequented spots in the country for migrating birds, and said to be one of the most important waterfowl nesting areas in North America. At least 18 species of ducks and geese flock here each autumn to feed before heading south for the long winter.

Northern Manitoba

Bird Cove ★, 16km east of Churchill, might be the area's best spot for observing the hundreds of bird species that pass through here, including possibly the rare Ross Gull. The wreck of the Ithaca, which sank in a storm on its way to Montreal in 1961 with a load of nickel ore, sits at the western tip of the cove. For addresses of polar bear-observation outfitters see p 522.

Water Sports

Eastern Manitoba

Gimli's best rental agency for water and land sports is **H2O Beach and Adventure Sports** (☎*642-9781*), located right on the sandy beach of **Lake Winnipeg**. It rents bicycles, in-line skates, sailboats, kayaks, beach volleyballs, windsurfing equipment and just about everything else one could want or need.

It's purely manufactured fun, but **Skinner's Wet 'n' Wild Waterslide Park** (☎*757-2623*) in Lockport keeps drawing crowds anyway. The attraction contains four big waterslides, two smaller slides, a giant hot tub, mini-golf, batting cages and lots more. It's impossible to miss the complex, situated at the west end of the Lockport bridge.

Accommodations

Bed and Breakfast of Manitoba (☎*661-0300, www.bedandbreakfast.mb.ca*) coordinates reservations for approximately 70 member B&Bs throughout the province.

The Manitoba Country Vacations Association (☎/⇄*667-3526, www.countryvacations.mb.ca*) in Winnipeg, provides a similar service but a different experience, booking rooms at farms or other rural vacation destinations.

Downtown Winnipeg

Guest House International Hostel
$14-$34
sb, ≡
168 Maryland St., R3G 1L3
☎***772-1272***
⇄***772-4117***
This is a quirky old house in a residential neighbourhood very close to downtown Winnipeg. However, be cautious when walking in this area at night. Walls feature art by Aboriginal children, and there are all kinds of rooming options. A game room in the somewhat crowded basement adds appeal, and the price is right.

Ivey House International Hostel
$14 members, $18 non-members
sb, tv, K
210 Maryland St., R3G 1L6
☎***772-3022***
⇄***784-1133***
This extremely friendly and well-run Hostelling International-member facility is situated close to downtown (and very close to the other hostel). A classy operation, featuring a big kitchen, great staff and rooms that sometimes include desks.

Casa Antigua
$50
sb
209 Chestnut St., Winnipeg
☎***775-9708***
This quiet and reasonably priced bed and breakfast, in a residential neighbourhood near the two hostels, was built in 1906 and is furnished with lovely antiques. Both English and Spanish are spoken here, and three bedrooms – all with a shared bathroom – are offered.

Ramada Marlborough
$89
⊙, *P*, 🐕, *tv*, ≡, ℜ
331 Smith St., R3B 2G9
☎***(800) 667-7666***
☎***942-6411***
⇄***942-2017***
With its central location and beautiful facade, the Ramada Marlborough makes a stunning first impression. While the sophisticated style is carried through in the hotel's wood-panelled dining room and the pleasant breakfast room, the guestrooms don't quite measure up, tending to be somewhat gloomy and cramped. Nevertheless, the place is comfortable.

Hotel Fort Garry
$119
tv, ≡, ⌂, ℜ, ≈, ⊛, ⊙
222 Broadway, R3C 0R3
☎***(800) 665-8088***
☎***942-8251***
⇄***956-2351***
One of the most recognizable hotels on the city's skyline, this big-shouldered, neo-Gothic building was built by the Canadian National Railway in 1913. The impressive lobby and function rooms welcome guests in high style, though the rooms themselves are somewhat disappointing for a hotel of this calibre. The place is currently undergoing extensive renovations that are to be completed by 2003.

The Radisson Winnipeg
$89-$119
🐕, ♿, *tv*, ≡, ℜ, ≈, ⌂, ⊛
288 Portage Ave., R3C 0B8
☎***(800) 268-1133***
☎***956-0400***
⇄***947-1129***
Smack in the downtown business district, this posh hotel features an haute-cuisine restaurant, child-care services and laundry service. Elegantly remodelled, the tastefully decorated rooms offer every comfort and excellent views. Very friendly and professional ser-

vice make this one of the best places to stay.

Place Louis-Riel All-Suite Hotel
$100 studio, $110 one bedroom
tv, ≡, *K*, ℜ
190 Smith St., R3C 1JB
☎***947-6961***
⇄***947-3029***
Every unit in this downtown high-rise is a suite, comprising several rooms and usually a kitchenette. Sixteen of the suites have two bedrooms. Ideal for longer visits.

Crowne Plaza Winnipeg Downtown
$99-$150
tv, ⊙, ♿, *P*, ≡, *K*, ℜ, ≈, ⊛, ⌂
350 St. Mary Ave., R3C 3J2
☎***942-0551***
☎***(800) 2CROWNE***
⇄***943-8702***
This centrally located hotel comes with all the frills: four restaurants, a dry cleaning service, a beautiful pool and recreation area and an attractive lobby. It even offers aerobic classes!

The Lombard
$89-$119
tv, ♿, ⊙, 🐕, ≡, ℜ, ≈, ⌂, ⊛, *K*
2 Lombard Place, R3B 0Y3
☎***957-1350***
☎***(800) 441-1414***
⇄***956-1791***
Under new ownership – it was formerly in the Westin chain – this landmark is among the top posh digs in the city. It's where the Rolling Stones stay when they're in town, though they sometimes get bumped by business conventions. Located at the busy and famous corner of Portage and Main.

St. Boniface

Gîte de la Cathédrale Bed and Breakfast
$50 bkfst incl
⊗, *P*, *sb*
581 Rue Langevin, St. Boniface
☎***233-7792***
Gîte de la Cathédrale Bed and Breakfast is located right across from Provencher Park in old St. Boniface. Five pleasant, flowery bedrooms are available; all are air-conditioned. Hostess Jacqueline Bernier's traditional French-Canadian breakfast might include pancakes with maple syrup, an omelette, or delicious French toast, served at a beautifully set table. Service is in French and very friendly.

Eastern Manitoba

Selkirk

Daerwood Motor Inn
$65
tv, *P*, 🐕, ♿, ≡
162 Main St., R1A 1R3
☎***482-7722***
☎***(800) 930-3888***
⇄***482-8655***
The Daerwood Motor Inn offers reasonably priced accommodations in central Selkirk, not far from several important local attractions. Rooms with kitchen units cost only $5 extra, and videocassette players are also available for an extra charge.

Riverton

Gull Harbour Resort
$90
♿, *P*, *tv*, ≡, ℜ, ≈, ⊛, ⌂, ⊙
Box 1000, B0C 2R0
☎***279-2041***
☎***(800) 267-6700***
⇄***279-2000***
A beautiful resort on the tip of an island. This convention centre is especially well known for the golf courses nearby, as well as the natural scenery of Hecla and Grindstone parks. It's also located close to the Hecla Island Heritage Home Museum.

Gimli

Lakeview Resort
$86
tv, *K*, ♿, 🐕, *P*, ≡, ℜ, ≈, ⌂
10 Centre St.
☎***(800) 456-4000***
☎***642-8565***
⇄***642-4400***
The Lakeview Resort is right on the harbour in Gimli. Guests can choose a country-style suite or a room overlooking the small town or the large lake from which the town derives most of its business. Breaking with the tradition of impersonal rooms in most big hotel chains, rooms here feature quilts, a fresh scent, hardwood floors and in-room mini bars; there is a cozy fireplace in the lobby. Each room has a balcony.

Southern Manitoba

Winkler

Winkler Inn
$70
tv, ≡, 🐕, ♿, ℜ, ≈, ⊛
851 Main St., R6W 4B1
☎***(800) 829-4920***
☎***325-4381***
⇄***325-9656***
The fertile Pembina Valley draws visitors to Winkler, and the Winkler Inn accommodates them with a wide variety of amenities, including queen-sized beds and a view of the pool. Also on site are a bar, restaurant, pool, and 10-person hot tub.

Central Manitoba

Wasagaming

New Chalet
$70
tv, P, ≈, ≡, ♿
CP 100, Wasagaming, R0J 2H0
☎***848-2892***
The New Chalet is open year-round and offers some of the best accommodations in the area. Pleasant and newly renovated, this well-kept establishment is centrally situated and offers guests the use of its outdoor swimming pool. It should be noted that since the hotel lies within park boundaries, guests must pay the park admission fee.

Lake Audy

Riding Mountain Guest Ranch
$75 per person, fb
sb
Box 11, 20km west of Clear Lake on Hwy. 354, R0J 0Z0
☎***848-2265***
One of the better guest ranch experiences in the province. Host Jim Irwin takes groups or individuals into his three-and-a-half storey ranch house, leading bison-viewing tours and serving meals in a dining room. Special touches here include a billiard table, a hot tub overlooking the fields, air conditioning in summer and a wood-heated sauna in winter. The ranch is quite close to Riding Mountain National Park, and the property also includes groomed trails for cross-country skiing and tobogganing. Irwin specializes in hosting group events. Minimum two-day stay, reservations recommended.

Roblin

Harvest Moon Inn
$64 bkfst incl.
tv, K, ♿, ≡
25 Commercial Dr., R0L 1P0
☎***937-3701***
☎***888-377-3399***
⇄***937-3701***
The Harvest Moon Inn is a new all-suite hotel with lots of room. Each suite includes a microwave, refrigerator, television and videocassette recorder; a small selection of free movies is available at the front desk. As a bonus, the family that runs the business is full of fishing advice and interesting stories about their travels.

Brandon

Comfort Inn by Journey's End
$78
tv, ≡, *P*, ♿
925 Middleton Ave., R7C 1A8
☎***727-6232***
☎***(800) 228-5150***
⇄***727-2246***
The Comfort Inn offers super rooms and professional management right on the Trans-Canada Facade north of downtown Brandon. Rooms here feature work tables and sofas, a bonus for business travellers; the only drawback is the place's popularity: it is often booked up months in advance.

Northern Manitoba

Churchill

Northern Lights Lodge
$88
tv, 🐕, ℜ
Box 70, R0B 0E0
☎***675-2403***
⇄***675-2011***
This northern outpost caters to those in search of the polar bears who can usually be seen frolicking on the shores of Hudson Bay. The inn is only open from June until November, and there is a restaurant on premises.

Polar Inn
$100
tv
15 Franklin St., R0B 0E0
☎675-8878
⇌675-2647
The presence of polar bears has inspired a whole slew of motels and inns in Churchill, including this one. Rooms have been recently updated and include all modern amenities like telephones and televisions. Mountain-bike rentals are a real bonus for outdoor types, and shoppers will find the on-site gift shop pleasant.

Restaurants

Downtown Winnipeg

Rogue's Gallery and Coffeehouse
$
closed Mon
432 Assiniboine Ave.
☎947-0652
www.roguesgallery.mb.ca
Rogue's Gallery and Coffeehouse occupies a large, rambling house on the river where young, hip Winnipeggers come for a coffee or a bite to eat. Works by local artists hang on the brightly coloured walls. The limited but diverse menu of dishes ranging from Italian chicken or pasta to rotis and falafel can be sampled in the various eclectically furnished rooms of this two-storey building or on the pretty summer patio. There is no table service.

Alycia's
$
559 Cathedral Ave.
☎582-8789
This is likely the most popular of Winnipeg's half-dozen or so Ukrainian eateries. "It sticks with you," say customers of the food here; and, indeed, the place is well-known around town for thick soups, hearty perogies, cabbage rolls and other warming fare. Red creamy sodas and decorations, such as Ukrainian Easter eggs and pictures of the Pope, add to the festive mood, and the owners also run a deli next door that offers takeout meats and side dishes.

Le Café Jardin
$
lunch only
340 Provencher Ave.
☎233-9515
Attached to the Franco-Manitoban Cultural Centre, this café serves French-Canadian cuisine as well as light meals and pastries baked on-site. The outdoor terrace is popular in summertime.

Nucci's Gelati
$
643 Corydon Ave.
☎475-8765
On a hot summer night, this ice cream parlour is the place to be. Don't be put off by the long line-up: the 30 flavours of delicious home-made gelato are well worth the wait! The huge servings will keep you cool as you stroll along Winnipeg's Italian strip, which comes alive with a festive atmosphere at night.

Blue Note Café
$-$$
875 Portage Ave.
☎774-2189
A local hangout where you can chow down on burgers, chili and other bar food. Groovy jazz plays on the sound system each night until about 9pm, when some local musical act takes the stage. There's history here, too – the original location, downtown on Main Street, was where music star Neil Young and Canadian heroes Crash Test Dummies both got their starts.

Carlos & Murphy's
$$
129 Osborne Ave.
☎284-3510
Right beside the Tap & Grill (see below), this small, dark restaurant has a real frontier feel to it – rough wooden boards are nailed to the wall in the pattern of a sunset, and saddles and other western gear decorate the interior. The Tex-Mex food comes in large portions, and is good with a lime Margarita or a Mexican beer.

Da Mamma Mia Ristorante
$$
631 Corydon Ave.
☎453-9210
One of the many Italian restaurants on Corydon Avenue, this one is worth visiting for its patio, fringed with basil and other herbs destined for the restaurant's kitchen. The terrace has the *de rigueur* colourful umbrellas, checkered tablecloths, and even a small fountain. The interior, on the other hand, is quite dark, and has an ornate gilded and slightly kitschy decor – so come here on a warm, sunny day. Simple meals of pasta, pizza and salad are served.

Elephant and Castle
$$
350 St. Mary Ave.
☎942-5555
Located in the lobby of the well-appointed Holiday Inn Crown Centre, this handsome English-style pub serves up the expected fare – turkey pot pie, bangers and mash, fish and chips, soups and sandwiches. The food is tasty and served with a smile. The dessert selection is especially good, including mousse, sherry trifle, deep-dish apple crisp, home-made pies and more. There's a full bar selection, as well.

Tap & Grill
$$
closed Sun
137 Osborne St.
☎284-7455
Located in the trendy Osborne Village, this restaurant has a relaxed Mediterranean atmosphere. Wicker chairs, shutters and ceramic tile floors create a cool, southern interior. There is an outdoor terrace in the back, surrounded by trellises and plants; an idyllic and very popular spot in the summertime. The menu includes meat dishes, seafood, pasta and a selection of fresh salads. Lemon, garlic and sun-dried tomatoes are the dominant flavours.

Hy's Steak Loft
$$$
216 Kennedy St.
☎942-1000
The brick-warehouse appearance of this downtown institution is quite deceiving; it's one of those places where smoky backroom deals are forged over Alberta prime rib. Politicians and other bigshots head for the wood-panelled steak room to watch the beef char-grilled to order on an open grill right before their eyes. Those with real clout ask for one of the Loft's private dining rooms and discuss changes in insurance laws or whatever else needs to be arranged out of the public's earshot. There's also a smoking room and lounge on the premises, good for relaxing before and after the big meal.

Orlando's Seafood Grill
$$$
709 Corydon Ave.
☎477-5899
For something a little more upscale, try this elegant Portuguese restaurant with a contemporary indoor decor and a charming deck patio. It is known for its expertly prepared fish dishes, such as, on occasion, such delicacies as shark. Attentive and knowledgeable service.

The Velvet Glove
$$$$
2 Lombard Ave.
☎985-6255
Located in the prestigious Lombard Hotel, this restaurant caters to Winnipeg's high rollers. Entrees might include choices of the chef's latest creations in beef, seafood or lamb; whatever's cooking, though, all meals begin with a simple soup and salad.

Eastern Manitoba

Gimli

Seagull's Restaurant
$-$$$
10 Centre St.
☎642-4145
This restaurant's biggest draw is its patio located right on the beach. Items like battered fish and gyros are served in a large dining room, and you can try some Icelandic Vinetarta for

dessert. Although there is nothing special about this place, it's the best sit-down restaurant in town.

Central Manitoba

Brandon

Humpty's
$
Hwy. 1
☎729-1902
This restaurant, located in a gas station on a Brandon service road running parallel to the Trans-Canada, serves up solid stick-to-your-ribs food such as burgers, eggs and lots of filling sandwiches. Locals swear by it.

Casteleyn Cappuccino Bar
$
closed Sun
908 Rosser Ave.
☎727-2820
This place is an oasis on the prairie, well worth a detour to Brandon. The Belgian Casteleyn family has been making hand-dipped chocolates here for seven years; last year they opened a bright new space and added gelato, Italian sodas and a cappuccino bar. This place is more of a coffeehouse than a restaurant, but there's a tasty selection of meat and vegetable focaccia sandwiches each day. Other dessert options include Grand Marnier truffles, amaretto cheesecake and peach chocolate gateau. A wonderful lunch or snack experience.

Over the Moon
$$
934 Rosser Ave.
☎727-1448
Several noteworthy restaurants can be found on Rosser Avenue, between 9th and 10th Sts. Among these, Over the Moon serves appetizing pastas and fusion fare in its contemporary dining room or on the lovely patio with hanging geraniums.

St.François-Xavier

The Nun's Kitchen
$$
1033 Hwy. 26
☎864-2300
Located in – what else – a former convent, this restaurant serves good food in a little French village outside of Winnipeg. Entrees include buffalo, quiche, chicken, ribs and the like; prices are surprisingly reasonable. The sunny dining room has lovely views of the surrounding countryside.

The Medicine Rock Café
$$$
990 Hwy. 26, St. Francis-Xavier
☎864-2451
Located in a large, new log building with comfortable booths and lots of windows, this place features one of the most interesting menus in the province. Dishes include ostrich, emu, boar and rabbit. Reservations are recommended, as this restaurant is often crowded.

Shellmouth

The Church Caffe
$$
Box 15; head north 25km from Russel on Hwy. 83, 10km west on Hwy. 482 and north again on Hwy. 549
☎564-2626
Housed in a former United Church, this place serves Austrian dinners in a scintillating lakeside location. It takes a bit of searching to find it, but the reward is a selection of beef, pork and turkey entrees that come with soup and salad. The restaurant won the Flavour of Rural Manitoba Award in 1995.

Wasagaming

T.R. McKoy's Italian Restaurant
$-$$
on Wasagaming St.
☎848-4653
This is an unexpected gem, serving well-prepared pasta, pizza and grill dishes in a friendly and relaxed ambiance.

Entertainment

Winnipeg

Bars and Pubs

Times Change Blues Bar
Thu to Sun
234 Main St.
☎957-0982
Little seems to have changed at the Times Change Blues Bar, a small, intimate club that keeps on playing... the blues.

Centre Culturel
340 Provencher Blvd.
☎233-8972
A lively crowd gathers Tuesdays at the Centre Culturel for an evening of Mardi Jazz. Live music is also presented on Thursday and Friday nights.

King's Head Pub
120 King St.
☎957-7710
This might be Winnipeg's best bar. Located in the Exchange District, it features lots of imported beers and a wide selection of scotch, plus darts and pool. Food is also available.

Toad in the Hole
112 Osborne St.
☎284-7201
In funky Osborne Village, this is a good pub with plenty of pints of various imported brews. Darts and pool are available here, as well.

Cultural Events

Royal Winnipeg Ballet
380 Graham Ave.
☎(800) 667-4792
☎956-2792
The Royal Winnipeg Ballet is Canada's best-known dance company, housed in its own performance building right downtown. The ballet company won a gold medal at the International Ballet Competition and sometimes hosts tours of its facility, in addition to regular performances.

The **Winnipeg Fringe Festival** (*held in Jul; ☎956-1340, fringe@mtc.mb.ca*) is one of the largest theatre festivals of its kind, featuring a mix of local talent and international groups who perform in various small downtown venues. Real discoveries are to be made among the wide variety of shows, which range from family entertainment to experimental works. Free outdoor performances are held at Old Market Square (see p 510) throughout the festival.

Folkorama
(*☎800-665-0234 or 982-6210*), Winnipeg's huge annual summer bash, lasts two weeks each August and covers a lot of ground: representatives of the city's many cultures – French, Ukrainian, Hungarian, Chinese, Japanese, East Indian, to name a few – cook the food, sing the songs and dance the dances of their homelands in the many pavilions that spring up around the city for this event.

Some 30,000 folkies converge on **Bird's Hill Park** for one fun-filled weekend each July to sing, dance, or simply enjoy the **Winnipeg Folk Festival** (***☎231-0096***), one of North America's finest festivals of its kind. The extravaganza draws talented musicians from around the world to play on outdoor stages for enthusiastic crowds of all ages.

Gaming

Club Regent
1425 Regent Ave. W.
☎957-2700
Palm trees and waterfalls set a Caribbean theme for the Club Regent casino. The emphasis here is on electronic gaming: bingo, poker and Keno. There are slot machines here, as well.

St. Boniface

The **Festival du Voyageur** (*768 Ave. Taché, St. Boniface; ☎237-7692; voyageur@festivalvoyageur.mb.ca*) is a giant annual street party in St. Boniface each February, celebrating winter and the voyageurs who settled the province. Action at the big outdoor pavilion includes dog-sled races, snow sculptures and children's activities, while musical performers entertain the crowds at night.

The **Cercle Molière** (*340 Provencher Blvd. and 825 Rue St-Joseph; ☎233-8055*) is Canada's oldest permanent theatre company, staging three major productions and the smaller "série Café-Théâtre" every year. Performances are in French.

Eastern Manitoba

Gimli

Islendingadagurinn (the Icelandic Festival of Manitoba) takes place during three days in late August, celebrating the local heritage from that far-off land right in downtown Gimli. The festival includes a parade, music, poetry, Icelandic food and more.

Southern Manitoba

Altona

The **Manitoba Sunflower Festival** celebrates the tall yellow flower for three days each July in Altona with Mennonite foods, parades, dancing in the street and the like.

Morris

The **Morris Stampede and Exhibition** turns Morris, an otherwise slowpoke town, into rodeo central for five days in early July. It is Canada's second-largest rodeo (after Calgary), and features chuckwagon and chariot races, an agricultural fair, and (of course) bullriding and other rodeo contests.

Central Manitoba

Dauphin

The hugely popular **National Ukrainian Festival** (*119 Main St. S., Dauphin; ☎638-5645; ⇛638-5851*) takes place in Dauphin for three days each mid-summer, beginning on a Friday morning. Heritage village festivities include a bread-baking competition, embroidery contests, an Easter-egg decorating competition, folk arts, lots of dancing and a beer garden.

Brandon

The whole town of Brandon puckers up for the **International Pickle Festival**, held downtown each September. Besides the obvious pickle-tastings, attractions include expanded musical stages, classic car shows, kickboxing contests, and a full slate of children's events such as the "Oodles of Onions Contest." Truly quirky, but a real slice of small-town prairie life nevertheless.

Portage La Prarie

In Portage La Prairie, the annual **Strawberry Festival** draws visitors from all over the province. Held in mid-July, it features lots of street dances, entertainment and a flea market in addition to strawberry treats.

Northern Manitoba

The Pas

The **Northern Manitoba Trappers' Festival** in The Pas runs for five days each February. Festivities here include a famous dog-sled race.

Shopping

Winnipeg

Shopping is concentrated in the downtown area: The Eaton Centre, Hudson's Bay Company and the North West Company – are within a few blocks of each other. They are connected by a series of covered elevated walkways that are especially appreciated in wintertime. The library and other buildings are also linked via these "skywalks."

Winnipeg's **Hudson's Bay Company** (*Portage Ave. and Memorial Blvd.*) was once the flagship of the illustrious chain, founded as a trading company in 1610. Now a modern department store, it still sells the original Hudson's Bay Blankets and other unique merchandise.

Eaton Place (*downtown at 234 Donald St.*), has more than 100 shops connected by the walkways. **Portage Place** is another downtown mall spanning three blocks; it contains 160 shops or so, an IMAX theatre and an in-house theatre company. **Polo Park**, (1485 Portage Ave., on the way to the airport), contains more than 180 shops and leans toward upscale department stores. Among other stores downtown, The **Bayat Gallery** (*163 Stafford St., ☎888-88 INUIT or 475-5873*) is particularly interesting; it is the city's best of Inuit art gallery.

Osborne Village has a number of great little boutiques that should not be left unexplored. Jewellery, paperware, gifts, clothes, cookingware and more can be found in shops along Osborne Street between River and Stradbrook Avenue.

Toad Hall (*54 Arthur St.; ☎956-2195 or 888-333-TOAD*) is a place that most children can only dream of. Shelves brimming with quality toys, both contemporary and traditional, line the walls of this store, which has a whimsical atmosphere that will transport children and adults alike into the magical realms of the imagination. Everything from complete handmade Czech puppet theatres to electric train sets, colourful kites and magic sets are sold.

McNally Robinson (*1120 Grant Ave.; ☎475-0483, info@mcnallyrobinson.ca*) is by far the best bookstore in the city. It has a huge selection in every field, with special emphasis on prairie writing. A spiral staircase winds around a massive tree trunk, leading to the children's section on the second floor. Its restaurant, Café au Livre, serves light lunches and desserts.

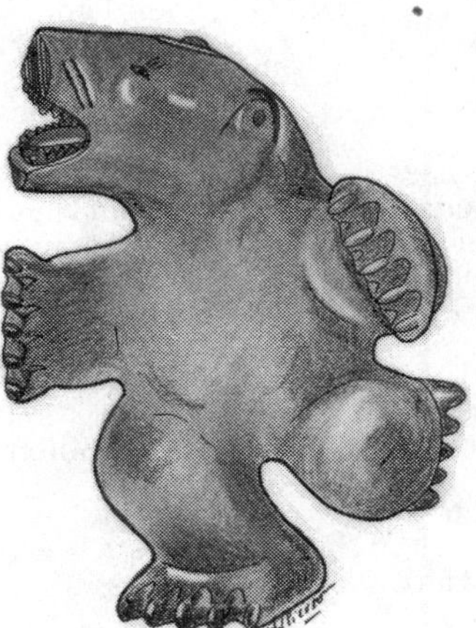

Index

Index

Index

Index

Order Form

ULYSSES TRAVEL GUIDES

☐ Atlantic Canada .... $24.95 CAN $17.95 US
☐ Bahamas .... $24.95 CAN $17.95 US
☐ Beaches of Maine .... $12.95 CAN $9.95 US
☐ Bed & Breakfasts in Québec .... $13.95 CAN $10.95 US
☐ Belize .... $16.95 CAN $12.95 US
☐ Calgary .... $17.95 CAN $12.95 US
☐ Canada .... $29.95 CAN $21.95 US
☐ Chicago .... $19.95 CAN $14.95 US
☐ Chile .... $27.95 CAN $17.95 US
☐ Colombia .... $29.95 CAN $21.95 US
☐ Costa Rica .... $27.95 CAN $19.95 US
☐ Cuba .... $24.95 CAN $17.95 US
☐ Dominican Republic .... $24.95 CAN $17.95 US
☐ Ecuador and Galapagos Islands .... $24.95 CAN $17.95 US
☐ El Salvador .... $22.95 CAN $14.95 US
☐ Guadeloupe .... $24.95 CAN $17.95 US
☐ Guatemala .... $24.95 CAN $17.95 US
☐ Honduras .... $24.95 CAN $17.95 US
☐ Jamaica .... $24.95 CAN $17.95 US
☐ Lisbon .... $18.95 CAN $13.95 US
☐ Louisiana .... $29.95 CAN $21.95 US
☐ Martinique .... $24.95 CAN $17.95 US
☐ Miami .... $9.95 CAN $12.95 US
☐ Montréal .... $19.95 CAN $14.95 US
☐ New Orleans .... $17.95 CAN $12.95 US
☐ New York City .... $19.95 CAN $14.95 US
☐ Nicaragua .... $24.95 CAN $17.95 US
☐ Ontario .... $27.95 CAN $19.95US
☐ Ottawa .... $17.95 CAN $12.95 US
☐ Panamá .... $24.95 CAN $17.95 US
☐ Peru .... $27.95 CAN $19.95 US
☐ Portugal .... $24.95 CAN $16.95 US
☐Puerto Rico .... $24.95 CAN $17.95 US
☐ Provence - Côte d'Azur .... $29.95 CAN $21.95US
☐ Québec .... $29.95 CAN $21.95 US
☐ Québec and Ontario with Via .... $9.95 CAN $7.95 US
☐ Seattle .... $17.95 CAN $12.95 US
☐ Toronto .... $18.95 CAN $13.95 US
☐ Vancouver .... $17.95 CAN $12.95 US
☐ Washington D.C. .... $18.95 CAN $13.95 US
☐ Western Canada .... $29.95 CAN $21.95 US

ULYSSES DUE SOUTH

☐ Acapulco .... $14.95 CAN $9.95 US
☐ Los Cabos and La Paz .... $14.95 CAN $10.95 US
☐ Cancún & Riviera Maya .... $19.95 CAN $14.95 US
☐ Cancun Cozumel .... $17.95 CAN $12.95 US
☐ Puerto Vallarta .... $14.95 CAN $9.95 US
☐ Huatulco - Oaxaca Puerto Escondido .... $17.95 CAN $12.95 US
☐ Cartagena (Colombia) .... $12.95 CAN $9.95 US
☐ Belize .... $16.95 CAN $12.95 US
☐ St. Martin and St. Barts .... $16.95 CAN $12.95 US
☐ Guadalajara .... $17.95 CAN $12.95 US

ULYSSES GREEN ESCAPES

☐ Cycling in France .... $22.95 CAN
$16.95 US

☐ Cycling in Ontario .... $22.95 CAN
$16.95 US

☐ Biking Montréal .... $3.95 CAN

☐ Hiking in the Northeastern U.S. .... $19.95 CAN
$13.95 US

☐ Hiking in Québec .... $19.95 CAN
$13.95 US

ULYSSES CONVERSATION GUIDES

☐ French for Better Travel .... $9.95 CAN
$6.95 US

☐ Spanish for Better Travel ... $9.95 CAN
$6.95 US

ULYSSES TRAVEL JOURNAL

☐ Ulysses Travel Journal (Colours) .. $9.95 CAN
$7.95 US

☐ Ulysses Travel Journal 80 Days ... $14.95 CAN
$9.95 US

TITLE	QUANTITY	PRICE	TOTAL

Name ....

Address ....

....

....

Telephone ....

Fax ....

E-mail ....

Payment : ☐ Money Order ☐ Visa ☐ MasterCard

Card Number ....

Expiry date ....

Signature ....

Sub-total	
Postage & Handling	$4.00
Sub-total	
G.S.T. in Canada 7%	
TOTAL	

ULYSSES TRAVEL GUIDES

4176 St-Denis
Montréal, Québec, H2W 2M5
tel (514) 843-9447 fax (514) 843-9448
Toll free: 1-877-542-7247
www.ulyssesguides.com
info@ulysses.ca